Ford Pick-ups & Bronco Automotive Repair Manual

Dennis Yamaguchi
and **J H Haynes** Member of the Guild of Motoring Writers

Models covered

F-100, F-150, F-250, F-350 and Bronco with 240 and 300 cu in six-cylinder in-line and 302, 351, 360, 390, 400 and 460 cu in V8 engines; Manual and automatic transmissions. 1973 through 1979

ISBN 0 85696 788 2

© **Haynes North America, Inc. 1983**
With permission from J.H. Haynes & Co. Ltd.

Printed in the USA

ABCDE

2

 (2Y7 – 36054)
(788)

Haynes Publishing Group
Sparkford Nr Yeovil
Somerset BA22 7JJ England

Haynes North America, Inc
861 Lawrence Drive
Newbury Park
California 91320 USA

Acknowledgements

Special thanks are due to Ford Motor Company for the supply of technical information and certain illustrations. Champion Spark Plug Company supplied the illustrations showing the various spark plug conditions. The bodywork repair photos were provided by Holt Lloyd Limited.

About this manual

Its purpose

The purpose of this manual is to help you get the best value from your vehicle. It can do so in several ways. It can help you decide what work must be done even if you choose to get it done by a dealer service department or a repair shop; it provides information and procedures for routine maintenance and servicing; and it offers diagnostic and repair procedures to follow when trouble occurs.

It is hoped that you will use the manual to tackle the work yourself. For many simpler jobs, doing it yourself may be quicker than arranging an appointment to get the vehicle into a shop and making the trips to leave it and pick it up. More importantly, a lot of money can be saved by avoiding the expense the shop must pass on to you to cover its labor and overhead costs. An added benefit is the sense of satisfaction and accomplishment that you feel after having done the job yourself.

Using the manual

The manual is divided into Chapters. Each Chapter is divided into numbered Sections, which are headed in bold type between horizontal lines. Each Section consists of consecutively numbered paragraphs.

The two types of illustrations used (figures and photographs) are referenced by a number preceding their captions. Figure reference numbers denote Chapter and numerical sequence in the Chapter; i.e. Fig. 12.4 means Chapter 12, figure number 4. Figure captions are followed by a Section number which ties the figure to a specific portion of the text. All photographs apply to the Chapter in which they appear, and the reference number pinpoints the pertinent Section and paragraph.

Procedures, once described in the text, are not normally repeated. When it is necessary to refer to another Chapter, the reference will be given as Chapter and Section number; i.e. Chapter 1/16. Cross reference given without use of the word 'Chapter' apply to Sections and/or paragraphs in the same Chapter. For example, 'see Section 8' means in the same Chapter.

Reference to the left or right of the vehicle is based on the assumption that one is sitting in the driver's seat facing forward.

Even though extreme care has been taken during the preparation of this manual, neither the publisher nor the author can accept responsibility for any errors in, or omissions from, the information given.

Introduction to the Ford Pick-ups and Bronco

The Ford F100, F250, 350 and Bronco are available in a variety of trim options.

Engine options include the 240 and 300 cubic inch six and V8 engines of 302, 351, 360, 390, 400 and 460 cubic inch displacement.

Chassis layout is conventional with the engine mounted at the front and the power being transmitted through either a manual or automatic transmission by a driveshaft to the solid rear axle on 2-wheel drive models. On 4-wheel drive vehicles, a transfer case transmits power to the front axle by way of a driveshaft. Models are equipped with three or four speed manual or three speed automatic transmissions.

Front suspension is either coil or leaf spring and telescopic shock absorbers and rear suspension is by leaf springs and telescopic shock absorbers. Manual steering is of the recirculating ball or worm and roller type with power assist as an option.

Brakes are self-adjusting drum-type with disc at the front on later models and vacuum assist as an option.

Contents

1976 Ford F100 2-wheel drive pick-up

1977 Ford F100 Custom 2-wheel drive pick-up

1977 Ford Bronco 4-wheel drive

1979 Ford Bronco Custom 4-wheel drive

1979 Ford F100 Custom 4-wheel drive pick-up

1978 Ford Bronco Ranger XLT 4-wheel drive

General dimensions

Wheelbase

F100	117, 133, 138.8 and 155 in
F150	117, 133, 138 and 155 in
F250	133, 139.8, 150.3 and 155 in
F350	104, 122, 137, 140, 161, 165.5 and 166.5 in
Bronco	92.0 in

Spare parts and vehicle identification numbers

Buying spare parts

Replacement parts are available from many sources, which generally fall into one of two categories – authorized dealer parts departments and independent retail auto parts stores. Our advice concerning these parts is as follows:

Retail auto parts stores: Good auto parts stores will stock frequently needed components which wear out relatively fast, such as clutch components, exhaust systems, brake parts, tune-up parts, etc. These stores often supply new or reconditioned parts on an exchange basis, which can save a considerable amount of money. Discount auto parts stores are often very good places to buy materials and parts needed for general vehicle maintenance such as oil, grease, filters, spark plugs, belts, touch-up paint, bulbs, etc. They also usually sell tools and general accessories, have convenient hours, charge lower prices and can often be found not far from home.

Authorized dealer parts department: This is the best source for parts which are unique to the vehicle and not generally available elsewhere (such as major engine parts, transmission parts, trim pieces, etc.).

Warranty information: If the vehicle is still covered under warranty, be sure that any replacement parts purchased – regardless of the source – do not invalidate the warranty!

To be sure of obtaining the correct parts, have engine and chassis numbers available and, if possible, take the old parts along for positive identification.

Vehicle identification numbers

Regardless from which source parts are obtained, it will be necessary to provide correct information concerning the vehicle model and year of manufacture plus the engine serial number and the vehicle identification number (VIN).

The Vehicle Certification Label, which is attached to the rear face of the driver's door or the rear door pillar, contains the VIN as well as other valuable information. In addition, each vehicle is equipped with a rating plate which includes the VIN number. On F-series trucks the rating plate is attached to the rear face of the driver's door lock panel. On Broncos the rating plate is attached to the inside panel of the glove compartment door. For title and registration purposes, the official VIN is stamped into the right front frame rail and is usually visible from inside the engine compartment.

Engine identification numbers

For specific and exact engine identification a decal type label is attached to each engine. This label is attached to the front of the rocker arm cover on six cylinder engines and the front of the *right* rocker arm cover on V8 engines. **Note:** *Exceptions may occur if brackets or equipment would prevent an unobstructed view of the label.*

Always refer to this label when replacement parts are required, as parts often are different within engine families.

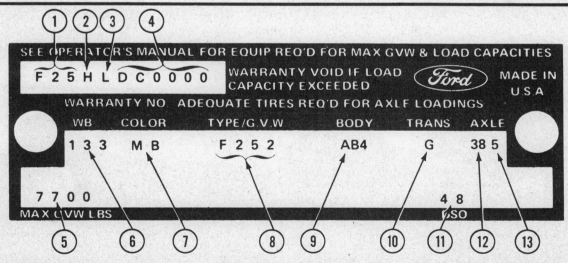

Usually located on the driver's door rear pillar, the Vehicle Certification Label contains the following information:

1 Truck series code
2 Engine code
3 Assembly plant code   } VIN
4 Serial and warranty number
5 Recommended maximum
   gross vehicle weight rating

6 Wheelbase
7 Paint codes
8 Model code and gross
   vehicle weight
9 Interior and seat and body/cab type

10 Transmission code
11 District and special order codes
12 Rear axle code
13 Front axle (if equipped) code

Maintenance techniques, tools and working facilities

Basic maintenance techniques

There are a number of techniques involved in maintenance and repair that will be referred to throughout this manual. Application of these techniques will enable the home mechanic to be more efficient, better organized and capable of performing the various tasks properly, which will ensure that the repair job is thorough and complete.

Fasteners

Fasteners, basically, are nuts, bolts, studs and screws used to hold two or more parts together. There are a few things to keep in mind when working with fasteners. Almost all of them use a locking device of some type; either a lock washer, locknut, locking tab or thread adhesive. All threaded fasteners should be clean and straight, with undamaged threads and undamaged corners on the hex head where the wrench fits. Develop the habit of replacing damaged nuts and bolts with new ones. Special locknuts with nylon or fiber inserts can only be used once. If they are removed, they lose their locking ability and must be replaced with new ones.

Rusted nuts and bolts should be treated with a penetrating fluid to ease removal and prevent breakage. Some mechanics use turpentine in a spout-type oil can, which works quite well. After applying the rust penetrant, let it "work" for a few minutes before trying to loosen the nut or bolt. Badly rusted fasteners may have to be chiseled or sawed off or removed with a special nut breaker, available at tool stores.

If a bolt or stud breaks off in an assembly, it can be drilled and removed with a special tool commonly available for this purpose. Most automotive machine shops can perform this task, as well as other repair procedures (such as repair of threaded holes that have been stripped out).

Flat washers and lock washers, when removed from an assembly, should always be replaced exactly as removed. Replace damaged washers with new ones. Always use a flat washer between a lock washer and any soft metal surface (such as aluminum), thin sheet metal or plastic.

Fastener sizes

For a number of reasons, automobile manufacturers are making wider and wider use of metric fasteners. Therefore, it is important to be able to tell the difference between standard (sometimes called U.S., English or SAE) and metric hardware, since they cannot be interchanged.

All bolts, whether standard or metric, are sized according to diameter, thread pitch and length. For example, a standard $\frac{1}{2}$ – 13 x 1 bolt is $\frac{1}{2}$ inch in diameter, has 13 threads per inch and is 1 inch long. An M12 – 1.75 x 25 metric bolt is 12 mm in diameter, has a thread pitch of 1.75 mm (the distance between threads) and is 25 mm long. The two bolts are nearly identical, and easily confused, but they are not interchangeable.

In addition to the differences in diameter, thread pitch and length, metric and standard bolts can also be distinguished by examining the bolt heads. To begin with, the distance across the flats on a standard bolt head is measured in inches, while the same dimension on a metric bolt is measured in millimeters (the same is true for nuts). As a result, a standard wrench should not be used on a metric bolt and a metric wrench should not be used on a standard bolt. Also, standard bolts have slashes radiating out from the center of the head to denote the grade or strength of the bolt (which is an indication of the amount of torque that can be applied to it). The greater the number of slashes, the greater the strength of the bolt (grades 0 through 5 are commonly used on automobiles). Metric bolts have a property class (grade) number, rather than a slash, molded into their heads to indicate bolt strength. In this case, the higher the number the stronger the bolt (property class numbers 8.8, 9.8 and 10.9 are commonly used on automobiles).

Strength markings can also be used to distinguish standard hex nuts from metric hex nuts. Standard nuts have dots stamped into one side, while metric nuts are marked with a number. The greater the number of dots, or the higher the number, the greater the strength of the nut.

Metric studs are also marked on their ends according to property class (grade). Larger studs are numbered (the same as metric bolts), while smaller studs carry a geometric code to denote grade.

It should be noted that many fasteners, especially Grades 0 through 2, have no distinguishing marks on them. When such is the case, the only way to determine whether it is standard or metric is to measure the thread pitch or compare it to a known fastener of the same size.

Since fasteners of the same size (both standard and metric) may have different strength ratings, be sure to reinstall any bolts, studs or nuts removed from your vehicle in their original locations. Also, when replacing a fastener with a new one, make sure that the new one has a strength rating equal to or greater than the original.

Tightening sequences and procedures

Most threaded fasteners should be tightened to a specific torque value (torque is basically a twisting force). Over-tightening the fastener can weaken it and lead to eventual breakage, while under-tightening can cause it to eventually come loose. Bolts, screws and studs, depending on the materials they are made of and their thread diameters, have specific torque values (many of which are noted in the Specifications Section at the beginning of each Chapter). Be sure to follow the torque recommendations closely. For fasteners not assigned a specific torque, a general torque value chart is presented here as a guide. As was previously mentioned, the size and grade of a fastener determine the amount of torque that can safely be applied to it. The figures listed here are approximate for Grade 2 and Grade 3 fasteners (higher grades can tolerate higher torque values).

	ft-lb	Nm
Metric thread sizes		
M-6	6 to 9	9 to 12
M-8	14 to 21	19 to 28
M-10	28 to 40	38 to 54
M-12	50 to 71	68 to 96
M-14	80 to 140	109 to 154
Pipe thread sizes		
$\frac{1}{8}$	5 to 8	7 to 10
$\frac{1}{4}$	12 to 18	17 to 24
$\frac{3}{8}$	22 to 33	30 to 44
$\frac{1}{2}$	25 to 35	34 to 47
U.S. thread sizes		
$\frac{1}{4}$ - 20	6 to 9	9 to 12
$\frac{5}{16}$ - 18	12 to 18	17 to 24
$\frac{5}{16}$ - 24	14 to 20	19 to 27
$\frac{3}{8}$ - 16	22 to 32	30 to 43
$\frac{3}{8}$ - 24	27 to 38	37 to 51
$\frac{7}{16}$ - 14	40 to 55	55 to 74
$\frac{7}{16}$ - 20	40 to 60	55 to 81
$\frac{1}{2}$ - 13	55 to 80	75 to 108

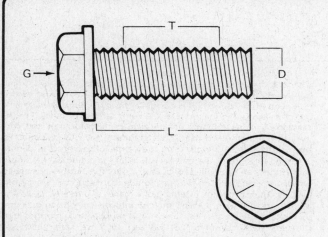

Standard (SAE) bolt dimensions/grade marks

G – Grade marks (bolt strength)
L – Length (in inches)
T – Thread pitch (number of threads per inch)
D – Nominal diameter (inches)

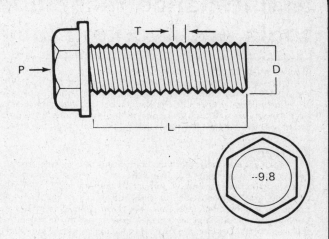

Metric bolt dimensions/grade marks

P – Property class (bolt strength)
L – Length (in millimeters)
T – Thread pitch (distance between threads; in millimeters)
D – Nominal diameter (in millimeters)

Grade	Identification
Hex Nut Grade 5	3 Dots
Hex Nut Grade 8	6 Dots

Standard hex nut strength markings

Class	Identification
Hex Nut Property Class 9	Arabic 9
Hex Nut Property Class 10	Arabic 10

Metric hex nut strength markings

Fasteners laid out in a pattern (i.e. cylinder head bolts, oil pan bolts, differential cover bolts, etc.) must be loosened and tightened in a definite sequence to avoid warping the component. Initially, the bolts or nuts should be assembled finger-tight only. Next, they should be tightened one full turn each, in a criss-cross or diagonal pattern. After each one has been tightened one full turn, return to the first one and tighten them all one half turn, following the same pattern. Finally, tighten each of them one-quarter turn at a time until they all have been tightened to the proper torque value. To loosen and remove them the procedure would be reversed.

Component disassembly

Component disassembly should be done with care and purpose to help ensure that the parts go back together properly. Always keep track of the sequence in which parts are removed. Make note of special characteristics or markings on parts that can be installed more than one way (such as a grooved thrust washer on a shaft). It is a good idea to lay the disassembled parts out on a clean surface in the order

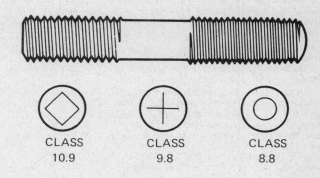

Metric stud strength markings

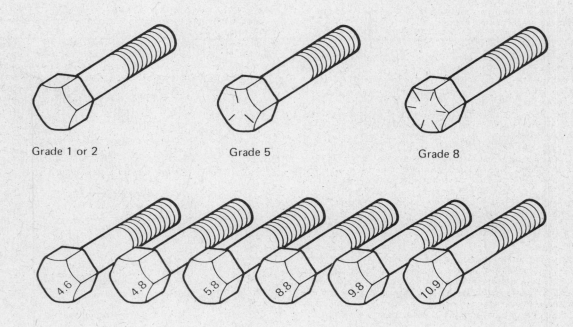

Bolt strength markings (top – standard: bottom – metric)

that they were removed. It may also be helpful to make simple sketches or take instant photos of components before removal.

When removing fasteners from an assembly, keep track of their locations. Sometimes threading a bolt back in a part, or putting the washers and nut back on a stud, can prevent mixups later. If nuts and bolts cannot be returned to their original locations, they should be kept in a compartmented box or a series of small boxes. A cupcake or muffin tin is ideal for this purpose, since each cavity can hold the bolts and nuts from a particular area (i.e. oil pan bolts, valve cover bolts, engine mount bolts, etc.). A pan of this type is especially helpful when working on assemblies with very small parts (such as the carburetor, alternator, valve train or interior dash and trim pieces). The cavities can be marked with paint or tape to identify the contents.

Whenever wiring looms, harnesses or connectors are separated, it's a good idea to identify them with numbered pieces of masking tape so that they can be easily reconnected.

Gasket sealing surfaces

Throughout any vehicle, gaskets are used to seal the mating surfaces between two parts and keep lubricants, fluids, vacuum or pressure contained in an assembly.

Many times these gaskets are coated with a liquid or paste-type gasket sealing compound before assembly. Age, heat and pressure can sometimes cause the two parts to stick together so tightly that they are very difficult to separate. Often the assembly can be loosened by striking it with a soft-faced hammer near the mating surfaces. A regular hammer can be used if a block of wood is placed between the hammer and the part. Do not hammer on cast parts or parts that could be easily damaged. With any particularly stubborn part, always recheck to see that every fastener has been removed.

Avoid using a screwdriver or bar to pry apart an assembly, as they can easily mar the gasket sealing surfaces of the parts (which must remain smooth). If prying is absolutely necessary, use an old broom handle, but keep in mind that extra clean-up will be necessary if the wood splinters.

After the parts are separated, the old gasket must be carefully scraped off and the gasket surfaces cleaned. Stubborn gasket material can be soaked with rust penetrant or treated with a special chemical to soften it so that it can be easily scraped off. A scraper can be fashioned from a piece of copper tubing by flattening and sharpening one end. Copper is recommended because it is usually softer than the surfaces to be scraped, which reduces the chance of gouging the part. Some gaskets can be removed with a wire brush, but regardless of the method used, the mating surfaces must be left clean and smooth. If for some reason the gasket surface is gouged, then a gasket sealer thick enough to fill scratches will have to be used upon reassembly of the components. For most applications, a non-drying (or semi-drying) gasket sealer should be used.

Hose removal tips

Caution: *If equipped with air conditioning, do not ever disconnect any of the a/c hoses without first de-pressurizing the system.*

Hose removal precautions closely parallel gasket removal precautions. Avoid scratching or gouging the surface that the hose mates against or the connection may leak. This is especially true for radiator hoses. Because of various chemical reactions, the rubber in hoses can bond itself to the metal spigot that the hose fits over. To remove a hose, first loosen the hose clamps that secure it to the spigot. Then, with slip joint pliers, grab the hose at the clamp and rotate it around the spigot. Work it back and forth until it is completely free, then pull it off (silicone or other lubricants will ease removal if they can be applied between the hose and the spigot). Apply the same lubricant to the inside of the hose and the outside of the spigot to simplify installation.

If a hose clamp is broken or damaged, do not re-use it. Do not re-use hoses that are cracked, split or torn.

Tools

A selection of good tools is a basic requirement for anyone who plans to maintain and repair his or her own vehicle. For the owner who has few tools, if any, the initial investment might seem high, but when compared to the spiraling costs of professional auto maintenance and repair, it is a wise one.

To help the owner decide which tools are needed to perform the tasks detailed in this manual, the following tool lists are offered: *Maintenance and minor repair, Repair and overhaul* and *Special*. The newcomer to practical mechanics should start off with the *Maintenance and minor repair* tool kit, which is adequate for the simpler jobs performed on a vehicle. Then, as his confidence and experience grow, he can tackle more difficult tasks, buying additional tools as they are needed. Eventually the basic kit will be expanded into the *Repair and overhaul* tool set. Over a period of time, the experienced do-it-yourselfer will assemble a tool set complete enough for most repair and overhaul procedures and will add tools from the *Special* category when he feels the expense is justified by the frequency of use.

Maintenance and minor repair tool kit

The tools in this list should be considered the minimum for performance of routine maintenance, servicing and minor repair work. We recommend the purchase of combination wrenches (box end and open end combined in one wrench); while more expensive than open-ended ones, they offer the advantages of both types of wrench.

Combination wrench set ($\frac{1}{4}$ in to 1 in or 6 mm to 19 mm)
Adjustable wrench – 8 in
Spark plug wrench (with rubber insert)
Spark plug gap adjusting tool
Feeler gauge set
Brake bleeder wrench
Standard screwdriver ($\frac{5}{16}$ in x 6 in)
Phillips screwdriver (No. 2 x 6 in)
Combination pliers – 6 in

Hacksaw and assortment of blades
Tire pressure gauge
Grease gun
Oil can
Fine emery cloth
Wire brush
Battery post and cable cleaning tool
Oil filter wrench
Funnel (medium size)
Safety goggles
Jackstands (2)
Drain pan

Note: *If basic tune-ups are going to be a part of routine maintenance, it will be necessary to purchase a good quality stroboscopic timing light and a combination tachometer/dwell meter. Although they are included in the list of Special tools, they are mentioned here because they are absolutely necessary for tuning most vehicles properly.*

Repair and overhaul tool set

These tools are essential for anyone who plans to perform major repairs and are in addition to those in the *Maintenance and minor repair tool kit*. Included is a comprehensive set of sockets which, though expensive, will be found invaluable because of their versatility (especially when various extensions and drives are available). We recommend the $\frac{1}{2}$ in drive over the $\frac{3}{8}$ in drive. Although the larger drive is bulky and more expensive, it has the capability of accepting a very wide range of large sockets (ideally, the mechanic would have a $\frac{3}{8}$ in drive set and a $\frac{1}{2}$ in drive set).

Socket set(s)
Reversible ratchet
Extension – 10 in
Universal joint
Torque wrench (same size drive as sockets)
Ball pein hammer – 8 oz
Soft-faced hammer (plastic/rubber)
Standard screwdriver ($\frac{1}{4}$ in x 6 in)
Standard screwdriver (stubby – $\frac{5}{16}$ in)
Phillips screwdriver (No. 3 x 8 in)
Phillips screwdriver (stubby – No. 2)
Pliers – vise grip
Pliers – lineman's
Pliers – needle nose
Pliers – snap-ring (internal and external)
Cold chisel – $\frac{1}{2}$ in
Scriber
Scraper (made from flattened copper tubing)
Center punch
Pin punches ($\frac{1}{16}$, $\frac{1}{8}$, $\frac{3}{16}$ in)
Steel rule/straight edge – 12 in
Allen wrench set ($\frac{1}{8}$ to $\frac{3}{8}$ in or 4 mm to 10 mm)
A selection of files
Wire brush (large)
Jackstands (second set)
Jack (scissor or hydraulic type)
Note: *Another tool which is often useful is an electric drill motor with a chuck capacity of $\frac{3}{8}$ in (and a set of good quality drill bits).*

Valve spring compressor

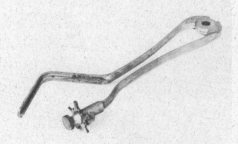

Piston ring groove cleaning tool

Piston ring compressor

Piston ring removal/installation tool

Cylinder ridge reamer

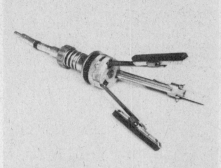

Cylinder surfacing hone

Cylinder bore gauge

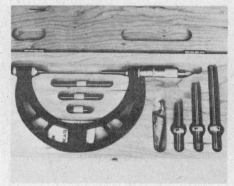

Micrometer set

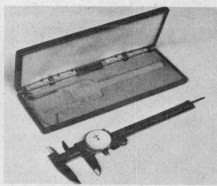

Dial caliper

Hydraulic lifter removal tool

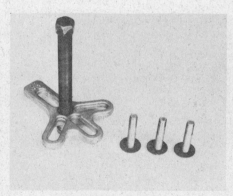

Universal-type puller

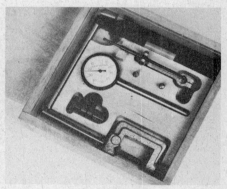

Dial indicator set

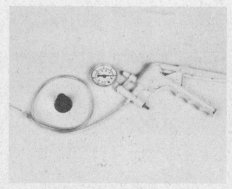

Hand-operated vacuum pump

Brake shoe spring tool

Special tools

The tools in this list include those which are not used regularly, are expensive to buy, or which need to be used in accordance with their manufacturer's instructions. Unless these tools will be used frequently, it is not very economical to purchase many of them. A consideration would be to split the cost and use between yourself and a friend or friends. In addition, most of these tools can be obtained from a tool rental shop on a temporary basis.

This list contains only those tools and instruments widely available to the public, and not those special tools produced by vehicle manufacturers for distribution to dealer service departments. Occasionally, references to the manufacturer's special tools are included in the text of this manual. Generally, an alternative method of doing the job without the special tool is offered. However, sometimes there is no alternative to their use. Where this is the case, and the tool cannot be purchased or borrowed, the work should be turned over to the dealer, a repair shop or an automotive machine shop.

Valve spring compressor
Piston ring groove cleaning tool
Piston ring compressor
Piston ring installation tool
Cylinder compression gauge
Cylinder ridge reamer
Cylinder surfacing hone
Cylinder bore gauge
Micrometer(s) and/or dial calipers
Hydraulic lifter removal tool
Balljoint separator
Universal-type puller
Impact screwdriver
Dial indicator set
Stroboscopic timing light (inductive pickup)
Hand-operated vacuum/pressure pump
Tachometer/dwell meter
Universal electrical multi-meter
Cable hoist
Brake spring removal and installation tools
Floor jack

Buying tools

For the do-it-yourselfer who is just starting to get involved in vehicle maintenance and repair, there are a couple of options available when purchasing tools. If maintenance and minor repair is the extent of the work to be done, the purchase of individual tools is satisfactory. If, on the other hand, extensive work is planned, it would be a good idea to purchase a modest tool set from one of the large retail chain stores. A set can usually be bought at a substantial savings over the individual tool prices (and they often come with a tool box). As additional tools are needed, add-on sets, individual tools and a larger tool box can be purchased to expand the tool selection. Building a tool set gradually allows the cost of the tools to be spread over a longer period of time and gives the mechanic the freedom to choose only those tools that will actually be used.

Tool stores will often be the only source of some of the special tools that are needed, but regardless of where tools are bought, try to avoid cheap ones (especially when buying screwdrivers and sockets) because they won't last very long. The expense involved in replacing cheap tools will eventually be greater than the initial cost of quality tools.

Care and maintenance of tools

Good tools are expensive, so it makes sense to treat them with respect. Keep them in a clean and usable condition and store them properly when not in use. Always wipe off any dirt, grease or metal chips before putting them away. Never leave tools lying around in the work area. Upon completion of a job, always check closely under the hood for tools that may have been left there (so they don't get lost during a test drive).

Some tools, such as screwdrivers, pliers, wrenches and sockets, can be hung on a panel mounted on the garage or workshop wall, while others should be kept in a tool box or tray. Measuring instruments, gauges, meters, etc. must be carefully stored where they cannot be damaged by weather or impact from other tools.

When tools are used with care and stored properly, they will last a very long time. Even with the best of care, tools will wear out if used frequently. When a tool is damaged or worn out, replace it; subsequent jobs will be safer and more enjoyable if you do.

Working facilities

Not to be overlooked when discussing tools is the workshop. If anything more than routine maintenance is to be carried out, some sort of suitable work area is essential.

It is understood, and appreciated, that many home mechanics do not have a good workshop or garage available, and end up removing an engine or doing major repairs outside (it is recommended that the overhaul or repair be completed under the cover of a roof).

A clean, flat workbench or table of suitable working height is an absolute necessity. The workshop should be equipped with a vise that has a jaw opening of at least four inches.

As mentioned previously, some clean, dry storage space is also required for tools, as well as the lubricants, fluids, cleaning solvents, etc. which soon become necessary.

Sometimes waste oil and fluids, drained from the engine or transmission during normal maintenance or repairs, present a disposal problem. To avoid pouring oil on the ground or into the sewage system, simply pour the used fluids into large containers, seal them with caps and deliver them to a local recycling center or disposal facility. Plastic jugs (such as old anti-freeze containers) are ideal for this purpose.

Always keep a supply of old newspapers and clean rags available. Old towels are excellent for mopping up spills. Many mechanics use rolls of paper towels for most work because they are readily available and disposable. To keep the area under the vehicle clean, a large cardboard box can be cut open and flattened to protect the garage or shop floor.

Whenever working over a painted surface (such as when leaning over a fender to service something under the hood), always cover it with an old blanket or bedspread to protect the finish. Vinyl covered pads, made especially for this purpose, are available at auto parts stores.

Jacking and towing

Jacking

The jack supplied with the vehicle should only be used for raising it for the purpose of changing a tire or placing jackstands under the frame. Under no circumstances should work be performed beneath the vehicle or the engine started while this jack is being used as the only means of support.

All vehicles are supplied with a screw-type jack for lifting the axle nearest to the tire being changed.

The vehicle should be on level ground with the wheels blocked and the transmission in Park (automatic) or Reverse (manual) and the parking brake applied. Pry off the hub cap (if equipped) using the tapered end of the lug wrench. Loosen the wheel nuts one half turn and leave them in place until the wheel is raised off the ground.

Place the jack under the axle or radius rod and use the jack handle to turn the jackscrew clockwise until the wheel is raised off the ground. Remove the wheel nuts, pull off the wheel and replace it with the spare.

With the beveled side in, replace the wheel nuts and tighten them until snug. Lower the vehicle by turning the jackscrew counter-clockwise. Remove the jack and tighten the nuts in a diagonal pattern. Replace the hubcap by placing it into position and using the heel of your hand or a rubber mallet to seat it.

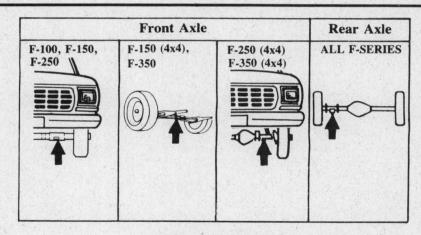

Pick-up truck jacking points

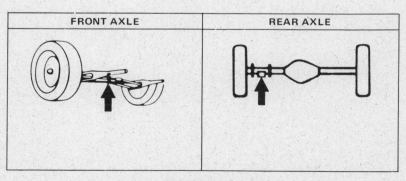

Bronco jacking points

Wheel lug nut tightening sequence

Towing

Vehicles with automatic transmissions can be towed with all four wheels on the ground with the selector in Neutral, provided speeds do not exceed 30 mph and the distance is not over 15 miles. For distances over 15 miles, the vehicle must be either towed with the rear wheels off the ground or the driveshaft must be disconnected from the axle.

4-wheel drive vehicles which are towed from the front must have the front wheels raised off the ground and the rear driveshaft removed. If towed with the front wheels on the ground, the free-running hubs (if equipped) must be unlocked or the front driveshaft removed.

Towing equipment specifically designed for this purpose should be used and should be attached to the main structural members of the vehicle and not the bumper or brackets.

Safety is a major consideration when towing and all applicable state and local laws must be obeyed. A safety chain system must be used for all towing.

While towing, the parking brake should be fully released and the transmission should be in Neutral. The steering must be unlocked (ignition switch in the Off position). Remember that power steering and power brakes will not work with the engine off.

Automotive chemicals and lubricants

A number of automotive chemicals and lubricants are available for use in vehicle maintenance and repair. They represent a wide variety of products ranging from cleaning solvents and degreasers to lubricants and protective sprays for rubber, plastic and vinyl.

Contact point/spark plug cleaner is a solvent used to clean oily film and dirt from points, grime from electrical connectors and oil deposits from spark plugs. It is oil free and leaves no residue. It can also be used to remove gum and varnish from carburetor jets and other orifices.

Carburetor cleaner is similar to contact point/spark plug cleaner but it is a stronger solvent and may leave a slight oily residue. It is not recommended for cleaning electrical components or connections.

Brake system cleaner is used to remove grease or brake fluid from brake system components (where clean surfaces are absolutely necessary and petroleum-based solvents cannot be used); it also leaves no residue.

Silicone based lubricants are used to protect rubber parts such as hoses, weatherstripping and grommets, and are used as lubricants for hinges and locks.

Multi-purpose grease is an all purpose lubricant used whenever grease is more practical than a liquid lubricant such as oil. Some multi-purpose grease is colored white and specially formulated to be more resistant to water than ordinary grease.

Bearing grease/wheel bearing grease is a heavy grease used where increased loads and friction are encountered (i.e. wheel bearings, universal joints, etc.).

High temperature wheel bearing grease is designed to withstand the extreme temperatures encountered by wheel bearings in disc brake equipped vehicles. It usually contains molybdenum disulfide, which is a 'dry' type lubricant.

Gear oil (sometimes called gear lube) is a specially designed oil used in differentials, manual transmissions and manual gearboxes, as well as other areas where high friction, high temperature lubrication is required. It is available in a number of viscosities (weights) for various applications.

Motor oil, of course, is the lubricant specially formulated for use in the engine. It normally contains a wide variety of additives to prevent corrosion and reduce foaming and wear. Motor oil comes in various weights (viscosity ratings) of from 5 to 80. The recommended weight of the oil depends on the seasonal temperature and the demands on the engine. Light oil is used in cold climates and under light load conditions; heavy oil is used in hot climates and where high loads are encountered. Multi-viscosity oils are designed to have characteristics of both light and heavy oils and are available in a number of weights from 5W-20 to 20W-50.

Oil additives range from viscosity index improvers to slick chemical treatments that purportedly reduce friction. It should be noted that most oil manufacturers caution against using additives with their oils.

Gas additives perform several functions, depending on their chemical makeup. They usually contain solvents that help dissolve gum and varnish that build up on carburetor and intake parts. They also serve to break down carbon deposits that form on the inside surfaces of the combustion chambers. Some additives contain upper cylinder lubricants for valves and piston rings.

Brake fluid is a specially formulated hydraulic fluid that can withstand the heat and pressure encountered in brake systems. Care must be taken that this fluid does not come in contact with painted surfaces or plastics. An opened container should always be resealed to prevent contamination by water or dirt.

Undercoating is a petroleum-based tar-like substance that is designed to protect metal surfaces on the under-side of a vehicle from corrosion. It also acts as a sound deadening agent by insulating the bottom of the vehicle.

Weatherstrip cement is used to bond weatherstripping around doors, windows and trunk lids. It is sometimes used to attach trim pieces as well.

Degreasers are heavy duty solvents used to remove grease and grime that accumulate on engine and chassis components. They can be sprayed or brushed on and, depending on the type, are rinsed with either water or solvent.

Solvents are used alone or in combination with degreasers to clean parts and assemblies during repair and overhaul. The home mechanic should use only solvents that are non-flammable and that do not produce irritating fumes.

Gasket sealing compounds may be used in conjunction with gaskets, to improve their sealing capabilities, or alone, to seal metal-to-metal joints. Many gasket sealers can withstand extreme heat, some are impervious to gasoline and lubricants, while others are capable of filling and sealing large cavities. Depending on the intended use, gasket sealers either dry hard or stay relatively soft and pliable. They are usually applied by hand, with a brush, or are sprayed on the gasket sealing surfaces.

Thread cement is an adhesive locking compound that prevents threaded fasteners from loosening because of vibration. It is available in a variety of types for different applications.

Moisture dispersants are usually sprays that can be used to dry out electrical components such as the distributor, fuse block and wiring connectors. Some types can also be used as treatment for rubber and as a lubricant for hinges, cables and locks.

Waxes and polishes are used to help protect painted and plated surfaces from the weather. Different types of paint may require the use of different types of wax or polish. Some polishes utilize a chemical or abrasive cleaner to help remove the top layer of oxidized (dull) paint in older vehicles. In recent years, many non-wax polishes (that contain a wide variety of chemicals such as polymers and silicones) have been introduced. These non-wax polishes are usually easier to apply and last longer than conventional waxes and polishes.

Safety first!

Regardless of how enthusiastic you may be about getting on with the job at hand, take the time to ensure that your safety is not jeopardized. A moment's lack of attention can result in an accident, as can failure to observe certain simple safety precautions. The possibility of an accident will always exist, and the following points should not be considered a comprehensive list of all dangers. Rather, they are intended to make you aware of the risks and to encourage a safety conscious approach to all work you carry out on your vehicle.

Essential DOs and DON'Ts

DON'T rely on a jack when working under the vehicle. Always use approved jackstands to support the weight of the vehicle and place them under the recommended lift or support points.

DON'T attempt to loosen extremely tight fasteners (i.e. wheel lug nuts) while the vehicle is on a jack — it may fall.

DON'T start the engine without first making sure that the transmission is in Neutral (or Park where applicable) and the parking brake is set.

DON'T remove the radiator cap from a hot cooling system — let it cool or cover it with a cloth and release the pressure gradually.

DON'T attempt to drain the engine oil until you are sure it has cooled to the point that it will not burn you.

DON'T touch any part of the engine or exhaust system until it has cooled sufficiently to avoid burns.

DON'T siphon toxic liquids such as gasoline, antifreeze and brake fluid by mouth, or allow them to remain on your skin.

DON'T inhale brake lining dust — it is potentially hazardous (see Asbestos below)

DON'T allow spilled oil or grease to remain on the floor — wipe it up before someone slips on it.

DON'T use loose fitting wrenches or other tools which may slip and cause injury.

DON'T push on wrenches when loosening or tightening nuts or bolts. Always try to pull the wrench toward you. If the situation calls for pushing the wrench away, push with an open hand to avoid scraped knuckles if the wrench should slip.

DON'T attempt to lift a heavy component alone — get someone to help you.

DON'T rush or take unsafe shortcuts to finish a job.

DON'T allow children or animals in or around the vehicle while you are working on it.

DO wear eye protection when using power tools such as a drill, sander, bench grinder, etc. and when working under a vehicle.

DO keep loose clothing and long hair well out of the way of moving parts.

DO make sure that any hoist used has a safe working load rating adequate for the job.

DO get someone to check on you periodically when working alone on a vehicle.

DO carry out work in a logical sequence and make sure that everything is correctly assembled and tightened.

DO keep chemicals and fluids tightly capped and out of the reach of children and pets.

DO remember that your vehicle's safety affects that of yourself and others. If in doubt on any point, get professional advice.

Asbestos

Certain friction, insulating, sealing, and other products — such as brake linings, brake bands, clutch linings, torque converters, gaskets, etc. — contain asbestos. *Extreme care must be taken to avoid inhalation of dust from such products since it is hazardous to health.* If in doubt, assume that they *do* contain asbestos.

Fire

Remember at all times that gasoline is highly flammable. Never smoke or have any kind of open flame around when working on a vehicle. But the risk does not end there. A spark caused by an electrical short circuit, by two metal surfaces contacting each other, or even by static electricity built up in your body under certain conditions, can ignite gasoline vapors, which in a confined space are highly explosive. Do not, under any circumstances, use gasoline for cleaning parts. Use an approved safety solvent.

Always disconnect the battery ground (–) cable *at the battery* before working on any part of the fuel system or electrical system. Never risk spilling fuel on a hot engine or exhaust component.

It is strongly recommended that a fire extinguisher suitable for use on fuel and electrical fires be kept handy in the garage or workshop at all times. Never try to extinguish a fuel or electrical fire with water.

Torch (flashlight in the US)

Any reference to a "torch" appearing in this manual should always be taken to mean a hand-held, battery-operated electric light or flashlight. It DOES NOT mean a welding or propane torch or blowtorch.

Fumes

Certain fumes are highly toxic and can quickly cause unconsciousness and even death if inhaled to any extent. Gasoline vapor falls into this category, as do the vapors from some cleaning solvents. Any draining or pouring of such volatile fluids should be done in a well ventilated area.

When using cleaning fluids and solvents, read the instructions on the container carefully. Never use materials from unmarked containers.

Never run the engine in an enclosed space, such as a garage. Exhaust fumes contain carbon monoxide, which is extremely poisonous. If you need to run the engine, always do so in the open air, or at least have the rear of the vehicle outside the work area.

If you are fortunate enough to have the use of an inspection pit, never drain or pour gasoline and never run the engine while the vehicle is over the pit. The fumes, being heavier than air, will concentrate in the pit with possibly lethal results.

The battery

Never create a spark or allow a bare light bulb near a battery. They normally give off a certain amount of hydrogen gas, which is highly explosive.

Always disconnect the battery ground (–) cable *at the battery* before working on the fuel or electrical systems.

If possible, loosen the filler caps or cover when charging the battery from an external source (this does not apply to sealed or maintenance-free batteries). Do not charge at an excessive rate or the battery may burst.

Take care when adding water to a non maintenance-free battery and when carrying a battery. The electrolyte, even when diluted, is very corrosive and should not be allowed to contact clothing or skin.

Always wear eye protection when cleaning the battery to prevent the caustic deposits from entering your eyes.

Mains electricity (household current in the US)

When using an electric power tool, inspection light, etc., which operates on household current, always make sure that the tool is correctly connected to its plug and that, where necessary, it is properly grounded. Do not use such items in damp conditions and, again, do not create a spark or apply excessive heat in the vicinity of fuel or fuel vapor.

Secondary ignition system voltage

A severe electric shock can result from touching certain parts of the ignition system (such as the spark plug wires) when the engine is running or being cranked, particularly if components are damp or the insulation is defective. In the case of an electronic ignition system, the secondary system voltage is much higher and could prove fatal.

Troubleshooting

Contents

Engine

1 Engine will not rotate when attempting to start

1 Battery terminal connection loose or corroded. Check the cable terminals at the battery; tighten or clean corrosion as necessary.
2 Battery discharged or faulty. If the cable connectors are clean and tight on the battery posts, turn the key to the On position and switch on the headlights and/or windshield wipers. If these fail to function, the battery is discharged.
3 Automatic transmission not fully engaged in Park or manual transmission clutch not fully depressed.
4 Broken, loose or disconnected wiring in the starting circuit. Inspect all wiring and connectors at the battery, starter solenoid (at lower right side of engine) and ignition switch (on steering column).
5 Starter motor pinion jammed on flywheel ring gear. If manual transmission, place gearshift in gear and rock the vehicle to manually turn the engine. Remove starter (Chapter 5) and inspect pinion and flywheel (Chapter 5) at earliest convenience.
6 Starter solenoid faulty (Chapter 5).
7 Starter motor faulty (Chapter 5).
8 Ignition switch (Chapter 12).

2 Engine rotates but will not start

1 Fuel tank empty.
2 Battery discharged (engine rotates slowly). Check the operation of electrical components as described in previous Section (see Chapter 1).
3 Battery terminal connections loose or corroded. See previous Section.
4 Carburetor flooded and/or fuel level in carburetor incorrect. This will usually be accompanied by a strong fuel odor from under the hood. Wait a few minutes, depress the accelerator pedal all the way to the floor and attempt to start the engine.
5 Choke control inoperative (Chapter 4).
6 Fuel not reaching carburetor. With ignition switch in Off position, open hood, remove the top plate of air cleaner assembly and observe the top of the carburetor (manually move choke plate back if necessary). Have an assistant depress accelerator pedal fully and check that fuel spurts into carburetor. If not, check fuel filter (Chapters 1 and 4), fuel lines and fuel pump (Chapter 4).
7 Excessive moisture on, or damage to, ignition components (Chapter 5).
8 Worn, faulty or incorrectly adjusted spark plugs (Chapter 1).
9 Broken, loose or disconnected wiring in the starting circuit (see previous Section).
10 Distributor loose, thus changing ignition timing. Turn the distributor as necessary to start the engine, then set ignition timing as soon as possible (Chapter 1).
11 Ignition condenser faulty (Chapter 1).
12 Broken, loose or disconnected wires at the ignition coil, or faulty coil (Chapter 5).

3 Starter motor operates without rotating engine

1 Starter pinion sticking. Remove the starter (Chapter 5) and inspect.
2 Starter pinion or engine flywheel teeth worn or broken. Remove the inspection cover at the rear of the engine and inspect.

4 Engine hard to start when cold

1 Battery discharged or low. Check as described in Section 1.
2 Choke control inoperative or out of adjustment (Chapter 1).
3 Carburetor flooded (see Section 2).
4 Fuel supply not reaching the carburetor (see Section 4).
5 Carburetor worn and in need of overhauling (Chapter 4).

5 Engine hard to start when hot

1 Choke sticking in the closed position (Chapter 1).
2 Carburetor flooded (see Section 2).

3 Air filter in need of replacement (Chapter 1).
4 Fuel not reaching the carburetor (see Section 4).

6 Starter motor noisy or excessively rough in engagement

1 Pinion or flywheel gear teeth worn or broken. Remove the inspection cover at the rear of the engine and inspect.
2 Starter motor retaining bolts loose or missing.

7 Engine starts but stops immediately

1 Loose or faulty electrical connections at distributor, coil or alternator.
2 Insufficient fuel reaching the carburetor. Disconnect the fuel line at the carburettor and remove the filter (Chapter 1). Place a container under the disconnected fuel line. Observe the flow of fuel from the line. If little or none at all, check for blockage in the lines and/or replace the fuel pump (Chapter 4).
3 Vacuum leak at the gasket surfaces or the intake manifold and/or carburetor. Check that all mounting bolts (nuts) are tightened to specifications and all vacuum hoses connected to the carburetor and manifold are positioned properly and are in good condition.

8 Engine 'lopes' while idling or idles erratically

1 Vacuum leakage. Check mounting bolts (nuts) at the carburetor and intake manifold for tightness. Check that all vacuum hoses are connected and are in good condition. Use a doctor's stethoscope or a length of fuel line hose held against your ear to listen for vacuum leaks while the engine is running. A hissing sound will be heard. A soapy water solution will also detect leaks. Check the carburetor and intake manifold gasket surfaces.
2 Leaking EGR valve or plugged PCV valve (see Chapter 6).
3 Air cleaner clogged and in need of replacement (Chapter 1).
4 Fuel pump not delivering sufficient fuel to the carburetor (see Section 7).
5 Carburetor out of adjustment (Chapter 4).
6 Leaking head gasket. If this is suspected, take the vehicle to a repair shop or dealer where this can be pressure checked without the need to remove the heads.
7 Timing chain or gears worn and in need of replacement (Chapter 2).
8 Camshaft lobes worn, necessitating the removal of the camshaft for inspection (Chapter 2).

9 Engine misses at idle speed

1 Spark plugs faulty or not gapped properly (Chapter 1).
2 Faulty spark plug wires (Chapter 1).
3 Carburetor choke not operating properly (Chapter 1).
4 Sticking or faulty emissions systems.
5 Clogged fuel filter and/or foreign matter in fuel. Remove the fuel filter (Chapter 1) and inspect.
6 Vacuum leaks at carburetor, intake manifold or at hose connections. Check as described in Section 8.
7 Incorrect speed (Chapter 1) or idle mixture (Chapter 1).
8 Incorrect ignition timing (Chapter 1).
9 Uneven or low cylinder compression. Remove plugs and use compression tester as per manufacturer's instructions.

10 Engine misses throughout driving speed range

1 Carburetor fuel filter clogged and/or impurities in the fuel system (Chapter 1). Also check fuel output at the carburetor (see Section 7).
2 Faulty or incorrectly gapped spark plugs (Chapter 1).
3 Incorrectly set ignition timing (Chapter 1).
4 Check for a cracked distributor cap, disconnected distributor wires or damage to the distributor components (Chapter 5).
5 Leaking spark plug wires (Chapter 1).
6 Emission system components faulty (Chapter 6).

7   Low or uneven cylinder compression pressures. Remove spark plugs and test compression with gauge (Chapter 1).
8   Weak or faulty ignition system (see Chapter 5).
9   Vacuum leaks at carburetor, intake manifold or vacuum hoses (see Section 8).

11 Engine stalls

1   Carburetor idle speed incorrectly set (Chapter 1).
2   Carburetor fuel filter clogged and/or water and impurities in the fuel system (Chapter 1).
3   Choke improperly adjusted or sticking (Chapter 1).
4   Distributor components damp, points out of adjustment or damage to distributor cap, rotor etc. (Chapter 5).
5   Emission system components faulty.
6   Faulty or incorrectly gapped spark plugs (Chapter 1). Also check spark plug wires (Chapter 1).
7   Vacuum leak at the carburetor, intake manifold or vacuum hoses. Check as described in Section 8.
8   Valve lash incorrectly set (Chapter 2).

12 Engine lacks power

1   Incorrect ignition timing (Chapter 1).
2   Excessive play in distributor shaft. At the same time check for worn or maladjusted contact rotor, faulty distributor cap, wires, etc. (Chapter 5).
3   Faulty or incorrectly gapped spark plugs (Chapter 1).
4   Carburetor not adjusted properly or excessively worn (Chapter 4).
5   Weak coil or condensor (Chapter 5).
6   Faulty system coil (Chapter 5).
7   Brakes binding (Chapter 1).
8   Automatic transmission fluid level incorrect, causing slippage (Chapter 1).
9   Manual transmission clutch slipping (Chapter 8).
10 Fuel filter clogged and/or impurities in the fuel system (Chapter 1).
11 Emission control system not functioning properly (Chapter 6).
12 Use of sub-standard fuel. Fill tank with proper octane fuel.
13 Low or uneven cylinder compression pressures. Test with compression tester, which will detect leaking valves and/or blown head gasket (Chapter 1).

13 Engine backfires

1   Emission system not functioning properly (Chapter 6).
2   Ignition timing incorrect (Chapter 1).
3   Carburetor in need of adjustment or worn excessively (Chapter 4).
4   Vacuum leak at carburetor, intake manifold or vacuum hoses. Check as described in Section 8.
5   Valve lash incorrectly set, and/or valves sticking (Chapter 2).

14 Pinging or knocking engine sounds on hard acceleration or uphill

1   Incorrect grade of fuel. Fill tank with fuel of the proper octane rating.
2   Ignition timing incorrect (Chapter 1).
3   Carburetor in need of adjustment (Chapter 4).
4   Improper spark plugs. Check plug type with that specified on tune-up decal located inside engine compartment. Also check plugs and wires for damage (Chapter 1).
5   Worn or damaged distributor components (Chapter 5).
6   Faulty emission system (Chapter 6).
7   Vacuum leak. (Check as described in Section 8).

15 Engine 'diesels' (continues to run) after switching off

1   Idle speed too fast (Chapter 1).
2   Electrical solenoid at side of carburetor not functioning properly (not all models, see Chapter 4).

3   Ignition timing incorrectly adjusted (Chapter 1).
4   Air cleaner valve not operating properly (Chapter 4).
5   Excessive engine operating temperatures. Probable causes of this are: malfunctioning thermostat, clogged radiator, faulty water pump (see Chapter 3).

Engine electrical

16 Battery will not hold a charge

1   Alternator drivebelt defective or not adjusted properly (Chapter 1).
2   Electrolyte level too low or too weak (Chapter 1).
3   Battery terminals loose or corroded (Chapter 1).
4   Alternator not charging properly (Chapter 5).
5   Loose, broken or faulty wiring in the charging circuit (Chapter 10).
6   Short in vehicle circuitry causing a continual drain on battery.
7   Battery defect internally.

17 Ignition light fails to go out

1   Fault in alternator or charging circuit (Chapter 5).
2   Alternator drivebelt defective or not properly adjusted (Chapter 1)

18 Ignition light fails to come on when key is turned

1   Ignition light bulb faulty (Chapter 10).
2   Alternator faulty (Chapter 5).
3   Fault in the printed circuit, dash wiring or bulb holder (Chapter 10).

Engine fuel system

19 Excessive fuel consumption

1   Dirty or choked air filter element (Chapter 1).
2   Incorrectly set ignition timing (Chapter 1).
3   Choke sticking or improperly adjusted (Chapter 1).
4   Emission system not functioning properly (not all vehicles, see Chapter 6).
5   Carburetor idle speed and/or mixture not adjusted properly (Chapter 1).
6   Carburetor internal parts excessively worn or damaged (Chapter 4).
7   Low tire pressure or incorrect tire size (Chapter 1).

20 Fuel leakage and/or fuel odor

1   Leak in a fuel feed or vent line (Chapter 4).
2   Tank overfilled. Fill only to automatic shut-off.
3   Emission system filter in need of replacement (Chapter 6).
4   Vapor leaks from system lines (Chapter 4).
5   Carburetor internal parts excessively worn or out of adjustment (Chapter 4).

Engine cooling system

21 Overheating

1   Insufficient coolant in system (Chapter 1).
2   Fan belt defective or not adjusted properly (Chapter 1).
3   Radiator core blocked or radiator grille dirty and restricted (Chapter 3).
4   Thermostat faulty (Chapter 3).
5   Fan blades broken or cracked (Chapter 3).
6   Radiator cap not maintaining proper pressure. Have cap pressure tested by gas station or repair shop.
7   Ignition timing incorrect (Chapter 1).

22 Overcooling

1 Thermostat faulty (Chapter 3).
2 Inaccurate temperature gauge (Chapter 10).

23 External water leakage

1 Deteriorated or damaged hoses. Loose clamps at hose connections (Chapter 3).
2 Water pump seals defective. If this is the case, water will drip from the 'weep' hole in the water pump body (Chapter 3).
3 Leakage from radiator core or header tank. This will require the radiator to be professionally repaired (see Chapter 3 for removal procedures).
4 Engine drain plugs or water jacket freeze plugs leaking (see Chapters 2 and 3).

24 Internal water leakage

Note: *Internal coolant leaks can usually be detected by examining the oil. Check the dipstick and inside of valve cover for water deposits and an oil consistency like that of a milkshake.*
1 Faulty cylinder head gasket. Have the system pressure-tested professionally or remove the cylinder heads (Chapter 1) and inspect.
2 Cracked cylinder bore or cylinder head. Dismantle engine and inspect (Chapter 2).
3 Intake manifold gasket faulty.

25 Water loss

1 Overfilling system (Chapter 3).
2 Coolant boiling away due to overheating (see causes in Section 15).
3 Internal or external leakage (see Sections 22 and 33).
4 Faulty radiator cap. Have the cap pressure tested.

26 Poor coolant circulation

1 Inoperative water pump. A quick test is to pinch the top radiator hose closed with your hand while the engine is idling, then let it loose. You should feel the surge of water if the pump is working properly (Chapter 3).
2 Restriction in cooling system. Drain, flush and refill the system (Chapter 3). If it appears necessary, remove the radiator (Chapter 3) and have it reverse-flushed or professionally cleaned.
3 Fan drivebelt defective or not adjusted properly (Chapter 1).
4 Thermostat sticking (Chapter 3).

Clutch

27 Fails to release (pedal pressed to the floor – shift lever does not move freely in and out of reverse

1 Improper linkage adjustment (Chapter 8).
2 Clutch fork off ball stud. Look under the car, on the left side of transmission.
3 Clutch disc warped, bent or excessively damaged (Chapter 8).

28 Clutch slips (engine speed increases with no increase in road speed)

1 Linkage in need of adjustment (Chapter 8).
2 Clutch disc oil soaked or facing worn. Remove disc (Chapter 8) and inspect.
3 Clutch disc not seated in. It may take 30 or 40 normal starts for a new disc to seat.

29 Grabbing (juddering) on take-up

1 Oil on clutch disc facings. Remove disc (Chapter 8) and inspect. Correct any leakage source.
2 Worn or loose engine or transmission mounts. These units move slightly when clutch is released. Inspect mounts and bolts.
3 Worn splines on clutch gear. Remove clutch components (Chapter 8) and inspect.
4 Warped pressure plate or flywheel. Remove clutch components and inspect.

30 Squeal or rumble with clutch fully engaged (pedal released)

1 Improper adjustment; no lash (Chapter 8).
2 Release bearing binding on transmission bearing retainer. Remove clutch components (Chapter 8) and check bearing. Remove any burrs or nicks, clean and relubricate before reinstallation.
3 Weak linkage return spring. Replace the spring.

31 Squeal or rumble with clutch fully disengaged (pedal depressed)

1 Worn, faulty or broken release bearing (Chapter 8).
2 Worn or broken pressure plate springs (or diaphragm fingers) (Chapter 8).

32 Clutch pedal stays on floor when disengaged

1 Bind in leakage or release bearing. Inspect linkage or remove clutch components as necessary.
2 Linkage springs being over-traveled. Adjust linkage for proper lash. Make sure proper pedal stop (bumper) is installed.

Manual transmission
Note: *All the following contained within Chapter 7 unless noted.*

33 Noisy in Neutral with engine running

1 Input shaft bearing worn.
2 Damaged main drive gear bearing.
3 Worn countergear bearings.
4 Worn or damaged countergear anti-lash plate.

34 Noisy in all gears

1 Any of the above causes, and/or:
2 Insufficient lubricant (see checking procedures in Chapter 1).

35 Noisy in one particular gear

1 Worn, damaged or chipped gear teeth for that particular gear.
2 Worn or damaged synchronizer for that particular gear.

36 Slips out of high gear

1 Transmission loose on clutch housing.
2 Shift rods interfering with engine mounts or clutch lever.
3 Shift rods not working freely.
4 Damaged mainshaft pilot bearing.
5 Dirt between transmission case and clutch housing, or misalignment of transmission.
6 Worn or improperly adjusted linkage.

37 Difficulty in engaging gears

1   Clutch not releasing fully (see clutch adjustment, Chapter 1).
2   Loose, damaged or maladjusted shift linkage. Make a thorough inspection, replacing parts as necessary. Adjust as described in Chapter 1.

38 Fluid leakage

1   Excessive amount of lubricant in transmission (see Chapter 1) for correct checking procedures. Drain lubricant as required).
2   Side cover loose or gasket damaged.
3   Rear oil seal or speedometer oil seal in need of replacement (Section 6).

Automatic transmission

Note: *Due to the complexity of the automatic transmission, it is difficult for the home mechanic to properly diagnose and service this component. For problems other than the following, the vehicle should be taken to a reputable mechanic.*

39 Fluid leakage

1   Automatic transmission fluid is a deep red color, and fluid leaks should not be confused with engine oil which can easily be blown by air flow to the transmission.
2   To pinpoint a leak, first remove all built-up dirt and grime from around the transmission. Degreasing agents and/or steam cleaning will achieve this. With the underside clean, drive the vehicle at low speeds so that air flow will not blow the leak far from its source. Raise the vehicle and determine where the leak is coming from. Common areas of leakage are:

   a)   Fluid pan: tighten mounting bolts and/or replace pan gasket as necessary (see Chapter 7)
   b)   Rear extension: tighten bolts and/or replace oil seal as necessary (Chapter 7)
   c)   Filler pipe: replace the rubber seal where pipe enters transmission case
   d)   Transmission oil lines: tighten connectors where lines enter transmission case and/or replace lines
   e)   Vent pipe: transmission over-filled and/or water in fluid (see checking procedures, Chapter 7)
   f)   Speedometer connector: replace the O-ring where speedometer cable enters transmission case

40 General shift mechanism problems

1   Chapter 7 deals with checking and adjusting the shift linkage on automatic transmissions. Common problems which may be attributed to poorly adjusted linkage are:

   a)   Engine starting in gears other than Park or Neutral
   b)   Indicator on quandrant pointing to a gear other than the one actually being used
   c)   Vehicle will not hold firm when in Park position
Refer to Chapter 7 to adjust the manual linkage.

41 Transmission will not downshift with accelerator pedal pressed to the floor

1   Chapter 7 deals with adjusting the downshift cable or downshift switch to enable the transmission to downshift properly.

42 Engine will start in gears other than Park or Neutral

1   Chapter 7 deals with adjusting the various linkages used with automatic transmissions.

43 Transmission slips, shifts rough, is noisy or has no drive in forward or reverse gears

1   There are many probable causes for the above problems, but the home mechanic should concern himself only with one possibility: fluid level.
2   Before taking the vehicle to a specialist, check the level of the fluid and condition of the fluid as described in Chapter 1. Correct fluid level as necessary or change the fluid and filter if needed. If problem persists, have a professional diagnose the probable cause.

Driveshaft

44 Leakage of fluid at front of driveshaft

1   Defective transmission rear oil seal. See Chapter 7 for replacing procedures. While this is done, check the splined yoke for burrs or a rough condition which may be damaging the seal. If found, these can be dressed wth crocus cloth or a fine dressing stone.

45 Knock or clunk when transmission is under initial load (just after transmission is put into gear)

1   Loose or disconnected rear suspension components. Check all mounting bolts and bushings (Chapter 11).
2   Loose driveshaft bolts. Inspect all bolts and nuts and tighten to torque specifications (Chapter 8).
3   Worn or damaged universal joint bearings. Test for wear (Chapter 8).

46 Metallic grating sound consistent with road speed

1   Pronounced wear in the universal joint bearings. Test for wear (Chapter 8).

47 Vibration

Note: *Before it can be assumed that the driveshaft is at fault, make sure the tires are perfectly balanced and perform the following test.*
1   Install a tachometer inside the vehicle to monitor engine speed as the vehicle is driven. Drive the vehicle and note the engine speed at which the vibration (roughness) is most pronounced. Now shift the transmission to a different gear and bring the engine speed to the same point.
2   If the vibration occurs at the same engine speed (rpm) regardless of which gear the transmission is in, the driveshaft is NOT at fault since the driveshaft speed varies.
3   If the vibration decreases or is eliminated when the transmission is in a different gear at the same engine speed, refer to the following probable causes.
4   Bent or dented driveshaft. Inspect and replace as necessary (Chapter 8).
5   Undercoating or built-up dirt, etc, on the driveshaft. Clean the shaft throroughly and test.
6   Worn universal bearings. Remove and inspect (Chapter 8).
7   Driveshaft and/or companion flange out of balance. Check for missing weights on the shaft. Remove driveshaft (Chapter 8) and reinstall 180° from original position. Retest. Have driveshaft professionally balanced if problem persists.

Rear axle

48 Noise – same when in drive as when vehicle is coasting

1   Road noise. No corrective procedures available.
2   Tire noise. Inspect tires and tire pressures (Chapter 11).
3   Front wheel bearings loose, worn or damaged (Chapter 11).

49 Vibration

1   See probable causes under *Driveshaft*. Proceed under the guide-

lines listed for the driveshaft. If the problem persists, check the rear wheel bearings by raising the rear of the car and spinning the wheels by hand. Listen for evidence of rough (noisy) bearings. Remove and inspect (Chapter 8).

50 Oil leakage

1   Pinion oil seal damaged (Chapter 8).
2   Axle shaft oil seals damaged (Chapter 8).
3   Differential inspection cover leaking. Tighten mounting bolts or replace the gasket as required (Chapter 8).

Brakes

Note: *Before assuming a brake problem exists, check; that the tires are in good condition and are inflated properly (see Chapter 1); the front end alignment is correct; and that the vehicle is not loaded with weight in an unequal manner.*

51 Vehicle pulls to one side under braking

1   Defective, damaged or oil contaminated disc pad on one side. Inspect as described in Chapter 9.
2   Excessive wear of brake pad material or disc on one side. Inspect and correct as necessary.
3   Loose or disconnected front suspension components. Inspect and tighten all bolts to specifications (Chapter 11).
4   Defective caliper assembly. Remove caliper and inspect for stuck piston or damage (Chapter 8).

52 Noise (high-pitched squeak without brake applied)

1   Front brake pads worn out. This noise comes from the wear sensor rubbing against the disc (does not apply to all vehicles). Replace pads with new ones immediately (Chapter 9).

53 Excessive brake pedal travel

1   Partial brake system failure. Inspect entire system (Chapter 9) and correct as required.
2   Insufficient fluid in master cylinder. Check (Chapter 9) and add fluid and bleed system if necessary.
3   Rear brakes not adjusting properly. Make a series of starts and stops while the vehicle is in Reverse. If this does not correct the situation remove drums and inspect self-adjusters (Chapter 9).

54 Brake pedal feels spongy when depressed

1   Air in hydraulic lines. Bleed the brake system (Chapter 9).
2   Faulty flexible hoses. Inspect all system hoses and lines. Replace parts as necessary.
3   Master cylinder mountings insecure. Inspect master cylinder (nuts) and torque-tighten to specifications.
4   Master cylinder faulty (Chapter 9).

55 Excessive effort required to stop vehicle

1   Power brake servo not operating properly (Chapter 9).
2   Excessively worn linings or pads. Inspect and replace if necessary (Chapter 9).
3   One or more caliper pistons (front wheels) or wheel cylinders (rear wheels) seized or sticking. Inspect and rebuild as required (Chapter 9).
4   Brake linings or pads contaminated with oil or grease. Inspect and replace as required (Chapter 9).
5   New pads or linings fitted and not yet 'bedded in'. It will take awhile for the new material to seat against the drum (or rotor).

56 Pedal travels to floor with little resistance

1   Little or no fluid in the master cylinder reservoir caused by; leaking wheel cylinder(s); leaking caliper piston(s); loose, damaged or disconnected brake lines. Inspect entire system and correct as necessary.

57 Brake pedal pulsates during brake application

1   Wheel bearings not adjusted properly or in need of replacement (Chapter 11).
2   Caliper not sliding properly due to improper installation or obstructions. Remove and inspect (Chapter 9).
3   Rotor not within specifications. Remove the rotor (Chapter 9) and check for excessive lateral run-out and parallelism. Have the rotor professionally machined or replace it with a new one.

Suspension and steering

58 Vehicle pulls to one side

1   Tire pressures uneven (Chapter 11).
2   Defective tire (Chapter 11).
3   Excessive wear in suspension or steering components (Chapter 11).
4   Front end in need of alignment. Take vehicle to a qualified specialist.
5   Front brakes dragging. Inspect braking system as described in Chapter 9.

59 Shimmy, shake or vibration

1   Tire or wheel out of balance or out of round. Have professionally balanced.
2   Loose, worn or out of adjustment wheel bearings (Chapter 11).
3   Shock absorbers and/or suspension components worn or damaged (Chapter 11).

60 Excessive pitching and/or rolling around corners or during braking

1   Defective shock absorbers. Replace as a set (Chapter 11).
2   Broken or weak springs and/or suspension components. Inspect as described in Chapter 11.

61 Excessively stiff steering

1   Lack of lubricant in steering box (manual) or power steering fluid reservoir (Chapter 11).
2   Incorrect tire pressures (Chapter 11).
3   Lack of lubrication at steering joints (Chapter 11).
4   Front end out of alignment.
5   See also Section 63 *Lack of power assistance.*

62 Excessive play in steering

1   Loose wheel bearings (Chapter 11).
2   Excessive wear in suspension or steering components (Chapter 11).
3   Steering gear out of adjustment (Chapter 11).

63 Lack of power assistance

1   Steering pump drivebelt faulty or not adjusted properly (Chapter 11).
2   Fluid level low (Chapter 11).

3   Hoses or pipes restricting the flow. Inspect and replace parts as necessary.
4   Air in power steering system. Bleed system (Chapter 11).

64 Excessive tire wear (not specific to one area)

1   Incorrect tire pressures (Chapter 11).
2   Tires out of balance. Have professionally balanced.
3   Wheels damaged. Inspect and replace as necessary.
4   Suspension or steering components excessively worn (Chapter 11).

65 Excessive tire wear on outside edge

1   Inflation pressures not correct (Chapter 11).
2   Excessive speed on turns.

3   Front end alignment incorrect (excessive toe-in). Have professionally aligned.
4   Suspension arm bent or twisted.

66 Excessive tire wear on inside edge

1   Inflation pressures incorrect (Chapter 11).
2   Front end alignment incorrect (toe-out). Have professionally aligned.
3   Loose or damaged steering components (Chapter 11).

67 Tire tread worn in one place

1   Tires out of balance. Balance tires professionally.
2   Damaged or buckled wheel. Inspect and replace if necessary.
3   Defective tire.

Chapter 1 Tune-up and routine maintenance

Contents

1

Specifications

Note: *Additional specifications and torque recommendations can be found in each individual Chapter.*

Recommended lubricants and fluids

Engine oil type .... SAE grade SE or better

Automatic transmission fluid type
    C6 transmission .... Dexron II Series D (Ford no. ESP-M2C138-CJ)
    All others .... Type F (Ford no. ESW-M2C33-F)
Manual transmission and transfer case lubricant .... SAE 140W gear oil (Ford no. ESO-M2C83-C)
Engine coolant .... Ethylene-glycol based (Ford no. ESE-M97B18-C)
Differential lubricant
    Dana and Ford (non-locking) .... SAE 90W gear oil (Ford no. ESW-M2C105-A)
    Dana (limited slip) .... Add friction modifier EST-M2C118-A to the above fluid during refill (4 oz. to the rear and 2 oz. to the front – if so equipped)
    Ford (Traction-Lok) .... SAE 90W gear oil (Ford no. ESW-MZC 119-A)

Chassis lubrication, clutch linkage, parking brake
linkage, steering column U-joints, driveshaft U-joints
front and rear wheel bearings (except rear F-100 and F150)
and transmission linkage .... Lithium based grease NLGI no. 2 (Ford no. ESA-M1C75B)
Manual steering gear and front free-running hubs (4 X 4) ...... Ford no. ESW-M1C87-A steering gear lubricant or equivalent
Steering gear (F-150 4 X 4) manual steering .... SAE 90W EP gear oil (Ford no. ESW-MZC105-A)
Steering linkage, upper and lower king pin bearing
(F-250 4 X 4 4500 lb front axle) .... Molybdenum disulphide grease NLGI no. 2 (Ford no. ESA-M1C92-A Type II)
Brake and clutch master cylinder .... DOT 3 heavy duty brake fluid (Ford no. ESA-M6C25-A)
Power steering rservoir .... Type F automatic transmission fluid (Ford no. ESW-MZC33-F)

Engine oil capacity (with new filter)
F100, F150, F250 and F350 (1973 and 1974)

	US qts
240 cu in six cylinder	5.0
300 cu in six cylinder	6.0
302 cu in V8	6.0
360 cu in V8	6.0
390 cu in V8	6.0

460 cu in V8	7.0
1975 thru 1979 (all)	6.0
Bronco (1973 and 1974)	
six cylinder	7.0
1975 thru 1979 (all)	5.0

Coolant capacity – pick-ups

	US qts
1973 thru 1975	
240 cu in six cylinder	
F100 2-wheel drive, manual	14.1
F100 2 and 4-wheel drive, manual and automatic	14.4
F100 2-wheel drive, automatic with extra-cooling radiator	16.3
F100 4-wheel drive manual	16.7
300 cu in six cylinder F250 and F350 manual and automatic	14.4
F250 manual and automatic with extra-cooling radiator	16.3
F250 and F350 manual and automatic with extra-cooling	
radiator	16.7
F350 with single rear wheels and extra-cooling radiator	13.3
F350 manual and automatic with extra-cooling radiator	18.3
302 cu in V8 engine	
F100 4-wheel drive automatic	14.8
F100 4-wheel drive with manual and extra-cooling radiator	17.1
F100 4-wheel drive manual and automatic with air conditioning .	17.5
360 cu in V8 engine	
F100, F150 and F250 manual and automatic	19.6
F100, F150 and F250 with extra-cooling radiator	21.9
F100, F150 and F250 with air conditioning	22.3
390 cu in V8 engine	
F100, F150 and F250 2-wheel drive	19.6
F100, F150, F250 and F350	22.3
F100, F150, F250 and F350 with air conditioning and	
super-cooling options	23.9
460 cu in V8 engine	
F100, F150, F250 and F350	21.0
F100, F150, F250 and F350 with extra-cooling radiator	22.6
F100, F150, F250 and F350 with air conditioning	23.9
1976	**US qts**
300 cu in six cylinder engine	
F100, F150 and F250	
2-wheel drive standard cooling	12.5
2-wheel drive extra-cooling	14.5
4-wheel drive standard cooling	14.5
4-wheel drive extra-cooling	16.5
F350 (all)	14.5
302 cu in V8 engine	
Manual transmission	15.0
Automatic transmission	17.5
360 cu in V8 engine	
F100, F150 and F350	
Standard cooling	22.5
Air conditioning and super-cooling	24.0
Heavy duty trailer towing package	24.5
390 cu in V8 engine	
F100, F150, F250 and F350	
Standard cooling	22.5
Air conditioning	24.0
Heavy duty trailer towing package	24.5
460 cu in engine	
F150, F250 and F350	22.5
1977	**US qts**
300 cu in six cylinder engine	
Standard cooling (all models)	14.0
Air conditioned models	17.0
302 cu in V8 engine	
Manual transmission	22.0
Super-cooling option	24.0
351 cu in V8 engine	
F150 and F250	
Standard cooling	20.0
Air conditioning and extra-cooling	22.0
Super-cooling option	24.0
400 cu in V8 engine	
F100, F150, F250 and F350 standard cooling	22.0
F100, F150, F250 and F350 super-cooling	24.0
460 cu in V8 engine	
All models	23.0

1978 and 1979	US qts
300 cu in six cylinder engine	
Manual transmission	13.0
Automatic transmission	14.0
Super-cooling option	18.0
302 cu in V8 engine	
Standard	15.0
Air conditioning and super-cooling option	18.0
351 cu in V8 engine	
F150, F250 and F350 standard cooling	15.0
F100 standard cooling	17.0
F100, F150, F250 and F350 super-cooling	24.0
F100, F150, F250 and F350 air conditioning	18.0
400 cu in V8 engine	
Standard cooling	18.0
Super-cooling option	24.0
460 cu in V8 engine – all	24.0

Coolant capacity – Bronco

1973	US qts
Six cylinder	9.0
V8	15.0
1974 thru 1977	
Six cylinder	15.0
V8	17.0
1978 and 1979	
351 cu in V8 engine	
Standard cooling	20.0
Extra-cooling	22.0
Super-cooling	24.0
400 cu in V8 engine	
Standard cooling	22.0
Super-cooling	24.0

1

Fuel tank capacity (standard) – Pick-ups

	US gal
1973 thru 1976	
F100 2- and 4-wheel drive	19.2
F150 2- and 4-wheel drive	19.2
F250 crew cab and 4-wheel drive	19.3
F250 crew cab and 4-wheel drive (California)	17.5
F350 stake, chassis-cab and platform bed	19.3
F350 stake, chassic-cab and platform bed (California)	17.5
F350 cowl mounted tank	22.5
F350 cowl mounted tank (California)	20.2
F350 Super Camper Special	20.6
F350 Super Camper Special (California)	19.3
F100, F250 and F350 Super cab	19.2
1977	
F100 2-wheel drive	19.2
F150 and F250 2-wheel drive and F150 and F250 4-wheel drive	19.2
F250 crew cab and 4-wheel drive	19.3
F250 crew cab and 4-wheel drive (California)	17.5
F350 stake, chassis-cab and platform bed	19.3
F350 stake, chassis-cab and platform bed (California)	17.5
F350 Camper Special	20.6
F350 Camper Special (California)	19.3
F100, F250 and F350 Super cab	19.2
1978	
F100, F150, F250 and crew cab 2 and 4-wheel drive	19.2
F350 stake, chassis cab and platform bed and F250 and 350 2-wheel drive and crew cab	20.2
F350 Camper Special	21.0
F350 Camper Special (California)	19.0
F100, F250 and F350 Super cab	19.2
1979	
F100 2-wheel drive	19.2
F150 and F250 2-wheel drive	19.2
F250 and F350 4-wheel drive and crew cab	20.2
F350 Styleside	19.0
F100, F150, F250 and F350 and Super cab	19.2

Fuel tank capacity (standard) – Bronco

	US gal
1973 thru 1976	12.25
1977	14.0
1978	25.5
1979	25.0

Manual transmission capacity – Pick-ups

	US pts
1973 thru 1975	
3-speed (Ford)	3.5
3-speed heavy duty (Warner T-87G)	5.5
4-speed (Warner T-18B)	7.0
4-speed (New Process 435)	7.0
4-speed (New Process 435 without extension)	6.5
1976 and 1977	
3-speed (Ford)	3.5
4-speed (Warner T18B)	8.0
4-speed (New Process 435)	7.0
4-speed (New Process 435 without extension)	6.5
1978 thru 1979	
3-speed (Ford)	3.5
4-speed (Warner T18B)	7.0
4-speed (New Process 435)	7.0
4-speed (New Process 435 without extension)	6.5
4-speed overdrive	4.5

Automatic transmission capacity – Pick-ups

	US pts
1973	
Heavy-duty Cruise-o-matic	22
C4	20.5
C6	25.5
1974	
FMX	22
C4	20.5
C6	28
C6 4-wheel drive	26.5
1975 thru 1977	
FMX	22
C4 (300 cu in six cylinder engine)	
1975	20.5
1976 and 1977	20.0
C4 (302 cu in V8 engine)	17.5
C6 (360 and 390 cu in V8 engines)	24.5
C6 (460 cu in V8 engine)	27.5
C6 (4-wheel drive)	27.5
1978	
C4	20.0
C6	23.5
C6 (4-wheel drive)	27.0
1979	
C4	20.0
C6	23.8
C6 (4-wheel drive)	26.4

Transfer case capacity – Pick-ups

	US pt
1973 and 1974	
F100 4-wheel drive	1.25
F250 single-speed	4.5
1975 and 1976	
F100 Dana single speed with manual transmission	1.25
New Process part-time	4.5
New process full-time (except crew cab)	9.0
1977 thru 1979	
New Process 2-speed part-time	4.0
New Process full-time	9.0

Driving axles capacity – Pick-ups

	US pts
1973 thru 1975	
Ford 3300 (F100)	6.5
Ford 3600 (F100)	6.5
Ford 3750 (F100)	7.0
Dana 44-6CF (F250 4-wheel drive)	4.0*
Dana 44-6CF HD (F250 4-wheel drive)	4.0**

Dana 44-7F (F100 4-wheel drive front axle)	4.75
Dana 60 (F250 rear axle)	6.0
Dana 61 (F250 rear axle)	6.0
Dana 70 (F350 rear axle)	6.5
Dana 60F (F250 front axle)	6.0

*Add 1 pint for each steering knuckle on 1973 models and 5 oz for 1974 and 1975 models.

**Add 1 pint for each steering knuckle on 1973 models and 15 oz on 1974 and 1975 models.

1976

Ford (F100 and F150 2-wheel drive)	6.5
Ford (F100 and F150 4-wheel drive)	7.0
Dana 44-7F front axle (F100 2-wheel drive)	4.75
Dana 44-6F HD (F250 4-wheel drive)	4.0
Dana 60 and 61 (F250)	6.0
Dana 61-2 (F250)	5.0
Dana 60F front axle (F250 crew cab)	6.0
Dana 70 rear axle (F350)	6.5

1977 thru 1979

Ford (F100 and F150)	6.5
Ford (F150 4-wheel drive)	6.5
Dana 44-3 (F100 and F150 2-wheel drive)	3.5
Dana 44-9F front axle (F150)	
Part-time	4.0
Full-time	5.8
Dana 44-9F (F250)	5.6
Dana 44-7F (F150)	
Part-time	4.0
Full-time	5.8
Dana 60 (F250)	6.0
Dana 70 (1977 F350)	6.5

1978 and 1979

Dana 61 (F250)	7.0
Dana 60 rear axle (F250)	6.0
Dana 61-2 (F250 and F350)	5.0
Dana 60-7F (F250 heavy duty)	6.0
Dana 70 (F350 super and regular cab)	7.0

Manual transmission — Bronco

	US pts
1973 thru 1977 all	3.5
1978 all	6.5
1979 all	7.0

Automatic transmission — Bronco

	US qts
1973 and 1974	11.0
1975	8.75
1976 and 1977	11.0
1978	13.5
1979	13.2

Transfer case — Bronco

	US pts
1973 thru 1977	2.75
1978 and 1979	
Part-time	4.0
Full-time	9.0

Driving axles — Bronco

	US pts
1973 thru 1977	
Front axle	3.5
Rear axle	9.0
1978 and 1979	
Front axle	5.8
Rear axle	6.5

Ignition

Spark plug type and gap*

	Type (Motorcraft)	Gap
Six-cylinder engines		
1973 through 1974		
light duty	BSF42C or equivalent	.035 inch
heavy duty	BSF3 or equivalent	.030 inch
1975 through 1979	BSF42C or equivalent	.044 inch
V8 engines		
1973		
302, 360, 390	BSF42C or equivalant	.035 inch
460	ASF52C or equivalent	.044 inch
1974 (all)	BSF42C or equivalent	.044 inch
1975		
302, 351W, 460	ASF42C or equivalent	.044 inch
(all others)	BSF42C or equivalent	.044 inch

Cylinder numbering and distributor location

Firing order and rotation

Clockwise

Front

Firing order 1-5-3-6-2-4

Six cylinder in-line engines

Cylinder numbering and distributor location

Front — Distributor

Firing order and rotation

Counterclockwise

Front

302, 360, 390, 460   351/400

Firing order

1-5-4-2-6-3-7-8   1-3-7-2-6-5-4-8

V8 engines

1976
302	ASF52C or equivalent	.044 inch
351W	ASF32C or equivalent	.044 inch
360, 390 (F100)	BSF82C or equivalent	.044 inch
(all others)	BSF42C or equivalent	.044 inch
1977 (all)	ASF42C or equivalent	.044 inch
1978 (all)	ASF42C or equivalent	.044 inch
1979 (all except 351)	ASF42C or equivalent	.044 inch
351	ASF52C or equivalent	.044 inch

Refer to the Vehicle Emission Control Label in the engine compartment and follow the information on the label if it differs from that shown here.

Distributor type
1973 and 1974	Mechanical breaker point type
1975 thru 1979	Breakerless, Dura-spark

Distributor direction of rotation
Six-cylinder engines	Clockwise
V8 engines	Counterclockwise

Firing order
Six cylinder engines	1-5-3-6-2-4
302, 360, 390, 460 engines	1-5-4-2-6-3-7-8
351, 400 engines	1-3-7-2-6-5-4-8
Ignition timing	See Tune-up decal in engine compartment

Ignition breaker point gap (point-type ignitions only)
Six cylinder engines	0.027 in
V8 engines	0.017 in

Ignition dwell angle (point-type ignitions only)
Six cylinder engines	35 to 39 degrees
V8 engines	24 to 30 degrees

Drivebelt tension (with Burroughs-type gauge)
$\frac{1}{4}$ in belts
During maintenance	30 lbs
Installation used (over 10 minute engine operation)	60 lbs
Installation new	80 lbs

3/8, 15/32, or 1/2 in belts
During maintenance	50 lbs
Installation used (over 10 minutes engine operation)	110 lbs
Installation new	140 lbs

Clutch pedal free-play ... $\frac{3}{4}$ to $1\frac{1}{2}$ in

Brakes
Front disc brake pad minimum thickness (from surface of pad to backing plate	$\frac{1}{32}$ in
Front disc brake pad minimum thickness (above rivet heads)	0.030 in
Brake shoe minimum thickness (from surface to rivet head)	$\frac{1}{32}$ in

Torque specifications   **ft-lb**
Spark plug-to-cylinder head	10 to 15

Wheel lug nut
$\frac{1}{2}$ in nut	90
$\frac{9}{16}$ in nut (single rear wheels)	145
$\frac{9}{16}$ in nut (dual rear wheels)	220
Front wheel bearing adjusting nut (4 x 2 only)	22 to 25 (back-off $\frac{1}{8}$ turn)
Front hub bearing inner adjusting nut (4 x 4 models only)	50 (back-off $\frac{1}{4}$ turn)
Front hub outer locknut (4 x 4 only)	50 to 80
Rear wheel bearing inner adjusting nut (full-floating models only)	50 to 80 (back-off $\frac{3}{8}$ turn)
Rear wheel bearing outer locknut (full floating models only)	90 to 110
Oil pan drain plug	15 to 25
Transmission filler plug (manual)	10 to 20
Transmission pan retaining bolts (automatic)	12 to 16
Transfer case filler plug (4 x 4 only)	25 to 35
Torque converter drain plug (automatic)	14 to 28
Filter screen-to-main body (automatic)	40 to 55 in-lb

1 Introduction

This Chapter was designed to help the home mechanic maintain his or her vehicle for peak performance, economy, safety and longevity.

On the following pages you will find a maintenance schedule along with Sections which deal specifically with each item on the schedule. Included are visual checks, adjustments and item replacements.

Servicing your vehicle using the time/mileage maintenance schedule and the sequenced sections will give you a planned program of maintenance. Keep in mind that it is a full plan, and maintaining only a few items at the specified intervals will not give you the same results.

You will find as you service your vehicle that many of the procedures can, and should, be grouped together due to the nature of the job at hand. Examples of this are as follows:

If the vehicle is fully raised for a chassis lubrication, for example, this is the ideal time for the following checks: manual transmission fluid, exhaust system, suspension, steering and the fuel system.

If the tires and wheels are removed, as during a routine tire rotation, go ahead and check the brakes and wheel bearings at the same time.

If you must borrow or rent a torque wrench, it would be advisable to service the spark plugs and repack (or replace) the wheel bearings all in the same day to save time and money.

The first step of this or any maintenance plan is to prepare yourself before the actual work begins. Read through the appropriate sections for all work that is to be performed before you begin. Gather together all necessary parts and tools. If it appears you could have a problem during a particular job, don't hesitate to ask advice from your local parts man or dealer service department.

2   Routine maintenance intervals

The following recommendations are given with the assumption that the vehicle owner will be doing the maintenance or service work (as opposed to a dealer service department). They are based on factory service/maintenance recommendations, but the time and/or mileage intervals have been shortened in most cases, to ensure that the service is thorough and complete. Not all maintenance checks or operations apply to every vehicle.

When the vehicle is new, it should be serviced initially by a factory authorized dealer service department to protect the factory warranty. In most cases the initial maintenance check is done at no cost to the owner.

Every 250 miles (400 km), weekly, and before long trips

Steering
    Check tire pressures (cold) (Sec 9)
    Inspect tires for wear and damage (Sec 5)

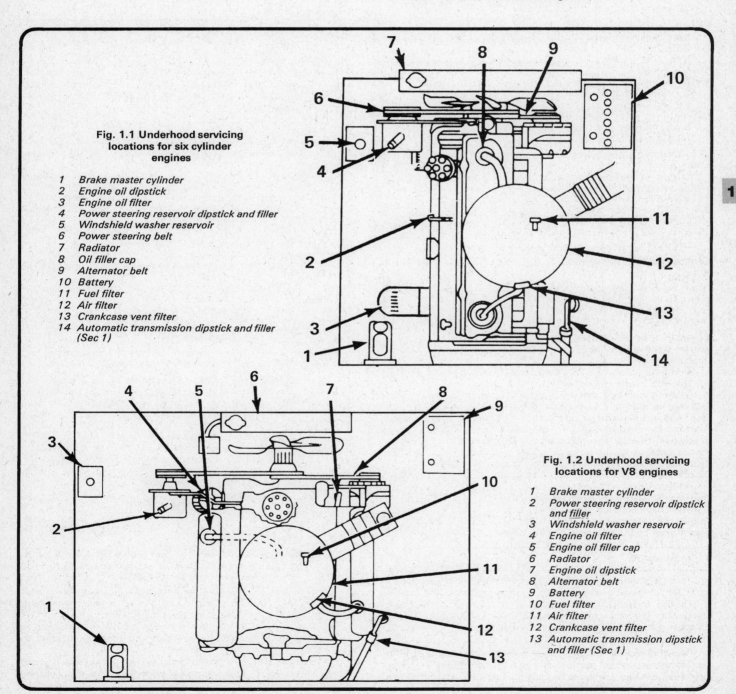

Fig. 1.1 Underhood servicing locations for six cylinder engines

    1   Brake master cylinder
    2   Engine oil dipstick
    3   Engine oil filter
    4   Power steering reservoir dipstick and filler
    5   Windshield washer reservoir
    6   Power steering belt
    7   Radiator
    8   Oil filler cap
    9   Alternator belt
    10 Battery
    11 Fuel filter
    12 Air filter
    13 Crankcase vent filter
    14 Automatic transmission dipstick and filler
        (Sec 1)

Fig. 1.2 Underhood servicing locations for V8 engines

    1   Brake master cylinder
    2   Power steering reservoir dipstick
        and filler
    3   Windshield washer reservoir
    4   Engine oil filter
    5   Engine oil filler cap
    6   Radiator
    7   Engine oil dipstick
    8   Alternator belt
    9   Battery
    10 Fuel filter
    11 Air filter
    12 Crankcase vent filter
    13 Automatic transmission dipstick
        and filler (Sec 1)

1

Check power steering reservoir level (Sec 3)
Check steering for smooth and accurate operation (Sec 9)

Brakes
Check the level in the brake fluid reservoir, if fluid level has
dropped noticeably since the last check inspect all brake lines and
hoses for leakage (Sec 7)
Check for satisfactory brake operation (Sec 7)

Lights, wipers, horns, instruments
Check all lights for proper operation
Check the operation of the windshield wipers and washers
Check the windshield wiper blade element condition (Sec 14)
Check the horn operation
Check the operation of all instruments

Engine
Check the oil level, add oil as required (Sec 3)
Check the radiator coolant level and add coolant as required (Sec
3)
Check the battery electrolyte level, adding water as necessary
(Sec 3)

Every 3000 miles (5000 km) or 3 months, whichever comes first

Change the engine oil and filter (Sec 16)
Check the TPS or throttle solenoid valve (Chapter 6)
Check the exhaust heat control valve operation (Chapter 6)
Check and replace if necessary, the air cleaner filter element (Sec 15).
Clean and refill the oil bath-type air cleaner (Sec 15).
Check the curb idle speed (Sec 33).
Check the fast idle speed (Sec 33).

Every 6000 miles (10 000 km) or 6 months, whichever comes first

Check carburetor TPS 'off' idle speed (Chapter 4)
Lubricate the universal joints and slip yoke (if equipped with
grease fittings) (Sec 19)
Lubricate the steering column universal joints (4-wheel drive) (Sec 19)
Check cooling system clamps and hoses (Sec 12)
Lubricate the front axle spindle pins (2-wheel drive) (Sec 19)
Check the exhaust system for loose or damaged components (Sec 8)
Check the power steering fluid level, adding fluid as necessary (Sec 3)
Lubricate the steering linkage (Sec 19)
Lubricate the clutch linkage (Sec 19)
Check the disc brake linings, piston boots and pivot pins (Sec 7)
Check the front axle lubricant level (4-wheel drive), adding oil
as necessary (Sec 3)
Check the rear axle lubricant level, adding oil as necessary (Sec 3)
Check the transfer case lubricant level (4-wheel drive), adding oil as
necessary (Sec 3)
Check the clutch linkage free-play, and adjust as necessary (Sec 20)
Check the manual transmission lubricant level and clean the breather,
adding oil as necessary (Sec 3)
Check all drivebelts for proper tension (Sec 6)
Inspect the drivebelts for wear and damage, replacing as necessary
(Sec 6)
Check the deceleration fuel valve (Sec 32)
Check the automatic transmission bands (Chapter 7)
Adjust the ignition timing (conventional distributor) (Sec 31)
Inspect the conventional distributor points, adjusting or replacing as
necessary (Sec 28)
Check the carburetor throttle, choke and deceleration valves, adjusting
or replacing as necessary (Chapters 4 and 6)
Adjust the idle fuel mixture (if applicable) (Sec 33)
Replace the fuel filter element (Sec 17)

Every 12 000 miles (20 000 km) or 12 months, whichever comes first

Lubricate the parking brake linkages, pivots and clevises (Sec 19)
Clean and repack with the specified grease, the front free running hubs
(4-wheel drive) (Chapter 8)

Check the spark plug wires (Sec 26)
Check the operation of the EGR system and delay valve (if equipped)
(Chapter 6)
Check the operation of the spark control system (if equipped) (Chapter
6)
Replace the spark plugs (engines using leaded fuel) (Sec 29)
Check and clean the crankcase breather cap (Sec 13)
Inspect the drum brake lining, lines and hoses (Sec 7)
Check the PCV valve, replacing it as necessary (Sec 13)
Drain the chassis mounted fuel filter system (Sec 17)
Check the engine coolant condition (Sec 12)
Check the operation of the temperature controlled air cleaner (Chapter
6)

Every 18 000 miles (30 000 km) or 18 months, whichever comes first

Replace the spark plugs (engines using unleaded fuel) (Sec 29)
Adjust the ignition timing (breakerless distributor) (Sec 31)
Check the distributor cap and rotor (breakerless distributor) (Sec 27)
Tighten the intake manifold nuts and bolts to the specified torque
(Chapter 2)
Check the Thermactor system (Chapter 6)
Replace the crankcase ventilation filter (Sec 13)
Check the choke system (Sec 32)
Add oil to the distributor shaft oil cup (if so equipped) (Sec 28)

Every 24 000 miles (40 000 km) or 24 months, whichever comes first

Drain and refill the cooling system with the specified coolant (Sec 24)
Repack and adjust rear wheel bearings (Dana axles) (Chapter 8)
Drain and refill the manual transmission with the specified lubricant
(Sec 21)
Drain the refill the front axle (4-wheel drive) (Sec 23)
Drain and refill the transfer case (4-wheel drive) (Sec 21)
Drain and refill the rear axle (Sec 23)
Check the evaporative system hoses, vapor line and fuel filler cap (Sec
18)
Check the evaporative emissions canister, replacing it as necessary
(Sec 18)
Check the engine compression (Sec 30)

Severe operating conditions

Severe operating conditions are defined as follows:

a)   Extended periods of idling or low-speed operation
b)   Towing any trailers up to 1000 lb (450 kg) for long distances
c)   Operating when the outside temperatures remain below
     10°F (-12°C) for 60 days or more and most trips are less
     than 10 miles 816 km)
d)   Operation in severe dust conditions
e)   The automatic transmission is also considered to be part of
     the systems under severe operating conditions and must be
     serviced at closer intervals on vehicles which accumulate
     2000 miles (3200 km) per month

If your vehicle falls into the severe operating conditions category,
the maintenance schedule must be amended as follows:

a)   Change engine oil and filter every 2 months or 2000 miles
     (3200 km)
b)   Check, clean and regap spark plugs every 4000 miles (6400
     km)
c)   Service the automatic transmission bands every 5000 miles
     (8000 km) (Chapter 7) and drain and refill the transmission
     with fresh fluid every 20 000 miles (32 000 km)
d)   Dana rear axles must be drained and refilled every 6000
     miles if a Class II or III trailer is towed
e)   Check the oil bath-type air cleaner and change the oil at 6000
     miles (9600 km). Check the paper-type air cleaner element
     frequently
f)   Lubricate the universal joints, slip yoke, front axle spindle
     pins, steering linkage, spring shackles and pins daily or as

soon as possible when operating in mud and/or water or every 1000 miles (1600 km) when operating off road

g) Check and replace the cartridge-type fuel filter frequently when operating in dusty conditions

3 Fluid levels check

1 There are a number of components on a vehicle which rely on the use of fluids to perform their job. Through the normal operation of the car, these fluids are used up and must be replenished before damage occurs. See the *Recommended Lubricants* Section for the specific fluid to be used when adding is required.
When checking fluid levels it is important that the vehicle is on a level surface.

Engine oil

2 The engine oil level on six-cylinder engine equipped vehicles is checked with a dipstick located on the left side of the engine block between the fuel pump and the distributor. On all V8 engines except for 360-390 cu in and 4-wheel drive models, the dipstick is located on the right front of the engine directly in front of the cylinder head. On 4-wheel drive and 360-390 cu in engine equipped trucks, the dipstick is located on the left front of the engine directly adjacent to the front spark plug.

3 The oil level should be checked when the vehicle is cold or, at least 10 minutes after the vehicle has been shut off. Make sure that the vehicle is sitting on level ground. Any deviations in level can cause a major variation in the actual fluid check.

4 Pull the dipstick from the tube and wipe all the oil from the end with a clean rag. Insert the dipstick all the way back into the oil pan and pull it out again. Check the dipstick at the end and note the oil level in relationship to the marks on the dipstick. Some dipsticks have an Add followed by a number mark to help indicate how much oil to add to the engine. In any case, the oil should be kept within the safe reading on the dipstick (Fig. 1.3).

5 Oil is added to the engine by removing the cap located on the rocker arm cover. Use an oil spout or funnel to reduce any chance of oil being poured on the outside of the engine.

6 Checking the oil level can also be an important preventative maintenance step. If the oil level is dropping abnormally, this indicates an oil leakage or internal engine wear problems which should be checked and corrected. If there are water droplets in the oil, or if it has a milky-looking color, this also indicates internal engine problems that should be looked into immediately.

7 The condition of the oil is also important and can be checked when checking the level. With the dipstick removed from the engine, take your thumb and index finger and wipe oil from the dipstick onto your fingers. Look for small dirt particles or engine filings which will show up on the dipstick or feel gritty to the touch. This is an indication that the oil should be drained and fresh oil added. If this condition persists, there is something wearing inside of the engine abnormally and this condition should be checked.

Automatic transmission

8 The fluid inside the transmission must be at normal operating temperature to get an accurate reading on the dipstick. This is done by driving the car for several miles, making frequent starts and stops to allow the transmission to shift through all gears.

9 Park the car on a level surface, place the selector lever in 'Park' and leave the engine running at an idle.

10 Remove the transmission dipstick (located on the right side, near the rear of the engine) and wipe all the fluid from the end of the dipstick with a clean rag (photo).

11 Push the dipstick back into the transmission until the cap seats firmly on the dipstick tube. Now remove the dipstick again and observe the fluid on the end. The uppermost level of the fluid should be between the 'Add' and 'Don't Add' marks (Fig. 1.4).

12 If the fluid level is at or below the 'Add' mark on the dipstick, add sufficient fluid to raise the level to the 'Don't Add' mark. One pint of fluid will raise the level to this point. Fluid should be added directly into the dipstick guide tube, using a funnel to prevent spills.

13 It is important that the transmission not be overfilled. Under no

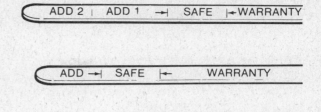

Fig. 1.3 Typical oil dipstick markings (Sec 3)

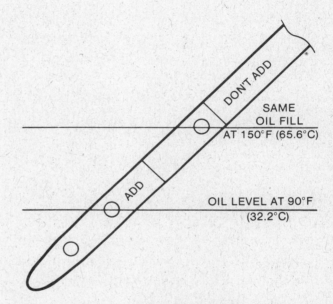

Fig. 1.4 Automatic transmission fluid levels at varying temperatures (Sec 3)

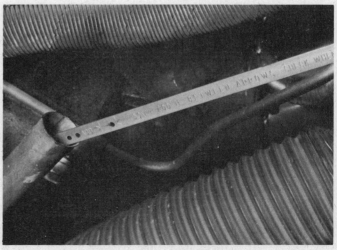

3.10 The automatic transmission dipstick as it is seen during a fluid check

circumstances should the fluid level be above the 'Don't Add' mark on the dipstick, as this could cause internal damage to the transmission. The best way to prevent overfilling is to add fluid a little at a time, driving the car and checking the level between additions.

14 Use only transmission fluid specified by Ford. This information can be found in the *Recommended Lubricants* portion of the specifications.

15 The condition of the fluid should also be checked along with the level. If the fluid at the end of the dipstick is dark reddish-brown color, or if the fluid has a 'burnt' smell, the transmission fluid should be changed. If you are in doubt about the condition of the fluid, purchase some new fluid and compare the two for color and smell.

Manual transmission

16 To check a manual transmission for fluid, access to the transmission must be made under the vehicle.

17 Locate the filler plug at the side of the transmission case. Clean all dirt from the area adjacent to the filler plug. Slowly withdraw the filler plug. If fluid starts to come out as the filler plug is withdrawn, immediately re-insert it back into the transmission as the level is correct.

18 Remove the filler plug if the fluid does not run out, and check that the fluid level is up to the bottom of the filler plug hole. If it is not, fill the transmission through this hole to the correct level.

19 Visually check the transmission for any signs of leakage at either the front or rear seals or near such components as the speedometer drive.

Transfer case (4 x 4)

20 To check the fluid level in the transfer case, (if so equipped) locate the filler plug on the side just as you did for the transmission.

21 Check the transfer case level in the same manner as the manual transmission fluid was checked.

Differential

22 Differentials are checked by withdrawing the filler plug from either the rear cover (Dana differentials) or from the side of the removeable differential assembly (all others). Use the same procedure as was used to check the fluid level in the manual transmissions (photo).

Engine coolant

Caution: *Do not attempt to check the engine coolant under any circumstances while the engine is running or immediately after it has been run.* Damage to the cooling system, and to the engine, and personal injury can result from attempting to check the coolant while the engine is hot. If the engine has been run, turn it off and wait until it has cooled. Use extreme caution when removing the radiator cap even after an engine has cooled, as steam and pressure can be released from the cooling system.

23 To check the engine coolant with a non-recovery type system, remove the radiator cap. Check the coolant level by looking down the neck and observing the fluid level below the cap seat. Add sufficient coolant to bring the level between $\frac{3}{4}$ and $1\frac{1}{2}$ inches below the neck (Fig. 1.5).

24 If the vehicle is equipped with a closed cooling system, the radiator cap should not be removed for checking. A coolant reservoir located to the side of the radiator should indicate a level within itself. If the level in the reservoir is between the Low and Full marks it is correct. If the level is below the low mark check the radiator after the system has completely cooled. For this check, the radiator cap must be removed.

25 If the radiator is very low on fluid, check the cooling system for any leaks using a pressure-type checker.

Brake fluid

26 Remove any accumulation of dirt or loose particles from the cover. The brake fluid reservoir is located directly above the brake master cylinder which is attached to either the firewall at the left of the engine or to the brake vacuum booster in that same location. If checking the brake fluid on a vehicle with water or snow on it, be sure to clean the

3.22 The inspection/fill plug found on the rear cover of the differential assembly

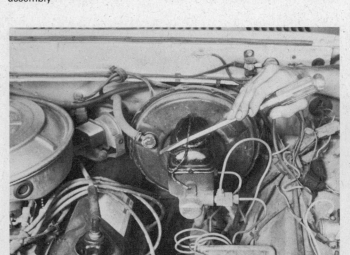

3.27 Prying the retaining clip off the master cylinder

3.29 Removing the master cylinder cap to check the brake fluid level

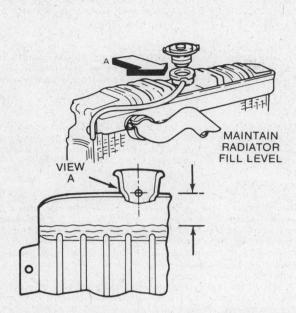

Fig. 1.5 Method of measuring cooling system fluid level in non-closed cooling system (Sec 3)

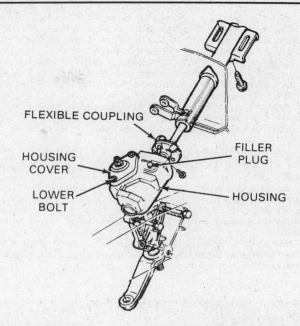

Fig. 1.6 Steering box components for fluid level check (Sec 3)

1

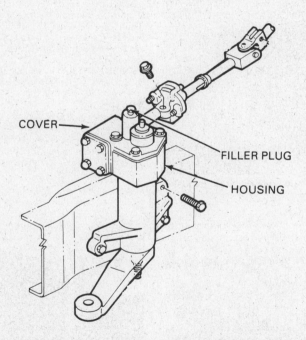

Fig. 1.7 Steering box components for fluid level check (F-150 4 x 4 and Bronco) (Sec 3)

hood and cowling area completely of any liquid. Serious contamination of the brake fluid can result if even one drop of water is allowed to enter the brake fluid reservoir.

27 Snap the retaining clip to the side to release the cover from the master cylinder reservoir (photo).

28 Remove the cover being very careful not to let any type of contamination enter the reservoir.

29 Observe the fluid level inside of the dual chambers. Check that it is within one-quarter inch of the top of the cylinder (photo).

30 Small amounts of fluid can be added to the system to make up for any fluid lost due to either evaporative conditions or to brake component wear. If a large amount of fluid is necessary to bring the system back up to the proper level, check the system for any signs of leakage. Loss of braking can result from leakage in the brake hydraulic system.

31 Clean the cover carefully and replace it back onto the cylinder. Be careful not to allow any contaminants to fall into the reservoir.

32 Snap the retaining clip back into place.

3.33 The dipstick for checking the power steering fluid is attached to the inside of the screw-on cap

4.12 Cleaning corrosion from the battery posts and cable connectors using a special wire cleaning tool

Power steering

33 The power steering pump is located to the left front of the engine. The dipstick for the power steering system is located in the cap to the filler neck of the power steering pump (photo).
34 With the engine at its normal operating temperature, turn the steering wheel in both directions to the end of the stops several times to stabilize the fluid level within the system.
35 Stop the engine and check the fluid level. Remove the cap from the pump and check that the fluid shows between the bottom of the dipstick and the full mark on the 'Full-Hot' side of the dipstick. If the fluid is being checked when the vehicle is cold, check the fluid on the 'Full-Cold' side.

Steering box

F100, F250 and F350 (4 x 2)
36 To check the steering box lubricant on these models, first center the steering wheel.
37 Remove the filler plug from the steering gear housing (Fig. 1.6).
38 Remove the bolt that attaches the lower cover to the steering gear housing.
39 With a clean punch or a similar tool, remove the loose lubricant from the filler plug hole and from the cover-to-housing attaching bolt hole.
40 Turn the steering wheel to the left stop slowly. Lubricant should rise to the level of the cover bolt hole.
41 Turn the steering wheel to the right stop.
42 Lubricant should rise to the filler plug hole. If the lubricant does not rise to the level of the holes, add lubricant and repeat the procedure.
43 When the lubricant has performed as described in the above steps, install the lower cover-to-housing attaching bolt. Next install the filler plug.
F150 (4 x 4) and Bronco
44 Remove the filler plug from the sector shaft cover (Fig. 1.7).
45 Observe that the lubricant is visible through the filler plug tower. If the lubricant is visible, the level is correct. Reinstall the filler plug. If the lubricant is not visible, add steering gear lubricant until the level is approximately one inch from the top of the hole in the filler plug tower. Install the filler plug.
F250 (4 x 4)
46 On models F250 (4 x 4) remove the filler plug from the top of the steering gear housing.
47 Check the level and see that it is below the filler plug hole.
48 Add fluid if necessary to raise the level to the bottom of the filler plug hole. Do not use any type of pressurized filling system to perform this addition.

Windshield washer fluid

49 Check the clear windshield washer reservoir for the proper level.

50 Fill the windshield washer reservoir if necessary with water in warm climates or with a special cleaning and anti-freeze washer solution for climates where the temperature gets below freezing.

4   Battery – servicing

Checking

1   Certain precautions must be followed when checking or servicing the battery. Hydrogen gas, which is highly flammable, is always present in the battery cells so keep lighted tobacco or any other open flames away from the battery. The electrolyte inside the battery is actually diluted sulfuric acid, which can be hazardous to your skin and cause damage if splashed in the eyes. It will also ruin clothes and painted surfaces.
2   Check the battery case for cracks and evidence of leakage.
3   To check the electrolyte level in the battery, remove all vent caps. If the battery water level is low, add distilled water until the level is above the cell plates. There is an indicator in each cell to help you judge when enough water has been added. Do not overfill.
4   Periodically check the specific gravity of the electrolyte with a hydrometer. This is especially important during cold weather. If the reading is below the specification, the battery should be recharged.
5   Check the tightness of the battery terminals to ensure good electrical connections. The terminals can be cleaned with a stiff wire brush. Corrosion can be kept to a minimum by applying a layer of petroleum jelly or grease to the terminal and cable connectors after they are assembled.
6   Inspect the entire length of the battery cables for corrosion, cracks and frayed conductors.
7   Check that the rubber protector over the positive terminal is not torn or missing. It should completely cover the terminal.
8   Make sure that the battery is securely mounted.
9   The battery case and caps should be kept clean and dry. If corrosion is evident, clean the battery as described below.
10 If the vehicle is not being used for an extended period, disconnect the battery cables and have it charged approximately every six weeks.

Cleaning

11 Corrosion on the battery hold-down components and inner fender panels can be removed by washing with a solution of water and baking soda. Once the area has been thoroughly cleaned, rinse it with clear water.
12 Corrosion on the battery case and terminals can also be removed with a solution of water and baking soda and a stiff brush. Be careful that none of the solution is splashed into your eyes or onto your skin (wear protective gloves). Do not allow any of the baking soda and water solution to get into the battery cell. Rinse the battery thoroughly once it is clean.

13 To thoroughly clean a battery cable terminal, the connections must be removed. When removing and installing the battery terminal connectors, always use a battery terminal puller tool as the battery poles can be easily damaged through twisting or pulling actions on the terminal connectors. After removing the terminal connectors, thoroughly clean both the battery posts and the insides of the terminal connectors with a special battery cleaning tool (photo).

14 Metal parts of the vehicle which have been damaged by spilled battery acid should be painted with a zinc-based primer and paint. Do this only after the area has been thoroughly cleaned and dried.

Charging

15 As was mentioned before, if the battery's specific gravity is below the specified amount, the battery must be recharged.

16 If the battery is to remain in the vehicle during charging, disconnect the cables from the battery to prevent damage to the electrical system.

17 When batteries are being charged, hydrogen gas, which is very explosive and flammable is produced. Do not smoke or allow an open flame near a charging or a recently charged battery. Also, do not plug in the battery charger until the connections have been made at the battery posts.

18 The average time necessary to charge a battery at the normal rate is from 12 to 16 hours (sometimes longer). Always charge the battery slowly. A quick charge or boost charge is hard on a battery and will shorten its life. Use a battery charger that is rated at no more than $3\frac{1}{2}$ amperes.

19 Remove all of the vent caps and cover the vent holes with a clean cloth to prevent the spattering of electrolyte. Hook the battery charger leads to the battery posts (positive to positive, negative to negative), then plug in the charger. Make sure it is set at 12 volts if it has a selector switch.

20 Watch the battery closely during charging to make sure that it does not overheat.

21 The battery can be considered fully charged when it is gassing freely and there is no increase in specific gravity during three successive readings taken at hourly intervals.

22 Overheating of the battery during charging at normal charging rates, excessive gassing and continual low specific gravity readings are an indication that the battery should be replaced with a new one.

5 Tires and wheels – checking and rotation

Checking

1 Periodically inspecting the tires can not only prevent you from being stranded with a flat tire, but can also give you clues as to possible problems with the steering and suspension systems before major damage occurs.

2 Proper tire inflation adds miles to the life of the tires, allows the vehicle to achieve maximum gas mileage and contributes to overall riding comfort.

3 When inspecting the tire, first check the wear on the tread. Irregularities in the tread pattern (cupping, flat spots, more wear on one side than the other) are indications of front end alignment and/or balance problems. If any of these conditions are found, you should take the vehicle to a wheel alignment shop to correct the problem. Tires with tread marker indicators showing should be replaced. Truck tires without tread markers should be replaced if there is less than $\frac{1}{32}$ inch of tread left on any part of the tire.

4 Also check the tread area for cuts or punctures. Many times a nail or tack will imbed itself into the tire tread and yet the tire will hold its air pressure for a short time. In most cases, a repair shop or gas station can repair the punctured tire.

5 It is also important to check the sidewalls of the tire, both inside and outside. Check for the rubber being deteriorated, cut or punctured. Also inspect the inboard side of the tire for signs of brake fluid leakage, indicating a thorough brake inspection is needed immediately (Section 7).

6 Incorrect tire pressure cannot be determined merely by looking at the tire. This is especially true for radial tires. A tire pressure gauge must be used. If you do not already have a reliable gauge, it is a good idea to purchase one and keep it in the glove box. Built-in pressure gauges at gas stations are often unreliable. If you are in doubt as to the accuracy of your gauge, many repair shops have 'master' pressure gauges which you can use for comparison purposes.

7 Always check tire inflation when the tires are cold. Cold, in this case, means that the vehicle has not been driven more than one mile after sitting for three hours or more. It is normal for the pressure to increase 4 to 8 pounds or more when the tires are hot.

8 Unscrew the valve cap protruding from the wheel and firmly press the gauge onto the valve stem. Observe the reading on the gauge and check this figure against the recommended tire pressure for your vehicle.

9 The recommended pressures are listed on a tag attached to the driver's door latch post under the striker plate or in the back of your owner's manual. Be sure to set the pressure in accordance with both the size of tire on your particular vehicle and with the load you are planning to carry with it. These specifications will vary widely so be careful when looking them up. Overloaded and/or underinflated tires on a truck are one of the most common areas of break-down as well as being potentially dangerous.

10 Check all tires and add air as necessary to bring all tires up to the recommended pressure levels. Do not forget the spare tire. Be sure to reinstall the valve caps, which will keep dirt and moisture out of the valve stem mechanism.

11 Carefully inspect the wheels for damage or any signs of deterioration. Wheels that have been scraped or hit against a curb are especially susceptible to cracking or bending. If a wheel is damaged in any way it is a good idea to replace it with a new one.

12 Check the wheel lug nuts for tightness. Wheels should be torqued to the correct specification with a torque wrench and this is always true when dealing with aluminum alloy wheels. If the bolt holes have become elongated or flattened, replace the wheel. Torque the lug nuts in the proper sequence as shown in Figure 1.9.

13 A very thorough examination of the wheel/tire unit requires removal of the wheel from the vehicle. If the assembly has been balanced on the vehicle, mark one wheel stud and one bolt hole on the wheel so the assembly can be installed in the same relative position.

14 Clean the inner surface of the wheel and pay particular attention to the mating face of the wheel where it contacts the brake drum or hub assembly. Any corrosion on this surface can prevent the wheel from seating flat against the drum or hub.

15 Some F250 and F350 model trucks will have two-piece or 'split-rim' type wheels. Check these types of wheels very carefully for any signs of incorrect seating between the outer ring and the main center of the wheel. This type of wheel can come apart with the power of a small explosion and has been known to cause injury and even death. If you have a wheel of this type that appears to be incorrectly

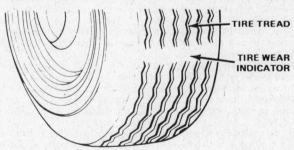

Fig. 1.8 Tread wear marker on tire (Sec 5)

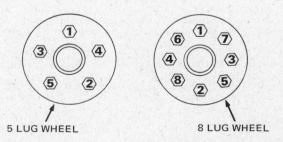

Fig. 1.9 Correct lug nut tightening sequence (Sec 5)

assembled or is coming apart, take it immediately to a truck-tire service facility. Do not attempt to do any type of work on these wheels as they require a safety cage as well as other special equipment to be handled properly.

Rotation

16 The tires should be rotated at the specified intervals and whenever uneven wear is noticed. Tire rotation can contribute significantly to increased life from a set of tires. Tires should be rotated only if they are the same size, tread type, ply rating and load range. All of this information can be read from the raised printing on the sidewall of the tire.

17 Since the vehicle will be raised and the tires removed anyway, this is a good time to check the brakes (Sec 7) and/or repack the wheel bearings (Chapter 9). Read these Sections through first to determine if you will be performing these operations at the same time you rotate the tires.

18 The position of each tire in the rotation sequence depends on the type of tire used on your car. Radial tires use a different rotation pattern from conventional type tires (Fig. 1.10). Do not use any other rotation pattern than the type shown or else handling, ride and other problems can occur, particularly with radial type tires.

19 See the information in *Jacking and Towing* at the front of this manual for the proper procedures to follow in raising the car and changing a tire; however, if the brakes are to be checked, do not apply the parking brake as stated. Make sure the tires are blocked to prevent the vehicle from rolling.

20 Preferably, the entire vehicle should be raised at the same time. This can be done on a hoist or by jacking up each corner of the vehicle and then lowering it onto jack stands placed under the frame rails. Always use four jack stands and make sure the vehicle is firmly supported all around.

21 After rotation, check and adjust the tire pressures as necessary and be sure to check wheel nut tightness.

---

6 Engine drive belt(s) – check and adjustment

1 The drive belts, or V-belts as they are sometimes called, at the front of the engine play an important role in the overall operation of the vehicle and its components. Due to their function and material make-up, the belts will wear and stretch after a period of time and should be inspected and adjusted periodically to prevent major engine damage.

2 The number of belts used on a vehicle depends on the accessories installed. Drive belts are used to turn: the alternator; air pump; power steering pump; water pump; fan; and air conditioning compressor. Depending on the pulley arrangement, a single belt may be used for more than one of these ancillary components.

3 With the engine off, open the hood and locate the various belts at the front of the engine. Using your fingers (and a flashlight if necessary), move along the belts checking for cracks or separation. Also check for fraying and for glazing which gives the belt a shiny appearance. Both sides of the belts should be inspected, which means you will have to twist the belt to check the underside.

4 Drive belt tension should be checked using a special gauge designed for this purpose. On dual belt systems, check one belt at a time. Compare the reading on the drive belt gauge with Specifications at the front of the Chapter.

5 If space limitations do not permit the use of a tensioning tool, drive belt tension can be checked by pushing on the belt at a distance halfway between the pulleys. Push firmly with your thumb and see how much the belt moves downward (deflects). A rule of thumb is that if the distance (pulley center to pulley center) is between 7 inches and 11 inches, the belt should deflect $\frac{1}{4}$ inch. If the belt is longer and travels between pulleys spaced 12 inches to 16 inches apart, the belt should deflect $\frac{1}{2}$ in.

6 If it is found necessary to adjust the belt tension, either to make the belt tighter or looser, this is done by moving the belt-driven accessory on its bracket.

7 For each component there will be an adjustment or strap bolt and a pivot bolt. Both bolts must be loosened slightly to enable you to move the component.

8 After the two bolts have been loosened, move the component away from the engine (to tighten the belt) or toward the engine (to loosen the belt). Hold the accessory in this position and check the belt

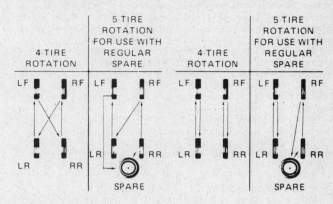

TIRE ROTATION DIAGRAM

BIAS & BIAS BELTED TIRES   RADIAL PLY TIRES

Fig. 1.10 Tire rotation sequence for conventional and radial ply tires (Sec 5)

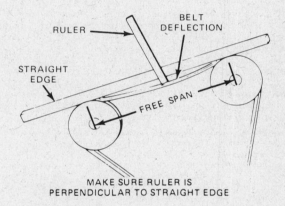

MAKE SURE RULER IS PERPENDICULAR TO STRAIGHT EDGE

Fig. 1.11 Method for checking engine drivebelt tension (Sec 6)

tension. If it is correct, tighten the two bolts until snug, then recheck the tension. If it is alright, fully tighten the two bolts.

9 It will often be necessary to use some sort of pry bar to move the accessory while the belt is adjusted. If this must be done to gain the proper leverage, be very careful not to damage the component being moved, or the part being pried against.

---

7 Brake system – inspection and adjustment

1 The brakes should be inspected at the specified intervals, as well as every time the wheels are removed or whenever a problem is suspected. Indications of a potential problem in the braking systems are: the car pulls to one side when the brake pedal is depressed; noises coming from the brakes when they are applied; excessive brake pedal travel; pulsating pedal; and leakage of fluid (usually seen on the inside of the tire or wheel).

Disc-brakes – inspection

2 Loosen the lug nuts on the front wheels, but do not remove them.

3 Raise the front end of the vehicle and support it with jack stands securely. Be sure the parking brake is set. (See *Jacking and Towing* in the front of this book).

4 Remove the front wheel.

5 Turn the front steering all the way to the right to enable the brake inspection hole of the left brake to be observed more easily. The inspection hole appears as an oval-shaped window squarely in the center of the brake caliper bracket. We recommend that the brake pads be replaced if they are worn within the tolerances listed at the

beginning of this Chapter. It is also advisable to replace them if any difference in wear is apparent between the two sides.

6 If there is a question about whether to replace the pads or not, a more accurate measurement can be made by removing the pads as described in Chapter 9. Remember, disc brake pads are relatively inexpensive and easy to replace, other brake parts such as discs are not.

7 Perform the same inspection on the right front brake system after turning the steering all the way to the left for better viewing access. If any deviation is noted between the four front brake pads (two per side), all of the pads should be replaced at the same time. Do not mix different types of replacement pads or use pads of a different material type than original equipment.

8 While checking the pad linings, also inspect the rotor surface for scoring or hot spots indicated by small discolored blemishes. Light scoring is acceptable but if the damage is excessive, the rotor should be resurfaced or replaced with a new one. Always replace rotors in pairs.

Hydraulic lines and parking brake cables

9 Before installing the wheels, check for any leakage around the brake hose connections leading to the caliper. Also check for damage (cracking, splitting, etc.) to the brake hose and lines.

10 Replace the hose, lines or fittings if any sign of hydraulic leakage is present.

11 Inspect the hydraulic system throughout the vehicle by first supporting the vehicle to allow access to the undercarriage. Trace the hydraulic lines from the master cylinder to the brake equalizing chamber and then out to each individual wheel. Pay particular attention to the rubber-coated brake hoses that lead to the front calipers and to the flexible rubber line that connects the brake line at the rear of the vehicle's frame to tee fitting located on the rear axle housing.

12 Carefully observe the parking brake system, cables, linkage and connecting points. If any fraying or damage is noted to any of the cables, replace the necessary parts.

Drum brakes – inspection and cleaning

Note: *The following procedure requires a special large deep socket if your vehicle is equipped with the full-floating type of axle hub (identified by 8-lug wheels and a protruding center hub). Additionally you will need new lock washers for the axle retaining nuts as well as a new gasket and axle bearing nut lock washer.*

13 The brake drum must be removed in order to inspect the condition of the linings and hardware.

14 Loosen the lug nuts approximately $\frac{1}{2}$ turn. On models with full-floating axle hubs, loosen the axle retaining bolts on the center hub.

15 Raise the vehicle and support it securely.

16 Remove the lug nuts and the wheel(s).

17 On vehicles equipped with semi-floating axles (5-lug wheels and no protruding center hub) unthread the spring clips from the lug studs and pull the drum off the axle flange. Note: If the drum will not come off of the flange easily, check to make sure the emergency brake is fully released. If the drum still won't come off, it will be necessary to back off the brake shoe adjustment.

Note: *Steps 18 through 24 below apply to full-floating hubs only. Refer to Fig. 1.12 for component identification.*

18 Heavy-duty vehicles equipped with full-floating rear axles require removal of the axle. Remove the previously loosened axle retaining nuts and washers and remove the axle and gasket.

19 Use a chisel and hammer to bend the tabs of the lock washer away from the flats of the locknut.

20 Remove the locknut from the hub using a deep socket of the correct size.

Caution: *Never use a chisel to remove the lock nut or wheel bearing adjusting nut.*

21 Remove the lock washer.

22 Remove the wheel bearing adjusting nut with the deep socket.

23 Pull the drum off the spindle approximately 2 to 3 inches and then push it back on. This will pull the outer wheel bearing out onto the spindle for easier removal. (See Chapter 9 for instructions on backing off the brake adjustment for drum removal if it won't pull off easily).

24 Remove the brake drum. Notice that the inner wheel bearing will

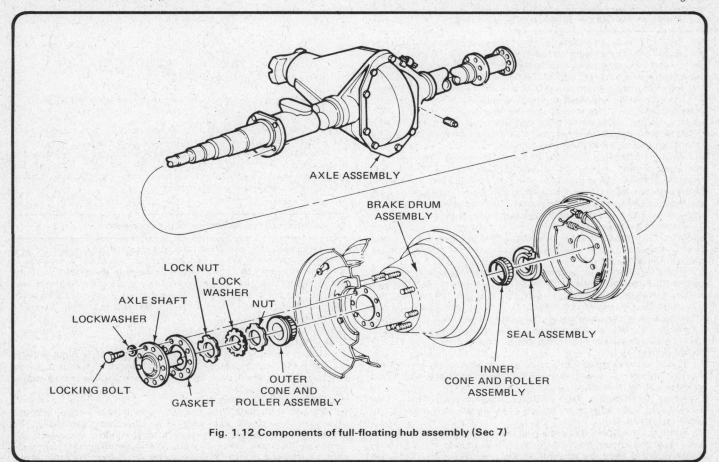

Fig. 1.12 Components of full-floating hub assembly (Sec 7)

be retained to the drum with the inner wheel bearing seal. Use caution not to damage this seal.

25 With the drum removed, carefully vacuum or brush away any accumulations of brake lining material and dust. Do not blow this material out with compressed air as asbestos is hazardous to breathe.

26 Check the thickness of the lining material. If the thickness is at the minimum specification or close to it, the brake shoes should be replaced with new ones. The shoes should also be replaced if they are cracked, glazed (shiny surface) or wet from brake fluid or oil.

27 Check the brake return springs, parking brake cable (rear brakes), and self-adjusting brake mechanisms for condition and position.

28 Carefully check the brake components for any signs of fluid leakage. Use your finger to carefully pry back the lip of the rubber wheel cylinder cups. These are located at the top of the brake assembly (photo). Any leakage at these cups is an indication that the wheel cylinders should be overhauled immediately (Chapter 9). Also check the connections at the rear of the brake backing plate for any signs of leakage or deterioration.

29 If the wheel cylinders are dry and there are signs of grease or oil in the brake assembly area, the axle seal is defective and should be replaced. Grease or oil will ruin asbestos and rubber parts so any accumulation of grease or oil requires replacement of the brake shoes and/or rubber parts affected by it. See Chapter 9 for seal replacement procedures.

30 Wipe off the inside of the drum with a clean rag and brake cleaning solvent or denatured alcohol. Again, be careful not to breathe or spread the dangerous asbestos dust.

31 Check the inside of the drum for cracks, scores, deep grooves or hard spots which will appear as small discolored spots. If these imperfections cannot be removed with fine emery cloth and light rubbing, the drum must be taken to an automotive machine shop, parts house or brake specialist with the equipment necessary to machine the drums.

32 If, after the inspection and cleaning process, all parts are in good working condition, reinstall the brake drum, retaining clips and wheel (semi-floating axle type only).

33 On full floating-type axle assemblies only, the following steps 34 through 43 should be followed.

34 Install the drum(s) after carefully inspecting the hub seal and wear surface of the spindle. Make sure the inner wheel bearing has plenty of lubricant and the bearing area is free or dust or asbestos. If the bearing is dirty or dry, the seal will have to be removed with a seal removing tool or two screwdrivers. Discard the seal after comparing it to its replacement. Remove the bearing, clean it along with the housing and repack the bearing with the proper lubricant. Install the bearing and seal into the drum assembly (Chapter 9).

35 As a temporary means of protection, wrap the threads of the spindle with tape.

36 Very carefully slide the complete hub/drum assembly over the spindle so as not to damage the inner seal. After the drum assembly is positioned fully onto the spindle, remove the tape.

37 Install the outer bearing (making sure that it is clean and packed with the correct lubricant) and start the large retaining nut by hand. Tighten the nut with the special deep socket to the specified torque setting and back off the nut the specified amount.

38 Use a new lock washer and install it onto the spindle. Notice that it is two-sided and that the smooth side should be installed facing outward.

39 Install the locknut and tighten it to the specified torque setting.

40 Check that the drum/hub assembly rotates freely and under no circumstances should the bearings be preloaded. Due to the high capacity weight rating of this type of axle assembly, this installation process must be adhered to exactly. Damage to the bearings, spindle or even loss of the wheel assembly can result from improper installation procedures.

41 Bend the tabs of the lock washer over at least two of the flats on the locknut.

42 Install the axle using a new gasket. Use new lock washers and install the axle retaining bolts. Torque the retaining bolts to the correct specification.

43 Check the end play of the hub and drum assembly with a dial indicator. If you do not own this checking equipment, it can be rented from most rental outlets. The correct end play is 0.001 to 0.010 inch. If not correct, repeat the previous steps, commencing with a loose bearing.

7.28 During the brake inspection, the wheel cylinders should be carefully checked for leakage

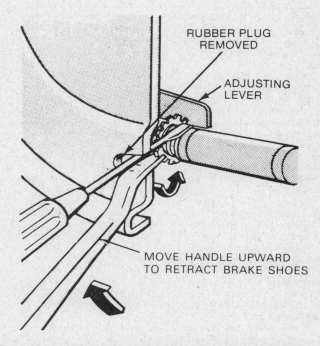

RUBBER PLUG REMOVED

ADJUSTING LEVER

MOVE HANDLE UPWARD TO RETRACT BRAKE SHOES

Fig. 1.13 A small screwdriver and special brake adjusting tool are used to back off the shoes for drum removal or adjustment (Sec 7)

Drum brake adjustment

44 Adjust the brakes (if they have been replaced or had to be retracted for removal purposes) by removing the rubber plug at the rear of the brake backing plate.

45 Use a brake adjustment tool inserted through the slot in the backing plate to rotate the star wheel adjuster until the brakes drag against the drums. You will need to keep rotating the wheel assembly while you are performing this operation.

46 Finally, loosen the star wheel adjuster to a point where the dragging just stops. If the drum drags heavily in one spot, it is egg-shaped and will need to be resurfaced or replaced for proper braking operation.

47 Install the wheel(s) and torque the retaining nuts in order to the correct specification. Lower the vehicle to the ground and pump the brake pedal several times to ascertain correct brake operation and 'feel' before attempting to drive the vehicle.

8   Exhaust system – inspection

1   With the exhaust system cold (at least three hours after being driven), check the complete exhaust system from its starting point at the engine to the end of the tailpipe. This is best done on a hoist where full access is available.

2   Check the pipes and their connections for signs of leakage and/or corrosion indicating a potential failure. Check that all brackets and hangers are in good condition and are tight.

3   At the same time, inspect the underside of the body for holes, corrosion, open seams, etc. which may allow exhaust gases to enter the passenger compartment. Seal all body openings with silicone or body putty.

4   Rattles and other driving noises can often be traced to the exhaust system, especially the mounts and hangers. Try to move the pipes, muffler and catalytic converter (if equipped). If the components can come into contact with the body or driveline parts, secure the exhaust system with new mountings.

5   This is also an ideal time to check the running condition of the engine by inspecting the very end of the tailpipe. The exhaust deposits here are an indication of engine tune. If the pipe is black and sooty or bright white deposits are found, the engine is in need of a tune-up including a thorough carburetor inspection and adjustment.

9   Suspension and steering – inspection

1   Whenever the front of the vehicle is raised for service it is a good idea to visually check the suspension and steering components for wear.

2   Indications of a fault in these systems are: excessive play in the steering wheel before the front wheels react; excessive sway around corners or body movement over rough roads; binding at some point as the steering wheel is turned.

3   Before the vehicle is raised for inspection, test the shock absorbers by pushing downward to rock the vehicle at each corner. If you push the vehicle down and it does not come back to a level position without one or two bounces, the shocks are worn and need to be replaced. As this is done, check for squeaks and strange noises from the suspension components. Information on shock absorber and suspension components can be found in Chapter 11.

4   Now raise the front end of the vehicle and support it firmly on jack stands placed under the frame rail. Because of the work to be done, make sure the vehicle cannot fall from the stands.

5   Grab the top and bottom of the front tire with your hands and rock the tire/wheel on its spindle. If there is any play or looseness, the wheel bearings should be serviced (see Chapter 9).

6   Crawl under the vehicle and check for loose bolts, broken or disconnected parts and deteriorated rubber bushings on all suspension and steering components. Look for grease or fluid leaking from around the steering box. Check the power steering hoses and their connections for leaks.

7   If the wheel bearings have been adjusted or determined to be adjusted properly, again grasp the wheel assembly and move it up and down and side to side to check the spindle bushings (4 x 2) or king pin joints (4 x 4) for looseness. Any play or looseness in these components requires disassembly and usually replacement. Improper lubrication usually causes failure of these components. If they are loose, steering control, shimmying at the steering wheel and other problems often crop up. Do not ignore these components as they are the major connecting points of the wheel/spindle assembly to the suspension of the vehicle.

10   Glass and mirrors – inspection

1   Vehicle cab glass as well as mirrors, particularly in vehicles with loads or bodies that restrict vision, are very important safety factors of a truck. All the glass should be examined and cleaned before each day's operation of the vehicle. If any glass within the driver's viewing area is cracked or broken, it is a good idea to replace it as soon as possible.

2   Mirrors play an important part in the operation of a truck, especially when high, wide loads restrict the driver's vision. Make sure that all mirrors are in good condition. Clean them daily. Make sure that the adjustment is correct and that all brackets and mounting hardware are tight.

11   Lighting system – inspection and adjustment

1   It is easiest to inspect the lighting system at night in an enclosed garage (do not run the engine inside an enclosed area).

2   First, turn on the lights to the first position on the headlight switch. This should activate all of the parking lights and various marker lights. Carefully walk around the vehicle and make sure that all lights are working properly. Trucks depend on certain marker light systems to indicate their size and height to other vehicles in traffic situations. It is a safety factor to keep these lighting systems working correctly.

3   If a light is found to be inoperative, check the bulb to determine if that is the problem. If a bulb replacement does not remedy the situation, see Chapter 10.

4   Turn the light switch on to the full headlight position. All the lights that were previously illuminated should still be lit along with the headlights. Make sure that the high beam works on the headlight system as well as the normal driving beam. Check the headlight aim for proper range and side angle. Adjust the headlights with a special headlight aimer or with the following temporary method, if necessary.

Headlight adjustment

5   You will need a screwdriver and a flat wall to shine your headlights on.

6   Park your vehicle approximately three feet from the wall you have selected (a garage door works well for this purpose). It is easier to do this at dusk or dark for clear definition of where the lights are shining.

7   Mark the outlines of the beam pattern on the wall with a pencil or tape. Move the vehicle back about twenty-five feet from the wall. The top of the low beam should be no higher than the top of the circles you have enscribed on the wall. They should also be no lower than the center of the circles.

8   If the beam shines outside of the circle, use the screwdriver and locate one of the two headlight adjustment screws which are accessible through slots provided in the headlight molding (the piece of plastic trim surrounding the headlight). These adjustment screws have tension springs. One screw will raise and lower the light beam and the other one will rotate it from side to side. Experiment with each screw until you move the beams in the direction that you want them to go.

9   Adjust the high beams in a similar manner. If you have a four-light system, the bright beams (center) are adjusted so the center of the beam is aimed at the top of the low beam marks.

10   As this procedure is less than perfect, it it best to have the headlights adjusted by a professional as soon as possible.

12   Cooling system – inspection

1   Many major engine failures can be attributed to a faulty cooling system. If equipped with an automatic transmission, the cooling system also plays an integral role in transmission longevity.

2   The cooling system should be checked with the engine cold. Do this before the vehicle is driven for the day or after it has been shut off for one or two hours.

3   Remove the radiator cap and thoroughly clean the cap (inside and out) with clean water. Also clean the filler neck on the radiator. All traces of corrosion should be removed.

4   Carefully check the upper and lower radiator hoses along with the smaller diameter heater hoses. Inspect their entire length, replacing any hose which is cracked, swollen or shows signs of deterioration. Cracks may become more apparent if the hose is squeezed.

5   Also check that all hose connections are tight. A leak in the cooling system will usually show up as white or rust colored deposits on the areas adjoining the leak.

6   Use compressed air or a soft brush to remove bugs, leaves etc. from the front of the radiator or air conditioning condensor. Be careful not to damage the delicate cooling fins, or cut yourself on the sharp fins.

1

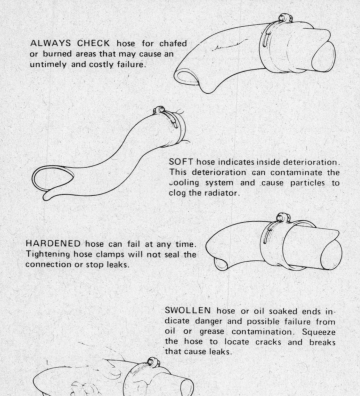

ALWAYS CHECK hose for chafed or burned areas that may cause an untimely and costly failure.

SOFT hose indicates inside deterioration. This deterioration can contaminate the cooling system and cause particles to clog the radiator.

HARDENED hose can fail at any time. Tightening hose clamps will not seal the connection or stop leaks.

SWOLLEN hose or oil soaked ends indicate danger and possible failure from oil or grease contamination. Squeeze the hose to locate cracks and breaks that cause leaks.

Fig. 1.14 Various cooling system hose deterioration conditions (Sec 12)

7   If a fault is suspected in the cooling system, a special pressure test can be performed. Most service stations and repair facilities can do this for a minimal charge.

13 PCV system – inspection and valve replacement

Inspection

Note: *The following tests are to be performed with the engine idling and at normal operating temperature.*

1   Remove the PCV valve from the gasket located in the rocker arm cover. Make sure the connection to the PCV valve at the inlet side remains connected.
2   Check for a strong suction which will be accompanied by a hissing noise at the valve. You can place a finger over the valve inlet to feel the suction. At the same time the finger is blocking the valve, any vacuum leaks should become apparent in the connections and the hose.
3   Install the PCV valve back into its correct position.
4   Loosely plug the air inlet hose after removing it from the air cleaner connection. Use a small piece of stiff paper over the opening to block it. After approximately a minute, the paper should be held against the hose opening by a strong suction.
Note: *The following tests will be made with the engine shut off.*
5   Remove the PCV valve from its grommet and shake it. It should make a clicking, metallic noise which indicates the valve is operating.
6   Observe the hose leading to the PCV valve as well as the air inlet connections, PCV valve grommet and air inlet gasket at the oil filler cap (if so equipped). If any loose connections are found, tighten the connections or replace the clamps.
7   If the hoses are found to be leaking, replace the hoses.

Valve replacement

8   Replace the PCV valve if it fails any of the above tests. Make sure that the replacement valve is equal to the original equipment. An

exception to this rule occurs after high mileage when a special high-flow PCV valve is recommended in the maintenance chart.
9   Remove the valve from the gasket and remove the clamp securing the valve to the hose.
10   Insert the PCV valve into the grommet in the valve cover.
11   Connect the hose linking the crankcase or manifold to the top of the PCV valve. Make sure the hose is not cracked or leaking. Install the clamp over the hose end.
12   Start the engine and make sure that the PCV system functions properly as discussed previously.
13   On V8 engines, the PCV valve is attached to the crankcase breather/oil filler cap. Be sure to remove, clean (with solvent) and replace the cap whenever PCV valve maintenance is required.
14   Replace the crankcase ventilation filter in the air cleaner housing. To do this, remove the air cleaner top plate, lift out the filter (it is a small, rectangular filter) and replace it with a new one.

14 Windshield wipers – inspection and blade replacement

1   Windshield wiper blades will need replacement depending on the amount of use, weather conditions, chemical reactions from environmental conditions and age. Keep the blades clean and lubricated with a light silicone spray.
2   If the wiper blades cease to do an effective job of wiping the windshield clean, make sure that the blade and the windshield are cleaned properly before replacement. Look at the blades closely while they are still installed on the vehicle without manually moving the wiper arms across the windshield. Make sure that the blades are in good condition and have not started to deteriorate or split.
3   If the windshield wiper blades do not prove effective and they have been cleaned along with the windshield (a film-like coating on the windshield can also cause streaking or poor wiping) replace the blades with new ones.
4   To replace the windshield wiper blades, press down on the arm while depressing the tab located underneath the saddle clip.
5   Pull the blade and blade saddle off of the windshield wiper arm.
6   Most wiper blade elements can be replaced without replacing the entire wiper blade assembly. Due to the differences in various manufacturer's retaining techniques, you will need to refer to each individual manufacturer's instructions to replace the rubber blade element. Generally, a retaining clip is used at the end of the assembly and the blade slides out of the blade frame lever.
7   Install the completed blade frame assembly back on to the wiper arm. The tab will automatically snap into place when the blade saddle is positioned correctly. Under no conditions should the arm be removed or pulled across the windshield while the wiper assembly is stationery. If easier access to the wiper blade is required, turn the wiper system on and turn the ignition switch to the 'Off' position when the blades arrive at the most accessible position.

15 Air filter

1   At the specified intervals, the air filter should be replaced with a new one. A thorough program of preventative maintenance would call for the filter to be inspected periodically between changes.
2   The air filter is located inside the air cleaner housing on the top of the engine. To remove the filter, unscrew the wing nut at the top of the air cleaner and lift off the top plate (photo). If the top plate is connected to emissions control devices, tilt it back far enough to allow access to the filter element.
3   While the top plate is off, be careful not to drop anything down into the carburetor.
4   Lift the air filter out of the housing.
5   To check the filter, hold it up to strong sunlight, or place a flashlight or droplight on the inside of the ring-shaped filter. If you can see light coming through the paper element, the filter is all right. Check all the way around the filter.
6   Wipe the inside of the air cleaner housing with a rag. Be careful not to drop any debris down the carburetor.
7   Place the old filter (if in good condition) or the new filter (if specified interval has elapsed) back into the air cleaner housing. Make sure it seats properly in the bottom of the housing.
8   Reinstall the top plate with the wing nut.

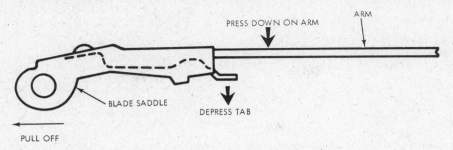

PRESS DOWN ON ARM

ARM

BLADE SADDLE

DEPRESS TAB

PULL OFF

Fig. 1.15 Components of wiper blade assembly (Sec 14)

15.2 Lifting away the air cleaner top plate to reveal the filter within

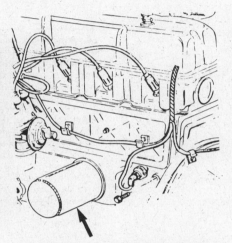

Fig. 1.16 Typical oil filter location on six cylinder engines (Sec 16)

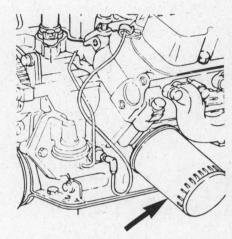

Fig. 1.17 Typical oil filter location on V8 engines (Sec 16)

16 Engine oil and filter change

1   Frequent oil changes may be the best form of preventative maintenance available for the home mechanic. When engine oil ages, it gets diluted and contaminated which ultimately leads to premature parts wear.

2   Although some sources recommend oil filter changes every other oil change, we feel that the minimal cost of an oil filter and the relative ease with which it is installed dictates that a new filter be used whenever the oil is changed.

3   The tools necessary for a normal oil and filter change are: a wrench to fit the drain plug at the bottom of the oil pan; an oil filter wrench to remove the old filter; a container with at least an eight quart capacity to drain the old oil into; and a funnel or oil can spout to help pour fresh oil into the engine.

4   In addition, you should have plenty of clean rags and newspapers handy to mop up any spills. Access to the underside of the vehicle is greatly improved if it can be lifted on a hoist, driven onto ramps or supported by jack stands. Do not work under a vehicle which is supported only by a bumper, hydraulic or scissors-type jack.

5   If this is your first oil change, it is a good idea to crawl underneath and familiarize yourself with the locations of the oil drain plug and the oil filter. Since the engine and exhaust components will be warm during the actual work, it is best to figure out any potential problems before the vehicle and its accessories are hot.

6   Allow the engine to warm up to normal operating temperature. If the new oil or any tools are needed, use this warm-up time to gather everything necessary for the job. The correct type of oil to buy for your application can be found in *Recommended Lubricants* near the front of this Chapter.

7   With the engine oil warm (warm engine oil will drain better and more built-up sludge will be removed with the oil), raise the vehicle for

access beneath. Make sure it is firmly supported. If jack stands are used they should be placed towards the front of the frame rails.

8   Move all necessary tools, rags and newspaper under the vehicle. Postion the drain pan under the drain plug. Keep in mind that the oil will initially flow from the pan with some force, so place the pan accordingly.

9   Being careful not to touch any of the hot exhaust pipe components, use the wrench to remove the drain plug near the bottom of the oil pan. Depending on how hot the oil has become, you may want to wear gloves while unscrewing the plug the final few turns.

10   Allow the old oil to drain into the pan. It may be necessary to move the pan further under the engine as the oil flow reduces to a trickle.

11   After all the oil has drained, clean the drain plug thoroughly with a clean rag. Small metal filings may cling to this plug which could immediately contaminate your new oil.

12   Clean the area around the drain plug opening and reinstall the drain plug. Tighten the plug securely with your wrench. If a torque wrench is available, torque the drain plug to the proper specification.

13   Move the drain pan in position under the oil filter.

14   Now use the filter wrench to loosen the oil filter. Chain or metal band-type filter wrenches may distort the filter canister, but don't worry too much about this as the filter will be discarded anyway.

15   Sometimes the oil filter is on so tight it cannot be loosened, or it is positioned in an area which is inaccessible with a filter wrench. As a last resort, you can punch a metal bar or long screwdriver directly through the bottom of the canister and use this as a T-bar to turn the filter. If this must be done, be prepared for oil to spurt out of the canister as it is punctured.

16   Completely unscrew the old filter. Be careful, it is full of oil. Empty the old oil inside the filter into the drain pan.

17   Compare the old filter with the new one to make sure they are of the same type.

18   Use a clean rag to remove all oil, dirt and sludge from the area

where the oil filter mounts to the engine. Check the old filter to make sure the rubber gasket is not stuck to the engine mounting surface. If this gasket is stuck to the engine (use a flashlight if necessary), remove it.

19 Open one of the cans of new oil and fill the new filter with fresh oil. Also smear a light coat of this fresh oil onto the rubber gasket of the new oil filter.

20 Screw the new filter to the engine following the tightening directions printed on the filter canister or packing box. Filter manufacturers recommend against using a filter wrench due to possible overtightening or damage to the canister.

21 Remove all tools, rags, etc. from under the car, being careful not to spill the oil in the drain pan. Lower the vehicle off its support devices.

22 Move to the engine compartment and locate the oil filler cap on the engine. In most cases there will be a twist off cap on the rocker arm cover or a cap at the end of a fill tube at the front of the engine.

23 If an oil can spout is used, push the spout into the top of the oil can and pour fresh oil through the filler opening. A funnel placed into the opening may also be used.

24 Pour about 3 qts. of fresh oil into the engine. Wait a few minutes to allow the oil to drain to the pan, then check the level on the oil dipstick (see Section 3 if necessary). If the oil level is at or near the lower 'Add' mark, start the engine and allow the new oil to circulate.

25 Run the engine for only about a minute and then shut it off. Immediately look under the car and check for leaks at the oil pan drain plug and around the oil filter. If either is leaking, tighten with a bit more force.

26 With the new oil circulated and the filter now completely full, recheck the level on the dipstick and add enough oil to bring the level to the safe mark on the dipstick.

27 During the first few trips after an oil change, make a point to check for leaks and also the oil level.

28 The old oil drained from the engine cannot be reused in its present state and should be disposed of. Oil reclamation centers, auto repair shops and gas stations will normally accept the oil which can be refined and used again. After the oil has cooled, it can be drained into a suitable container (capped plastic jugs, topped bottles, milk cartons, etc.) for transport to one of these disposal sites.

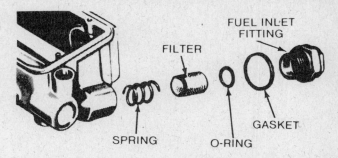

Fig. 1.18 Components of fuel filter (internal inlet housing type) (Sec 17)

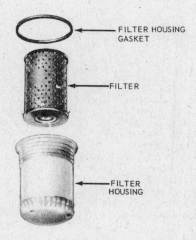

Fig. 1.19 Components of fuel filter (integral with pump type) (Sec 17)

17 Fuel filter – replacement

1 Fuel filters need to be replaced according to the maintenance interval suggestions as well as when a blockage in the fuel line occurs due to excessive foreign material in the fuel.

2 When a fuel filter is replaced, precautions should be exercised considering the volatile nature of gasoline. This work should be done on a cool engine. Never smoke or have any open flames around the work area. Do not work within an enclosed area. When removing a fuel system component, take care to clean up any spills which will inevitably occur when gasoline under pressure is released. Make sure that gasoline does not puddle or stand anywhere in the engine compartment or work area. Clean any spilled gasoline off the vehicle as well as yourself as it can burn your skin.

3 Fuel filters are located in a number of different positions depending on the year, engine size and weight rating of the vehicle. Most fuel filters can be found in-line somewhere between the fuel pump and the carburetor.

4 If a fuel filter is located in-line between the carburetor and the fuel pump, it is usually connected with rubber hoses. Release the clamps on the rubber hoses and slowly remove the filter from the system. Use caution in this step as gasoline will be under pressure at this point.

5 After removing the filter, drain it of gasoline and discard it in a non-incendiary refuse container. Replace the filter with an exact replacement duplicate and push it in to new rubber connecting hoses which should be provided with the filter. Also replace the clamps if they appear weak.

6 Tighten all clamps. Start the vehicle and check for leaks.

7 If the filter is the type located in the inlet of the carburetor, first remove the line leading to the inlet by unthreading it if it has a fitting or by removing the clamp and hose if it is so equipped.

8 Carefully unscrew the carburetor inlet/filter unit from the carburetor. Be careful not to damage the threads in the carburetor.

9 Some filters in the carburetor are integral with the inlet connec-

tion. If this type is being replaced, simply screw in a new filter/inlet assembly.

10 If an internal filter is located inside the carburetor inlet, the spring, gasket and filter must be removed after the inlet is unscrewed.

11 Assemble the new filter, seal and spring in the reverse order of their removal.

12 Carefully screw in the inlet connector using caution not to damage the threads in the carburetor.

13 Some fuel filters are located in the bottom of the fuel pump. To remove this type of filter, unscrew the canister from the bottom of the fuel pump in the same way that an oil filter is removed.

14 Slowly drop the canister and filter assembly off the bottom of the fuel pump, being careful not to spill the gasoline contained within it.

15 Empty the container of gasoline and then remove the filter and gasket assembly.

16 Insert a new filter and gasket assembly.

17 Screw the filter and filter housing assembly back on to the base of the fuel pump.

18 Start the vehicle and check the filter and surrounding area for leaks.

18 Evaporative emissions system – inspection

1 The evaporative emissions system consists of the charcoal carbon canister, the lines connecting the canister to the carburetor air cleaner and to the fuel tank, and the fuel tank filler cap.

2 Inspect the fuel filler cap(s) and make sure the gasket sealing the cap is in good condition. It should not be cracked, broken or show signs of leakage.

3 Inspect the lines leading to the charcoal carbon canister from the fuel tank. They should be in good shape and the rubber should not show signs of cracking, checking or leakage.

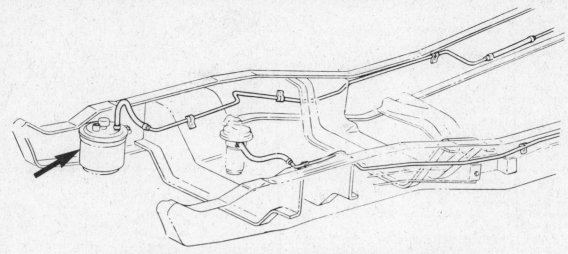

Fig. 1.20 Typical carbon canister location at front of frame rail (Sec 18)

4 Check all of the clamps and make sure they are sealing the system. Check the carbon-filled canister for any signs of leakage, over-filling or damage. In most cases, a carbon canister will last the lifetime of the vehicle; however, certain situations will require replacement. If the carbon canister shows signs of leakage or damage, replace it, as it is not a serviceable unit.
5 Check all the lines leading from the carbon canister to the air cleaner. In some cases there will be two lines, one leading from the carburetor fuel bowl to vent it, and one line leading from the carbon canister to the air cleaner for burning of the accumulated vapors.
6 Replace any lines in questionable condition and exercise the same precautions as are necessary when dealing with fuel lines or the fuel filter.

19 Lubrication – chassis, body and driveline components

1 A grease gun filled with the proper grease (see *Recommended Lubricants* near the front of this Chapter) and some wiping rags are the main pieces of equipment necessary to lubricate the chassis and steering components. Notice that different components require different types of grease so a grease gun with changeable cartridges or several grease-guns will be necessary to correctly perform the lubrication process.
2 Carefully look over Figs 1.21 or 1.22 for the location of the lubrication fittings on the chassis and steering linkage. After you have familiarized yourself with these locations, look under the vehicle and relate the chart to the grease fittings, many of which are visible from under the front of the vehicle's front bumper.
3 Easier access to some of these fittings will require raising and supporting the vehicle with a jack and jack stands. Be sure the vehicle is firmly supported with jack stands and read the information on jacking instructions at the front of this book if you are unfamiliar with the correct procedures.
4 Before you do any greasing, force a little of the grease out the nozzle to remove any dirt from the end of the gun. Wipe the nozzle clean with a rag.
5 With the grease gun, plenty of clean rags and the location diagram, go under the vehicle to begin lubricating the components.
6 Wipe the grease fitting nipple clean and push the nozzle firmly over the fitting nipple. Squeeze the trigger on the grease gun to force grease into the component. **Note:** *When lubricating the steering linkage joints, pump only enough lubricant to fill the rubber cup to a firm to the touch capacity.* If you pump in too much grease, the cups can rupture allowing grease to leak out and dirt to enter the joint. For all other suspension and steering fittings, continue pumping grease into the nipple until grease seeps out of the joint between the two components. If the grease seeps out around the grease gun nozzle, the nipple is clogged or the nozzle is not fully seated around the fitting nipple. Re-secure the gun nozzle to the fitting and try again. If necessary, replace the fitting. Make sure the king pins have plenty of grease of the correct type.

7 Wipe the excess grease from the components and the grease fitting.
8 Check the universal joints on the driveshaft; some have fittings, some are factory sealed. About two pumps is all that is required for grease-type universal joints. While you are under the vehicle clean and lubricate the parking brake cable along with its cable guides and levers. This can be done by smearing some of the chassis grease onto the cable and its related parts with your fingers. Place a few drops of light engine oil on the transmission and transfer case (if 4X4 or Bronco) shifting linkage rods and swivels.
9 Lower the vehicle to the ground for the remaining body lubrication process.
10 Open the hood and smear a little chassis grease on the hood latch mechanism. If the hood has an inside release, have an assistant pull the release knob from inside the vehicle as you lubricate the cable at the latch.
11 Lubricate all the hinges (door, hood, tailgate) with a few drops of light engine oil to keep them in proper working order.
12 The key lock cylinders can be lubricated with spray-on graphite which is available at auto parts stores.
13 Spray silicone lubricant on the door seals to keep them pliable and effective.
14 Lubricate the accelerator linkage pivots with a multi-purpose lubricant, usually available in small spray cans.
15 Lubricate the clutch linkage (if the vehicle is stick-shift equipped) with the grease gun through the fitting provided on the cross-shaft linkage.
16 Use a rust penetrant and inhibitor on the manifold exhaust heat control valve if the vehicle is so equipped.
17 Spray some multi-purpose lubricant on the brake pedal (and clutch pedal) pivot shafts under the dash area for smooth, quiet operation of these pedal(s). Be sure to wipe off any excess so that the operator's shoes and clothing do not pick up any extra lubricant.
18 Some universal joints, particularly those found on 4 X 4 equipped vehicles, will require the use of a special 'needle' lubrication adapter for your grease gun. Do not overlook this part of the drive-line lubrication as it is important for the continued service of these joints and they are relatively expensive and difficult to replace should they fail.

20 Clutch adjustment

Note: *On 1973 through 1976 Broncos, clutch pedal total travel must be adjusted first as described in Chapter 7.*
1 To adjust the clutch pedal free play, two measurements will have to be taken.
2 The first measurement is taken with the pedal fully released. The distance between the face of the clutch pedal and the bottom of the steering wheel should be taken for a base measurement.
3 Depress the clutch pedal until all of the free play is taken up and

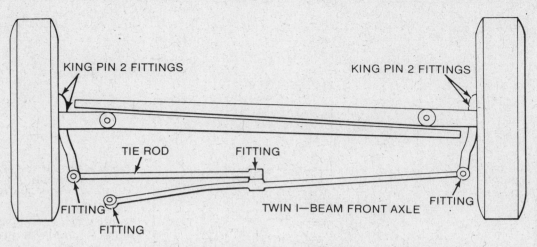

KING PIN 2 FITTINGS

KING PIN 2 FITTINGS

TIE ROD

FITTING

FITTING

FITTING

FITTING

TWIN I—BEAM FRONT AXLE

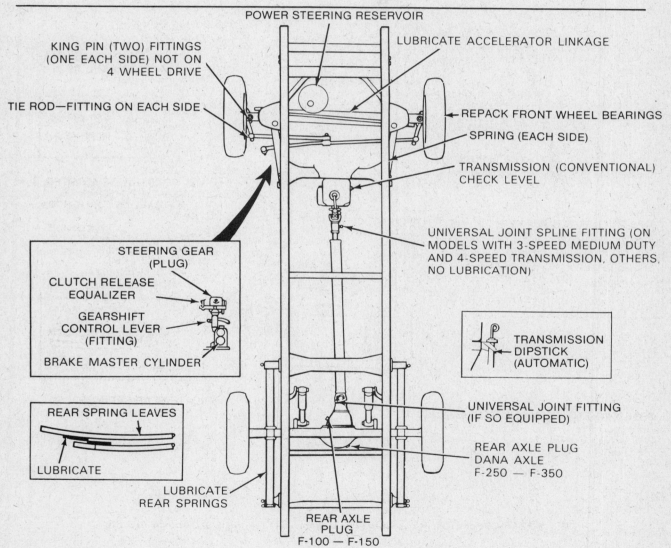

POWER STEERING RESERVOIR

KING PIN (TWO) FITTINGS (ONE EACH SIDE) NOT ON 4 WHEEL DRIVE

LUBRICATE ACCELERATOR LINKAGE

TIE ROD—FITTING ON EACH SIDE

REPACK FRONT WHEEL BEARINGS

SPRING (EACH SIDE)

TRANSMISSION (CONVENTIONAL) CHECK LEVEL

UNIVERSAL JOINT SPLINE FITTING (ON MODELS WITH 3-SPEED MEDIUM DUTY AND 4-SPEED TRANSMISSION, OTHERS, NO LUBRICATION)

STEERING GEAR (PLUG)

CLUTCH RELEASE EQUALIZER

GEARSHIFT CONTROL LEVER (FITTING)

BRAKE MASTER CYLINDER

TRANSMISSION DIPSTICK (AUTOMATIC)

REAR SPRING LEAVES

LUBRICATE

UNIVERSAL JOINT FITTING (IF SO EQUIPPED)

REAR AXLE PLUG DANA AXLE F-250 — F-350

LUBRICATE REAR SPRINGS

REAR AXLE PLUG F-100 — F-150

Fig. 1.21 Chassis and suspension lubrication locations for 4 x 2 trucks (Sec 18)

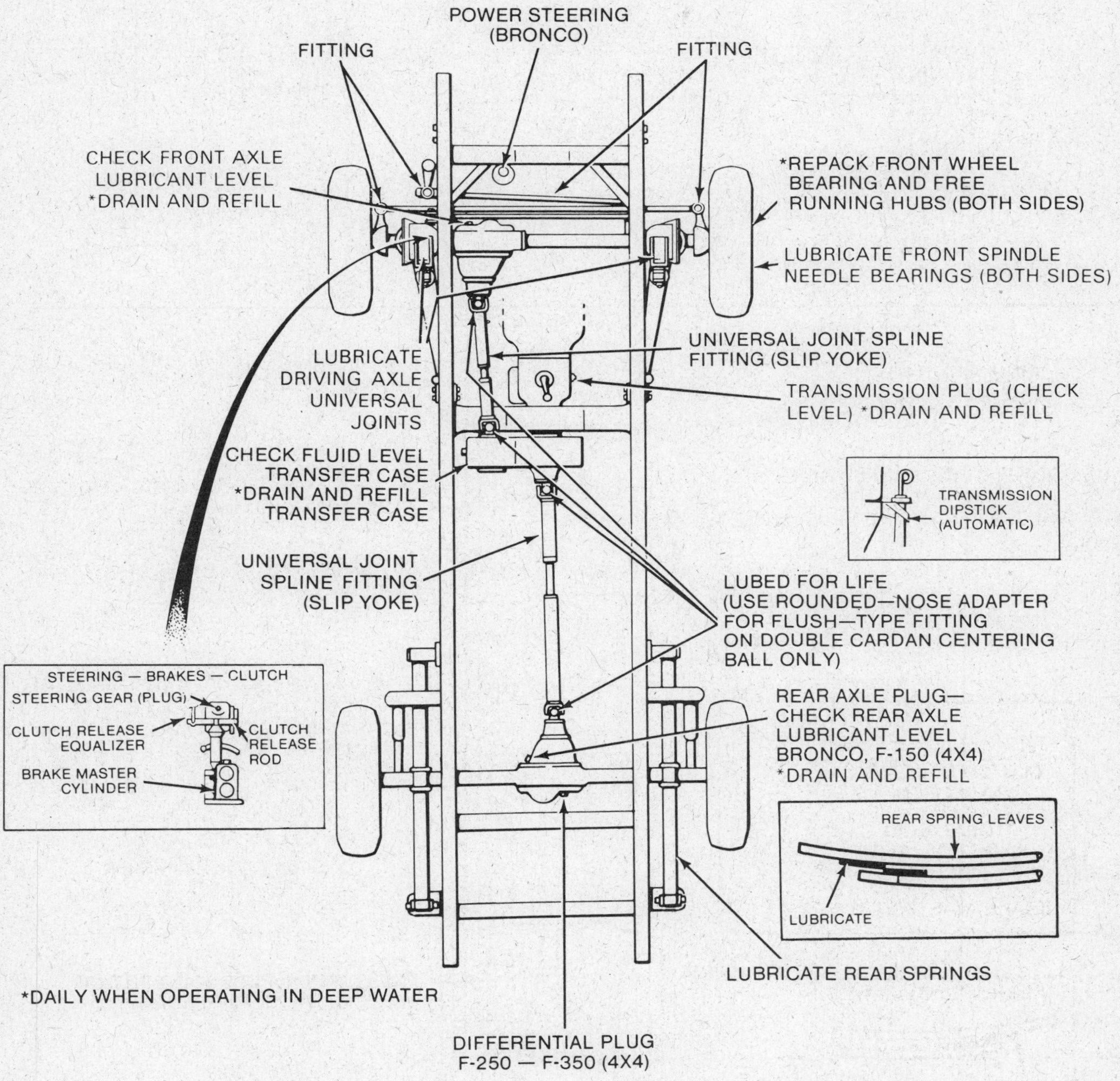

POWER STEERING
(BRONCO)

FITTING

FITTING

CHECK FRONT AXLE
LUBRICANT LEVEL
*DRAIN AND REFILL

*REPACK FRONT WHEEL
BEARING AND FREE
RUNNING HUBS (BOTH SIDES)

LUBRICATE FRONT SPINDLE
NEEDLE BEARINGS (BOTH SIDES)

LUBRICATE
DRIVING AXLE
UNIVERSAL
JOINTS

UNIVERSAL JOINT SPLINE
FITTING (SLIP YOKE)

TRANSMISSION PLUG (CHECK
LEVEL) *DRAIN AND REFILL

CHECK FLUID LEVEL
TRANSFER CASE
*DRAIN AND REFILL
TRANSFER CASE

TRANSMISSION
DIPSTICK
(AUTOMATIC)

1

UNIVERSAL JOINT
SPLINE FITTING
(SLIP YOKE)

LUBED FOR LIFE
(USE ROUNDED—NOSE ADAPTER
FOR FLUSH—TYPE FITTING
ON DOUBLE CARDAN CENTERING
BALL ONLY)

STEERING — BRAKES — CLUTCH

STEERING GEAR (PLUG)

CLUTCH RELEASE
EQUALIZER

CLUTCH
RELEASE
ROD

BRAKE MASTER
CYLINDER

REAR AXLE PLUG—
CHECK REAR AXLE
LUBRICANT LEVEL
BRONCO, F-150 (4X4)
*DRAIN AND REFILL

REAR SPRING LEAVES

LUBRICATE

LUBRICATE REAR SPRINGS

*DAILY WHEN OPERATING IN DEEP WATER

DIFFERENTIAL PLUG
F-250 — F-350 (4X4)

Fig. 1.22 Chassis and suspension lubrication locations for 4 x 4 trucks and Bronco (Sec 19)

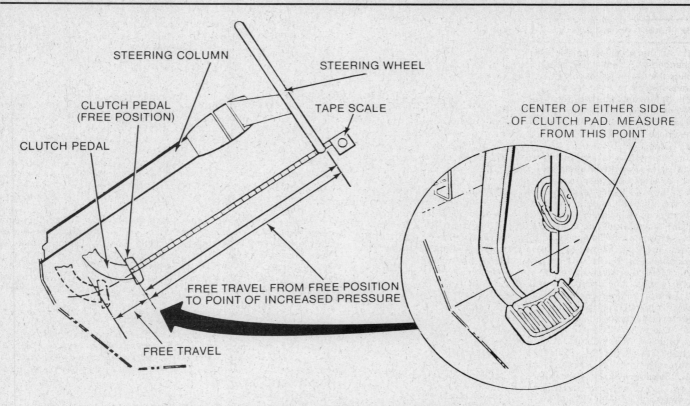

Fig. 1.23 Method of measuring clutch free travel (Sec 20)

additional resistance is felt. This point is the beginning of the clutch being actuated at the release bearing.

4   In this depressed position, again measure the distance between the base of the steering wheel and the clutch pedal face. Subtract this distance from the original base measurement to find the clutch pedal free travel.

5   If the clutch pedal free travel is more than the maximum, or, less than the minimum specifications, the clutch must be adjusted to prevent either premature failure of the throw-out bearing or damage to the clutch.

6   To adjust the clutch, remove the retracting spring at the clutch linkage near the bellhousing next to the clutch release lever.

7   Loosen the two jam nuts on the clutch release rod and back off both of the nuts several turns.

8   Turn the first jam nut against the swivel until the correct free travel is achieved. Notice that one turn of the jam nut will move the travel approximately $\frac{3}{8}$ in.

9   Hold the first jam nut with an open end wrench, and tighten the second jam nut against the first. This locks the adjustment. Re-check your measurement.

10   Reinstall the clutch linkage retracting spring.

---

21   Manual transmission and/or transfer case – fluid change

1   The transmission and transfer case (4x4 models only) use the same type of fluid and are drained and filled in the same way.

2   Drive the vehicle for at least 15 minutes in city-type stop-and-go traffic to warm the fluid in the case(s). If the 4x4 transfer case fluid is being changed, perform this driving cycle with the transfer case engaged in 4-wheel drive (hubs unlocked on selective-type models). If the vehicle is equipped with a full time 4x4 system, the previous step does not apply. Use all of the gears including Reverse during this driving cycle to ensure that the oil is sufficiently warm to drain completely.

3   Raise the vehicle to a level position using either a suitable lift or four jack stands (see *Jacking and Towing* at the front of this book). Remove the drain plug from the unit you wish to change the fluid in. Allow plenty of time for the oil to drain.

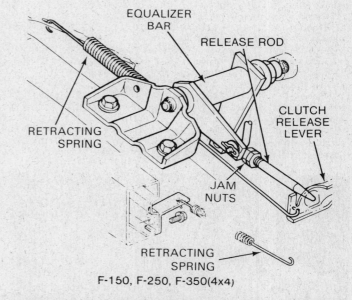

Fig. 1.24 Components of the clutch linkage system (Sec 20)

4   After all of the oil has been drained, replace and re-torque the case drain plug.

5   Using the proper grade and type of hypoid gear oil, refill the transmission and/or transfer case until the fluid reaches the filler hole level.

6   Replace the filler plug(s) and tighten the plug(s) to the correct torque specification. Drive the vehicle for a short distance and re-check the level in the unit being serviced. In some cases a small amount of additional fluid will have to be added if the circulation has taken up some of the fluid.

7   After driving the vehicle through a normal cycle procedure, re-check the drain and filler plugs for any signs of leakage.

22 Automatic transmission fluid change

1   At the specified time intervals, the transmission fluid should be changed and the filter replaced with a new one. Since there is no drain plug, the transmission oil pan must be removed from the bottom of the transmission to drain the fluid.

2   Before any draining, purchase the specified transmission fluid (see *Recommended Lubricants* near the front of this Chapter) and a new filter. The necessary gaskets should be included with the filter; purchase an oil pan gasket and a strainer-to-valve body gasket.

3   Other tools necessary for this job include: jack stands to support the vehicle in a raised position; wrench to remove the oil pan bolts; standard screwdriver; drain can capable of holding at least 30 pints; newspapers and clean rags.

4   The fluid should be drained immediately after the vehicle has been driven. This will remove any built-up sediment better than if the fluid were cold. Because of this, it may be wise to wear protective gloves (fluid temperature can exceed 350° in a hot transmission).

5   After the vehicle has been driven to warm up the fluid, raise it and place it on jack stands for access underneath. Make sure it is firmly supported by the four stands placed on the frame rails.

6   Move the necessary equipment under the vehicle, being careful not to touch any of the hot exhaust components.

7   Place the drain pan under the transmission oil pan and remove the oil pan bolts along the rear and sides of the pan. Loosen, but do not remove, the bolts at the front of the pan.

8   Carefully pry the pan downward at the rear, allowing the hot fluid to drain into the drain pan. If necessary, use a screwdriver to break the gasket seal at the rear of the pan; however, do not damage the pan or transmission in the process.

9   Support the pan and remove the remaining bolts at the front of the pan. Lower the pan and drain the remaining fluid into the drain receptacle. As this is done, check the fluid for metal particles which may be an indication of internal failure.

10 Now visible on the bottom of the transmission is the filter/strainer held in place by screws (photo).

11 Remove the screws, the filter and its gasket.

12 Thoroughly clean the transmission oil pan with solvent. Inspect for metal particles or foreign matter. Dry with compressed air, if available. It is important that all remaining gasket material be removed from the oil pan mounting flange. Use a gasket scraper or putty knife for this.

13 Clean the filter mounting surface on the valve body. Again, this surface should be smooth and free of any leftover gasket material.

14 Place the new filter into position, with a new gasket between it and the transmission valve body. Install the mounting screws and tighten securely.

15 Apply a bead of gasket sealant around the oil pan mounting surface, with the sealant to the inside of the bolt holes. Press the new gasket into place on the pan, making sure all bolt holes line up.

22.10 The automatic transmission filter and its attaching screws (arrows)

16 Lift the pan up to the bottom of the transmission and install the mounting bolts. Tighten the bolts in a diagonal fashion, working around the pan. Using a torque wrench, tighten the bolts to the specified torque.

17 Lower the vehicle off the jack stands.

18 Open the hood and remove the transmission fluid dipstick from its guide tube.

19 Since fluid capacities vary between the various transmission types, it is best to add a little fluid at a time, continually checking the level with the dipstick. Allow the fluid time to drain into the pan. Add fluid until the level just registers on the end of the dipstick. In most cases, a good starting point will be 4 to 5 pints added to the transmission through the filler tube (use a funnel to prevent spills).

20 With the selector lever in 'Park' apply the parking brake and start the engine without depressing the accelerator pedal (if possible). Do not race the engine at a high speed; run at slow idle only, for at least two minutes.

21 Depress the brake pedal and shift the transmission through each gear. Place the selector in the 'Neutral' position and check the level on the dipstick (with the engine still idling). Look under the vehicle for leaks around the transmission oil pan mating surface.

22 Add more fluid through the dipstick tube until the level on the dipstick. Do not allow the fluid level to go above this point, as the transmission would then be overfilled, necessitating the removal of the pan to drain the excess fluid.

23 Push the dipstick firmly back into its tube and drive the vehicle to reach normal operating temperature (15 miles of highway driving or its equivalent in the city). Park on a level surface and check the fluid level on the dipstick with the engine idling and the transmission in 'Neutral'. The level should now be at the 'Don't add' mark on the dipstick. If not, add more fluid as necessary to bring the level up to this point. Again, do not overfill.

23 Differentials – fluid change

Note: *Carefully read through this procedure before undertaking this process. You will need to purchase the correct type and amount of differential lubricant before draining the old fluid out of the vehicle. In some cases you will also need a differential cover gasket and an additive.*

1   The vehicle should be driven for several minutes before draining the rear axle fluid. This practice will warm up the fluid and ensure complete drainage.

2   Move a drain pan, rags, newspapers, and tools under the vehicle. With the drain pan under the differential, remove the drain plug from the bottom of the housing. If no drain plug is provided, remove the fluid through the fill plug with a suction gun or syringe. On Dana-type differentials no drain plug is provided which necessitates that the differential cover be removed to drain the fluid. Remove the inspection/fill plug to help vent the drainage procedure on non-Dana type differentials.

3   After the fluid has completely drained, wipe the area around the drain hole with a clean rag and install the drain plug. Reinstall the differential cover with a new gasket on Dana-type differentials. Torque the cover retaining bolts to the proper specification.

4   Fill the housing (through the inspectin hole) with the recommended lubricant until the level is even with the bottom of the inspection hole. Check the manufacturer's tag on the driver's door latch post or the tag attached to the differential to determine if your vehicle is equipped with a locking or equal-lock type of differential. These differentials require the use of an additional additive to supplement the normal differential lubricant. Add the prescribed amount of this additive at this time. Install the inspection plug after cleaning it and the threads in the case or cover.

5   After driving the vehicle, check for leaks at the drain and inspection plugs.

6   When the job is complete, check for metal filings or chips in the drained fluid, which indicate that the differential should be thoroughly inspected and repaired (see Chapter 8 for more information).

24 Cooling system servicing (draining, flushing and refilling

1   Periodically, the cooling system should be drained, flushed and refilled. This is to replenish the antifreeze mixture and prevent rust and

corrosion which can impair the performance of the cooling system and ultimately cause engine damage.

2   At the same time the cooling system is serviced, all hoses and the fill cap should be inspected and replaced if faulty (see Section 12).

3   As antifreeze is a poisonous solution, take care not to spill any of the cooling mixture on the vehicle's paint or your own skin. If this happens, rinse immediately with plenty of clear water. Also it is advisable to consult your local authorities about the dumping of antifreeze before draining the cooling system. In many areas reclamation centers have been set up to collect automobile oil and drained antifreeze/water mixtures rather than allowing these liquids to be added to the sewage and water facilities.

4   With the engine cold, remove the radiator pressure fill cap.

5   Move a large container under the radiator to catch the water/antifreeze mixture as it is drained.

6   Drain the radiator. Most models are equipped with a drain plug at the bottom of the radiator which can be opened using a wrench to hold the fitting while the petcock is turned to the open position. If this drain has excessive corrosion and cannot be turned easily, or the radiator is not equipped with a drain, disconnect the lower radiator hose to allow the coolant to drain. Be careful that none of the solution is splashed on your skin or in your eyes.

7   If accessible, remove the two engine drain plugs. There is one plug on each side of the engine, about halfway back and on the lower edge near the oil pan rail. These will allow the coolant to drain from the engine itself.

8   On systems with an expansion reservoir, disconnect the overflow pipe and remove the reservoir. Flush it out with clean water.

9   Place a cold water hose (a common garden hose is fine) in the radiator filler neck at the top of the radiator and flush the system until the water runs clean at all drain points.

10   In severe cases of contamination or clogging of the radiator remove (see Chapter 3) and reverse flush it. This involves simply inserting the cold pressure hose in the bottom radiator outlet to allow the clear water to run against the normal flow, draining through the top. A radiator repair shop should be consulted if further cleaning or repair is necessary.

11   Where the coolant is regularly drained and the system refilled with the correct antifreeze/inhibitor mixture there should be no need to employ chemical cleaners or descalers.

12   To refill the system, reconnect the radiator hoses and install the drain plugs securely in the engine. Special thread sealing tape (available at auto parts stores) should be used on the drain plugs going into the engine block. Install the expansion reservoir and the overflow hose where applicable.

13   On vehicles without an expansion reservoir, refill the system through the radiator filler cap until the water level is about three inches below the filler neck.

14   On vehicles with an expansion reservoir, fill the radiator to the base of the filler neck and then add more coolant to the expansion reservoir so that it reaches the 'FULL COLD' mark.

15   Run the engine until normal operating temperature is reached and with the engine idling, add coolant up to the correct level (see Section 3), then fit the radiator cap so that the arrows are in alignment with the overflow pipe. Install the reservoir cap.

16   Always refill the system with a mixture of high quality antifreeze and water in the proportion called for on the antifreeze container or in your owner's manual. Chapter 3 also contains information on antifreeze mixture.

17   Keep a close watch on the coolant level and the various cooling hoses during the first few miles of driving. Tighten the hose clamps and/or add more coolant mixture as necessary.

25 Wheel bearing check and repack (4x2 models)

Note: *This procedure applies only to 2-wheel drive vehicles. Information on 4x4s and Broncos can be found in Chapter 8.*

1   In most cases, the front wheel bearings will not need servicing until the brake pads are changed. However, these bearings should be checked whenever the front wheels are raised for any reason.

2   With the vehicle securely supported on jack stands, spin the wheel and check for noise, rolling resistance or free play. Now grab the top of the tire with one hand and the bottom of the tire with the other. Move the tire in and out on the spindle. If it moves more than 0.005 in, the bearings should be checked, then repacked with grease or replaced if necessary.

3   To remove the bearings for replacing or repacking, begin by removing the hub cap and wheel.

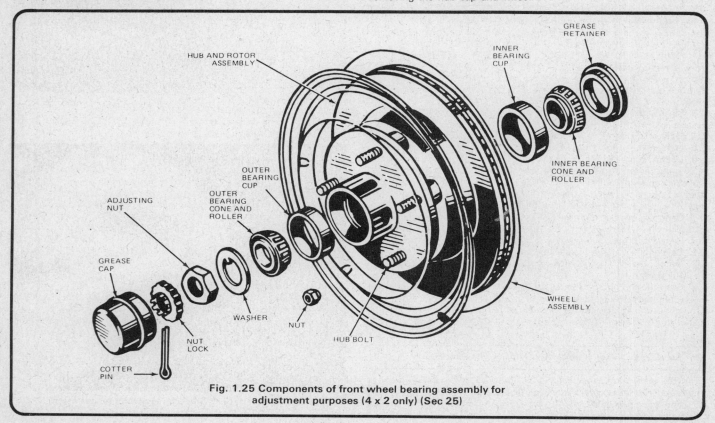

Fig. 1.25 Components of front wheel bearing assembly for
adjustment purposes (4 x 2 only) (Sec 25)

4   Remove the brake caliper as described in Chapter 9.
5   Use wire to hang the caliper assembly out of the way. Be careful not to kink or damage the brake hose.
6   Pry the hub grease cap off the hub using a screwdriver. This cap is located at the center of the hub.
7   Use needle-nose pliers to straighten the bent ends of the cotter pin and then pull the cotter pin out of the locking nut. Discard the cotter pin, as a new one should be used on reassembly.
8   Remove the spindle nut and its washer from the end of the spindle.
9   Pull the hub assembly outward slightly and then push it back into its original position. This should force the outer bearing off the spindle enough so that it can be removed with your fingers. Remove the outer bearing, noting how it is installed on the end of the spindle.
10 Now the hub assembly can be pulled off the spindle.
11 On the rear side of the hub, use a screwdriver to pry out the inner bearing lip seal. As this is done, note the direction in which the seal is installed.
12 The inner bearing can now be removed from the hub, again noting how it is installed.
13 Use clean parts solvent to remove all traces of the old grease from the bearings, hub and spindle. A small brush may prove useful; however, make sure no bristles from the brush embed themselves inside the bearing rollers. Allow the parts to air dry.
14 Carefully inspect the bearings for cracks, heat discoloration, bent rollers, etc. Check the bearing races inside the hub for cracks, scoring, or uneven surfaces. If the bearing races are in need of replacement this job is best left to a repair shop which can press the new races into position.
15 Use an approved high temperature front wheel bearing grease to pack the bearings. Work the grease fully into the bearings, forcing the grease between the rollers, cone and cage.
16 Apply a thin coat of grease to the spindle at the outer bearing seat, inner bearing seat, shoulder and seal seat.
17 Put a small quantity of grease inboard of each bearing race inside the hub. Using your fingers, form a dam at these points to provide extra grease availability and to keep thinned grease from flowing out of the bearing.
18 Place the grease-packed inner bearing into the rear of the hub and put a little more grease outboard of the bearings.
19 Place a new seal over the inner bearing and tap the seal with a flat plate and a hammer until it is flush with the hub.
20 Carefully place the hub assembly onto the spindle and push the grease-packed outer bearing into position.
21 Install the washer and spindle nut. Tighten the nut only slightly (17 to 25 ft-lbs of torque).
22 In a forward direction, spin the hub to seat the bearings and remove any grease or burrs which would cause excessive bearing play later.
23 Put a little grease outboard of the outer bearing to provide extra grease availability.
24 Now check that the spindle nut is still tight (17 to 25 ft-lbs).
25 Loosen the spindle nut $\frac{1}{8}$ turn.
26 Using your hand (not a wrench of any kind), tighten the nut until it is snug. Install a new cotter pin through the hole in the spindle and spindle nut. If the nut slits do not line up, loosen the nut slightly until they do. From the hand-tight position the nut should not be loosened any more than one-half flat to install the cotter pin.
27 Bend the ends of the new cotter pin until they are flat against the nut. Cut off any extra length which could interfere with the dust cap.
28 Install the dust cap, tapping it into place with a rubber mallet.
29 Reinstall the brake caliper as described in Chapter 9.
30 Install the tire/wheel assembly to the hub and tighten the mounting nuts.
31 Grab the top and bottom of the tire and check the bearings in the same manner as described at the beginning of this Section.
32 Lower the vehicle to the ground and fully tighten the wheel nuts. Install the hub cap, using a rubber mallet to fully seat it.

26 Spark plug wires – inspection and replacement

1   The spark plug wires should be checked at the recommended intervals or whenever new spark plugs are installed.
2   The wires should be inspected one at a time to prevent mixing up the order which is essential for proper engine operation. Each original spark plug wire is numbered to help identify its location. If any number is illegible, a piece of masking tape can be marked with the correct number and wrapped around the spark plug wire.
3   Disconnect the plug wire from the spark plug. A removal tool can be used for this, or you can grab the rubber boot, twist slightly and then pull the wire free. Do not pull on the wire itself, only on the rubber boot (photo).
4   Inspect inside the boot for corrosion, which will look like a white crusty powder (photo). Some vehicles use a conductive white grease which should not be mistaken for corrosion. **Note:** *When any spark plug wire on an electronic ignition system is detached from a spark plug, distributor or coil terminal, silicone grease (Ford No. D7AZ-19A331-A or equivalent electronic application grease) should be applied to the interior surface of the boot before reinstalling the wire onto the component.*
5   Now push the wire and boot back onto the end of the spark plug. It should be a tight fit on the plug end. If not, remove the wires and use a pair of pliers to carefully crimp the metal connector inside the wire boot until the fit is secure.
6   Now using a clean rag, clean the wire its entire length. Remove all built-up dirt and grease. As this is done, inspect for burns, cracks or any other form of damage.
7   Disconnect the wire at the distributor (again, pulling and twisting only on the rubber boot). Check for corrosion and a tight fit in the same manner as the spark plug end.

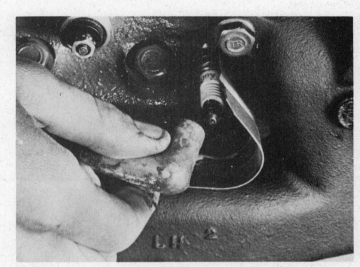

26.3 Remove the spark plug wire by grasping the boot rather than the wire itself

26.4 Inspecting the inside of the spark plug boot for corrosion

8   Check the remaining spark plug wires in the same way, making sure they are securely fastened at the distributor and spark plug.

9   A visual check of the spark plug wires can also be made. In a darkened garage (make sure there is ventilation), start the engine and observe each plug wire. Be careful not to come into contact with any moving engine parts. If there is a break or fault in the wire, you will be able to see arcing or a small spark at the damaged area.

10   Additional information can be found in Chapter 5.

11   Spark plug wires suspected of non-conducting or poor conducting qualities can also be checked using a multi-meter. No special training other than possession of this tool is required for this test. These meters are usually available from parts houses or electronic-supply stores. Remove any wire suspected of failure or high resistance from the vehicle. (It is wise to test the entire set, one wire at a time, during the process of a tune-up). Set the meter to measure resistance. Use a test lead connected to each end of the wire and measure the amount of resistance through the wire. Compare it to the specifications found at the front of this Chapter. Replace any wires with a higher than specification resistance factor.

12   An electronic engine oscilloscope is probably the most effective method of determining true 'on vehicle' spark plug operating condition; however, these are expensive and must be operated by experienced, trained personnel. Local tune-up shops and service centers are usually equipped with these units and will generally test a vehicle's entire ignition system in a short amount of time for a nominal fee. If a test of this type reveals defective spark plug wire(s), you can then purchase a set or wire from a local auto supply source and replace them yourself.

13   If it is decided the spark plug wires are in need of replacement, purchase a new set for your specific engine model. Wire sets can be purchased which are pre-cut to the proper size and with the rubber boots already installed. Remove and replace each wire individually to prevent mix-ups in the firing sequence.

27   Distributor cap and rotor – inspection and replacement

1   To check the distributor cap and rotor, first release the two clips retaining the distributor cap to the distributor body (or to the adapter on electronic ignition equipped vehicles). Lift the cap from the distributor and turn it over to observe the contacts on the inside surface. Wipe the cap clean with a dry, anti-static cloth and check that the contact points are not burned or scored. Also, carefully inspect, using a high-powered light if necessary, for any signs of carbon tracking which look like black pencil lines on the inside of the cap surface. If any of these conditions exist, replace the distributor cap with a new one.

2   Check the carbon contact located at the center of the cap and make sure that it is not worn down. It should protrude from the cap a small amount in order to make contact with the corresponding spring blade of the rotor.

3   Lift the rotor off of the distributor cam and check that the spring on the top of the rotor arm is effective and that the contact point is clean. It may be necessary to use a small cleaning file to brush away some of the carbon but do not wear away any of the metal. Check the outer rotating end of the contact on the rotor. Make sure that no excessive pitting, scoring or erosion is present. If any of these conditions exist, replace the rotor with a new one.

4   Installation of the rotor requires aligning the tang on the inside of the rotor with the corresponding notch on the distributor shaft. Push the rotor firmly onto the shaft until it bottoms on its seat once the notch and tang are aligned.

5   Install the cap over the top of the distributor (or the adapter on electronic ignition equipped models) and make sure that the notch in the cap fits the tang which protrudes on the side of the body (adapter) of the distributor. Clip the two retaining clips to each side of the cap and make sure that all of the wires are securely inserted into their respective terminals.

28   Distributor – servicing and contact points replacement

Servicing
Note: *The servicing of all distributors will be the same with the exception of later model vehicles factory equipped with electronic*

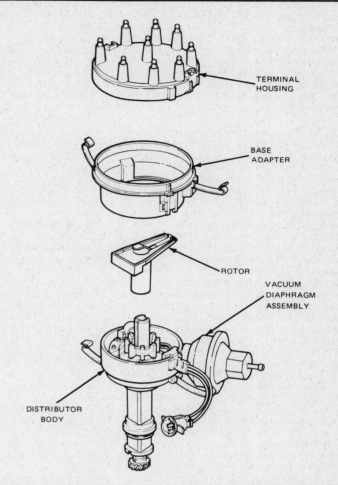

Fig. 1.26 Components of electronic ignition distributor (Sec 27)

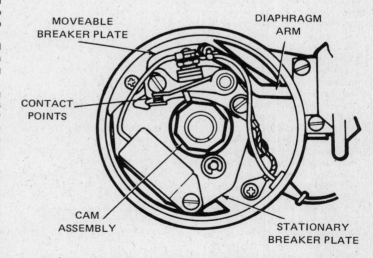

Fig. 1.27 Components of distributor with breaker points (Sec 28)

ignitions. Electronic-type distributors require no servicing other than checking the cap and rotor as described in the previous Section.

1   Remove the distributor cap and rotor as described in the previous Section.

2   Apply a drop or two of engine oil onto the felt lubricating pad. This pad will provide lubricant to the bearings and spindle when the engine is running.

3   Lubricate the automatic timing control by dropping no more than two drops of oil through the hole in the contact plate. Apply one drop of oil to the pivot post of the contact breaker points if so equipped. Clean and wipe away any excess oil on the inside of the distributor and make sure all wires, connections and screws are tight and in good condition. If the distributor is equipped with an oil cup (on the shaft housing), lift up on the spring-loaded cap and fill the cup with engine oil. This oil lubricates the shaft and bushings and prevents premature wear.

Contact points replacement and adjustment

4   The ignition points need to be replaced at regular service intervals on vehicles not equipped with electronic ignition. Occasionally the rubbing block on the points will wear sufficiently to require readjustment.
5   After removing the distributor cap and rotor, the points may be examined by gently prying them open to reveal the condition of their surfaces. If they are rough, pitted or dirty they should be replaced. **Note**: *The following procedures require the removal and installation of small screws which can easily fall down into the distributor, thereby necessitating a total tear-down. Use a magnetized screwdriver and exercise caution.*
6   To replace the cylinder-shaped condensor (which should be replaced along with the points), remove the screw that secures the condensor to the point plate. Loosen the nut or screw retaining the condenser connecting lead and low tension lead to the body of the points assembly. Remove the condensor and its mounting bracket. Installation of a new condensor is the reverse of removal.
7   Remove the two point assembly retaining screws, then disconnect the condensor lead from the points as described in the previous step.
8   Loosen the retaining nut or screw on the point assembly and remove the primary ignition lead from the assembly.
9   Remove the point assembly from the distributor.
10 Lubricate the heel of the point assembly with a small amount of approved distributor point lube. Do not use oil or ordinary lubricating grease.
11 Install the new point assembly onto the distributor base plate utilizing the two hold-down screws. Notice that the ground lead is attached to the rear hold-down screw.
12 Install the condensor as described in step 6.
13 Install the primary ignition lead and the condensor lead to the points assembly using the retaining nut. Make sure that the forked connectors for the primary ignition and the condensor do not touch the base plate or any other grounded surface.
14 Two adjusting methods are available for setting the points. The first and most effective method is through the use of a dwell meter.
15 Connect the dwell meter to the primary ignition terminal of the points assembly or to the distributor terminal of the coil. Connect the other lead of the dwell meter to the engine ground. (Note some dwell meters may have different connecting instructions so always follow the instrument manufacturer's directions).
16 Have an assistant crank the engine over or use a remote starter and crank the engine with the ignition switch turned to On.
17 Observe the dwell reading on the meter and compare it to the specifications found at the front of this Chapter or on the engine tune-up decal. If the dwell reading is incorrect, adjust it by first loosening the two point assembly hold-down screws a small amount.
18 Move the point assembly plate with a screwdriver inserted into the slot provided next to the points. Closing the gap on the points will increase the dwell reading while opening will decrease it.
19 Tighten the hold-down screws after the correct reading is obtained and recheck the setting before reinstalling the rotor and cap.
20 If a dwell meter is unavailable, a feeler gauge can be used to set the points.
21 Have a helper crank the engine in short intervals until the heel of the point rests on a high point of the cam assembly. The heel must be exactly on the apex of one of the cam lobes for correct point adjustment. (It may be necessary to rotate the front pulley of the engine with a socket and handle to position the cam lobe exactly).
22 Measure the gap between the contact points with a correct sized feeler gauge. If the gap is incorrect, loosen the two hold-down screws and move the point assembly until the correct gap is achieved.
23 Retighten the hold-down screws and recheck the gap one more time before installing the distributor cap and rotor. Be sure to check the cap and rotor as described in the previous Section.

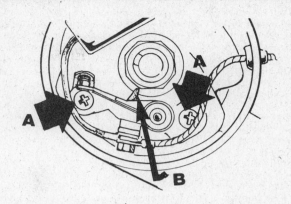

Fig. 1.28 Breaker point assembly retaining screws (A), and lubrication location at rubbing block (B) (Sec 28)

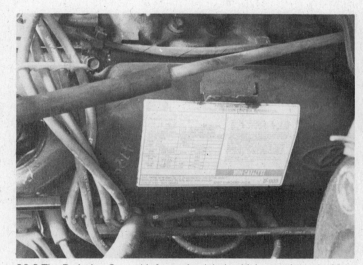

29.3 The Emission Control Information label, which contains valuable information pertaining to the specific vehicle

29 Spark plug replacement

1   The spark plugs are located on the left side of the engine (6 cylinders) or on both sides (V8 engines).
2   In most cases the tools necessary for a spark replacement job are: a plug wrench or spark plug socket which fits onto a ratchet wrench (this special socket will be insulated inside to protect the porcelain insulator) and a feeler gauge to check and adjust the spark plug gap.
3   The best policy to follow when replacing the spark plugs is to purchase the new spark plugs beforehand, adjust them to the proper gap and then replace each plug one at a time. When buying the new spark plugs it is important that the correct plug is purchased for your specific engine. This information can be found on the tune-up decal located under the hood of your vehicle or in the factory owner's manual. If differences exist between these sources, purchase the spark plug type specified on the tune-up decal as this information was printed for your specific engine. If equipped with electronic-type ignition (late 1974 on), Ford specifies that a special silicone grease (Ford part no. D7AZ-19A331-A) be applied inside the wire boot whenever one of the high tension cables is disconnected.
4   With the new spark plugs at hand, allow the engine to thoroughly cool before attempting the removal. During this cooling time, each of the new spark plugs can be inspected for defects and the gap can be checked.
5   The gap is checked by inserting the proper thickness gauge between the electrodes at the tip of the plug. The gap between these

electrodes should be the same as that given on the tune-up decal. The wire should just touch each of the electrodes. If the gap is incorrect, use the notched adjuster on the feeler gauge body to bend the curved side electrode slightly until the proper gap is achieved. Also, at this time check for cracks in the spark plug body indicating the spark plug should be replaced with a new one. If the side electrode is not exactly over the center one, use the notched adjuster to align the two.

6   Cover the fenders of the vehicle to prevent damage to exterior paint.

7   With the engine cool, remove the spark plug wire from one spark plug. Do this by grabbing the boot at the end of the wire, not the wire itself (see photo 26.3). Sometimes it is necessary to use a twisting motion while the boot and plug wire are pulled free. Using a plug wire removal tool is the easiest and safest method.

8   If compressed air is available, use this to blow any dirt or foreign material away from the spark plug area. A common bicycle pump will also work. The idea here is to eliminate the possibility of material falling into the engine cylinder as the spark plug is removed.

9   Now place the spark plug wrench or socket over the plug and remove it from the engine by turning in a counter-clockwise motion.

10   Compare the spark plugs with those shown in the photographes on page 137 to get an indication of the overall running condition of the engine.

11   Carefully insert one of the new plugs into the spark plug hole and tighten it by hand. Be especially careful not to cross-thread the spark plug in the hole. If resistance is felt as you thread the spark plug in by hand, back it out and start again. *Do not under any circumstances, force the spark plug into the hole with a wrench or socket.*

12   Finally tighten the spark plug with the wrench or socket. It is best to use a torque wrench for this to ensure the plug is seated correctly. The correct torque figure is given in Specifications.

13   Before pushing the spark plug wire onto the end of the plug, inspect it following the procedures outlined in Section 26. Using a clean screwdriver, apply a thin layer of the silicone grease to the inside of the spark plug boot.

14   Install the plug wire to the new spark plug, again using a twisting motion on the boot until it is firmly seated on the spark plug. Make sure the wire is routed through the loom clips.

15   Follow the above procedures for the remaining spark plugs, replacing each one at a time to prevent mixing up the spark plug wires.

30 Compression check

1   A compression check will tell you what mechanical condition the engine is in. Specifically, it can tell you if the compression is down due to leakage caused by worn piston rings, defective valves and seats or a blown head gasket. Make sure that the engine oil is of the correct viscosity and that the battery has a correct amount of charge in it.

2   Operate the engine for a minimum of one-half an hour at 1200 rpm or at a normal operating schedule until all operating temperatures have stabilized at their usual level.

3   Turn the engine off. Set the carburettor throttle plates to the wide-open position.

4   Remove all spark plug wires from the spark plugs after marking them for position. Clean the area around the spark plugs before you remove them. This will keep dirt from falling into the cylinders while you are performing the compression test. Remove the spark plugs.

5   Install the compression gauge in the number one cylinder spark plug hole.

Note: *Make sure that the ignition switch is Off or the ignition coil is disconnected before proceeding with the next step.*

6   Crank the engine for approximately five revolutions with a remote starter or with an assistant operating the ignition switch from the driver's seat.

7   Observe the number of compression strokes required to reach the highest reading of compression. Also, observe the pattern that the engine takes in building up to its highest reading of compression (the compression should build up quickly in a healthy engine). Low compression on the first stroke, followed by gradually increasing pressure on successive strokes, indicates worn piston rings. A low compression reading on the first stroke, which does not build up during successive strokes, indicates leaking valves or a defective head gasket. Record the highest gauge reading obtained. Repeat the procedure for

the remaining cylinders and compare the results. The compression is considered normal if the lowest cylinder reading is within 75% of the highest cylinder reading.

9   Variations exceeding 75% are a good indication of internal engine component problems. To further diagnose the engine using the compression gauge, select the low reading cylinder(s) for a further 'wet' compression test.

10   To perform a 'wet' compression test, pour a couple of teaspoons of engine oil (a squirt can works well) into each cylinder, through the spark plug hole, and repeat the test.

11   If the compression increases after the oil is added, the piston rings are definitely worn. If the compression does not increase significantly the leakage is occurring at the valves or head gasket.

12   If two adjacent cylinders have equally low compression, there is a strong possibility that the head gasket between them is blown. The appearance of coolant in the combustion chambers of the crankcase would verify this condition.

13   If the compression is higher than normal, the combustion chambers are probably coated with carbon deposits. If that is the case, the cylinder head (or heads) should be removed and decarbonized.

14   If compression is way down, or varies greatly between cylinders, it would be a good idea to have a 'leak-down' test performed by a reputable automotive repair shop. This test will pinpoint exactly where the leakage is occurring and how severe it is.

31 Ignition timing – checking and adjustment

Note: *The process for checking and adjusting ignition timing requires the use of a stroboscopic type timing light. These are available at auto parts stores as well as from rental agencies. Static timing procedures (covered in Chapter 5) or timing an engine 'by ear' are not acceptable with today's tight emissions controls and should only be used to initially start and run an engine after it has been disassembled or the distributor has been removed.*

1   Start the engine and bring it to running temperature by driving it through a driving cycle until the temperature gauge indicates normal operating temperature or for 20 minutes if the vehicle is not equipped with a gauge.

2   Shut the engine off and connect the stroboscopic type timing light as per the manufacturer's instructions. At the same time, refer to the emissions control decal (located inside the engine compartment) for the proper specifications to set the engine timing. Make sure the wiring leads for the timing light are not contacting any heat source such as an exhaust manifold and that they are routed away from any moving parts such as the vehicle's cooling fan.

3   Remove any block and vacuum hoses leading to the distributor if this is dictated by the instructions on the tune-up or emissions control

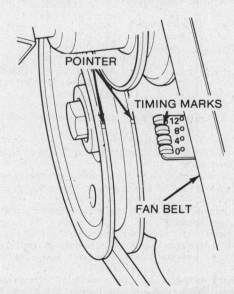

Fig. 1.29 Typical six cylinder engine timing marks and pulley (Sec 31)

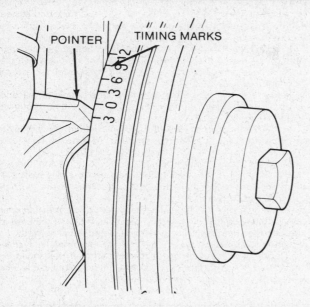

Fig. 1.30 Typical V8 engine timing marks and pulley (Sec 31)

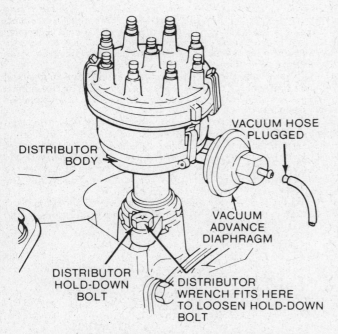

Fig. 1.31 Distributor hold-down bolt location (Sec 31)

decal. Use a golf-tee, pencil or other similar device to block off any removed vacuum lines.

Caution: *Make sure that you have no dangling articles of clothing such as ties or jewelry which can be caught in the moving components of the engine.*

4   Start the engine, make sure it is operating correctly and bring the idle to the proper speed.

5   Aim the timing light at the timing marks. If the timing marks do not show up clearly, it may be necessary to stop the engine and clean the timing pointer and crankshaft pulley with a rag and a cleaning agent.

6   Compare the setting of the timing marks with the proper specification for your vehicle. If the marks line up, the ignition timing is correct and no adjustment is necessary. If the marks are incorrect, turn off the engine.

7   Loosen the distributor hold-down bolt with a wrench or special distributor bolt tool (Fig. 1.31).

8   Re-start the engine and rotate the distributor in either direction while pointing the timing light at the timing marks.

9   Be sure that the timing marks are aligned correctly and turn off the engine.

10 Tighten the distributor hold-down bolts.

11 Re-start the engine and check the timing to make sure it has not moved while tightening down the clamp bolt.

12 Re-check the idle speed to make sure it is not changed significantly. If the idle speed has changed, re-set the idle speed and re-check the timing, as timing will vary with engine rpm.

13 Reconnect all vacuum hoses and other connections removed for checking purposes.

32 Carburetor and choke system – inspection

Carburetor check

1   The first step in inspection of the carburetor is the removal of the air cleaner. The following instructions will apply to most vehicles, however some variations may be encountered.

2   Remove the wing nut in the center of the top cover.

3   Remove the clamp and rubber fresh air inlet hose from the air cleaner duct and valve assembly.

4   Remove the hose clamp and flexible hot air tube from the bottom of the duct and valve assembly. Be careful in this step if the engine is warm as this hose is used to duct hot air from the exhaust manifold area up to the carburetor.

5   Remove any hoses (vacuum) attached to the bottom of the air cleaner assembly. Mark them carefully so they may be re-attached in the correct positions. Plug these hoses with a golf tee, pencil, or similar item to prevent vacuum leaks.

6   Remove the rocker cover vent hose from the side of the air cleaner (at the elbow). This is a rubber hose leading from the rocker cover and PCV valve.

7   Remove the flexible air purge hose leading from the charcoal canister to the air cleaner.

8   Lift the air cleaner assembly off of the carburetor.

Note: *Make sure that the gasket at the base of the air cleaner assembly either remains with the air cleaner or stays on the inlet flange of the carburetor. It sometimes can come loose and fall into the engine or carburetor intake as the air cleaner is removed.*

9   The air cleaner lid may be set to the side of the engine compartment if it is connected to one or two vacuum hoses (optional). If you do this, place the air cleaner lid where it will not be damaged or contact hot engine parts.

10 Once the air cleaner has been removed, a visible inspection of the carburetor is possible. The main item to look for is decaying and/or leaking hoses. It is not necessary to remove any hoses to check their condition, but flexing them with the fingers will usually reveal telltale cracks or splits. Check the carburetor body itself for any signs of leakage and/or built up sludge which could hamper the operation of any moving parts. Take care not to knock loose any large pieces of residue which will fall down into the carburetor inlet and finally end up in the engine. If excessively dirty, the carburetor should be removed and thoroughly cleaned (see Chapter 4).

11 While looking for leaks, check the carburetor top plate hold-down screws for tightness. Often times vibration and time will cause these screws to loosen up creating a major source of gasoline and vacuum leakage. If a leak is suspected at any other point of the carburetor system, but it is not readily identifiable, clean the entire area and then prepare to run the vehicle without the air cleaner.

Note: *Do not drive the vehicle in this condition as the engine is heavily dependent on filtered air for its continued service. This is a test procedure and should be performed only long enough to pinpoint any leaks which may occur under pressure or with the engine running.* Before starting the engine, disconnect and plug the small vacuum hose(s) which connect to the base of the air cleaner. Place these hoses out of the way from any heat sources or from the drive belts and pulleys.

12 Check the accelerator linkage or the cable that connects the carburetor to the accelerator pedal. A helper working the throttle from the driver's position will allow you to make close observation of the

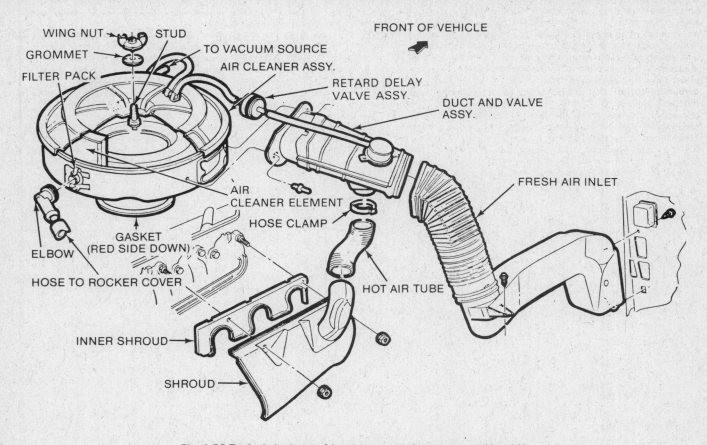

Fig. 1.32 Typical air cleaner (dry element type) components (Sec 32)

moving components of the accelerator system. Perform this procedure with the engine off.

13 Have an assistant slowly depress the accelerator to its full travel, then allow it to return while observing the cable or linkage and attending moving parts. Lubrication of these parts can be accomplished at the same time. Use a light weight penetrating oil for the cable and pivot points.

14 If any major leaks or problems are noticed in the carburetor, refer to Chapter 4 for further information.

Note: *Always use caution to see that nothing is dropped or lost into the carburetor air intake, as it will eventually end up in the engine and cause serious damage.*

Choke system check

15 The choke only operates when the engine is cold, so this check should be performed before the vehicle has been started for the day. The vehicle should be allowed to sit at least four hours at a temperature under 68°F since the last time it was run.

16 The air cleaner need not be removed for this check, but the top plate must be opened up. Take the top plate off by removing the wing nut and washer. Set the top cover aside, making sure you place it in a position where it is out of the way of any moving parts and is not in contact with any heat sources.

17 Look at the top of the carburetor at the center of the air cleaner housing. You will notice a flat plate at the carburetor opening.

18 Have an assistant press the accelerator pedal to the floor. The plate should close off the inlet fully. (On 4-barrel carburetors, the plate covers only the front 2 barrels of the carburetor). Start the engine while you observe the plate at the carburetor inlet. Do not position your face directly over the carburetor, as the engine could backfire, causing serious burns. When the engine starts, the choke plate should open slightly.

19 Allow the engine to continue running at a fast idle speed. As the engine warms up to operating temperature, the plate should slowly open, allowing more air to enter through the top of the carburetor. Some vehicles will not fully open the plate unless the accelerator pedal is once again quickly pushed to more than its half-way position and released. If, after a few moments, you notice that the plate is not moving, try this quick depression of the accelerator pedal to see if it does release the choke linkage.

20 After a few minutes of operation, the choke plate should be fully opened to the vertical position once the engine has warmed up to operating temperature. You will notice that the engine speed corresponds with the plate opening. With the plate fully closed, the engine should run at a fast idle speed. As the plate opens, the engine speed should decrease and eventually arrive at its normal curb idle operation level.

21 If during the above checks a fault is detected, refer to Chapter 4 for specific information on adjusting and servicing the choke components. Chapter 6 also contains information on emission control systems related to the carburetor.

33 Idle speed and mixture adjustment

1   Anti-pollution laws in this country have dictated that strict tune-up rules are applied to light duty vehicles including trucks. Idle speed and especially idle mixtures are covered under these regulations and strict adherence to the correct method of adjustment is required. Due to the wide range of vehicles, models and power train combinations covered in this book, it is impractical to describe every method of idle speed and mixture adjustment. Additionally, certain areas require that these adjustments be made only by qualified technicians using expensive, specialized exhaust sampling equipment.

2   If you feel that you are qualified to make these adjustments,

please refer to Chapter 4 for the correct procedure involving your vehicle. The data for your particular vehicle should be clearly displayed on a decal or metal plate inside the engine compartment. Various devices such as throttle positioners, dash pots or solenoids and the connecting or disconnecting of vacuum lines to them are all variables which must be controlled while making idle speed adjustments. Do not under any circumstances attempt to make any adjustments on carburetors or attempt to disable the limiter type devices on the idle mixture screws in an effort to modify your vehicle's idle or performance characteristics. Following the factory designated procedures is the best way to achieve a satisfactory performing engine and comply with Federal and local motor vehicle laws.

3   If you are equipped to handle the correct procedure for adjusting idles, be sure to adhere strictly to the procedure involved for the vehicle and to the data provided on the emissions control decal.

34 Valves – adjustment

All Ford truck light duty engines are equipped with hydraulic valve lifters. Under normal circumstances these lifters maintain the ideal valve adjustment clearance for the valve train. Therefore, no adjustment is necessary.

In some instances, especially when repeated valve jobs have been performed on an engine, the valve clearance will have to be manually set. In these cases, a special procedure is required to bleed down the hydraulic lifter, check the clearance and replace the actual pushrod with a longer or shorter service unit. If you have a vehicle which is suspected of this condition, see Chapter 2 for the correct procedure to install a different sized service unit (pushrod) for correct valve lash adjustment.

1

Chapter 2 Part A Engine general

Contents

Specifications

Note: *All engine Specifications are located in Chapter 2B (six cylinder in-line engines) and 2C (V8 engines). Refer to the appropriate Chapter for Specifications applicable to your engine.*

1 General information

A wide variety of engines were installed in Ford pick-ups and Broncos, ranging from economical in-line six cylinder engines to large displacement, high-powered V8's. All engines have cast iron blocks with cylinder bores machined directly into the block. Forged crankshafts run in replaceable bearing inserts.

Lubrication for these power plants is handled by full pressure oiling systems supplied by an oil pump driven from the base of the distributor. A flow-through oil filter with provision for oil bypass is part of this system.

The pistons are of the three-ring type with two compression rings and one oil control ring. Connecting rods have replaceable bearings in the big end (crankshaft) and replaceable bushings at the small end (piston).

These engines have cast iron cylinder heads with replaceable valve guide inserts. The valves are activated by a camshaft which runs within the block in replaceable bearings. Hydraulic lifters ride on the camshaft lobes and provide motion to the pushrods, which in turn act on rocker arms to move the valves.

These power plants are all durably constructed for long service life and are fully serviceable for rebuilding.

2 Engine repair operations – general note

The following engine repair operations can be performed with the engine installed and still bolted to its mounts:

Removal of the intake and exhaust manifolds
Removal of the valve mechanism
Removal of the cylinder heads
Removal of the damper, crankcase front cover (timing cover), front oil seal, timing chain and timing gears.
Removal of the flywheel (with the transmission removed)
Removal of the camshaft

The following engine repair operations can be performed with the engine installed but raised slightly off its mounts:

Removal of the oil pan
Removal of the oil pump
Removal of the rear main oil seal
Removal of the pistons, connecting rods and bearings
Removal of the engine mounts

The following engine repair operations can be performed only after the engine has been completely removed from the vehicle:

Removal of the crankshaft
Removal of the main and camshaft bearings

Whenever engine work is required, there are some basic steps which the home mechanic should perform before any work is begun. These preliminary steps will help prevent delays during the operation. They are as follows:

a) Read through the appropriate Sections in this manual to get an understanding of the processes involved, tools necessary and replacement parts which will be needed.

b) Contact your local dealer or auto parts store to check on replacement parts availability and cost. In many cases, a decision must be made beforehand whether to simply remove the faulty component and replace it with a new or rebuilt unit or to overhaul the existing part.

c) If the vehicle is equipped with air conditioning, it is absolutely necessary that a qualified specialist de-pressurize the system (if required to perform the necessary engine repair work). The home mechanic should never disconnect any of the air conditioning system lines while it is still pressurized, as this can cause serious personal injury as well as damage to the air conditioning system. Determine if de-pressurization is necessary while the vehicle is still operational.

3 Engine overhaul – general note

1 It is not always easy to determine when, or if, an engine should be completely overhauled, as a number of factors must be considered.

2 High mileage is not necessarily an indication that an overhaul is needed, while low mileage, on the other hand, does not preclude the need for an overhaul. Frequency of servicing is probably the single most important consideration. An engine that has regular (and frequent) oil and filter changes, as well as other required maintenance, will most likely give many thousands of miles of reliable service. Conversely, a neglected engine may require an overhaul very early in its life.

3 Excessive oil consumption is an indication that piston rings and/or valve guides are in need of attention (make sure that oil leaks are not responsible before deciding that the rings and guides are bad). Have a cylinder compression or leak-down test performed by an experienced tune-up mechanic to determine for certain the extent of the work required.

4 If the engine is making obvious 'knocking' or rumbling noises, the connecting rod and/or main bearings are probably at fault. Check the oil pressure with a gauge (installed in place of the oil pressure sending unit) and compare it to the Specifications. If it is extremely low, the bearings and/or pump are probably worn out.

5 Loss of power, rough running, excessive valve train noise and high fuel consumption rates may also point to the need for an overhaul (especially if they are all present at the same time). If a complete tune-up does not remedy the situation, major mechanical work is the only solution.

6 An engine overhaul generally involves restoring the internal parts to the specifications of a new engine. During an overhaul, the piston rings are replaced and the cylinder walls are reconditioned (rebored and/or honed). If a rebore is done, then new pistons are also required. The main and connecting rod bearings are replaced with new ones and, if necessary, the crankshaft may be reground to restore the journals. Generally, the valves are serviced as well, since they are usually in less-than-perfect condition at this point. While the engine is being overhauled, other components such as the carburetor, the distributor, the starter and the alternator can be rebuilt also. The end result should be a like-new engine that will give as many trouble-free miles as the original.

7 Before beginning the engine overhaul, read through the entire procedure to familiarize yourself with the scope and requirements of the job. Overhauling an engine is not that difficult, but it is time-consuming. Plan on the vehicle being tied up for a considerable period of time, especially if parts must be taken to an automotive machine shop for repair or reconditioning. Most work can be done with typical shop hand tools, although a number of precision measuring tools are required for inspecting parts to determine if they must be replaced. Often a reputable automotive machine shop will handle the inspection of parts and offer advice concerning reconditioning and replacement. As a general rule, time is the primary cost of an overhaul, so it doesn't pay to install worn or sub-standard parts.

8 As a final note, to ensure maximum life and minimum trouble from a rebuilt engine, everything must be assembled with care in a spotlessly clean environment.

4 Engine rebuilding alternatives

1 The home mechanic is faced with a number of options when performing an overhaul. The decision to replace the engine block, piston/rod assemblies and crankshaft depends on a number of factors with the number one consideration being the condition of the block. Other considerations are: cost, availability of machine shop facilities, parts availability, time available to complete the project and experience.

2 Some of the rebuilding alternatives are as follows:

Individual parts – If the inspection procedures prove that the engine block and most engine components are in reusable condition, this may be the most economical alternative. The block, crankshaft and piston/rod assemblies should all be inspected carefully. Even if the block shows little wear, the cylinder bores should receive a finish hone; a job for a machine shop.

Master kit (crankshaft kit) – This rebuild package usually consists of a reground crankshaft and a matched set of pistons and connecting rods. The pistons will come already installed on the connecting rods. Piston rings and the necessary bearings may or may not be included in the kit. These kits are commonly available for standard cylinder bores, as well as for engine blocks which have been bored to a regular oversize.

Short block – A short block consists of an engine block with a crankshaft and piston/rod assemblies already installed. All new bearings are incorporated and all clearances will be within tolerances. Depending on where the short block is purchased, a guarantee may be included. The existing camshaft, valve mechanism, cylinder heads and external parts can be bolted to this short block with little or no machine shop work necessary for the engine overhaul.

Long block – A long block consists of a short block plus oil pump, oil pan, cylinder head(s), valve cover(s), camshaft and valve mechanism, camshaft gear, timing gear, timing chain and crankcase front cover. All components are installed with new bearings, seals and gaskets incorporated throughout. The installation of manifolds and external parts is all that is necessary. Some form of guarantee is usually included with purchase.

3 Give careful thought to which method is best for your situation and discuss the alternatives with local automotive machine shops, auto parts dealers or dealership partsmen.

5 Engine overhaul – disassembly sequence

1 The Sections in this Chapter deal with removal, inspection, overhaul and installation of the various engine components. Reference should be made to the appropriate Chapters for removing and servicing the external engine components. These parts include the alternator, water pump, carburetor, etc.

2 If the engine is removed from the vehicle for major overhaul, the entire engine should be stripped. The exact order in which the engine parts are removed is to some degree a matter of personal preference. However, the following sequence can be used as a guide:

   a) Alternator (Chapter 5).
   b) Accessory drivebelts and pulleys (if not previously removed).
   c) Water pump and related hoses (Chapter 3).
   d) Fuel pump and filter assembly (Chapter 4).
   e) Distributor and coil (Chapter 5).
   f) Carburetor and fuel lines (Chapter 4).
   g) Clutch, pressure plate and disc (Chapter 7).
   h) Oil dipstick and dipstick tube (4-wheel drive and 360-390 engines only).
   i) Spark plugs (Chapter 1).

3 With these components removed, the engine sub-assemblies can be removed, serviced and installed in the following order:

   a) Exhaust manifold(s).
   b) Intake manifold.
   c) Rocker arm covers.
   d) Rocker arms and pushrods.
   e) Lifters.
   f) Cylinder head assembly.
   g) Front pulley and vibration damper assembly.
   h) Timing cover, timing chain and gears.
   i) Camshaft.
   j) Oil pan.
   k) Oil pump and pickup assembly.
   l) Piston and rod assemblies.
   m) Crankshaft and bearings.

6 Engine removal – methods and precautions

If it has been decided that an engine needs to be removed for overhaul or major repair work, certain preliminary steps should be taken.

Locating a suitable work area is of greatest importance. A shop is, of course, the most desirable place to work. Adequate work space along with storage space for the vehicle is very important. If a shop or garage is not available, at the very least, a flat, level, clean work surface made of concrete or asphalt is required.

Cleaning of the engine compartment and engine prior to removal will help you keep tools clean and organized.

2A

A hoist such as an engine A-frame will also be necessary. Make sure that the equipment is rated in excess of the combined weight of the engine and its accessories. Safety is of primary importance, considering the potential hazards involved in lifting the engine out of the vehicle.

If the engine is being removed by a novice, a helper should be available. Advice and aid from someone more experienced would also be helpful. There are many instances when one person cannot simultaneously perform all of the operations which will be required when lifting the engine out of the vehicle.

Plan the operation ahead of time. Arrange for or obtain all of the tools and equipment you will need prior to beginning the job. Some of the equipment necessary to perform engine removal and installation safely and with relative ease are (in addition to an engine hoist) a heavy duty floor jack, complete sets of wrenches and sockets as described in the front of this book, wooden blocks and plenty of rags and cleaning solvent for mopping up the inevitable spills. If the hoist is to be rented, make sure that you arrange for it in advance and perform all of the operations possible without it beforehand. This will save you money and time.

Plan for the vehicle to be out of use for a considerable amount of time. A machine shop will be required to perform some of the work which the home mechanic cannot accomplish due to a lack of special equipment. These shops often have a busy schedule and it would be wise to consult them prior to removing the engine in order to accurately estimate the amount of time required to service or repair components that may need work.

Always use extreme caution when removing and installing the engine; serious injury can result from careless actions. Plan ahead. Take your time and a job of this nature, although major, can be accomplished successfully.

7   Engine – removal and installation

Note: *The engine must be removed alone, with the transmission left in place in the vehicle. Also, due to the wide range of vehicle models and engines covered by this manual, the following instructions are of a general nature and may cover some steps not applicable to your vehicle. If a step doesn't apply to your vehicle, move on to the next one.*

1   Remove the negative battery cable from the battery.

2   Mark the position of the hood with a scribe or marking pen so it can be installed in the same position relative to the hinges and latch. Remove the hood. Cover the fenders for protection.

3   Remove the air cleaner along with the related emissions control and supply hoses from the carburetor. Cover the inlet of the carburetor with a clean cloth.

4   Remove all vacuum lines from the intake manifold area. Some of these lines will connect the automatic transmission modulator, speed control and emission control related systems. Clearly mark all lines to prevent confusion when the engine is installed.

5   Remove the fuel feed hose from the fuel pump. Use caution when performing this step as gasoline is flammable and all precautions pertaining to flammable liquids should be observed. Plug the feed hose with a clamp and bolt if the fuel tank level is above the fuel feed line level. **Note**: *Mark any electrical wires for proper installation before disconnecting them.*

6   Disconnect the electrical connection(s) at the rear of the engine. In most cases, this will be a large multi-plug connector(s). However, some vehicles will be equipped with individual wires leading to components such as the engine operating sensors, ignition coil and emissions control related items like throttle positioners and choke heaters. Remove the starter cable from the starter. Position this cable out of the way. Remove the spark plug wires and the distributor cap as a unit.

7   Remove the speed control actuating cable from the carburetor linkage.

8   Remove the choke cable from the carburetor at its hold-down clamp and connecting linkage.

9   Disconnect the transmission kick-down cable or linkage from its connecting point at the carburetor linkage and at the transmission bellcrank connector.

10   Remove the throttle linkage from the carburetor connecting point and from the throttle pedal bellcrank (in some cases this is a cable system which will have a cable hold-down clamp on the intake manifold and a connector at the carburetor linkage). Remove the throttle linkage return spring.

11   Drain the engine oil and remove the engine oil filter.

12   Drain the coolant from the engine and radiator drain plugs.

13   Remove the heater hoses from their connecting points at the water pump and intake manifold. Position these heater hoses out of the way and secure them to the fender well.

14   Remove the radiator hoses from the engine. Remove the radiator hoses from the radiator if there is not enough clearance for the radiator to be removed with the hoses still in place.

15   Remove the fan shroud from the radiator and slide it back over the fan assembly.

16   Remove the transmission cooler lines from the chamber at the bottom of the radiator.

17   Loosen the alternator adjusting bolt and remove the drivebelt from the pulleys. Remove all other drivebelts attached to the water pump/fan drive pulley.

18   Remove the bolts retaining the fan and spacer (or fan clutch drive assembly) to the water pump.

19   Remove the assembly and fan shroud by lifting them straight up and out of the engine compartment.

20   Remove the radiator-to-radiator saddle retaining bolts.

21   Remove the radiator from the vehicle from the top of the engine compartment. Remove the alternator retaining bolt and position the alternator and wiring out of the way. It is important to secure the alternator in place with a wire or rope to prevent damage to the wiring connector at the rear of the alternator. Never allow the alternator to hang from the wiring.

22   In some cases the air conditioning system will not need discharging, since the hoses are long enough leading to the compressor unit for it to be swung out of the way and secured to the fender well. *Disconnect the air conditioning hoses only if the system has been discharged.*

23   Remove the air conditioning compressor from the mounting brackets and secure it out of the way.

24   Remove the power steering pump belt.

25   Remove the power steering pump from the mounting bracket, position it out of the way and secure it.

Note: *The following steps will be performed with the vehicle raised. Make sure that the vehicle is supported securely.*

26   Remove the starter (Chapter 5).

27   Remove the automatic transmission dipstick tube retaining bolt from the rear of the cylinder head or from the rear of the bellhousing retaining lug. Remove the automatic transmission dipstick and tube.

28   Remove the lower bellhousing retaining bolts.

29   Remove the engine mount-to-frame insulator retaining nuts and washers.

30   Support the transmission assembly securely using retaining straps and/or cables. It is possible to support the transmission with blocks or jacks but it also must be secured to prevent it from moving side-to-side.

31   Remove the flywheel inspection cover.

32   Remove the torque converter drain plug cover.

33   Remove the torque converter-to-flexplate retaining nuts. They will be at the front of the torque converter flexplate and the crankshaft will need to be rotated 90° to position each retaining nut for removal.

34   Remove the bolt(s) retaining the inlet pipe(s) to the exhaust manifold(s). Remove the exhaust inlet pipe(s) from the exhaust manifold(s).

35   Remove the upper bellhousing-to-engine retaining bolts.

36   Lower the vehicle and make sure the transmission is supported solidly.

37   Install an engine lifting sling or chain. There are several methods which can be used to accomplish this. Metal eye hooks can be attached with bolts positioned at diagonally opposite corners of the cylinder heads on V8 engines. Six cylinder engine diagonal mounting can be achieved by using a manifold-to-cylinder head retaining bolt at the right front of the engine and the accessory mounting boss at the left rear of the engine block to retain the eye hooks or bracket. A sling can be fashioned from a short piece of chain connected to open-end hooks. A cable and bracket arrangement would also work well.

38   Raise the engine high enough for the engine mount studs to clear the frame bracket insulators.

39   Double check all attachment points to ensure that all of the retaining bolts holding the engine to the transmission have been removed.

40 Separate the engine from the bellhousing (or torque-converter housing) making sure that the flywheel/clutch assembly (torque-converter flexplate) pulls straight out of the housing without binding. You may need to adjust the engine height and angle for the two components to separate cleanly. A small wedge-type tool can be used between the housing and the engine block to separate them. However, if resistance is felt, check to make sure no retaining bolts are left in the engine. Do not force any parts during this removal procedure. If the engine is stuck to the transmission assembly, a fastener is probably holding them together.

41 Pull the engine straight forward and away from the transmission. Take care not to damage the transmission input shaft while performing this step.

42 When the transmission input shaft or torque converter has completely cleared the clutch assembly or flexplate, raise the engine and remove it from the engine compartment. There should be no connections between the engine and the vehicle.

8 Engine mounts – replacement (engine in vehicle)

1 Disconnect the throttle linkage from the carburetor on vehicles equipped with mechanical linkage.
2 Disconnect the fuel supply hose from the fuel tank line at the fuel pump. **Caution:** *Observe all precautions for working with flammable liquids (gasoline) when performing this operation.*
3 Disconnect the negative battery cable from the battery.
4 On vehicles equipped with an automatic transmission, remove the transmission cooler lines from their mounting clips located on the side of the engine block. Make sure that the lines are free from the engine, as it will need to be raised several inches to replace the mounts. Disconnect the clutch cross-shaft on manual transmission equipped vehicles.
5 Disconnect the lower radiator hose from the radiator.
6 Disconnect the upper radiator hose from the radiator.
7 Disconnect the engine mount retaining nuts from the connecting studs at the insulator.

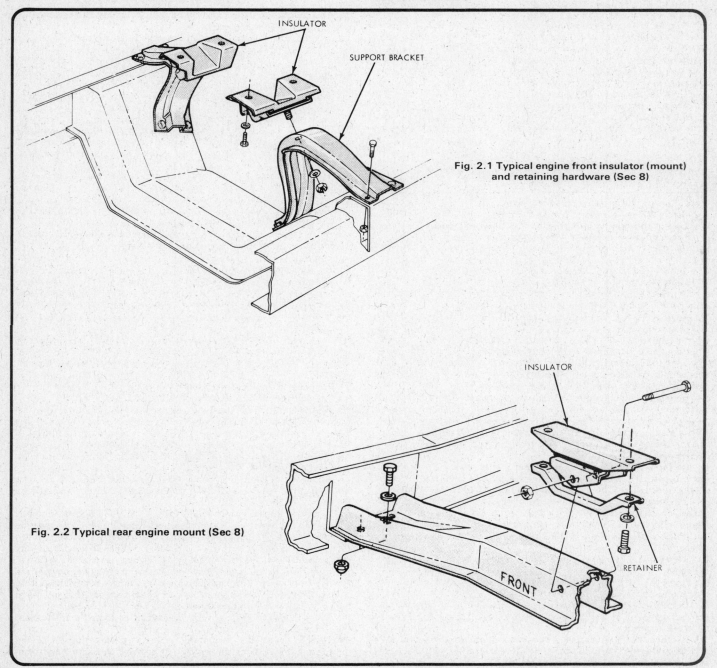

Fig. 2.1 Typical engine front insulator (mount) and retaining hardware (Sec 8)

2A

Fig. 2.2 Typical rear engine mount (Sec 8)

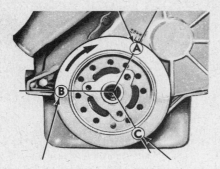

Fig. 2.3 Vibration damper marks (arrows) for valve adjustment on 1973 thru 1978 six cylinder engines (Sec 9)

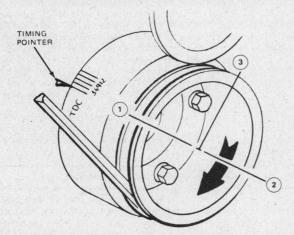

Fig. 2.4 Vibration damper marks for valve adjustment on V8 engines and 1979 six cylinder engines (Sec 9)

POSITION 1

No. 1 Intake No. 1 Exhaust
No. 7 Intake No. 5 Exhaust
No. 8 Intake No. 4 Exhaust

POSITION 2

No. 5 Intake No. 2 Exhaust
No. 4 Intake No. 6 Exhaust

POSITION 3

No. 2 Intake No. 7 Exhaust
No. 3 Intake No. 3 Exhaust
No. 6 Intake No. 8 Exhaust

Fig. 2.5 Vibration damper position and valve adjustment order for 302, 351W and 460 engines (Sec 9)

POSITION 1

No. 1 Intake No. 1 Exhaust
No. 4 Intake No. 3 Exhaust
No. 8 Intake No. 7 Exhaust

POSITION 2

No. 3 Intake No. 2 Exhaust
No. 7 Intake No. 6 Exhaust

POSITION 3

No. 2 Intake No. 4 Exhaust
No. 5 Intake No. 5 Exhaust
No. 6 Intake No. 8 Exhaust

Fig. 2.6 Vibration damper position and valve adjustment order for 351M and 400 engines (Sec 9)

8   If the rear mount is being changed, make sure that the speedometer cable, driveshaft, transmission linkage and transfer case linkage (if so equipped) will not bind or contact the body as the transmission is being raised.

9   Raise the engine (or transmission) using a jack and a block of wood underneath the oil pan. Make sure that the engine mounts do not bind as the engine is raised up off the insulator assembly.

10 Disconnect the engine mounts from the engine.

11 Install the new mounts onto the engine making sure that the bolts are tightened to the proper torque.

12 Lower the engine back onto the insulators making sure that the mount stud lines up with and falls into the hole provided in the engine mount insulator located on the frame crossmember.

13 Attach the insulator retaining nut and lock washer. Tighten this nut to the proper torque.

14 Assembly is the reverse of disassembly. Make certain that all linkages are attached securely and adjusted properly.

9   Valve adjustment

Six cylinder engines (1973 through 1978 only)

1   Connect an auxiliary starter switch to the starter solenoid.

2   Mark the vibration damper pulley with two chalk marks spaced 120° on either side of the timing mark.

3   Position the piston in the number one cylinder at top dead center (TDC) on the compression stroke. To do this, remove all of the spark plugs from the engine, then locate the number one cylinder spark plug wire and trace it back to the distributor. Make a mark on the distributor body directly below the terminal where the number one spark plug wire attaches to the distributor cap, then remove the cap and wires from the distributor. Slip a wrench or socket over the large bolt at the front of the crankshaft and slowly turn it in a clockwise direction (viewed from the front) until the notch in the crankshaft pulley is aligned with the O on the timing mark tag. At this point the rotor should be pointing at the mark you made on the distributor body. If it is not, turn the crankshaft one complete revolution (360°) in a clockwise direction. If the rotor is now pointing at the mark on the distributor body, then the number one piston is at TDC on the compression stroke.

4   Remove the rocker arm cover.

5   Using a torque wrench, check the break-away torque required to turn the locknut for the number one cylinder's rocker arms counterclockwise. If the break-away torque is less than specified, replace the locknuts with new ones.

6   Adjust the intake and exhaust valve clearance for the number one cylinder by first loosening the rocker arm stud nut until there is clearance between the rocker arm and pushrod. You can keep a finger on the pushrod while loosening the rocker arm retaining nut, and feel the point at which tension is relieved from the pushrod.

7   Tighten the nut slowly until the rocker arm just begins to touch the pushrod and valve (zero clearance). Note the exact position of your ratchet or socket handle.

Fig. 2.7 Checking valve clearances on a V8 engine using the special tool (arrow) and a feeler gauge (Sec 9)

8 Turn the locating nut in exactly one turn to place the hydraulic lifter plunger in the desired operating range.
9 Repeat this procedure for the number one exhaust valve.
10 Rotate the engine exactly 120° clockwise (to the chalkmark) and adjust the number five intake and exhaust valves.
11 Rotate the engine 120° farther and adjust the number three intake and exhaust valves.
12 Rotate the engine 120° (back to the top dead center point) and adjust the number six intake and exhaust valves.
13 Again, rotate the engine 120° and adjust the number two intake and exhaust valves.
14 Finally, rotate the engine 120° more and adjust the number four intake and exhaust valves.
15 Attach a new rocker arm cover gasket and install the cover.
16 Connect all components and lines previously removed to obtain access to the rocker arms.
17 Start the engine and allow it to reach normal operating temperature. Check that the engine is operating smoothly and that there is no roughness (which could be caused by a tight valve). Also listen for valve lifter noise which could be caused by a loose valve. If any of these problems occur, recheck the valve adjustments.

V8 engines (all) and 1979 six cylinder engines
Note: *Since no provision is made for valve adjustments on these engines, service pushrods are available 0.060 in shorter and 0.060 in longer than standard pushrods to provide adjustment capability. Normally, these engines do not need any valve adjustments as the lash is taken care of by the hydraulic lifter. If major engine work is done, such as a valve job, which will alter the relationship between valve train components, the following valve checking procedure is provided. If you have a running engine that has symptoms of valve clearance problems (such as excessive noise from a lifter), check for a defective part. Normally an engine will not reach a point where it needs a valve adjustment unless a component malfunction has occurred. Hydraulic lifter failure or excessive rocker arm wear are two likely examples of component failure.*
18 Make sure that the lifter is compressed (not pumped up with oil). This is accomplished during engine assembly by installing new lifters or by compressing the lifter and relieving it of all internal oil pressure. If you are compressing a lifter that is pumped up from use, a special tool will be necessary.
19 Position the number one piston at top dead center on the compression stroke (refer to Step 3). Note that V8 engines have the ignition timing numbers on the pulley and a pointer on the engine. Finding TDC is accomplished in the same way.
All engines except 360-390 CID
20 With the crankshaft in this position, mark a line all the way through the crankshaft (center) and another line 90° from the timing mark as shown in the accompanying illustration.
21 On six cylinder engines, divide the pulley into 120° increments as described in Step 2, then proceed to steps 25 and 26 for the valve adjustment sequence.
22 With the number one piston at TDC, check the gaps between the number one cylinder's rocker arms and valve stems with a feeler gauge. Compare the results to the Specifications. Make sure the hydraulic lifter is fully compressed. If the clearance is less than specified, install a shorter service pushrod. If the clearance is greater than specified, install a longer service pushrod.
23 Rotate the engine 180° clockwise to position number two, as shown in the accompanying illustration. Check the valve clearance for the cylinders indicated (make sure the directions apply to your specific engine type).
24 Rotate the engine 270° clockwise to position number three and adjust the corresponding valves.

25 For six cylinder engines, adjust both valves for cylinder number one at position A (see accompanying illustration). Rotate the crankshaft to position B. Adjust both valves for cylinder number five. Rotate the crankshaft 120° to position C and adjust both valves for cylinder number three.
26 Rotate the crankshaft 120° back to position A and adjust both valves for cylinder number six. Repeat the above process and adjust both valves for cylinder number two at position B. Finally complete the procedure by adjusting both valves for cylinder number four at position C.
360-390 CID engines
27 These engines have a valve adjustment procedure that requires only one full revolution of the crankshaft. Position the number one piston at TDC on the compression stroke (see Step 3). Check the adjustment for both valves of cylinders one and eight. Check the intake valves on cylinders three and seven. Also check the exhaust valves on cylinders four and five.
28 Now turn the crankshaft 360° (or one full revolution) and locate the timing marker back at TDC. Check the adjustment of both valves for cylinders two and six. Check the clearance on the intake valves for cylinders four and five. Finally, complete the procedure by checking the gap on the exhaust valves of cylinders three and seven.
29 After completion of the entire valve adjustment procedure, install the remaining engine components and run the engine. It may be necessary for an engine to run several minutes for the clearance in the valve train to be taken up completely by the hydraulic lifter(s), particularly if new lifters were installed.
30 If the components are all in good shape and a valve lash problem is indicated by excessive noise or rough engine idling, use the special service tool to compress the lifter to recheck the valve clearance.

10 Engine start-up after major repair or overhaul

1 With the engine in place in the vehicle and all components connected, make a final check that all lines and wiring have been connected and that no rags or tools have been left in the engine compartment.
2 Connect the negative battery cable. If it sparks or arcs, power is being drawn from someplace and all accessories and wiring should be checked.
3 Fill the cooling system with the proper mixture and amount of coolant (Chapter 3).
4 Fill the crankcase with the correct quantity and grade of oil (Chapter 1).
5 Check the tension of all drivebelts (Chapter 1).
6 Remove the high tension wire from the center tower of the distributor cap to prevent the engine from starting. Now crank the engine over for about 15 to 30 seconds. This will allow the oil pump to distribute oil and the fuel pump to start pumping fuel to the carburetor.
7 Now connect the high tension lead at the distributor and start the engine. Immediately check all gauges and warning lights for proper readings and check for leaks of coolant or oil.
8 If the engine does not start immediately, check to make sure fuel is reaching the carburetor. This may take a while.
9 After allowing the engine to run for a few minutes at low speed, turn it off and check the oil and coolant levels.
10 Start the engine again and check the ignition timing, emission control settings and carburetor idle speeds (Chapter 1).
11 Run the vehicle easily during the first 500 to 1000 miles (break-in period) then check the torque settings on all major engine components, particularly the cylinder heads. Tighten any bolts which may have loosened.

2A

Chapter 2 Part B Six cylinder in-line engines

Contents

Specifications

240 CID engine (1973 models)
General

Bore and stroke	4.00 x 3.18 in
Compression ratio	8.5:1
Compression pressure	Lowest cylinder must be within 75% of highest cylinder

Engine block
Cylinder bore

Diameter	4.000 to 4.0036 in
Taper limit	0.010 in
Out-of-round limit	0.005 in
Deck warpage limit	0.003 in per 6 in or 0.007 in overall

Pistons and rings
Piston

Diameter	
Coded red	3.9984 to 3.9990 in
Coded blue	3.9996 to 4.0002 in
Oversize available	0.003 in
Piston-to-cylinder bore clearance	
Standard	0.0014 in
Service limit	0.0022 in
Piston ring-to-groove side clearance	
Standard	
Top ring	0.002 to 0.004 in
2nd ring	0.0025 to 0.004 in
Oil ring	Snug fit in groove
Service limit	
Top ring	0.006 in
2nd ring	0.006 in
Piston ring end gap	
Top ring	0.010 to 0.020 in
2nd ring	0.010 to 0.020 in
Oil ring	0.015 to 0.055 in
Piston pin diameter (standard)	0.9750 to 0.9753 in
Piston pin-to-piston clearance	0.0002 to 0.0004 in
Piston pin-to-connecting rod fit	Interference fit

Cylinder numbering
and distributor location

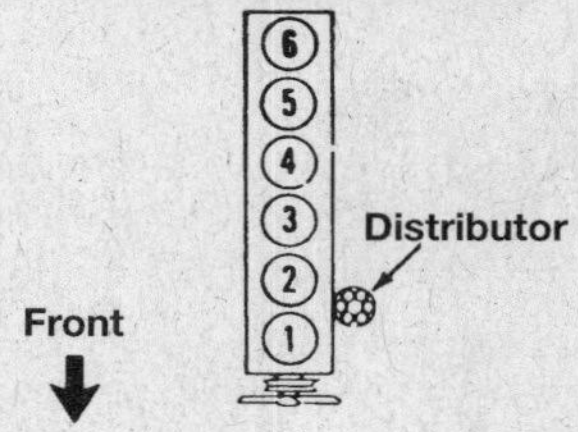

Front

Distributor

Firing order and rotation

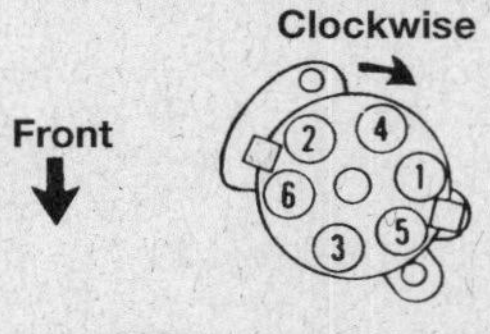

Clockwise

Front

Firing order 1-5-3-6-2-4

Six cylinder in-line engines

Crankshaft and flywheel
Main journal
    Diameter .... 2.3982 to 2.3990 in
    Taper limit .... 0.0003 in
    Out-of-round limit .... 0.0004 in
    Runout limit .... 0.002 in
Main bearing oil clearance
    Standard .... 0.0005 to 0.0015 in
    Service limit .... 0.0022 in
Connecting rod journal
    Diameter .... 2.1228 to 2.1236 in
    Taper limit .... 0.0003 in
    Out-of-round limit .... 0.0004 in
Connecting rod bearing oil clearance
    Standard .... 0.0008 to 0.0015 in
    Service limit .... 0.0024 in
Connecting rod side clearance
    Standard .... 0.006 to 0.013 in
    Service limit .... 0.018 in
Crankshaft endplay
    Standard .... 0.004 to 0.008 in
    Service limit .... 0.012 in
Flywheel clutch face runout limit .... 0.010 in
Flywheel ring gear lateral runout limit
    Manual transmission .... 0.045 in
    Automatic transmission .... 0.040 in

Camshaft
Bearing journal
    Diameter .... 2.0170 to 2.0180 in
    Out-of-round limit .... 0.0005 in
Bearing oil clearance
    Standard .... 0.001 to 0.003 in
    Service limit .... 0.006 in
Lobe lift
    Intake .... 0.2490 in
    Exhaust .... 0.2490 in
Runout limit .... 0.008 in
Endplay
    Standard .... 0.001 to 0.007 in
    Service limit .... 0.009 in
Cam gear-to-crankshaft gear backlash .... 0.002 to 0.004 in
Cam gear runout limit (assembled) .... 0.006 in TIR
Crankshaft gear runout limit (assembled) .... 0.003 in TIR

Cylinder head and valve train
Head warpage limit .... 0.006 in per 6 in or 0.007 in overall
Valve seat angle .... 45°
Valve seat width
    Intake .... 0.060 to 0.080 in
    Exhaust .... 0.070 to 0.090 in
Valve seat runout limit .... 0.0015 in
Valve face angle .... 44°
Valve face runout limit .... 0.002 in
Valve margin width .... 1/32 in min
Valve stem diameter
    Intake .... 0.3416 to 0.3423 in
    Exhaust .... 0.3416 to 0.3423 in
Valve guide diameter
    Intake .... 0.3433 to 0.3443 in
    Exhaust .... 0.3433 to 0.3443 in
Valve stem-to-guide clearance
    Intake
        Standard .... 0.0010 to 0.0027 in
        Service limit .... 0.0055 in
    Exhaust
        Standard .... 0.0010 to 0.0027 in
        Service limit .... 0.0055 in
Valve spring free length
    Intake .... 1.99 in (approx.)
    Exhaust .... 1.87 in (approx.)
Valve spring pressure (lbs. @ specified length)
    Intake (1st check)
        Standard .... 76 to 84 @ 1.700 in
        Service limit .... 68 @ 1.700 in
    Intake (2nd check)
        Standard .... 187 to 207 @ 1.300 in

2B

Service limit .... 166 @ 1.300 in
Exhaust (1st check)
    Standard .... 77 to 85 @ 1.580 in
    Service limit .... 69 @ 1.580 in
Exhaust (2nd check)
    Standard .... 182 to 202 @ 1.180 in
    Service limit .... 162 @ 1.180 in
Valve spring installed height
    Intake .... $1\frac{11}{16}$ to $1\frac{19}{32}$ in
    Exhaust .... $1\frac{9}{16}$ to $1\frac{23}{32}$ in
Valve spring out-of-square limit .... 0.078 ($\frac{5}{64}$) in
Collapsed lifter gap
    Allowable .... 0.074 to 0.174 in
    Desired .... 0.124 in
Lifter diameter .... 0.8740 to 0.8745 in
Lifter bore diameter .... 0.8752 to 0.8767 in
Lifter-to-bore clearance
    Standard .... 0.0007 to 0.0027 in
    Service limit .... 0.005 in
Pushrod runout limit .... 0.015 in
Oil pump
Outer race-to-housing clearance .... 0.001 to 0.013 in
Rotor assembly end clearance .... 0.0010 to 0.0040 in
Driveshaft-to-housing bearing clearance .... 0.0015 to 0.0029 in
Relief spring tension .... 20.6 to 22.6 lbs. @ 2.490 in
Relief valve clearance .... 0.0015 to 0.0029 in

240 CID engine (1974 models)

Note: *For all Specifications not listed here, refer to the 1973 240 CID engine Specifications. The items included here are only the ones that are different.*

Cylinder bore
    Diameter .... 4.000 to 4.0048 in

Crankshaft
Main journal
    Out-of-round limit .... 0.0006 in
Connecting rod journal
    Out-of-round limit .... 0.0006 in
Camshaft
Bearing journal
    Out-of-round limit .... 0.0005 in
Cylinder head and valve train
Valve seat runout limit .... 0.002 in
Valve spring pressure (lbs @ specified length)
    Intake (1st check)
        Standard .... 76 to 84 @ 1.700 in
        Service limit .... 68 @ 1.700 in
    Intake (2nd check)
        Standard .... 187 to 207 @ 1.300 in
        Service limit .... 168 @ 1.300 in
    Exhaust (1st check)
        Standard .... 76 to 84 @ 1.690 in
        Service limit .... 68 @ 1.690 in
    Exhaust (2nd check)
        Standard .... 182 to 202 @ 1.180 in
        Service limit .... 164 @ 1.180
Collapsed lifter gap
    Allowable .... 0.100 to 0.200 in
    Desired .... 0.100 to 0.150 in

300 CID engine (all years)

Note: *For all Specifications not listed here, refer to the 1973 240 CID engine Specifications. The items included here are only the ones that are different.*
General
Bore and stroke .... 4.00 x 3.98 in

Engine block
Cylinder bore
    Diameter .... 4.000 to 4.0048 in
Deck warpage limit .... 0.003 in per 6 in or 0.006 in overall
Pistons and rings
Piston ring-to-groove clearance
    Top ring
        1973 thru 1976 .... 0.002 to 0.004 in
        1977 thru 1979 .... 0.0019 to 0.0036 in
    2nd ring (all) .... 0.002 to 0.004 in

Oil ring end gap (1977 and 1979 only)	0.010 to 0.003 in
Piston pin-to-piston clearance	
1977 and 1978 heavy duty only	0.0003 to 0.0005 in
Crankshaft and flywheel	
Main journal	
Taper limit	0.0005 in
Out-of-round limit	0.0006 in
Main bearing oil clearance	
Standard	0.0008 to 0.0015 in
Service limit	
Light duty	0.0026 in
Heavy duty	0.0028 in
Connecting rod journal	
Taper limit	0.0006 in
Out-of-round limit	0.0006 in
Connecting rod bearing oil clearance	
Service limit (1973 thru 1976 only)	0.0027 in
Flywheel ring gear lateral runout limit	
Manual transmission	
1973 and 1974	0.045 in
All others	0.040 in
Automatic transmission	
1973 and 1974	0.040 in
All others	0.060 in
Camshaft	
Bearing journal	
Out-of-round limit	0.0005 in
Cam gear runout limit (assembled)	
1977 thru 1979 only	0.005 in TIR
Crankshaft gear runout limit (assembled)	
1977 thru 1979 only	0.005 in TIR
Cylinder head and valve train	
Valve seat runout limit (All except 1973)	0.002 in
Valve spring pressure	
1973 and 1975 thru 1979	Same as 1973 240 CID engine
1974 only	Same as 1974 240 CID engine
Collapsed lifter gap (1974 thru 1979 only)	
Allowable	0.100 to 0.200 in
Desired	0.125 to 0.175 in

Torque specifications

	ft-lb
Cylinder head bolts	
1973	70 to 75
1974 thru 1979	70 to 85
Main bearing cap bolts	
1974 only	65 to 72
All others	60 to 70
Connecting rod cap nuts	40 to 45
Exhaust manifold-to-cylinder head	
1973 thru 1976	23 to 28
1977 thru 1979	28 to 33
Intake-to-exhaust manifold	28 to 32
Intake manifold-to-cylinder head	
1973 thru 1976	23 to 28
1977 thru 1979	22 to 32
Oil pump-to-engine block bolts	12 to 15
Oil pump cover plate bolts	
1973	9 to 15
All others	6 to 14
Flywheel/flexplate bolts	75 to 85
Vibration damper bolt	130 to 150
Water pump bolts	15 to 20
Oil pickup tube	12 to 15
Rocker arm cover bolts	4 to 7
Oil pan bolts	10 to 12
Rocker arm stud adjusting nut break-away torque	4.5 to 15
Rocker arm stud nut (1979 only)	17 to 23

2B

11 General information

The Ford six cylinder engines come in three versions for light duty truck applications. The 240 cubic inch version was offered through production year 1974. The 300 cubic inch light duty engine and the 300 heavy duty engine were offered in all vehicles (heavy duty engines are not available in California). All six cylinder engines use an engine block made of a special high grade cast iron. The crankshaft is supported by seven main bearings. The 240 and 300 cubic inch light duty engines have a nodular iron crankshaft, while the 300 heavy duty engine crankshaft is made of forged alloy steel. Pistons are made of an aluminum alloy with integral steel struts cast in. The rocker arms are ball pivot stud mounted with positive stop rocker arm studs being added in 1978. Lifters are hydraulic and self-adjusting. The timing gears are the helical cut type. The 300 cubic inch engines have

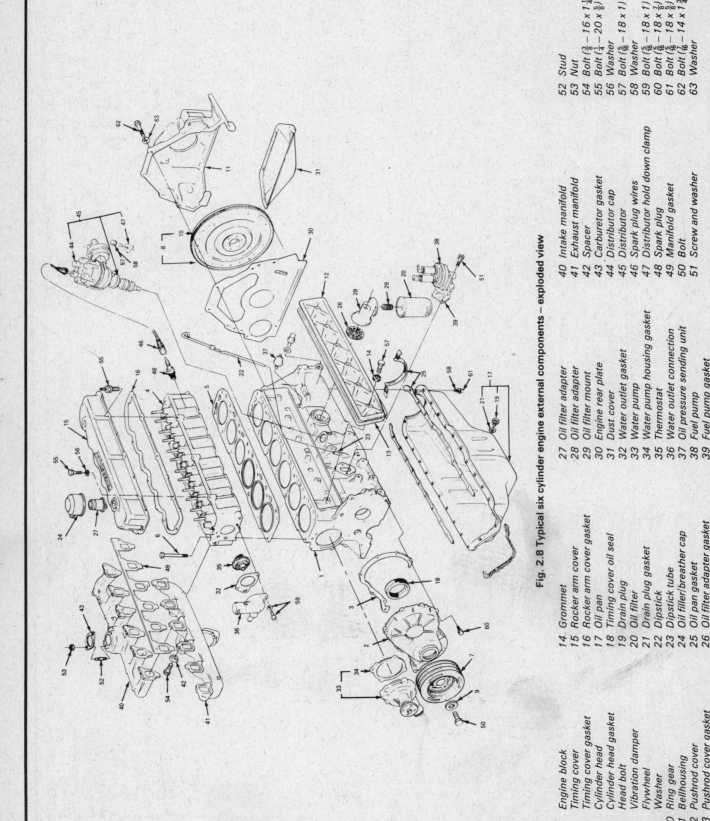

Fig. 2.8 Typical six cylinder engine external components — exploded view

1 Engine block
2 Timing cover
3 Timing cover gasket
4 Cylinder head
5 Cylinder head gasket
6 Head bolt
7 Vibration damper
8 Flywheel
9 Washer
10 Ring gear
11 Bellhousing
12 Pushrod cover
13 Pushrod cover gasket

14 Grommet
15 Rocker arm cover
16 Rocker arm cover gasket
17 Oil pan
18 Timing cover oil seal
19 Drain plug
20 Oil filter
21 Drain plug gasket
22 Dipstick
23 Dipstick tube
24 Oil filler/breather cap
25 Oil pan gasket
26 Oil filter adapter gasket

27 Oil filter adapter
28 Oil filter adapter
29 Oil filter mount
30 Engine rear plate
31 Dust cover
32 Water outlet gasket
33 Water pump
34 Water pump housing gasket
35 Thermostat
36 Water outlet connection
37 Oil pressure sending unit
38 Fuel pump
39 Fuel pump gasket

40 Intake manifold
41 Exhaust manifold
42 Spacer
43 Carburetor gasket
44 Distributor cap
45 Distributor
46 Spark plug wires
47 Distributor hold down clamp
48 Spark plug
49 Manifold gasket
50 Bolt
51 Screw and washer

52 Stud
53 Nut
54 Bolt $(\frac{3}{8} - 16 \times 1\frac{1}{4})$
55 Bolt $(\frac{1}{4} - 20 \times \frac{5}{8})$
56 Washer
57 Bolt $(\frac{5}{16} - 18 \times 1)$
58 Washer
59 Bolt $(\frac{5}{16} - 18 \times 1)$
60 Bolt $(\frac{5}{16} - 18 \times \frac{7}{8})$
61 Bolt $(\frac{5}{16} - 18 \times \frac{5}{8})$
62 Bolt $(\frac{7}{16} - 14 \times 1\frac{3}{4})$
63 Washer

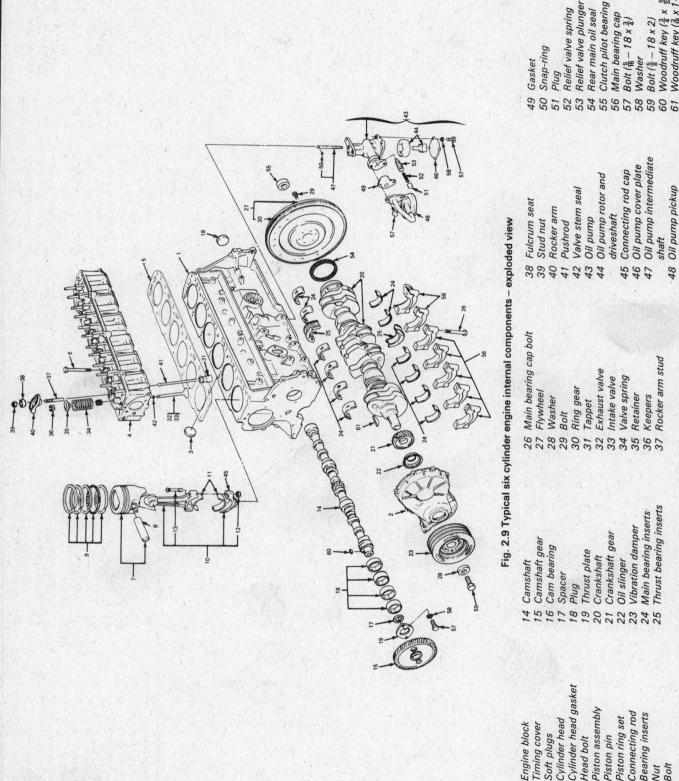

Fig. 2.9 Typical six cylinder engine internal components — exploded view

1 Engine block
2 Timing cover
3 Soft plugs
4 Cylinder head
5 Cylinder head gasket
6 Head bolt
7 Piston assembly
8 Piston pin
9 Piston ring set
10 Connecting rod
11 Bearing inserts
12 Nut
13 Bolt

14 Camshaft
15 Camshaft gear
16 Cam bearing
17 Spacer
18 Plug
19 Thrust plate
20 Crankshaft
21 Crankshaft gear
22 Oil slinger
23 Vibration damper
24 Main bearing inserts
25 Thrust bearing inserts

26 Main bearing cap bolt
27 Flywheel
28 Washer
29 Bolt
30 Ring gear
31 Tappet
32 Crankshaft
33 Intake valve
34 Valve spring
35 Retainer
36 Keepers
37 Rocker arm stud

38 Fulcrum seat
39 Stud nut
40 Rocker arm
41 Pushrod
42 Valve stem seal
43 Oil pump
44 Oil pump rotor and
   driveshaft
45 Connecting rod cap
46 Oil pump cover plate
47 Oil pump intermediate
   shaft
48 Oil pump pickup

49 Gasket
50 Snap-ring
51 Plug
52 Relief valve spring
53 Relief valve plunger
54 Rear main oil seal
55 Clutch pilot bearing
56 Main bearing cap
57 Bolt ($\frac{5}{16}$ – 18 x $\frac{3}{4}$)
58 Washer
59 Bolt ($\frac{5}{8}$ – 18 x 2)
60 Woodruff key ($\frac{3}{4}$ x $\frac{5}{32}$)
61 Woodruff key ($\frac{3}{16}$ x $1\frac{3}{4}$)

2B

exhaust valve rotators. The heavy duty 300 engine is the same as the light duty engine except for heavy duty pistons, intake and exhaust valves and radiator.

12 Valve spring, retainer and seal — replacement (on vehicle)

Note: *Broken valve springs, retainers or defective valve stem seals can be replaced without removing the cylinder head (on engines that have no damage to the valves or valve seats). Two special tools and a compressed air source are required to perform this operation, so read through this Section carefully and rent or buy the tools before beginning this job.*

1   Remove the air cleaner.
2   Remove the accelerator cable return spring.
3   Remove the accelerator cable linkage at the carburetor.
4   Disconnect the choke cable at the carburetor connecting point.
5   Remove the PCV valve from the rocker arm cover and remove the rocker arm cover.
6   Remove the spark plug from the cylinder which has the bad component.
7   Crank the engine until the piston in the cylinder with the bad component is at top dead center on the compression stroke (refer to Step 3 of Section 9 in Chapter 2A). Note that the distributor should be marked opposite the appropriate terminal; not necessarily number one.
8   Install a special air line adapter which will screw into the spark plug hole and connect to a compressed air source. Remove the valve rocker arm stud nut, fulcrum seat, rocker arm and pushrod.
9   Apply compressed air to the cylinder in question. If the engine rotates until the piston is at bottom dead center, be very careful that you do not drop the valve into the cylinder as it will fall all the way in. Do not release the air pressure or the valve will drop through the guide.
10 Compress the valve spring with the special tool designed for this purpose.
11 Remove the keepers, spring retainer and valve spring, then remove the valve stem seal. **Note:** *If air pressure fails to hold the valve in the closed position during this operation, there is apparently damage to the seat or valve. If this condition exists, remove the cylinder head for further repair operations.*
12 If air pressure has forced the piston to the bottom of the cylinder, wrap a rubber band, tape or string around the top of the valve stem so that the valve will not fall through into the combustion chamber if it is dropped. Release the air pressure.
13 Inspect the valve stem for damage. Rotate the valve in its guide and check the valve stem tip for eccentric movement (which would indicate a bent valve).
14 Move the valve up and down through its normal travel and check that the valve guide and stem do not bind. If the valve stem binds, either the valve is bent and/or the guide is damaged and the head will have to be removed for repair.
15 Reapply air pressure to the cylinder to retain the valve in the closed position.
16 Lubricate the valve stem with engine oil and install a new valve stem seal.

17 Install the spring in position over the valve. Make sure that the closed coil end of the spring is correctly positioned next to the cylinder head.
18 Install the valve spring retainer. Compress the valve spring, using the valve spring compressor, and install the valve spring keepers. Remove the compressor tool and make sure that the valve spring keepers are installed correctly.
19 Apply engine oil to both ends of the pushrod.
20 Install the pushrod in position.
21 Apply engine oil to the tip of the valve stem.
22 Apply engine oil to the fulcrum seats and socket.
23 Install the rocker arm, fulcrum seat and stud nut. Adjust the valve clearance following the procedure in Chapter 2A (No adjustment is necessary on 1979 models; torque the valve fulcrum nut to the specified torque).
24 Remove the air source and the adapter from the spark plug hole.
25 Install the spark plug and connect the spark plug wire to it.
26 Install a new rocker arm cover gasket and attach the rocker arm cover to the engine.
27 Connect the accelerator cable to the carburetor at its connecting point.
28 Install the accelerator cable return spring. Connect the choke cable to the carburetor.
29 Install the PCV valve in the rocker arm cover and make sure that the line connected to the PCV valve is positioned correctly on both ends.
30 Install the air cleaner.
31 Start and run the engine, making sure that there are no oil leaks and that there are no unusual sounds coming from the valve assembly.

13 Manifolds — removal and installation

Removal

1   Remove the air cleaner and related air cleaner attachments.
2   Disconnect the choke cable at its linkage connecting point at the carburetor.
3   Disconnect the accelerator cable or linkage at the connecting point of the carburetor. Remove the accelerator return spring.
4   Remove the kick-down rod return spring and the kick-down shaft from its linkage at the carburetor.
5   Disconnect the fuel inlet line from the carburetor.
6   Disconnect the vacuum advance line for the distributor from the carburetor.
7   Disconnect the muffler inlet pipe from the exhaust manifold and support it out of the way.
8   Disconnect the power brake booster vacuum line from the intake manifold.
9   Remove the ten bolts and three nuts retaining the manifolds to the cylinder head. Lift the manifold assemblies away from the engine.
10 Remove and scrape the gaskets from the mating surface of the manifolds. If the manifolds are to be replaced or changed, remove the nuts connecting the intake manifold to the exhaust manifold.

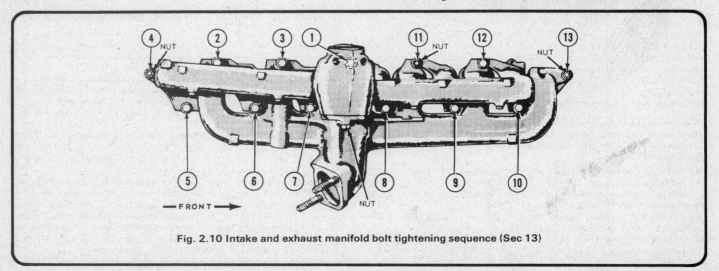

Fig. 2.10 Intake and exhaust manifold bolt tightening sequence (Sec 13)

Installation

11 Install new studs in the exhaust manifold for the inlet pipe.
12 If the intake and the exhaust manifolds have been separated, coat the mating surfaces with graphite grease. Place the exhaust manifold over the studs on the intake manifold. Connect the two with the lock washers and nuts. Tighten the nuts finger tight.
13 Install a new intake manifold-to-head gasket.
14 Coat the mating surfaces lightly with graphite grease. Place the manifold assemblies against the mating surface of the cylinder head, making sure that the gaskets are positioned correctly. Install the attaching washers, bolts and nuts finger tight and make sure everything is positioned and aligned correctly. Tighten the nuts and bolts to the proper torque in the order shown. Tighten the exhaust-to-intake manifold nuts to the proper torque (if they were removed).
15 Attach a new gasket to the inlet pipe and fasten the pipe to the exhaust manifold. Tighten the nuts to the proper torque.
16 Install the crankcase vent hose to the intake manifold inlet tube and tighten the hose clamp.
17 Attach the fuel inlet line to the carburetor.
18 Install the distributor vacuum line on the fitting at the carburetor.
19 Connect the accelerator cable to the carburetor and install the return spring. Connect the choke cable to the carburetor and adjust the choke.
20 Install the bellcrank assembly and kick-down rod return spring.
21 Adjust the transmission control kick-down linkage as specified in Chapter 7.
22 Install the air cleaner. Readjust the engine idle speed and idle fuel mixture as described in Chapter 4.

14 Flywheel – removal, inspection and installation

Note: *These instructions are valid only if the engine has been removed from the vehicle. If the engine is still in the vehicle, the transmission, the bellhousing and clutch assembly must be removed to expose the flywheel (refer to Chapter 7). Automatic transmission equipped vehicles are equipped with a flexplate rather than a flywheel. It can be separated from the crankshaft by removing the mounting bolts. If the ring gear teeth are worn or damaged or if the flexplate is damaged, replace it with a new one and tighten the mounting bolts to the specified torque.*
1 Mark the flywheel and the crankshaft end with a center punch to ensure installation in the same relative position.
2 To keep the crankshaft from turning, wedge a large screwdriver or pry bar between the ring gear teeth and the engine block (it must be positioned so that as the crankshaft moves, the tool bears against the block). Make sure that the tool is not pushing against the oil pan. Another method of preventing crankshaft rotation involves holding the front pulley retaining bolt with a large wrench or socket and breaker bar. This method may require a helper. **Caution:** *Support the flywheel before performing the following step as it could fall off and be damaged or cause injury.*
3 Remove the flywheel retaining bolts from the crankshaft flange.
4 Remove the flywheel from the crankshaft by pulling straight back on it.
5 Inspect the flywheel clutch disc mating surface for scoring, heat marks, cracks and warpage. If any of these conditions exist, the flywheel should be taken to an automotive machine shop to be resurfaced (or replaced with a new one). If the flywheel is cracked, it must be replaced with a new one.
6 Installation is the reverse of removal. The retaining bolts should be coated with a thread-locking compound and tightened in a criss-cross pattern to the prescribed torque.

15 Rocker arm and pushrod covers – removal and installation

Removal

1 Remove the positive crankcase ventilation hose from the top of the rocker arm cover.
2 Disconnect the air vent tube from the oil filler cap and remove the filler cap and tube from the rocker arm cover.
3 Disconnect the fuel supply hose at the fuel pump and at the carburetor. Remove the fuel supply hose.
4 Bring the engine to top dead center for the number one piston and mark the distributor as described in Chapter 5. Remove the distributor from the engine.

5 Remove the ignition coil and bracket from the side of the engine.
6 Remove the retaining screws holding the rocker arm cover to the cylinder head.
7 Remove the rocker arm cover from the cylinder head and clean the old gasket from the mating surfaces.
8 Remove the retaining bolts for the pushrod cover at the left side of the engine.
9 Remove the pushrod cover from the side of the engine and clean the old gasket from the cover and engine block.

Installation

10 Install a new gasket on the pushrod cover. RTV-type gasket sealant will keep it positioned.
11 Place the pushrod cover on the engine and tighten the retaining bolts.
12 Install a new rocker arm cover gasket in the rocker arm cover. RTV-type gasket sealant will hold it in place.
13 Install the rocker arm cover on the cylinder head, making sure that the bolt holes line up.
14 Install the rocker arm cover retaining bolts and tighten them to the proper torque.
15 Install the components listed in Steps 1 through 5 in reverse order.
16 After the engine has been started, run it until it reaches normal operating temperature. Check the pushrod cover and rocker arm cover for leaks.

16 Rocker arms and pushrods – removal, inspection and installation

1 Remove the rocker arm cover as described in the previous Section.
2 Remove the rocker arm stud nut, fulcrum seat and rocker arm from each cylinder. Keep them in order or mark them if they are to be re-installed so they can be replaced in their original positions.
3 Inspect the rocker arm cover bolt holes for worn or damaged seals where the bolt heads meet the cover.
4 Inspect the rocker arm for signs of excessive wear, galling or damage. Make sure the oil hole at the pushrod end of the rocker arm is open.
5 Inspect the rocker arm fulcrum for galling and check for wear on its face. If any of these conditions exist, replace the rocker arm and fulcrum as an assembly.
6 To remove the pushrods, pull them straight up through the cylinder head and out of the lifter pocket.
7 Inspect the pushrods to see if they are bent, cracked or excessively worn. If any of these conditions exist, replace the pushrods with new ones.
8 Apply engine oil or assembly lube to the top of the valve stem and the pushrod guide in the cylinder head.
9 Apply lubricant to the rocker arm fulcrum seat and the fulcrum seat socket in the rocker arm.
10 Install the pushrod (with lubricant applied to both ends).
11 Install the valve rocker arm, fulcrum seat and stud nut and tighten the stud nut to the proper torque.
12 Replace the rocker arm cover and gasket as described in the previous Section.

17 Valves – servicing

1 Because of the complex nature of the job and the special tools and equipment required, servicing of the valves, the valve seats and the valve guides (commonly known as a 'valve job') is best left to a professional.
2 The home mechanic can remove and disassemble the head(s), do the initial cleaning and inspection, then reassemble and deliver the head to a dealer service department or a reputable automotive machine shop for the actual valve servicing.
3 The dealer service department, or automotive machine shop, will remove the valves and springs, recondition or replace the valves and valve seats, recondition or replace the valve guides, check and replace the valve springs, spring retainers and keepers (as necessary), replace the valve seals with new ones, reassemble the valve components and make sure the installed spring height is correct. The cylinder head gasket surface will also be resurfaced if it is warped.
4 After the valve job has been performed by a professional, the head

2B

will be in like-new condition. When the head is returned, be sure to clean it again, very thoroughly (before installation on the engine), to remove any metal particles and abrasive grit that may still be present from the valve service or head resurfacing operations. Use compressed air, if available, to blow out all the holes and passages.

18 Cylinder head – removal, inspection and installation

Removal

Note: *If the engine has been removed from the vehicle, you may skip Steps 1 through 14 and begin with Step 15.*

1   Drain the cooling system.
2   Remove the air cleaner and connections leading to the air cleaner.
3   Disconnect the PCV valve from the rocker arm cover and remove the valve.
4   Disconnect the vent hose from the intake manifold inlet tube and remove it.
5   Disconnect and remove the carburetor fuel inlet line leading from the fuel pump.
6   Disconnect and remove the distributor vacuum line at the carburetor.
7   Disconnect the choke cable at its connection point to the carburetor and position the choke cable and housing out of the way. Secure the cable and housing to the firewall or fender well.
8   Disconnect the accelerator cable or accelerator linkage from the carburetor connecting point. Remove the accelerator return spring.
9   Disconnect the kick-down link at the carburetor connecting point.
10 Disconnect and remove the upper radiator hose from the thermostat outlet.
11 Remove the heater hose at the coolant outlet elbow.
12 Remove the nuts securing the muffler inlet pipe to the exhaust manifold and support the pipe out of the way.
13 Mark the wires leading to the coil and disconnect them. Remove the coil bracket attaching bolt. Secure the coil and bracket out of the way.
14 Remove the rocker arm cover.
15 Loosen the rocker arm stud nuts so that the rocker arms can be rotated to one side.
16 Remove the pushrods in sequence and label them so they can be installed in their original locations. A numbered box or rack will keep them properly organized.
17 Disconnect the spark plug wires at the spark plugs.
18 Remove the cylinder head retaining bolts. If you have an engine hoist or similar device handy, attach eyelet bolts at the two ends of the cylinder head in the holes provided and lift the cylinder head off of the engine block. If equipment of this nature is not available, use a helper and pry the cylinder head up off of the engine block. **Caution:** *Do not wedge any tools between the cylinder head and block gasket mating surfaces.*
19 Turn the cylinder head upside down and secure it on a work bench or cylinder head holding device. **Note:** *New and rebuilt cylinder heads are commonly available for engines at dealerships and auto parts stores. Due to the fact that some specialized tools are necessary for the dismantling and inspection of the heads, and replacement parts may not be readily available, it may be more practical and economical for the home mechanic to purchase replacement heads and install them.*
20 Another alternative at this point is to take the cylinder heads to a competent automotive machine shop or shop specializing in cylinder heads and exchange them or leave your heads for the overhaul process.
21 If the complete engine is being overhauled at the same time, it may be wise to wait until the other components have been inspected.
22 If you are attempting to repair a part of the cylinder head assembly or you wish to inspect the components yourself, read the following procedure first to gain an understanding of the steps involved and the tools and replacement parts necessary for the job. Proceed as follows.
23 Using a valve spring compressor (available at tool or auto parts stores), compress each of the valve springs and remove the valve keepers. Work on one valve at a time, removing the keepers, then releasing the spring and removing the retainer, valve rotator (if equipped), spring and spring damper. Place these components together on the numbered box or rack used during cylinder head removal. All valve mechanism components must be kept separate so they can be returned to their original locations.

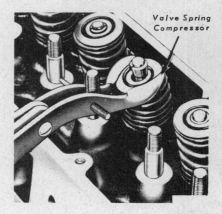

Fig. 2.11 Compressing the valve spring with a valve spring compressor to remove the keepers (Sec 18)

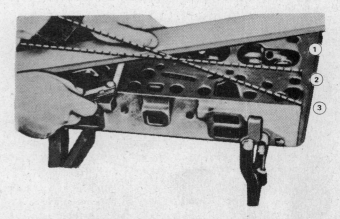

Fig. 2.12 Checking the cylinder head gasket surface for warpage with a straightedge and feeler gauge (check with the straightedge in three positions) (Sec 18)

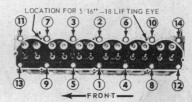

Fig. 2.13 Cylinder head bolt tightening sequence (Sec 18)

24 Remove the oil seals fom the stem of each valve. New seals should be used during reassembly.
25 Remove any spring shims used at the bottom of the valve spring.
26 Remove each valve, in turn, and place them in the numbered box or rack to complete the valve mechanism removal. Place the valve components in an area where they will not be mixed up.
27 Clean all old gasket material or sealant from the head gasket mating surface. Be careful not to scratch this sealing surface.
28 Clean the threads on all cylinder head attaching bolts thoroughly.

Inspection

29 Inspect each of the valve springs and dampers. Replace any spring which is deformed, cracked or broken. Check the valve spring tension using a special tool designed for this purpose. If you don't have access to this tool, take the springs to a shop that does. Weak valve springs may appear all right but can cause a poor running engine.
30 Carefully inspect the head for cracks around and inside the exhaust ports, combustion chambers or external cracks to the water jackets.

31 Check the cylinder head for warpage. Do this by placing a straightedge across the length of the head and measuring any gaps between the straightedge and the head surface with a feeler gauge. This should be done at three points across the head gasket surface and also in a diagonal fashion across this surface.

32 If warpage exceeds the specified limit at any point, when a straightedge which spans the entire head is used, the cylinder head should be resurfaced.

33 At this point, even if you are doing the work yourself, you will have to take your cylinder head and related components to a shop with the necessary equipment for valve service work. If you choose not to reassemble the head yourself, omit steps 35 through 40 and begin the procedure at step 41 to reinstall the head on the engine block.

34 Make sure all valve mechanism components are perfectly clean and free from carbon and dirt. The bare cylinder head should also be clean and free from abrasive agents which may have been used for valve grinding, reaming, etc.

35 Insert a valve in the proper port. Install a new oil seal over the valve stem, using engine oil for lubricant.

36 Assemble the valve spring assembly for that cylinder. This will include the spring, seat, retainer and valve rotator (if so equipped). Notice the closed coil end of the spring mates to the seat on the cylinder head.

37 Use the valve spring compressor to hold the spring assembly over the valve stem.

38 Install the valve keepers and release the compressor. Make sure the keepers seat properly in the upper groove of the valve stem.

39 Tap the retainers to ensure that the keepers are seated correctly.

40 Check the installed height of the valve springs using a caliper. Measure from the top of the shim (if present) or the spring seat to the top of the valve spring. Set the calipers next to a scale. Compare the spring height on the scale to the Specifications. If the springs are too long, shims can be used under the valve spring to bring the spring to the proper height. Shims are used to correct springs which are too high, as the shims will act to compress the springs slightly. At no time should the spring be shimmed to give an installed height under the minimum specified length.

Installation

41 Make sure that the cylinder head and cylinder block mating surfaces are clean, flat and prepared for the new cylinder head gasket. Clean the exhaust manifold and muffler inlet pipe gasket surfaces.

42 Position the gasket over the dowel pins on the cylinder block, making sure that it is facing the right direction and that the correct surface is exposed. Gaskets are often marked 'front' and 'this side up' to aid the installer.

43 Using the previously installed lifting hooks (or two people) carefully lower the cylinder head into place on the block in its correct position. Take care not to move the head sideways or to scrape it across the surface as it can dislodge the gasket and/or damage the mating surfaces.

44 Coat the cylinder head retaining bolts with light engine oil and thread the bolts into the block. Tighten the bolts using the cylinder head bolt tightening sequence shown in the accompanying illustration. Work up to the final torque in three steps to avoid warping the head.

45 Apply a coat of engine oil to the rocker arm fulcrum seats and sockets in the rocker arms.

46 Install the pushrods, the rocker arms, the rocker arm fulcrum seats and the retaining nuts.

47 Install the rocker arm cover. The remaining steps are the reverse of the removal procedure.

48 Start the engine and allow it to reach operating temperature. Shut it off, allow it to cool down and retorque the head bolts.

---

19 Timing cover and gears – removal and installation

Note: *The following procedure requires the use of a gear puller and gear installation tools.*

Removal

1 Drain the cooling system.

2 Remove the fan shroud and the radiator (Chapter 3).

3 Remove the alternator adjustment bolt.

4 Loosen the drivebelt and swing the adjusting arm up out of the way.

5 Remove the fan, drivebelts, fan spacer and pulley.

6 Remove the large bolt and washer from the crankshaft nose. It may be necessary to prevent the crankshaft from rotating by putting the transmission in gear (if the engine is still in the vehicle) or by holding the flywheel or crankshaft flange with a suitable tool if the engine is out of the vehicle.

7 Remove the vibration damper using a suitable puller.

8 Remove the front oil pan attaching bolts.

9 Remove the timing cover attaching bolts.

10 Remove the cover and scrape the old gasket from the mating surfaces of the cover and the engine block.

11 Remove the crankshaft oil seal by pushing it out of the front cover with a suitable sized drift. Be careful not to damage the front cover while performing this operation.

12 Remove any chemical sealants from the seal bore of the cover. Check the bore carefully for anything that would prevent the new seal from seating properly in the cover.

13 Before removing the gears, the camshaft endplay, timing gear backlash and timing gear runout should be inspected as described in Section 20.

14 Turn the crankshaft and/or camshaft until the timing marks of both gears can be aligned as shown in the accompanying illustration. **Caution:** *If the heads, valves and pistons remain in the engine while the gears are being installed, do not turn either the crankshaft or camshaft while the gears are removed. Serious internal engine damage can result from rotating either assembly independent of the other.*

15 Install a suitable gear puller and remove the gear from the camshaft.

16 Using a suitable puller, remove the timing gear from the crankshaft.

Installation

17 Make sure that the camshaft endplay, timing gear backlash and timing gear runout are within Specifications. Do not install the camshaft gear until all of these camshaft related tolerances are correct.

18 Align the key spacer and thrust plate before installing the camshaft drive gear onto the camshaft. Make sure that the timing marks are properly aligned.

19 Install the crankshaft gear using the special drive tool. A substitute special tool can be fashioned by using a bolt and nut with a thread that matches the thread of the vibration damper retaining bolt. Use a bolt approximately $2\frac{1}{2}$ inches long. Place the crankshaft gear on the crankshaft. Position the damper onto the crankshaft. Thread the bolt (with the nut run all the way up the bolt) into the crankshaft nose. After the bolt is threaded into the crankshaft as far as possible, use the nut

2B

Fig. 2.14 Crankshaft and camshaft timing gear marks properly aligned (Sec 19)

to drive the damper onto the crankshaft. Make sure the damper is correctly aligned with the key on the crankshaft and check the internal bore of the damper as well as the outside surface of the crankshaft if resistance is felt. The damper will drive the crankshaft gear into position. Remove the damper with a puller. A large deep socket (if you have access to one) can also be used to drive the gear onto the crankshaft and will save having to pull the damper back off.

20 Install the crankshaft oil slinger in front of the crankshaft drive gear. Note that the cupped side faces away from the engine.

21 Coat the outside edge of the new crankshaft oil seal with grease and install the seal in the cover using an appropriate drive tool. Make sure the seal is seated completely in the bore.

22 If the oil pan is still on the engine, cut the old front oil pan seal flush at the cylinder block-to-pan junction. Remove the old seal.

23 Clean all gasket surfaces on the camshaft cover, block and oil pan.

24 If the oil pan is in place, cut and install a new pan seal so that it is flush with the engine block-to-oil pan junction.

25 Align the pan seal locating tabs with the holes in the oil pan. Make sure that the seal tabs pull all the way through so that the seal is completely seated. Apply RTV-type gasket sealant to the block and pan mating surfaces (particularly to the corner junctions of the block, oil pan and cover).

26 Position the cover over the end of the crankshaft and onto the cylinder block. Start the cover and pan retaining screws by hand.

27 Slide an alignment tool over the crank stub to make sure that the cover is located correctly before tightening the retaining bolts. If no alignment tool is available, try to locate a pipe to center the seal over the nose of the crankshaft. If the seal is not centered, the high spots will cause oil leakage around the vibration damper.

28 Tighten the retaining bolts for the cover and oil pan to the correct torque.

29 Install the alternator adjusting arm and tighten all the oil pan and front cover screws.

30 Make sure that the oil pan screws are tightened first to compress the pan seal so that the alignment of the cover is retained.

31 Lubricate the nose of the crankshaft, the inner hub of the vibration damper and the seal surface with engine oil.

32 Align the damper keyway with the key on the crankshaft and install the damper.

33 Install the bolt and washer retaining the damper and tighten it to the proper torque.

34 Install the pulley(s), drivebelt(s), spacer and fan.

35 Adjust all drivebelt tensions.

36 Install the fan shroud, radiator and hoses.

37 Fill the cooling system.

38 Fill the engine with oil if the oil has been drained.

39 Start and operate the engine at a fast idle and check for leaks of any type.

Fig. 2.15 Removing the camshaft gear with a gear puller (Sec 19)

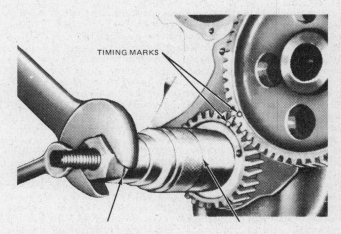

Fig. 2.16 Installing the crankshaft gear with the timing marks properly aligned (note special tools (arrows) being used) (Sec 19)

20 Camshaft and lifters – removal, inspection and installation

Removal

1 Remove the air cleaner.

2 Remove the PCV valve from the rocker arm cover.

3 Disconnect the choke cable at the connecting point of the carburetor.

4 Disconnect the throttle cable at the carburetor connecting point. Remove the accelerator return spring.

5 Remove the coil bracket retaining bolt and swing the coil out of the way. Support it securely and do not let it hang from the wires.

6 Remove the rocker arm cover.

7 Disconnect the spark plug wires from the spark plugs and the coil wire from the coil.

8 Remove the distributor cap and spark plug wire assembly.

9 Remove the pushrod cover from the side of the block.

10 Loosen the rocker arm stud nuts until the rocker arms are free of the pushrods. Turn the rocker arms to the side and remove the pushrods. Make sure that the pushrods are numbered or marked so that they can be installed in the same locations.

11 Remove the valve lifters with a special magnetic valve lifter tool.

12 Drain the cooling system and the oil from the crankcase.

13 Remove the radiator.

14 Remove the front timing cover.

15 Remove the oil pump and oil pan.

Fig. 2.17 Removing the tappets with a magnetic tool (arrow) (Sec 20)

Fig. 2.18 Checking camshaft endplay with a dial indicator (Sec 20)

16 Disconnect the fuel lines at the fuel pump. Remove the fuel pump retaining bolts and secure the fuel pump out of the way.

17 Disconnect the vacuum line at the distributor and remove the vacuum line from the carburetor. **Note:** *The following checking procedures require the use of a magnetic base dial indicator.*

18 Check the camshaft endplay by pushing the camshaft all the way to the rear of its travel in the block.

19 Install a dial indicator so that the indicator stem is on the camshaft sprocket retaining bolt. Zero the dial indicator in this position.

20 Using a large screwdriver between the camshaft gear and the block, pull the camshaft forward and release it. The reading on the dial indicator will give you the endplay measurement. Compare it to the Specifications. If the endplay is excessive, check the spacer for correct installation. If the spacer is correctly installed, and the endplay is too great, replace the thrust plate with a new one.

21 Check the timing gear backlash by installing a dial indicator on the cylinder block and positioning the stem against the timing gear.

22 Zero the pointer on the dial indicator.

23 While holding the crankshaft still, move the camshaft timing gear until it takes up the slack in the gear train.

24 Read the dial indicator to obtain the gear backlash.

25 Compare the results to the Specifications.

26 If the backlash is excessive, replace the timing gear and the crankshaft gear with new ones.

27 To check the timing gear runout, install a dial indicator on the engine block with the stem touching the face of the timing gear.

28 Hold the camshaft gear against the camshaft thrust plate and zero the indicator.

29 Rotate the crankshaft to turn the camshaft while holding the camshaft gear against the thrust plate.

30 Rotate the gear through one complete revolution of the camshaft. Observe the reading on the dial indicator during this revolution.

31 If the runout exceeds the Specifications, remove the camshaft gear and check for foreign objects or burrs between the camshaft and gear flanges. If this condition does not exist and the runout is excessive, the gears must be replaced with new ones. Use a similar procedure to check the crankshaft gear runout. Make sure that the crankshaft is situated against one end of the thrust bearing (this will prevent you from obtaining a crankshaft endplay measurement as opposed to the actual runout of the crankshaft gear).

32 Turn the crankshaft until the timing marks are directly adjacent to each other.

33 Remove the camshaft thrust plate retaining screws.

34 Carefully withdraw the camshaft from the engine block, being careful that the lobes do not catch on the camshaft bearings (they can scrape and damage them easily).

35 Remove the camshaft from the gear using a special hydraulic press. This procedure will have to be handled by a suitably equipped automotive machine shop.

36 Remove the key, the thrust plate and the spacer.

Inspection

37 Visually inspect the hydraulic lifters for cupping on the camshaft mating face and for signs of excessive wear, galling or cracking.

38 The hydraulic valve lifter is tested using a special lifter tester and special testing fluid. This procedure must be handled by a suitably equipped automotive machine shop.

39 If you suspect that a lifter is defective, you will have to replace the lifter with a new one. It is not necessary to test the new lifter before installation.

40 Check the lift of each camshaft lobe in a special V-block cradle. Again, this is a procedure which should be handled by a suitably equipped machine shop.

41 Also, check the camshaft bearing surfaces for any signs of galling or excesive wear. If any of these conditions exist, replace the camshaft with a new one. If the bearing journals of the camshaft show any signs of wear or damage, check the cam bearings in the engine block. Do not install any camshaft in worn or damaged bearings.

Installation

42 Make sure that the camshaft endplay, timing gear backlash and/or timing gear runout are within Specifications before installing the camshaft.

43 oil the camshaft bearing journals and apply engine assembly lubricant to all of the lobes.

44 Install the key, spacer and thrust plate into position on the front of

Fig. 2.19 Checking timing gear backlash with a dial indicator (Sec 20)

Fig. 2.20 Checking timing gear runout with a dial indicator (Sec 20)

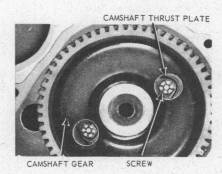

Fig. 2.21 The camshaft thrust plate bolts can be removed by inserting a socket through the holes in the gear (Sec 20)

2B

the camshaft. Install the gear onto the camshaft using the special tool. An alternative is to use a bolt that will fit the threaded hole in the end of the camshaft. Put a nut and large flat washer on the bolt. Thread the bolt into the camshaft with the gear in place. Hold the bolt stationary and turn the nut down the bolt to push the gear into place on the camshaft. Remove the bolt and nut combination after the cam gear is in place.

45 Install the camshaft into the engine. Be careful not to nick or damage the camshaft bearings. Install the camshaft retaining bolts, making sure the camshaft gear is aligned with the crankshaft gear.

46 Tighten the camshaft thrust plate bolts to the proper torque, using the access holes provided in the camshaft gear.

47 Install the timing cover as described in Section 19.
48 Do not turn the engine until the distributor is installed, as the timing marks must remain aligned.
49 Install the oil pump and oil pan.
50 Lubricate the bottom of the lifters with engine assembly lube and install them into their proper positions. Install the pushrods, align the rocker arms and tighten the nuts, install the rocker arm and pushrod covers and hook up the throttle cable.
51 Install the distributor as described in Chapter 5.
52 Install the fuel pump as described in Chapter 4.
53 Install the vacuum line connecting the distributor to the carburetor.
54 Connect the fuel outlet line and the fuel feed line to the fuel pump.
55 Fill the crankcase with oil.
56 Install the radiator and fill the cooling system with the correct coolant.
57 Start the engine and check for oil and fuel leaks.
58 Adjust the ignition timing.
59 Adjust the carburetor idle speed and mixture.

21 Oil pan – removal and installation

Note: *This procedure is for removal and installation of the oil pan with the engine in the vehicle only. If the engine has been removed for an overhaul, use only Step 10 and steps 14 through 26.*

Removal

1 Drain the engine oil and disconnect the negative battery cable from the battery.
2 Drain the cooling system.
3 Remove the radiator as described in Chapter 3.
4 Raise the vehicle and support it securely. Disconnect the starter cable at the starter.
5 Remove the starter from the bellhousing. It is attached with three bolts.
6 Remove the engine front insulator-to-support bracket retaining nuts and washers.
7 Raise the front of the engine with a jack. Place a thick wooden block between the jack and the oil pan.

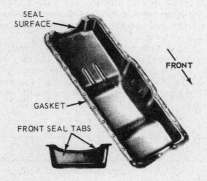

Fig. 2.22 Oil pan gasket installation details (Sec 21)

SEAL SURFACE
FRONT
GASKET
FRONT SEAL TABS

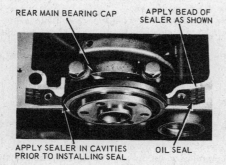

REAR MAIN BEARING CAP
APPLY BEAD OF SEALER AS SHOWN
APPLY SEALER IN CAVITIES PRIOR TO INSTALLING SEAL
OIL SEAL

Fig. 2.23 Rear oil pan seal installation details (Sec 21)

8 Place one inch wood blocks between the front support insulators and the support brackets.
9 Lower the engine onto the spacer blocks and remove the jack.
10 Remove the oil pan attaching bolts.
11 Lower the pan to the crossmember.
12 Remove the two oil pump inlet tube-to-oil pump retaining bolts and washers.
13 Remove the oil pump inlet assembly and allow it to rest in the oil pan.
14 Remove the oil pan from the vehicle. It may be necessary to rotate the crankshaft so that the counterweights clear the pan.
15 Clean all gaskets from the mating surfaces of the engine block and the pan.

Installation

16 Remove the rear main bearing cap-to-oil pan seal.
17 Remove the timing cover-to-oil pan seal.
18 Clean all mating surfaces and seal grooves.
19 Install new oil pan-to-cylinder front cover oil seals.
20 Install a new rear main bearing cap-to-oil pan seal.
21 Install new oil pan side gaskets on the block. Apply a thin, even coat of RTV-type gasket sealer to both sides of the gaskets.
22 Make sure the tabs of the front and rear seal fit properly into the mating slots on the oil pan side seals. A small amount of RTV-type gasket sealer at each mating junction will help prevent any leaks from these critical spots.
23 Clean the inlet tube and screen assembly and place it in the oil pan.
24 Position the oil pan underneath the engine.
25 Lift the inlet tube and screen assembly from the oil pan and secure it to the oil pump with a new gasket. Tighten the two retaining bolts to the proper torque.
26 Attach the oil pan to the engine block and install the retaining bolts. Tighten the bolts starting from the center and working outward in each direction.
27 Raise the engine with a jack and a block of wood underneath the oil pan and remove the wood spacers previously installed under the support brackets.
28 Lower the engine to the correct installed position and install the washers and nuts on the insulator studs. Tighten the nuts securely.
29 Install the starter and connect the starter cable.
30 Lower the vehicle.
31 Install the radiator according to the instructions found in Chapter 3.
32 Fill the cooling system with coolant and check for leaks.
33 Fill the engine crankcase with oil and hook up the negative battery cable.
34 Start the engine and check carefully for leaks at the oil pan gasket sealing surfaces.

22 Oil pump – removal and installation

1 Remove the oil pan as described in Section 21.
2 Remove the bolts retaining the oil pump to the block.
3 Remove the oil pump assembly.
4 Clean the mating surfaces of the oil pump and the block.
5 Before installation, prime the pump by filling the inlet opening with oil and rotating the pump shaft until the oil spurts out of the outlet.
6 Attach the oil pump to the engine block using the two retaining bolts.
7 Tighten the bolts to the proper torque.
8 Install the oil pan by referring to Section 21.

23 Oil pump – disassembly, inspection and reassembly

1 Remove the two bolts securing the pick-up to the oil pump, then remove the pick-up.
2 Clean the oil pump with solvent and dry it thoroughly with compressed air.
3 Remove the oil pump housing cover. It is retained by four bolts.
4 Use a brush to clean the inside of the pump housing and the pressure relief valve chamber. Make sure that the interior of the oil pump is clean.
5 Visually check the inside of the pump housing and the outer race and rotor for excessive wear, scoring or damage. Check the mating

Fig. 2.24 Checking the oil pump outer race-to-housing clearance
(Sec 23)

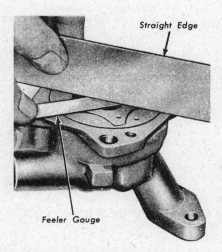

Fig. 2.25 Checking the oil pump rotor assembly end clearance
(Sec 23)

24.2 Removing the cylinder wear ridge with a ridge reaming tool
(follow the manufacturer's directions for the tool)

surface of the pump cover for wear, grooves or damage. If any of these conditions exist, replace the pump with a new one.
6   Measure the outer race-to-housing clearance with a feeler gauge.
7   Using a straightedge and feeler gauge, measure the end plate-to-rotor assembly clearance.
8   Check the driveshaft-to-housing bearing clearance by measuring the inside diameter of the housing bearing and subtracting that figure from the outside diameter of the driveshaft.
9   If any components fail the checks mentioned, replace the entire oil pump, as the components are not serviced as separate parts.
10   Inspect the relief valve spring for wear or a collapsed condition.
11   Check the relief valve piston for scoring, damage and free operation within its bore.
12   If the relief valve fails any of the above tests, replace the entire relief valve assembly with a new one.
13   Install the rotor, outer housing and race into the oil pump.
14   Install the rotor housing cover and the four retaining bolts and tighten them to the proper torque.
15   Attach the pick-up tube to the oil pump body using a new gasket. Tighten the bolts to the proper torque.

24 Piston/connecting rod assembly – removal

1   Prior to removing the piston/connecting rod assemblies, remove the cylinder head, the oil pan, and the oil pump by referring to the appropriate Sections.
2   Using a ridge reamer, completely remove the ridge at the top of each cylinder (photo) (follow the manufacturer's instructions provided with the ridge reaming tool). Failure to remove the ridge before attempting to remove the piston/connecting rod assemblies will result in piston breakage.
3   Mark each of the connecting rods and connecting rod bearing caps to ensure that they are properly mated during reassembly.
4   Loosen each of the connecting rod cap nuts approximately $\frac{1}{2}$ turn each. Remove the number one connecting rod cap and bearing insert. Do not drop the bearing insert out of the cap. Slip a short length of plastic or rubber hose over each connecting rod cap bolt (to protect the crankshaft journal when the piston is removed) and push the connecting rod/piston assembly out through the top of the engine. Use a wooden tool to push on the upper bearing insert in the connecting rod. If resistance is felt, double-check to make sure that all of the ridge was removed from the cylinder.
5   Repeat the procedure for the remaining cylinders. After removal, reassemble the connecting rod caps and bearing inserts to their respective connecting rods and install the cap nuts finger tight. Leaving the old bearing inserts in place until reassembly will help prevent the connecting rod bearing surfaces from being accidentally nicked or gouged.

25 Crankshaft and main bearings – removal

Note: *The crankshaft may be removed only after the engine has been removed from the vehicle.*
1   Remove the spark plugs from the cylinder head. Remove the cylinder head if the entire engine is going to be dismantled.
2   Remove the oil level dipstick.
3   Remove the bolt and lock washer retaining the vibration damper to the front of the crankshaft.
4   Remove the vibration damper with a suitable puller. Remove the pulley spacer on all engines except the 300 cid six (and 351M thru 400M V8's).
5   Remove the timing cover and gasket as described elsewhere in this Chapter .
6   Remove the flywheel.
7   Remove the engine rear cover plate.
8   Remove the oil pan and gaskets.
9   Remove the oil pump and inlet tube assembly.
10   Visually check all of the main bearing and rod bearing caps to see that they are marked for location. If they are not, mark them with a numbered die or a center punch.
11   If the engine is being entirely dismantled, remove the piston and rod assemblies.
12   If the crankshaft only is being removed from the engine, remove

2B

the connecting rod cap and bearing from the number one cylinder and then rotate it to the top dead center position. **Note:** *Use caution when turning the crankshaft for further connecting rod cap removal as the rod bolts can come in contact with the crankshaft bearing surfaces and damage the crank pin journals. It is a very good idea to slip a short section of rubber hose over each rod bolt to protect the journals.*

13 Follow the procedure in Step 12 for each remaining connecting rod cap and bearing.

14 Remove the main bearing caps and retaining bolts.

15 Remove the rear main bearing oil seal.

16 Remove the lower main bearing inserts if they did not stay with the main bearing caps.

17 Carefully lift the crankshaft out of the engine block taking care that all of the crank pins clear the exposed connecting rod bolts.

18 Replace the main bearings and caps in the block and tighten the bolts finger tight.

26 Engine block – cleaning and inspection

1 Remove the soft plugs from the engine block. To do this, knock the plugs into the block (using a hammer and punch), then grasp them with large pliers and pull them back through the holes.

2 Using a gasket scraper, remove all traces of gasket material from the engine block. Be very careful not to nick or gouge the gasket sealing surfaces.

3 Remove the main bearing caps and separate the bearing inserts from the caps and the engine block. Tag the bearings according to which cylinder they were removed from (and whether they were in the cap or the block) and set them aside.

4 Using a hex wrench of the appropriate size, remove the threaded oil gallery plugs from the front and back of the block.

5 If the engine is extremely dirty, it should be taken to an automotive machine shop to be steam cleaned or hot tanked.

6 After the block is returned, clean all oil holes and oil galleries one more time (brushes for cleaning oil holes and galleries are available at most auto parts stores). Flush the passages with warm water (until the water runs clear), dry the block thoroughly and wipe all machined surfaces with a light rust-preventative oil. If you have access to compressed air, use it to speed the drying process and to blow out all of the oil holes and galleries.

7 If the block is not extremely dirty or sludged up, you can do an adequate cleaning job with warm soapy water and a stiff brush. Take plenty of time and do a thorough job. Regardless of the cleaning method used, be very sure to thoroughly clean all oil holes and galleries, dry the block completely and coat all machined surfaces with light oil.

8 The threaded holes in the block must be clean to ensure accurate torque readings during reassembly. Run the proper size tap into each of the holes to remove any rust, corrosion, thread sealant or sludge and to restore any damaged threads. If possible, use compressd air to clear the holes of debris produced by this operation. Now is a good time to thoroughly clean the threads on the head bolts and the main bearing cap bolts as well.

9 Reinstall the main bearing caps and tighten the bolts finger tight.

10 After coating the sealing surfaces of the new soft plugs with a good quality gasket sealer, install them in the engine block. Make sure they are driven in straight and seated properly, or leakage could result. Special tools are available for this purpose, but equally good results can be obtained using a large socket (with an outside diameter slightly larger than the outside diameter of the soft plug) and a large hammer.

11 Double-check to make sure that the ridge at the top of the cylinders has been competely removed.

12 Visually check the block for cracks, rust and corrosion. Look for stripped threads in the threaded holes. It is also a good idea to have the block checked for hidden cracks by an automotive machine shop that has the special equipment to do this type of work. If defects are found, have the block repaired, if possible, or replaced.

13 Check the cylinder bores for scuffing and scoring.

14 Using the appropriate precision measuring tools, measure each cylinder's diameter at the top (just under the ridge), center and bottom of the cylinder bore, parallel to the crankshaft axis. Next, measure each cylinder's diameter at the same three locations across the crankshaft axis. Compare the results to the Specifications. If the cylinder walls are badly scuffed or scored, or if they are out-of-round or tapered beyond the limits given in the Specifications, have the engine block rebored and honed at an automotive machine shop. If a rebore is done, oversized pistons and rings will be required as well.

15 If the cylinders are in reasonably good condition and not worn to the outside of the limits, and if the piston-to-cylinder clearances can be maintained properly, then they do not have to be rebored; honing is all that is necessary.

16 Before honing the cylinders, install the main bearing caps (without the bearings) and tighten the bolts to the specified torque.

17 To perform the honing operation, you will need the proper size flexible hone (with fine stones), plenty of light oil or honing oil, some rags and an electric drill motor. Mount the hone in the drill motor, compress the stones and slip the hone into the first cylinder. Lubricate the cylinder thoroughly, turn on the drill and move the hone up and down in the cylinder at a pace which will produce a fine crosshatch pattern on the cylinder walls (with the crosshatch lines intersecting at approximately a 60° angle). Be sure to use plenty of lubricant, and do not take off any more material than is absolutely necessary to produce the desired finish. Do not withdraw the hone from the cylinder while it is running. Instead, shut off the drill and continue moving the hone up and down in the cylinder until it comes to a complete stop, then compress the stones and withdraw the hone. Wipe the oil out of the cylinder and repeat the procedure on the remaining cylinders. Remember, do not remove too much material from the cylinder wall. If you do not have the tools or do not desire to perform the honing operation, most automotive machine shops will do it for a reasonable fee.

18 After the honing job is complete, chamfer the top edges of the cylinder bores with a small file so that the rings will not catch when the pistons are installed.

19 Check the cylinder head mating surface (top deck) of the block using a straightedge and a feeler gauge. Have the deck surface of the block machined if the warpage exceeds the Specifications.

20 Next, the entire engine block must be thoroughly washed again with warm soapy water to remove all traces of the abrasive grit produced during the honing operation. Be sure to run a brush through all oil holes and galleries and flush them with running water. After rinsing, dry the block and apply a coat of light rust preventative oil to all machined surfaces. Wrap the block in a plastic trash bag to keep it clean and set it aside until reassembly.

27 Crankshaft and bearings – inspection

1 Clean the crankshaft with solvent (be sure to clean the oil holes with a stiff brush and flush them with solvent) and dry it thoroughly. Check the main and connecting rod bearing journals for uneven wear, scoring, pitting and cracks. Check the remainder of the crankshaft for cracks and damage.

2 Using an appropriate size micrometer, measure the diameter of the main and connecting rod journals (photo) and compare the results

27.2 Measuring a crankshaft main bearing journal's diameter with a micrometer

to the Specifications. By measuring the diameter at a number of points around the journal's circumference, you will be able to determine whether or not the journal is worn out-of-round. Take the measurement at each end of the journal, near the crank throw, to determine whether the journal is tapered.

3 If the crankshaft journals are damaged, tapered, out-of-round or worn beyond the limits given in the Specifications, have the crankshaft reground by a reputable automotive machine shop. Be sure to use the correct undersize bearing inserts if the crankshaft is reconditioned.

4 Even though the main and connecting rod bearings should be replaced with new ones during the engine overhaul, the old bearings should be retained for close examination, as they may reveal valuable information about the condition of the engine.

5 Bearing failure occurs mainly because of lack of lubrication, the presence of dirt or other foreign particles, overloading the engine and/or corrosion. Regardless of the cause of bearing failure, it must be corrected before the engine is reassembled to prevent it from happening again.

6 When examining the bearings, remove them from the engine block, the main bearing caps, the connecting rods and the rod caps and lay them out on a clean surface in the same general position as their location in the engine. This will enable you to match any noted bearing problems with the corresponding crankshaft journal.

7 Dirt and other foreign particles get into the engine in a variety of ways. It may be left in the engine during reassembly, or it may pass through filters or breathers. It may get into the oil, and from there into the bearings. Metal chips from machining operations and normal engine wear are often present. Abrasives are sometimes left in engine components after reconditioning, especially when parts are not thoroughly cleaned using the proper cleaning methods. Whatever the source, these foreign objects often end up embedded in the soft bearing material and are easily recognized. Large particles will not embed in the bearing and will score or gouge the bearing and shaft. The best prevention for this cause of bearing failure is to clean all parts thoroughly and keep everything spotlessly clean during engine assembly. Frequent and regular changes of engine oil, and oil filter, are also recommended.

8 Lack of lubrication (or lubrication breakdown) has a number of interrelated causes. Excessive heat (which thins the oil), overloading (which squeezes the oil from the bearing face) and oil leakage or throw-off (from excessive bearing clearances, worn oil pump or high engine speeds) all contribute to lubrication breakdown. Blocked oil passages, which usually are the result of misaligned oil holes in a bearing shell, will also oil-starve a bearing and destroy it. When lack of lubrication is the cause of bearing failure, the bearing material is wiped or extruded from the steel backing of the bearing. Temperatures may increase to the point where the steel backing turns blue from overheating.

9 Driving habits can have a definite effect on bearing life. Full-throttle low-speed operation (or 'lugging' the engine) puts very high loads on bearings, which tends to squeeze out the oil film. These loads cause the bearings to flex, which produces fine cracks in the bearing face (fatigue failure). Eventually the bearing material will loosen in pieces and tear away from the steel backing. Short-trip driving leads to corrosion of bearings, as insufficient engine heat is produced to drive off the condensed water and corrosive gases produced. These products collect in the engine oil, forming acid and sludge. As the oil is carried to the engine bearings the acid attacks and corrodes the bearing material.

10 Incorrect bearing installation during engine assembly will lead to bearing failure as well. Tight-fitting bearings, which leave insufficient bearing oil clearance, result in oil starvation. Dirt or foreign particles trapped behind a bearing insert result in high spots on the bearing which lead to failure.

28 Piston/connecting rod assembly – inspection

1 Before the inspection process can be carried out, the piston/connecting rod assemblies must be cleaned and the old piston rings removed from the pistons.

2 Using a piston ring installation tool, carefully remove the rings from the pistons. Do not nick or gouge the pistons in the process.

3 Scrape all traces of carbon from the top (or crown) of the piston. A hand-held wire brush or a piece of fine emery cloth can be used once the majority of the deposits have been scraped away. Do not, under

any circumstances, use a wire brush mounted in a drill motor to remove deposits from the pistons. The piston material is soft and will be eroded away by the wire brush.

4 Use a piston ring groove cleaning tool to remove any carbon deposits from the ring grooves. If a tool is not available, a piece broken off the old ring will do the job. Be very careful to remove only the carbon deposits. Do not remove any metal and do not nick or scratch the sides of the ring grooves.

5 Once the deposits have been removed, clean the piston/rod assemblies with solvent and dry them thoroughly. Make sure that the oil hole in the big end of the connecting rod and the oil return holes in the back side of the ring groove are clear.

6 If the pistons are not damaged or worn excessively, and if the engine block is not rebored, new pistons will not be necessary. Normal piston wear appears as even vertical wear on the piston thrust surfaces and slight looseness of the top ring in its groove. New piston rings, on the other hand, should always be used when an engine is rebuilt.

7 Carefully inspect each piston for cracks around the skirt, at the pin bosses and at the ring lands.

8 Look for scoring and scuffing (on the thrust faces of the skirt), holes (in the piston crown) and burned areas (at the edge of the crown). If the skirt is scored or scuffed, the engine may have been suffering from overheating and/or abnormal combustion, which caused excessively high operating temperatures. The cooling and lubrication systems should be checked thoroughly. A hole in the piston crown, an extreme to be sure, is an indication that abnormal combustion (preignition) was occurring. Burned areas at the edge of the piston crown are usually evidence of spark knock (detonation). If any of the above problems exist, the causes must be corrected or the damage will occur again.

9 Corrosion of the piston (evidenced by pitting) indicates that coolant is leaking into the combustion chamber and/or the crankcase. Again, the cause must be corrected or the problem may persist in the rebuilt engine.

10 Measure the piston ring side clearance by laying a new piston ring in the ring groove and slipping a feeler gauge in beside it. Check the clearance at three or four locations around the groove. Be sure to use the correct ring for each groove; they are different. If the side clearance is greater than specified, new pistons will have to be used and the block rebored to accept them.

11 Check the piston-to-bore clearance by measuring the bore and the piston diameter. Make sure that the pistons and bores are correctly matched. Measure the piston on the thrust faces (at a 90° angle to the piston pin) at the piston pin centerline (photo). Subtract the piston diameter from the bore diameter to obtain the clearance. If it is greater than specified, the block will have to be rebored and new pistons and rings installed. Check the piston pin-to-rod clearance by twisting the piston and rod in opposite directions. Any noticeable play indicates that there is excessive wear, which must be corrected. The piston/connecting rod assemblies should be taken to an automotive

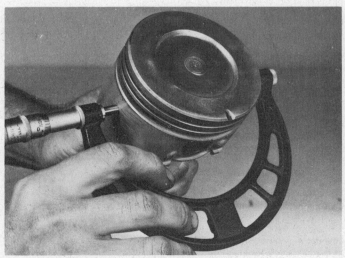

28.11 Measuring piston diameter with a micrometer

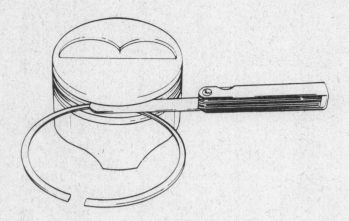

Fig. 2.26 Checking piston ring-to-groove clearance (Sec 28)

29.8 Comparing the width of the crushed Plastigage to the scale on the container to obtain the bearing oil clearance

29.13 Checking connecting rod endplay with a feeler gauge

machine shop to have the new piston rings installed and the pistons and connecting rods rebored.

12 If the pistons must be removed from the connecting rods, such as when new pistons must be installed, or if the piston pins have too much play in them, they should be taken to an automotive machine shop. While they are there, it would be convenient to have the connecting rods checked for bend and twist, as automotive machine shops have special equipment for this purpose.

13 Check the connecting rods for cracks and other damage. Temporarily remove the rod caps, lift out the old bearing inserts, wipe the rod and cap bearing surfaces clean and inspect them for nicks, grooves and scratches. After checking the rods, replace the old bearings, slip the caps in place and tighten the nuts finger tight. Unless new pistons or connecting rods must be installed, do not disassemble the pistons from the connecting rods.

29 Main and rod bearings – checking clearances

1 **Note:** *There are three precautions to observe when working with Plastigage. These are:*

   a) *Plastigage is soluble in oil, so all oil and grease should be removed from the crankshaft and bearing surfaces before the check is done*

   b) *Do not rotate the crankshaft while the Plastigage is installed, as this may cause damage to the crankshaft or bearing surfaces*

   c) *Remove all traces of the Plastigage when the check is complete. Be very careful not to damage the crankshaft or bearing surfaces as the Plastigage is removed. Do not use sharp tools or abrasive cleaners, instead, remove the used Plastigage with your fingernail or a blunt wood stick*

2 Whenever an engine is overhauled, the bearing clearances should be checked. This should be done for reused bearings as well as for new bearings.

3 The procedure is basically the same for both the main bearings and the connecting rod bearings.

4 With the crankshaft set into the engine block, install the main bearings into the engine block and the main bearing caps.

5 Remove all oil, grime and foreign materials from the crankshaft and bearing surfaces.

6 Place a piece of Plastigage (available at most auto supply shops) along the length of each main bearing journal on the crankshaft.

7 Install each main bearing cap and tighten the attaching bolts to the specified torque. The arrow on each cap should face toward the front of the engine.

8 Now remove each bearing cap and measure the width of the Plastigage strip which will have flattened out when the caps were tightened (photo). A scale is provided on the Plastigage envelope for measuring the width of the Plastigage strip, and thus, bearing clearance.

9 If the Plastigage is flattened more at the ends than in the middle, or vice versa, this is an indication of journal taper which can be checked in the Specifications Section.

10 To test for an out-of-round condition, remove all traces of the Plastigage (be careful not to damage the crankshaft or bearing surfaces) and rotate the crankshaft 90 degrees. With the crankshaft rotated to this point, use the Plastigage to check the clearances again. Compare these measurements with those taken previously to arrive at eccentricity or out-of-round.

11 To check connecting rod bearing clearances, install each piston/rod assembly and use the Plastigage as described above.

12 Connecting rod side clearance can be checked with the piston/rod assemblies temporarily installed for bearing clearance checking.

13 With the piston/rod assemblies installed and the bearing caps tightened to the specified torque, use feeler gauges to check the clearance between the sides of the connecting rods and the crankshaft throws (photo).

14 If the clearance at this point is below the minimum tolerance, the rod may be machined for more clearance at this area.

15 If the clearance is excessive, a new rod must be used or the crankshaft must be replaced with a new one.

16 If the bearings have shown to be within all tolerances, they may be installed following the steps outlined in the appropriate Sections.

17 If not within Specifications, the bearings should be replaced with

the correctly sized bearings. Upper and lower bearings should always be replaced as an assembly.

30 Crankshaft oil seals – replacement

Front crankshaft seal

Note: *The following operation requires a special tool for proper seal installation.*

1 Drain the cooling system and crankcase.
2 Remove the radiator.
3 Remove the crankshaft and the timing cover.
4 Drive out the oil seal with a pin punch.
5 Clean out the recess in the cover.
6 Coat the outer edge of the new seal with grease and install it using the special tool designed for this operation. As an alternative, a large piece of pipe can be used to push the new seal in. However, use extreme caution as the seal can be damaged easily with this method. Drive in the seal until it is fully seated in the recess. Make sure that the spring is properly positioned within the seal.
7 Install the timing cover on the engine as described in Section 19.

Rear crankshaft seal

Note: *If rear crankshaft oil seal replacement is the only operation being performed, it can be accomplished with the engine in the vehicle. If, however, the oil seal is being replaced along with the rear main bearing, the engine must be removed.*

8 Disconnect the negative battery cable from the battery, then remove the starter.
9 Remove the transmission (Chapter 7).
10 On manual transmission equipped vehicles, remove the pressure plate, disc and clutch assembly. On automatic transmission equipped vehicles, remove the flexplate.
11 Remove the flywheel attaching bolts and remove the flywheel and engine rear cover plate.
12 Use an awl to punch two holes in the crankshaft rear oil seal.
13 Punch the holes on opposite sides of the crankshaft, just above the bearing cap-to-engine block junction.
14 Thread a sheet metal screw into each punched hole.
15 Use two large screwdrivers or small pry bars and pry against both screws at the same time to remove the crankshaft rear oil seal. A block or blocks of wood placed against the engine will provide additional leverage.
16 Be very careful when performing this operation that you do not damage the crankshaft oil seal contact surfaces.
17 Clean the oil recess in the rear of the engine block and main bearing cap surface of the crankshaft.
18 Inspect, clean and polish the oil seal contact.
19 Coat the new oil seal with a light film of engine oil.
20 Coat the crankshaft with a light film of engine oil.
21 Start the seal into the cavity in the back of the engine with the seal lip facing forward and install it with the special drive tool. Make sure that the tool stays in alignment with the crankshaft until the tool contacts the block. See step 6 for seal installation alternatives.
22 Make sure that the seal has been installed correctly after removing the tool.
23 Install the engine rear cover plate.
24 Attach the flywheel (or flexplate) to the crankshaft.
25 Install the clutch assembly.
26 Install the transmission as described in Chapter 7.
27 Install the starter and hook up the battery cable.

31 Crankshaft and main bearings – installation

1 Crankshaft installation is generally one of the first steps in engine reassembly; it is assumed at this point that the engine block and crankshaft have been cleaned and inspected and repaired or reconditioned.
2 Position the engine so that the bottom is facing up.
3 Remove the main bearing cap bolts and lift out the caps. Lay them out in the proper order to help ensure that they are installed correctly.
4 If they are still in place, remove the old bearing inserts from the block and the main bearing caps. Wipe the main bearing surfaces of

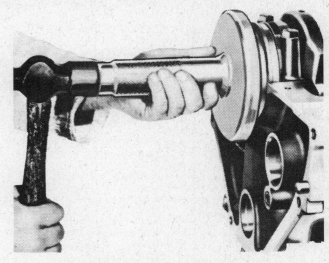

Fig. 2.27 Installing the rear main oil seal using a drift-type tool (Sec 30)

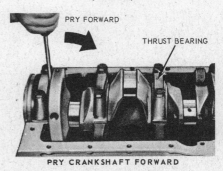

Fig. 2.28 Before tightening the thrust bearing cap bolts, pry the crankshaft forward ...

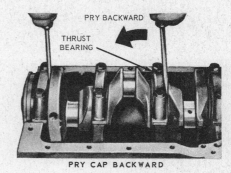

Fig. 2.29 ... pry the bearing cap backwards ...

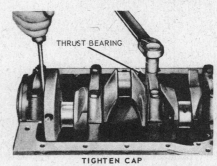

Fig. 2.30 ... then tighten the cap bolts to the specified torque while holding the crankshaft in the forward position (Sec 31)

2B

the block and caps with a clean, lint-free cloth (they must be kept spotlessly clean).

5   Clean the back side of the new main bearing inserts and lay one bearing half in each main bearing saddle (in the block) and the other bearing half from each bearing set in the corresponding main bearing cap. Make sure that the tang on the bearing insert fits into the notch in the block or cap. Also, the oil holes in the block and cap must line up with the oil holes in the bearing insert. Do not hammer the bearing into place and do not nick or gouge the bearing faces.

6   The flanged thrust bearing must be installed in the number five cap and saddle.

7   Clean the faces of the bearings in the block and the crankshaft main bearing journals with a clean, lint-free cloth. Check or clean the oil holes in the crankshaft, as any dirt here can only go one way — straight through the new bearings.

8   Once you are certain that the crankshaft is clean, lubricate the main bearings in the block with clean engine oil and carefully lay the crankshaft in position (an assistant would be very helpful here) in the main bearings.

9   Lubricate the bearings in the caps with clean engine oil, then install the caps in their respective positions in the block. **Note:** *Do not install the thrust bearing cap (number five) at this time.*

10 Install the bolts and tighten them to the specified torque. Work up to the final torque in three steps.

11 Rotate the crankshaft a number of times by hand and check for any obvious binding.

12 Install the thrust bearing cap and bolts and tighten the bolts finger tight.

13 Using a large screwdriver, pry the crankshaft forward against the thrust surface of the upper bearing half.

14 Hold the crankshaft in this position and pry the thrust bearing cap to the rear. This will align the thrust surfaces of both halves of the bearing.

15 While holding the crankshaft forward, tighten the thrust bearing cap bolts to the specified torque. Again, work up to the final torque in three steps.

16 Check the crankshaft endplay with a dial indicator setup. To do this, mount the indicator so that the stem rests against the crankshaft flange, parallel to the crankshaft. Pry the crankshaft as far as possible to the rear, then zero the dial indicator. Pry the crankshaft forward and note the indicator reading (which represents the endplay). If it is less than the minimum allowed, check the thrust bearing faces for scratches, nicks and dirt. If the bearing is not damaged or dirty, make sure it is the correct bearing for your engine and, reinstall it by following steps 12 through 15. Recheck the endplay after it is installed.

32 Piston rings – installation

1   Before installing the new piston rings, the ring end gaps must be checked.

2   Lay out the piston/connecting rod assemblies and the new ring sets so that the rings will be matched with the same piston and cylinder during the end gap measurement and engine assembly.

3   Insert the top (number one) ring into the first cylinder and square it up with the cylinder walls by pushing it in with the top of the piston. The ring should be at the bottom of the cylinder, just below the lower limit of the ring travel. To measure the end gap, slip a feeler gauge between the ends of the ring. Compare the measurement to the Specifications.

4   If the gap is larger or smaller than specified, double-check to make sure that you have the correct rings before proceeding.

5   If the gap is too small, it must be enlarged or the ring ends may come in contact with each other during engine operation, which can cause serious damage to the engine. The end gap can be increased by filing the ring ends very carefully with a fine file. Mount the file in a vise equipped with soft jaws, slip the ring over the file so that the ends contact the file face and slowly move the ring to remove material from the ends. When performing this operation, file only from the outside in.

6   Excess end gap is not critical unless it is greater than 0.040 in (1 mm). Again, double-check to make sure you have the correct rings for your engine.

7   Repeat the procedure for each ring that will be installed in the first cylinder and for each ring in the remaining cylinder. Remember to keep rings, pistons and cylinders matched up.

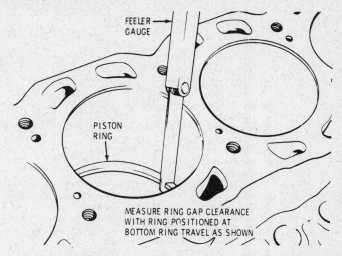

Fig. 2.31 Checking piston ring end gap (Sec 32)

8   Once the ring end gaps have been checked/corrected, the rings can be installed on the pistons.

9   The oil control ring (lowest one on the piston) is installed first. It is composed of three separate components. Slip the spacer expander into the groove then install the upper side rail. Do not use a piston ring installation tool on the oil ring side rails, as they may be damaged. Instead, place one end of the side rail into the groove between the spacer expander and the ring land, hold it firmly in place and slide a finger around the piston while pushing the rail into the groove. Next, install the lower side rail in the same manner.

10 After the three oil ring components have been installed, check to make sure that both the upper and lower side rails can be turned smoothly in the ring groove.

11 The number two (middle) ring is installed next. Use a piston ring installation tool and fit the ring into the middle groove on the piston. Do not expand the ring any more than is necessary to slide it over the piston.

12 Finally, install the number one (top) ring in the same manner.

13 Repeat the procedure for the remaining pistons and rings.

33 Piston/connecting rod assembly – installation

1   Before installing the piston/connecting rod assemblies, the cylinder walls must be perfectly clean, the top edge of each cylinder must be chamfered, and the crankshaft must be in place.

2   Remove the connecting rod cap from the end of the number one connecting rod. Remove the old bearing inserts and wipe the bearing surfaces of the connecting rod and cap with a clean, lint-free cloth (they must be spotlessly clean).

3   Clean the back side of the new upper bearing half, then lay it in place in the connecting rod. Make sure the tang on the bearing fits into the notch in the rod. Also, the oil holes in the rod and bearing insert must line up. Do not hammer the bearing insert into place, and be very careful not to nick or gouge the bearing face. Do not lubricate the bearing at this time.

4   Clean the back side of the other bearing insert half and install it in the rod cap. Again, make sure the tang on the bearing fits into the notch in the cap, and do not apply any lubricant. It is critically important to ensure that the mating surfaces of the old bearing and connecting rod are perfectly clean and oil-free when they are assembled together.

5   Position the piston ring gaps as shown in the accompanying illustration, then slip a section of plastic or rubber hose over each connecting rod cap bolt.

6   Lubricate the piston and rings with clean engine oil and install a piston ring compressor on the piston. Leave the skirt protruding about $\frac{1}{4}$ in to guide the piston into the cylinder. The rings must be compressed as far as possible.

7   Rotate the crankshaft so that the number one connecting rod

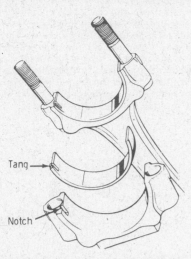

Fig. 2.32 Make sure that the tang on the bearing insert fits into the notch in the rod or cap when attaching the piston/connecting rod assembly to the crankshaft (Sec 33)

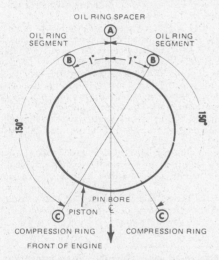

Fig. 2.33 Space the piston ring end gaps as shown before installing the piston in the block (Sec 33)

33.10 Installing a piston

journal is as far from the number one cylinder as possible (bottom dead center), and apply a uniform coat of engine oil to the number one cylinder walls.

8   With the notch on top of the piston pointing to the front of the engine, gently place the piston/connecting rod assembly into the number one cylinder bore and rest the bottom edge of the ring compressor on the engine block. Tap the top edge of the ring compressor to make sure it is contacting the block around its entire circumference.

9   Clean the number one connecting rod journal on the crankshaft and the bearing faces in the rod.

10   Carefully tap on the top of the piston with the end of a wooden hammer handle while guiding the end of the connecting rod into place on the crankshaft journal (photo). The piston rings may try to pop out of the ring compressor just before entering the cylinder bore, so keep some downward pressure on the ring compressor. Work slowly, and if any resistance is felt as the piston enters the cylinder, stop immediately, find out what is hanging up and fix it before proceeding. Do not, for any reason, force the piston into the cylinder, as you will break a ring and/or the piston.

11   Once the piston/connecting rod assembly is installed, the connecting rod bearing oil clearance must be checked before the rod cap is permanently bolted in place. Use Plastigage to check the clearance as described in Section 29. If the clearance is not correct, service bearings are available in 0.001 and 0.002 inch under sizes. Try using one half of an undersize bearing set as this will often be sufficient to bring connecting rod bearing clearance up to Specifications. Under no circumstances should you use shims or shave any material from a bearing insert. Once the proper clearance has been achieved, proceed to the next step.

12   Carefully scrape all traces of the Plastigage material off the rod journal and/or bearing face (be very careful not to scratch the bearing). Make sure the bearing faces are perfectly clean, then apply a uniform layer of clean, high quality multi-purpose grease (or engine assembly lube) to both of them. You will have to push the piston into the cylinder to expose the face of the bearing insert in the connecting rod; be sure to slip the protective hoses over the rod bolts first.

13   Slide the connecting rod back into place on the journal, remove the protective hoses from the rod cap bolts, install the rod cap and tighten the nuts to the specified torque. Again, work up to the torque in three steps.

14   Follow the above procedure for the remaining cylinders. Keep the back sides of the bearing inserts and the inside of the connecting rod and cap perfectly clean when assembling them. Make sure you have the correct piston for the cylinder and that the arrow on the piston points to the front of the engine when the piston is installed. Remember, use plenty of oil to lubricate the piston before installing the ring compressor, and be sure to match up the mating marks on the conencting rod and rod cap. Also, when installing the rod caps for the final time, be sure to lubricate the bearing faces adequately.

15   After all the piston/connecting rod assemblies have been properly installed, rotate the crankshaft a number of times by hand and check for any obvious binding.

16   As a final step, the connecting rod big end side clearance must be checked (Section 29).

34 Engine – final assembly and pre-oiling after overhaul

1   After the crankshaft, piston/rod assemblies and the various associated bearings have been installed in the engine block, the remainder of the components (cylinder head(s), oil pump, camshaft, etc.) can be installed following the installation procedures located in the various Sections of this Chapter.

2   Follow the engine disassembly sequence in the reverse order, using new gaskets where necessary.

3   Adjust the valve lash as described in Chapter 2A.

4   After a major overhaul it is a good idea to pre-oil the engine before it is installed and initially started. This will tell you if there are any faults in the oiling system at a time when corrections can be made easily and without damage. Pre-oiling the engine will also allow the parts to be lubricated thoroughly in a normal fashion, but without heavy loads placed upon them.

5   The engine should be assembled completely with the exception of the distributor and the rocker arm cover(s).

2B

6   A modified distributor will be needed for this job. This pre-oil tool is a distributor body with the bottom gear ground off and the counterweight assembly removed from the top of the shaft.

7   Place the pre-oiler into the distributor shaft access hole at the front of the intake manifold or on the left side of the block (six cylinder engines) and make sure the bottom of the shaft mates with the oil pump. Clamp the modified distributor into place just as you would an ordinary distributor. Now attach an electric drill motor to the top of the shaft.

8   With the oil filter installed, all oil galleries plugged (oil pressure sending unit installed) and the crankcase full of oil as shown on the dipstick, rotate the pre-oiler with the drill. Make sure the rotation is counterclockwise for V8 engines and clockwise for six cylinder engines. Soon, oil should start to flow from the rocker arms, signifying that the oil pump and oiling system is functioning properly. It may take two or three minutes for the oil to flow to each rocker arm. Allow the oil to circulate throughout the engine for a few minutes.

9   Check for oil leaks at all locations and correct as necessary.

10   Remove the pre-oiler and install the normal distributor and rocker arm cover(s).

Chapter 2 Part C V8 engines

Contents

Specifications

302 CID engine
General

Bore and stroke	4.00 x 3.00 in
Compression pressure	Lowest cylinder must be within 75% of highest cylinder

Engine block

Cylinder bore

Diameter	
1973	4.0004 to 4.0036 in
1974 on	4.0004 to 4.0052 in
Taper limit	0.010 in
Out-of-round limit	0.005 in
Deck warpage limit	0.003 in per 6 in or 0.006 in overall

Pistons and rings

Piston

Diameter	
Coded red	3.9984 to 3.9990 in
Coded blue	3.9996 to 4.0002 in
Oversizes available	0.003 in
Piston-to-cylinder bore clearance	
Standard	0.0018 in
Service limit	0.0026 in
Piston ring-to-groove clearance	
Standard	
Top ring (1973 thru 1976)	0.002 to 0.004 in
Top ring (1977 thru 1979)	0.0019 to 0.0036 in
2nd ring	0.002 to 0.004 in
Oil ring	Snug fit in groove
Service limit	
Top ring (1973 thru 1976)	0.006 in
Top ring (1977 thru 1979)	0.0056 in
2nd ring	0.006 in
Piston ring end gap	
Top ring	0.010 to 0.020 in
2nd ring	0.010 to 0.020 in
Oil ring (1973 thru 1978)	0.015 to 0.055 in
Oil ring (1979 only)	0.015 to 0.035 in

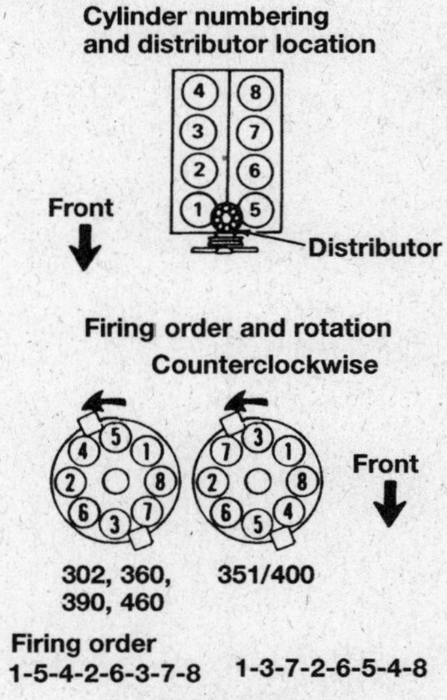

Cylinder numbering and distributor location

```
    [4] [8]
    [3] [7]
    [2] [6]
    [1] [5]
Front           — Distributor
  ↓
```

Firing order and rotation
Counterclockwise

302, 360, 390, 460   351/400

Front
  ↓

Firing order
1-5-4-2-6-3-7-8   1-3-7-2-6-5-4-8

V8 engines

2C

Piston pin diameter (standard)	0.9120 to 0.9123 in
Piston pin-to-piston clearance	
Heavy duty	0.0003 to 0.0005 in
All others	0.0002 to 0.0004 in
Piston pin-to-connecting rod fit	Interference fit

Crankshaft and flywheel

Main journal	
Diameter	2.2482 to 2.2490 in
Taper limit	
1973 and 1974	0.0003 in
1975 and 1976	0.0006 in
1977 thru 1979	0.0005 in
Out-of-round limit	
1973	0.0004 in
1974 thru 1979	0.0006 in
Runout limit	
1973	0.004 in
1974 thru 1979	0.002 in
Main bearing oil clearance	
Standard	
No 1 bearing	0.0001 to 0.0015 in
All others	0.0005 to 0.0015 in
Service limit	
No 1 bearing	0.002 in
All others	0.0024 in
Connecting rod journal	
Diameter	2.1228 to 2.1236 in
Taper limit	
1973 and 1974	0.0004 in
1975 thru 1979	0.0006 in
Out-of-round limit	
1973	0.0004 in
1974 thru 1979	0.0006 in
Connecting rod bearing oil clearance	
Standard	0.0008 to 0.0015 in
Service limit	
1973 thru 1976	0.0026 in
1977 thru 1979	0.0024 in
Connecting rod side clearance	
Standard	0.010 to 0.020 in
Service limit	0.023 in
Crankshaft endplay	
Standard	0.004 to 0.008 in
Service limit	0.012 in
Flywheel clutch face runout limit	0.010 in
Flywheel ring gear lateral runout limit	
Manual transmission	
1973 and 1974	0.040 in
1975 thru 1979	0.030 in
Automatic transmission	0.060 in

Camshaft

Bearing journal diameter	
No. 1	2.0805 to 2.0815 in
No. 2	2.0655 to 2.0665 in
No. 3	2.0505 to 2.0515 in
No. 4	2.0355 to 2.0365 in
No. 5	2.0205 to 2.0215 in
Bearing oil clearance	
Standard	0.001 to 0.003 in
Service limit	0.006 in
Lobe lift	
Intake	
1973 thru 1976	0.2303 in
1977 thru 1979	0.2375 in
Exhaust	
1973 thru 1976	0.2375 in
1977 thru 1979	0.2474 in
Runout limit	0.005 in
Endplay	
Standard	0.001 to 0.007 in
Service limit	0.009 in
Timing chain deflection limit	0.500 in

Crankshaft sprocket runout limit (assembled)
1973 thru 1975	0.006 in
1976 thru 1979	0.005 in

Cylinder head(s) and valve train
Head warpage limit	0.003 in per 6 in or 0.006 in overall
Valve seat angle	45°

Valve seat width
Intake	0.060 to 0.080 in
Exhaust	0.060 to 0.080 in
Valve seat runout limit	0.0015 in
Valve face angle	44°
Valve face runout limit	0.002 in
Valve margin width	$\frac{1}{32}$ in min

Valve stem diameter
Intake	0.3416 to 0.3423 in
Exhaust	0.3411 to 0.3418 in

Valve guide diameter
Intake	0.3433 to 0.3443 in
Exhaust	0.3433 to 0.3443 in

Valve stem-to-guide clearance
Intake
Standard	0.0010 to 0.0027 in
Service limit	0.0055 in

Exhaust
Standard	0.0015 to 0.0032
Service limit	0.0055 in

Valve spring free length
Intake
1973 thru 1978	1.94 in
1979	2.04 in

Exhaust
1973	1.94 in
1974 thru 1979	1.85 in

Valve spring pressure (lbs @ specified length)
Intake and exhaust – 1973 thru 1976 (1st check)
Standard	76 to 84 @ 1.69 in
Service limit	68 @ 1.69 in

Intake and exhaust – 1973 thru 1976 (2nd check)
Standard	190 to 210 @ 1.31 in
Service limit	171 @ 1.31 in

Intake – 1977 and 1978
1st check	77 to 85 @ 1.58 in
2nd check	190 to 210 @ 1.31 in

Exhaust – 1977 and 1978
1st check	76 to 84 @ 1.60 in
2nd check	190 to 210 @ 1.20 in

Intake – 1979
1st check	74 to 82 @ 1.78 in
2nd check	192 to 212 @ 1.36 in

Exhaust – 1979
1st check	76 to 84 @ 1.60 in
2nd check	190 to 210 @ 1.20 in

Valve spring installed height
Intake
1973 thru 1978	$1\frac{43}{64}$ to $1\frac{45}{64}$ in
1979	$1\frac{43}{64}$ to $1\frac{51}{64}$ in

Exhaust
1973	$1\frac{43}{64}$ to $1\frac{45}{64}$ in
1974 thru 1979	$1\frac{19}{32}$ to $1\frac{39}{64}$ in
Valve spring out-of-square limit	0.078 ($\frac{5}{64}$) in

Collapsed tappet gap
Allowable
1973 thru 1976	0.090 to 0.190 in
1977 thru 1979	0.071 to 0.193 in

Desired
1973 and 1974	0.090 to 0.140 in
1975 and 1976	0.115 to 0.165 in
1977 thru 1979	0.096 to 0.165 in
Lifter diameter	0.8740 to 0.8745 in
Lifter bore diameter	0.8752 to 0.8767 in

Lifter-to-bore clearance
Standard	0.0007 to 0.0027 in
Service limit	0.005 in
Pushrod runout limit	0.015 in

2C

Oil pump

Outer race-to-housing clearance	0.001 to 0.013 in
Rotor assembly end clearance	0.001 to 0.004 in
Driveshaft-to-housing bearing clearance	0.0015 to 0.0030 in
Relief spring tension	10.6 to 12.2 lbs @ 1.704 in
Relief valve clearance	0.0015 to 0.0030 in

Torque specifications

	ft-lb
Cylinder head bolts	65 to 72
Main bearing cap bolts	60 to 70
Connecting rod nuts	19 to 24
Oil pan bolts	
$\frac{1}{4}$ – 20	7 to 9
$\frac{5}{16}$ – 18	9 to 11
Intake manifold-to-cylinder head	
1973 and 1974	17 to 25
1975 thru 1979	23 to 25
Exhaust manifold-to-cylinder head	
1973 and 1974	12 to 16
1975 thru 1979	18 to 24
Oil pump-to-engine block	22 to 32
Oil pump pickup tube	10 to 15
Flywheel/flexplate bolts	75 to 85
Vibration damper bolt	70 to 90
Rocker arm stud nut	17 to 23
Rocker arm cover bolts	3 to 5
Water pump bolts	12 to 15
Camshaft sprocket bolts	40 to 45
Timing cover bolts	12 to 15

351 (W) CID engine

Note: *For all Specifications not listed here, refer to the 302 CID engine Specifications. The items included here are only the ones that are different.*

General

Bore and stroke	4.00 x 3.50 in

Engine block

Cylinder bore diameter	4.000 to 4.0048 in

Pistons and rings

Piston diameter	
Coded red	3.9978 to 3.9984 in
Coded blue	3.9990 to 3.9960 in
Piston-to-cylinder bore clearance (1977 thru 1979 only)	
Standard	0.0022 in
Service limit	0.0030 in

Crankshaft and flywheel

Main journal	
Diameter	2.9994 to 3.002 in
Taper limit	0.0005 in
Out-of-round limit	0.0006 in
Runout limit	0.002 in
Main bearing oil clearance	
Standard	
No. 1 bearing	0.0005 to 0.0015 in
All others	0.0008 to 0.0015 in
Service limit	
No. 1 bearing	0.0005 to 0.0024 in
All others	0.0008 to 0.0026 in
Connecting rod journal	
Diameter	2.3103 to 2.3111 in
Taper limit	0.0006 in
Out-of-round limit	0.0006 in
Connecting rod bearing oil clearance service limit	0.0026 in

Camshaft

Lobe lift	
Intake (1977 thru 1979)	0.2600 in
Exhaust (1977 thru 1979)	0.2600 in

Cylinder head(s) and valve train

Valve seat runout limit	0.002 in

Valve spring free length
  Intake
    1973 thru 1978 .... 2.06 in
    1979 .... 2.04 in
  Exhaust
    1973 thru 1976 .... 2.12 in
    1977 and 1978 .... 1.87 in
    1979 .... 1.85 in
Valve spring pressure (lbs @ specified length)
  Intake – 1977 and 1978 only
    1st check .... 71 to 79 @ 1.79 in
    2nd check .... 190 to 210 @ 1.34 in
  Exhaust – 1977 and 1978 only
    1st check .... 76 to 84 @ 1.80 in
    2nd check .... 190 to 210 @ 1.20 in
Valve spring installed height
  Intake
    1973 thru 1978 .... $1\frac{49}{64}$ to $1\frac{13}{16}$ in
    1979 .... $1\frac{43}{64}$ to $1\frac{51}{64}$ in
  Exhaust
    1973 thru 1976 .... $1\frac{13}{16}$ to $1\frac{27}{32}$ in
    1977 and 1978 .... $1\frac{19}{32}$ to $1\frac{39}{64}$ in
    1979 .... $1\frac{37}{64}$ to $1\frac{39}{64}$ in
Collapsed tappet gap
  Allowable
    1973 thru 1976 .... 0.106 to 0.206 in
    1977 thru 1979 .... 0.098 to 0.198 in
  Desired
    1973 thru 1976 .... 0.131 to 0.181 in
    1977 thru 1979 .... 0.123 to 0.173 in

Oil pump
Relief spring tension .... 18.2 to 20.2 lbs @ 2.490 in

Torque specifications
          ft-lb
Cylinder head bolts (1977 thru 1979) .... 105 to 112
Main bearing cap bolts (1977 thru 1979) .... 95 to 105
Connecting rod nuts (1977 thru 1979) .... 40 to 45

360 and 390 CID engines
General
Bore and stroke
  360 engine .... 4.05 x 3.50 in
  390 engine .... 4.05 x 3.78 in
Compression pressure .... Lowest cylinder must be within 75% of highest cylinder

Engine block
Cylinder bore
  Diameter .... 4.0500 to 4.0536 in
  Taper limit .... 0.010 in
  Out-of-round limit .... 0.005 in
  Deck warpage limit .... 0.003 in per 6 in or 0.006 in overall

Pistons and rings
Piston
  Diameter
    Coded red .... 4.0484 to 4.0490 in
    Coded blue .... 4.0496 to 4.0502 in
  Oversizes available .... 0.003 in
Piston-to-cylinder bore clearance
  Standard .... 0.0015 in
  Service limit .... 0.0023 in
Piston ring-to-groove clearance
  Standard
    Top ring .... 0.002 to 0.004 in
    2nd ring .... 0.002 to 0.004 in
    Oil ring .... Snug fit in groove
  Service limit
    Top ring .... 0.006 in
    2nd ring .... 0.006 in
Piston ring end gap
  Top ring .... 0.015 to 0.023 in
  2nd ring .... 0.010 to 0.020 in
  Oil ring .... 0.015 to 0.055 in

2C

Piston pin diameter
    1973 and 1974 .... 0.9750 to 0.9753 in
    1975 and 1976 .... 0.9749 to 0.9754 in
Piston pin-to-piston clearance .... 0.0001 to 0.0003 in
Piston pin-to-connecting rod clearance
    1973 and 1974 .... 0.0001 to 0.0003 in
    1975 and 1976 .... 0.0002 to 0.0005 in

Crankshaft and flywheel
Main journal
    Diameter .... 2.7484 to 2.7492 in
    Taper limit
        1976 only .... 0.0005 in
        All others .... 0.0003 in
    Out-of-round limit
        1973 only .... 0.0004 in
        All others .... 0.0006 in
Main bearing oil clearance
    Standard
        1974 only .... 0.001 to 0.0015 in
        All others .... 0.0005 to 0.0015 in
    Service limit .... 0.0025 in
Connecting rod journal
    Diameter .... 2.4380 to 2.4388 in
    Taper limit
        1973 only .... 0.0003 in
        1974 only .... 0.0004 in
        All others .... 0.0005 in
    Out-of-round limit .... 0.0005 in
Connecting rod bearing oil clearance
    Standard .... 0.0008 to 0.0015 in
    Service limit .... 0.0025 in
Connecting rod side clearance
    Standard .... 0.008 to 0.025 in
    Service limit .... 0.030 in
Crankshaft endplay
    Standard .... 0.004 to 0.010 in
    Service limit
        1973 only .... 0.014 in
        All others .... 0.012 in
Flywheel clutch face runout limit .... 0.010 in
Flywheel ring gear lateral runout limit
    Manual transmission
        1973 and 1974 .... 0.030 in
        1975 and 1976 .... 0.040 in
    Automatic transmission .... 0.075 in

Camshaft
Bearing journal
    Diameter .... 2.1238 to 2.1248 in
    Runout limit .... 0.005 in
    Out-of-round limit .... 0.0005 in
Bearing oil clearance
    Standard .... 0.001 to 0.003 in
    Service limit .... 0.006 in
Lobe lift
    Intake .... 0.2470 in
    Exhaust .... 0.2490 in
Endplay .... 0.001 to 0.007 in
Timing gears runout limit .... 0.005 in TIR
Timing chain deflection limit .... 0.500 in

Cylinder head(s) and valve train
Head warpage limit .... 0.003 in per 6 in or 0.006 in overall
Valve seat angle .... 45°
Valve seat width
    Intake .... 0.060 to 0.080 in
    Exhaust .... 0.070 to 0.090 in
Valve seat runout limit
    1973 and 1974 .... 0.002 in
    1975 and 1976 .... 0.0015 in
Valve face angle .... 44°
Valve face runout limit .... 0.002 in
Valve margin width .... $\frac{1}{32}$ in min.

Valve stem diameter	
Intake	0.3711 to 0.3718 in
Exhaust	0.3706 to 0.3713 in
Valve guide diameter	
Intake	0.3728 to 0.3738 in
Exhaust	0.3728 to 0.3738 in
Valve stem-to-guide clearance	
Intake	
Standard	0.0010 to 0.0027 in
Service limit	0.0055 in
Exhaust	
Standard	0.0015 to 0.0032
Service limit	0.0055 in
Valve spring free length	
Intake	2.12 in
Exhaust	
F100 only	2.00 in
All others	2.12 in
Valve spring pressure (lbs @ specified length)	
Intake — (F100) and intake and exhaust (all others) (1st check)	
Standard	85 to 95 @ 1.820 in
Service limit	77 @ 1.820 in
Intake — (F100) and intake and exhaust (all others) (2nd check)	
Standard	209 to 231 @ 1.38 in
Service limit	186 @ 1.38 in
Exhaust — F100 only (1st check)	
Standard	76 to 84 @ 1.670 in
Service limit	69 @ 1.670 in
Exhaust — F100 only (2nd check)	
Standard	175 to 194 @ 1.240 in
Service limit (1973 only)	163 @ 1.240 in
Service limit (1974 thru 1976)	157 @ 1.240 in
Valve spring installed height	
F100 intake only and all others intake and exhaust	$1\frac{13}{16}$ to $1\frac{27}{32}$ in
F100 exhaust only	$1\frac{21}{32}$ to $1\frac{11}{16}$ in
Collapsed lifter gap	
Allowable	0.119 to 0.219 in
Desired	
1973 and 1974	0.119 to 0.169 in
1975 and 1976	0.144 to 0.184 in
Lifter diameter	0.8740 to 0.8745 in
Lifter bore diameter	0.8752 to 0.8767 in
Lifter-to-bore clearance	
Standard	0.0005 to 0.002 in
Service limit	0.005 in
Rocker arm shaft diameter	0.839 to 0.840 in
Rocker arm bore diameter	0.8425 to 0.8440 in
Rocker arm-to-shaft clearance	
Standard	0.002 to 0.005 in
Service limit	0.0065 in
Pushrod runout limit	
1973 only	0.015 in
All others	0.020 in

Oil pump

Outer race-to-housing clearance	0.001 to 0.013 in
Rotor assembly end clearance	0.001 to 0.004 in
Driveshaft-to-housing bearing clearance	0.0015 to 0.0029 in
Relief spring tension	8.7 to 9.5 lbs @ 1.560 in
Relief valve clearance	0.0015 to 0.0029 in

Torque specifications

	ft-lb
Cylinder head bolts	80 to 90
Main bearing cap bolts	95 to 105
Connecting rod cap nuts	40 to 45
Exhaust manifold-to-cylinder head	12 to 18
Intake manifold-to-cylinder head	40 to 45
Oil pump cover plate	9 to 14
Oil pump-to-engine block	17 to 27
Water pump bolts	20 to 25
Timing cover	
$\frac{3}{8}$ − 16 bolts	
1973 and 1974	26 to 34
1975 and 1976	19 to 27

2C

$\frac{5}{16}$ – 18 bolts
    1973 and 1974 .... 13 to 21
    1975 and 1976 .... 10 to 15
Fuel pump bolts .... 20 to 25
Camshaft sprocket bolts
    1973 and 1974 .... 34 to 45
    1975 and 1976 .... 45 to 57
Camshaft thrust plate bolts .... 12 to 15
Rocker arm shaft support .... 40 to 45
Rocker arm cover bolts .... 4 to 7
Flywheel/flexplate bolts .... 75 to 85
Vibration damper bolt
    1973 and 1974 .... 70 to 90
    1975 and 1976 .... 130 to 150

351 (M) and 400 CID engines

Note: *For all Specifications not listed here, refer to the 302 CID engine Specifications. The items included here are only the ones that are different.*

General
Bore and stroke
    351 (M) engine .... 4.00 x 3.50 in
    400 engine .... 4.00 x 4.00 in

Engine block
Cylinder bore diameter .... 4.0000 to 4.0048 in

Pistons and rings
Piston diameter
    Coded red .... 3.9982 to 3.9988 in
    Coded blue .... 3.9994 to 4.000 in
Piston-to-cylinder bore clearance
    Standard .... 0.0014 in
    Service limit .... 0.0022 in
Piston ring-to-groove clearance
    Standard
        Top ring .... 0.0019 to 0.0036 in
    Service limit
        Top ring .... 0.0056 in
Piston ring end gap
    Oil ring
        1978 only .... 0.015 to 0.055 in
        All others .... 0.010 to 0.035 in
Piston pin diameter (standard) .... 0.9745 to 0.9754 in
Piston pin-to-piston clearance .... 0.0003 to 0.0005 in

Crankshaft and flywheel
Main journal
    Diameter .... 2.9994 to 3.0002 in
    Runout limit .... 0.005 in
    Taper limit .... 0.0005 in
    Out-of-round limit .... 0.0006 in
Main bearing oil clearance
    Standard .... 0.0008 to 0.0015 in
    Service limit .... 0.0008 to 0.0026 in
Connecting rod journal diameter .... 2.3103 to 2.3111 in

Camshaft
No. 1 bearing journal diameter .... 2.1248 to 2.1328 in
Lobe lift (1977 and 1978)
    351 (M) engine
        Intake .... 0.235 in
        Exhaust .... 0.235 in
    400 engine
        Intake .... 0.2474 in
        Exhaust .... 0.250 in
Lobe lift (1979)
    Intake .... 0.250 in
    Exhaust .... 0.250 in

Cylinder head(s) and valve train
Valve seat width (exhaust) .... 0.070 to 0.090 in
Valve seat runout limit .... 0.002 in
Valve stem-to-guide clearance
    Service limit (intake and exhaust) .... 0.005 in

Valve spring free length
    Intake .... 2.06 in
    Exhaust
        1977 and 1978 .... 2.06 in
        1979 .... 1.93 in
Valve spring pressure (lbs @ specified length)
    1977 — intake and exhaust (all engines)
        1st check .... 76 to 84 @ 1.82 in
        2nd check .... 215 to 237 @ 1.39 in
    1978 and 1979 351 (M) engine — intake
        1st check .... 76 to 84 @ 1.82 in
        2nd check .... 215 to 237 @ 1.39 in
    1978 351 (M) engine — exhaust
        1st check .... 79 to 87 @ 1.65 in
        2nd check .... 215 to 237 @ 1.25 in
    1978 400 engine — intake
        1st check .... 76 to 84 @ 1.82 in
        2nd check .... 218 to 240 @ 1.39 in
    1978 400 engine — exhaust
        1st check .... 76 to 84 @ 1.68 in
        2nd check .... 218 to 240 @ 1.25 in
    1979 351 (M) engine — exhaust
        1st check .... 79 to 87 @ 1.68 in
        2nd check .... 215 to 237 @ 1.39 in
    1979 400 engine — intake
        1st check .... 76 to 84 @ 1.82 in
        2nd check .... 215 to 237 @ 1.39 in
    1979 400 engine — exhaust
        1st check .... 79 to 87 @ 1.68 in
        2nd check .... 215 to 237 @ 1.39 in
Valve spring installed height
    Intake .... $1\frac{13}{16}$ to $1\frac{27}{32}$ in
    Exhaust
        1979 only .... $1\frac{11}{16}$ to $1\frac{27}{32}$ in
        All others .... $1\frac{13}{16}$ to $1\frac{27}{32}$ in

Oil pump
Relief spring tension .... 20.6 to 22.6 lbs @ 2.49 in

2C

Torque specifications
                                                                         ft-lb
Cylinder head bolts .... 95 to 105
Main bearing cap bolts
    1977 .... 35 to 45
    1978 and 1979 .... 95 to 105
Connecting rod nuts .... 40 to 45
Intake manifold-to-cylinder head
    $\frac{5}{16}$ in bolt .... 17 to 25
    $\frac{3}{8}$ in bolt .... 22 to 32
Rocker arm stud nut .... 18 to 25
Camshaft thrust plate bolts .... 9 to 12

460 CID engine
Note: *For all Specifications not listed here, refer to the 302 CID engine Specifications. The items included here are only the ones that are different.*

General
Bore and stroke .... 4.360 x 3.850 in

Engine block
Cylinder bore diameter .... 4.3600 to 4.3636 in

Pistons and rings
Piston diameter
    Coded red .... 4.3585 to 4.3591 in
    Coded blue .... 4.3597 to 4.3603 in
Piston-to-cylinder bore clearance
    Standard .... 0.0022 in
    Service limit .... 0.0030 in
Piston ring-to-groove standard clearance (top and 2nd ring)
    1973 thru 1976 .... 0.002 to 0.004 in
    1977 and 1978 .... 0.0025 to 0.0045 in
    1979
        Top ring .... 0.0019 to 0.0036 in
        2nd ring .... 0.002 to 0.004 in

Piston ring end gap (oil ring only)
1973 thru 1976	0.015 to 0.055 in
1977 and 1978	0.010 to 0.030 in
1979	0.010 to 0.035 in
Piston pin diameter (standard)	1.0399 to 1.0402 in

Crankshaft and flywheel
Main journal diameter	2.9994 to 3.0002 in

Main bearing oil clearance (1973 and 1974)
Standard
No. 1 bearing	0.0004 to 0.0015 in
All others	0.0012 to 0.0015 in

Service limit
No. 1 bearing	0.0020 in
All others	0.0028 in

Main bearing oil clearance (1975 thru 1979)
Standard
No. 1 bearing	0.0008 to 0.0015 in
All others	0.0008 to 0.0026 in

Service limit
No. 1 bearing	0.0020 in
All others	0.0026 in
Connecting rod journal diameter	2.4992 to 2.500 in
Connecting rod bearing oil clearance service limit	0.0028 in

Camshaft
Bearing journal diameter	2.1238 to 2.1248 in

Lobe lift
Intake	0.2530 in
Exhaust	0.2780 in

Endplay (standard)
1977	0.003 to 0.007 in
1978 and 1979	0.001 to 0.006 in
Timing sprocket runout limit (assembled)	0.005 in

Cylinder head(s) and valve train
Valve stem diameter (exhaust)	0.3416 to 0.3423 in
Valve stem-to-guide standard clearance (exhaust)	0.010 to 0.027 in

Valve spring free length
Intake	2.03 in

Exhaust
1973 thru 1976	2.03 in
1977 thru 1979	2.068 in

Valve spring pressure (lbs @ specified length)
1973 thru 1976 (1st check)
Standard	76 to 84 @ 1.81 in
Service limit	68 @ 1.81 in

1973 thru 1976 (2nd check)
Standard	240 to 265 @ 1.33 in
Service limit	216 @ 1.33 in

1977 thru 1979
1st check	76 to 84 @ 1.81 in
2nd check	218 to 240 @ 1.33 in

Valve spring installed height
Intake	$1\frac{51}{64}$ to $1\frac{53}{64}$ in
Exhaust	$1\frac{51}{64}$ to $1\frac{53}{64}$ in

Collapsed tappet gap
Allowable	0.075 to 0.175 in

Desired
1973 and 1974	0.075 to 0.125 in
1975 thru 1979	0.100 to 0.150 in

Oil pump
Relief spring tension	20.6 to 22.6 @ 2.49 in

Torque specifications

	ft-lb
Cylinder head bolts	130 to 140
Main bearing cap bolts	95 to 105
Connecting rod nuts	40 to 45
Intake manifold-to-cylinder head	25 to 32
Exhaust manifold-to-cylinder head	28 to 33
Oil pump-to-engine block	20 to 25
Oil pump cover bolts	6 to 10
Rocker arm stud nut	18 to 25
Camshaft thrust plate bolts	9 to 12
Timing cover bolts	15 to 20

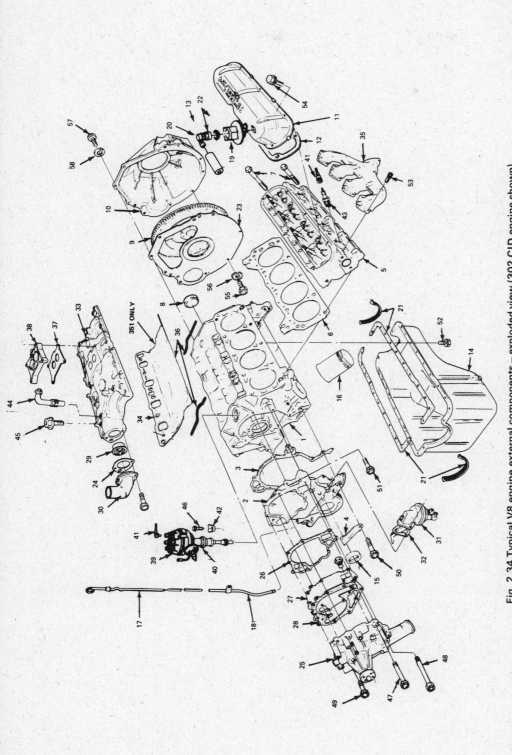

2C

Fig. 2.34 Typical V8 engine external components — exploded view (302 CID engine shown)

1	Engine block	13	PCV valve assembly	25	Water pump	35	Exhaust manifold
2	Timing cover	14	Oil pan	26	Water pump housing	36	Manifold gasket set
3	Timing cover gasket	15	Timing cover oil seal		gasket	37	Carburetor gasket
4	Timing reference pointer	16	Oil filter	27	Water pump cover	38	Spacer
5	Cylinder head	17	Dipstick	28	Water pump cover gasket	39	Distributor cap
6	Head gasket	18	Dipstick tube	29	Thermostat	40	Distributor
7	Head bolt	19	Oil filler cap	30	Water outlet connection	41	Spark plug wires
8	Soft plug (camshaft bore)	20	PCV hose	31	Fuel pump	42	Distributor clamp
9	Flywheel	21	Oil pan gasket and seal	32	Fuel pump mounting	43	Spark plug
10	Bellhousing	22	Grommet		gasket	44	Elbow
11	Rocker arm cover	23	Engine rear plate	33	Intake manifold	45	Bolt ($\frac{5}{16}$ – 18 x $\frac{7}{8}$)
12	Rocker arm cover gasket	24	Water outlet gasket	34	Seal	46	Bolt ($\frac{5}{16}$ – 18 x 1)

47	Bolt ($\frac{5}{16}$ – 18 x $3\frac{5}{8}$)
48	Bolt ($\frac{5}{16}$ – 18 x 5)
49	Bolt ($\frac{5}{16}$ – 18 x $2\frac{1}{2}$)
50	Bolt ($\frac{5}{16}$ – 18 x 2)
51	Bolt or screw
	($\frac{5}{16}$ – 18 x 1)
52	Bolt ($\frac{5}{16}$ – 18 x $1\frac{7}{8}$)
53	Bolt ($\frac{3}{8}$ – 16 x $1\frac{7}{8}$)
54	Bolt ($\frac{1}{4}$ – 20 x $\frac{5}{8}$)
55	Bolt ($\frac{5}{16}$ – 18 x $\frac{3}{4}$)
56	Lock washer
57	Bolt ($\frac{7}{16}$ – 14 x $1\frac{3}{4}$)
58	Lock washer

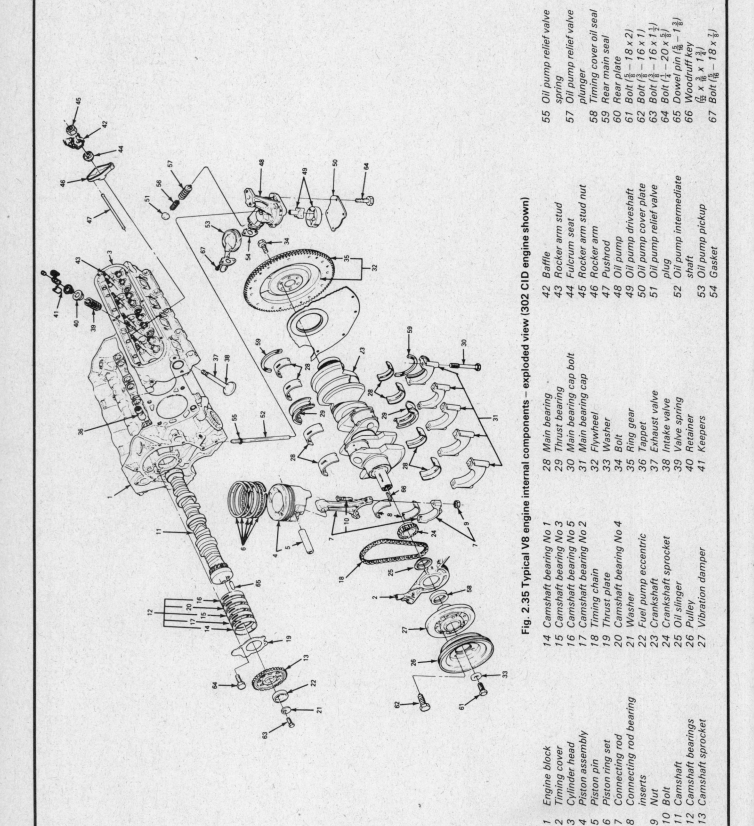

Fig. 2.35 Typical V8 engine internal components – exploded view (302 CID engine shown)

1 Engine block
2 Timing cover
3 Cylinder head
4 Piston assembly
5 Piston pin
6 Piston ring set
7 Connecting rod
8 Connecting rod bearing inserts
9 Nut
10 Bolt
11 Camshaft
12 Camshaft bearings
13 Camshaft sprocket

14 Camshaft bearing No 1
15 Camshaft bearing No 3
16 Camshaft bearing No 5
17 Camshaft bearing No 2
18 Timing chain
19 Thrust plate
20 Camshaft bearing No 4
21 Washer
22 Fuel pump eccentric
23 Crankshaft
24 Crankshaft sprocket
25 Oil slinger
26 Pulley
27 Vibration damper

28 Main bearing
29 Thrust bearing
30 Main bearing cap bolt
31 Main bearing cap
32 Flywheel
33 Washer
34 Bolt
35 Ring gear
36 Tappet
37 Exhaust valve
38 Intake valve
39 Valve spring
40 Retainer
41 Keepers

42 Baffle
43 Rocker arm stud
44 Fulcrum seat
45 Rocker arm stud nut
46 Rocker arm
47 Pushrod
48 Oil pump
49 Oil pump driveshaft
50 Oil pump cover plate
51 Oil pump relief valve plug
52 Oil pump intermediate shaft
53 Oil pump pickup
54 Gasket

55 Oil pump relief valve spring
57 Oil pump relief valve plunger
58 Timing cover oil seal
59 Rear main seal
60 Rear plate
61 Bolt ($\frac{5}{8}$ – 18 x 2)
62 Bolt ($\frac{3}{8}$ – 16 x 1)
63 Bolt ($\frac{3}{8}$ – 16 x 1$\frac{1}{2}$)
64 Bolt ($\frac{1}{4}$ – 20 x $\frac{5}{8}$)
65 Dowel pin ($\frac{5}{16}$ – 1$\frac{3}{8}$)
66 Woodruff key ($\frac{1}{32}$ x $\frac{3}{16}$ x 1$\frac{3}{4}$)
67 Bolt ($\frac{5}{16}$ – 18 x $\frac{7}{8}$)

35 General information

Ford Motor Company was the first truck company to offer V8 engines in their light duty trucks and the model years covered in this book reflect the large percentage of vehicles sold with these power-plants.

These V8 engines are gasoline fueled with overhead valves actuated by hydraulic lifters. All V8's have five main bearing supported crankshafts.

A number of different V8 engines have been offered during the model years covered by this manual. The 302 cubic inch displacement engine has been offered in all model years 1973 through 1979 and is a lightweight, thin-wall, cast iron block engine. F-100 through F-250 trucks as well as the Bronco have all used this engine.

1973 through 1976 vehicles had the 360 and 390 cubic inch displacement V8 engines offered as an option on all series except Broncos. The F-350 trucks were often equipped with one of these two deep-skirt, heavy wall powerplants. The Y configuration of the cast iron block is one of the distinguishing characteristics of this engine. This design results in rigid crankshaft encasement and corresponding durability.

Starting in 1977, 351 and 400 M-series engines were optional in all F-series vehicles and standard equipment in Broncos. Both of these engines feature thin-wall, special high grade cast iron blocks with auto-thermic, aluminum alloy tin-plated pistons. The 400 engine is totally "square" in that it has exactly the same bore and stroke dimensions. The 351 engine is more conventional in design with its larger bore than stroke specifications.

One of the largest engines available in light duty trucks is the 460 cubic inch displacement engine offered in all F-series trucks, 1973 through 1979 model years. It is a favorite option of trailer-towers and others who need high torque pulling power in a light duty truck. The block is lightweight design, cast iron construction and the rocker arms are positive stop type, pedestal mounted.

These engines are durably designed and will give long life with proper maintenance. Accessibility to these engines in F-series trucks is very good and they can be serviced easily within the confines of the chassis. These engines are all three point mounted with two side mounts at the front and one crossmember mount underneath the transmission. The engine can be removed from the vehicle with a normal amount of preparatory work when overhaul or other major operations are necessary.

36 Valve spring, retainer and seal – replacement (on vehicle)

Note: *Broken valve springs, retainers or defective valve stem seals can be replaced without removing the cylinder head involved on engines that have no damage to the valves or valve seats. Two special tools are required for this operation, so read through the instructions carefully and rent or purchase the tools before starting work on the engine.*
1   Remove the air cleaner and related components.
2   Remove the accelerator cable return spring.
3   Remove the accelerator cable linkage at the carburetor.
4   Disconnect the choke cable at the carburetor connecting point.
5   Remove the PCV valve from the rocker arm cover and remove the rocker arm cover.
6   Remove the spark plug from the cylinder which has the bad component.
7   Crank the engine until the piston in the cylinder with the bad component is at top dead center on the compression stroke (refer to Step 3 of Section 9 in Chapter 2A. Note that the distributor should be marked opposite the appropriate terminal; not necessarily number one.
8   Install a special air line adapter which will screw into the spark plug hole and connect to an air source such as a compresser. Remove the rocker arm stud nut, fulcrum seat, rocker arm and pushrod on all engines except the 360 and 390. For 360 and 390 engines, the rocker arm shaft bolts should be loosened a little at a time until there is enough clearance to move the rocker arm aside on the valve needing work. If the valve is on the end, the rocker arm assembly will have to be removed after withdrawing the cotter pin and washer.
9   Apply compressed air to the cylinder in question. If the engine rotates until the cylinder is at bottom dead center, be very careful that you do not drop the valve into the cylinder as it will fall all the way in.

Do not release the air pressure or the valve will drop through the guide.
10 Compress the valve spring with a compressor designed to work with the head still on the vehicle.
11 Remove the keepers, spring retainer and valve spring. Remove the valve stem seal. **Note:** *If air pressure fails to hold the valve in the closed position during this operation, there is apparently damage to the seat or the valve. If this condition exists, remove the cylinder head for further repair.*
12 If air pressure has forced the piston to the bottom of the cylinder, wrap a rubber band, tape or string around the top of the valve stem so that the valve will not drop through into the combustion chamber. Release the air pressure.
13 Inspect the valve stem for damage. Rotate the valve in its guide and check the valve stem tip for eccentric movement which would indicate a bent valve.
14 Move the valve up and down through its normal travel and check that the valve guide and stem do not bind. If the valve stem binds, either the valve is bent and/or the guide is damaged and the head will have to be removed for repair.
15 Reapply air pressure to the cylinder to retain the valve.
16 Lubricate the valve stem with engine oil and install a new valve stem seal.
17 Install the spring in position over the valve. Make sure that the closed coil end of the spring is located next to the cylinder head.
18 Install the valve spring retainer. Compress the valve spring using the valve spring compressor and install the keepers. Remove the compressor tool and make sure that the keepers are installed correctly.
19 Apply engine oil or assembly lube to both ends of the pushrod.
20 Install the pushrod in position.
21 Apply engine oil or assembly lube to the tip of the valve stem.
22 Apply engine oil to the fulcrum seats and socket. On 360 and 390 engines, lubricate the rocker arm and slide it back into position. Install the rocker arm, fulcrum seat and stud nut. Adjust the valve clearance following the procedure in Chapter 2A. Be sure to tighten the rocker arm shaft assembly bolts on 360 and 390 engines.
23 Remove the air source and the adapter from the spark plug hole.
24 Install the spark plug and connect the spark plug wire to it.
25 Attach a new rocker arm cover gasket to the cover and install the rocker arm cover.
26 Connect the accelerator cable to the carburetor at its connecting point.
27 Install the accelerator cable return spring. Connect the choke cable to the carburetor.
28 Install the PCV valve in the rocker arm cover and make sure that the line connected to the PCV valve is connected on both ends.
29 Install the air cleaner.
30 Start and run the engine. Make sure that there are no leaks and that there are no unusual sounds coming from the valve assembly.

37 Manifolds – removal and installation

Intake manifold

Note: *Due to the weight and bulk of the large displacement engine intake manifolds, it is recommended that an engine hoist or puller device coupled with lifting hooks available from hardware stores be used to lift these manifolds from the engine. They can be removed by hand. However, the aid of a helper is suggested to avoid damaging engine components and/or causing personal injury.*
1   Drain the cooling system.
2   Remove the air cleaner and intake duct assemblies.
3   Carefully mark and remove any emissions control connections at the air cleaner.
4   Disconnect the upper radiator hose from the thermostat housing located at the top of the engine. Locate this hose out of the way.
5   Disconnect the heater hose and the water pump by-pass hose at the intake manifold connections.
6   Remove the right rocker arm cover on 460 engines. Remove both rocker arm covers, rocker arm assemblies and pushrod assemblies from 360 and 390 engines.
7   Disconnect the spark plug wires at the spark plugs. Unclip and remove the distributor cap together with the spark plug wires.
8   Disconnect the primary wiring leads to the coil and mark them so they can be reinstalled correctly.
9   Remove the coil mounting bracket and mounting bolt.

2C

10 Remove the carburetor fuel inlet line from the carburetor and position it out of the way. It may be necessary to disconnect the line or loosen it at the fuel pump in order to perform this operation if the line is constructed of steel.

11 Disconnect the vacuum advance hose(s) from the distributor and mark them for proper installation.

12 Remove the distributor hold down bolt and mark the position of the distributor, and the distributor rotor for correct installation. It is a good idea to position the number one piston at top dead center when performing this operation (Section 9, Chapter 2A).

13 Remove the distributor from the engine, taking care that the distributor-to-oil pump driveshaft remains in the engine and connected to the oil pump.

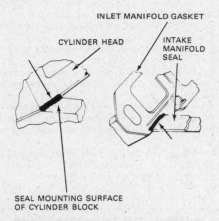

Fig. 2.36 Apply RTV-type sealant to the areas indicated (arrows) when installing the intake manifold and gaskets (302, 351W, 360, 390 and 460 engines) (Sec 37)

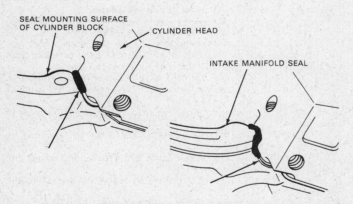

Fig. 2.37 Apply RTV-type sealant to the areas indicated (arrows) when installing the intake manifold and gaskets (351M and 400 engines) (Sec 37)

14 Remove the wire from the coolant temperature sender unit.

15 Remove the wire(s) from any sensors mounted in the intake manifold and/or the upper thermostat housing.

16 Remove the throttle cable or linkage connection at the carburetor.

17 Remove the kick-down cable at the carburetor if the vehicle is equipped with an automatic transmission.

18 Remove the pull cable and activating unit from the intake manifold if the vehicle is equipped with a cruise control unit.

19 Remove the vacuum hose leading to the power brake booster from the intake manifold. Secure this hose to the firewall out of the way.

20 Remove the carburetor from the intake manifold if the carburetor is to be serviced separately.

21 Remove any wiring leading to components located on the intake manifold. Locate the wires where they won't be damaged.

22 Disconnect the crankcase vent hose leading from the manifold to the rocker arm cover.

23 Remove the bolts retaining the intake manifold to the cylinder heads.

24 Attach the lifting hooks at opposite corners and lift the intake manifold from the engine. It may be necessary to pry the intake manifold away from the cylinder heads but be careful to avoid damaging the mating surfaces.

25 Clean the mating surfaces of the intake manifold and cylinder heads. Take care not to get any material down into the intake ports.

26 Remove the end gaskets from the top of the engine block.

27 Remove the oil gallery splash pan from the engine (if so equipped). **Note**: *302 engines are not equipped with this particular pan. 460 engines have the splash pan incorporated into the intake manifold main gasket.*

28 Apply a bead of RTV-type gasket sealant to the mating points at the junctions of the cylinder heads and engine block.

29 Position new seals on the engine block and press the seal locating tabs into the holes in the mating surface. This is a very critical step as correct intake manifold sealing depends on the quality of the installation of these gaskets.

30 Apply RTV-type gasket sealant to the opposite ends of the intake manifold seal on 351 and 400 engines.

31 On 350 and 390 engines, install the oil splash pan underneath the locating tabs on the cylinder head gaskets. It may be necessary to bend the pan slightly to get it to fit under the gaskets.

32 Position the intake manifold gasket onto the block and cylinder head with the alignment notches fitting into the dowels on the block. Be sure that all of the holes in the gasket are aligned with the corresponding holes in the cylinder head.

33 Lower the intake manifold into position using either a lift or two people, being careful not to disturb or dislocate the intake manifold gasket(s).

34 Install the intake manifold retaining bolts finger tight. Tighten the intake manifold bolts in the sequence shown in the accompanying illustration (note that different engines have different bolt tightening sequences). Work up to the final torque in three steps to avoid warping the manifold.

35 Install the remaining components in the reverse order of removal.

36 Start and run the engine and allow it to reach operating temperature. After it has reached operating temperature, check carefully for leaks.

37 Shut the engine off and retighten the manifolds while the engine is still warm.

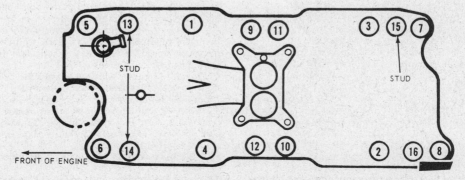

Fig. 2.38 Intake manifold bolt tightening sequence (302 and 351W engines) (Sec 37)

Exhaust manifold

38 If the right-hand exhaust manifold is being removed, remove the air cleaner, intake duct and heat stovepipe.
39 If the left-hand exhaust manifold is being removed, remove the engine oil filter.
40 On vehicles equipped with a column selector and automatic transmission, disconnect the cross lever shaft for the automatic transmission selector to provide the clearance necessary to remove the manifold.

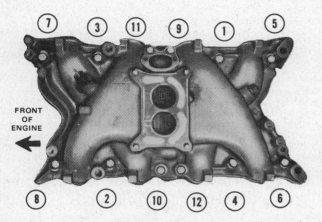

Fig. 2.39 Intake manifold bolt tightening sequence (351M and 400 engines) (Sec 37)

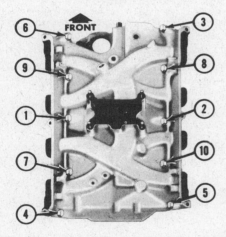

Fig. 2.40 Intake manifold bolt tightening sequence (360 and 390 engines) (Sec 37)

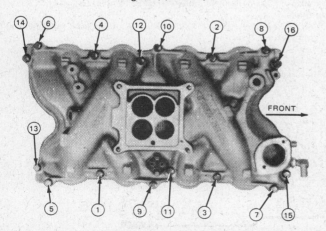

Fig. 2.41 Intake manifold bolt tightening sequence (460 engine) (Sec 37)

41 Disconnect the retaining bolts holding the inlet pipe(s) to the exhaust manifold(s).
42 Remove the spark plug heat shields if so equipped.
43 Remove the exhaust manifold retaining bolts.
44 Remove the exhaust manifold.
45 Clean the mating surfaces of the exhaust manifold and the cylinder head.
46 Clean the mounting flange of the exhaust manifold and the inlet pipe.
47 Apply graphite grease to the mating surface of the exhaust manifold.
48 Position the exhaust manifold on the head and install the attaching bolts. Tighten the bolts to the specified torque in three steps, working from the center to the ends.
49 If so equipped, install the spark plug heat shields.
50 Install the gasket or spacer between the inlet pipe and the exhaust manifold outlet.
51 Connect the inlet pipe to the exhaust manifold using new retaining nuts.
52 Tighten the retaining nuts to the proper torque making sure that the exhaust inlet pipe is situated squarely in the exhaust manifold outlet.
53 Install the oil filter if the left exhaust manifold was removed.
54 Install the automatic transmission selector cross shaft at the chassis and the engine block if the vehicle is equipped with a column shifter.
55 If the right exhaust manifold was replaced, install the air cleaner heat stovepipe, air cleaner and intake duct.
56 Start the engine and check for exhaust leaks.

38 Flywheel – removal, inspection and installation

Refer to Section 14 of Chapter 2B for this procedure.

39 Rocker arm covers – removal and installation

1 Remove the air cleaner and intake duct assembly.
2 Remove the crankcase ventilation hoses and lines where applicable. Make sure that all lines and hoses have been removed from the rocker arm covers and position them out of the way.
3 Remove the PCV valve from the oil filler cap or rocker arm cover.
4 Remove the vacuum line and electric solenoid on 302 engines only.
5 Remove the vacuum solenoid mounted on the left-hand cover (if so equipped).
6 Disconnect the spark plug wires. Mark them so they can be installed in their original locations.
7 Remove the spark plug wires clipped to the rocker arm covers and position them out of the way.
8 Remove the clips retaining the wiring looms running along the left-hand cover.
9 Remove the rocker arm cover retaining bolts.
10 Remove the rocker arm cover(s).
11 Remove all old gasket material and sealant from the rocker arm cover and cylinder head gasket surfaces.
12 Make sure the gasket surfaces of the rocker arm covers are flat and smooth, particularly around the bolt holes. Use a hammer and a block of wood to flatten them out if they are deformed.
13 Attach a new rocker arm cover gasket to the cover. Notice that there are tabs provided in the cover to retain the gasket. It may be necessary to apply RTV-type gasket sealant to the corners of the cover to retain the gasket there.
14 Install the rocker arm cover onto the cylinder head, making sure that the bolt holes are aligned correctly.
15 Install the rocker arm cover retaining bolts finger tight.
16 Working from the center of the rocker arm cover, tighten the retaining bolts to the correct torque. **Caution:** *Do not overtighten the bolts or the valve covers will warp and the gaskets will be pushed out of position, causing leaks.*
17 The remainder of the installation procedure is the reverse of removal.
18 Start the engine and run it until it reaches normal operating temperature, then make sure that there are no leaks.

2C

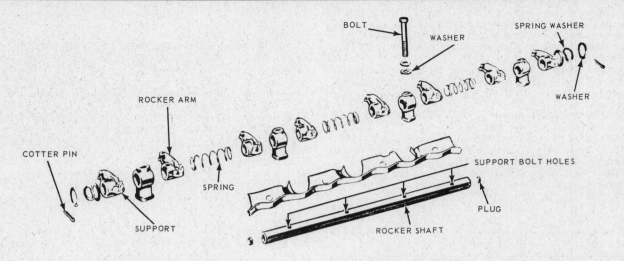

Fig. 2.42 Rocker arm shaft components – exploded view (360 and 390 engines) (Sec 40)

40 Rocker arms and pushrods – removal, inspection and installation

Removal – all engines except 360-390 CID
1   Remove the rocker arm covers as described in Section 39.
2   Remove the rocker arm fulcrum bolt.
3   Remove the oil deflector (351-400M and 460 engines only), fulcrum seat(s), fulcrum guides (302 engines only), and the rocker arms. If the pushrods only are being removed, loosen the fulcrum retaining bolts and rotate the rocker arms out of the way of the pushrods.

Removal – 360-390 CID engines
4   Starting at the number four cylinder, loosen the right bank rocker arm shaft support bolts in sequence. Start by turning the bolts two turns at a time. After the bolts are all loosened, remove the rocker arm shaft assembly and oil baffle plate.
5   Starting at the number five cylinder on the left rocker arm shaft, proceed in the same way as above. This procedure must be followed exactly to avoid damaging the rocker arm shaft.
6   If all of the rocker arms and/or pushrods are being removed, mark them so that they can be installed in the same locations.
7   To remove the pushrods, pull them straight up through the cylinder head and out of the lifter pocket.

Inspection – all engines
8   Inspect the rocker arms for signs of excessive wear, galling or damage.
9   On individual rocker arm type engines (302, 351-400 and 460) inspect the oil hole at the pushrod end of the rocker arm and make sure that it is open.
10 Inspect the rocker arm fulcrum face for galling or checking. If any of these conditions exist, replace the rocker arm and fulcrum as an assembly with new parts.
11 The rocker arm shaft assembly must be disassembled for further inspection.
12 Remove the cotter pin from the end of each rocker arm shaft.
13 Remove the flat washer and spring washer from each end of the shaft.
14 Slide the rocker arms springs and supports off the shaft, making sure that you keep them in order on a bench or table top so they can be reinstalled in their exact same locatons.
15 If it is necessary, remove the plugs from the end of each shaft. Do so by piercing or drilling the end of one plug. Insert a steel rod through the drilled plug and knock out the plug on the opposite end.
16 Working from the open end, knock out the remaining plug.
17 Clean the rocker arm shaft, baffle, rocker arms, stands, springs and installing hardware with solvent and dry them thoroughly.
18 Inspect the rocker arm shaft for any signs of galling or excessive

Fig. 2.43 Proper installation position of rocker arm shaft (360 and 390 engines) (Sec 40)

wear. If this condition exists, replace the rocker arm shaft with a new one.
19 Inspect the internal bores of the rocker arms for signs of galling or excessive wear. If wear is evident, replace the rocker arms with new ones.

Installation – all engines except 360-390 CID
20 Inspect the pushrods for bending, excessive wear at either ball end or cracking. If any of these conditions exist, replace the pushrods with new ones.
21 Apply engine oil or assembly lube to the top of the valve stem and the pushrod guide in the cylinder head.
22 Apply engine oil to the rocker arm fulcrum seat and the fulcrum seat socket in the rocker arm.
23 Install the pushrods in the correct positions with lubricant supplied to both ends.
24 Install the fulcrum guides (302 engines only), rocker arms, fulcrum seats, oil deflector (351-400M and 460 engines only) and fulcrum bolts.
25 Tighten the fulcrum bolts to the proper torque.
26 Replace the rocker arm cover and gasket as described in Section 39.
27 Start and run the engine and check for roughness, and/or noise. Refer to Section 9 of Chapter 2A for any corrections that may need to be made for either a rough running engine or excessive noise in the valve train.

Installation – 360-390 CID engines
28 Lubricate all of the moving parts of the rocker arms and shaft with engine oil. Apply engine assembly lube to the pads of the rocker arms.

29 If the plugs were removed from the ends of the shafts, use a correct size tool with the same inside diameter or a pin punch to press the plugs (cap side out) into each end of the rocker arm shaft.

30 Install the rocker arms, supports and springs in the order shown in the accompanying illustration. Make sure that the oil holes in the shaft are facing down. Notice that when the properly assembled shaft is correctly installed, the identification notch on the end of the shaft will face down and toward the front on the right bank and toward the rear on the left bank.

31 Install the remaining flat washers, spring washers and cotter pins.

32 Install the pushrods into the lifter pockets.

33 Install the rocker arm shaft assembly onto the engine and tighten the bolts finger tight. Make sure the rocker arms are positioned correctly over each pushrod. Tighten the bolts gradually, two turns at a time, in sequence, until the final torque is attained. Make sure that you follow this procedure exactly, or damage can occur to the rocker arm shaft assembly.

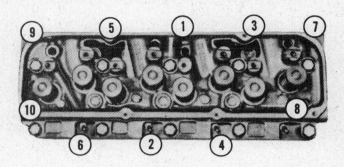

Fig. 2.44 Cylinder head bolt tightening sequence (Sec 42)

41 Valves – servicing

Refer to Section 17 of Chapter 2B.

42 Cylinder heads – removal, inspection and installation

Removal

1 Remove the intake manifold and carburetor as an assembly as described previously.

2 Remove the rocker arm cover(s) by referring to the appropriate Section.

3 If the left cylinder head is being removed on a vehicle equipped with factory air conditioning, remove the compressor and support it securely to the side of the engine compartment. **Caution:** *Do not disconnect the air conditioning hoses, as serious injury or damage to the system will result.*

4 If the left cylinder head is being removed and the vehicle is equipped with power steering, remove the power steering bracket retaining bolt from the left cylinder head.

5 Position the power steering pump out of the way so it will not leak fluid.

6 If the right cylinder head is being removed, remove the alternator mounting bracket through bolt.

7 Remove the air cleaner inlet tube (if so equipped) from the right cylinder head.

8 Remove the ground wire connected to the rear of the cylinder head.

9 Disconnect the exhaust manifold retaining bolts from the exhaust manifolds.

10 Remove the rocker arms or rocker arm assemblies as described previously. Remove the pushrods. Be sure to mark them, as they will need to be reinstalled in their original locations.

11 Loosen the cylinder head retaining bolts by reversing the order shown in the tightening sequence diagram, then remove the bolts from the heads. Keep them in order so they can be installed in their original locations.

12 Using a hoist (or two people), carefully remove the cylinder head from the block, using care to avoid damaging the gasket mating surfaces.

Inspection

13 Refer to Chapter 2B, Secton 18, Step 19 for cylinder head disassembly and inspection procedures.

Installation

14 Make sure that the cylinder head and engine block mating surfaces are clean, flat and prepared properly for the new cylinder head gasket.

15 Position the head gasket over the dowel pins on the block. Make sure that the head gasket is facing the right direction and that the correct surface is exposed. Gaskets are sometimes marked 'front' and 'top' to help clarify their installation position.

16 Using a hoist (or two people), carefully lower the cylinder head(s) into place on the block in the correct position. Take care not to move the head sideways or scrape it across the block as it can dislodge the gasket and/or damage the gasket surfaces.

17 Coat the cylinder head retaining bolts with light engine oil and thread the bolts into the engine block through the head.

18 Tighten the bolts finger tight.

19 Tighten the bolts in the sequence shown in the accompanying illustration. Work up gradually in three steps to the final torque, going through the pattern completely on each step.

20 Apply engine oil to the rocker arm fulcrum seat and sockets or the rocker arm assemblies.

21 Install the pushrods as described earlier.

22 Install the rocker arm covers.

23 The remainder of the installation procedure is the reverse of removal.

24 Start and run the engine and check it carefully for leaks and unusual noises.

43 Timing chain and cover – removal and installation

Removal

1 Drain the cooling system.

2 Remove the screws attaching the radiator shroud to the radiator.

3 Remove the bolts attaching the fan to the water pump shaft.

4 Remove the fan and the radiator shroud.

5 Disconnect the upper radiator hose at the thermostat housing.

6 Disconnect the lower radiator hose at the water pump outlet.

7 Disconnect the transmission oil cooler lines at the radiator (if so equipped).

8 Loosen the alternator mounting and adjusting bolts to relieve the tension on the drivebelt. If the vehicle is equipped with air conditioning, loosen the air conditioning idler pulley.

9 Remove the air pump.

10 Remove the drivebelts and the water pump pulley.

11 Remove the bolt attaching the air conditioning compressor support, water pump and compressor. Remove the compressor support. **Caution:** *Do not loosen or remove the air conditioning hoses, as serious personal injury or damage to the system could result.*

12 On 360 and 390 engines, remove the water pump.

13 Remove the bolts and washers retaining the crankshaft pulley to the vibration damper. Remove the crankshaft pulley.

14 Remove the large bolt and washer retaining the vibration damper to the crankshaft.

15 Remove the vibration damper with a puller.

16 Remove the crankshaft pulley spacer.

17 Remove the bypass hose from the top of the water pump.

18 Disconnect the heater return hose or tube at the water pump.

19 Remove and plug the fuel inlet line at the fuel pump.

20 Disconnect the fuel line at the carburetor. Remove the fuel feed line from the fuel pump.

21 Remove the fuel pump.

22 Remove the retaining bolts holding the timing cover to the engine block.

23 Use a thin bladed knife or similar tool to cut the oil pan seal flush with the engine block mating surface.

24 Remove the timing cover and water pump as an assembly (except

2C

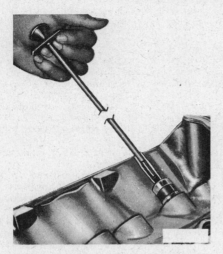

Fig. 2.45 Removing a tappet (Sec 43)

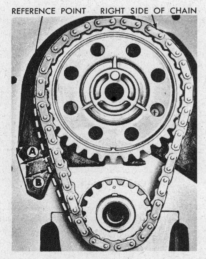

Fig. 2.46 Measuring timing chain deflection (distance A minus distance B equals deflection) (Sec 43)

Fig. 2.47 Correct timing mark alignment (Sec 43)

on 360 and 390 engines). Remove the water pump and the cover separately on 360 and 390 engines.

25 Remove the timing cover gasket and oil pan seal.

26 Remove the water pump from the timing cover if the cover is being replaced with a new one.

27 Check the timing chain deflection by rotating the crankshaft in a counterclockwise direction to take up the slack on the left side of the chain (as you view the engine from the front).

28 Establish a reference point on the block and use a ruler to check the distance from the reference point to the left side of the chain.

29 Rotate the crankshaft in the opposite direction to take up the slack on the opposite (or right side) of the chain.

30 Force the left side of the chain out and measure the distance between the reference point and the chain. This will give you the deflection. If the deflection exceeds the Specifications, the timing chain and sprockets will need replacement with new parts.

31 If the timing chain and sprockets are being removed, turn the engine until the timing marks are aligned as shown in the accompanying illustration.

32 Remove the camshaft sprocket retaining bolt, washer, fuel pump eccentric (two-piece on 460 engines) and front oil slinger from the crankshaft.

33 Slide the timing chain and sprockets forward and off of the camshaft and crankshaft as an assembly.

Installation

34 Assemble the timing chain and sprockets so that the timing marks are in alignment as shown in the accompanying illustration.

35 Install the chain and sprockets onto the camshaft and crankshaft as an assembly. Make sure that the timing marks remain in proper alignment during the installation procedure.

36 Install the oil slinger over the nose of the crankshaft.

37 Install the fuel pump eccentric, camshaft sprocket retaining bolt and washer. Tighten the retaining bolt to the proper torque. Lubricate the timing chain and gears with engine oil.

38 Clean the old gasket material from the gasket mating surface on the oil pan.

39 Coat the gasket surface of the oil pan with RTV-type gasket sealant. Cut and position the required sections of new front cover-to-oil pan seal on the oil pan.

40 Apply sealant at the corners of the mating surfaces.

41 Coat the gasket surfaces of the cover with sealant and install a new gasket. Coat the mating surface on the block with sealant.

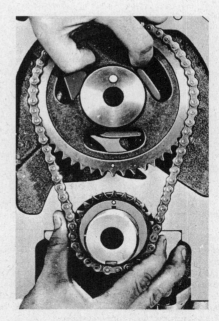

Fig. 2.48 Installing timing sprocket and chain as an assembly (note alignment of timing marks) (Sec 43)

42 Position the timing cover on the block after installing a new front crankshaft seal as described in Section 54.
43 Use care when installing the cover to avoid damaging the front crankshaft seal.
44 Install the cover alignment tool to position the cover properly. If no alignment tool is available, you will have to use the crankshaft pulley to position the seal. It may be necessary to force the cover down slightly to compress the oil pan seal. This can be done by inserting a punch in the retaining bolt holes.
45 Coat the threads of the retaining bolts with RTV-type sealant and install the retaining bolts. Note that on 360 and 390 engines two different sizes of retaining bolts are used.
46 While holding the cover in alignment, tighten the oil pan-to-front cover retaining bolts.
47 Remove the alignment punch.
48 Tighten the retaining bolts holding the cover to the engine block.
49 Apply a thin coat of grease to the vibration damper seal contact surface.
50 Install the crankshaft spacer.
51 Install the Woodruff key onto the crankshaft and slide the vibration damper into position.
52 Install the vibration damper retaining bolt and washer.
53 This bolt may be used to push the damper onto the crankshaft if the proper installation tool is not available.
54 Attach the crankshaft pulley to the damper and install the pulley retaining bolts.
55 Attach a new fuel pump gasket to the fuel pump and install the fuel pump.
56 Connect the fuel lines to the fuel pump.
57 The remainder of the installation procedure is the reverse of removal. Make sure that all bolts are tightened securely.
58 After filling the cooling system, install a new oil filter and add oil to the engine.
59 Start and run the engine at a fast idle and check for coolant and oil leaks.
60 Check the engine idle speed and ignition timing.

44 Camshaft and lifters – removal, inspection and installation

Removal

1 Remove the air cleaner.
2 Remove the intake manifold.
3 Remove the rocker arm cover.
4 Remove the rocker arm assemblies and pushrods on 360 and 390 engines.
5 On all other engines, loosen the rocker arm nuts and rotate the rocker arms to the side.
6 Mark the pushrods if they are to be reused and remove them from the engine.
7 Remove the valve lifters from the engine using a special tool designed for this purpose. Sometimes they can be removed with a magnet if there is no varnish build up or wear on them. If they are stuck in their bores, you will have to obtain a special tool designed for grasping lifters internally and work them out.
8 Remove the timing cover, chain and gears.
9 Remove the grille if the engine is in the vehicle.
10 Remove the retaining bolts securing the camshaft and thrust plate to the engine block.
11 Slowly withdraw the camshaft from the engine, being careful not to damage the bearings with the cam lobes.

Inspection

12 Visually inspect the hydraulic valve lifters for cupping on the camshaft mating face and for signs of excessive wear, galling, or cracking.
13 The hydraulic valve lifters must be tested using special equipment. This procedure must be handled by a suitably equipped automotive machine shop.
14 If you suspect that a lifter is defective, replace it with a new one. It is not necessary to test a new lifter before installation.
15 Check the camshaft lobe lift on a special V-block cradle with a dial indicator. Again, this is a procedure which should be handled by a suitably equipped automotive machine shop.
16 Visually check the camshaft bearing surfaces for any signs of galling or excessive wear. If any of these conditions are present, or if

there is a question about the camshaft (and you have no access to testing or measurement equipment), replace it with a new one.

Installation

17 Lubricate the camshaft journals with engine oil and apply engine assembly lube to the cam lobes.
18 Slide the camshaft into position, being careful not to scrape or nick the bearings.
19 Install the camshaft thrust plate. Tighten the thrust plate retaining bolts to the proper torque.
20 Check the camshaft endplay by pushing it toward the rear of the engine.
21 Install a dial indicator so that the stem is on the camshaft sprocket attaching bolt. Zero the dial indicator.
22 Position a large screwdriver between the camshaft gear and the block. **Note:** *Do not pry against aluminum or nylon camshaft sprockets when any type of valve train load is on the camshaft, as damage to the sprocket can result.*
23 Pull the camshaft forward with the screwdriver and release it.
24 Compare the dial indicator reading to the Specifications.
25 If the endplay is excessive, check the spacer for correct installation before it is removed. If the spacer is installed correctly, replace the thrust plate. Notice that the thrust plate has a groove on it; it should face in on all engines except 360 and 390.
26 Check the timing chain deflection as described in Section 43.
27 Install the hydraulic valve lifters in their original bores if the old ones are being used. Make sure they are coated with engine assembly lube. Never use old lifters with a new camshaft.
28 The remainder of the installation procedure is the reverse of removal.

45 Oil pan – removal and installation

Refer to Section 21 of Chapter 2B for this procedure.

46 Oil pump – removal and installation

Refer to Section 22 of Chapter 2B.

47 Oil pump – disassembly, inspection and reassembly

Refer to Section 23 of Chapter 2B.

48 Piston/ connecting rod assembly – removal

Refer to Section 24 of Chapter 2B for this procedure.

49 Crankshaft and main bearings – removal

Refer to Section 25 of Chapter 2B.

50 Engine block – cleaning and inspection

Refer to Section 26 of Chapter 2B.

51 Crankshaft and bearings – inspection

Refer to Section 27 of Chapter 2B for this procedure.

52 Piston/connecting rod assembly – inspection

Refer to Section 28 of Chapter 2B.

53 Main and rod bearings – checking clearances

Refer to Section 29 of Chapter 2B.

2C

54 Crankshaft oil seals – replacement

Front seal

1 Remove the timing chain cover.
2 On all engines except 351-400M Series, tap the front crankshaft seal out using a drive tool. **Note:** *The front oil seal should be replaced with a new one whenever the cover is removed or leakage is apparent.*
3 Clean the grooves in the front cover.
4 Install the new front oil seal using a special drive tool (or a large drift if the drive tool is not available). If you are using a large drift, be

Fig. 2.49 A special tool (arrows) is required to remove ...

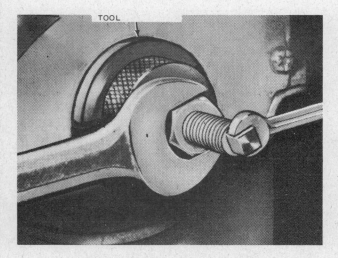

Fig. 2.50 ... and install the timing cover crankshaft oil seal on 351M and 400 engines (Sec 54)

very careful not to damage the front seal. Make sure that the spring remains positioned inside the front seal.
5 On 351-400M engines, remove the front seal using the special puller as shown in the accompanying illustration.
6 Clean the groove which the crankshaft front seal sits in.
7 Install the new seal using the special drive tool.

Rear seal

8 The crankshaft rear seal can be replaced with the engine in the vehicle. However, the transmission, clutch assembly (if so equipped) and flywheel must be removed first. Also, remove the oil pan and oil pump.
9 Loosen the main bearing cap bolts slightly to allow the crankshaft to drop no more than $\frac{1}{32}$ inch.
10 Remove the rear main bearing cap and detach the oil seal from the cap. To remove the portion of the rear main seal housed in the block, install a small sheet metal screw in one end of the seal and pull on the screw to rotate the seal out of the groove. Exercise extreme caution during this procedure to prevent scratching or damaging the crankshaft seal surfaces.
11 Carefully clean the seal grooves in the cap and block with a brush dipped in solvent.
12 Dip both seal halves in clean engine oil.
13 Carefully install the upper seal (engine block) into the groove with the lip of the seal toward the front of the engine.
14 It will be necessary to rotate it into the seal seat if the crankshaft is still in the engine. Make sure that $\frac{3}{8}$ inch of the seal protrudes on one side below the parting surface of the bearing cap.
15 Install the remaining half of the crankshaft seal into the main bearing cap. Make sure that $\frac{3}{8}$ in protrudes on the opposite side of the main bearing cap parting surface. Make sure that no rubber has been shaved from the outside diameter of the seal by the groove in the block or the crankshaft main bearing cap.
16 Tighten all but the rear main bearing cap bolts to the specified torque.
17 Install the rear main bearing cap and make sure that the parting surfaces of the seals meet each other as shown in the accompanying illustration.
18 Apply a thin coat of RTV-type gasket sealant to the rear main bearing cap at the top of the mating surface.
19 Tighten the cap bolts to the specified torque, making sure that no sealant has worked its way forward of the seal side groove.
20 On 360 and 390 engines, dip the main bearing cap side seals in engine oil and install them immediately into the grooves of the rear main bearing cap.
21 Make sure that no sealant is allowed to get on these seals as they work best when expanded with oil only. It may be necessary to tap these seals in for about the last $\frac{1}{2}$ inch of travel. Do not cut off the projecting seal ends.
22 Install the oil pan and oil pump.
23 The remainder of the installation procedure is the reverse of removal.

55 Crankshaft and main bearings – installation

1 Thoroughly clean the groove in the cylinder block and the rear main bearing cap that houses the rear main oil seal.
2 Make sure that the inside surfaces of the main bearing caps are clean and free of burrs, scratches or nicks which could prevent the bearing inserts from seating correctly.
3 Install new crankshaft main bearing upper inserts. Be certain that the inserts installed are the correct size. If the crankshaft has been ground undersized, then corresponding correct size bearing inserts should be supplied for proper clearance at the crankshaft journal. Refer to Chapter 2B, Section 29 for bearing oil clearance checking procedures.
4 Make sure that the crankshaft bearing upper inserts fit into the alignment slot provided, and that the groove and hole line up correctly in the main bearing saddle.
5 On 302 V8 engines only, make sure that the pin which located the rear oil seal on the rear main bearing saddle groove is removed. The new split, lip-type seal does not require this pin.
6 Dip the lip-type seal halves in clean engine oil. Install the upper engine oil seal in the bearing cap with the undercut side of the seal facing the front of the engine as shown in the accompanying

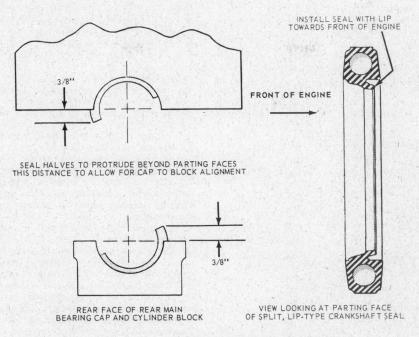

INSTALL SEAL WITH LIP
TOWARDS FRONT OF ENGINE

3/8''

FRONT OF ENGINE

SEAL HALVES TO PROTRUDE BEYOND PARTING FACES
THIS DISTANCE TO ALLOW FOR CAP TO BLOCK ALIGNMENT

3/8''

REAR FACE OF REAR MAIN
BEARING CAP AND CYLINDER BLOCK

VIEW LOOKING AT PARTING FACE
OF SPLIT, LIP-TYPE CRANKSHAFT SEAL

Fig. 2.51 Rear main oil seal installation details (Sec 54)

2C

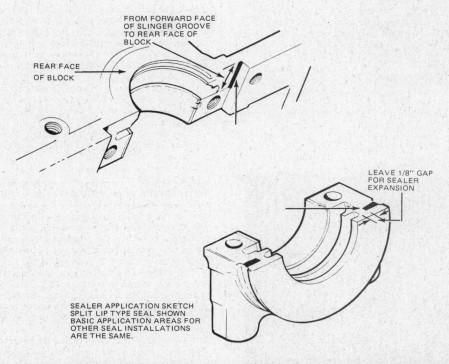

FROM FORWARD FACE
OF SLINGER GROOVE
TO REAR FACE OF
BLOCK

REAR FACE
OF BLOCK

LEAVE 1/8'' GAP
FOR SEALER
EXPANSION

SEALER APPLICATION SKETCH
SPLIT LIP TYPE SEAL SHOWN
BASIC APPLICATION AREAS FOR
OTHER SEAL INSTALLATIONS
ARE THE SAME.

Fig. 2.52 Apply RTV-type sealant to the areas indicated (arrows) before installing the rear main bearing cap (Sec 54)

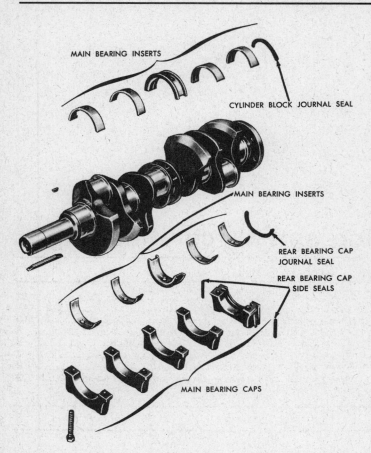

MAIN BEARING INSERTS

CYLINDER BLOCK JOURNAL SEAL

MAIN BEARING INSERTS

REAR BEARING CAP
JOURNAL SEAL

REAR BEARING CAP
SIDE SEALS

MAIN BEARING CAPS

Fig. 2.53 Crankshaft and main bearing components – exploded view (360 and 390 engines) (note rear bearing cap side seal locations) (Sec 55)

illustration. Also note that the upper half of the bearing cap seal is allowed to protrude $\frac{3}{8}$ inch on one side to mate with the corresponding upper main bearing cap oil seal.

7   Carefully lower the crankshaft into place making sure that no

bearing surfaces are allowed to touch either the block or connecting rods (if they are still installed in the block).

8   Check the clearance of each main bearing using Plastigage as described in the appropriate Section.

9   Apply RTV-type sealant to each side of the rear main bearing cap and apply sealant to the block as shown in the accompanying illustration.

10 Apply engine oil to the crankshaft journals and bearings.

11 Install all of the bearing caps except the thrust bearing cap. Make sure that the main bearing caps are all installed in their original positions, as numbered during disassembly.

12 Tighten the main bearing cap bolts to the proper torque.

13 Install the thrust bearing cap with the bolts finger tight.

14 Pry the crankshaft forward against the thrust surface of the upper half of the thrust bearing (see illustrations in Chapter 2B).

15 While holding the crankshaft forward, pry the thrust bearing cap to the rear. This procedure aligns the thrust surfaces of both halves of the thrust bearing in relationship to the crankshaft.

16 Keep applying forward pressure on the crankshaft and tighten the thrust bearing cap bolts to the proper torque.

17 Check the crankshaft endplay with a dial indicator setup. To do this, mount the dial indicator so that the stem rests against the crankshaft flange, parallel to the crankshaft. Force the crankshaft as far as possible to the rear, then zero the dial indicator. Push the crankshaft forward and note the indicator reading (the reading represents crankshaft endplay). If the play is greater than specified, install a new thrust bearing. If it is less than the minimum allowed, check the thrust bearing faces for scratches, nicks and dirt. If the faces are not damaged or dirty, reinstall the bearing by following the alignment procedure in Steps 11 thru 16. Recheck the endplay.

56 Piston rings – installation

Refer to Section 32 of Chapter 2B.

57 Piston/connecting rod assembly – installation

Refer to Section 33 of Chapter 2B.

58 Engine – final assembly and pre-oiling after overhaul

Refer to Section 34 of Chapter 2B for this procedure.

Chapter 3 Cooling, heating and air conditioning

Contents

Specifications

Radiator
Type
    Pick-ups and 1978 thru 1979 Bronco .... Vertical-flow with integral upper and lower tanks.
    1973 thru 1977 Bronco .... Cross-flow with integral side tanks and separate expansion tank.

Water pump
Type .... Centrifugal, impeller type
Drivebelt tension .... See Chapter 1 Specifications

Thermostat
Type .... Wax pellet
Location
    V8 engines .... Front of intake manifold
    Six cylinder engines .... Front of cylinder head
Opening temperature
    Low temperature .... 170° F
    Medium temperature .... 180° F
    High temperature .... 210° F

Heater
Blower motor amperage draw
    Pick-up .... 8.0 amps max.
    Bronco .... 7.0 amps max.

Torque specifications
	ft-lbs
Radiator clamp-to-radiator support (Bronco 1973 thru 1977)	5 to 8
Radiator-to-radiator support (Pick-ups and 1978 thru 1979 Bronco)	10 to 15
Fan shroud-to-radiator (Pick-ups and 1978 thru 1979 Bronco)	5 to 8
Fan shroud-to-radiator (1973 thru 1977 Bronco)	1 to 2
Fan-to-water pump	12 to 18
Thermostat housing retaining bolts	
Intake six-cylinder engine	12 to 15
302 V8 engine	9 to 12
All other V8 engines	23 to 28
Water pump-to-housing retaining bolts	
All engines except 460 cid	12 to 18
460 cid	15 to 21

3

1 General information

Ford light duty trucks and 1978 through 1979 Broncos have a cooling system consisting of a vertical flow radiator, thermostat for temperature control and an impeller-type water pump driven by a belt from the crankshaft pulley.

The radiator cooling fan is mounted on the front of the water pump. Certain vehicles with extra heavy-duty cooling systems incorporate an automatic clutch which disengages the fan at high road speeds or when the outside temperature is sufficient to maintain a low radiator temperature. On some models, a fan shroud is mounted to the rear face of the radiator to increase cooling efficiency.

The 1973 through 1977 Broncos are equipped with a type of cooling system similar to that above. The only difference is in the use of a cross-flow radiator and coolant recovery system on the 1973 through 1977 models. After 1977, the Bronco was equipped with an identical cooling system to light duty Ford trucks.

The cooling system is pressurized by means of a spring-loaded radiator filler cap. Cooling efficiency is improved by raising the boiling point of the coolant through increased cooling system pressure. If the coolant temperature rises above the boiling point, the extra pressure in the system forces the radiator cap internal spring-loaded valve off its seat and exposes the overflow pipe or the coolant recovery bottle connecting tube to allow the displaced coolant a path of escape.

The cooling sytem functions as follows: Cold water from the radiator circulates up the lower radiator hose to the water pump where it is pumped into the cylinder block around the water passages to cool the engine. The coolant then travels up into the cylinder head, around the combustion areas of the cylinders and valve seats, absorbing heat before it finally passes out through the thermostat. When the engine is running at its correct temperature the water flow from the cylinder head(s) diverges to flow through the intake manifold, car interior heater (when activated) and the radiator.

When the engine is cool (below its normal operating temperature), the thermostat valve is closed, thus preventing the coolant from flowing into the radiator and restricting the flow to the engine. The restriction in the flow of coolant enables the engine to quickly warm to its correct operating temperature.

The coolant temperature is monitored by a sender mounted in either the cylinder head or the intake manifold. The sender, together with the gauge on the instrument panel, gives a continuous indication of coolant temperature to the operator.

Normal maintenance consists of checking the level of fluid in the radiator at regular intervals, inspecting the hoses and connections for signs of leakage or material deterioration, and checking the cooling fan drivebelt tension and condition.

2 Cooling system inspection

Refer to Chapter 1 for the various cooling system checking procedures.

3 Cooling system servicing (draining, flushing and refilling)

Refer to Chapter 1 for complete information on cooling system servicing procedures.

4 Antifreeze

1   It is recommended that the cooling system contain a water/ethylene glycol based antifreeze solution which will give protection down to at least −20°F at all times. This provides protection against corrosion and increases the coolant boiling point. When handling antifreeze, take care that it is not spilled on the vehicle paint, since it will invariably cause damage if not removed immediately.
2   The cooling system should be drained, flushed and refilled at least twice a year. The use of antifreeze solutions for periods longer than the specified intervals can cause damage and encourage the formation of rust and scale due to the corrosion inhibitors gradually losing their efficiency.
3   Before adding antifreeze to the system, check all hose connections and check for signs of leakage around the thermostat and water pump.

4   The exact mixture of antifreeze-to-water which you should use depends upon the relative weather conditions. Consult the information provided by the antifreeze manufacturer on the container label. A good general guide is water and antifreeze mixed in a 50/50 ratio.

5 Thermostat – removal, inspection and installation

Removal

1   Partially drain the radiator to a level below the thermostat housing. The thermostat is located at the end of the upper radiator hose, opposite the radiator. It is contained within a housing bolted to the cylinder head on six cylinder engines or to the intake manifold on V8 engines.
2   Loosen the top radiator hose from the thermostat housing and remove the hose. Remove the bypass hose on 302 cu in engines. Disconnect any vacuum or electrical lines from any sensor(s) located on the housing. Mark them for re-installation purposes.
3   Remove the bolts and lock-washers retaining the thermostat housing to the cylinder head or intake manifold.
4   Lift the thermostat housing from the cylinder head or intake manifold.
5   Remove the thermostat from the housing, taking careful note of which direction it is installed.
6   Clean the mating faces of the thermostat housing and of the cylinder head or intake manifold.

Testing

7   Due to the minimal cost of a replacement thermostat, it is usually better to purchase a new unit rather than attempt a test. However, the following procedure can be used to detect a faulty thermostat.
8   Heat a pan of water over the kitchen stove until the temperature nears those listed at the front of this Chapter. A thermometer used in the making of candy can be used to monitor the temperature.
9   Using wire, suspend the thermostat into the hot water. The valve should open approximately $\frac{1}{4}$ inch at the specified temperature.
10 If the thermostat does not react to temperature variations as stated above, or if there are any visible signs of defect (corrosion, cracks, etc.), the thermostat should be replaced with a new one.

Installation

11 After cleaning both mating surfaces of the thermostat housing, install a new thermostat housing gasket to the housing.
12 Install the thermostat into the housing making sure it faces the right direction. The copper element should face the engine and the bridge or flange should face the radiator. If there is a locking recess in the housing turn the thermostat until the corresponding tang fits into the recess.
13 Install the housing, thermostat and gasket to the head or manifold.

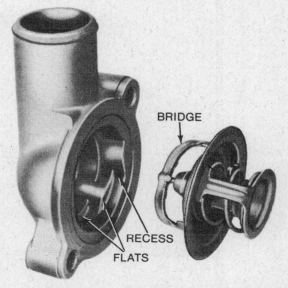

Fig. 3.1 Thermostat installation into housing (Sec 5)

14 Install the thermostat housing retaining bolts and torque them to the proper specification.

15 Install the radiator hose back onto the thermostat housing and tighten the clamp.

16 Refill the cooling system and test the system for leaks after the engine has been run.

17 Observe the temperature on the instrument panel gauge (if equipped) and check that the thermostat is operating correctly. The engine should reach normal operating temperature within a few minutes of running. Also, check that the heater is putting out warm air. This is a good indication of the coolant temperature.

6 Radiator – removal, inspection and installation

Note: *Refer to Chapter 1 for preliminary checks of the cooling system.*

Removal

1 Drain the radiator using the draincock located near the bottom of the radiator. See the information given in Chapter 1 pertaining to this.

2 Remove the lower radiator hose and clamp from the radiator. Be careful not to put excess pressure on the outlet tube, as it can easily break away.

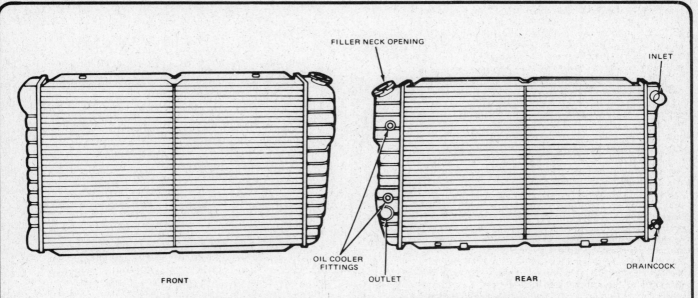

Fig. 3.2 A typical cross-flow radiator as used on 1973 thru 1977 Broncos (Sec 6)

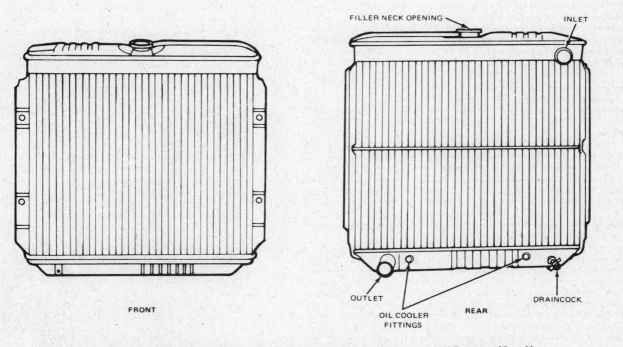

Fig. 3.3 A typical down-flow radiator as used on all pick-ups and late-model Broncos (Sec 6)

3   Remove the upper radiator hose and clamp from the radiator top tank.
4   If equipped with an automatic transmission, remove the transmission cooler lines from the bottom of the radiator taking care not to twist the lines or damage the fittings. It is best to use a fitting wrench for this particular job. Plug the ends of the disconnected lines to prevent leakage and stop dirt from entering the system.
5   Remove the bolts which attach the fan shroud to the radiator support. Place the shroud over the fan, allowing space for radiator removal. In some cases the fan itself will have to be removed. Once the fan is out of the way, the shroud and radiator can be lifted together straight up and out of the engine compartment.

Inspection
6   Inspect the radiator for signs of leakage, deterioration and/or rust. Inspect the cooling fins for bending and/or damage. In most cases a reputable radiator repair shop should be consulted for repairs.

Installation
7   Installation is the reverse of removal. Take care to install the radiator into the vehicle with caution as the cooling fins along with the radiator itself are fragile and can be damaged easily by mishandling or contact with the fan or radiator support. Make sure that the radiator is mounted securely with the proper retaining bolts and that all hoses and clamps are in good condition before you connect them to the radiator.
8   After remounting all components related to the radiator, start and run the engine and allow it to reach normal operating temperature. Visually check for leaks.

7   Water pump – checking

1   A water pump that is in need of replacement will usually give indications through noise from the bearing and/or leakage.
2   Visually check the water pump for leakage. Pay special attention to the area around the front pump seal at the outlet of the driveshaft and at the drain hole.
3   The front bearing in the water pump can be checked for roughness or excessive looseness by first removing the drivebelt and grasping the fan by hand to check for movement. Attempt to move the fan up and down as well as circularly to test for a loose bearing.
4   Visually check the sealing surfaces where the water pump mates to the front cover (or to the cylinder block on 360 and 390 engines) for signs of leakage.
5   If any of the above indications are present, the water pump will have to be removed for further checking and/or replacement.

8   Water pump – removal and installation

1   With the engine cold, drain the cooling system.
2   Remove the fan shroud retaining bolts.
3   Remove the fan retaining bolts from the nose of the water pump and remove the shroud, fan and spacer.
4   If equipped, loosen the power steering pump attaching bolt(s). Slacken the power steering pump drivebelt by releasing the adjustment bolt and allowing the power steering pump to move toward the engine. If the power steering pump bracket is retained at the water pump, the power steering pump should be completely removed and laid to one side to facilitate removal of the bracket.
5   If equipped with air conditioning, **do not** disconnect any of the hoses or lines. The following procedures can be performed by moving, not disconnecting, the a/c compressor. Loosen the air conditioning compressor top bracket retaining bolts. Remove the bracket on engines that have it secured to the pump. Remove the air conditioner idler arm and assembly.
6   Remove the air compressor and power steering pump drivebelt.
7   If equipped, remove the air pump pulley hub bolts and remove the bolt and pulley. Remove the air pump pivot bolt, bypass hose and air pump.
8   Loosen the alternator pivot bolt.
9   Remove the retaining bolt and spacer for the alternator.
10 Remove the adjustment arm bolt, pivot bolt and alternator drive belt.

11 Remove the alternator bracket if it is retained at the water pump.
12 Disconnect the lower radiator hose from the water pump inlet.
13 Disconnect the heater hose from the water pump.
14 Disconnect the bypass hose from the water pump.
15 Remove the water pump retaining bolts and remove the water pump from the cylinder front cover or the engine block, (depending on engine type). Take note of the installed positions of the various-sized bolts.
16 Remove the separator plate from the water pump (460 engine only).
17 Remove the gaskets from the mating faces of the water pump and from the cylinder front cover or cylinder block.
18 Before installation, remove and clean all gasket material from the water pump, cylinder front cover, separator plate mating surfaces and/or cylinder block.
19 Position new gaskets onto the water pump and coat them on both sides with water resistant sealer.
20 Carefully install the water pump onto the cylinder front cover (or cylinder block).
21 Install the retaining bolts finger-tight and make sure that all gaskets are in place and that the hoses line up in the correct position. It may be necessary to transfer some hose ports and/or fittings from the old pump if you are replacing it with a new pump.
22 Tighten the retaining bolts to the proper torque specifications.
23 Connect the radiator lower hose and clamp.
24 Connect the heater return hose and clamp.
25 Connect the bypass hose to the water pump.
26 If equipped, install the top air conditioning compressor bracket and idler pulley assembly.
27 Install the remaining components to the water pump and engine in the reverse order of removal.
28 Adjust all of the belts for the alternator, air pump, power steering, air conditioning compressor and other drive accessories (if equipped).
29 Fill the cooling system with the proper coolant mixture.
30 Start the engine and make sure there are no leaks. Check the level frequently during the first few weeks of operation to ensure there are no leaks and the level in the system is stable.

9   Water temperature sender – checking and replacement

Checking
1   The water temperature indicating system consists of a sending unit which is screwed into the cylinder head or manifold and a corresponding temperature gauge mounted in the instrument panel. When the coolant temperature of the engine is low, the resistance of the sending unit is high and thus sends a restrictive flow of current to the gauge. This causes the pointer to move only a short distance. As the temperature of the engine increases, the resistance at the sending unit decreases and thus causes an increased flow of current and movement at the gauge.
Note: *Do not apply 12 volt current directly to the temperature sender terminal at any time, as the voltage will damage the unit.*
2   Start the engine and allow it to run with a thermometer placed in the radiator neck until a minimum temperature of 180°F is read.
3   The gauge in the instrument panel should indicate within the normal band of the reading scale.
4   If the gauge does not indicate correctly, disconnect the gauge lead from the terminal at the sender unit.
5   Connect the lead of a 12 volt test light or the positive lead of a voltmeter to the gauge lead that was disconnected.
6   Connect the other test lead to an engine ground.
7   With the ignition switch set to the On or Accessory position, a flashing light or fluctuating voltage should indicate that the instrument voltage regulator is operating and the gauge circuit is not grounded.
8   If the light stays on or the voltage reading is steady, the instrument voltage regulator is bad. If no voltage is indicated by the voltmeter or test light, check for an open circuit in the system.
9   If all of the above readings check out correctly yet the gauge does not work properly, the gauge sender needs replacement.

Replacement
10 Disconnect the battery ground cable.
11 Disconnect the temperature sending unit wire at the sending unit.

12 Remove the temperature sending unit from the cylinder head by using the proper socket.
13 Prepare the new temperature sending unit for installation by applying electrically-conductive thread sealing tape or sealer such as spray-on copper sealer to the threads.
14 Install the temperature sending unit into the cylinder head or intake manifold.
15 Connect the wire to the temperature gauge sending unit.
16 Connect the negative battery cable.
17 Start the engine and check that the temperature sending unit is operating correctly.

10 Heater core – removal and installation

Note: *The following procedure is intended for vehicles without air*

conditioning. The addition of a/c complicates the procedure to the point where it is beyond the scope of the home mechanic.
1 Disconnect the negative battery cable from the battery.
2 Disconnect the temperature control and the air door control cables from the heater housing. Carefully position the cables out of the way to prevent any damage from occurring to them.
3 Disconnect the electrical wires from the blower resistor and the blower motor.
4 Remove the retaining screws holding the air inlet vent duct to the main body of the heater housing.
5 Disconnect the wires from the heater blower on the engine side of the firewall.
6 Drain the water from the radiator and remove the heater hoses from the heater core on the engine side of the firewall.
7 Remove the heater body retaining nuts from the studs on the engine side of the firewall.

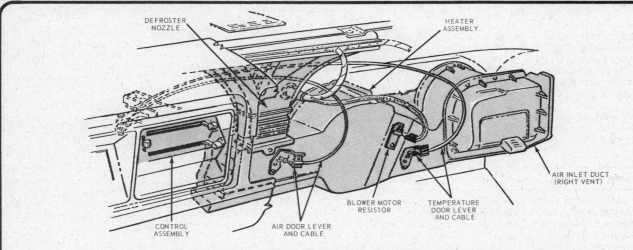

Fig. 3.4 Typical heater control components of F-150, F-350 trucks with standard heater (Sec 10)

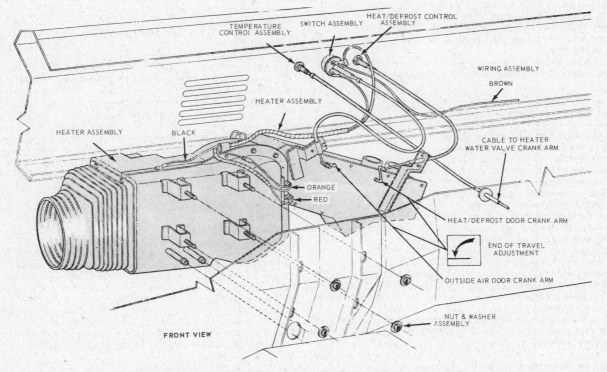

Fig. 3.5 Typical heater control components of Bronco (Sec 10)

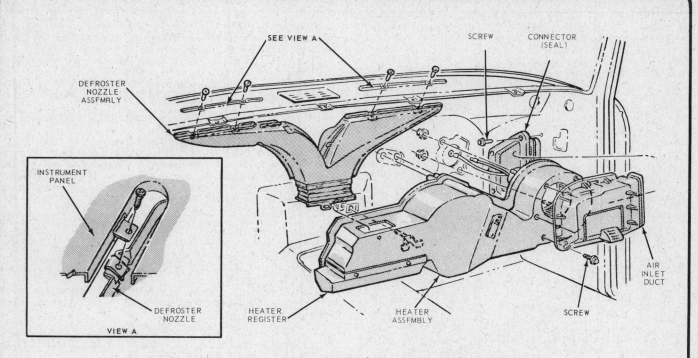

Fig. 3.6 Heater core and related components of F-150/F-350 trucks (Sec 10)

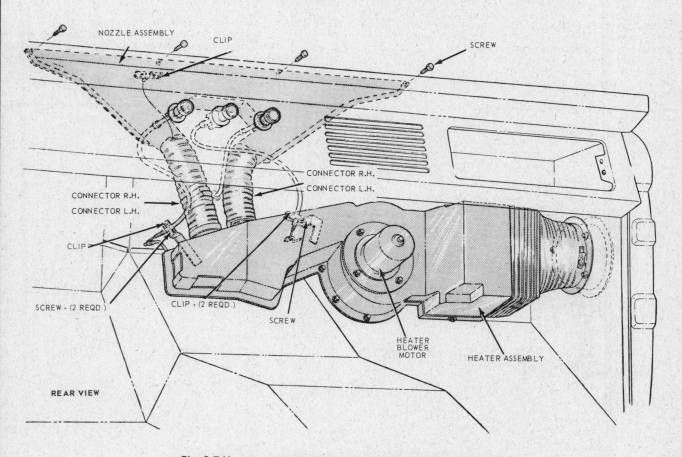

Fig. 3.7 Heater core and related components of Bronco (Sec 10)

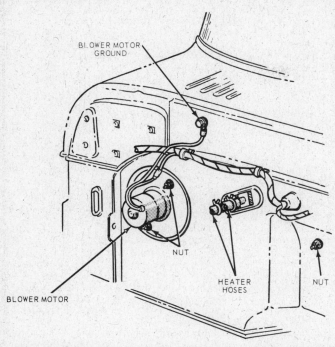

Fig. 3.8 F-100/F-350 heater unit retaining nuts for firewall side (Sec 10)

8   Remove the heater assembly from the passenger side of the firewall.
9   Remove the gasket situated between the heater hose end and the dash panel where the core inlet and outlet tubes pass through.
10 Remove the heater core cover and gasket.
11 Pull the heater core and lower support from the main heater assembly.

Installation

12 Install the foam gaskets onto the heater core and place the heater core into the heater assembly.
13 Install the cover plate and core seal gasket with the retaining screws.
14 Position the main heater assembly into the vehicle and push the studs through the firewall. Put the nuts on the studs and tighten them to retain the heater assembly.
15 Connect the heater hoses to the heater core tubes and refill the cooling system.
16 Reconnect the blower motor wires.
17 Position the defroster nozzle onto the heater assembly so that the defroster and heater openings are in the Up position and make sure that the seal is carefully situated around the duct to avoid leakage.
18 Install the air inlet vent duct to the heater. Make sure the duct is firmly placed against the seal on the side cowl and tighten the retaining screws.
19 Connect the wires to the blower motor resistor and connect the wires to the blower motor.
20 Connect the temperature cable and the air door cable to the heater and adjust the cables as described in Section 12.
21 Reinstall the gasket between the heater hose ends and the dash panel at the core end.
22 Start and run the engine. Make sure the cooling system is full. Check the heater for operation and check for any signs of coolant leakage.

11 Heater control – removal and installatiom

Removal
1   Disconnect the negative battery cable.
2   Pull the two knobs off each radio control shaft.
3   Use a hook tool to release the knobs on the fuel gauge switch (if so equipped), heater control switches and the wiper-washer knob.
4   Remove the knob and shaft from the light switch as described in Chapter 10.
5   Remove the nut and washer from each radio control shaft and remove the radio faceplate.

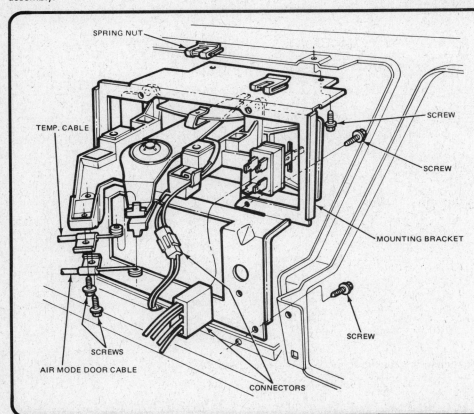

Fig. 3.9 Rear view of F-100 through F-350 heater control panel (Sec 11)

6   Remove the screws retaining the instrument cluster bezel. Remove the entire instrument cluster bezel.
7   Disconnect the illumination light from the bezel between the light and wiper-washer switch.
8   Remove the four heater control attaching screws and pull the control unit away from the mounting bracket.
9   Remove the two vacuum port connector blocks on vehicles equipped with factory air conditioning.
10 Disconnect the blower switch and illumination light wires.
11 Disconnect the two bottom cables from the control assembly if equipped with a heater only. Disconnect the one air blend door cable from vehicles equipped with factory air conditioning.

Installation

12 Install the cables on the control assembly. The pigtail of the cable must point away from the control lever.
13 Plug in the wires for the light illuminating the heater controls.
14 Connect the blower wire connectors to the blower switch.
15 Position the control assembly to the mounting plate and install the remaining retaining screws.
16 Install the instrument cluster face, radio face and all of the control knobs.
17 Connect the ground cable of the battery and check the operation of the controls.
18 Turn on the instrument lights and make sure they are operating.
19 Turn the ignition switch to Accessory or On position and make sure the blower operates on all of its speed settings.
20 Check the air flow blows in the correct directions when the controls are set to Heat or Defrost position. If they are not operating correctly, adjust the controls as described in the following Section.

12 Heater control – adjustment

Note: *When checking the adjustment, make sure the heater control temperature switch travels all the way through the span from the Cool to the Warm position. Also check the heater mode control for correct operation from the Off through the Heat and on to the Defrost position. If these conditions do not exist, the cables must be adjusted as follows:*

1   To adjust the air door mode control cable, loosen the cable clamp screw located on the distributor housing plenum.
2   Place the mode control lever in the Defrost position.
3   Push the air door crank to the extreme right position and tighten the cable clamp attaching screw in this position.
4   To adjust the temperature control cable, loosen the cable clamp located on the heater housing.
5   Place the temperature control lever at the Warm position.
6   Push the temperature door crank to the extreme right position and tighten the cable clamp attaching screw in this position.

13 Heater blower – checking

1   Connect the positive lead of an ammeter to the positive post of a 12 volt battery.
2   Connect the negative lead of the ammeter to the disconnected power wire of the heater blower. The remaining wire at the blower should be properly grounded.
3   This will operate the heater blower independently of the control switch and wiring.
4   The motor should run under these conditions. The current drawn by the motor will be indicated on the ammeter. Make sure the current drawn meets the specification for the blower.
5   If the heater blower does not operate under these conditions, it is defective and needs to be replaced with a new one.
6   If the heater blower does operate under these conditions, but does not operate when connected to the vehicle system, the wiring, fuse, connections or switch are defective and should be traced using standard electrical system procedures.

14 Heater blower – removal and installation

Removal

1   Disconnect the temperature control and the air door control cables

from the heater housing. Carefully position the cables out of the way to prevent any damage from occurring to them.
2   Disconnect the electrical wires from the blower resistor and the blower motor.
3   Remove the retaining screws holding the air inlet vent duct to the main body of the heater housing.
4   Disconnect the wires from the heater blower on the engine side of the firewall.
5   Drain the water from the radiator and remove the heater hoses from the heater core on the engine side of the firewall.
6   Remove the heater body retaining nuts from the studs on the engine side of the firewall.
7   Remove the heater assembly from the passenger side of the firewall.
8   Remove the gasket situated between the heater hose end and the dash panel through which the core inlet and outlet tubes pass.
9   Remove the screws and nuts retaining the heater blower to the heater assembly.
10 Remove the blower fan from the motor shaft.
11 Remove the motor from the mounting plate.

Installation

12 Install the motor onto the mounting plate.
13 Install the blower fan onto the motor shaft.
14 Install the blower and motor into the heater assembly.
15 Position the main heater assembly into the vehicle and push the studs through the firewall. Connect the nuts to the studs and tighten them to retain the heater assembly.
16 Connect the heater hoses to the heater core tubes and refill the cooling system.
17 Reconnect the blower motor wires.
18 Position the defrost nozzle onto the heater assembly so that the defroster and heater openings are in the Up position and make sure the seal is carefully situated around the duct to avoid leakage.
19 Install the air inlet vent duct to the heater. Make sure the duct is firmly situated against the seal on the side cowl and tighten the retaining screws.
20 Connect the wires to the blower motor resistor and connect the wires to the blower motor.
21 Connect the temperature cable and the air door cable to the heater and adjust the cables as described in Section 12.
22 Reinstall the gasket between the heater hose ends and the dash panel at the core ends.
23 Start and run the engine. Make sure the cooling system is full. Check the heater for operation and check for any signs of coolant leakage.

15 Air conditioning – general description

Caution: *The air conditioning system contains refrigerant under high pressure. Any attempt to disconnect fittings without depressurizing the*

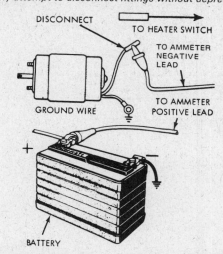

Fig. 3.10 Test connections for checking the heater blower motor (Sec 13)

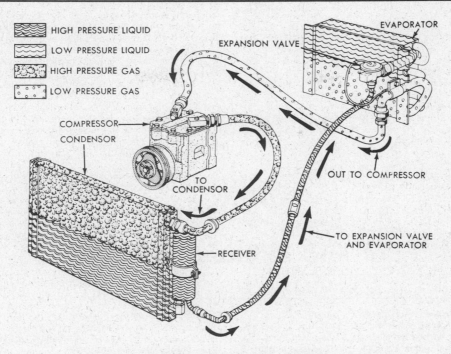

HIGH PRESSURE LIQUID

LOW PRESSURE LIQUID

HIGH PRESSURE GAS

LOW PRESSURE GAS

EVAPORATOR

EXPANSION VALVE

COMPRESSOR

CONDENSOR

TO
CONDENSOR

OUT TO COMPRESSOR

RECEIVER

TO EXPANSION VALVE
AND EVAPORATOR

**Fig. 3.11 Basic operational components and flow chart for a
typical air conditioning system (Sec 15)**

*system can cause serious injury. It is recommended that repairs be left
to a Ford dealer or other qualified repair shop.*

Ford light duty trucks come with factory, dealer-installed and a
number of aftermarket air conditioning systems. This book deals only
with the factory system, as all other manufacturers of air conditioning
systems have their own data and specifications which will apply to
their units.

The Ford light duty trucks use a straight-forward air conditioning
system which consists of a receiver which holds the liquid refrigerant
R-12 for use, a supply line leading to the expansion valve, an
evaporator located inside the passenger compartment, a return line
leading to the inlet of the compressor, a compressor and a feed line
leading back to the condenser.

The refrigerant (R-12) is pumped through the system by the air
compressor which is actuated by the thermostatic (de-icing) switch
located within the evaporator. As the temperature rises in the
evaporator and the switch is activated through the air conditioning
control in the cab, the thermostatic switch alternately activates and
de-activates the magnetic clutch located in the compressor to provide
a uniform flow of refrigerant throughout the system. The air conditioning system is fully serviceable and can be recharged, checked and
serviced by qualified personnel.

16 Air conditioning – checking and maintenance

Caution: *The air conditioning system contains refrigerant under high
pressure. Any attempt to disconnect fittings without depressurizing the*

*system can cause serious injury. It is recommended that repairs be left
to a Ford dealer or other qualified repair shop.*

1   Checking and maintenance of the air conditioning system will be
limited to visual inspection. Check for obstructed air passages,
disconnected or broken wires leading to the air compressor magnetic
clutch, loose or broken mounting brackets for the air conditioning
compressor and/or a loose magnetic clutch.
2   Visually inspect all of the connecting lines for signs of leakage
and/or deterioration.
3   Most factory systems are equipped with a sight glass which is on
the high pressure refrigerant line between the receiver and the
expansion valve. The sight glass can be used to check for adequate
refrigerant level in the system.
4   Clean the sight glass before checking for proper charge. Turn the
air conditioner on and set the controls for maximum cooling. Observe
the sight glass for bubbles with the engine running at approximately
1500 rpm. If the sight glass shows continuous bubbles, an under-
charge of refrigerant is probably the cause. If the system is under-
charged, it should also be checked for leaks using the specialized
equipment that an air conditioning service center has. Also, watch the
sight glass after the A/C clutch is engaged. If no bubbles appear
directly after A/C clutch engagement, there may be too much
refrigerant or no refrigerant at all.
5   If any problems are found in the air conditioning system, take it to
an air conditioning shop or dealership specializing in this type of work
and have the repair or maintenance work done. It is normal for an air
conditioning system to need a slight recharge after each season. The
air conditioning system should be cycled by the operator at least once
a month, even during the cold weather season.

3

Chapter 4 Fuel and exhaust systems

Contents

Specifications

Fuel pump

Type	Mechanical, driven from camshaft
Pressure	
Six cylinder engines	5.0 to 7.0 psi
Eight cylinder engines	6.0 to 8.0 psi
Volume (at idle rpm)	
1973 models	1 pint in 30 seconds
1974 models	1 pint in 15 seconds
1975 thru 1979 models	1 pint in 20 seconds

Torque specifications

	ft-lb
Fuel	
Fuel pump retaining bolts	
302, 360-390 and 460 cid engines	19 to 27
351M-400 cid engines (bolt)	10 to 15
351M-400 cid engines (nut)	14 to 20
Carburetor retaining nuts	12 to 15
Fuel filter-to-carburetor	
All engines except 460 cid	80 to 100 in-lbs
460 cid engines	29 to 37 in-lbs
Exhaust system	
Exhaust bracket-to-frame cross-member	23 to 32
Exhaust bracket-to-frame side rail	
5/16 - 18 fastener	12 to 17
3/8 - 16 fastener	23 to 32
Exhaust pipe joint U-bolt	25 to 36
Inlet pipe-to-exhaust manifold	25 to 38
Inlet pipe U-bolt	25 to 36
Outlet pipe U-bolt clamps	10 to 15
Hanger bracket screw	7 to 11
The following torque ranges are to be used for fittings or fasteners not indicated above	
$\frac{5}{16}$ in diameter bolt or nut	12 to 17
$\frac{3}{8}$ in diameter bolt or nut	31 to 42
$\frac{7}{16}$ in diameter bolt or nut	50 to 70
$\frac{1}{2}$ in diameter bolt or nut	75 to 105

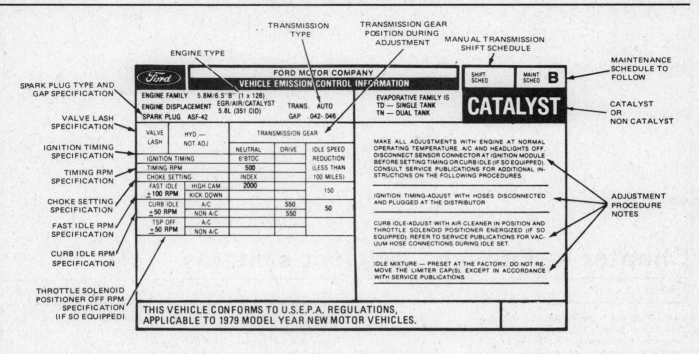

Labels around the decal (clockwise/by position):

- ENGINE TYPE
- TRANSMISSION TYPE
- TRANSMISSION GEAR POSITION DURING ADJUSTMENT
- MANUAL TRANSMISSION SHIFT SCHEDULE
- MAINTENANCE SCHEDULE TO FOLLOW
- CATALYST OR NON CATALYST
- ADJUSTMENT PROCEDURE NOTES
- SPARK PLUG TYPE AND GAP SPECIFICATION
- VALVE LASH SPECIFICATION
- IGNITION TIMING SPECIFICATION
- TIMING RPM SPECIFICATION
- CHOKE SETTING SPECIFICATION
- FAST IDLE RPM SPECIFICATION
- CURB IDLE RPM SPECIFICATION
- THROTTLE SOLENOID POSITIONER OFF RPM SPECIFICATION (IF SO EQUIPPED)

FORD MOTOR COMPANY
VEHICLE EMISSION CONTROL INFORMATION

SHIFT SCHED   MAINT SCHED   B

ENGINE FAMILY   5.8M/6.5''B'' (1 x 128)
ENGINE DISPLACEMENT   EGR/AIR/CATALYST   TRANS. AUTO
5.8L (351 CID)   GAP .042-.046
SPARK PLUG ASF-42

EVAPORATIVE FAMILY IS
TD — SINGLE TANK
TN — DUAL TANK

CATALYST

VALVE LASH	HYD — NOT ADJ	TRANSMISSION GEAR		
		NEUTRAL	DRIVE	IDLE SPEED
IGNITION TIMING		6°BTDC		REDUCTION
TIMING RPM		500		(LESS THAN
CHOKE SETTING		INDEX		100 MILES)
FAST IDLE ±100 RPM	HIGH CAM	2000		150
	KICK DOWN			
CURB IDLE ±50 RPM	A/C		550	50
	NON A/C		550	
TSP OFF ±50 RPM	A/C			
	NON A/C			

MAKE ALL ADJUSTMENTS WITH ENGINE AT NORMAL OPERATING TEMPERATURE. A/C AND HEADLIGHTS OFF. DISCONNECT SENSOR CONNECTOR AT IGNITION MODULE BEFORE SETTING TIMING OR CURB IDLE (IF SO EQUIPPED). CONSULT SERVICE PUBLICATIONS FOR ADDITIONAL INSTRUCTIONS ON THE FOLLOWING PROCEDURES.

IGNITION TIMING-ADJUST WITH HOSES DISCONNECTED AND PLUGGED AT THE DISTRIBUTOR

CURB IDLE-ADJUST WITH AIR CLEANER IN POSITION AND THROTTLE SOLENOID POSITIONER ENERGIZED (IF SO EQUIPPED). REFER TO SERVICE PUBLICATIONS FOR VACUUM HOSE CONNECTIONS DURING IDLE SET.

IDLE MIXTURE — PRESET AT THE FACTORY. DO NOT REMOVE THE LIMITER CAP(S), EXCEPT IN ACCORDANCE WITH SERVICE PUBLICATIONS.

THIS VEHICLE CONFORMS TO U.S.E.P.A. REGULATIONS, APPLICABLE TO 1979 MODEL YEAR NEW MOTOR VEHICLES.

Fig. 4.1 A typical emissions control information decal as attached inside the engine compartment (Sec 2)

1 General information

The fuel system on all models consists of a fuel tank(s) mounted in a variety of locations on the chassis, a mechanically-operated fuel pump, and a carburetor with air cleaner for filtering purposes. A combination of metal and rubber fuel hoses are used to connect these three components and in the case of some vehicles which have auxiliary tanks, a fuel flow control valve which is located between the tanks and the fuel pump in the system.

The carburetor is a single, dual or four-venturi downdraft type depending on the engine displacement and year of production.

The fuel system (especially the carburetor) is heavily inter-related with the emissions control system on all vehicles produced for sale in the United States. Certain modifying components of the emissions control system are described in Chapter 6.

2 Carburetor – servicing and overhaul

1 A thorough road test and check of carburetor adjustments should be done before any major carburetor service. Specifications for some adjustments are listed on the *vehicle emission control information label* found in the engine compartment.

2 Some performance complaints directed at the carburetor are actually a result of loose, misadjusted or malfunctioning engine or electrical components. Others develop when vacuum hoses leak, are disconnected or are incorrectly routed. The proper approach to analyzing carburetor problems should include a routine check of the following areas:

  a) Inspect all vacuum hoses and actuators for leaks and proper installation (see Chapter 6, *Emission control systems*).
  b) Tighten the intake manifold nuts and carburetor mounting nuts evenly and securely.
  c) Perform a cylinder compression test.
  d) Clean or replace the spark plugs as necessary.
  e) Test the resistance of the spark plug wires.
  f) Inspect the ignition primary wires and check the vacuum advance operation. Replace any defective parts.
  g) Check the ignition timing according to the instructions listed on the *emissions control label*.
  h) Set the carburetor idle mixture.

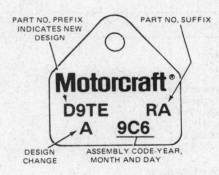

PART NO. PREFIX INDICATES NEW DESIGN

PART NO. SUFFIX

Motorcraft®
D9TE   RA
A   9C6

DESIGN CHANGE

ASSEMBLY CODE-YEAR, MONTH AND DAY

Fig. 4.2 An identification tag similar to this will be attached to the carburetor. Use this number when ordering replacement parts or a new (rebuilt) carburetor (Sec 2)

  i) Check the fuel pump pressure as described in Section 9.
  j) Inspect the heat control valve in the air cleaner for proper operation.
  k) Remove the carburetor air filter element and blow out any dirt with compressed air. If the filter is extremely dirty, replace it with a new one.
  l) Inspect the crankcase ventilation system.

3 Carburetor problems usually show up as flooding, hard starting, stalling, severe backfiring, poor acceleration and lack of response to idle mixture screw adjustments. A carburetor that is leaking fuel and/or covered with wet-looking deposits needs attention.

4 Diagnosing carburetor problems may require that the engine be started and run with the air cleaner removed. While running the engine without the air cleaner it is possible that it could backfire. A backfiring situation is likely to occur if the carburetor is malfunctioning, but removal of the air cleaner alone can lean the air/fuel mixture enough to produce an engine backfire. Perform this type of testing for as short a time as possible and be especially watchful for the potential of backfire and the possibility of starting a fire. Do not position your face or any portions of your body directly over the carburetor during inspection or servicing procedures.

4

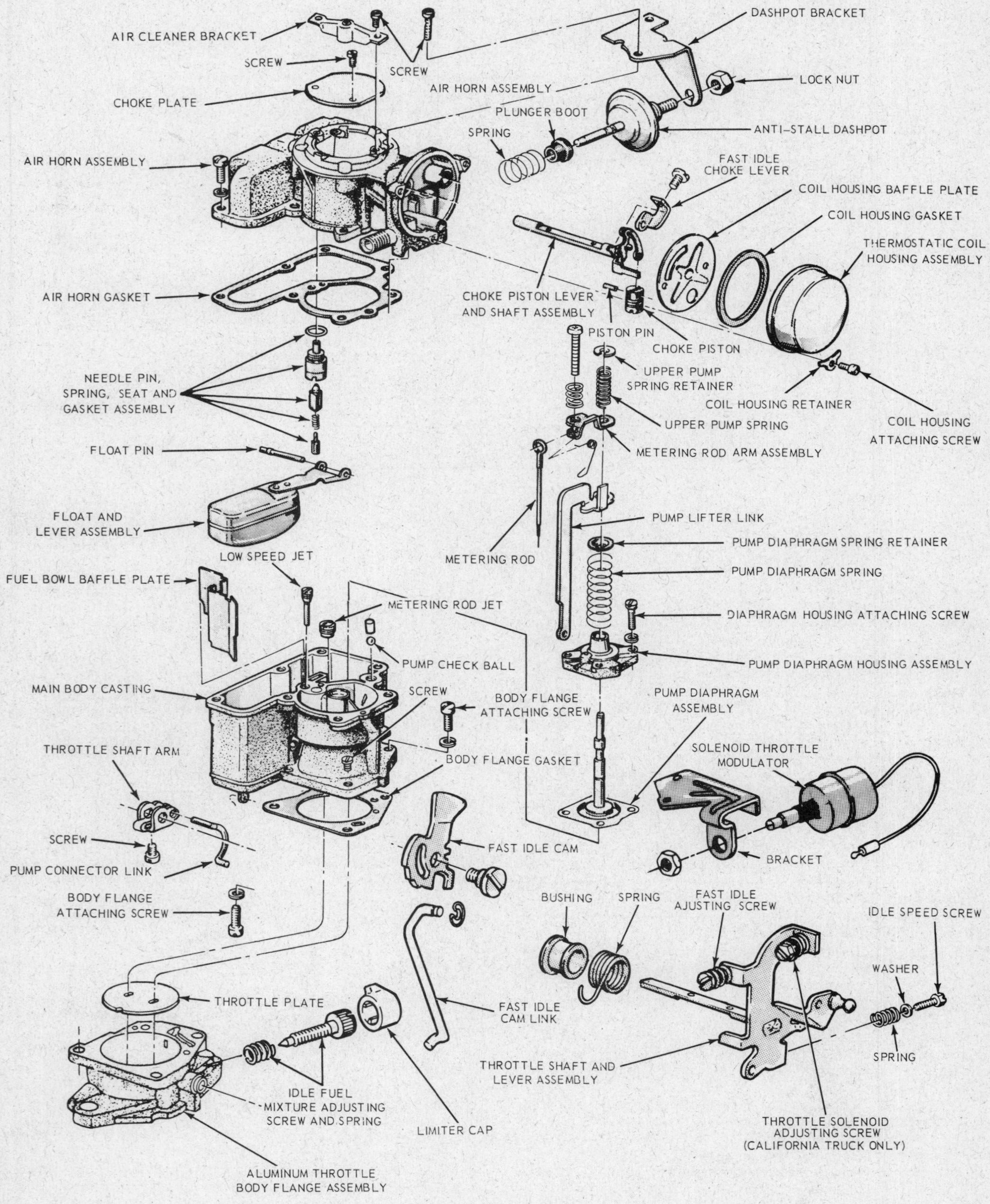

AIR CLEANER BRACKET

SCREW

SCREW

DASHPOT BRACKET

LOCK NUT

CHOKE PLATE

AIR HORN ASSEMBLY

PLUNGER BOOT

SPRING

ANTI-STALL DASHPOT

AIR HORN ASSEMBLY

FAST IDLE CHOKE LEVER

COIL HOUSING BAFFLE PLATE

COIL HOUSING GASKET

THERMOSTATIC COIL HOUSING ASSEMBLY

AIR HORN GASKET

CHOKE PISTON LEVER AND SHAFT ASSEMBLY

PISTON PIN

CHOKE PISTON

COIL HOUSING RETAINER

COIL HOUSING ATTACHING SCREW

NEEDLE PIN, SPRING, SEAT AND GASKET ASSEMBLY

UPPER PUMP SPRING RETAINER

UPPER PUMP SPRING

METERING ROD ARM ASSEMBLY

FLOAT PIN

FLOAT AND LEVER ASSEMBLY

PUMP LIFTER LINK

PUMP DIAPHRAGM SPRING RETAINER

PUMP DIAPHRAGM SPRING

LOW SPEED JET

METERING ROD

FUEL BOWL BAFFLE PLATE

METERING ROD JET

DIAPHRAGM HOUSING ATTACHING SCREW

PUMP CHECK BALL

PUMP DIAPHRAGM HOUSING ASSEMBLY

MAIN BODY CASTING

SCREW

BODY FLANGE ATTACHING SCREW

PUMP DIAPHRAGM ASSEMBLY

THROTTLE SHAFT ARM

BODY FLANGE GASKET

SOLENOID THROTTLE MODULATOR

SCREW

FAST IDLE CAM

BRACKET

PUMP CONNECTOR LINK

BODY FLANGE ATTACHING SCREW

BUSHING

SPRING

FAST IDLE AJUSTING SCREW

IDLE SPEED SCREW

WASHER

THROTTLE PLATE

FAST IDLE CAM LINK

SPRING

IDLE FUEL MIXTURE ADJUSTING SCREW AND SPRING

LIMITER CAP

THROTTLE SHAFT AND LEVER ASSEMBLY

THROTTLE SOLENOID ADJUSTING SCREW (CALIFORNIA TRUCK ONLY)

ALUMINUM THROTTLE BODY FLANGE ASSEMBLY

Fig. 4.3 Carter YF 1-V carburetor (1973 shown) as used on 6-cylinder engines (Sec 2)

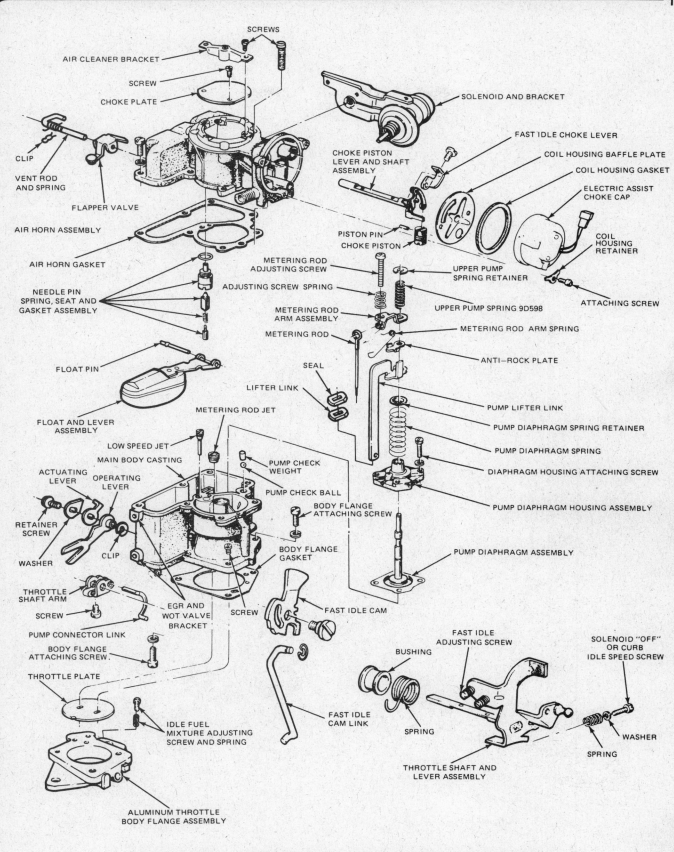

SCREWS

AIR CLEANER BRACKET

SCREW

CHOKE PLATE

SOLENOID AND BRACKET

FAST IDLE CHOKE LEVER

COIL HOUSING BAFFLE PLATE

COIL HOUSING GASKET

ELECTRIC ASSIST CHOKE CAP

CLIP

VENT ROD AND SPRING

FLAPPER VALVE

AIR HORN ASSEMBLY

AIR HORN GASKET

CHOKE PISTON LEVER AND SHAFT ASSEMBLY

PISTON PIN

CHOKE PISTON

COIL HOUSING RETAINER

ATTACHING SCREW

NEEDLE PIN SPRING, SEAT AND GASKET ASSEMBLY

METERING ROD ADJUSTING SCREW

ADJUSTING SCREW SPRING

METERING ROD ARM ASSEMBLY

METERING ROD

UPPER PUMP SPRING RETAINER

UPPER PUMP SPRING 9D598

METERING ROD ARM SPRING

ANTI-ROCK PLATE

FLOAT PIN

FLOAT AND LEVER ASSEMBLY

LOW SPEED JET

MAIN BODY CASTING

ACTUATING LEVER

OPERATING LEVER

RETAINER SCREW

WASHER

CLIP

THROTTLE SHAFT ARM

SCREW

PUMP CONNECTOR LINK

BODY FLANGE ATTACHING SCREW.

THROTTLE PLATE

SEAL

LIFTER LINK

METERING ROD JET

PUMP CHECK WEIGHT

PUMP CHECK BALL

BODY FLANGE ATTACHING SCREW

BODY FLANGE GASKET

SCREW

EGR AND WOT VALVE BRACKET

FAST IDLE CAM

PUMP LIFTER LINK

PUMP DIAPHRAGM SPRING RETAINER

PUMP DIAPHRAGM SPRING

DIAPHRAGM HOUSING ATTACHING SCREW

PUMP DIAPHRAGM HOUSING ASSEMBLY

PUMP DIAPHRAGM ASSEMBLY

FAST IDLE CAM LINK

IDLE FUEL MIXTURE ADJUSTING SCREW AND SPRING

ALUMINUM THROTTLE BODY FLANGE ASSEMBLY

BUSHING

SPRING

FAST IDLE ADJUSTING SCREW

THROTTLE SHAFT AND LEVER ASSEMBLY

SOLENOID "OFF" OR CURB IDLE SPEED SCREW

WASHER

SPRING

4

Fig. 4.4 Carter YF 1-V carburetor (1979 shown) as used on 6-cylinder engines (Sec 2)

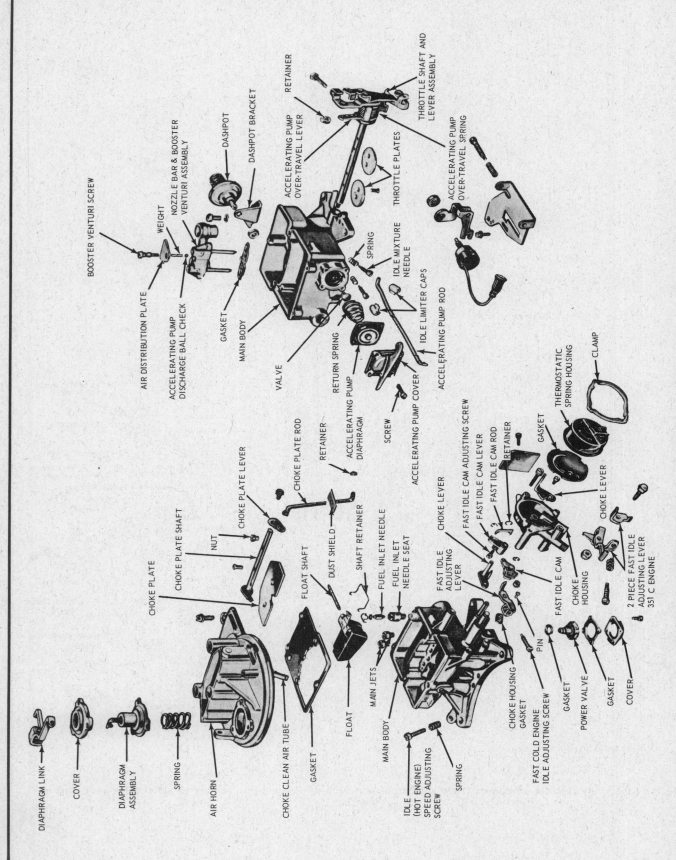

Fig. 4.5 Motorcraft 2100-D 2-V carburetor (1973 shown) as used on various 8-cylinder engines (Sec 2)

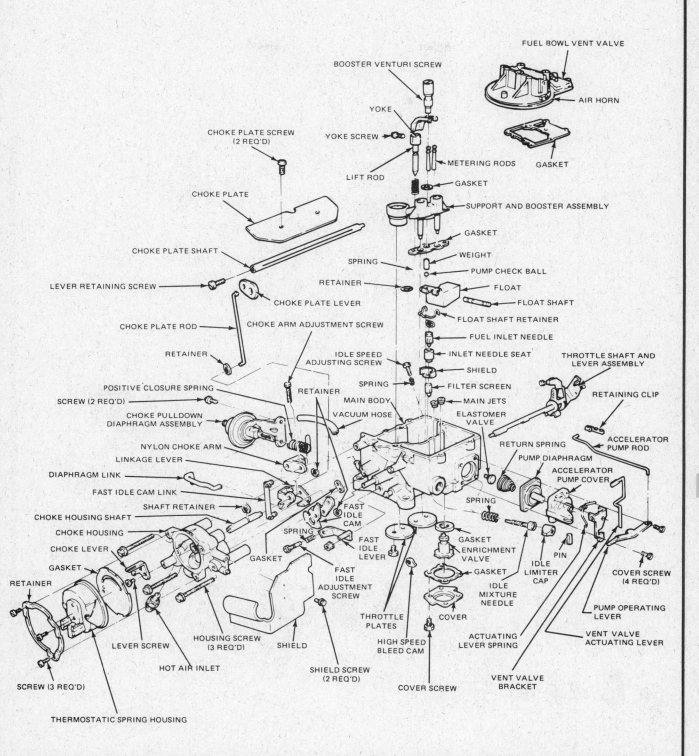

Fig. 4.6 Motorcraft 2150 2-V carburetor (1979 shown), without altitude compensator, as used on various 8-cylinder engines (Sec 2)

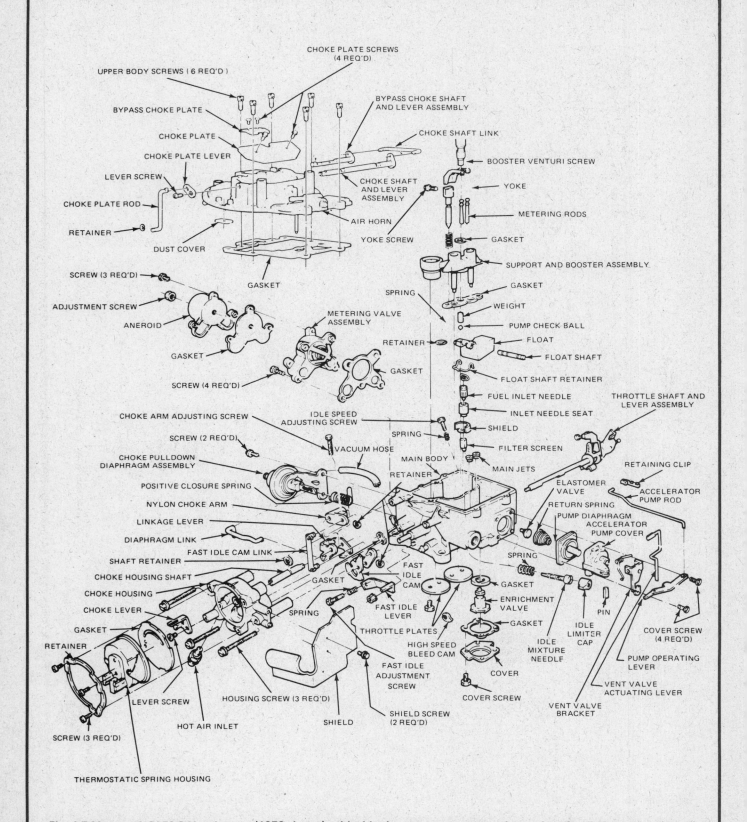

Fig. 4.7 Motorcrafr 2150 2-V carburetor (1979 shown), with altitude compensator, as used on various 8-cylinder engines (Sec 2)

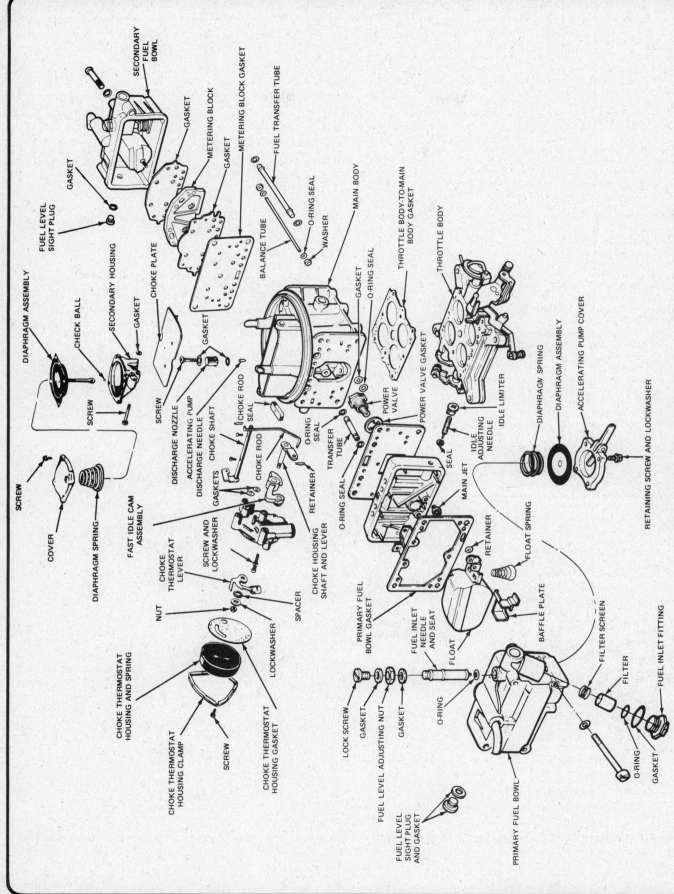

Fig. 4.8 Holley 4180 C 4-V carburetor (1979 shown) as used on various 8-cylinder engines (Sec 2)

SECONDARY FUEL BOWL

GASKET

GASKET

METERING BLOCK

GASKET

METERING BLOCK GASKET

FUEL TRANSFER TUBE

O-RING SEAL

WASHER

MAIN BODY

GASKET

O-RING SEAL

THROTTLE BODY-TO-MAIN BODY GASKET

THROTTLE BODY

FUEL LEVEL SIGHT PLUG

GASKET

DIAPHRAGM ASSEMBLY

CHECK BALL

SECONDARY HOUSING

GASKET

CHOKE PLATE

BALANCE TUBE

SCREW

SCREW

DISCHARGE NOZZLE

ACCELERATING PUMP DISCHARGE NEEDLE

CHOKE SHAFT

CHOKE ROD SEAL

GASKETS

CHOKE ROD

O-RING SEAL

TRANSFER TUBE

RETAINER

O-RING SEAL

POWER VALVE

POWER VALVE GASKET

SEAL

IDLE ADJUSTING NEEDLE

IDLE LIMITER

DIAPHRAGM SPRING

DIAPHRAGM ASSEMBLY

ACCELERATING PUMP COVER

RETAINING SCREW AND LOCKWASHER

SCREW

COVER

DIAPHRAGM SPRING

FAST IDLE CAM ASSEMBLY

CHOKE THERMOSTAT LEVER

SCREW AND LOCKWASHER

CHOKE HOUSING SHAFT AND LEVER

MAIN JET

NUT

SPACER

LOCKWASHER

CHOKE THERMOSTAT HOUSING AND SPRING

CHOKE THERMOSTAT HOUSING CLAMP

SCREW

CHOKE THERMOSTAT HOUSING GASKET

FUEL LEVEL ADJUSTING NUT

LOCK SCREW

GASKET

GASKET

O-RING

FLOAT

PRIMARY FUEL BOWL GASKET

FUEL INLET NEEDLE AND SEAT

RETAINER

FLOAT SPRING

BAFFLE PLATE

FILTER SCREEN

FILTER

O-RING

GASKET

FUEL INLET FITTING

FUEL LEVEL SIGHT PLUG AND GASKET

PRIMARY FUEL BOWL

5   Once it is determined that the carburetor is in need of work or an overhaul, several alternatives should be considered. If you are going to attempt to overhaul the carburetor yourself, first obtain a good quality carburetor re-build kit which will include all necessary gaskets, internal parts, instructions and a parts list. You will also need carburetor cleaning solvent and some means of blowing out the internal passages of the carburetor with air.

6   Due to the many configurations and variations of carburetors offered on the range of vehicles listed in this book, it is not feasible for us to do a step-by-step overhaul of each type. You will find a good, detailed instruction list with any quality carburetor overhaul kit and it will apply in a more specific manner to the carburetor you have.

7   Another alternative available is to obtain a new or rebuilt carburetor. These are readily available from dealers and auto parts stores for all engines covered in this manual. The important fact when purchasing one of these units is to make sure your exchange carburetor is identical to the one you are returning. Often times a tag is screwed to the top plate of your carburetor which will aid your parts man in determining the exact type of carburetor you have. When obtaining a rebuilt carburetor or a re-build kit, take time to ascertain that the kit or carburetor matches your application exactly. Seemingly insignificant differences can make a large amount of difference in the overall running condition of your engine.

8   If you choose to overhaul your own carburetor, allow enough time to disassemble the carburetor carefully, soak the necessary parts in the cleaning solvent (usually for at least one half day or according to the time instructions listed on the carburetor cleaner) and reassemble which will usually take you much longer than disassembly. When you are disassembling a carburetor, take care to match each part with the illustration listed in your carburetor kit, and use a clean work space with an orderly display of each removed part to help you reassemble the carburetor correctly. Overhauls by amateurs sometimes result in a vehicle which runs less well or not at all compared to the original condition. To avoid this happening to you, use care and patience when disassembling your carburetor so that you can reassemble it to its exact, original condition.

3   Carburetor – removal and installation

Caution: *There are a number of safety steps to follow when working with gasoline. Refer to 'Safety First' near the front of this manual.*

1   Disconnect the negative battery cable. Remove the hose connections leading to the air cleaner. Mark these with coded pieces of tape to help in reassembly.

2   Remove the air cleaner assembly.

3   Use a small catch-can and disconnect the fuel feed line from the carburetor. Plug the end of this hose to prevent further leakage.

4   Disconnect any electrical leads from any emission control devices connected to the carburetor. Mark these connections so they can be installed in the proper position.

5   Remove any vacuum lines from the carburetor. Mark them for installation purposes.

6   Disconnect the kick-down lever or cable from the carburetor (if equipped).

7   Disconnect the throttle cable or linkage from the carburetor.

8   Disconnect any under-carburetor heater hoses that may be connected to the carburetor.

9   Disconnect any coolant transfer hoses that may be connected to the choke system.

10   Remove the carburetor retaining nuts from the studs in the intake manifold.

11   Lift off the carburetor, spacer plate (if equipped), and gasket(s). Place a piece of cardboard over the intake manifold surface to prevent debris from falling into the engine while the carburetor is removed.

12   Before installation, carefully clean the mating surfaces of the intake manifold, spacer plate (if equipped), and the base of the carburetor of any old gasket material. These surfaces must be perfectly clean and smooth to prevent vacuum leaks.

13   Install a new gasket(s).

14   Install the carburetor and spacer plate (if equipped) over the studs on the intake manifold.

15   Install the retaining nuts and torque them to the proper specification. Be careful not to over-torque these retaining nuts as they can warp the base plate of the carburetor.

16   Perform Steps 1 through 9 in reverse order, making sure that all hoses, wiring, etc are returned to their original positions.

4   Carburetor – external adjustments

Note: *All carburetors on US vehicles come equipped with adjustment limiters or limiter stops on the carburetor idle mixture screws. All adjustments to these mixture screws are to be made only within the range provided by the limiter devices. In addition, the following procedures are intended for general use only. The information given on the emissions control decal located under the hood is specific for your engine and should be followed.*

The main adjustments available for carburetors operating on the vehicle are idle, fuel (idle) mixture, and fast idle (with the choke). The following procedures are provided for the mechanic to adjust a carburetor on a running vehicle. They are not intended to supersede the instructions provided on the *emissions control decal* affixed to the engine or engine compartment nor are they designed to provide a proper mixture and idle adjustment if an emissions control analyzer is called for in the adjustment. They will however, provide a way to make the vehicle run satisfactorily until it can be serviced or adjusted by a proper dealership or service center with the correct emissions control sampling equipment.

Note: *All necessary adjustments and/or inspection procedures discussed in Section 2 should be performed before carburetor service begins.*

Idle speed (preliminary)

1   Set the fuel mixture screws to the full counterclockwise position allowed by the limiter caps.

2   Back off the idle speed adjusting screw until the throttle bore plates are seated in the throttle bore. Some vehicles are equipped with either a dashpot or a solenoid-type idle valve to hold the linkage open. Make sure these devices are not holding the idle up when making this adjustment.

3   Turn the idle adjusting screw inward until it initially contacts the throttle stop. Turn the screw an additional one and one half turns to establish a preliminary idle speed adjustment.

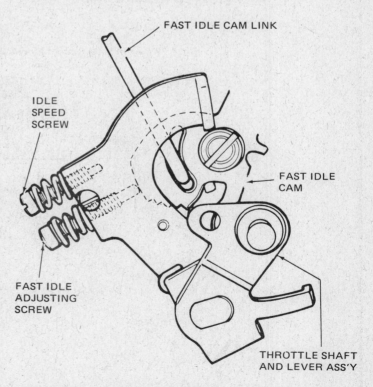

Fig. 4.9 Idle adjustment – TF series (1 barrel carburetor) (Sec 4)

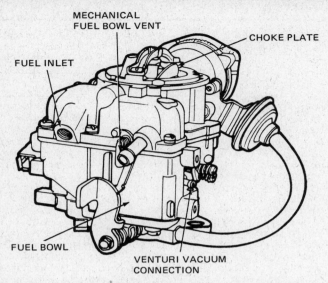

MECHANICAL
FUEL BOWL VENT

FUEL INLET

CHOKE PLATE

FUEL BOWL

VENTURI VACUUM
CONNECTION

Fig. 4.10 Overall view of Carter YF – 1 barrel carburetor
(Sec 4)

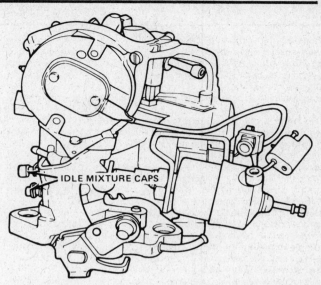

IDLE MIXTURE CAPS

Fig. 4.11 Idle mixture adjustment – YF series (1 barrel
carburetor) (Sec 4)

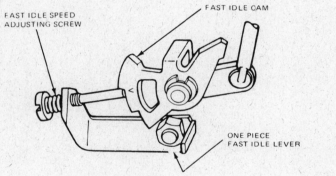

FAST IDLE SPEED
ADJUSTING SCREW

FAST IDLE CAM

ONE PIECE
FAST IDLE LEVER

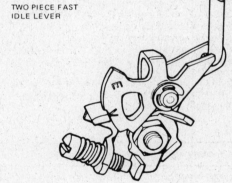

TWO PIECE FAST
IDLE LEVER

Fig. 4.12 Fast idle adjustment screws 2150 – (2 barrel carburetor) (Sec 4)

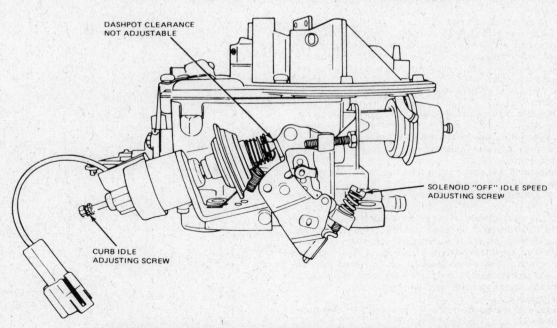

DASHPOT CLEARANCE
NOT ADJUSTABLE

SOLENOID "OFF" IDLE SPEED
ADJUSTING SCREW

CURB IDLE
ADJUSTING SCREW

Fig. 4.13 Solenoid-dashpot throttle positioner (2150 2 barrel carburetor) (Sec 4)

4

Idle speed (engine running)

4   Set the parking brake and block the wheels to prevent movement. If equipped with an automatic transmission, have an assistant apply the brakes as a further safety precaution during the following procedures.

5   Start the engine and allow the engine to achieve normal operating temperature.

6   Ensure that the ignition timing is set as described in Chapter 1.

7   On a vehicle with a manual shift transmission, the idle should be set with the transmission in Neutral. On vehicles with automatic transmissions, the idle setting is made with the transmission in Drive.

8   Make sure the choke plate is fully opened.

9   Make sure the air conditioning is turned off.

10 Use a tachometer of known accuracy and connect it to the vehicle according to the manufacturer's instructions.

11 Adjust the engine curb idle rpm to the specifications given on the *emissions control label*. Make sure the air cleaner is installed for this adjustment.

12 If so equipped, turn the solenoid assembly to obtain the specified curb idle rpm with the solenoid activated.

13 Set the automatic transmission to Neutral.

14 Disconnect the power to the solenoid lead wire at the connector.

15 Adjust the carburetor throttle stop screw to obtain 500 rpm in Neutral.

16 Connect the solenoid power wire and open the throttle slightly by hand. The solenoid plunger should hold the throttle lever in the extended position and move the rpm range up.

Idle mixture adjustment

17 Turn the idle mixture adjusting screw(s) inward all the way.

18 Back the screw(s) out slowly until the smoothest idle is obtained. If equipped with two mixture screws, they should be turned in equal amounts.

19 Take the vehicle to an approved service center with the correct exhaust analyzing equipment and have the mixture adjusting set according to the exhaust content specifications.

Fast idle adjustment

20 The fast idle adjusting screw is provided to maintain engine idle rpm while the choke is operating and the engine has a limited air supply during its cold running cycle. As the choke plate moves through its range of travel from the closed to the open position, the fast idle cam rotates to allow decreasingly slower idle speeds until the normal operating temperature and correct curb idle rpm is reached.

21 Before adjusting the fast idle make sure the curb idle speed and mixture are adjusted as previously discussed.

22 With the engine at normal operating temperature and the tachometer attached, manually rotate the fast idle cam until the fast idle adjusting screw rests on the specified step of the cam (see *emissions control label* for proper step).

23 Turn the fast idle adjusting screw inward or outward to obtain the specified fast idle rpm.

---

5   Automatic choke – inspection and adjustment

Note: *Choke checking procedures can be found in Chapter 1.*

1   Remove the air cleaner with the engine cold and not running.

2   Rotate the throttle (or have an assistant depress the gas pedal) to the open position and observe that the choke plate freely shuts tightly in the opening of the upper body air horn. With the accelerator held open, check that the choke plate can be freely moved and is not hanging up due to deposits of varnish. If the choke plate has excessive deposits or varnish, it will have to be either cleaned with a commercial spray-on carburetor cleaner or the carburetor will need to be dismantled and overhauled or replaced (see Section 2). A spray-on type of carburetor cleaner will remove any surface varnish which may be causing sticky or erratic choke plate action, however care must be used to prevent sediment from entering the throttle venturis.

3   Start the vehicle. If equipped with an electric choke, use a voltmeter to check that the electric assist on the side of the choke thermostat housing has voltage. Voltage should be constantly supplied to the temperature sensing switch as long as the engine is running. If no voltage is present, circuit check the system to determine the problem.

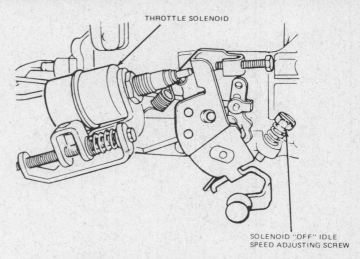

Fig. 4.14 Throttle positioner system (2150 2 barrel carburetor) (Sec 4)

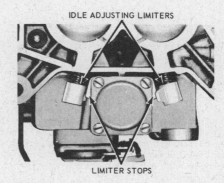

Fig. 4.15 Bottom view of idle mixture screws and limiter caps (2150 2 barrel carburetor) (Sec 4)

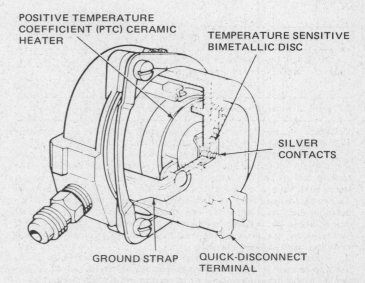

Fig. 4.16 Typical electric choke installation (Sec 5)

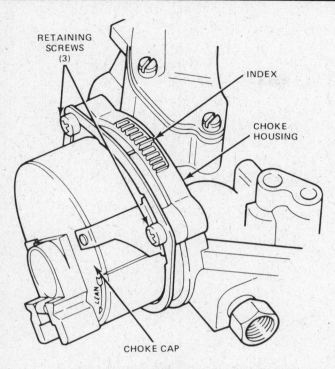

Fig. 4.17 Choke housing adjustment – YF series 1 barrel carburetor (Sec 5)

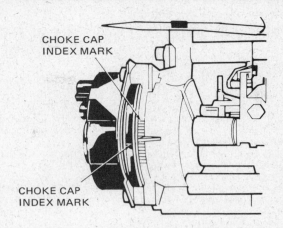

Fig. 4.18 Choke housing adjustment – 2150 2 barrel carburetor (Sec 5)

4 Some automatic chokes will come equipped with a thermostatic spring housing which controls the choke action. To adjust this type of housing, loosen the three clamp screws that attach the thermostatic spring housing to the choke housing. The spring housing can now be turned to vary the setting on the choke. Set the spring housing to the specified mark (see *emissions control label* in the engine compartment) and tighten the retaining screws. Do not try to compensate for poor choke operation by varying the index setting from the specified spot. If the choke is not operating properly, the spring inside the housing may be worn, broken or other problems may exist in the choke system. If this situation exists, the spring and housing will need to be replaced.

5 Allow the vehicle to completely cool (at least four hours – preferably overnight) and check for proper operation as described in Chapter 1.

6 Fuel filter – removal and installation

Since fuel filter replacement is a part of normal periodic maintenance, the procedure can be found in Chapter 1.

7 Fuel lines and valves – routing and replacement

Caution: *There are a number of safety steps to follow when working with gasoline. Refer to 'Safety First' near the front of this manual.*

1 The fuel lines of these vehicles are generally made of metal with short lengths of rubber hose connecting critical flex points such as the tank or fuel pump. The metal fuel lines are retained to the body and frame with various clips and brackets. They generally will require no service; however, if they are allowed to come loose from their retaining brackets they can vibrate and eventually be chafed through. If a fuel line needs to be replaced, it would be best to leave this service to a dealership or specialist in this field as it requires special flaring and crimping tools to build the lines.

2 If a short section of fuel line is damaged, rubber fuel hose can be used to replace it if it is no longer than 12 in. Cut a length of fuel quality rubber hose longer than the section to be replaced and use a tubing cutter to remove the damaged portion of the metal line. Install

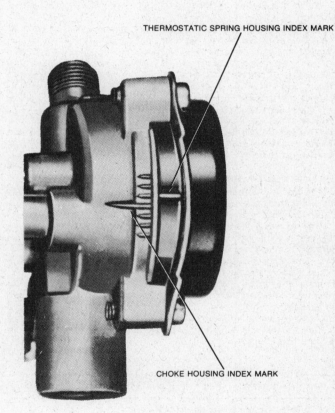

Fig. 4.19 Choke housing adjustment – 4180 4 barrel carburetor (Sec 5)

the rubber fuel line using two hose clamps and check to make sure no leaks are present.

3 If new fuel lines are necessary, they must be cut, formed and flared out of fuel system tubing. If you have the equipment to do so, remove the old fuel line from the vehicle and duplicate the bends and length of the system off of the vehicle.

4 Install the new section of tubing and be careful to install new clamps and/or brackets where needed. Make sure the replacement tubing is of the same diameter, shape and quality as the original one. Make sure all flared ends conform to the same type as the original fuel line. Make sure fuel lines connected to fuel pumps or other fittings are of the double flare type. Make sure all metal shavings are removed from inside the tubing before installation.

5   Always check rubber hoses for any signs of leakage or deterioration.

6   If a rubber hose needs replacing, it is advisable to also replace the clamp.

7   If the vehicle is equipped with two tanks, it will also have a switching valve somewhere in the system. If a factory auxiliary tank is installed, the switching valve will be located next to the heater controls and will be electrically operated. If this valve is being replaced, be sure to remove the battery cable before replacement as sparks can ignite gasoline when removing the connection to the auxiliary fuel tank switching valve.

8   Fuel pump – description and testing

Caution: *There are a number of safety steps to follow when working with gasoline. Refer to 'Safety First' near the front of this manual.*

1   All vehicles are equipped with a single-action mechanical fuel pump.

2   The fuel pump on six cylinder engines is located on the lower left portion of the cylinder block, midway between the front of the block and the distributor.

3   The fuel pump on V8 engines is mounted on the left side of the front cylinder cover.

4   All fuel pumps are of the permanently-sealed design and are non-serviceable or re-buildable.

5   All fuel pumps are actuated mechanically by a rocker arm on the fuel pump, operating off an eccentric lobe on the nose of the camshaft.

Testing (preliminary)

6   Before suspecting the fuel pump as being faulty, check all fuel hoses and lines and the fuel filter (Chapter 1).

7   Disconnect the fuel pipe at the carburetor inlet union and the high tension lead to the ignition coil (to prevent the engine from actually starting).

8   Place a suitable container at the end of the disconnected pipe and have an assistant crank the engine over from the driver's seat. A good spurt of gasoline should emerge from the end of the pipe every second revolution.

Testing (pressure)

9   Remove the air cleaner assembly.

10   Disconnect the fuel line at the carburetor or at the fuel filter.

11   Connect a pressure gauge with a flexible hose between the fuel delivery line and the carburetor. Make sure the inside diameter of the hose is no smaller than the diameter of the pressure hose.

12   Connect a T fitting into the pressure hose so the fuel line can be connected to the carburetor and the pressure gauge.

13   Make sure the engine has been run and the idle and operating temperatures are set to specification.

14   Start and run the engine. Observe the fuel pressure on the gauge. It should be within the specifications listed at the front of this Chapter.

Testing (volume)

15   To check the fuel pump for volume, a T fitting must be inserted into the fuel line with a flexible hose leading to a graduated fuel container. Graduated volume marks should show clearly on the container you use.

16   Install a hose restricter, valve or other control device on the outlet line to allow the fuel to be shut off to the test container.

17   Start and run the engine with the fuel restrictor or valve shut.

18   Open the restrictor and allow the fuel to run into the container. At the end of the specified test time, close the restrictor and measure the volume of fuel in the container. Compare the volume and time with that given in the Specifications at the front of this Chapter.

19   If the volume is below the specified amount, install a new auxiliary fuel supply onto the inlet side of the fuel pump. A small gas can with a hose tightly fit into the cap can be used as an auxiliary fuel supply. This will eliminate the possibility of a clogged tank and/or a delivery lines. Repeat the test and check the volume. If the volume has changed or now reaches specification, the fuel lines and/or tank(s) are clogged. If the volume is still low, the fuel pump must be replaced with a new one.

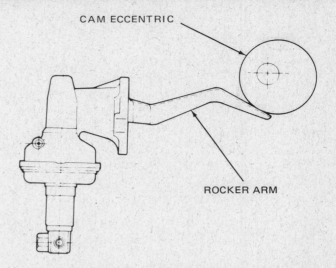

Fig. 4.20 The fuel pump is a mechanical type, operated via a rocker arm from the camshaft (Sec 8)

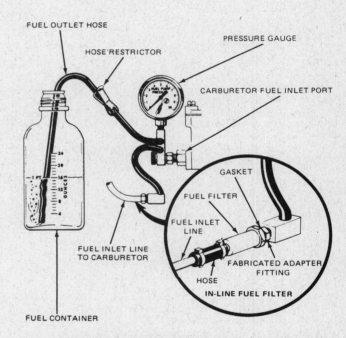

Fig. 4.21 Connections and equipment necessary to test the fuel pump for pressure and volume (Sec 8)

9   Fuel pump – removal and installation

Caution: *Use extreme caution when working around the fuel pump as the lines leading to and from the pump will be full of gasoline under pressure. It is advisable to keep wet rags and a catch-can available to try and keep the amounts of residual gasoline and spray to a minimum. Never smoke or use any type of electrical equipment around the fuel pump when removing or installing it. Use caution not to remove or install the fuel pump in an enclosed area and especially where an open flame is present such as around a water heater. Further safety precautions can be found in 'Safety First' near the front of this manual.*

1   Disconnect the negative battery cable and then remove the inlet line at the fuel pump.

2   Plug the end of the line to prevent further leakage and possible contamination from dirt.

3   Remove the outlet pipe at the fuel pump and allow it to drain into the catch-can.

4   Remove the two bolts and washers securing the fuel pump to the timing cover (or to the block on six cylinder engines).

5   Remove the fuel pump and gasket (on some models a spacer plate may be positioned for heat insulation properties).

6   Clean the mating surfaces of the fuel pump, timing cover (engine block), and spacer (if so equipped). The mating surfaces must be perfectly smooth for a good gasket seal upon re-installation.

7   Install a new gasket on the fuel pump mating surface using an oil-resistant sealer.

8   After cleaning the surfaces and applying the gasket, apply oil-resistant sealer to the other side of the gasket and to the threads on the retaining bolts.

9   After installing the pump onto the engine block, make sure the rocker arm of the fuel pump is positioned correctly on the camshaft eccentric. It may be necessary to rotate the engine until the eccentric is at its low position to facilitate easier fuel pump installation.

10 Holding the fuel pump tightly against its mounting surface, install the retaining bolts and new lock washers.

11 Torque the retaining bolts to the proper specifications.

12 Remove the plug from the inlet line and connect the inlet line to the fuel pump.

13 Connect the outlet line to the fuel pump. Connect the negative battery cable.

14 Start and run the engine and check it for fuel and/or oil leaks.

10 Fuel tank – description and warning

Note: *When working with fuel tanks observe all cautions listed previously in this Chapter and in 'Safety First' near the front of this manual. Fuel tank repairs requiring an open flame (welding, soldering, etc) should never be performed by a home mechanic.*

1   The fuel tank(s) of these vehicles are made of galvanized metal and located in various positions. The vehicles usually come with a rear-mounted fuel tank located between the frame rails behind the rear axle. Some vehicles (4-wheel drive and F-350) come equipped with an in-cab, behind-the-seat fuel tank.

2   An auxiliary tank is offered as an option on most vehicles and is generally located between the frame rails on the left side of the vehicle between the driveline and the left frame rail in front of the rear axle. If an auxiliary tank is fitted to the vehicle, a switching valve assembly is also included to switch the fuel flow as well as the level reading from one tank to another. Some Broncos come equipped with an auxiliary fuel tank manufactured of a special high-density polyethylene plastic. This tank is non-repairable and if damaged, should be replaced.

11 Fuel tank – removal and installation

Note: *See the previous Section and all cautions given in this Chapter and 'Safety First' near the front of this manual.*

In cab

1   Disconnect the negative battery cable and then use a siphon to drain the fuel tank through the filler neck into a suitable container. Do not start the siphoning action with your mouth.

2   Move the seat to the full forward position on its track and tilt the seat back forward.

3   Disconnect the fuel gauge sending unit wire.

4   Disconnect the fuel line from the fuel tank. Plug this line to prevent leakage and contamination to the system. Mark it with coded tape to ease reinstallation.

5   Disconnect the evaporative emissions vapor return line(s), if equipped. Again, plug and mark as above.

6   Disconnect the fuel return line(s), plugging and coding as above.

7   Loosen the clamp retaining the filler neck to the tank inlet.

8   Pull the filler neck up through the cab hole and away from the tank.

9   Remove the fuel tank retaining bolts and nuts.

10 Lift the tank up and out of the cab.

11 If the tank is being replaced with a new one, remove the fuel gauge sending unit and pressure relief tube.

12 Remove the gasket from the sending unit.

13 If the fuel tank has been replaced, cleaned or serviced, install the fuel gauge sending unit and pressure relief tube using a new gasket.

14 If required, glue new anti-rattling insulation material onto the fuel tank.

15 If required, glue three new rubber pads in place in the bottom channel of the tank.

16 If required, glue new washers to the body at the mounting bolt holes.

17 Position the tank inside the cab and install the cap screws at the bottom of the tank.

18 Install the nuts at the top of the tank.

19 Follow Steps 3 through 12 in reverse order.

20 Check the fuel lines for leakage after filling the tank.

Bronco

21 Using a siphon, drain the fuel tank through the filler neck into a suitable container. Do not start the siphoning action with your mouth.

22 Raise the rear of the vehicle and support it securely.

23 Disconnect the battery ground cable.

24 Disconnect the fuel gauge sending unit wire from the fuel tank sender.

25 Loosen the clamp on the fuel filler pipe hose at the filler inlet and disconnect the hose from the pipe.

26 Loosen the hose clamps and slide the clamps forward to disconnect the fuel hose from the fuel gauge sending unit. Plug the end of this hose and mark it with coded tape to help in installation.

27 If the fuel gauge sending unit is to be removed, turn the unit retaining ring counterclockwise and remove it.

28 Remove the sending unit retaining ring gasket.

29 Remove the fuel tank mounting strap retaining nut and swing the strap down and position it out of the way. Use a floor jack or similar device with a block of wood and lower the tank just enough to gain access to the fuel tank vent hose at the top of the tank.

30 Disconnect the fuel tank vent hose from the top of the fuel tank, plugging and marking it as above.

31 Disconnect the fuel tank lines leading to the fuel tank separator at the fuel tank fitting. Again, plug and mark them.

32 Lower the fuel tank carefully and remove it from the vehicle.

33 Installation is the reverse of removal. Be careful to position the forward edge of the tank at its mounting lug in the frame crossmember and connect the hoses before raising it into place.

Frame-mounted behind axle

34 Raise the rear of the vehicle and support it securely.

35 Disconnect the ground cable from the battery.

36 Disconnect the fuel gauge sending unit from the fuel gauge sending unit wire.

37 Remove the fuel drain plug or siphon the fuel out of the tank into a suitable storage container. Do not start the siphoning action with your mouth.

38 Loosen the fuel feed line hose clamps and slide the clamps forward.

39 Disconnect the fuel line at the fuel gauge sending unit. Plug the end of this hose to prevent leakage and/or contamination. Also mark it with coded tape to help during installation.

40 If the fuel gauge sending unit is being removed, turn the unit retaining ring counterclockwise and remove the sending unit, retaining ring and gasket.

41 Loosen the clamps on the fuel filler inlet pipe and remove the pipe hose from the tank.

42 Loosen the clamps on the vent hose and remove the vent hose from the tank. Plug and mark it as above.

43 Support the tank with a floor jack and block of wood or similar device.

44 Remove the bolts retaining the tank supports to the frame.

45 Carefully lower the tank until the vent tube is exposed and disconnect the vent tube from the emission control valve at the top of the tank. Plug and mark it as above.

46 Remove the filler pipe and vent hose and position them completely out of the way.

47 Carefully lower the tank and remove it from beneath the vehicle.

48 Disassemble the skid plate from the bottom of the tank, if equipped.

49 Installation is the reverse of removal.

Note: *When attaching vent and fuel line(s) make sure the lines are in good condition. If they are in need of replacement, be sure to replace them with fuel hose of the same quality and size.*

4

Under cab auxiliary

50 Drain the fuel tank using a siphon through the filler neck. Do not start the siphoning action with your mouth.

51 Remove the clamps and disconnect the feed hoses attached to the fuel tank. Plug each hose to prevent leakage and/or contamination. Mark each hose with coded pieces of tape to help during installation.

52 Remove the evaporative emission control vapor lines from the emission control valve. Plug and mark each hose as above.

53 Support the tank with a jack and a block of wood or similar apparatus.

54 Remove the nuts and bolts from the retaining straps and carefully lower the tank to the floor.

55 Installation is the reverse of removal. Be sure to connect all hoses and inspect them before connection.

Bronco auxiliary

56 The procedure for removal and installation of this fuel tank is the same as *Under cab auxiliary* above with the following important difference.

57 Since this tank is made of high-density polyethylene plastic, it is important that the securing locknuts are not over-tightened, as this could crack the plastic. The locknuts should be assembled onto the J-bolts until 1.25 inches of thread is exposed below the nut. This applies to vehicles with and without skid plates.

12 Fuel tank – cleaning and repair

1 If a fuel tank shows that it has a build-up of sediment or rust in the bottom, it must be removed and cleaned.

2 When the tank is removed it should be flushed out with hot water and detergent or sent to a radiator shop for chemical flushing which is preferable.

3 Never attempt to weld, solder or make any type of repairs on an empty fuel tank. Leave this work to an authorized repair shop.

4 The use of a chemical type sealer for on-vehicle repairs is advised only in case of emergency and the tank should be removed and sent to a shop for more permanent repairs as soon as possible.

5 Never store a gas tank in an enclosed area where gas fumes could build up and cause an explosion and/or fire.

13 Exhaust system – general information

The exhaust systems used on these vehicles vary according to the engine, wheelbase, gross vehicle weight rating and emissions controls. Many vehicles use a catalytic converter which is covered in Chapter 6. All vehicles use a single muffler and tailpipe. All exhaust systems are retained with a combination of metal and rubber clamps and some exhaust systems are equipped with heat shields when excessive exhaust temperatures are encountered due to the installation of emissions control equipment.

Due to the high temperatures inherent in the exhaust system, any attempt to inspect or repair it should be done only after the entire system has cooled. This may take several hours.

14 Exhaust system – parts replacement

1 Inspection of the exhaust system consists of visually checking the inlet pipe(s), outlet pipe and mufflers for broken welds, split joints or corrosion damage resulting in leakage. Also inspect the clamps, insulators and brackets for cracks and stripped, corroded or missing fasteners. The exhaust system should be free from leaks, binding, vibration or contact points other than the hangers. If loose, broken or mis-aligned clamps, shields, brackets or pipes are encountered, replacement of the defective exhaust system component will be necessary.

2 Alignment of the exhaust components is also important as mis-aligned exhaust components will allow parts of the system to contact portions of the body and/or frame causing noise, wear and transfer of heat. If this situation is encountered, the exhaust system will need to be loosened and re-aligned or components will need to be replaced.

3 If brush shields are noted to be loose, bent or missing they will need re-alignment or replacement. Check the exhaust shield to make sure that any combustible matter such as brush or debris is not caught within the mesh.

4 If your inspection reveals the exhaust system, or portions of it need to be replaced, first secure the proper parts needed to repair the system. The components of the exhaust system can generally be split at their major divisions such as the inlet pipe from the muffler or the muffler from the tailpipe. However, if corrosion is the cause or need for replacement, it is probably necessary to replace the entire exhaust system.

5 Raise and support the vehicle securely.

6 Make sure the exhaust system is cool.

7 Apply some rust penetrant solvent to the retainer bolts for the exhaust inlet pipe flange.

8 Remove the exhaust inlet pipe flange retaining nuts.

9 Remove the shields from the catalytic converter, if equipped.

10 Remove the clamps retaining the muffler or converter to the inlet pipe(s).

11 Remove the hanger supporting the muffer and/or catalytic converter from the vehicle.

12 Remove the clamps retaining the rear of the muffler to the tailpipe.

13 Remove the section(s) necessary for replacement. It may be necessary to allow the axle to hang free from the rear frame in order to get the curved section of the tailpipe over the rear axle housing. Be sure to support the vehicle's frame securely before removing the support from the axle.

14 Installation is the reverse of removal. Always use new gaskets and retaining nuts whenever the system is being replaced. It is also a good idea to use new hangers and/or retaining brackets when replacing the exhaust system.

15 Start the vehicle and check for exhaust leaks and/ or rattles caused by misalignment.

Chapter 5 Engine electrical systems

Contents

Specifications

Distributor
Type
    1973 through late 1974 .... Contact breaker point type
    Late 1974 through 1979 .... Solid state, breakerless
Automatic advance .... Vacuum and centrifugal
Direction of rotation
    Six cylinder engines .... Clockwise
    Eight cylinder engines .... Counter-clockwise
Contact breaker point gap (1973-1974)
    Six cylinder engines .... 0.027 in
    Eight cylinder engines .... 0.017 in
Contact breaker point dwell angle (1973-1974)
    Six cylinder engines .... 35 to 39 degrees
    Eight cylinder engines .... 24 to 30 degrees

Firing order
Six cylinder engines 1-5-3-6-2-4
302, 360, 390, 460 engines 1-5-4-2-6-3-7-8
351, 400 engines 1-3-7-2-6-5-4-8

Ignition timing
.... See tune-up decal located under hood

Spark plug wire resistance
.... Not to exceed 5000 Ohms per inch

Ignition coil
.... 8 volt, oil filled

Alternator brush length
New .... $\frac{1}{2}$ in
Wear limit .... $\frac{5}{16}$ in

Torque specifications
                                                                      ft-lb
Alternator pulley nut .... 60 to 100
Starter motor mounting bolts .... 15 to 20
Starter motor through bolts .... 55 to 75 in-lb
Spark plugs .... 10 to 15

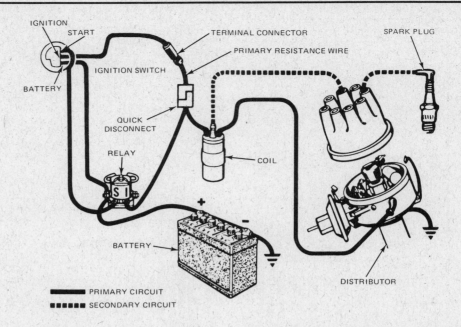

Fig. 5.1 Typical ignition system circuit as used on conventional (1973-1974) point-type systems (Sec 3)

1   General information

The engine electrical systems include the ignition, charging and starting components. They are considered separately from the rest of the electrical system (lighting, etc) because of their proximity and importance to the engine and its prime function in the vehicle.

Exercise caution when working around any of these components for several reasons. The components are easily damaged if tested, connected or stressed incorrectly. The alternator is driven by an engine drivebelt which could cause serious bodily harm if your fingers or hands become entangled in it with the engine running. Both the starter and alternator are sources of direct battery voltage which could arc or even cause a fire if over-loaded or shorted.

Never leave the ignition switch on for long periods of time with the engine not running. Do not disconnect the battery cable(s) while the engine is running. Be especially careful not to cross-connect battery cables from another source such as another car when jump-starting.

Don't ground either of the ignition coil terminals, even momentarily. When hooking up a test tachometer/dwell meter to the terminal(s) of the coil, make sure it is compatible with the type of ignition system on the vehicle. If equipped with electronic-type ignition (late 1974 on), special silicone grease (Ford part no. D7AZ-19A331-A) must be applied to the inside of any disconnected high-tension cable. A clean screwdriver should be used to apply a thin layer of this grease to the inside of the wire at the spark plug, distributor terminal and coil. Additional safety-related information can be found in *Safety First* near the front of this manual.

2   Battery

The battery is the ultimate source for engine (and vehicle) electrical power. It must be kept in good condition and serviced regularly. See Chapter 1 for servicing and charging procedures for the battery.

3   Ignition system – description

Two types of ignition systems are used on Ford pick-ups and Broncos. 1973 and 1974 vehicles use a breaker-point type ignition system along with a standard ignition coil and resistor. Late production run 1974 vehicles through 1979 use an electronic-type ignition system which couples a magnetic signal-triggering type distributor to

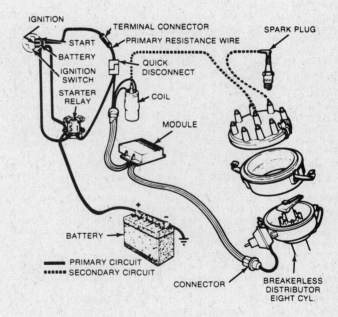

Fig. 5.2 Typical ignition system circuit as used on pointless (1975-1979) systems (Sec 3)

an electronic control box which triggers a high voltage coil. This type of system is relatively trouble-free and requires little maintenance along with long spark plug life.

Both types of ignitions fire spark plugs of different gaps through the secondary ignition system. Coil, coil high tension lead, distributor cap and spark plug wires are of the standard design. The electronic ignition system uses a special anti-conducting cap, spacer and rotor while the breaker point-type system uses the more standard black carbolic-type components.

Both types of ignitions have diaphragm-type vacuum advance unit(s) attached to the distributor. Some distributors use a double vacuum diaphragm unit as described in Chapter 6. All distributors have mechanical advance units utilizing centrifugal weight and governor springs internally mounted.

4   Ignition system – inspection and testing

Note: *Initial checking procedures for many ignition components can be found in Chapter 1.*

The ignition system consists of two separate systems as described in the previous Section. Secondary ignition system problems and diagnosis are best handled through the use of an automotive electronic oscilloscope. An experienced operator and an electronic oscilloscope can pinpoint such problems as worn spark plugs, high-resistance spark plug wires, damaged or cracked distributor cap and/or rotor, leakage between spark plug wires and other similar problems.

Primary ignition problems can also be determined through the use of an oscilloscope. However, the main components sometimes require special test apparatus, procedures and operations.

A preliminary diagnosis of an ignition system can reveal such things as poor or disconnected wires and/or leaking problems from the coil or the distributor.

With electronic ignition, the complexity of the design and testing procedures prevents in-field diagnosis of the system by the average home mechanic. If a preliminary overall visual check reveals no obvious problems such as disconnected, broken or cracked components, the vehicle will have to be taken to an authorized service center to have the components diagnosed and repaired. If the module is diagnosed as defective, replacements are available from aftermarket manufacturers as well as dealerships.

5   Spark plugs

1   Properly functioning spark plugs are a necessity if the engine is to perform properly. At the intervals specified in Chapter 1 or your owner's manual, the spark plugs should be replaced with new ones. Removal and installation information can be found in the *Tune-up and Maintenance* Chapter.
2   It is important to replace spark plugs with new ones of the same heat range and type. A series of numbers and letters are stamped on the spark plug to help identify each variation.
3   The spark plug gap is of considerable importance as, if it is too large or too small, the size of the spark and its efficiency will be seriously impaired. To set it, measure the gap with a feeler gauge, and then bend open, or close, the outer plug electrode until the correct gap is achieved. The center electrode should never be bent as this may crack the insulation and cause plug failure, if nothing worse.
4   The condition and appearance of the spark plugs will tell much about the condition and tune of the engine. If the insulator nose of the spark plug is clean and white with no deposits, this is indicative of a weak mixture, or too hot a plug (a hot plug transfers heat away from the electrode slowly – a cold plug transfers it away quickly).
5   If the tip and insulator nose are covered with hard black looking deposits, then this is indicative that the mixture is too rich. Should the plug be black and oily, then it is likely the engine is fairly worn, as well as the mixture being too rich.
6   If the insulator nose is covered with light tan to greyish brown deposits, then the mixture is correct and it is likely the engine is in good condition.
7   If there are any traces of long brown tapering stains on the outside of the white portion of the plug, then the plug will have to be replaced with a new one, as this shows there is a faulty joint between the plug body and the insulator, and compression is being allowed to leak away.
8   Always tighten a spark plug to the specified torque – no tighter.

6   Ignition timing

The ignition timing procedures are provided in Chapter 1. Refer to these procedures as well as the *emissions control decal* located on the vehicle's valve cover, engine area or glovebox door.

7   Spark plug wires

Spark plug wires are tested as described in Section 4. Be careful when testing any spark plug wires that you do not puncture them or use any type of adapters that will cause shorting of the spark path through the spark plug boot, cap or wire. Be very careful when testing the engine for spark with a spark plug wire off as there is high voltage present and extended testing can cause damage to emissions control systems.

For point-type ignition systems only, the secondary wire resistance may be checked by using an ohmmeter and measuring the resistance from one end of the spark plug wire to the other. The wire must be removed from the vehicle to accomplish this and the probes for the ohmmeter should be inserted onto the metal contacts on each end of the wire and not pierced or punctured into the wire or boot. If excessive resistance is found past the Specification listed at the front of this Chapter, the wire should be replaced with a new one.

For further information on spark plug wire removal-installation, see Chapter 1.

8   Ignition coil – checking and replacement

Checking
1   The ignition coil cannot be satisfactorily tested without the proper electronic diagnostic equipment. If a fault is suspected in the coil, have it professionally checked by a dealer or repair shop specializing in electrical repairs. The coil can be replaced with a new one using the following procedure.

Replacement
2   Disconnect the negative battery cable.
3   Using coded strips of tape, mark each of the wires at the coil to help return the wires to their original positions during re-installation.
4   Remove the primary coil-to-distributor high tension lead.
5   Remove the connections at the coil. On electronic ignitions, these connections may be of the push-lock connector type. Withdraw them from the coil by releasing the tab at the bottom of the connector.
6   Remove the retaining bolt(s) holding the coil bracket to the cylinder head or intake manifold.
7   Remove the coil from the coil bracket by loosening the clamp bolt.
8   Installation is the reverse of removal; however, if equipped with electronic-type ignition (late 1974 on), apply a thin layer of silicone grease to the inside of the coil-to-distributor high tension lead (see Section 1 for more information).

9   Distributor – inspection and servicing

Refer to Chapter 1 for inspection and servicing procedures for the distributor and its components.

10   Distributor – removal and installation

Removal
1   Disconnect the negative battery cable and remove the air cleaner and related hoses (V-8 engines only).
2   Release the spring clips or hold-down screws and remove the distributor cap. Secure the cap out of the way. Disconnect the vacuum hose(s) leading to the advance chamber on the side of the distributor.
3   Crank the engine until the rotor points to the number one cylinder terminal (marked on the distributor cap) and the pointer on the crankshaft is at the TDC mark (see *Ignition timing* in Chapter 1 if necessary).
4   Scribe a mark on the distributor body and the intake manifold (V-8 engines) or engine block (6-cylinder engines) to indicate the position of the rotor and distributor body. The distributor must be re-installed in this exact same position – so take care marking it.
5   Remove the clamp bolt and clamp from the distributor base.
6   Disconnect the primary ignition wire from points-type distributors or remove the wiring harness connector on electronic ignition distributors.
7   Lift the distributor out of the engine. In most cases the hexagonal oil pump drive will stay in the oil pump and in the engine. If it pulls up with the distributor, make sure you don't drop it into the engine. If the distributor seems hard to remove, pull on the body gently as it is made of aluminum and can be easily damaged. **Note:** *Do not rotate the engine while the distributor is removed.*

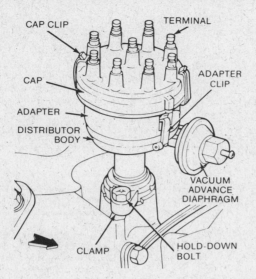

Fig. 5.3 Breakerless electronic distributor and external components (Sec 10)

Installation

8　Installation is the reverse of removal. Make sure you get the marks on the body, and the block or manifold aligned before installing the distributor cap. Time the engine as described in Chapter 1.

9　If the engine was rotated while the distributor was out or if it is being assembled after major work, the following steps will enable you to install the distributor correctly.

10　Remove the number one spark plug. Hold your finger over the hole and manually crank the engine until compression pressure is felt. Rotate the engine until the timing pointer at the crankshaft points to top dead center (TDC).

11　Install the distributor in the block with the rotor pointing at the number one spark plug terminal of the distributor cap. If the vehicle is equipped with factory electronic ignition, align the armature spokes.

12　If the distributor will not fully engage, it may be necessary to crank the engine over with the starter after the distributor drive gear is engaged to allow the oil pump intermediate shaft to seat in the bottom of the distributor. If you have to do this, crank the engine back to the compression stroke TDC position for the number one cylinder and make sure all of the marks line up.

13　Install the remaining items in Steps 1 through 6 in reverse order and time the engine with a stroboscopic timing light as described in Chapter 1.

11　Charging system – general information

The electrical charging system is used to replenish the battery voltage which is drained from the use of accessories and the running requirements of the engine's ignition system. An alternator provides electrical power and is driven by a V-belt and pulley drive system. It is generally located on the right side of the engine in varying positions depending on vehicle accessories. Maintenance of the drivebelt tension, along with battery terminal service are the two primary maintenance items in the charging system. Details are provided in Chapter 1. The charging output is regulated by an external regulator mounted on the fender well or radiator support. The regulator is connected to the alternator through the use of a wiring loom utilizing quick-release connectors. The system is protected from circuit overloading through the use of fusible links and the alternator is connected to the system with heavy gauge wire. A charge indicator light or gauge is provided. Circuit diagrams for the charging system are provided at the end of Chapter 10.

12　Charging system – check

1　If a malfunction occurs in the charging circuit, don't automatically assume the alternator is causing the problem. First check the following items:

a)　Check the drivebelt tension and condition (see Chapter 1). Replace it if it's worn or deteriorated.

b)　Make sure the alternator mounting and adjustment bolts are tight.

c)　Inspect the alternator wiring harness and the connectors at the alternator and voltage regulator. They must be in good condition and tight.

d)　Check the fusible link (if equipped) located between the starter solenoid and the alternator. If it's burned, determine the cause, repair the circuit and replace the link (the vehicle won't start and/or the accessories won't work if the fusible link blows). Sometimes a fusible link may look good, but still be bad. If in doubt, remove it and check it for continuity.

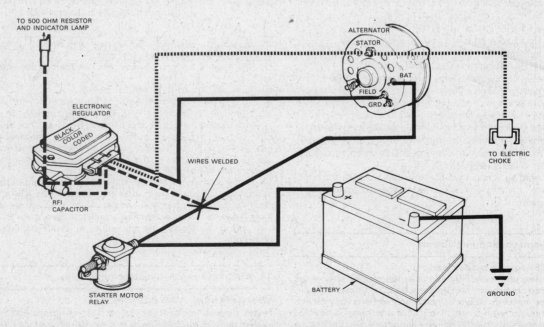

Fig. 5.4 Charging system with electronic regulator and warning lamp indicator – 1979 shown (Sec 11)

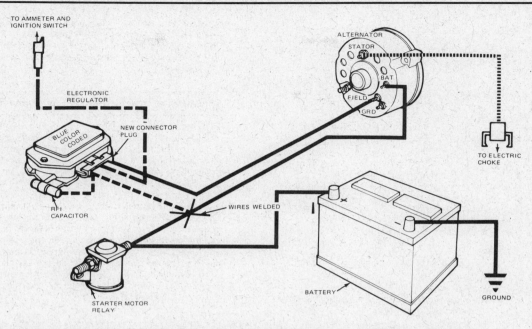

Fig. 5.5 Charging system with electronic regulator and ammeter gauge – 1979 shown (Sec 11)

e) Start the engine and check the alternator for abnormal noises (a shrieking or squealing sound indicates a bad bearing).

f) Check the specific gravity of the battery electrolyte. If it's low, charge the battery (doesn't apply to maintenance free batteries).

g) Make sure the battery is fully charged (one bad cell in a battery can cause overcharging by the alternator).

h) Disconnect the battery cables (negative first, then positive). Inspect the battery posts and the cable clamps for corrosion. Clean them thoroughly if necessary (see Chapter 1). Reconnect the cable to the positive terminal.

i) With the key off, connect a test light between the negative battery post and the disconnected negative cable clamp.

   1) If the test light does not come on, reattach the clamp and proceed to the next Step.

   2) If the test light comes on, there is a short (drain) in the electrical system of the vehicle. The short must be repaired before the charging system can be checked.

   3) Disconnect the alternator wiring harness.

      a) If the light goes out, the alternator is bad.

      b) If the light stays on, pull each fuse until the light goes out (this will tell you which component is shorted).

2 Using a voltmeter, check the battery voltage with the engine off. It should be approximately 12-volts.

3 Start the engine and check the battery voltage again. It should now be approximately 14 to 15-volts.

4 Turn on the headlights. The voltage should drop, and then come back up, if the charging system is working properly.

5 If the voltage reading is more than the specified charging voltage, the voltage regulator is faulty (see Section 15).

6 If the voltage reading is less than the specified voltage, the alternator diode(s), stator or rectifier may be bad or the voltage regulator may be malfunctioning.

---

13 Alternator – removal and installation

1 Disconnect the negative battery lead.

2 Carefully note the terminal connections at the rear or side of the alternator and disconnect them. Most connections will have a retaining nut and washer on them, however some connections may have a plastic snap-fit connector with a retaining clip. If a terminal is covered by a slip-on plastic cover, be careful when pulling the cover back so as not to damage the terminal or connector.

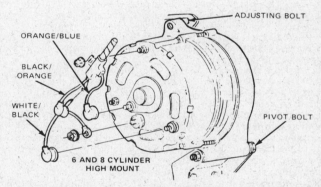

Fig. 5.6 Typical rear terminal type alternator with wire harness connections (Secs 13 and 14)

3 Loosen the alternator adjustment arm bolt.

4 Loosen the alternator pivot bolt.

5 Pivot the alternator to allow the drivebelt to be removed from the pulleys.

6 Remove the belt(s) from the pulley.

7 Remove the adjustment arm bolt and pivot the arm out of the way.

8 Remove the pivot bolt and spacer and carefully lift the alternator up and out of the engine compartment. Be careful not to drop or jar the alternator in any way as this can damage the delicate electronic internal parts. **Note:** *If purchasing a new or rebuilt alternator, take the original one with you to the dealer or parts store so the two can be compared side-by-side.*

9 Installation is the reverse of removal. Be careful when connecting all terminals at the rear or side of the alternator. Make sure they are clean, tight and all terminal ends are tight on the wires. If you find any loose terminal ends, make sure you install new ones to the wiring, as any arcing or shorting at the wires or terminals can damage the alternator.

---

14 Alternator brush – replacement

Rear terminal type alternator

Note: *Internal replacement parts for alternators may not be readily available in your area. Check into availability before proceeding.*

1 Remove the alternator as described in Section 13.

2   Scribe a line across the length of the alternator housing to ensure correct reassembly.
3   Remove the housing through-bolts and the nuts and insulators from the rear housing. Make a careful note of all insulator locations.
4   Withdraw the rear housing section from the stator, rotor and front housing assembly.
5   Remove the brushes and springs from the brush holder assembly which is located inside the rear housing.
6   Check the length of the brushes against the wear dimensions given in Sepcifications at the beginning of the Chapter and replace with new ones if necessary.
7   Install the springs and brushes into the holder assembly and retain them in place by inserting a piece of stiff wire through the rear housing and brush terminal insulator. Make sure enough wire protrudes through the rear housing so it may be withdrawn at a later stage.
8   Install the rear housing rotor and front housing assembly to the stator, making sure the scribed marks are aligned.
9   Install the housing through-bolts and rear end insulators and nuts but do not tighten at this time.
10 Carefully extract the piece of wire from the rear housing and check that the brushes are seated on the slip ring. Tighten the through-bolts and rear housing nuts.
11 Install the alternator as described in Section 13.

Side terminal type alternator
12 Remove the alternator as described in Section 13 and scribe a mark on both end housings and the stator for ease of reassembly.
13 Remove the through-bolts and separate the front housing and rotor from the rear housing and stator. Be careful that you do not separate the rear housing and stator.
14 Use a soldering iron to unsolder and disengage the brush holder from the rear housing. Remove the brushes and springs from the brush holders.
15 Remove the two brush holder attaching screws and lift the brush holder from the rear housing.
16 Remove any sealing compound from the brush holder and rear housing.
17 Inspect the brushes for damage and check their dimensions against Specifications. If they are out of specification, replace them with new ones.
18 To reassemble, install the springs and brushes in the brush holders, inserting a piece of stiff wire to hold them in place.
19 Place the brush holder in position to the rear housing, using the wire to retract the brushes through the hole in the rear housing.
20 Install the brush holder attaching screws and push the holder toward the shaft opening as you tighten the screws. **Caution:** *The rectifier can be overheated and damaged if the soldering is not done quickly.* Press the brush holder lead onto the rectifier lead and solder in place.
21 Place the rotor and front housing in position in the stator and rear housing. After aligning the scribe marks, install the through-bolts.
22 Turn the fan and pulley to check for binding in the alternator.
23 Withdraw the wire which is retracting the brushes and seal the hole with waterproof cement.

15   Regulator – removal and installation

1   Remove the negative battery terminal from the battery.
2   Locate the voltage regulator. It will usually be positioned on the radiator wall or the fender well near the front of the vehicle.
3   Push the two tabs on either side of the quick-release clip retaining the wiring loom to the regulator. Pull the quick-release clip straight out from the side of the regulator.
4   Remove the two regulator retaining screws. Notice that one screw will locate the ground wire terminal.
5   Remove the regulator.
6   Installation is the reverse of removal. Make sure you get the wiring clip positioned firmly onto the regulator terminals and that both clips click into place.

16   Starting system – general information

The starting system consists of an electric starter motor with an integral positive engagement drive, the battery, a starter switch

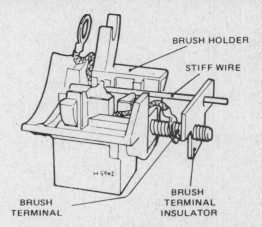

Fig. 5.7 Method of retracting brushes prior to installing on rear terminal alternator (Sec 14)

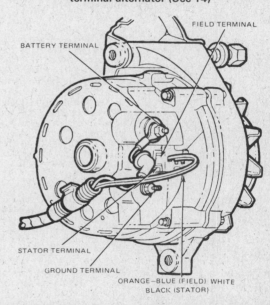

Fig. 5.8 Typical side terminal type alternator with wire harness connections (Secs 13 and 14)

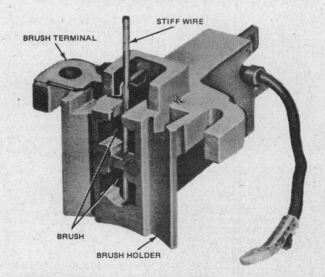

Fig. 5.9 Method of retracting brushes prior to installing brush holder on side terminal alternator (Sec 14)

CARBON DEPOSITS

Symptoms: Dry sooty deposits indicate a rich mixture or weak ignition. Causes misfiring, hard starting and hesitation.

Recommendation: Check for a clogged air cleaner, high float level, sticky choke and worn ignition points. Use a spark plug with a longer core nose for greater anti-fouling protection.

OIL DEPOSITS

Symptoms: Oily coating caused by poor oil control. Oil is leaking past worn valve guides or piston rings into the combustion chamber. Causes hard starting, misfiring and hesition.

Recommendation: Correct the mechanical condition with necessary repairs and install new plugs.

TOO HOT

Symptoms: Blistered, white insulator, eroded electrode and absence of deposits. Results in shortened plug life.

Recommendation: Check for the correct plug heat range, over-advanced ignition timing, lean fuel mixture, intake manifold vacuum leaks and sticking valves. Check the coolant level and make sure the radiator is not clogged.

PREIGNITION

Symptoms: Melted electrodes. Insulators are white, but may be dirty due to misfiring or flying debris in the combustion chamber. Can lead to engine damage.

Recommendation: Check for the correct plug heat range, over-advanced ignition timing, lean fuel mixture, clogged cooling system and lack of lubrication.

HIGH SPEED GLAZING

Symptoms: Insulator has yellowish, glazed appearance. Indicates that combustion chamber temperatures have risen suddenly during hard acceleration. Normal deposits melt to form a conductive coating. Causes misfiring at high speeds.

Recommendation: Install new plugs. Consider using a colder plug if driving habits warrant.

GAP BRIDGING

Symptoms: Combustion deposits lodge between the electrodes. Heavy deposits accumulate and bridge the electrode gap. The plug ceases to fire, resulting in a dead cylinder.

Recommendation: Locate the faulty plug and remove the deposits from between the electrodes.

NORMAL

Symptoms: Brown to grayish-tan color and slight electrode wear. Correct heat range for engine and operating conditions.

Recommendation: When new spark plugs are installed, replace with plugs of the same heat range.

ASH DEPOSITS

Symptoms: Light brown deposits encrusted on the side or center electrodes or both. Derived from oil and/or fuel additives. Excessive amounts may mask the spark, causing misfiring and hesitation during acceleration.

Recommendation: If excessive deposits accumulate over a short time or low mileage, install new valve guide seals to prevent seepage of oil into the combustion chambers. Also try changing gasoline brands.

WORN

Symptoms: Rounded electrodes with a small amount of deposits on the firing end. Normal color. Causes hard starting in damp or cold weather and poor fuel economy.

Recommendation: Replace with new plugs of the same heat range.

DETONATION

Symptoms: Insulators may be cracked or chipped. Improper gap setting techniques can also result in a fractured insulator tip. Can lead to piston damage.

Recommendation: Make sure the fuel anti-knock values meet engine requirements. Use care when setting the gaps on new plugs. Avoid lugging the engine.

SPLASHED DEPOSITS

Symptoms: After long periods of misfiring, deposits can loosen when normal combustion temperature is restored by an overdue tune-up. At high speeds, deposits flake off the piston and are thrown against the hot insulator, causing misfiring.

Recommendation: Replace the plugs with new ones or clean and reinstall the originals.

MECHANICAL DAMAGE

Symptoms: May be caused by a foreign object in the combustion chamber or the piston striking an incorrect reach (too long) plug. Causes a dead cylinder and could result in piston damage.

Recommendation: Remove the foreign object from the engine and/or install the correct reach plug.

5

located in the cab of the vehicle, a Neutral start switch (automatic transmission equipped vehicles only) a starter solenoid and wiring looms connecting these components.

When the ignition switch is turned to the Start position, the starter solenoid is energized through the starter control circuit. The solenoid then connects battery voltage to the starter motor.

Vehicles with an automatic transmission have a Neutral start switch in the starter control circuit which prevents operation of the starter if the selector lever is not in the N or P position.

When the starter is energized by the battery, current flows to the grounded field coil and operates the magnetic switch which drives the starter drive plunger forward to engage the flywheel ring gear.

When the drive plunger reaches its travel, the field coil grounding contacts open and the starter motor contacts engage, allowing the starter to turn.

A special holding coil is used to maintain the starter drive shoe in its fully-seated position while the starter is turning the engine.

When the battery voltage is released from the starter, a retracting spring withdraws the starter drive pinion from the flywheel and the motor contact is broken.

17 Starter – checking in vehicle

If the starter motor does not rotate when the starter switch is activated, check that the transmission selector lever is in N or P (automatic transmission vehicles only).

Check that the battery is well-charged and that all cables at the battery, starter solenoid and starter are tight and free of corrosion.

If the motor spins but the engine is not cranking, the starter drive is defective and the starter motor will have to be removed for drive replacement.

If the switch does not operate the starter at all but the drive can be heard engaging the flywheel with a loud "click", then the fault lies in the motor activating contacts within the motor itself. The motor will have to be removed and replaced or overhauled.

If the starter motor cranks the engine at an abnormally slow speed, ensure that the battery is fully charged and all terminal connections are tight. It is also necessary to check that the engine oil viscosity is not too thick and the resistance is not due to a mechanical problem within the engine.

A voltmeter connected to the starter motor terminal of the solenoid (positive) and to the ground (negative) will show the voltage being sent to the starter. If the voltage is adequate and the starter still turns slowly, the resistance is in the starter and the starter should be replaced or overhauled.

If a fault has been definitely traced to the starter, the original unit can be simply replaced by a rebuilt or new starter (Section 18) or the original starter can be overhauled (Section 19).

18 Starter – removal and installation

1   Disconnect the negative battery cable.
2   Disconnect the feed wire connecting the starter solenoid to the starter at the starter.
3   Remove the retaining bolts securing the starter to the bellhousing.
4   Pull the starter out of the bellhousing and lower it from the vehicle.
5   Installation is the reverse of removal. When inserting the starter into its opening of the bellhousing make sure it is situated squarely and the mating faces are flush. Tighten the retaining bolts to the proper Specification.

19 Starter brush – replacement

Note: *The starter assembly must be removed from the vehicle before the brushes can be replaced. Before attempting to replace the brushes in the starter make sure the problem you are having is related to the brushes. Oftentimes loose connections, poor battery condition or*

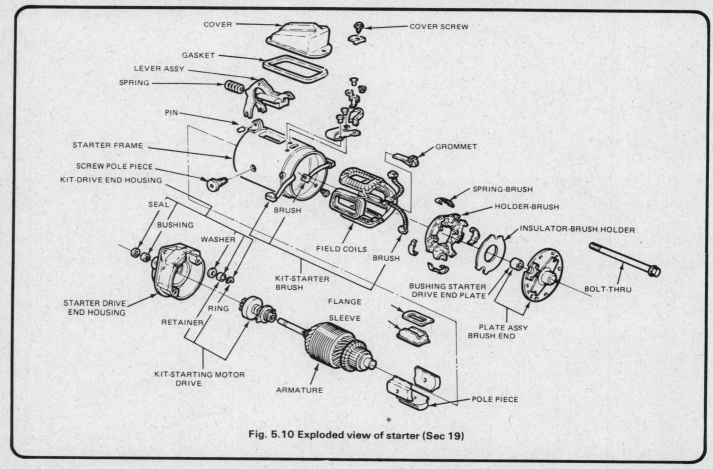

Fig. 5.10 Exploded view of starter (Sec 19)

wiring problems are a more likely cause of no start or poor starting conditions. Check on the availability of internal replacement parts before proceeding.

1   Remove the starter from the vehicle (Section 18).
2   Remove the two through-bolts from the starter frame.
3   Pull the brush end plate along with the brush springs and brushes from the holder.
4   Remove the ground brush retaining screws from the frame. Remove the brushes from the frame.
5   Cut the insulated brush leads from the field coils as close to the field connection point as possible.
6   Inspect the plastic brush holder for any signs of cracks or broken mounting pads. If these conditions exist, replace the plastic brush holder.
7   Place the new insulated field brush lead onto the field coil connection.
8   Crimp the clip provided with the brushes to hold the brush lead to the connection.
9   Using a low-heat soldering gun (300 Watts), solder the lead, clip and connection together using rosin-core solder.
10   Install the ground brush leads to the frame with the retaining screws.
11   Install the brush holder and insert the brushes into the holder.
12   Install the brush springs. Notice that the positive brush leads are positioned in their respective slots in the brush holder to prevent any chance of grounding the brushes.
13   Install the brush end plate in place. Make sure the end plate insulator is positioned correctly on the end plate.
14   Install the through-bolt to the starter frame and tighten to the correct torque Specification.
15   A battery can be used to check the starter by connecting a heavy cable such as jumper cables to the positive and negative battery posts.
16   Connect the ground lead to the starter.
17   Secure the starter in soft jaws of a vise or other similar clamping device.
18   Momentarily contact the starter connection with the positive cable from the battery.
19   The starter should spin and the solenoid drive should engage the gear in a forward position when this connection is completed.
20   If the starter operates correctly, install the starter in the vehicle as described in the previous Section.

20 Starter solenoid — removal and installation

1   Disconnect the negative battery cable followed by the positive cable from the battery.
2   Disconnect the positive battery cable and feed cable from the terminal on the starter solenoid. Mark them to prevent mix-ups during installation.
3   Disconnect the starter feed wire from the opposite feed terminal on the starter solenoid. Mark the feed wire as above.
4   Disconnect the two starter solenoid triggering wires from the top posts on the solenoid. Make sure you mark or indicate these wires as they can be cross-connected and damage the electrical system.
5   Remove the two starter solenoid-to-fender well retaining bolts.
6   Remove the starter solenoid.
7   Before installing the new or replacement solenoid, use a wire brush to carefully clean the mounting surface on the fender well for better grounding capability.
8   Install the starter solenoid to the fender well using the retaining bolts and tighten them securely. **Note**: *Use care when tightening these bolts as they are self-threading and can easily be stripped in the mounting hole.*
9   Reconnect all wires to their original positions.

5

Chapter 6 Emission control systems

Contents

Specifications

Torque specifications

	ft-lb
EGR valve-to-carburetor spacer or intake manifold	12 to 18
Thermactor pump pulley-to-hub	130 to 180 (in-lb)
Thermactor adjusting arm-to-pump	25 to 35
Thermactor pump pivot bolt	22 to 32

1 General information

In order to meet US Federal anti-pollution laws, vehicles are equipped with a variety of emission control systems, depending on the models and the states in which they are sold.

Since the emissions systems control so many of the engine's functions, driveability and fuel consumption, as well as conformance to the law, can be affected should any problems develop. Therefore, it is very important that the emissions systems be kept operating at peak efficiency.

This Chapter will describe all of the systems which may be installed in order to cover all models.

The Emission Control Information label located under the hood contains information important to properly maintaining the emissions control systems as well as for keeping the vehicle correctly tuned.

2 Positive crankcase ventilation (PCV) system – general information

The positive crankcase ventilation system is a closed recirculating system which is designed to prevent engine crankcase fumes from escaping into the atmosphere through the engine oil filler cap. The crankcase control system regulates these blow-by vapors by circulating them back into the intake manifold where they are burned with the incoming fuel and air mixture.

The air source for the crankcase ventilation system is in the carburetor air cleaner. Air passes through a filter located in the air cleaner to a hose connecting the air cleaner to the oil filler cap. The oil filler cap is sealed at the opening to prevent the entrance of outside air. From the oil filler cap the air flows into the rocker arm chamber, down past the pushrods and into the crankcase. The air then circulates from the crankcase up into another section of the rocker arm chamber. The air and crankcase gases then enter a spring-loaded regulator valve (PCV valve) that controls the amount of flow as operating conditions vary. Some engines have a fixed orifice PCV valve that meters a steady flow of gas mixture regardless of the extent of engine blow-by gases. In either case, the air and gas mixture is routed to the intake manifold through the crankcase vent hose tube and fittings. This process goes on continuously while the engine is running.

The main thing to pay attention to for correct operation of this system is proper maintenance of the hoses, fittings and valve. To check the system, see the instructions in Chapter 1.

3 Evaporative Emission Control (EEC) system – description and maintenance

1 The EEC system is designed to limit the emission of fuel vapors to the atmosphere. It consists of the fuel tank, pressure and vacuum sensitive fuel filler cap, a restrictor bleed orifice, charcoal canister and associated connecting hoses.

2 When the fuel tank is filled, vapors are discharged to the atmosphere through the filler tube and the space between the inner fuel filler tube and the outer neck. With this system, when fuel covers

VEHICLE EMISSION CONTROL INFORMATION

ENGINE FAMILY 2.3 CATALYST EGR/AIR (1CEF)			
ENGINE DISPLACEMENT CID 140 CID			
SPARK PLUG AGRF-52 GAP .032-.036			
DISTRIBUTOR—BREAKERLESS			
CHOKE HOUSING	MAN/TRANS 1 LEAN		
NOTCH SETTING	AUTO/TRANS 1 LEAN		
TRANSMISSION	AUTO NEUTRAL	AUTO DRIVE	MANUAL NEUTRAL
IGNITION TIMING	10° BTDC		6° BTDC
TIMING RPM	550		550
CURB IDLE A/C		750	900
RPM NO A/C		750	900
IDLE MIXTURE—ARTIFICIAL ENRICHMENT			
RPM GAIN		20-60	20-60
RPM RESET		40	40

THIS VEHICLE REQUIRES MAINTENANCE SCHEDULE "B"

MAKE ALL ADJUSTMENTS WITH ENGINE AT NORMAL OPERATING TEMPERATURES, A/C AND HEADLIGHTS OFF

CURB IDLE—ADJUST WITH THROTTLE SOLENOID POSITIONER ENERGIZED, THERMACTOR AIR ON, ALL VACUUM HOSES CONNECTED AND AIR CLEANER IN POSITION. WHENEVER CURB IDLE IS RESET, CHECK AND ADJUST THE DECEL VALVE ACCORDING TO THE SERVICE MANUAL

IDLE MIXTURE—PRESET AT THE FACTORY. DO NOT REMOVE THE LIMITER CAP(S). CONSULT THE SERVICE MANUAL FOR DESCRIPTION OF ARTIFICIAL ENRICHMENT METHOD OF IDLE MIXTURE ADJUSTMENT TO BE USED ONLY DURING TUNE-UPS AND MAJOR CARBURETOR REPAIRS. IDLE MIXTURE MUST BE MEASURED WITH THERMACTOR AIR OFF

INITIAL TIMING—ADJUST WITH HOSES DISCONNECTED AND PLUGGED AT THE DISTRIBUTOR

REFERENCE TO A/C, THROTTLE SOLENOID, THERMACTOR AIR AND DECEL VALVE APPLICABLE ONLY IF THE ENGINE IS SO EQUIPPED. CONSULT SERVICE PUBLICATIONS FOR FURTHER INSTRUCTIONS ON TIMING AND IDLE SET

THIS VEHICLE CONFORMS TO U.S.E.P.A. REGULATIONS APPLICABLE TO 1975 MODEL YEAR NEW MOTOR VEHICLES. THIS VEHICLE ALSO CONFORMS TO THE STATE OF CALIFORNIA CERTIFICATION STANDARDS APPLICABLE TO 1975 MODEL YEAR NEW MOTOR VEHICLES.

FORD MOTOR COMPANY

921

D52E-9C485-DA

Fig. 6.1 Typical Emission Control Information label located under the hood (Sec 1)

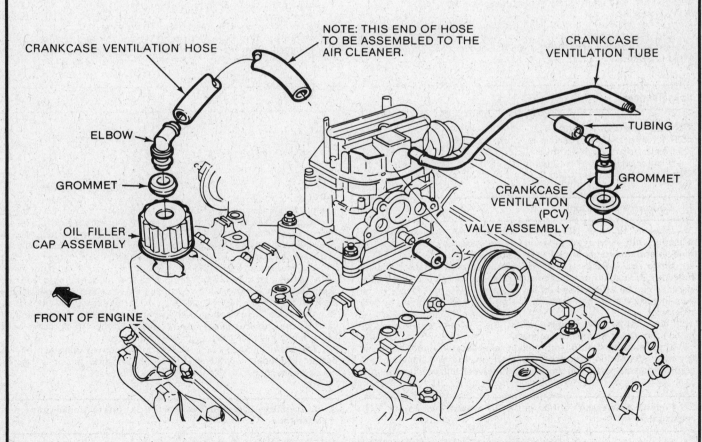

Fig. 6.2 Typical PCV system component layout (V8 engine shown) (Sec 2)

6

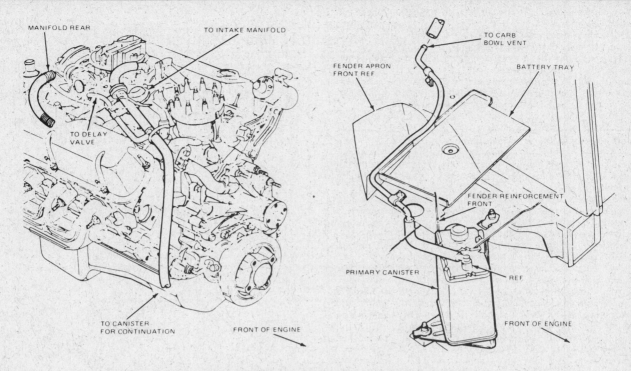

Fig. 6.3 Typical evaporative emission system component layout (Sec 3)

the filler control tube, vapors can no longer escape because a vapor lock is created by the orifice.

3   When thermal expansion occurs in the fuel tank, vapor is forced through the orifice and is drawn into the carburetor as soon as the engine is started.

4   Some models incorporate a fuel bowl vent valve to direct vapors which collect in the carburetor back into the charcoal canister when the engine is off.

5   Maintenance consists of inspecting the system for leaks and checking the purge valve of the canister for proper operation.

6   Further inspection and maintenance of this system is described in Chapter 1.

4   Exhaust gas recirculation (EGR) system – description and maintenance

1   An exhaust gas recirculation system is used on most engines to control NOx emissions. In this system, a vacuum operated EGR flow control valve regulates the flow of exhaust gas picked up from the crossover pipe or exhaust manifold to the inlet located in the intake manifold or below the carburetor.

2   A vacuum signal originating from the EGR vacuum port on the carburetor operates the EGR valve. This signal is often modified by valves located in series for delay purposes.

3   A coolant temperature sending valve is included in the vacuum circuit to prevent exhaust gas recirculation until the temperature of the coolant reaches a pre-set minimum.

4   A more complicated system, using two series valves, is sometimes needed to provide control of exhaust gas recirculation for engine operation at high speed cruise conditions. The second valve, called the high speed modulator valve, controls the exhaust gas recirculation flow as a function of vehicle speed.

5   Exhaust gas recirculation system malfunctions usually show up in the form of a poorly or non-operating EGR valve. This situation is easily observed by accelerating a warm engine and watching the operation of the EGR valve. If the EGR valve does not operate, a check of the supply line will determine whether the valve is stuck or inoperative or if vacuum is not reaching the valve. If the valve proves to be stuck or inoperative, it should be removed and cleaned or replaced. If the vacuum signal to the valve is not present or restricted, a thorough

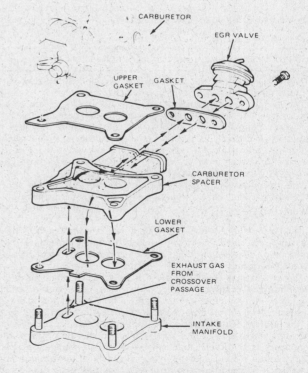

Fig. 6.4 Typical EGR valve installation (Sec 4)

systematic check of the EGR system hoses and valves will have to be performed by an experienced technician.

6   The EGR valve can be removed for cleaning and inspection. If the valve is found to be damaged, corroded or extremely dirty it should be replaced with a new unit of the proper type.

7   If the valve is to be cleaned, check that the orifice in the body is clear of obstructions and be careful not to enlarge it while cleaning.

The internal deposits can be removed with a small power-driven rotary wire brush. Deposits around the valve stem can be removed using a steel blade approximately 0.029 in (0.7 mm) thick in a sawing motion around the stem shoulder at both sides of the disc. Clean the cavity and passages in the main body, ensuring that the poppet valve wobbles axially before reassembly.

8   Some models use a tapered stem-type EGR valve which must be cleaned with sandblasting equipment. Others are of the exposed stem type which can be cleaned with a wire brush.

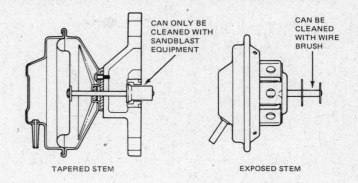

Fig. 6.5 Alternative types of EGR valves (Sec 4)

5   Spark control systems – description and testing

1   Numerous vacuum control systems are used to modify spark advance and retard (if equipped) through the vacuum diaphragms in the distributor.

2   These systems are fairly complex and have many valves, relays, amplifiers and other components built into them. Each vehicle will have a system peculiar to the model year, geographic region and gross vehicle weight rating. A schematic diagram located on the underside of the hood will detail the exact components and vacuum line routing of the particular system on your vehicle.

3   The two main checks that you can perform on this system are for vacuum leaks and operation of the diaphragms.

4   Visually check all vacuum hoses for cracks, splits or hardening. Next, remove the distributor cap and rotor. Apply a vacuum to the distributor advance port (and retard port, if so equipped) and see if the breaker point or relay plate inside of the distributor moves. The plate should move opposite the distributor direction of rotation when vacuum is applied to the advance port and should move in the direction of rotation if vacuum is applied to the retard port (if so equipped).

5   Checking of the temperature relays, delay valves or other modifiers of the spark timing systems is beyond the scope of the average home mechanic. Consult an expert if you suspect that you have other problems within the spark advance system.

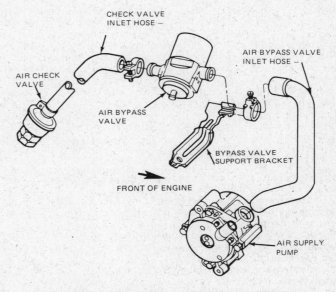

Fig. 6.6 Thermactor system components (Sec 6)

6   Thermactor system – general information

The Thermactor air injection system is installed on certain engines to reduce carbon monoxide and hydrocarbon emissions.

The system accomplishes this by injecting fresh air into the hot exhaust stream directly after it leaves the combustion chamber.

A pump supplies air under pressure to the exhaust port near the exhaust valve through internal or external passages in the cylinder head or exhaust manifold. The fresh air combines with the hot exhaust gases and promotes further combustion which converts these gases into carbon dioxide and water.

The major components of the Thermactor system are the air pump, distribution hoses, by-pass valve, idle vacuum valve, check valve and various clamps and brackets for mounting these components.

The air pump is driven by a belt from the crankshaft pulley. The by-pass valve diverts air from the system to the atmosphere during conditions of deceleration, or high exhaust gas flow. This valve also prevents backfiring.

The exhaust gas check valve is a one-way valve which permits air to flow into the exhaust port or prevents the reverse flow of exhaust gases into the manifold or air pump. The Thermactor idle valve controls the amount of time that the Thermactor pump air is cycled into the system. During periods of prolonged idle, cold running or decleration, this valve diverts air pump air to the atmosphere. Most components of the Thermactor system, although relatively simple in design, require testing equipment not available to the average home mechanic. If a visual inspection reveals any problems outside of a broken hose, inoperative pump or malfunctioning check valve, the system will have to be diagnosed and serviced by an expert.

7   Choke control system – general information

Various choke system modifiers include an electrically assisted heating coil, choke pull-down and choke pull-off assemblies. These systems are installed on carburetors to improve emissions control by matching engine fuel requirements at all temperatures more exactly and to improve driveability. All of these controls use some sort of engine coolant temperature sensing device. Various control units are mounted which monitor the engine temperature and the choke position to provide precise choke action relative to the engine's ability to run on lean fuel mixtures as it warms up. In addition, various linkages are connected between the modifying units and the choke linkage. All of these systems modify the choke openings by lessening the time that the choke plate is closed. Information on the Emission Control Information label and from a suitable carburetor rebuild kit can be used to service and adjust these choke modifying devices.

8   Temperature controlled air cleaner – description and testing

1   The air cleaner temperature control system is used to keep the air entering the carburetor at a warm and consistent temperature. The carburetor can then be calibrated much leaner for emissions reduction, improvement of warm-up and better driveability.

2   Two air flow circuits are used. They are controlled by various intake manifold vacuum and temperature sensing valves. A vacuum motor, which operates a heat control door in the air cleaner snorkel, is activated by these two previously mentioned circuits. When the under hood temperature is cold, air is drawn through the shroud which fits over the exhaust manifold, up through the heated air pipe and into the air cleaner. This provides warm air for the carburetor, resulting in better driveability and faster warm-up.

3   As the under hood temperature rises, the heat control door will be closed by the vacuum motor and the air that enters the air cleaner will be drawn through the cold air snorkel or duct. This provides a consistent intake air temperature.

4   Checking of this system should be done while the engine is cold. If the engine is equipped with a cold air inlet snorkel duct, remove the clamp and the duct so that you can view the heat control door through the air inlet snorkel. Start the vehicle and see if the heat control door moves down to allow hot air from the manifold shroud to enter the air cleaner. As the vehicle warms up, the vacuum motor should pull the heat control door open, eventually allowing cool air to enter through the snorkel. If this does not occur, any one of the many components in the system could be defective. Any obvious conditions such as a stuck air inlet door, faulty vacuum motor or leaking heat tube or hoses should be corrected by component replacement.

9   Deceleration and idle throttle control system – description and testing

1   A deceleration valve is used to provide an enriched mixture when the engine is coasting with the throttle closed. This valve is installed on the intake manifold and has two vacuum outlet ports. When the engine decelerates, a vacuum is applied to the control port and the valve opens, allowing additional fuel to enter the intake manifold. A throttle positioner solenoid, similar in appearance to a flashlight battery, is also used on the throttle shaft. This device, which is electrically powered, holds the throttle in a position to achieve a satisfactory idle speed while the engine is running. When the engine is turned off, and the electrical power to this solenoid is shut off, the throttle closes, preventing dieseling and the accompanying excessive emissions.

2   Some vehicles with automatic transmissions are equipped with a dashpot, which slows the throttle closing speed when decelerating. As the throttle is released by the driver, the dashpot plunger extends and slowly allows the throttle shaft to return to its normal idle position.

3   The deceleration valve cannot be checked without sophisticated equipment. The deceleration dashpot can be checked by opening the throttle with the engine shut off and allowing the throttle to return to its idle position. The dashpot should slow the throttle return speed.

4   The throttle positioner can be checked by observing the plunger at the solenoid when the ignition key is turned to On. It will be necessary to open the throttle slightly to allow the plunger to extend when the ignition switch is turned On. After the power is cut off by turning the ignition switch Off, the plunger should retract. If the plunger is inoperative, check for voltage at the solenoid terminal before replacing the assembly itself. If voltage is present and the plunger does not work, the assembly should be replaced with a new one.

10   Exhaust heat control system – description and maintenance

1   The exhaust heat control valve system found on Ford-built vehicles uses a valve which is controlled by a thermostat or vacuum. This valve is mounted between the exhaust manifold and one branch of the exhaust pipe. The system routes hot exhaust gases to the intake manifold heat riser during cold engine operation. Warming of this heat riser helps to eliminate any condensation of fuel on the cold surfaces of the intake system and provides better evaporation and distribution of the air-fuel mixture. The net result of this is better driveability and faster warm-up.

2   To check the operation of the thermostatic control valve located at the junction between the exhaust manifold and the exhaust head pipe, start the vehicle (it must be completely cool) and see if the exhaust valve closes and slowly starts to open as the engine warms up. If this action does not occur, manually check the valve for free movement. If the valve is stuck, it can sometimes be loosened with penetrating oil. It should be lubricated periodically with graphite grease.

3   If the valve is stuck and cannot be loosened up, it should be replaced as it can cause an over-heated engine if it is stuck shut or an engine that warms up too slowly if it is stuck open. No other service operations are required on this system. Occasionally the exhaust passage within the intake manifold becomes clogged. If this situation

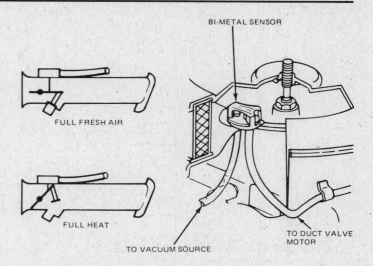

FULL FRESH AIR

FULL HEAT

BI-METAL SENSOR

TO VACUUM SOURCE

TO DUCT VALVE MOTOR

Fig. 6.7 Temperature controlled air cleaner operation (Sec 8)

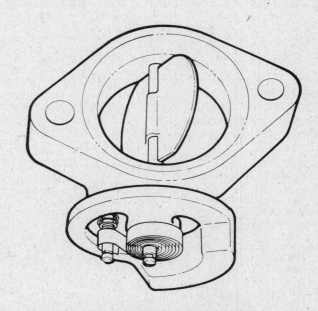

Fig. 6.8 Typical exhaust heat control valve (temperature controlled) (Sec 10)

occurs, the exhaust gas will not flow correctly and improper heating of the cold mixture is the result. The only way to alleviate this situation is to remove the manifold and have the manifold cleaned in a caustic bath (a procedure normally known as hot-tanking).

11   Catalytic converter – general information

The catalytic converter is generally located in the exhaust system, upstream of the muffler. The converter consists of a ceramic honey-comb-like core housed in a stainless steel pipe. The core is coated with a platinum and paladium catalyst which converts unburned carbon monoxide and hydrocarbons into carbon dioxide and water by a chemical reaction.

No special maintenance of the converter is required, but it can be damaged by the use of leaded fuels, engine misfire, excessive richness of the fuel mixture, incorrect operation of the Thermactor system or running out of gasoline.

Chapter 7A Clutch

Contents

Specifications

Torque specifications

	ft-lb
Pressure plate-to-flywheel bolts	15 to 20

1   Clutch – general information

The clutch assembly consists of a single dry plate 3-finger type pressure plate, a single friction disc and a bearing which pushes on the fingers of the pressure plate to release the clutch.

The pressure plate contains several springs which provide continuous surface pressure on the plate face for clutch engagement.

The clutch disc is splined and slides freely along the input shaft of the transmission. Friction lining material is riveted to the clutch disc. It has a spring-cushioned hub to absorb driveline shocks and provide smooth engagement.

The clutch is operated by a series of levers and cranks known as the linkage. This linkage transfers motion at the clutch pedal into movement at the throwout bearing arm. When the clutch pedal is depressed, the throwout bearing pushes on the arms of the pressure plate assembly, which in turn pulls the pressure plate friction disc away from the lining material of the asbestos-faced disc.

When the clutch pedal is released, the pressure plate springs force the pressure plate into contact with the lining on the clutch disc. Simultaneously, the clutch disc is pushed a fraction of an inch forward on the transmission splines by the pressure of the plate, which engages the disc with the flywheel. The clutch disc becomes firmly sandwiched between the pressure plate and the engine flywheel and engine power is transferred to the transmission.

2   Clutch – adjustment

1   See Chapter 1 for clutch free-play adjustment instructions. 1973 through 1976 Broncos require clutch total travel adjustment as described below.

2   Measure the total travel of the pedal from the resting point to the floor. If the total travel is less than $6\frac{3}{4}$ inches or more than 7 inches, adjustment must be made.

3   Loosen the locknut on the bolt holding the pedal bumper under the dash. Move the bumper up or down until the correct travel is achieved. Tighten the nut on the pedal bumper bolt.

3'   Clutch – inspection (in vehicle)

1   Some vehicles are equipped with a two-piece clutch housing. If your vehicle is so equipped, a removable cover can be found on the bottom of the clutch housing when viewed from under the vehicle. Be sure to raise and support the vehicle securely before attempting this procedure.

2   Remove the bolts retaining the cover to the bottom of the clutch housing. Remove the cover.

3   Inspect the clutch assembly from the bottom of the housing. Look for any broken, loose or worn parts. If no apparent defect is revealed, compare the thickness of the clutch disc (sandwiched between the pressure plate and the flywheel) to a new disc. This comparison will give you some idea of the clutch disc life left in your vehicle and the need for replacement.

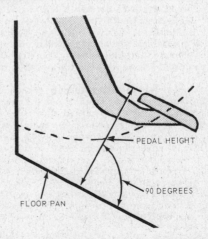

Fig. 7.1 Measuring Bronco clutch pedal total travel (Sec 2)

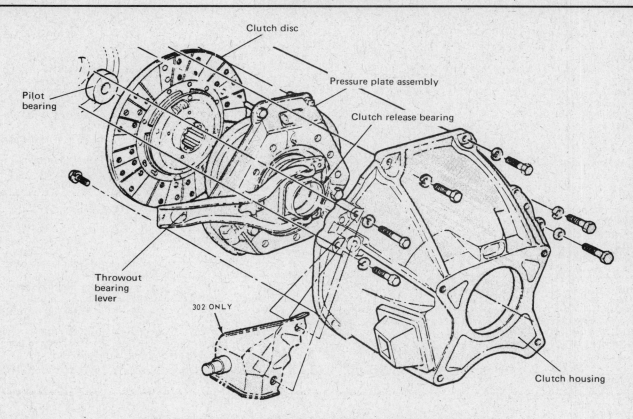

Fig. 7.2 Typical clutch assembly components – exploded view (Sec 4)

4   Clutch assembly – removal, inspection and installation

Removal

1   Remove the transmission (and transfer case if 4 x 4) as described in Chapter 7B.

2   Disconnect the clutch throwout bearing lever retracting spring and pushrod from the lever.

3   Remove the clutch housing inspection plate (if so equipped).

4   Remove the starter.

5   Remove the clutch housing retaining bolts from the rear of the engine. Remove the clutch housing. You can remove the clutch assembly on two-piece clutch housings from the bottom and leave the housing attached. However, it is usually easier to remove the entire housing because of reduced working room.

6   Scribe an indexing mark on the flywheel and pressure plate assembly if the pressure plate is to be reinstalled. This ensures that the two components are installed in the same position relative to each other.

7   Working in a pattern around the circumference of the pressure plate assembly, loosen the retaining bolts a little at a time. This procedure is necessary to prevent warpage of the pressure plate.

8   Remove the clutch throwout bearing release lever and throwout bearing if the clutch housing is not being removed. Remove the retaining bolts, pressure plate and disc.

Inspection

9   Closely check the clutch disc for glazing, cracking, warpage, the presence of oil or grease, broken hub springs or wear close to the rivets of the bonded facing. If any of these conditions exist, replace the clutch disc with a new one. Always replace the disc if a new pressure plate is being installed.

10   Check the pressure plate for any scoring, cracks, weak springs or heat marks (blue streaks on the friction surface). If any of these conditions exist, replace the pressure plate with a new one. If the clutch was chattering or rough in engagement while in operation, the clutch pressure plate and disc should be replaced.

11   Check the flywheel surface for any indications of scoring, cracks or heat marks. If these conditions exist, replace or resurface the flywheel (Section 5). Also check the pilot bearing at this time.

12   Check the clutch release bearing for roughness and excessive wear (where the surface pushes on the clutch pressure plate fingers). If any of these conditions exist, replace the release bearing assembly. It is usually a good idea to replace the release bearing any time the clutch is being serviced, as the cost is relatively small compared to the labor required to gain access to it.

Installation

13   Place the clutch disc on the flywheel with the correct side facing the flywheel. Make sure the disc is clean and free of any grease, oil or contaminates. Clean it off with an evaporative clutch and brake cleaner. Make sure the flywheel surface is clean and undamaged.

14   Position the clutch pressure plate over the disc and use a pilot tool to hold the clutch disc in correct alignment with the crankshaft axis.

15   Start the retaining bolts into the pressure plate and tighten them finger tight. Slowly begin to tighten these bolts, a little at a time, working around the circumference of the pressure plate. Tighten the bolts to the proper torque specification. Remove the clutch disc pilot tool.

16   The remainder of the installation procedure is the reverse of removal. Be sure to tighten all bolts securely.

5   Flywheel and pilot bearing – inspection and replacement

Inspection

1   Prior to inspecting the flywheel and pilot bearing, the transfer case (if 4 x 4), transmission, clutch housing and clutch assembly must be removed.

2   Visually inspect the flywheel for any signs of cracking, warpage, scoring or heat checking. If any of these conditions exist, the flywheel must be removed and replaced, or resurfaced at an automotive machine shop.

3   If the flywheel appears to be warped or has excessive runout

(indicated by high spots on the friction surface), install a dial indicator on the rear of the engine block. Hold the crankshaft forward (to take up any clearance in the crankshaft thrust bearing) and slowly turn the engine through one revolution by hand. Observe the reading on the dial indicator. If the runout exceeds the specification, replace the flywheel.

4 Carefully insert your finger into the inner race of the pilot bearing located in the center of the crankshaft flange. Check for any burrs or scoring. Rotate the bearing and feel for roughness or excessive play. If any of these conditions exist, replace the pilot bearing.

Replacement

5 Replace the flywheel as described in Chapter 2.
6 Remove the pilot bearing with a special inside puller designed for this purpose. You can purchase one from an auto parts store or they are often available from rental yards.
7 Replace the bearing using a suitable pusher tool. Always replace the bearing with the single-piece, bronze, oil impregnated bearing. If the bearing has been in stock for a long period of time, it would be a good idea to soak the bearing in 20W engine oil prior to installing it. Installation can be made easier by chilling the bearing in a freezer to shrink it enough to fit easily into the crankshaft.
8 Install the flywheel, making sure the retaining bolts are tightened to the proper torque specification.

6 Clutch linkage – removal and installation

1 The most likely source of wear in the clutch linkage is the equalizer shaft bushings.
2 To remove the shaft, jack up the front of the vehicle and support it on jackstands.

3 Disconnect the clutch release lever return spring.
4 Remove the spring retainer and washer and detach the clutch release rod from the equalizer shaft.
5 Remove the spring clip and washer from the end of the clutch relay rod and detach the rod from the equalizer shaft.
6 Remove the nuts and bolts securing the equalizer shaft mounting bracket to the side of the chassis member and slide the bracket and shaft assembly off the clutch housing mounting bracket.
7 Remove the bushings from inside the ends of the equalizer shaft and install new ones.
8 Install the equalizer shaft and clutch linkage by reversing the removal procedure.
9 Finally, adjust the clutch as described in Section 2.

7 Clutch pedal – removal and installation

1 From beneath the dash panel, remove the spring clip and disconnect the operating rod from the clutch pedal lever. Retrieve the bushing from the lever.
2 Remove the locknut securing the clutch lever to the clutch pedal shaft assembly and remove the lever.
3 Remove the shoulder bolt, bushing and locknut securing the master cylinder pushrod to the brake pedal.
4 Pull the clutch pedal and shaft out and remove them together with the brake pedal and bushing.
5 Examine the bushings and shaft and replace any worn parts.
6 Grease the shaft and bushings. Install the clutch and brake pedal assembly using the reverse of the removal procedure.
7 Finally, adjust the clutch and pedal height as described in Chapter 1.

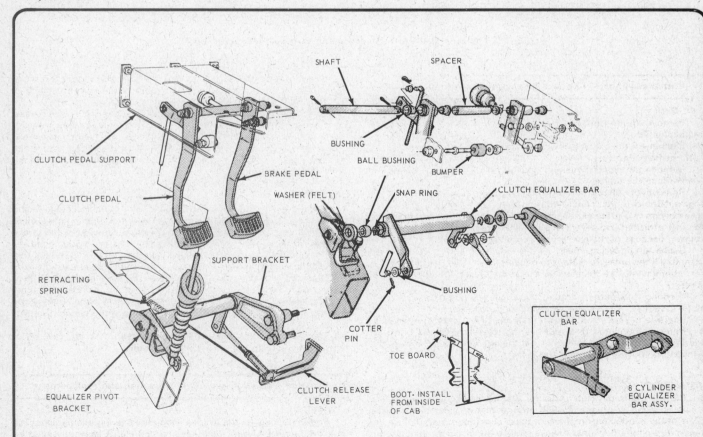

Fig. 7.3 Clutch pedal and linkage components – exploded view (Bronco shown; others similar) (Secs 6 and 7)

7A

Chapter 7B Transmission

Contents

Specifications

Torque specifications

Manual transmission	ft-lb
Linkage adjusting locknuts	18 to 23
Transmission-to-engine bolts	
3-speed	40 to 50
4-speed	35 to 45
Automatic transmission	
Linkage adjusting locknuts	12 to 18
Band adjusting screws	10
Band adjusting screw locknuts	35 to 45
Converter-to-flywheel bolts	23 to 28
Transmission-to-engine bolts	23 to 33
Oil pan-to-transmission bolts	12 to 16

8 Manual transmission – general information

Ford trucks are equipped with a 3-speed fully synchronized (except reverse gear) transmission as standard equipment.

A 4-speed transmission with a very low ratio unsynchronized first and reverse gears is a popular optional unit available with all engines except the 460 V8.

A 4-speed overdrive type transmission is available with either six cylinder or small V8 powerplants beginning with the 1978 model year.

All of these transmissions are housed in iron cases with external shift linkages except for the low-ratio 4-speed unit which comes with a floor shifter.

9 Manual transmission linkage – adjustment

1   All manual transmission shift linkages are adjusted in the same way, whether column- or floor-mounted type. The only exception is the 4-speed transmission with the tower-type stick emerging from the top of the transmission. This type of transmission has direct, non-adjustable linkage.

2   Place the transmission rods in the Neutral position. Use a $\frac{3}{16}$ inch gauge pin, for insertion into the alignment holes of the shifter. These holes can be found next to the steering column on the engine side of the firewall for 3-speed column shifted transmissions.

3   The alignment holes can be found on the three linkage arms below the shifter arm on 4-speed overdrive transmission-equipped vehicles.

4   Loosen the shift rod-to-arm retaining bolts (A and B in the accompanying illustration) on 3-speed models. Loosen the three shift arm retaining nuts at the transmission on 4-speed overdrive models.

5   Place all of the transmission arms in the Neutral position at the transmission.

6   Install the alignment pin into the holes on either type of linkage. If the linkage is out of adjustment, you may have to move one or more of the arms to get them all to line up.

7   Retighten the shift arm retaining nuts.

8   Check the linkage for correct operation.

10 Manual transmission – removal and installation

Removal

1   Drain the transmission lubricant into a suitable container. On vehicles equipped with a truck-type 4-speed transmission, remove the rubber boot, floor mat (and floor pad if necessary). On some vehicles it may be necessary to remove the seat and the transmission floor pan cover plate for clearance purposes.

2   Raise the vehicle and support it securely.

3   Disconnect the back-up light switch located on the rear of the transmission.

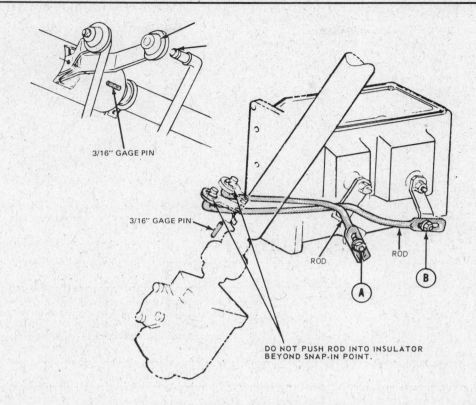

3/16" GAGE PIN

3/16" GAGE PIN

ROD

ROD

A

B

DO NOT PUSH ROD INTO INSULATOR
BEYOND SNAP-IN POINT.

Fig. 7.4 Typical transmission shift linkage adjustment details (Sec 9)

4   Remove the speedometer cable retaining bolt and remove the speedometer cable and gear assembly. Position the cable out of the way to avoid damage or contamination.

5   Disconnect the parking brake lever from its linkage and remove the cable from the crossmember.

6   Disconnect and remove the driveshaft or coupling shaft.

7   If the vehicle is a 4 x 4, remove the transfer case as described in Section 19.

8   Support the transmission with a transmission jack. Make sure the transmission is securely clamped to the jack.

9   Remove the shift linkage arms and assembly on 4-speed overdrive transmission equipped vehicles. Remove the gear shift housing on 4-speed truck transmission equipped vehicles. Remove the shift arms from vehicles equipped with a 3-speed transmission.

10 Remove the transmission rear mount retaining bolt(s) and remove the rear support crossmember (4 x 2 vehicles only). It may be necessary to raise the transmission slightly to allow the crossmember to clear the rear mount.

11 Remove the transmission retaining bolts from the rear of the clutch housing.

12 Slowly withdraw the transmission from the clutch housing, making sure you put no unnecessary pressure on the transmission input shaft. Once the input shaft has cleared the clutch housing, lower the transmission and remove it from beneath the vehicle.

Installation

13 Apply a light coating of C1AZ-19590-B lubricant or its equivalent to the clutch release lever fulcrum and fork. Apply this lubricant sparingly, as any excess will contaminate the clutch disc.

14 Secure the transmission to the transmission jack and raise it up to the level of the clutch housing face. Make sure the clutch is aligned with an alignment tool if it was removed and replaced. Make sure the clutch throwout bearing and hub are properly positioned on the release lever fork.

15 Install guide studs in the retaining holes of the clutch housing. These studs can be purchased or made from bolts (with the correct thread) about two to three inches long. Cut the head off the bolts and

grind off any burrs. A slot cut into the end of the bolt will enable you to thread it in and out with a screwdriver.

16 Raise the transmission and start the holes of the transmission face onto the guide studs. Slide the transmission forward on the studs until the input shaft engages the clutch splines. Continue to slide the transmission forward until the face of the case mates with the clutch housing face.

17 Remove the guide studs and install the retaining bolts.

18 The remaining steps are basically the reverse of removal.

11 Automatic transmission – general information

The automatic transmission is a popular option in Ford trucks and Broncos. This transmission is constructed in two main subassemblies.

a) A three-element hydrokinetic torque converter coupling, capable of torque multiplication at an infinitely variable ratio.

b) A torque/speed responsive and hydraulically-operated planetary gearbox providing three forward gears and one in reverse.

Due to the complexity of the automatic transmission unit, if performance is not up to standard, or overhaul is necessary, you should leave this job for a dealership or shop with the knowledge and special equipment for diagnosis and overhaul. The content of the following Sections is therefore confined to supplying general information and any service information and instructions that can be used by the owner.

The automatic transmission often installed in pick-ups and Broncos is manufactured by Ford and is either the C4 type for 302 engines and inline six cylinder engines or the C6 type for all other V8 engines. The FMX transmission was installed on some F350 vehicles until 1978. All of these transmissions are very similar, but some differences, are described in the following Sections. A transmission oil cooler is standard and ensures cooler operation of the transmission. A vacuum connection to the intake manifold provides smoother and more consistent downshifts under load.

7B

12 Automatic transmission – removal and installation

Note: *If the transmission being removed is in a 4 x 4 vehicle (except 1973 through 1976 F250 models), the transfer case must be removed prior to transmission removal.*

1　If possible, raise the vehicle on a hoist or place it over an inspection pit. Alternatively, raise the vehicle to obtain the maximum possible amount of working room underneath. Support it securely.

2　Place a large drain pan beneath the transmission oil pan. Then, working from the rear, loosen the attaching bolts and allow the fluid to drain. Remove all the bolts except the two front ones to drain as much fluid as possible, then temporarily install two bolts at the rear to hold it in place.

3　Remove the torque converter drain plug access cover and adapter plate bolts from the lower end of the converter housing.

4　Remove the flywheel-to-converter attaching nuts, turning the engine as necessary to gain access by means of a socket on the crankshaft pulley attaching bolt. **Caution**: *Do not rotate the engine backwards.*

5　Rotate the engine until the converter drain plug is accessible, then remove the plug, catching the fluid in the drain pan. Install and tighten the drain plug afterwards.

6　Remove the driveshaft by referring to Chapter 8. Place a polyethylene bag over the end of the transmission to prevent dirt from entering.

7　Detach the speedometer cable from the extension housing by removing the hold-down bolt and withdrawing the cable and gear.

8　Disconnect the shift rod at the transmission manual lever and the kickdown rod at the transmission downshift lever.

9　Remove the starter motor retaining bolts and position the motor out of the way.

10　Disconnect the Neutral safety switch leads.

11　Disconnect the vacuum lines from the vacuum modulator.

12　Position a transmission jack beneath the transmission and raise it so that it *just* begins to lift the transmission weight.

13　Remove the bolt and nut securing the rear mount to the crossmember.

14　Remove the four bolts securing the crossmember to the chassis members. Raise the transmission slightly on the jack and remove the crossmember.

15　Disconnect the inlet pipe flange(s) from the exhaust manifold(s).

16　Support the rear of the engine using a jack or suitable blocks of wood.

17　Disconnect the oil cooler lines at the transmission and plug them

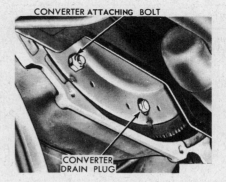

Fig. 7.5 Typical converter attaching bolt and converter drain plug locations (Sec 12)

to prevent dirt from entering. Use a fitting wrench to avoid rounding off the nuts.

18　Remove the lower converter housing-to-engine bolts and the transmission filler tube.

19　Make sure that the transmission is securely mounted on the jack, then remove the two upper converter housing-to-engine bolts.

20　Carefully move the transmission to the rear and down and away from the vehicle.

21　Installing the transmission is essentially the reverse of the removal procedure, but the following points should be noted:

a)　Rotate the converter to align the bolt drive lugs and drain plug with their holes in the flywheel.

b)　Do not allow the transmission to take a 'nose-down' attitude as the converter will move forward and disengage from the pump gear.

c)　When installing the flywheel-to-converter bolts, position the flywheel so the pilot hole is in the six o'clock position. First, install one bolt through the pilot hole and torque tighten it, followed by the remaining bolts. Do not attempt to install it in any other way.

d)　Adjust the kickdown rod and selector linkage as necessary.

e)　When the vehicle has been lowered to the ground, add sufficient fluid to bring the level up to the Max mark on the dipstick with the engine not running. Having done this, check and top-up the fluid level, as described in Chapter 1.

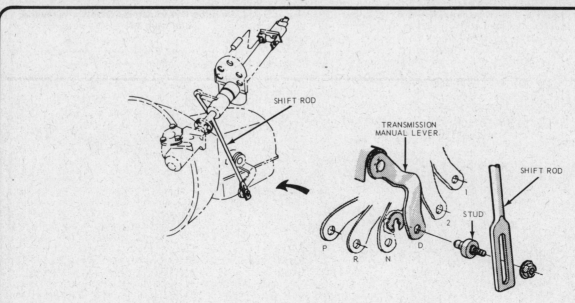

Fig. 7.6 Typical automatic transmission shift linkage adjustment details (Sec 13)

13 Automatic transmission – linkage adjustment

1   With the engine stopped, place the transmission shift lever in the Drive position and hold it against the 'D' stop by tying an eight pound weight to the end of the lever.
2   Loosen the shift rod locknut on the side of the transmission.
3   Place the selector lever on the side of the transmission in the Drive position by moving the lever to the rear as far as possible and then forward two clicks.
4   Hold the shift rod and lever stationary and tighten the nut to the correct torque specification.
5   Remove the weight from the shift lever and check the operation of all gear positions.

14 Automatic transmission – band adjustment

C-6 transmission and C-4 intermediate band
1   The intermediate or front band is used to hold the sun gear stationary to produce second gear. If it is not correctly adjusted, there will be noticeable slip during the first-to-second gear shift or on the downshift from high to second gear. The first symptoms of these problems will be very sluggish shifts instead of the usual crisp action.
2   To adjust the intermediate band, loosen and remove the locknut on the band adjustment screw (located on the left-hand side of the

case). Tighten the adjusting screw to the specified torque, then loosen it exactly $1\frac{1}{2}$ turns (C-4 $1\frac{3}{4}$ turns). Install a new locknut and tighten it to the specified torque while holding the adjustment screw to keep it from turning.

C-4 low and reverse band
3   The low and reverse band is operational when the selector lever is placed in the Low or Reverse positions. If it is not correctly adjusted, there will be no drive with the selector lever in Reverse (also associated with no engine braking with the selector lever in Low).
4   To adjust this band, remove the adjusting screw locknut from the screw (located on the right-hand side of the case). Tighten the adjusting screw to the specified torque, then loosen it exactly three turns. Install a new locknut and tighten it to the specified torque while holding the adjusting screw to keep it from turning.

15 Automatic transmission – downshift adjustment

1   Disconnect the downshift rod return spring and hold the throttle shaft lever in the wide open position.
2   Hold the kick-down rod against the through detent stop.
3   Loosen the locknut and adjust the downshift screw so as to provide a clearance between the screw top and the throttle shaft lever tab of 0.01 to 0.08 in (0.25 to 2.03 mm).
4   Reconnect the downshift rod return spring.

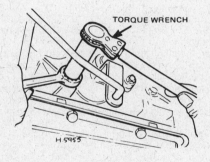

Fig. 7.7 Adjusting the C-4 (intermediate) and C-6 transmission bands (Sec 14)

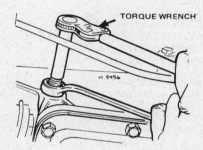

Fig. 7.8 Adjusting the C-4 transmission low and reverse band (Sec 14)

7B

Chapter 7C Transfer case

Contents

Specifications

Torque specifications

	ft-lb
Transfer case (New Process 205)	
Idler shaft locknut	200
Idler shaft cover bolts	18
Front output shaft front bearing retainer bolts	30
Front output shaft yoke locknut	200
Rear output shaft bearing retainer bolts	30
Rear output shaft yoke locknut	150
Power take-off cover bolts	15
Front output shaft rear bearing retainer bolts	30
Drain and filler plugs	30
Transfer case-to-frame bolts	130
Transfer case-to-adapter bolts	25
Adapter mount bolts	25
Transfer case bracket-to-frame nuts (upper)	30
Transfer case bracket-to-frame nuts (lower)	65
Adapter-to-transmission bolts (manual transmission)	22
Adapter-to-transmission bolts (automatic transmission)	35
Transfer case control mounting bolt	100
Transfer case (New Process 203)	
Adapter-to-transfer case attaching bolts	38
Adapter-to-transmission attaching bolts	40
Transfer case bracket-to-frame nuts (upper)	50
Transfer case bracket-to-frame nuts (lower)	65
Transfer case shift lever attaching nuts	25
Transfer case shift lever rod swivel locknuts	50
Transfer case shift lever locking arm nut	150
Skid plate attaching bolt retaining nuts	45
Crossmember support attaching bolt retaining nut	45
Adapter mount bolts	25
Intermediate case-to-range box bolts	30
Front output bearing retainer bolts	30
Output shaft yoke nuts	150
Front output rear bearing retainer bolts	30
Differential assembly screws	45
Rear output shaft housing	30
Poppet ball retainer nut	15
Power take-off cover bolts	15
Front input bearing retainer bolts	20
Filler plug	25

Transfer case (Dana 20)

Shift rail set screws	15
Front output shaft rear cover bolts	30
Front output shaft front bearing retainer	30
Front output shaft yoke locknut	150
Intermediate shaft lockplate bolt	15
Rear output shaft housing bolts	30
Rear output shaft yoke locknuts	150
Case bottom cover bolts	15
Transfer case-to-adapter bolts	45
Transfer case-to-frame bolts	45
Adapter mount bolts	25

16 Transfer case – general description

Ford trucks and Broncos use a manually-shifted transfer case containing either constant mesh helical gears (part-time 4-wheel drive) or a constant drive special Hy-vo chain (full-time 4-wheel drive). In 1973 only, a one-speed constant mesh transfer case was offered on F100 trucks only. All transfer cases are shifted from inside the passenger compartment with a shift lever connected to linkage attached to the transfer case. 1973 through 1976 F250 trucks and certain early Bronco model transfer cases have power fed to them through a separate driveshaft exiting from the rear of the transmission while all other vehicles are connected directly to the back of the transmission. Full-time four-wheel drive transfer cases have a differential built into their internal gears to compensate for the difference in road speed of the front and rear wheels, while part-time systems do not have this feature. The part-time systems are designed to be used in 4-wheel drive only on soft or loose road surfaces where the differences in road speed are taken up by the 'give' in the traction compound.

17 Fluid level – checking

For a description of checking fluid levels in the transmission or transfer case, refer to Chapter 1.

18 Transfer case and manual transmission – fluid change

Refer to Chapter 1, Routine maintenance, for the transfer case/manual transmission fluid change procedure.

19 Transfer case – removal and installation

1   Raise the vehicle on a lift. If this facility is not available, raise the vehicle with ramps, stands or jacks. Ensure that the vehicle is safely supported before starting work.
2   Drain the transfer case oil into a suitable container.
3   Disconnect the speedometer drive cable and the reverse light switch.
4   Using a suitable cradle or stand, support the transfer case and loosen and remove the bolts attaching the transfer case to the transmission adapter.
5   Remove the crossmember supports and, where necessary, remove the skid plate.
6   Disconnect the front and rear driveshafts and tie them up out of the way of the work area (see Chapter 8 for further information).
7   Disconnect the shift lever rod from the shift rail link. *On full-time four wheel drive models,* disconnect the shift levers at the transfer case.
8   Carefully move the transfer case to the rear, until the input shaft clears the adapter, and lower the assembly from the vehicle.
9   Installation is a reverse of removal but ensure all nuts and bolts are tightened to the specified torque. Be sure to fill the transfer case with the correct grade and quantity of oil.

20 Transfer case (New Process 205) – overhaul

Disassembly
Rear output shaft and yoke assembly
1   Loosen the rear output shaft yoke nut.

2   Loosen and remove the rear output shaft housing bolts and remove the housing and retainer assembly from the transfer case.
3   Remove the yoke retaining nut and the yoke from the shaft, then remove the shaft assembly from the housing.
4   Using a suitable pair of pliers, remove and discard the housing bearing snap-ring.
5   At the inside of the housing, remove the thrust washer and washer pin.
6   Remove the tanged bronze washer.
7   Remove the gear needle bearings (32 per row), spacer and second row of needle bearings.
8   Remove the tanged bronze washer from the shaft.
9   Remove the pilot rollers (15), retainer ring and washer.
10 Remove the oil seal retainer, ball bearings, speedometer gear and spacer. If required, the housing bearing may be pressed or tapped out.
11 Remove the oil seal from the retainer.
12 Discard all gaskets and place the parts in a safe place for inspection later on.

Front output shaft assembly
13 Loosen and remove the yoke locknut, lift away the washer and remove the yoke.
14 Loosen and remove the front bearing attaching bolts and remove the retainer.
15 Remove the front output shaft rear bearing retainer attaching bolts.
16 Using a soft-faced hammer, tap the end of the output shaft to remove the shaft, the gear assembly and the rear bearing retainer from the case.
17 Remove the sliding clutch from the output high gear, washer and bearing which will have remained in the case.
18 Using suitable snap-ring pliers, remove the gear retaining ring from the shaft.
19 Remove the thrust washer and pin from the shaft.
20 Slide off the front output low gear, needle bearings (32 per row) and the spacer from the front output shaft.
21 If it is necessary to replace the front output shaft rear bearing, support the cover and press the bearing from the cover. A new bearing is simply pressed into the case, but make sure that the force is applied to the outside diameter of the bearing only.

Shift rail and fork assemblies
22 Remove the two poppet nuts on top of the transfer case; lift out the two poppet springs and, using a magnet, remove the poppet balls.
23 Using a $\frac{1}{4}$ inch diameter punch, drive the cup plugs into the case.
24 Position both shift rails in Neutral. Using a long narrow punch, drive the shift fork pins through the shift rails into the case.
25 Remove the clevis pins and the shift rail connector link.
26 Remove the shift rails, upper (range) rail first, followed by the lower (4-wheel) rail.
27 Remove the shift forks and the sliding clutch from the case.
28 Remove the front output high gear, washer and bearing from the case.
29 Remove the shift rail cup plugs and pins that were driven into the case earlier.

Input shaft assembly
30 Using suitable snap-ring pliers, remove the snap-ring in front of the bearing. Use a soft-faced hammer to tap the shaft out of the rear of the case. Tap the bearing out of the front of the case.
31 Tip the case onto the power take off face and remove the two interlock pins from inside the case.

7C

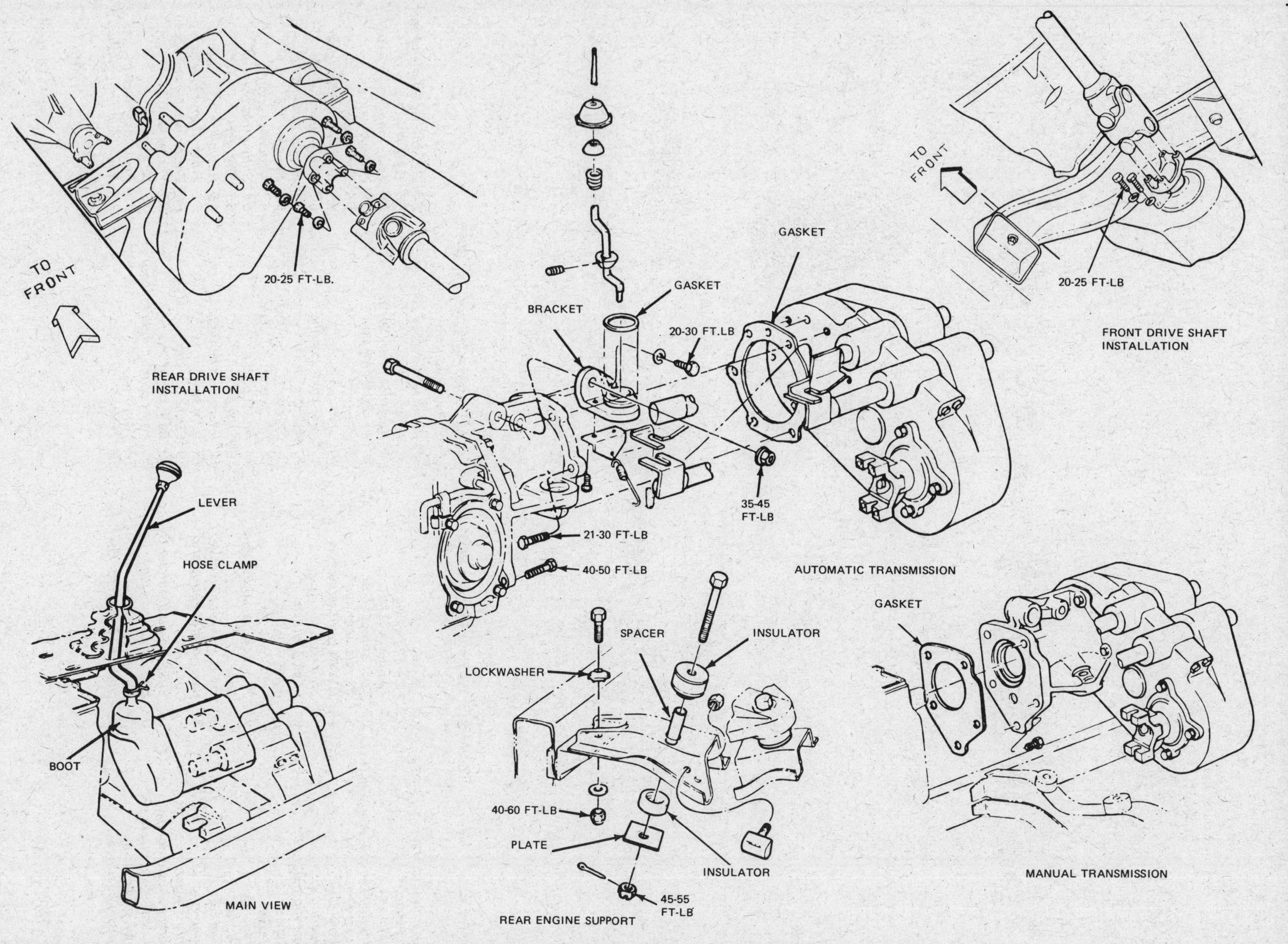

FRONT DRIVE SHAFT
INSTALLATION

20-25 FT-LB

TO
FRONT

MANUAL TRANSMISSION

GASKET

AUTOMATIC TRANSMISSION

GASKET

35-45
FT-LB

GASKET

20-30 FT-LB

INSULATOR

INSULATOR

SPACER

45-55
FT-LB

BRACKET

21-30 FT-LB

40-50 FT-LB

LOCKWASHER

40-60 FT-LB

PLATE

REAR ENGINE SUPPORT

20-25 FT-LB.

REAR DRIVE SHAFT
INSTALLATION

TO
FRONT

LEVER

HOSE CLAMP

BOOT

MAIN VIEW

Fig. 7.9 Typical transfer case mounting details (Sec 19)

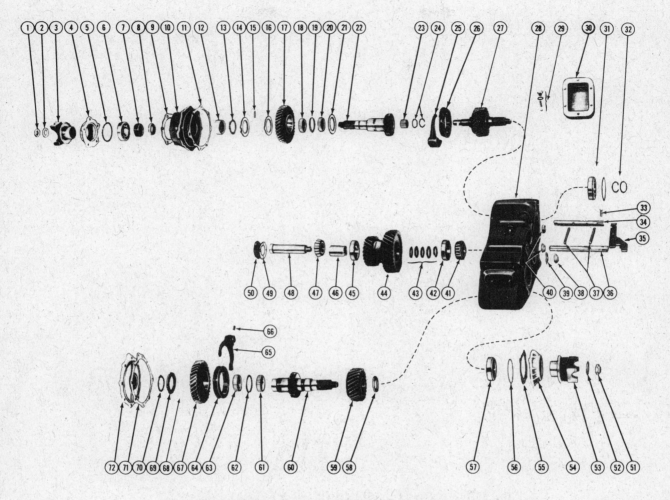

Fig. 7.10 New Process 205 transfer case – exploded view (Sec 20)

1	Rear output shaft locknut
2	Washer
3	Yoke
4	Bearing retainer and seal assembly
5	Snap-ring
6	Bearing
7	Speedometer gear
8	Spacer
9	Gasket
10	Housing
11	Gasket
12	Bearing
13	Snap-ring
14	Thrust washer
15	Thrust washer lock pin
16	Thrust washer (tanged)
17	Low-speed gear
18	Needle bearings
19	Spacer
20	Needle bearngs
21	Tanged washer
22	Rear output shaft
23	Needle bearings
24	Washer and retainer
25	Shift fork
26	Sliding clutch
27	Input shaft
28	Transfer case
29	Poppet plug, spring and ball
30	P.T.O. gasket and cover
31	Input shaft bearing and snap-ring
32	Snap-ring and rubber O-ring
33	Shift link clevis pin
34	Range shift rail
35	Shift rail connector link
36	Front wheel drive shift rail
37	Interlock pins
38	Rear idler locknut
39	Washer
40	Shift rail seals
41	Idler shaft bearing
42	Bearing cup
43	Shims
44	Idler gear
45	Bearing cup
46	Spacer
47	Idler shaft bearing
48	Idler shaft
49	Cover gasket
50	Rear cover
51	Front output shaft locknut
52	Washer
53	Yoke
54	Bearing retainer and seat
55	Gasket
56	Snap-ring
57	Front bearing
58	Thrust washer
59	Front wheel high gear
60	Front output shaft
61	Needle bearings
62	Spacer
63	Needle bearing
64	Sliding clutch gear
65	Shift fork
66	Roll pin
67	Front output low gear
68	Thrust washer lock pin
69	Thrust washer
70	Snap-ring
71	Rear cover gasket
72	Rear cover and bearing

7C

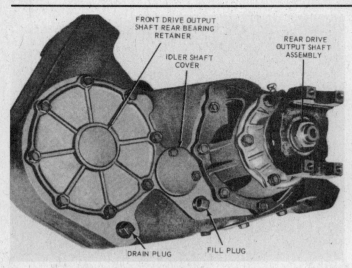

Fig. 7.11 Rear view of New Process 205 transfer case (Sec 20)

Fig. 7.12 Front view of New Process 205 transfer case (Sec 20)

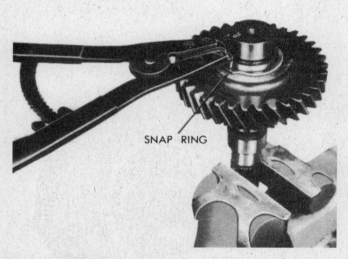

Fig. 7.13 Removing the front output shaft gear retaining snap-ring (Sec 20)

Fig. 7.14   Removing the front output shaft

Idler gear

32 Loosen and remove the idler gear shaft nut.

33 Loosen and remove the idler shaft rear cover attaching bolts. Lift away the cover.

34 Using a soft-faced hammer and a drift, drive out the idler gear shaft.

35 Remove the idler gear through the output shaft bore.

36 Remove the two bearing cups from the idler gear.

Cleaning and inspection

37 Thoroughly wash all components in solvent. Carefully inspect all bearings and rollers for evidence of chipping, cracks or worn spots. Inspect the shaft splines and gears for chipped teeth or excessive wear, replacing work or damaged components as necessary.

Reassembly
Idler gear

38 If previously removed, press the two bearing cups into the idler gear. Use suitably-sized tubing or pipe to perform this operation.

39 Assemble the two bearing cones, spacer, shims and idler gear on the shaft and check the endplay of the idler gear. It should be 0.000 to 0.002 inch. Adjust or replace shims as necessary to achieve this endplay.

40 Install the idler gear assembly into the transfer case. Install the large end first, through the front output bore.

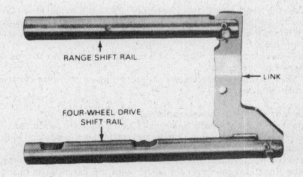

Fig. 7.15   Shift rails (Sec 20)

Fig. 7.16 Pressing a bearing cup into the idler gear with a drift (Sec 20)

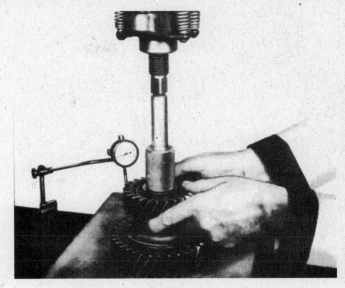

Fig. 7.17 Checking the idler gear endplay (Sec 20)

IDLER GEAR

Fig. 7.18 Installing the idler gear assembly (Sec 20)

41 Install the idler shaft from the large bore side and drive it through the idler gear with a soft-faced hammer.
42 Install the washer and a new locknut on the idler shaft. Check for the correct endplay again and make sure the assembly rotates freely. Tighten the idler shaft locknut to the specified torque.
43 Install the idler shaft cover (with a new gasket) in position and screw in the attaching bolts. Tighten the bolts to the specified torque. **Note:** *The flat on the idler shaft cover must be located next to the front output shaft rear cover.*

Shift rail and fork assemblies
44 Press the two rail seals, metal lip out, into the case.
45 Install the interlock pins through the large bore or power take off cover opening.
46 Start the front output drive shift rail into its bore in the case from the back, slotted end first, with the poppet notches up.
47 Install the shift fork (long end in) into the shift rail. Push the rail, through the shift fork, into the Neutral position.
48 Install the input shaft bearing and shaft into the case.
49 Start the range rail into its bore in the case from the front with the poppet notches up.
50 Install the sliding clutch onto the shift fork. Place the assembly over the input shaft in the case. Position the fork to receive the range shift rail. Push the range shift rail through the shift fork and into the Neutral position.
51 Install new lockpins through the holes at the top of the case and drive them into the forks.
Note: *When installing the range rail lockpin, place the case on the power take off opening.*

Front output shaft and gear assembly
52 Install two rows of needle bearings (32 on each rod), separated by the spacer in the front low output gear and retain them in position with a sufficient amount of grease.
53 Place the front output shaft, spline end down, in a soft jaw vise. Install the front low gear over the shaft, with the clutch gear facing down, and install the thrust washer pin and thrust washer. Hold these components in position with a new snap-ring. **Note:** *The snap-ring should be positioned so that the opening is opposite the pin.*
54 Position the front wheel high gear and washer into the case. Install the sliding clutch in the shift fork, then put the fork and rail in the front wheel drive (4-Hi) position, with the clutch teeth in mesh with the teeth of the front wheel high gear.

7C

IDLER SHAFT

Fig. 7.19 Installing the idler shaft (Sec 20)

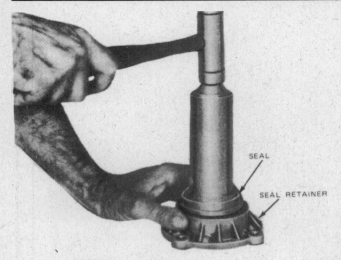

Fig. 7.20   Installing seal

Fig. 7.21 Installing the rear output shaft housing bearing (Sec 20)

Fig. 7.22 Installing the rear output shaft, spacer and speedometer gear (Sec 20)

55 Align the washer, high gear and the sliding clutch with the bearing bore. Insert the front output shaft and low gear assembly through the high gear assembly.
56 Using a piece of tubing, install a new seal in the bearing retainer. Install the front output bearing and retainer into the case.
57 Clean and grease the rollers in the front output rear bearing retainer. Install the retainer, using a new gasket. Apply thread sealant to the attaching bolts before tightening them to the specified torque.
58 Install the front output yoke, washer and locknut. Tighten the locknut to the specified torque.

Rear output shaft assembly
59 Install two rows of needle bearings (32 in each row), separated by the spacer, into the output low gear. Use grease to retain the needle bearings in position.
60 Install the thrust washer onto the rear output shaft, tang down in clutch gear groove. Install the output low gear onto the shaft with the clutch teeth facing down.
61 Install the thrust washer over the gear with the tab pointing up and away from the gear. Install the washer pin and also the large thrust washer over the shaft and pin. Rotate the washer until the tab fits into the slot approximately 90° away from the pin. Install the snap-ring to retain these components and check the endplay. It should be 0.002 to 0.027 inch.
62 Grease the pilot bore or the rear output shaft and install the needle bearings (15). Install the thrust washer and a new snap-ring.
63 Clean, grease and install a new bearing in the retainer housing.
64 Install the housing onto the output shaft assembly. Install the spacer and speedometer gear, then install the bearing.
65 Install the rear bearing retainer seal using a piece of suitable diameter tubing.
66 Install the bearing retainer assembly onto the housing with one or two gaskets, depending on the clearance. Tighten the retainer attaching bolts to the specified torque.
67 Install the yoke, washer and locknut to the output shaft. Tighten the yoke locknut to the specified torque.
68 Position the range rail in the high position and install the output shaft and retainer assembly on the transfer case.
69 Install the power take off cover and gasket.
70 Install the cup plugs at the rail pin holes.
71 Finally, install the shift rail cross link, clevis pins and lockpins.

21 Transfer case (New Process 203) – overhaul

Disassembly
1   Before attempting to disassemble the transfer case, make sure that all external surfaces are clean and free of grime. If the transfer case oil was not drained prior to removal, do it now.
2   Position the transfer case on a workbench or suitable work table.
3   Using the special tool, loosen the rear output shaft flange retaining nut. **Note:** *Tap the dust shield to the rear on the shaft (away from the bolts) to obtain the necessary clearance to remove the bolts from the flange and allow installation of the tool.*
4   Loosen and remove the bolts retaining the front output shaft front bearing retainer. Remove the bearing retainer and gasket from the transfer case.
5   With the assistance of a second person, position the assembly on suitable blocks.
6   Loosen and remove the bolts retaining the rear output shaft assembly to the transfer case and disengage the assembly from the case.
7   Carefully slide the carrier unit from the shaft. **Note:** *A 1½ to 2 inch diameter hose clamp may be installed on the input shaft at this time to prevent the loss of bearings when removing the input shaft assembly from the range box.*
8   Raise the shift rail and drive out the pin retaining the shift fork to the rail.
9   Loosen and remove the shift rail poppet ball plug. Lift out the spring and poppet ball from the case. A small magnet will simplify removal of the ball.
10 Push the shift rail down, lift up on the lockout clutch and remove the shift fork from the clutch assembly.
11 Loosen and remove the bolts retaining the front output shaft rear bearing retainer to the transfer case. Tap on the front of the shaft or

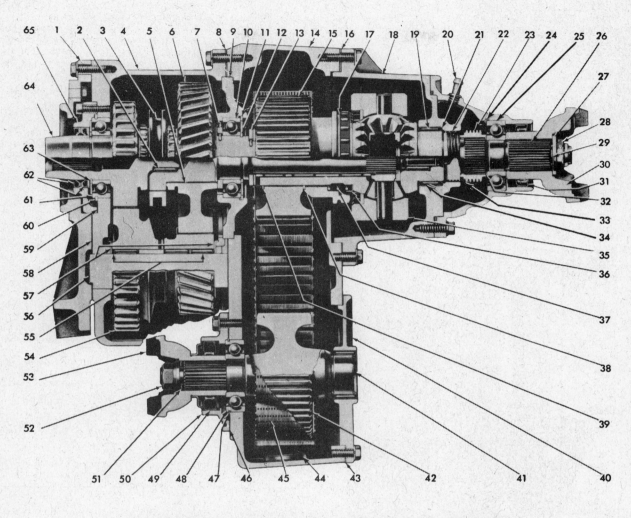

Fig. 7.23 Section view of the New Process 203 transfer case (Sec 21)

1 Adapter	14 Intermediate (chain housing)	32 Shims	48 Front output front bearing
2 Input drive gear pilot bearings	15 Drive shaft sprocket	33 Input shaft O-ring	49 Front output shaft seal
3 Range selector sliding clutch	16 Gasket	34 Input shaft pilot bearings	50 Front output bearing retainer
4 Range selector housing	17 Sliding lock clutch	35 Differential carrier assembly	51 Rubber spline seal
5 Low speed gear bushing	18 Rear output housing	36 Spring washer cup	52 Locknut
6 Low speed gear	19 Rear output front bearing	37 Lockout clutch spring	53 Front output yoke
7 Thrust washer and locating pin	20 Vent	38 Snap-ring	54 Countergear
8 Gasket	21 Oil seal	39 Snap-ring	55 Countergear spacers and bearing
9 Input bearing retainer	22 Oil pump	40 Front output rear bearing cover	56 Countergear spacers and bearing
10 Input bearing	23 Speedometer drive gear	41 Front output rear bearing	57 Countergear thrust washer
11 Bearing retaining ring	24 Bearing retainer ring	42 Front output drive sprocket	58 Gasket
12 Bearing retaining ring	25 Rear output rear bearing	43 Gasket	59 Bearing retainer gasket
13 Thrust washer, locating pin, lubricating washer, & spacer	26 Rear output shaft	44 Magnet	60 Bearing outer ring
	27 Washer	45 Drive chain	61 Input gear bearing
	28 Locknut	46 Gasket	62 Input gear seals (2)
	29 Rubber spline seal	47 Bearing outer ring	63 Bearing snap-ring
	30 Rear output yoke		64 Input gear
	31 Rear output seal		65 Input gear bearing retainer

7C

carefully pry the retainer away from the case. Remove the retainer from the shaft. Recover any roller bearings which may fall from the rear cover.

12 If it is necessary to replace the rear bearing, support the cover and press the bearing from the cover. When installing a new bearing, position it squarely and press it into the cover until it is flush with the opening.

13 From the lower side of the case, carefully pry the output shaft front bearing from its location.

14 Disengage the front output shaft from the cabin and remove the shaft from the transfer case.

15 Loosen and remove the bolts attaching the intermediate chain housing to the range box. Lift the intermediate housing from the range box.

16 Remove the chain from the intermediate housing.

17 Remove the locknut clutch, drivegear and input shaft assembly from the range box. Take care not to lose the roller bearings (see note in paragraph 7).

18 Pull up on the shift rail and disconnect the rail from the link.

19 Remove the input shaft assembly from the range box by lifting it up and away.

20 At this point the transfer case is completely disassembled into its subassemblies. Each of the subassemblies should then be dismantled, as described under *Subassembly repairs,* for cleaning and inspection.

Cleaning and inspection

Bearings: Place all bearings and rollers in cleaning solvent and allow them to remain long enough to loosen all accumulated lubricant, Inspect the bearings and rollers for evidence of chipping, cracks or worn areas. Replace any that are doubtful.

Shafts and gears: Thoroughly clean all shafts and gears. Inspect the shaft splines and bearing surfaces for signs of chipped teeth or excessive wear.

Case, cover and housings: The transfer case, cover and housings must be thoroughly cleaned and examined for cracks or damage.

Subassembly repairs

Differential carrier assembly

21 Remove the bolts from the carrier assembly and separate the carrier sections.

22 Lift the pinion gear and spider assembly from the carrier.

23 Remove the pinion thrust washers, pinion roller washers, pinion gears and roller bearings from the spider unit.

24 Clean and inspect all components, replacing worn or broken parts as necessary.

25 Begin reassembly by loading the roller bearings in the pinion gears. (132 rollers required, 33 in each pinion). Use petroleum jelly to hold them in position.

26 Install the pinion roller washer, pinion gear, roller washer and thrust washer on each leg of the spider.

27 Place the spider assembly into the front half of the carrier, with the undercut surface of the spider thrust surface facing down or toward the gear teeth.

28 Align the marks on the carrier sections and position the carrier halves together. Install the retaining bolts and tighten them to the specified torque.

Lockout clutch assembly:

29 Remove the front side gear from the input shaft assembly and remove the thrust washer, roller bearings (123) and spacers from the front side gear bore. Note the position of the spacers to simplify reassembly.

30 Using suitable snap-ring pliers, remove the snap-ring retaining the drive sprocket to clutch assembly. Slide the drive sprocket from the front side gear.

31 Remove the lower snap-ring, then remove the sliding gear, spring and spring cup washer from the front side gear.

32 Clean and inspect all components for signs of wear, replacing parts as necessary.

33 Install the spring cup washer, spring and sliding clutch gear on the front side gear.

34 Install the snap-ring that retains the sliding clutch to the front side gear.

35 Load the roller bearings (123) and spacers in the front side gear. Use petroleum jelly to hold the roller bearings in position.

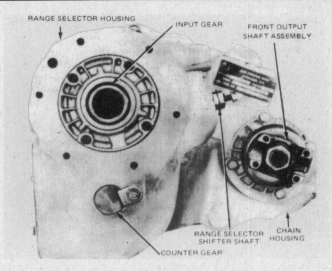

Fig. 7.24 Front view of the New Process 203 transfer case (Sec 21)

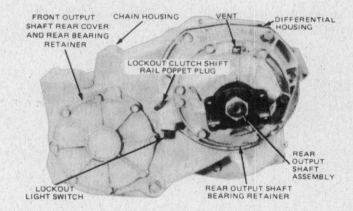

Fig. 7.25 Rear view of the New Process 203 transfer case (Sec 21)

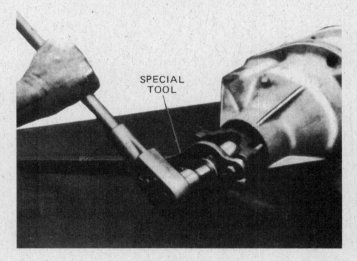

Fig. 7.26 Using a special tool to remove the rear output shaft flange nut (Sec 21)

Fig. 7.27 Removing the front output shaft front bearing retainer (Sec 21)

Fig. 7.28 Position the transfer case on wooden blocks before beginning disassembly (Sec 21)

Fig. 7.29 Removing the shaft fork roll pin (Sec 21)

36 Install the thrust washer in the gear end of the front side gear.
37 Slide the drive sprocket onto the clutch splines and install the retaining ring.

Input shaft assembly
38 Slide the thrust washer and spacer from the shaft.
39 Using snap-ring pliers, remove the snap-ring retaining the input bearing retainer assembly to the shaft and remove the bearing retainer assembly from the shaft.
40 Support the low speed gear (large gear) and tap the shaft from the gear and thrust washer.
41 Using a screwdriver, pry behind the open end of the large snap-ring, retaining the input bearing in the bearing retainer, and remove the snap-ring from the retainer. Tap the bearing from the retainer.
42 Remove the pilot roller bearings (15) from the end of the input shaft.
43 Remove and discard the O-ring from the end of the shaft.
44 Clean and inspect all components, replacing parts as necessary.
45 Begin reassembly by positioning the bearing on the retainer and tapping or pressing it into place. The ball loading slots should be toward the concave side of the retainer.
46 Install the large snap-ring to secure the bearing in the retainer. **Note:** *The snap-ring is a selective fit; to provide the tightest fit, four thicknesses (A, B, C or D) are available.*
47 Install the low speed gear onto the shaft, with the clutch end toward the gear end of the shaft.
48 Position the thrust washers on the shaft, aligning the slot in the washer with the pin in the shaft. Slide or tap the washer into position.
49 Position the input bearing retainer on the shaft and install a new snap-ring. **Note:** *The snap-ring is a selective fit. To provide the tightest fit four thicknesses (A, B, C or D) are available.*
50 Slide the spacer and thrust washer onto the shaft. Align the spacer with the location pin.
51 Install the roller bearings (15) in the end of the shaft and use a heavy grade grease to hold them in position.
52 Install a new O-ring on the end of the shaft.

Disassembly of range selector housing (range box)
Removing the shifter assembly
53 Remove the poppet plate spring, plug and gasket.
54 Disengage the sliding clutch gear from the input gear and remove the clutch fork and sliding gear from the case.
55 Loosen and remove the shift lever assembly retaining nut and the upper shift lever from the shifter shaft.
56 Remove the shift lever snap-ring and lower lever.
57 Push the shifter shaft assembly down and remove the lockout clutch connector link. **Note:** *The long end of the connector link engages the poppet plate.*
58 Remove the shifter shaft assembly from the case and separate the inner and outer shifter shafts. Remove and discard the O-rings.
59 Inspect the poppet plate for damage. If it is necessary to remove the poppet plate, drive the pivot shaft from the case. The poppet plate and spring should be removed from the bottom of the case.

Removing the input gear assembly
60 Remove the input gear bearing retainer and seal assembly.
61 Remove the large snap-ring from the bearing outer diameter.
62 Tap the input gear and bearing from the case.
63 Remove the snap-ring retaining the input shaft bearing to the shaft and remove the bearing from the input gear.

Removing the cluster gear assembly
64 From the intermediate case side, remove the countershaft from the cluster gear and the case. Use a bar of suitable diameter for this. Remove the cluster gear assembly from the case. **Note:** *Recover the roller bearings (72) from the gearcase and shaft.*
65 Remove the cluster gear thrust washers from the case.
66 Clean and inspect all components, replacing parts as necessary.

Reassembly of range selector housing
Installing the countergear assembly
67 Using a heavy grade grease, install the roller bearings (72) and spacers in the cluster gear bore. **Note:** *A special tool may be required for this operation.*
68 Using a heavy grade grease, position the countershaft thrust

7C

washers in the case. Engage the tabs on the washers with a slot in the case thrust surface.

69 Position the cluster gear assembly in the case and install the countershaft, through the front face of the range box, into the gear assembly. The countershaft face with the flat should face forward, and must be aligned with the case gasket.

Installing the input gear assembly

70 Install the bearing (without snap-ring) on the input gear shaft, positioning the snap-ring groove out, and install a new retaining ring on the shaft. Position the input gear and bearing in the housing. **Note:** *The snap-ring is a selective fit. To provide the tightest fit, four thicknesses (A, B, C or D) are available.*

71 Install the snap-ring in the outside diameter of the bearing.

72 Align the oil slot in the retainer with the drain hole in the case and install the input gear bearing retainer, gasket and retaining bolts. Tighten the bolts to the specified torque.

Installing the shifter shaft assembly

73 If removed, install the poppet plate and pivot pin assembly in the housing. Use a sealant on the pin.

74 Install new O-rings on the inner and outer shifter shafts. Lubricate the O-rings and assemble the inner shaft in the outer shaft.

75 Push the shifter shafts into the housing, engaging the long end of the lockout clutch connector link to the outer shifter shaft before the shaft assembly bottoms.

76 Install the lower shift lever and retaining ring.

77 Install the upper shift lever and shifter shaft retaining nut.

78 Install the shift fork and sliding clutch gear. Push the fork up into the shifter shaft assembly to engage the poppet plate, sliding the clutch gear forward onto the input shaft gear.

79 Install the poppet plate spring, gasket and plug in the top of the housing. Check the spring engagement with the poppet plate.

Input gear bearing replacement

80 Remove the bearing retainer attaching bolts, retainer and gasket from the housing.

81 Using suitable snap-ring pliers, remove the snap-ring retaining the bearing on the shaft.

82 Using a screwdriver or other suitable tool, pry the bearing from the case and remove it from the shaft.

83 Carefully inspect the input gear for burrs, scoring, heat discoloration, etc. Also inspect the condition of the seal in the bearing retainer. Replace components as necessary.

84 Install the bearing with the snap-ring on the input gear shaft. Position the bearing in the case and tap into place with a soft-faced hammer. **Note:** *The snap-ring is a selective fit. To provide the tightest fit, four thicknesses (A, B, C or D) are available.*

85 Install the snap-ring to retain the bearing on the shaft.

86 Position a new gasket and the bearing retainer on the housing. Install the retaining bolts, tightening them to the specified torque.

Input gear bearing retainer seal replacement

87 Remove the bearing retainer attaching bolts, retainer and gasket.

88 Pry the seal out of the retainer.

89 Position the new seal in the retainer, and install it using a length of tubing of suitable diameter.

90 Position the bearing retainer and gasket on the housing. Install the attaching bolts, tightening them to the specified torque.

Disassembly and reassembly of rear output shaft housing

91 Remove the speedometer driven gear from the housing.

92 If not removed during transfer case disassembly, remove the flange nut and washer. Remove the flange from the shaft.

93 Tap on the flange end of the pinion, with a soft-faced hammer, to remove the pinion from the carrier. If the speedometer gear is not on the pinion shaft, reach into the carrier and remove it from the housing.

94 Pry out the old seal from its bore.

95 Using a screwdriver, pry behind the open ends of the snap-ring and remove the snap-ring retaining the rear bearing in the housing.

96 Pull or tap the bearing from the housing.

97 To remove the front bearing, insert a long drift punch through the rear opening, and drive the bearing from the housing.

Fig. 7.30 Removing the poppet ball plug (Sec 21)

Fig. 7.31 Lifting off the intermediate (chain) housing (Sec 21)

SNAP RING

Fig. 7.32 Removing the input shaft bearing retainer assembly snap-ring (Sec 21)

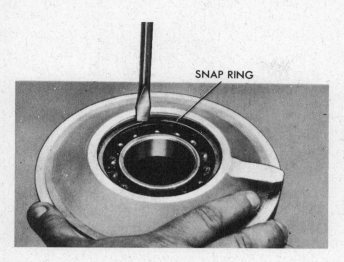

Fig. 7.33 Removing the input shaft bearing-to-retainer snap-ring (Sec 21)

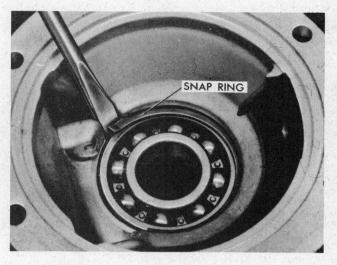

Fig. 7.34 Removing the rear output bearing retaining snap-ring (Sec 21)

98 Begin reassembly by positioning the rubber seal in the bearing bore. Use grease to hold it in place. Position the roller bearing in the bore and press it into place until it bottoms in the housing.
99 Position the rear bearing in the case and tap it into place.
100 Install the snap-ring to retain the bearing in the case. **Note:** *The snap-ring is a selective fit. To provide the tightest fit four thicknesses (A, B, C or D) are available.*
101 Position the rear seal in the bore and drive it into place, using a length of tubing of suitable diameter, until approximately $\frac{1}{8}$ to $\frac{3}{16}$ inch below the housing face.
102 Install the speedometer drive gear and shims on the output shaft. Install the shaft into the carrier through the front opening.
103 Install the flange, washer and retaining nut. Leave the nut loose until shim requirements are determined.
104 Install the speedometer driven gear in the case.

Front output shaft bearing retainer seal replacement
105 Pry, or drive out the existing seal from the retainer bore.
106 Apply a sealant to the outer diameter of the new seal.
107 Position the seal in the retainer bore and, using a piece of suitable diameter tubing, tap the seal into the retainer.

Front output shaft rear bearing replacement
108 Remove the rear cover from the transfer case.
109 Support the rear cover and press the bearing from the cover.
110 Position the new bearing on the outside face of the cover and, using a suitable piece of wood to cover the bearing, press it into the cover until it is flush with the opening.
111 Position the gasket and cover on the transfer case and tap into place.
112 Install the cover retaining bolts, tightening them to the specified torque.

Reassembly of transfer case
113 Place the range box on blocks, with the input gear side toward the bench.
114 Position the range box-to-transfer case housing gasket on the input housing.
115 Install the lockout clutch and drive sprocket assembly on the input shaft assembly. **Note:** *A 2 inch hose clamp may be installed on the end of the shaft to prevent loss of bearings from the clutch assembly.*
116 Install the input shaft, lockout clutch and drive sprocket assembly in the range box, aligning the tab on the bearing retainer with the notch in the gasket.
117 Connect the lockout clutch shift rail to the connector link, and

position the rail in the housing bore. Rotate the shifter shaft while lowering the shift rail into the housing, to prevent the link and rail from being disconnected.
118 Install the drive chain in the chain housing, positioning the chain around the outer wall of the housing.
119 Install the chain housing on the range box, engaging the shift rail channel of the housing to the shift rail. Position the chain on the input drive sprocket.
120 Install the front output sprocket in the case, engaging the drive chain to the sprocket. Rotate the clutch drive gear to assist in positioning the chain on the drive sprocket.
121 Install the shift fork to the clutch assembly and the shift rail, then push the clutch assembly fully into the drive sprocket. Install the roll pin, retaining the shift fork to the shift rod.
122 Install the front output shaft bearing.
123 Install the front output shaft bearing retainer, gasket and retaining bolts.
124 Install the front output shaft flange, gasket, seal, washer and retaining nut. Tap the dust shield back in place after installing the bolts in the flange.
125 Install the front output shaft rear bearing retainer, gasket and retaining bolts. **Note:** *If the rear bearing was removed, position the new bearing in the outside face of the cover, and press it into the cover until it is flush with the opening.*
126 Install the differential carrier assembly on the input shaft. The carrier bolt heads should face the rear of the shaft.
127 Install the rear output housing assembly, gasket and retaining bolts. Load the bearings in the pinion shaft.
128 Check the rear output shaft endplay. To do this, install a dial indicator on the rear housing so that it contacts the end of the output shaft. Holding the rear flange, rotate the front output shaft and determine the highest point of gear runout on the rear shaft. Zero the dial indicator and, with the rear shaft set at this point, pull up on the end of the shaft to determine the endplay.
129 Remove the dial indicator and install a shim pack onto the shaft, in front of the rear bearing, to control the endplay to within 0 to 0.005 inch. Hold the rear flange and rotate the front output shaft to check for binding of the rear output shaft.
130 Install the lockout clutch shaft rail poppet ball and spring. Screw the plug into the case.
131 Install the poppet plate spring, gasket and plug, if not installed during reassembly of the range box.
132 Install the shift levers on the range box shifter rail (if not left on the linkage in the vehicle).
133 Tighten all bolts, locknuts and plugs to the specified torque.
134 Fill the transfer case to the proper level, with the correct grade of oil; install and tighten the filler plug to the specified torque.

7C

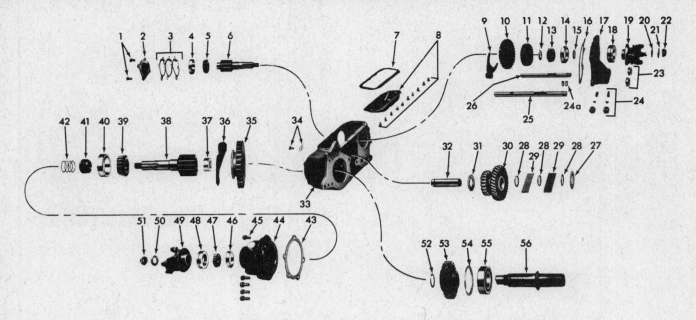

Fig. 7.35 Dana 20 transfer case – exploded view (Sec 22)

1　Cover bolts (4)
2　Front output shaft rear cover
3　Front output rear cover shims
4　Front output rear bearing cup
5　Front output rear bearing
6　Front output shaft
7　Bottom cover gasket
8　Bottom cover and bolts
9　Front wheel drive shift fork
10　Front output sliding gear
11　Front output gear
12　Thrust washer
13　Front output bearing

14　Front output bearing cup
15　Spacer
16　Front output bearing retainer gasket
17　Front output bearing retainer
18　Seal
19　Output yoke assembly
20　O-ring
21　Washer
22　Locknut
23　Shifter rail seals
24　Poppet ball, spring and cap screw
25　Rear wheel drive shift rail
26　Front wheel drive shift rail

27　Tanged thrust washer
28　Spacer
29　Needle bearings
30　Intermediate gears
31　Tanged thrust washer
32　Intermediate shaft
33　Transfer case
34　Intermediate shift lockplate and bolt
35　Rear wheel drive shift fork
36　Rear wheel sliding gear
37　Pilot bearing
38　Rear output shaft
39　Rear output front bearing
40　Rear output front bearing cup
41　Speedometer drive gear

42　Rear output shaft shims
43　Rear retainer gasket
44　Rear output bearing retainer
45　Rear retainer bolts (10)
46　Rear output rear bearing cup
47　Rear output rear bearing
48　Rear output retainer seal
49　Rear output yoke assembly
50　Spacer
51　Locknut
52　Snap-ring (input shaft)
53　Direct drive gear
54　Snap-ring (part of adapter assembly)
55　Bearing (part of adapter assembly)
56　Input shaft

22 Transfer case (Dana 20) – overhaul

Disassembly – general

1　Before disassembly begins, thoroughly clean all external surfaces of the transfer case with solvent.
2　Remove the cover from the bottom of the transfer case.
3　Remove the intermediate gear shaft lockplate at the rear side of the transfer case.
4　Using a soft drift and hammer, drive the intermediate shaft out of the rear of the case.
5　Remove the intermediate gear and thrust washers from the case.
6　Loosen and remove the bolts attaching the rear output shaft sub-assembly to the transfer case and remove the complete unit from the case.
7　Loosen and remove the locknut and washer from the front output shaft yoke (if not removed during unit removal from vehicle) and tap the yoke from the output shaft.
8　Loosen the dog set screw from the rear wheel drive shift fork. Rotate the shift rail to preload the poppet ball and pull the shift rail out of the housing. Remove the shift fork and clutch gear from the case. Remove the poppet ball and spring from the retainer.
9　Remove the front output shaft rear cover and shims.
10　Using a soft-faced hammer tap on the front end of the front output shaft, removing the shaft from the rear of the case. Remove the front

Fig. 7.36 Removing the intermediate gear shaft (Sec 22)

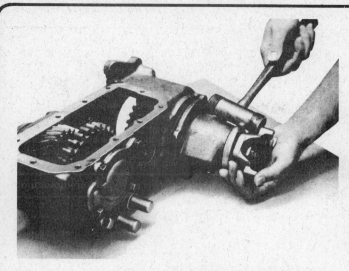

Fig. 7.37 Removing the rear output shaft sub-assembly (Sec 22)

Fig. 7.38 Removing the front output shaft (Sec 22)

Fig. 7.39 Removing the front output shaft rear bearing with a press (Sec 22)

Fig. 7.40 Removing the rear output shaft front bearing (Sec 22)

Fig. 7.41 Installing the rear output shaft pilot bearing (Sec 22)

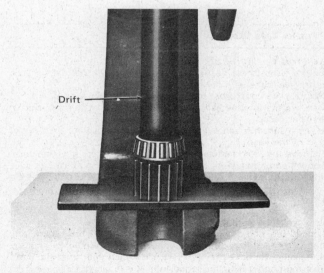

Fig. 7.42 Installing the rear output shaft front bearing (Sec 22)

7C

Fig. 7.43 Installing the rear output shaft front bearing cup (Sec 22)

Fig. 7.44 Installing the rear output shaft rear bearing cup (Sec 22)

Fig. 7.45 Installing the rear output shaft rear seal with a drift (Sec 22)

Fig. 7.46 Installing the front output shaft front bearing (Sec 22)

Fig. 7.47 Installing the front output shaft seal with a drift (Sec 22)

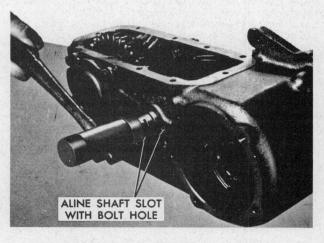

Fig. 7.48 Installing the intermediate shaft (Sec 22)

washer, front bearing, gear washer and the output gear from the case as they clear the shaft. This procedure will also remove the rear bearing cup. **Note:** *The front bearing cup can be removed, if required, by using a suitable puller or driver.*
11 Loosen the dog set screw at the front wheel drive shift fork. Swing the fork and gear toward the cover opening and lift out the gear. Rotate the shift rail to preload the poppet ball and pull the shift rail out of the retainer. Remove the fork as it clears the shift rail and remove the poppet ball and spring from the retainer.
12 Support the inner race of the rear bearing and press the bearing from the shaft.
13 Remove the front output shaft bearing retainer and gasket.
14 Using a suitable puller or pry bar, remove the shift rail lip seals.
15 Using a suitable puller or pry bar, remove the front bearing retainer seal.

Disassembly of the rear output shaft sub-assembly
16 Remove the speedometer driven gear from the rear retainer.
17 Support the yoke assembly in a soft jawed vise and remove the yoke locknut and washer.
18 Remove the assembly from the vise and, using a soft-faced hammer, tap the yoke from the shaft.
19 Support the rear face of the retainer and press the output shaft from the retainer.
20 Pry the seal from the housing bore.
21 Remove the tapered bearing and, using a suitable drift punch, drive the bearing cup from the housing rear bore.
22 Using a suitable brass drift, remove the bearing cup from the housing front bore.
23 Remove the shims and the speedometer gear from the shaft.
24 Using suitable bearing support remove the front bearing from the shaft.
25 Collapse and remove the pilot bearing from the output shaft pilot bore.

Cleaning and inspection
26 Thoroughly clean all components with solvent and dry with a lint-free cloth or dry compressed air.
27 Carefully inspect all bearings and rollers for evidence of chipping, cracks, or worn spots, replacing parts as necessary.
28 Closely examine all shafts, splines and gears for signs of chipped teeth or excessive wear, replacing parts as necessary.
29 Inspect the case, cover and bearing cups for any signs of cracking or damage.

Reassembly of the rear output shaft sub-assembly
30 Press a new pilot bearing into the bore of the rear output shaft using suitable pieces of tubing. **Note:** *The bearing identification should face out.*
31 Using a suitable guide, press the front bearing onto the shaft.
32 Install the front bearing cup in the front housing bore, using a suitable guide tool, until the cup seats in the housing.
33 Install the rear bearing and cup in the rear housing bore, using a suitable guide tool, until the cup seats in the housing.
34 Install the seal in the housing rear bore. Use a suitable piece of tubing.
35 Insert the output shaft into the front bore of the housing and position the yoke on the rear of the shaft. Support the front of the shaft and press the assembly together, seating the bearing on the shaft.
36 Support the yoke assembly in a soft jawed vise and install the washer and locknut. **Note:** *The locknut must be tightened to the specified torque before installing the driveshaft, during unit installation.*
37 Install the speedometer driven gear and the lockplate in the housing.

Reassembly – general
38 Position the front bearing cup and tap it into the bore until it is flush with the inner face.
39 Position the retainer and gasket on the case and install the attaching bolts.
40 If the shift rail seals were removed, position new seals in the retainer rail bores and press them into place with a block of wood or other suitable tool.
41 Install the poppet ball and spring (red) for the front wheel drive shift rail in the retainer.
42 Depress the poppet ball and push the shift rail through the retainer into the case. Install the shift fork on the shift rail and tighten the dog set screw. **Note:** *The shift fork set screw boss should face the front of the case.*
43 Install the poppet ball and spring (yellow) for the rear wheel drive shift rail in the retainer. **Note:** *Position the front wheel drive shift rail in Neutral, so that interlocks do not interfere with the second rail installation.*
44 Depress the poppet ball and install the shift rail through the retainer into the case. Install the shift fork on the rail and tighten the set screw.
45 Support the front output shaft and press the rear bearing onto the shaft. Use a suitable guide tool for this operation.
46 Place the front wheel drive clutch gear and drivegear in the shift fork with the collar toward the rear of the case.
47 Install the front output shaft through the rear of the case into the clutch gear, drivegear and spacer. Position the rear bearing cup in the case and tap it to within $\frac{1}{8}$ inch of the seat.
48 Position the front bearing on the shaft. Supporting the rear of the shaft, press the bearing into position using a suitable guide tool. Tap the front of the shaft to the rear to reposition the rear bearing cup.
49 Install the front output shaft rear bearing cover and shim pack.
50 Install the rear wheel drive clutch gear in the case and the shift fork. The gear shift collar should face the rear of the case.
51 Using a piece of suitable tubing, install the front output shaft retainer seal.
52 If the shift rail cups are damaged, or have been removed, position a new cup in the case bore and install by tapping on the end of the cup.
53 Install the front output shaft yoke, washer and locknut. **Note:** *The yoke locknut must be tightened to the specified torque before installing the driveshaft during unit installation.*
54 Using a dummy shaft, install the needle bearings and spacers in the intermediate gear. Position the thrust washers in the case, with the tang in the groove on the case and supporting the intermediate gear in the case. Install the intermediate shaft through the rear of the case. **Note:** *The intermediate shaft is press fit into the case front bore. Align the lockplate slot in the shaft with the bolt hole, before installing the shaft in the front bore. Take care not to damage the shaft O-ring.*
55 Install the intermediate shaft lockplate and bolt, and tighten to the specified torque.
56 Install the rear output shaft bearing assembly. Tighten the retaining bolts to the specified torque. **Note:** *Take care when engaging the input shaft to prevent damage to the pilot bearings.*
57 Install the rear output shaft yoke, washer and locknut (if not previously done during reassembly of the sub-assembly). **Note:** *The rear yoke locknut must be tightened to the specified torque before checking endplay, and before installing the rear driveshaft.*
58 Shift the transfer gears and check for satisfactory gear engagement and shift rail movement. The four wheel drive rail will have the greater poppet ball spring tension.
59 Position the bottom cover and gasket on the case, Install the cover bolts and tighten them to the specified torque.
60 After a major overhaul or rebuild, the front and rear output shafts should be checked for endplay. The endplay must be between 0.001 and 0.005 inch, and shims should be added or removed to achieve this.

7C

Chapter 8 Driveline – axles and driveshafts

Contents

Specifications

Rear axle

Type	Semi-floating (Ford) with removable carrier or full-floating (Dana) with integral carrier
Ratio	Varies – ratio stamped on metal tag attached to rear cover bolt
Endplay (full-floating)	0.001 to 0.010 in

Front axle

Type	Semi-floating (Dana 44) or full-floating (Dana 60)
Ratio	Varies – ratio stamped on metal tag attached to cover bolt
Endplay	0.001 to 0.010 in

Driveshaft

Type	One-piece or two-piece depending on wheelbase of vehicle (see Sec 17)

Torque specifications

Rear axle

Full-floating (Dana)

	ft-lb
Pinion shaft nut	250 to 270
Differential bearing cap bolts	80 to 90
Ring gear attaching bolts	110 to 115
Oil filler plug	20 to 30
U-joint bolts	15 to 20
Cover-to-housing bolts	30 to 40
Differential case bolts (Dana 70 two-piece case only)	55 to 75
Wheel bearing adjusting nut	50 to 80 (back off $\frac{3}{8}$ turn – see text)
Wheel bearing locknut	90 to 110
Axleshaft retaining bolt	40 to 50

Semi-floating (Ford)

Pinion retainer-to-carrier bolts	30 to 45
Ring gear attaching bolts	65 to 80
Bearing cap bolts	70 to 85
Carrier-to-housing bolts	25 to 40
Carrier-to-housing nuts	30 to 40
Axleshaft retaining nuts (bearing retainer plate)	50 to 75

Front axle

Pinion shaft nut (Dana 44)	200 to 220
Pinion shaft nut (Dana 60)	240 to 300
Differential bearing cap bolts	70 to 90
Ring gear attaching bolts (Dana 44)	45 to 65
Ring gear attaching bolts (Dana 60)	100 to 120
Cover-to-housing bolts	30 to 40
Oil filler plug	40
U-joint bolts	8 to 15
Wheel bearing adjusting nut	50 (back off 90 degrees – see text)
Wheel bearing locknut	
1973 thru 1976	80 to 100
1977 thru 1979	50 to 70

Driveshaft

Center bearing bracket-to-support	40 to 50
U-joint-to-rear yoke	90 to 110
U-joint adapter-to-rear axle	60 to 70

1 Rear axle – general information

The rear axle assembly consists of a straight, hollow housing enclosing a differential assembly and axleshafts. These axle assemblies support the vehicle through leaf springs attached to the frame.

The axleshaft bearings are of two distinctly different types. The main area of difference is in the design of the wheel bearings. As a general rule, trucks with Gross Vehicle Weight (GVW) ratings below 7000 pounds have semifloating axleshafts while those trucks with ratings above 7000 pounds have full-floating axle design. Full-floating axleshafts do not bear any of the vehicle's weight and can be removed independently of the tapered roller wheel bearings.

Both types of rear end designs use hypoid gears with the ring gear center line below the axleshaft center line. The lighter-duty type of rear axle has a 9-inch ring gear differential with a drop out type of housing. The heavier duty rear end is manufactured by Dana and has an integral carrier housing.

Due to the need for special tools and equipment, it is recommend-

ed that operations on these models be limited to those described in this Chapter. Where repair or overhaul is required, remove the axle assembly and take it to a rebuilder, or exchange it for a new or reconditioned unit. It is becoming increasingly rare to find individual axle components for local repair work as it is generally recognized that dismantling and rebuilding this unit is an 'in plant' job requiring special equipment and techniques.

Always make sure that an axle unit is changed for one of identical type and gear ratio.

Routine maintenance and minor repair procedures can be performed without removing the differential assembly from the axle housing or the rear axle assembly from the vehicle. The following components can be serviced as described above: axleshafts; wheel hubs; wheel hub bearings; wheel hub grease seals; wheel hub lugs.

2 Rear axle – fluid check

Refer to Chapter 1 for this procedure.

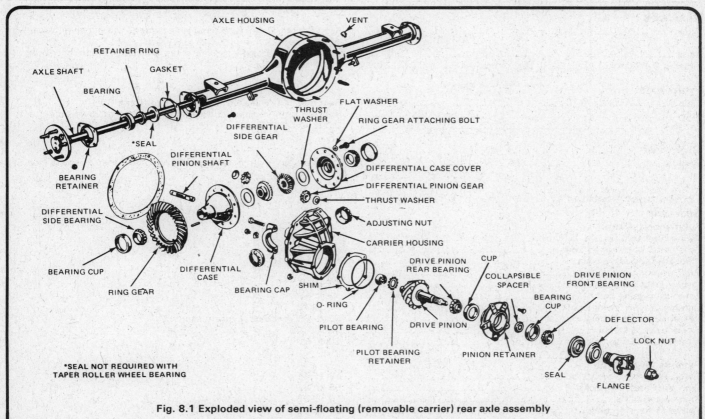

Fig. 8.1 Exploded view of semi-floating (removable carrier) rear axle assembly

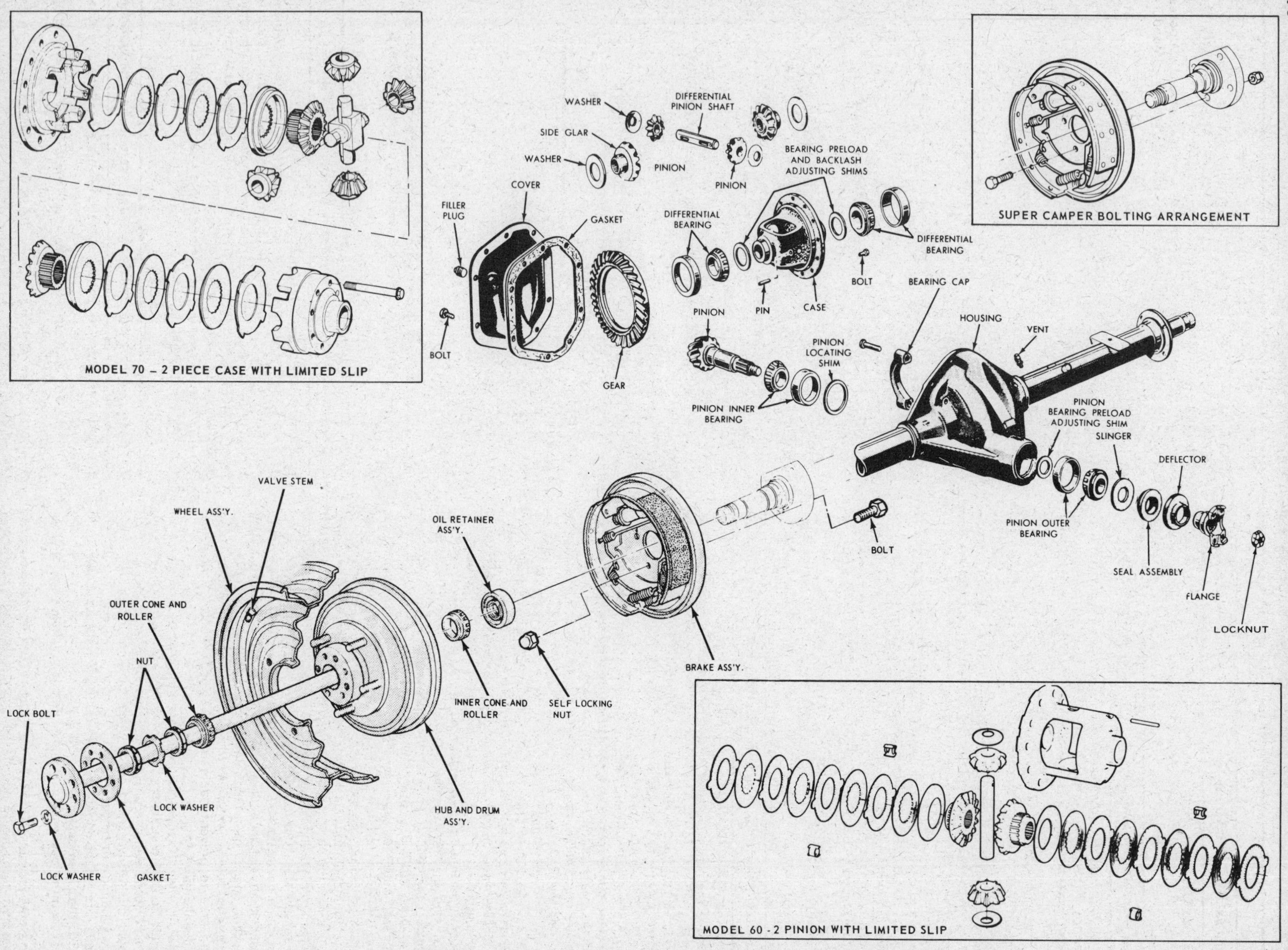

SUPER CAMPER BOLTING ARRANGEMENT

LOCKNUT

FLANGE

DEFLECTOR

SEAL ASSEMBLY

PINION BEARING PRELOAD ADJUSTING SHIM

SLINGER

PINION BEARING PRELOAD ADJUSTING SHIM

PINION OUTER BEARING

VENT

HOUSING

DIFFERENTIAL BEARING

BEARING CAP

BOLT

BOLT

MODEL 60 - 2 PINION WITH LIMITED SLIP

BEARING PRELOAD AND BACKLASH ADJUSTING SHIMS

PINION LOCATING SHIM

CASE

PIN

PINION INNER BEARING

DIFFERENTIAL PINION SHAFT

PINION

PINION

DIFFERENTIAL BEARING

WASHER

SIDE GEAR

WASHER

GASKET

GEAR

COVER

FILLER PLUG

BOLT

BRAKE ASS'Y.

SELF LOCKING NUT

OIL RETAINER ASS'Y.

INNER CONE AND ROLLER

HUB AND DRUM ASS'Y.

VALVE STEM

WHEEL ASS'Y.

OUTER CONE AND ROLLER

NUT

LOCK WASHER

LOCK WASHER

GASKET

LOCK BOLT

MODEL 70 – 2 PIECE CASE WITH LIMITED SLIP

Fig. 8.2 Exploded view of full-floating (integral carrier) rear axle assembly

3   Rear axle – fluid change

Refer to Chapter 1 for this procedure.

4   Rear axleshaft oil seal (semi-floating type) – replacement

Note: *The following procedure is for oil seal replacement of axles with ball bearings. Tapered roller bearings are used on certain semi-floating axles and require bearing removal for oil seal replacement (See Section 5).*
1   Remove the axleshaft as described in Section 8.
2   The axleshaft seal must be pulled out of the housing with a special slide hammer type puller.
3   Inspect the inner surface of the housing for any conditions that would prevent the new seal from fitting into its seat correctly. Remedy any problems of this type such as burrs, galling or rust before attempting to install the seal.
4   Smear a small amount of oil-resistant sealer on the outer edge of the seal. Do not allow the sealer to touch the sealing lip.
5   Drive the new seal into its bore. The seal must receive even pressure around its circumference, thus a tubular drift, large socket or special tool should be used for this. Push the seal into the housing until it seats.
6   Install the axleshaft.

5   Rear axle bearings and seal (full-floating type) – replacement

1   Raise the rear of the vehicle and support it securely.
2   Remove the rear wheels. Remove the axleshafts as described in Section 8.
3   Bend the tabs of the lock washer away from the wheel bearing locknut. Be careful not to damage the locknut. Use a special deep socket and remove the wheel bearing locknut.
4   Remove the lock washer. Remove the wheel bearing adjustment nut using the same socket as you used on the locknut.
5   Pull the brake drum and hub off the spindle. If the brake drum won't come off easily, it may be necessary to loosen the brake shoes slightly (Chapter 9).
6   Remove the outer bearing assembly from inside the hub.
7   Use a brass drift to drive the inner seal out of the hub assembly. Remove the inner bearing assembly from the hub.
8   Clean the inside of the wheel hub of all axle lubricant and grease. Clean the spindle.
9   Inspect the bearing assemblies for any signs of wear, pitting, galling or damage. Replace the bearings if any of these conditions exist. Inspect the bearing races for any signs of erratic wear, galling or damage. Drive out the bearing races with a brass drift if they need replacement. Install the new races with a suitable tool designed for this purpose. Never use a drift or punch for this operation as these races must be seated correctly and can be damaged easily.
10   Prior to installation, pack the inner and outer wheel bearing assemblies with the correct type of wheel bearing grease. If you do not have access to a bearing packer, pack each assembly carefully by hand and make sure the entire assembly is penetrated with lubricant.
11   Install the newly-packed inner wheel bearing into the brake drum hub. Install a new hub inner seal with a suitable drive tool (tubular drift, large socket, special tool) being careful not to damage the seal.
12   Wrap the spindle with electrician's tape around the end and threaded area to prevent damage to the inner wheel bearing seal during installation.
13   Carefully slide the hub and drum assembly over the spindle being very careful to keep it straight so as not to contact the spindle with the seal which would damage it. Remove the electrician's tape.
14   Install the newly-packed outer wheel bearing. Install the wheel bearing adjusting nut by hand.
15   While rotating the hub/drum assembly, tighten the adjusting nut to 50 to 80 ft-lb. Then back the nut off $\frac{3}{8}$ of a turn.
16   Coat the new lock washer with axle lube and install it smooth side out.
17   Install the locknut and torque it to 90 to 110 ft-lb. Make sure the hub assembly turns freely and has the correct amount of freeplay (0.001 to 0.010 inch) after the locknut is torqued. Bend two of the

lock tabs over the flats on the locknuts once the freeplay and turning of the hub has been checked.
18   Install the axleshaft and a new washer and torque the retaining bolts to the correct torque specification.
19   Adjust the brakes if they were loosened for removal purposes. Remove the support devices and lower the vehicle to the ground.

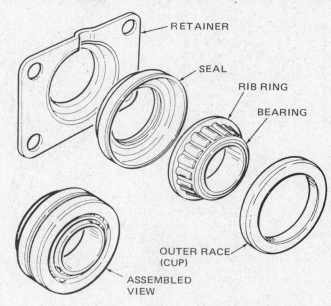

Fig. 8.3 Taper wheel bearings and oil seal (Sec 5)

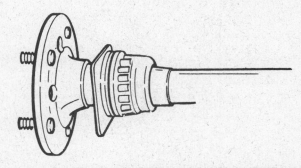

Fig. 8.4 The wheel bearing components must be pressed on and off the axleshaft, requiring a large hydraulic press (Sec 6)

6   Rear wheel bearing (semi-floating type) – replacement

1   Remove the axleshaft as described in Section 7.
2   Due to the requirement of a hydraulic press and various adapters, you must take your axleshaft(s) to an automotive machine shop or parts store with the equipment necessary to properly accomplish this task. On vehicles with tapered roller wheel bearings, the axleshaft seal should also be replaced at the same time.
3   After the new bearing has been pressed onto the axleshaft, install it as described in Section 7.

7   Rear axleshaft (semi-floating type) – removal and installation

1   Loosen the lug nuts on the wheel(s) for the side of the axle to be removed.
2   Raise and support the rear of the vehicle firmly on jackstands, blocking the front wheels to keep the vehicle from rolling.
3   Remove the wheel(s). Release the parking brake and remove the rear brake drum(s).
4   Loosen the axle retaining nuts by inserting a socket and extension

8

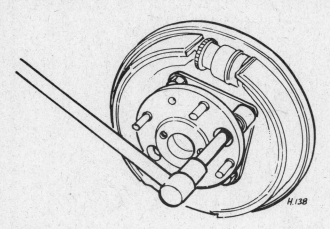

Fig. 8.5 Removing the axleshaft retaining nuts (Sec 7)

through the hole provided in the axle flange. Rotate the axle to allow access to all four nuts. Remove the nuts.

5   Remove the axleshaft by pulling on the flange. If the axle is stuck it can sometimes be removed by reinstalling the wheel assembly and using the greater leverage of the wheel to pull it out. When pulling out the axle, be careful not to damage the seal if you are reusing it although seals should always be replaced whenever an axle is removed. If both axles have been removed, take care not to mix them up as they are of different lengths. Secure the brake backing plate to the housing with one nut to make sure it doesn't fall off while you are performing other operations on the axleshaft or housing.

6   Installation is the reverse of removal. Install a new gasket between the brake backing plate and the axle housing flange. Be careful not to damage the inner lips of the axle seal when you are inserting the axleshaft into the housing (the splines on the end of the shaft are sharp). Torque the axleshaft retaining nuts to the correct specification. Torque the wheel assembly lug bolts to the correct specification.

8   Rear axleshaft (full-floating type) – removal and installation

1   Unscrew and remove the bolts which attach the axleshaft flange to the hub. There is no need to remove the tire and wheel or jack-up the vehicle.

2   Tap the flange with a soft-faced hammer to loosen the shaft and then grip the rib of the face of the flange with a pair of locking pliers; twist the shaft slightly in both directions and then withdraw it from the axle tube.

3   Installation is a reversal of removal but hold the axleshaft level in order to engage the splines at its inner end with those in the differential side gear. Always use a new gasket on the flange and keep both the flange and hub mating surfaces free from grease or oil.

9   Rear differential assembly (removable carrier type) – replacement

1   The differential assembly used in the light-duty axle housing is of the removable type. This unit must be removed for service operations including pinion seal replacement and gear lash preload to correct for noise or wear. This type of differential is used in conjunction with semi-floating axles.

2   Raise the vehicle and support the rear axle housing or frame securely.

3   Drain the rear axle housing using the plug under the center section.

4   Remove the axleshafts (Sec 2). It is not necessary to remove them totally but pull them out about ten inches to clear the differential side gears.

5   Remove the driveshaft.

6   Remove the carrier housing retaining nuts and washers around the entire circumference of the housing. Be careful not to lose the

identification tag retained by one of these nuts as it contains valuable information about the differential assembly.

7   Clean the area around the mating surfaces of the differential carrier housing.

8   Supporting the unit (a transmission jack is ideal), remove the differential assembly.

9   Clean the mating surface on the carrier housing and remove any old gasket material from the housing or the carrier assembly. Installation is the reverse of removal. Make sure you use a new gasket and that the mating faces of the housing and the carrier assembly are clean. Fill the differential with the correct type and grade of fluid (Chapter 1).

10   Rear axle assembly – removal and installation

1   Chock the front wheels, jack up the rear of the vehicle and support it on jackstands placed under the rear frame member.

2   Remove the wheels, brake drums and axleshafts as described in Sections 8 or 9.

3   Remove the driveshaft.

4   Disconnect the lower end of the shock absorbers from the axle housing.

5   Remove the brake vent tube (if equipped) from the brake pipe junction and retaining clamp.

6   Remove the brake pipes from the clips that retain them to the axle but do not disconnect any of the pipe unions.

7   Remove the brake linings and brake back plates and support them with wire to avoid straining the hydraulic brake lines which are still attached (See Chapter 9).

8   Support the weight of the axle on a jack and remove the nuts from the spring retaining U-bolts. Remove the bottom clamping plates.

9   Lower the axle assembly on the jack and withdraw it from the rear of the vehicle.

10   The axle assembly is installed using the reverse procedure to that of removal. Tighten the U-bolt and shock absorber nuts to the correct specification.

11   Front drive axle assembly (4 x 4) – general information

If your vehicle is equipped with four-wheel drive, it has a front axle that is a modified version of the rear axle manufactured by Dana. These axles incorporate a universal joint at the end of each axleshaft, inboard of the front brake assembly. These universal joints allow the front wheels to both drive and steer.

Light duty vehicles use a differential with an $8\frac{1}{2}$ inch ring gear while the front differential on heavier duty vehicles comes equipped with a $9\frac{3}{4}$ inch ring gear.

The front hubs come in two versions depending on what type of 4-wheel drive transfer case is used. 'Part time 4-wheel drive' transfer cases are coupled to free-wheeling (manually 'Locked' or 'Unlocked') hubs while 'full time 4-wheel drive' transfer cases are mated to permanently-locked front drive hubs.

12   Free-wheeling hub (front-wheel drive axle) – removal and installation

Internal-type

1   Turn the actuator lever to set the hub to the 'Lock' position.

2   Raise the vehicle on a suitable hoist or jack up the appropriate wheel.

3   Loosen and remove the six retaining plate bolts. Remove the retaining plate actuating knob and O-ring.

4   Using suitable pliers, remove the internal snap-ring outer clutch retaining ring and the actuating cam body.

5   Remove the axleshaft snap-ring.

6   Remove the pressure spring and spring retainer plate.

7   If further dismantling is required, remove the actuator knob and the O-ring from the retaining plate. Slide the inner clutch ring and bushing assembly from the axle sleeve and clutch ring assembly.

8   Wash all parts in solvent and dry with a lint-free cloth. Inspect all parts for signs of damage or wear, replacing as necessary.

9   Installation is the reverse of removal.

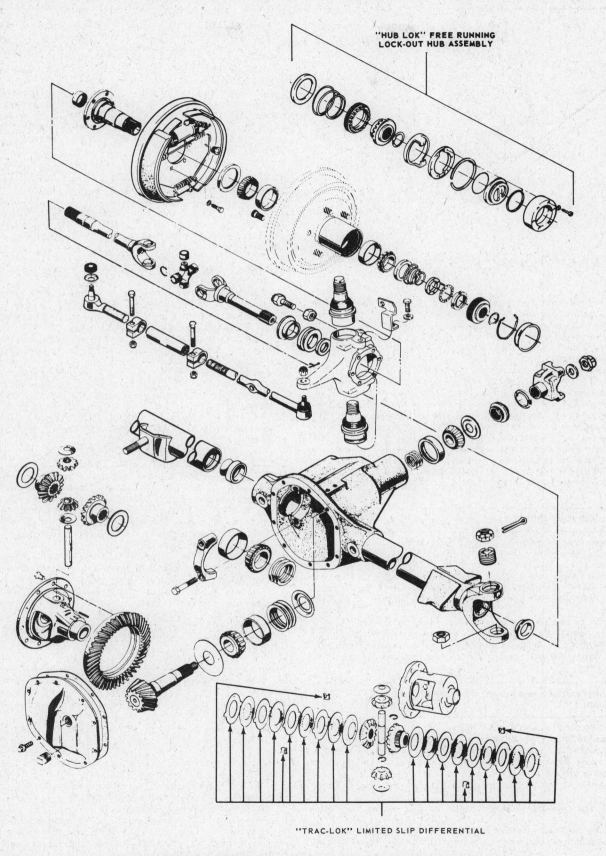

"HUB LOK" FREE RUNNING
LOCK-OUT HUB ASSEMBLY

"TRAC-LOK" LIMITED SLIP DIFFERENTIAL

Fig. 8.6 Exploded view of front driving axle assembly (1973 Bronco shown)

8

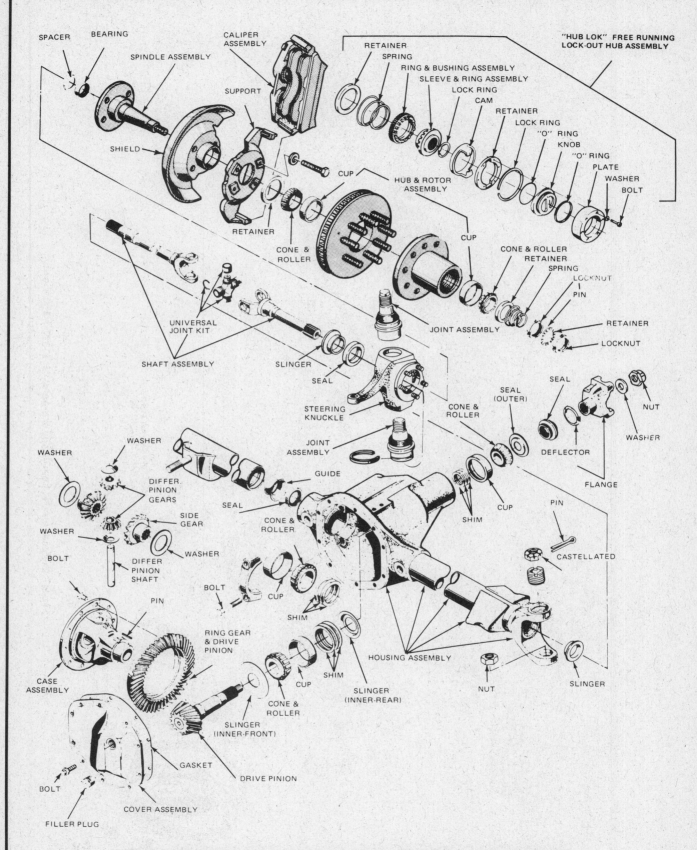

Fig. 8.7 Exploded view of front driving axle assembly (1979 Bronco, F 150, F 250 shown)

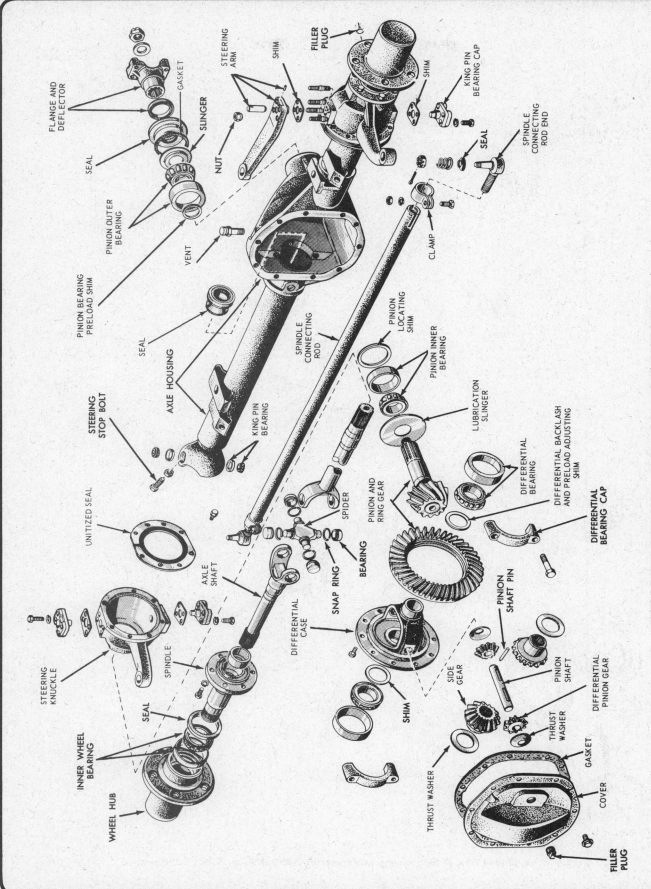

Fig. 8.8 Exploded view of front driving axle assembly (1973 F 250 shown)

FLANGE AND DEFLECTOR

SEAL

SLINGER

PINION OUTER BEARING

GASKET

STEERING ARM

NUT

SHIM

FILLER PLUG

SHIM

KING PIN BEARING CAP

SEAL

SPINDLE CONNECTING ROD END

PINION BEARING PRELOAD SHIM

SEAL

VENT

AXLE HOUSING

SPINDLE CONNECTING ROD

CLAMP

PINION LOCATING SHIM

PINION INNER BEARING

LUBRICATION SLINGER

DIFFERENTIAL BEARING

DIFFERENTIAL BACKLASH AND PRELOAD ADJUSTING SHIM

DIFFERENTIAL BEARING CAP

STEERING STOP BOLT

KING PIN BEARING

UNITIZED SEAL

AXLE SHAFT

SPIDER

PINION AND RING GEAR

SNAP RING

BEARING

STEERING KNUCKLE

SPINDLE

DIFFERENTIAL CASE

PINION SHAFT PIN

SEAL

SHIM

SIDE GEAR

PINION SHAFT

DIFFERENTIAL PINION GEAR

INNER WHEEL BEARING

THRUST WASHER

THRUST WASHER

GASKET

WHEEL HUB

COVER

FILLER PLUG

8

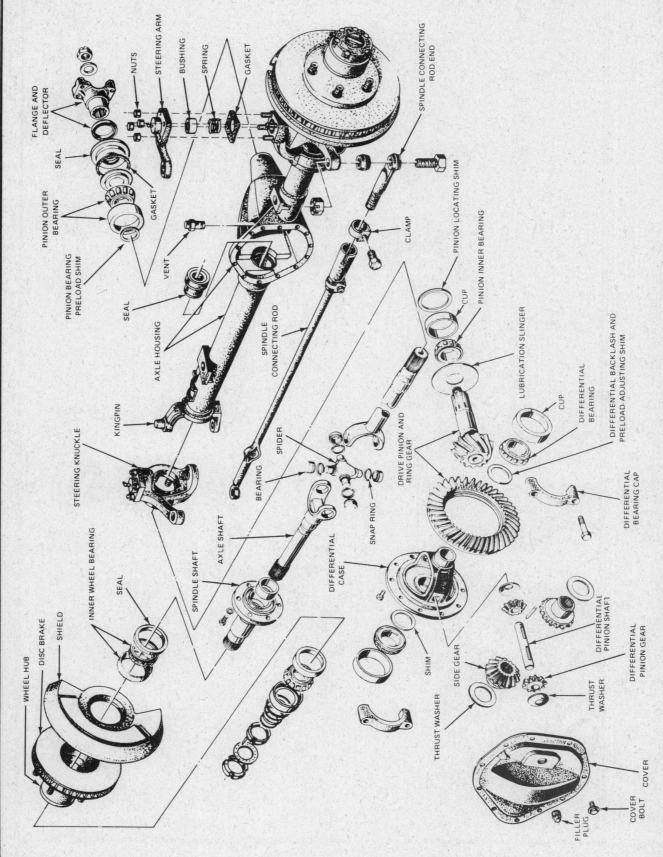

Fig. 8.9 Exploded view of front driving axle assembly (1979 F 250, F 350 shown)

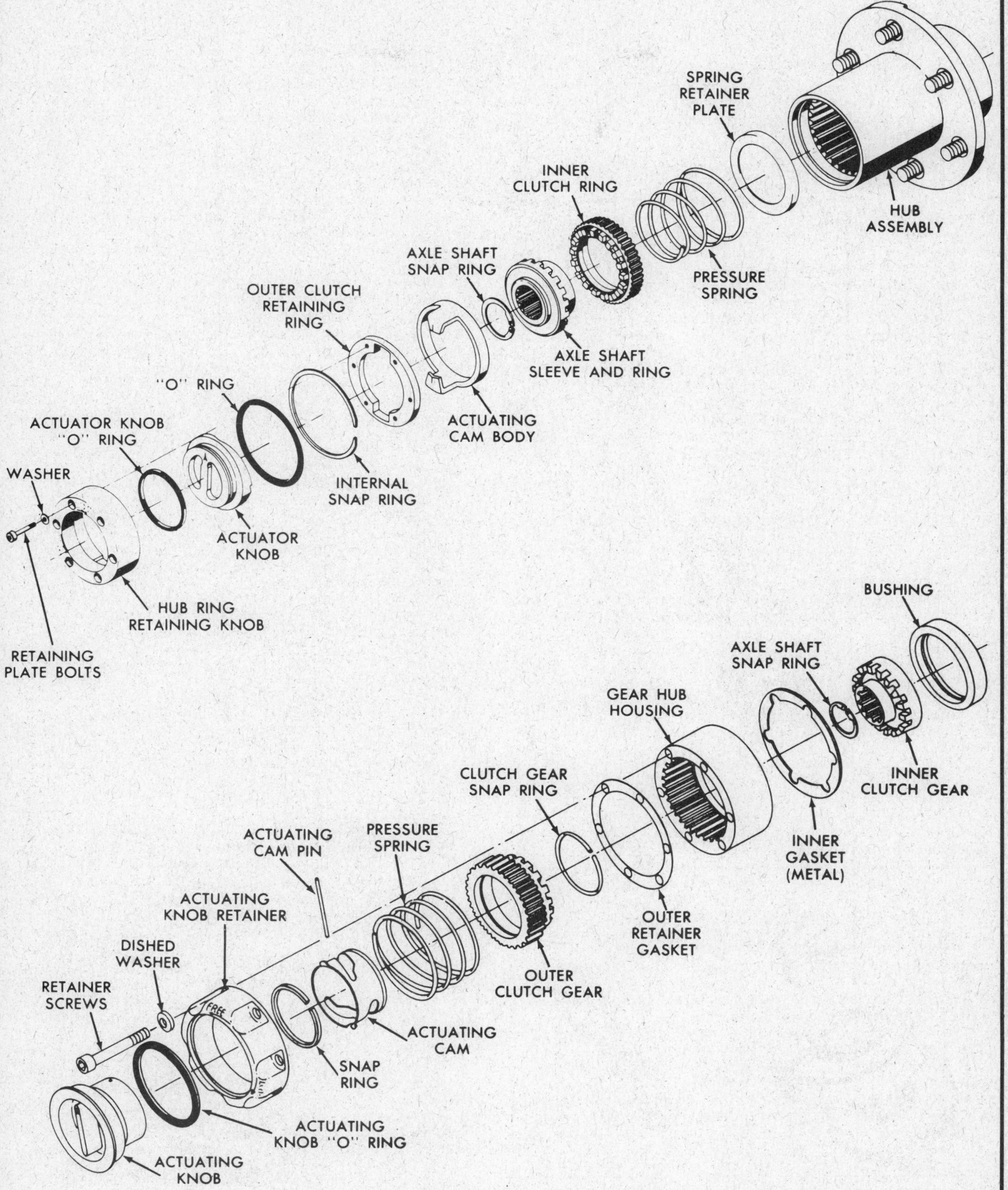

Fig. 8.10 Exploded views of the free-wheeling hubs used on 4 x 4 vehicles – internal-type (top) and external type (bottom) (Sec 12)

8

External-type

10 Place the vehicle on a suitable hoist, or jack up the appropriate wheel.

11 Turn the hub key knob to the 'Free' position.

12 Loosen and remove the Allen head bolts securing the retainer cap assembly to the wheel hub.

13 Roll off the hub cap assembly and gasket; also remove the exterior sleeve extension housing.

14 If further dismantling is required, turn the hub key knob to the locked position and drive out the key knob retainer roll pin.

15 Remove the outer clutch gear assembly.

16 Remove the lockring and the slotted adjustment sleeve. Remove the spring.

17 Remove the lockring securing the plastic key knob to the hub retainer cap.

18 Remove the O-ring from the plastic hub key knob.

19 Remove the snap-ring from the end of the axleshaft.

20 Pull off the internal clutch gear and collar.

21 Wash all parts in solvent and dry them with a lint-free cloth. Inspect all components for signs of wear or damage, replacing as necessary.

22 Begin reassembly by installing the internal clutch gear collar and gear. Install the lockring at the end of the axleshaft.

23 Install a pre-lubricated O-ring in the groove of the plastic hub key knob and insert this into the retainer cap.

24 Install the lockring securing the plastic key knob to the hub retainer cap. Check to see that the lockring is fully engaged into the slot by pushing outward on the plastic knob.

25 Install the slotted adjustment sleeve with the two tabs facing downward.

26 Install the key knob retaining roll pin with the knob in the 'Lock' position. Install the spring.

27 Place the outer clutch gear assembly on top of the spring, compress the spring and install the lockring at the sleeve end.

28 Turn the key knob to the 'Free' position. **Note:** *Before continuing to install the extension housing and the assembled cap assembly, remove the head from a 5 inch long, $\frac{3}{8}$ inch diameter bolt. Use this to align the assembly of the parts to the hub.*

29 Install this bolt into one of the hub housing bolt holes.

30 Install the exterior sleeve extension housing (with a new gasket) and the hub retainer cap assembly.

31 Install the Allen head bolts securing the retainer cap assembly to the wheel hub.

32 Turn the hub key knob to the 'Lock' position to ensure engagement.

33 Finally, install the wheel and lower the vehicle to the ground.

13 Locked hub (full-time 4 x 4 front drive axle) – removal and installation

1 Raise the front end of the vehicle and support it securely with stands.

2 Pry off the front grease cap.

3 Remove the snap-ring with snap-ring pliers.

4 Remove the splined driving hub. It may be necessary to pry slightly on this hub but be careful not to damage the hub or the inside of the wheel hub.

5 Remove the pressure spring. Notice which way this spring fits in the wheel hub. Remove the spring retainer.

6 Use a special tool designed to fit the locknut and wheel bearing adjustment nut and remove the locknut. Remove the lockring.

7 If further removal of the hub assembly is necessary, refer to Section 15.

8 Installation is the reverse of removal. When installing the grease cap, apply a small amount of non-hardening sealer before pressing the cap onto the hub assembly.

14 Front axle bearings and seals (4 x 4) – removal, adjustment and installation

Note: *Before disassembling your vehicle, purchase or rent the tool necessary to remove the locknut and adjusting nut from the spindle. Also obtain the parts necessary to replace the inner bearing seal as it*
should always be replaced whenever the entire front hub assembly is dismantled. If you cannot obtain the special tool necessary for the locknut and adjusting nut, this operation would be best handled by a dealership or shop specializing in this type of work.

1 Remove the free-wheeling or locked hub as described in the previous Sections.

2 Remove the wheel bearing locknut with the above listed special tool. Remove the lockring.

3 Remove the wheel bearing adjusting nut.

4 Remove the brake caliper assembly if the vehicle is equipped with disc brakes (Chapter 9).

5 Pull the hub and disc or drum assembly off the spindle. The outer wheel bearing will come out with the hub assembly so don't drop it.

6 Drive the grease retainer out of the back of the hub assembly. Remove the inside tapered roller bearing assembly from the back of the hub.

7 Clean the spindle, bearings and hub assembly with solvent.

8 Blow them dry with compressed air but do not 'dry-spin' the bearings. Inspect the bearings, inner races or cups and spindle for cracks, galling or any unusual wear patterns. Replace any component that shows signs of these conditions. If the bearing races (or cups) need replacement, the bearings must also be replaced.

9 Repack the bearings with the correct type and grade of wheel bearing lubricant (Chapter 1) using a bearing packer. If you don't have access to a packer, make sure you thoroughly penetrate the roller and cage assembly with lubricant.

10 If the bearing cups need replacement, drive out the old cups with a drift. Drive the new cups in with an approved tool (tubular drift, large socket) making sure that you don't damage the cups.

11 Insert the inner bearing assembly into the back of the hub. Pack the inside of the hub with wheel bearing grease but do not pack grease past the inside diameter of the bearing cups.

12 Install a new grease retainer or seal using an approved tool. Be careful not to damage the seal. Coat the inner lip of the seal with multi-purpose lubricant ESA-MIC75-B or equivalent.

13 Carefully install the hub assembly over the spindle being careful not to damage the seal or bearing with the sharp end of the spindle.

14 Install the outer bearing and adjusting nut.

15 Tighten the adjusting nut to 50 ft-lb while rotating the wheel/hub assembly to seat the bearings. Back the adjusting nut off approximately 90 degrees.

16 Install the lockring by turning the adjustment nut to the nearest notch for dowel pin installation. Install the outer locknut and torque it to specifications. Check the final endplay of the hub on the spindle and make sure it doesn't exceed the specification (0.001 to 0.010 in).

17 Install the free-wheeling or locked hub assembly as described previously.

15 Front axleshaft (4 x 4) – removal and installation

1 Remove the free-wheeling or locked hub as described previously.

2 Remove the front axle bearings and seal.

3 Remove the front brake backing plate (if the vehicle is equipped with drum brakes). Suspend the backing plate assembly out of the way to prevent damaging it.

4 If the vehicle is equipped with disc brakes, remove the nuts that retain the brake support bracket, dust shield and spindle to the steering knuckle (housing). Carefully remove the spindle.

5 Pull the axleshaft assembly from the axle housing, being very cautious as you pull the universal joint through the knuckle bore.

6 At this point the axle assembly can be serviced for universal joints, spindle bore seals, deflectors and spindle bore needle bearings.

7 Make sure all components mentioned in Step 6 are in good, serviceable condition.

8 Carefully insert the axle through the knuckle bore being careful not to damage the axle or seals. Engage the axle spline with the side gears of the differential and push the axle into its correct position.

9 Install the brake assembly, seals, bearings, and hub in the reverse order of removal. Tighten and fasten to the proper specification.

16 Front drive axle assembly (4 x 4) – replacement

1 Raise the front of the vehicle with a hoist or jack and support the

frame securely. Make sure that no vehicle weight is supported by the front axle.

2 Remove the front wheels.

3 Remove the front brake drums or brake caliper and discs if so equipped. Remove the brake backing plates. Suspend them out of the way to avoid damaging the brake parts or hoses.

4 Remove the steering drag link or Pitman arm from the steering arm using a suitable puller. Be careful not to damage the grease seal or connecting joint. Suspend the arm out of the way.

5 Remove the hydraulic brake line brackets from each end of the axle. Do not break the hydraulic connection to the brake lines. Remove the hydraulic lines from the clips and suspend the lines out of the way to prevent damaging them.

6 Disconnect the shock absorbers at both ends and compress them out of the way (F-250 and F-350 only).

7 Disconnect the front stabilizer bar at both ends (if so equipped). Pivot the bar up and out of the way.

8 Disconnect the front driveshaft at the flange and suspend it out of the way. Secure the universal joint caps so they do not fall off.

9 Support the front axle with a jack or other suitable device. It may take two jacks to do this safely as the offset of the front differential causes this assembly to be heavily weighted to one side.

10 For F-100, F-150 and Broncos, remove the bolts attaching the radius arm caps to the radius arms. Remove the radius arm caps but do not mix them up as they are matched to the radius arms (a number

1 through 100 is stamped on each arm and cap to help identify them). Remove the rubber insulators.

11 F-250 and F-350 front axle assemblies are suspended with leaf springs. Remove the nuts from the U-bolts retaining the axle housing to the spring clamp plates. Remove the U-bolts and the clamp plates.

12 Remove the front axle assembly from under the vehicle.

13 Installation is the reverse of removal. Be sure to tighten all retaining bolts and nuts to the correct torque specifications. If the differential or axle assemblies have been dismantled while the housing assembly was removed from the vehicle, make certain the axle is refilled with the correct amount and type of lubricant (Chapter 1).

14 Before test driving the vehicle, push on the brake pedal several times to ensure proper brake operation (particularly with disc brakes).

17 Driveshaft(s) – general information

The driveshaft is of tubular construction and may be of a one or two-section type according to the wheelbase of the vehicle.

On 4-wheel drive vehicles, the rear wheel driveline is very similar to that described above, but in order to drive the front wheels a driveshaft is incorporated between the transfer case and the front axle. This shaft is basically similar to the shafts used to drive the rear axle.

All driveshafts used to drive the rear wheels have needle bearing

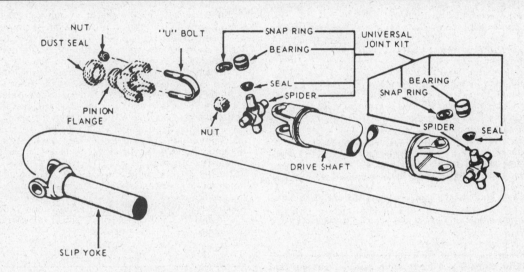

Fig. 8.11 One-piece driveshaft as used on most two-wheel drive, short-wheelbase trucks (Sec 17)

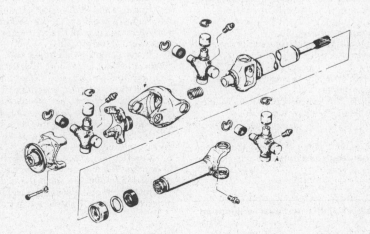

Fig. 8.12 Double Cardan type driveshaft as used on Bronco models (Sec 17)

8

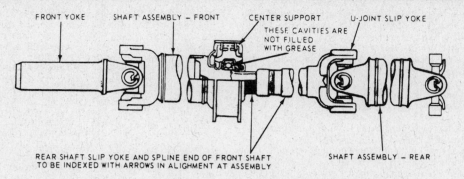

FRONT YOKE   SHAFT ASSEMBLY – FRONT   CENTER SUPPORT   U-JOINT SLIP YOKE

THESE CAVITIES ARE NOT FILLED WITH GREASE

REAR SHAFT SLIP YOKE AND SPLINE END OF FRONT SHAFT TO BE INDEXED WITH ARROWS IN ALIGHMENT AT ASSEMBLY

SHAFT ASSEMBLY – REAR

Fig. 8.13 Two-piece driveshaft with front slip yoke attachment (Sec 17)

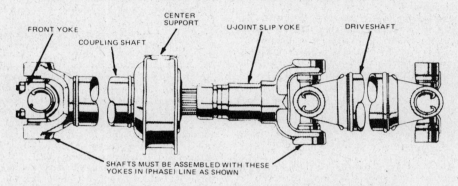

CENTER SUPPORT

FRONT YOKE   COUPLING SHAFT   U-JOINT SLIP YOKE   DRIVESHAFT

SHAFTS MUST BE ASSEMBLED WITH THESE YOKES IN (PHASE) LINE AS SHOWN

Fig. 8.14 Two-piece driveshaft with front flange attachment (Sec 17)

type universal joints. Single-section shafts have a splined sliding sleeve at the front end connecting to the output shaft of the transmission, while two-section shafts have a central slip joint. The purpose of these devices is to accommodate, by retraction or extension, the varying shaft length caused by the movement of the rear axle as the rear suspension deflects. On some 4-wheel drive models, due to the extent of the front driveshaft angle, a constant velocity joint is used at the transfer case end of the driveshaft.

Where a two-section shaft is used, the shaft is supported near its forward end on a ball bearing which is flexibly mounted in a bracket attached to the frame crossmember.

The attachment of the rear end of the driveshaft to the rear axle pinion flange (or the attachment of the front driveshaft to the front axle pinion flange) may be by U-bolt or bolted strap, according to the date of production and model.

The driveshaft is finely balanced during manufacture and it is recommended that care be used when universal joints are replaced to help maintain this balance. It is sometimes better to have the universal joints replaced by a dealership or shop specializing in this type of work. If you replace the joints yourself, mark each individual yoke in relation to the one opposite in order to maintain the balance. Do not drop the assembly during servicing operations.

18 Driveshaft(s) – balancing

1 Vibration of the driveshaft at certain speeds may be caused by any of the following:

    a) Undercoating or mud on the shaft
    b) Loose rear strap attachment bolts
    c) Worn universal joints
    d) Bent or dented driveshaft

2 Vibrations which are thought to be emanating from the driveshaft are sometimes caused by improper tire balance. This should be one of your first checks.

3 If the shaft is in a good, clean, undamaged condition, it is worth disconnecting the rear end attachment straps and turning the shaft 180 degrees to see if an improvement is noticed. Be sure to mark the

original position of each component before disassembly so the shaft can be returned to the same location.

4 If the vibration persists after checking for obvious causes and changing the position of the shaft, the entire assembly should be checked out by a professional shop or replaced.

19 Driveshaft(s) – removal and installation

Note:*On two-piece driveshafts, the rear shaft must be removed before the front shaft.*

1 Raise the vehicle and support it securely.

2 Use chalk or a scribe to 'index' the relationship of the driveshaft(s) to the mating flange. This ensures correct alignment when the driveshaft is reinstalled.

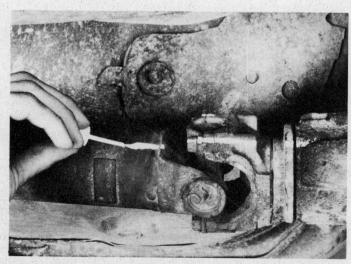

19.2 Marking the relationship of the driveshaft to the mating flange before removal

3   Remove the nuts or bolts securing the universal joint clamps to the flange. If the driveshaft has a spline on one end (either to the transmission or the center 'carrier' bearing) be sure to place marks on the mating flange or shaft to retain proper alignment on reinstallation.

4   Remove the nuts or bolts retaining the straps or universal joint to the flange on the opposite end of the driveshaft (if so equipped).

5   Pry the universal joint away from its mating flange and remove the shaft from the flange. be careful not to let the caps fall off of the universal joint which would cause contamination and loss of the needle bearings.

6   Repeat this process for the opposite end if it is equipped with a universal joint coupled to a flange.

7   If the opposite end is equipped with a sliding joint (spline), simply slide the yoke off the splined shaft.

8   If the shaft being removed is the front shaft of a two-piece unit, the rear is released by unbolting the two bolts securing the center bearing assembly. Again, make sure both ends of the shaft have been marked for installation purposes.

9   Installation is the reverse of removal. If the shaft cannot be lined up due to the components of the differential or transmission having been rotated, put the vehicle in Neutral or rotate one wheel to allow the correct alignment to be achieved. Always tighten the retaining nuts or bolts to the correct torque specification and make sure the universal joint caps are properly placed in the flange seat.

20 Driveshaft carrier bearing – checking and replacement

1   The carrier bearing can be checked in a similar manner as the universal joints are examined. Check for looseness or deterioration of the flexible rubber mounting.

2   Further examination of the carrier bearing can be made by running the vehicle in gear with the rear wheels raised in the air. However, this should be done only by an authorized dealer who can perform the tests safely.

3   Remove the driveshaft assembly.

4   With the driveshaft removed from the vehicle and the shaft sections separated at the center bearing, remove the bearing dust shield.

5   Remove the strap which retains the rubber cushion to the bearing support bracket.

6   Separate the cushion, bracket and bearing.

7   Pull the bearing assembly from the driveshaft.

8   Replace any worn components with new ones and reassemble. If the inner deflector was removed, install it to the shaft and stake it at two opposite points to ensure that it is a tight fit.

9   Pack the space between the inner dust deflector and the bearing with lithium base grease.

10   Carefully tap the bearing and slinger assembly onto the driveshaft journal until the components are tight against the shoulder on the shaft. Use a suitable piece of tubing to do this, taking care not to damage the shaft splines.

11   Install the dust shield (small diameter first) and press it up against the outer slinger.

12   Install the bearing rubber cushion, bracket and strap.

13   Reconnect the driveshafts making sure the previously made alignment marks align.

21 Driveshaft universal joints – general information

Universal joints are mechanical couplings which connect two rotating components that meet each other at different angles.

These joints are composed of a yoke on each side connected by a cross piece called a trunnion. Cups at each end of the trunnion contain needle bearings which provide smooth transfer of the torque load. Snap-rings either inside or outside of the bearing cups hold the assembly together.

Two main types of universal joints are used in Ford trucks with small differences in retention providing further variation.

The first type of universal joint is constructed with a single joint retained to its yoke with either internal or external snap-rings.

The second type referred to as 'double cardan' has two universal joints, a centering socket yoke and a center yoke. This type of coupling must be used in 4 x 4 vehicles where high torque loads and steep drive line angles are encountered (Broncos and some pick-ups).

22 Driveshaft universal joints – lubrication and checking

1   Refer to Chapter 1, for details on universal joint lubrication. Also see the routine maintenance schedule at the beginning of Chapter 1.

2   Wear in the needle roller bearings is characterized by vibration in the transmission, noise on acceleration, and in extreme cases of lack of lubrication, metallic squeaking and utlimately grating and shrieking sounds as the bearings disintegrate.

3   It is easy to check if the needle bearings are worn with the driveshaft in position, by trying to turn the shaft with one hand, the other hand holding the rear axle flange when the rear universal joint is being checked, and the front half coupling when the front universal joint is being checked. Any movement between the driveshaft and the front half couplings, and around the rear half couplings, is indicative of considerable wear. Another method of checking for universal joint wear is to use a pry bar inserted into the gap between the universal joint and the driveshaft or flange. Leave the vehicle in gear and try to pry the joint both radially and axially. Any looseness should be apparent with this method. A final test for wear is to attempt to lift the shaft and note any movement between the yokes of the joints.

4   If any of the above conditions exist, replace the universal joints with new ones.

23 Driveshaft universal joints – overhaul

Outer snap-ring type

1   With the driveshaft removed, mark the location of the joint yokes in relation to each other.

2   Extract the snap-rings from the ends of the bearing cups.

3   Using sockets or pieces of pipe of suitable diameter, use a vise to

23.2 Removing a snap-ring from one of the bearing cups

23.3a Two sockets and a vise are used to press the bearing cups out of the yoke. Note the socket on the right is slightly smaller than the cup and the one on the left is larger

23.3b Pliers are then used to twist the cup completely out of the yoke

8

press on the end of one cup and to displace the opposite one into the larger socket wrench or pipe. The bearing cup will not be fully ejected and it should be gripped with pliers and twisted completely out of the yoke.

4   Remove the first bearing cup by pressing the trunnion in the opposite direction, then repeat the operations on the other two cups.

5   Clean the yoke and inspect for damage or cracks.

6   Obtain the appropriate repair kit which will include, trunnion, cups, needle rollers, seals, washers and snap-rings.

7   Before beginning reassembly, pack the reservoirs in the ends of the trunnion with grease and work some into the needle bearings taking care not to displace them from their location around the inside of the bearing cups.

8   Position the trunnion in the yoke, partially install one cup into the yoke and insert the trunnion a little way into it. Partially install the opposite cup, center the trunnion, then, using the vise, press both cups into position using sockets of diameter slightly less than that of the bearing cups. Make sure that the needle bearings are not displaced and trapped during this operation.

9   Install the snap-rings.

10 Align the shaft yokes and install the other bearing cups in the same way.

Injected plastic (inner snap-ring) type

11 This type of universal joint will be found on some late model vehicles. Repair can be carried out after destroying the production line plastic retainers and fitting conventional snap-ring type repair kits.

12 Support the joint yoke in a press so that using a suitable forked pressing tool, pressure can be applied to two 'eyes' of the yoke to eject a bearing cup partially into a socket wrench of adequate diameter.

13 Repeat on all the cups and then twist the cups out of the yokes with a vise.

14 Clean away all trace of the plastic bearing cup retainers. This can be facilitated by probing through the plastic injection holes.

15 Obtain the appropriate repair kit which will include one pre-lubricated trunnion assembly, bearing cups, seals and other components.

16 Assemble the universal joint as described in paragraphs 8, 9 and 10 of this Section. Note that the snap-rings are installed on the inside of the yokes on this type of joint.

17 When reassembly is complete, if the joint is stiff to move, apply some hammer blows to the yoke which will free the bearing cups from the snap-rings.

Double cardan type constant velocity joint

18 An inspection kit containing two bearing cups and two retainers is available to permit the joint to be dismantled to the stage where the joint can be inspected. Before any dismantling is started, mark the flange yoke and coupling yoke to permit reassembly in the same position, then follow the procedure given previously for the snap-ring or injected plastic type, as applicable.

19 Disengage the flange yoke and trunnion from the centering ball. Pry the seal from the ball socket and remove the washers, spring and the three ball seats.

20 Clean the ball seat insert bushing and inspect for wear. If evident, the flange yoke and trunnion assembly must be replaced.

21 Clean the seal, ball seats, spring and washers and inspect for wear. If excessive wear is evident or parts are broken, a repair kit must be used.

22 Remove all plastic material from the groove of the coupling yoke (if applicable).

23 Inspect the centering ball, if damaged it must be replaced wth a new one.

24 Withdraw the centering ball from the stud using a suitable extractor.

25 Press a new ball onto the stud until it seats firmly on the stud shoulder. It is extremely important that no damage to the ball occurs during this stage.

26 Using the grease provided in the repair kit, lubricate all the parts and insert them into the ball seat cavity in the following order: spring, washer (small o.d.), three ball seats (largest opening outwards to receive the ball), washer (large o.d.) and the seal.

27 Lubricate the seal lips and press it (lip inwards) into the cavity. Fill the cavity with the grease provided.

28 Install the flange yoke to the centering ball, ensuring that the alignment marks are correctly positioned.

29 Install the trunnion caps as described previously for the snap-ring or injected plastic types.

Chapter 9 Brake system

Contents

Specifications

General

Brake fluid type	Ford ESA-M6C25 or DOT type 3 heavy duty
Pedal travel	Non-adjustable. If travel is excessive, or brakes drag, an internal adjustment to power booster is indicated. See Ford dealer.

Drum brakes

Drum wear limit	Specified on drum
Lining wear limit	$\frac{1}{32}$ inch above rivet head or metal shoe

Disc brakes

Rotor minimum thickness	
Light duty	1.12 in
Heavy duty	1.18 in
Rotor runout	
Integral hub and rotor	0.003 in
Separate hub and rotor	0.010 in
Pad lining wear limit	$\frac{1}{32}$ inch above rivet head or metal backing plate

Torque specifications

ft-lb

Drum brakes

Front brake backing plate-to-spindle	
$\frac{1}{2}$ x 13	55 to 70
$\frac{7}{16}$ x 14	30 to 50
$\frac{1}{2}$ x 20	55 to 75
Master cylinder-to-pedal bracket	12 to 17
Eccentric adjuster bolt	80 to 120 (in-lbs)

Disc brakes

Caliper key retaining screw	12 to 20
Piston housing-to-caliper	155 to 185
Spindle/anchor plate/dust shield-to-steering knuckle	50 to 60
Anchor plate-to-spindle	
1973 thru 1975	55 to 75
1976 thru 1979	74 to 102
Brake shoe mounting pins	17 to 23
Caliper mounting pins	17 to 23
Brake hose-to-caliper	17 to 25

1 General information

Ford light duty trucks (4 x 2 models) are equipped with disc brakes in the front and drum brakes in the rear. Ford light duty trucks (4 x 4 models) and Broncos are equipped with drum-type brakes on both front and rear wheels during the model years 1973 through 1975. Starting in 1976, Broncos and 4 x 4 light duty trucks were offered with disc brakes on the front and continued the use of drum-type brakes on the rear.

The hydraulic system has a dual master cylinder and separate front and rear brake line circuits. The master cylinder contains two hydraulic pistons (primary and secondary) fed by separate fluid reservoirs. A pressure differential valve and warning switch are incorporated into the hydraulic system. This valve provides a higher percentage of braking force to the front wheels to compensate for weight transfer when the brakes are applied. The warning switch indicates to the vehicle's operator when a failure has occurred in one of the braking circuits. If a failure in one of the circuits occurs, the other one will continue to operate the brakes, although total braking efficiency will be one-half of normal or less.

A vacuum brake booster provides servo assistance to the brake pedal and is optional on vehicles with drum-type front brakes. If the vehicle has disc brakes, the vacuum booster is standard equipment.

A parking brake system is provided and operates independently of the normal hydraulic brake system. A pedal on the driver's side of the cab operates a system of cables to activate the rear brake shoes only.

2 Braking system – inspection and adjustment

Refer to Chapter 1.

3 Drum brakes (light duty) – replacement

1 The braking system on F-100, F-150 and F-250 (standard) vehicles is considered light duty. In addition, the above models equipped with 4-wheel drive and Bronco models are classed as light duty.

2 Raise the vehicle and support it firmly with jackstands. Remove the wheel(s) and brake drum(s). If difficulty is encountered, see Step 3. **Note:** *It is advisable to service the brakes on one side of the vehicle at a time, leaving the other side fully assembled for reference if necessary.*

3 If the drum will not come off after removing the proper retaining components, the brake adjustment needs to be released. Start this procedure by removing the rubber cover from the slot provided in the brake backing plate. Insert a small screwdriver through the slot and hold the brake adjusting lever away from the adjusting screw. Use a brake adjustment tool to retract the automatic adjuster by turning the adjustment wheel downward with the tool. Once the shoes are retracted sufficiently, the brake drum can be removed. Be careful not to damage the brake adjustment wheel while performing this operation.

4 Install a brake cylinder clamp over the ends of the wheel cylinder cups. Be careful not to tear or damage the wheel cylinder boots. This will push in the ends of the wheel cylinder to relieve pressure on the brake system.

5 Release the adjusting lever from the adjusting screw by pivoting it backward. Retract the adjusting screw as far as possible.

6 Move the outboard side of the adjusting screw back and up off the pivot nut as far as possible. It will now be possible to pivot the hook assembly downward and rearward far enough to unhook the pivot from the rear brake shoe.

7 Remove the automatic adjusting spring and adjusting lever. Keep these parts together on the side of the vehicle you are working on as they are not designed to interchange from one side to the other.

8 Remove the secondary shoe retracting spring from the upper anchor with a brake tool designed for this purpose. Be careful, it is under a great deal of pressure.

9 Remove the primary shoe retracting spring from the upper anchor with the same special tool.

10 Remove the self-adjuster cable hook and the anchor pin plate (if so equipped) from the anchor pin.

11 Remove the self-adjuster cable guide from the rear shoe.

12 Remove the brake shoe hold-down caps, springs and pins from each shoe. This is done by depressing the spring, and then turning the pin until the head of the pin aligns with the slot in the cap. Keep these parts separate as they are often different for each shoe.

13 Remove each brake shoe. As you remove the shoes, the adjusting screw, pivot nut and pivot socket will fall free from the bottom of the shoes. Keep these parts together.

14 On rear brakes, the parking brake link and spring will be released from the top of the shoes as they are pulled free. Note which direction they fit and keep these parts together.

15 On rear brakes, pull the parking brake cable spring forward on the cable which will enable you to release the cable end from the hook on the parking brake lever. The parking brake lever can be removed from the secondary brake shoe by releasing the C-clip and then removing the lever and spring. Keep these parts together.

16 Clean all of the parts with brake cleaning solvent or rubbing alcohol. Do not use any other types of petroleum solvents or gasoline.

17 Clean the backing plate and other components with a vacuum cleaner. Do not use compressed air to blow the dust out because the flying asbestos brake particles are very hazardous to breathe and can irritate the skin. With the brake assembly dismantled to this point, now is the time to determine if wheel cylinder overhaul and brake drum servicing is required. If the wheel cylinder (brake cylinder) shows any signs of fluid leakage or if the rubber boots are damaged, it would be wise to overhaul the cylinder at this point (see Section 5). Inspect the inside of the brake drum for cracks, scores, deep scratches or 'hard spots' which will appear as small discolorations. If fine emery cloth will not bring the drum back to a smooth, even finish, the drums should be 'turned' (machined) at an automotive repair shop. Many mechanics have this done routinely as a part of the brake job – the cost is minimal.

18 Lubricate the brake shoe contact points (on the backing plate) with brake lube.

19 Assemble the parking brake lever to the rear brake shoe along with the spring. Use a new C-clip to retain the lever.

20 Place the primary brake shoe onto the backing plate and install the hold-down pin, spring and clip. Repeat the process for the rear brake shoe (after hooking the cable to the parking brake lever if it is on the rear wheel). Install the parking brake link, spring and washer if you are working on a rear brake.

21 Install the anchor pin plate (if so equipped). Install the self-adjuster cable end over the anchor pin with the crimped side facing inward.

22 Install the primary shoe retracting spring with the special brake spring tool. Crimp the end of the spring closer together after it is installed over the anchor pin if it has sprung open.

23 Install the flanged hole of the cable guide into the proper hole in the rear brake shoe web. Thread the cable around the groove in the cable guide.

24 Install the long rear shoe return spring with the brake tool. Again, crimp the end if the hook has opened up (don't crimp the spring end any tighter than a U shape). Recheck the adjuster cable end to make sure it isn't cocked or binding. It should sit squarely on the anchor pin and pivot freely behind the return springs.

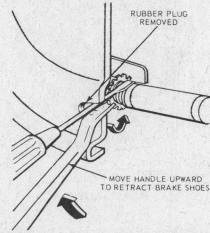

RUBBER PLUG REMOVED

MOVE HANDLE UPWARD TO RETRACT BRAKE SHOES

Fig. 9.1 The brake linings can be adjusted inward (away from the drum) by working through the access hole at the rear side of the brake assembly (Sec 3)

3.20 One of the brake shoe hold-down springs correctly retained by the pin (light duty brakes)

3.24 The secondary return spring and adjusting cable guide correctly installed (light duty brakes)

3.31 The self-adjuster assembly correctly installed (light duty brakes)

25 Remove the brake cylinder clamp after making sure the pins are correctly positioned between the wheel cylinder and the brake shoes.

26 Apply brake lubricant to the threads and socket end of the adjusting screw. Retract the adjusting screw to its minimum size and back it out $\frac{1}{2}$-turn. Notice that the socket end of the screw is stamped with an R or an L. This letter should correspond to the side of the vehicle you are working on (L on the left or driver's side or R on the right or passenger's side).

27 Assemble the adjusting socket to the adjustment screw and pivot nut and install this assembly between the brake shoes with the screw end closest to the secondary (rear) shoe.

28 Install the hooked end of the adjusting cable into the pivot hook from the backing plate side. Make sure you are using the correct adjusting lever as they are stamped L or R just as the adjusting screws are.

29 Place the hooked end of the adjuster spring into the large hole in the primary shoe web; then connect the loop end of the spring to the adjustment lever hole. Make sure that the adjustment cable is properly routed through the cable guide and is not caught on any springs or other brake components.

30 Pull the combination assembly (adjustment lever, cable end and spring) down toward the rear and engage the hook end of the pivot into the large hole of the secondary shoe web.

31 Check the operation of the self-adjusting mechanism by pulling the cable and cable pivot back far enough for the engagement tang on the pivot to ride up past one tooth on the adjusting screw and catch the tooth immediately above the original position. The spring action of the adjusting lever should pivot the adjusting screw as it springs back to its normal position. If this action checks out correctly, install the drum (and hub) assembly.

32 If the self-adjuster mechanism does not operate correctly, check the components for proper installation position and condition. Often

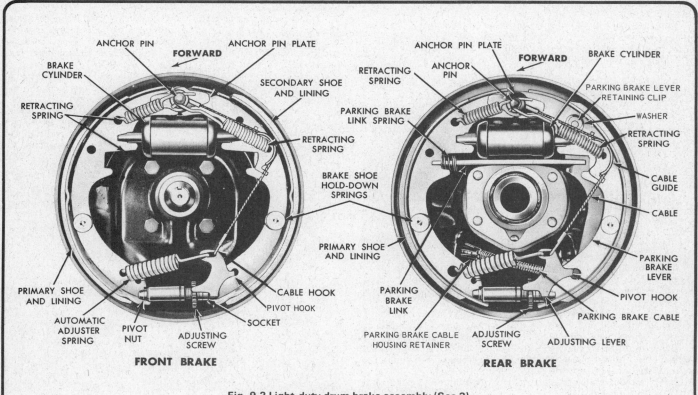

Fig. 9.2 Light-duty drum brake assembly (Sec 3)

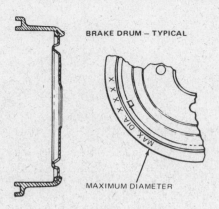
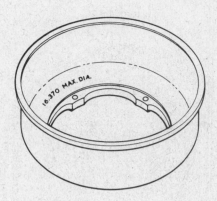

BRAKE DRUM – TYPICAL

MAXIMUM DIAMETER

Fig. 9.3 The maximum diameter of the brake drum is stamped on the drum. This indicates how much material can be removed in the 'turning' process before the drums require replacement (Sec 3)

times a stretched cable is the culprit in a non-operating system. Replace any components in questionable condition.

33 Manually adjust the brakes (by turning the adjustment screw) until there is a slight drag on the brake drum as it is slipped into place over the brake assembly.

34 Complete the assembly by installing the wheels and lowering the vehicle to the ground. Check the operation of the brakes before attempting to drive the vehicle. In some cases it will be necessary to adjust the brakes (Chapter 1) before road testing the vehicle.

4 Drum brakes (heavy duty) – replacement

1 Heavy duty drum brakes are found on F-250 models with higher Gross Vehicle Weight ratings and on F-350 series vehicles. Before beginning, observe the notes and cautions in Section 3.

2 Remove the wheel(s) from the vehicle after raising and supporting it securely. Refer to the appropriate Sections in Chapter 11 or Chapter 8 (4 x 4 models) for hub and drum assembly removal instructions.

3 If the drum will not come off after removing the proper retaining components, refer to Section 3, Step 3 of this Chapter for brake adjustment releasing instructions.

4 Remove the spring clip retainer holding the adjusting cable anchor fitting to the brake spring anchor pin (front brakes only).

5 Remove the parking brake lever assembly retaining nut from the rear of the backing plate (rear brakes only). Remove the parking brake lever assembly.

6 Remove the adjusting cable assembly from the anchor pin. Unthread it from the cable guide and disconnect the other end from the adjusting lever.

7 Remove the brake shoe retracting springs from both the primary and secondary brake shoes. Use the brake service tool for this operation.

8 Remove the brake shoe hold-down springs from both the primary and secondary brake shoes.

9 Remove the brake shoes. The adjusting screw assembly will fall loose at this time. Keep all parts of this assembly together.

10 Clean all of the springs and adjusting components with brake cleaner or rubbing alcohol. **Caution**: *Never use any petroleum solvents and never blow the parts clean with compressed air as fine asbestos dust is a serious health hazard if breathed.*

11 Clean the brake backing plate and hub components left on the vehicle. If the six ledge pads on the backing plate are corroded or rusty, sand them lightly to bare metal.

12 Apply a light coat of brake lube to the ledge pads. Apply a coating of lube to the retracting and hold-down spring contact points on the brake shoes and backing plate.

13 Dismantle and clean the pivot nut, adjusting screw, washer and socket. Take care not to mix these adjusting components from side-to-side as they are built for left or right side installation only. If these components become mixed, the adjusting lever and the socket end of the adjusting screw are stamped with the letter L or R. Carefully inspect the brake cylinder (wheel cylinder) and drum at this time. See Section 3 for further instructions.

4.8 Disconnecting one of the brake shoe hold-down springs (heavy duty brakes)

4.20 The self-adjuster assembly correctly installed (heavy duty brakes)

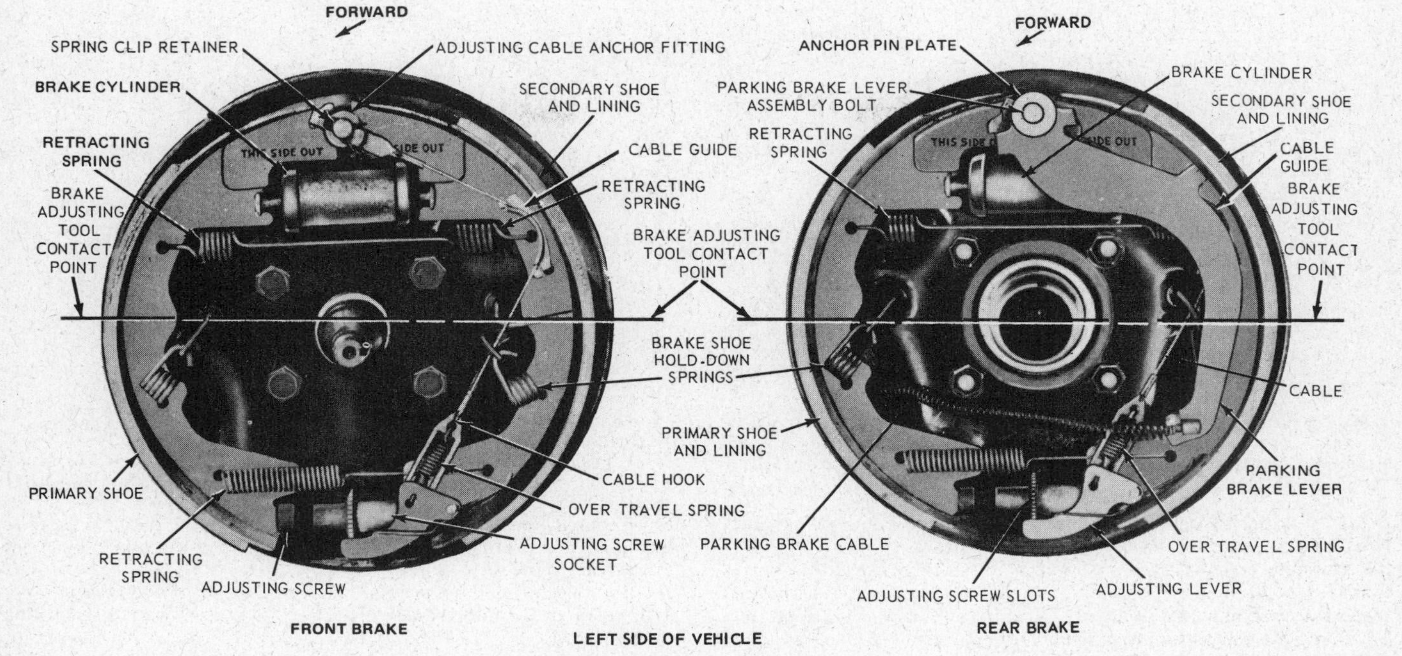

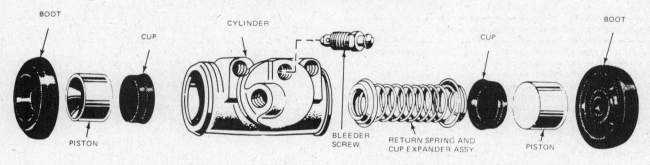

Fig. 9.4 Heavy duty drum brake assembly (Sec 4)

Labels (left, FRONT BRAKE): SPRING CLIP RETAINER, FORWARD, ADJUSTING CABLE ANCHOR FITTING, BRAKE CYLINDER, SECONDARY SHOE AND LINING, RETRACTING SPRING, THIS SIDE OUT, SIDE OUT, CABLE GUIDE, RETRACTING SPRING, BRAKE ADJUSTING TOOL CONTACT POINT, BRAKE ADJUSTING TOOL CONTACT POINT, PRIMARY SHOE, RETRACTING SPRING, ADJUSTING SCREW, CABLE HOOK, OVER TRAVEL SPRING, ADJUSTING SCREW SOCKET, BRAKE SHOE HOLD-DOWN SPRINGS

Labels (right, REAR BRAKE): ANCHOR PIN PLATE, FORWARD, PARKING BRAKE LEVER ASSEMBLY BOLT, BRAKE CYLINDER, RETRACTING SPRING, SECONDARY SHOE AND LINING, THIS SIDE, SIDE OUT, CABLE GUIDE, BRAKE ADJUSTING TOOL CONTACT POINT, PRIMARY SHOE AND LINING, CABLE, PARKING BRAKE LEVER, PARKING BRAKE CABLE, OVER TRAVEL SPRING, ADJUSTING SCREW SLOTS, ADJUSTING LEVER

FRONT BRAKE — LEFT SIDE OF VEHICLE — REAR BRAKE

Labels (Fig 9.5): BOOT, CUP, CYLINDER, BLEEDER SCREW, RETURN SPRING AND CUP EXPANDER ASSY, CUP, PISTON, BOOT, PISTON

Fig. 9.5 Exploded view of brake wheel cylinder (Sec 5)

14 Lubricate the threads of the adjustment components with brake lube and retract the adjustment to the smallest dimension.
15 Install the upper brake retracting spring between the two brake shoes and make sure you have the shoes positioned correctly.
16 Place the shoes and spring assembly into position on the backing plate and position the wheel cylinder pushrods into their proper slots on the brake shoe webbing.
17 Install both brake shoe hold-down springs.
18 Position the brake shoe adjustment screw assembly into place between the bottom of the brake shoes with the slot in the head of the adjusting screw pointed towards the primary shoe.
19 Install the lower brake shoe retracting spring.
20 Install the adjusting lever spring and the cable assembly to the adjusting lever. Position the adjusting lever onto the proper pin of the secondary shoe.
21 Place the adjusting lever cable into its proper position around the cable guide and hook the cable end to the anchor pin.
22 Install the spring clip retainer over the anchor pin and cable end on front brakes. Install the parking brake lever and retaining nut on rear brake assemblies.
23 Manually adjust the brakes (by turning the adjustment screw) until there is a slight drag on the brake drum as it is slipped into place over the brake assembly.
24 Install the brake drum and hub assembly. Adjust the bearings as described in Chapter 8 or Chapter 11. Install the wheels. Lower the vehicle from the stands or supports.

25 Check the brakes by applying them several times before attempting to drive the vehicle. Make sure they are adjusted by backing up and applying the brakes several times. Test drive the vehicle by making several light-effort slow speed stops to seat the brake linings. Avoid any high-speed or panic stops during the first brake applications.

5 Drum brake wheel cylinders – removal, overhaul and installation

Removal

1 The type of wheel cylinder and the method of removal is basically the same for all models. **Note:** *Obtain a wheel cylinder repair kit which will have all the necessary replacement parts.*
2 Refer to Section 3 or 4 as appropriate and remove the brake shoes.
3 Unscrew the brake pipe union from the rear of the wheel cylinder. Do not pull the metal tube from the cylinder as it will bend, making installation difficult.
4 Remove the two bolts securing the wheel cylinder to the brake backplate assembly.
5 Remove the wheel cylinder assembly.
6 Plug the end of the hydraulic pipe to stop the loss of too much hydraulic fluid and/or the entry of dirt.

9

Overhaul

7   Remove the rubber boots from the ends of the wheel cylinder.
8   Remove the pistons, cups and piston return spring. Remove the piston expander assembly from the cylinder.
9   Remove the bleeder screw from the cylinder.
10   Inspect the interior bore of the cylinder for scoring, corrosion or other damage. A very light film or accumulation can be cleaned out with a brake cylinder hone. However, if any question about the cylinder condition exists, it is best to replace it with a new one.
11   Clean the cylinder thoroughly with brake cleaning fluid.
12   Using brake assembly lubricant, coat all of the parts in the repair kit.
13   Install the piston return spring and a piston expander assembly between the two cups. Make sure the cups face wide-side inward. Install a piston into each end of the bore. Install the boot and link over each end of the cylinder. Clamp the pistons together with a brake clamp if necessary.

Installation

14   Place the completed brake cylinder onto the backing plate and install the retaining bolts and lock washers.
15   Install a new gasket on the brake line fitting and connect the line to the cylinder. Install the bleeder screw.
16   Refer to Sections 3 or 4 and install the brake shoes and hardware.
17   Bleed the hydraulic system as described in Section 14.

6   Disc brake pads (light duty) – replacement

Note: *Always replace disc brake pad sets in pairs. Never install pads on one wheel only. It is advisable to disassemble one side at a time, leaving the other side fully assembled for use as reference if necessary.*
1   Loosen the lug nuts on both front wheels. Chock the rear wheels. Set the parking brake. Raise the front of the vehicle and support it securely. Remove the front wheels.
2   Remove the retaining screw from the caliper retaining key.
3   Use a hammer and a soft drift to carefully tap the caliper retaining key and spring either inward or outward from the anchor plate. Use care so as not to damage the key.
4   Press the caliper assembly inward and upward against the caliper support springs and pivot the caliper off the rotor. Once the bottom of the caliper has cleared the anchor plate, pull it straight off the plate.
5   Use caution not to stretch or kink the flexible rubber brake hose and use wire to suspend the caliper from an upper suspension component out of the way.
6   If the pads are being reused, mark them for position so they can be installed in their original location.
7   Remove the pads from the anchor plate. The anti-rattle clips will come out with the pads as they are removed.
8   Clean the bracket, caliper and pads (if they are being reused) with brake cleaning solvent. Replace the pads if they measure less than the minimum thickness listed in the Specifications. Have the rotor resurfaced or replace it if it is scored, damaged or cracked.
9   If new pads are being installed, it is necessary to siphon some brake fluid from the large reservoir of the master cylinder to prevent overflow when the piston is compressed. Compress the piston with a special tool designed for this purpose. If you do not have access to this tool, the piston can be compressed as follows: Use a C-clamp and a 1-$\frac{3}{4}$ in by 1 in piece of wood placed between the leg of the clamp and a brake pad inserted into the caliper as shown in the accompanying Figure. Remove the clamp and pad after the piston is compressed.
10   Install the anti-rattle clips and pads onto the anchor plate. If the old pads are being reinstalled, make sure they are in their original position.
11   Detach the caliper from its supporting wire and position it against the anchor plate with the lower bevelled edge on top of the rear caliper support spring. Make sure the pads and clips remain in their correct position.
12   Carefully slide the caliper over the pads with a pivoting motion until the caliper upper bevelled edge can be pushed over the forward caliper support spring.
13   Use a large screwdriver or similar tool to hold the caliper over the upper caliper support spring and against the anchor plate.
14   Carefully install the caliper retaining key and spring. Remove the screwdriver and carefully tap the caliper key into its correct position.

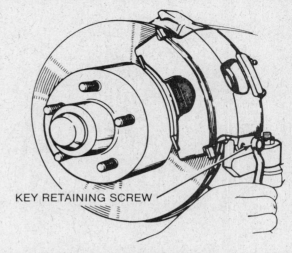

Fig. 9.6 Removing the caliper key retaining screw (Sec 6)

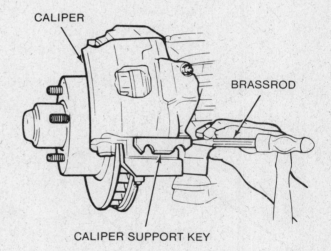

Fig. 9.7 Driving out the caliper support key (Sec 6)

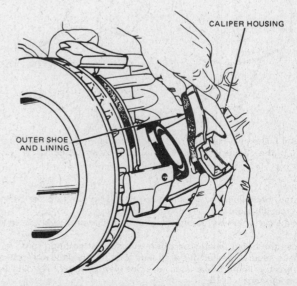

Fig. 9.8 Removing the outer shoe and lining from the caliper (Sec 6)

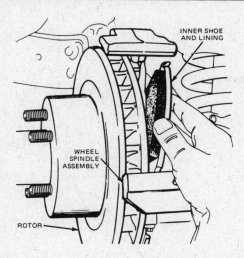

Fig. 9.9 Removing the inner shoe and lining (Sec 6)

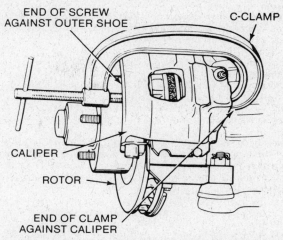

Fig. 9.10 Depressing the caliper piston to allow additional room for new (thicker) shoes (Sec 6)

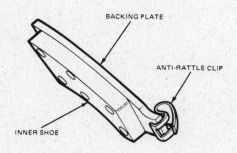

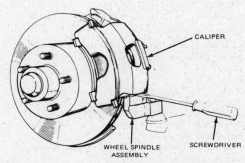

Fig. 9.12 Prying on the caliper assembly to ease support key installation (Sec 6)

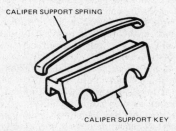

Fig. 9.13 Caliper support key and spring (Sec 6)

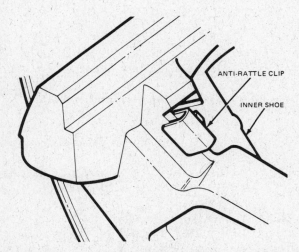

Fig. 9.11 The anti-rattle clip attached to the inner shoe (top) and the clip as it appears installed (bottom) (Sec 6)

15 Install the caliper key retaining screw and tighten it to the correct torque specification.

16 Install the wheel and tighten the lug nuts. Lower the vehicle to the ground.

17 Press the brake pedal several times before attempting to drive it. It will take several strokes of the brakes to bring the pads into contact with the rotor. If the brake hose was not disconnected, bleeding will not be necessary.

18 Test drive the vehicle and make the first several stops gentle ones to seat the brake pads.

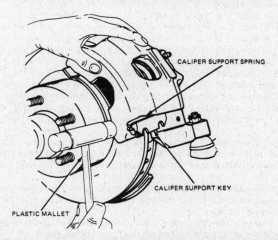

Fig. 9.14 Installing the caliper support key and spring into the caliper (Sec 6)

9

7 Disc brake pads (heavy duty) – replacement

Note: *See the note at the beginning of Section 6 before beginning.*

1973 through 1975 vehicles

1 Loosen the lug nuts on both front wheels. Chock the rear wheels. Set the parking brake, Raise the front of the vehicle and support it securely. Remove the wheels.
2 Remove the nuts from the brake pad retaining pins and withdraw the pins and anti-rattle coil springs.
3 Use a pair of thin-nosed pliers to withdraw the two brake pads from the caliper assembly.
4 Clean the inside of the caliper with brake cleaning solvent or alcohol and remove all dust and debris from the piston faces. **Caution:** *Do not use compressed air to blow this assembly clean as the flying asbestos dust is very dangerous to breathe.*
5 Siphon some brake fluid out of the large reservoir in the master cylinder. Use a piece of wood (a small hammer handle will work) and retract the pistons back into the caliper bores as far as possible. If you have disassembled both sides, block the opposite side pistons as they will pop out when you are compressing these pistons.
6 Install new pads into the caliper assembly. Make sure they are seated squarely. Insert the two retaining pins and anti-rattle springs. Make sure that the spring tangs engage the holes in the pad plates.
7 Install the pin retaining nuts and tighten them to the correct torque specification.
8 Pump the brake pedal several times to push the pads against the discs. Refill the master cylinder reservoir using new fluid.
9 Install the wheels and lower the vehicle to the ground.
10 Test drive the vehicle and apply the brakes lightly the first few times so that the pads will seat correctly.

1976 through 1979 vehicles

11 Perform step number 1.
12 Remove the retaining screw from the key.
13 Use a soft punch and a light hammer to drive out the key and spring.
14 Rotate the caliper out and away from the rotor by pulling on the key and spring end. Slide the opposite end of the caliper free of the slide in the support until the caliper clears the rotor. Support the caliper assembly with some wire from a suspension member. Be careful not to twist or stretch the flexible rubber brake hose.
15 Remove the large brake shoe anti-rattle spring.
16 Remove the inner and outer brake pads.
17 Clean the caliper and piston facings of dust or accumulated debris. Be especially watchful of the area on the support that the caliper slides on.
18 Position a C-clamp and one of the old disc brake pads into place on the caliper. Tighten the C-clamp to compress the pistons into the bottom of their bore. If both calipers have been removed, block the opposite side pistons to prevent them from popping out during this operation. Remove the clamp and pad.
19 Install the new shoes onto the support. Install the anti-rattle spring.
20 Place the bottom of the caliper assembly onto the support and rotate the assembly up into place over the pads and rotor.
21 Position the spring between the key and the caliper with the spring tangs overlapping the ends of the key. You may need a screwdriver or brake adjusting tool to support the caliper to start these pieces into their proper position.
22 Using the hammer and soft punch, tap the key and spring into place until the notch in the key lines up for the retaining screw.
23 Install the key retaining screw and torque it to the proper specification.
24 Perform Steps 8 through 10 of this Section.

8 Disc brake caliper (light duty) – overhaul

If hydraulic fluid is leaking from the caliper it will be necessary to install new seals. If brake fluid is found running down the side of the wheel, or if you notice that a pool of fluid forms alongside one wheel or the level in the master cylinder drops excessively, it is also indicative of seal failure. Obtain an overhaul kit which will contain all necessary parts.

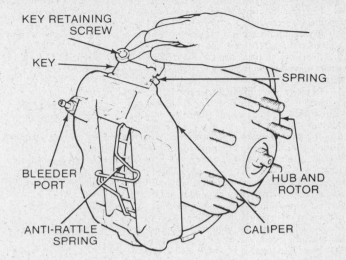

Fig. 9.15 Removing the key retaining screw on heavy duty 1976 – 1979 vehicles (Sec 7)

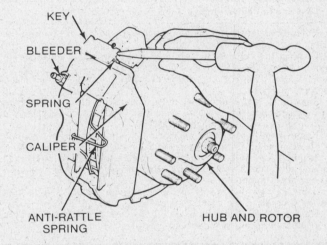

Fig. 9.16 Using a hammer and punch to remove the caliper key and spring (Sec 7)

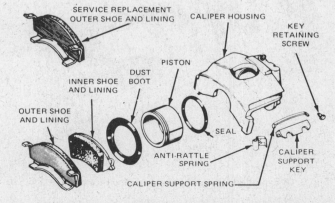

Fig. 9.17 Exploded view of light duty disc brake caliper (Sec 8)

1 Refer to Sections 6 or 7 and remove the caliper. Remove the flexible hose and plug it to prevent fluid loss or contamination.
2 Wrap a cloth around the caliper and, using compressed air at the hydraulic fluid port, carefully eject the pistons.
3 If the piston has seized in the bore, carefully tap around the piston while applying air pressure. **Caution:** *The piston will come out with force.*
4 Remove the rubber dust boot from the caliper assembly.
5 Carefully remove the rubber piston seal from the cylinder bore with a soft wood or plastic tool. Do not use a screwdriver as it could damage the bore.
6 Thoroughly wash all parts in brake cleaning solvent or alcohol. During reassembly, new rubber seals should be installed and they should be well lubricated with clean hydraulic fluid or brake assembly lube.
7 Inspect the piston and bore for signs of wear, score marks or other damage; if evident, a new caliper assembly will be necessary.
8 To reassemble, first place the new caliper piston seal into its groove in the cylinder bore. The seal must not become twisted.
9 Install a new dust boot and ensure that the flange seats correctly in the outer groove of the caliper bore.
10 Carefully insert the piston into the bore. When it is about three-quarters of the way in, spread the dust boot over the piston. Seat the dust boot in the piston groove and push the piston fully into the bore.
11 Reassembly is now complete and the unit is ready for installation on the vehicle.
12 After installing the caliper and pads to the vehicle, bleed the brakes as described in Section 14.

9 Disc brake caliper (heavy duty) – overhaul

1 Refer to Section 6 or 7 and remove the brake pads. Disconnect the flexible hose from the caliper.
2 Remove the calipers as described in Section 6 or 7. Obtain an overhaul kit which will contain all necessary parts.
3 Drain the brake fluid from the cylinders and secure the caliper assembly in a vise.
4 Place a 1⅛ in (29 mm) block of wood between the caliper and the cylinders and apply low pressure air to the brake hose inlet, forcing the pistons out against the wooden block.
5 Remove the wood block and pistons, remove the bolts securing the piston housing to the caliper and separate the components.
6 Remove and discard the rubber piston boots and seals and examine the pistons and bores for signs of wear or scoring. Replace any damaged components.
7 Lubricate new piston seals with brake assembly lube and fit them into the grooves in the cylinder bores.
8 Lubricate the cylinder bores with brake fluid and fit the lips of the rubber boots into the cylinder bore grooves.

9 Insert the pistons through the rubber boots and push them into the cylinder bores past the piston seals. Take great care not to damage or dislodge the piston seals from their groove in the cylinders.
10 Push both pistons all the way in using a block of wood.
11 Reinstall the piston housing to the caliper and tighten the retaining bolts to the specifications.
12 Install the calipers and pads as described in Section 6 or 7.
13 Bleed the brakes as described in Section 14.

10 Disc brake rotor – inspection

1 Refer to Section 6 or 7 and remove the disc brake pads and caliper assembly.
2 Inspect the rotor for any deep scratches, scoring or signs of cracking or breakage. If any of these conditions exist, the rotor must be removed for refinishing at a shop equipped for this type of machining work. If the rotor does not have any of the above-mentioned defects, measure the runout (especially if any signs of wobble such as a pulsating pedal exist).
3 Runout is measured with a dial indicator. These are available as rentals or they can be purchased. Attach the base of the indicator to some part of the suspension so that the indicator's stylus touches the rotor surface approximately 1 inch from the rotor's outer edge. Starting with the indicator set at zero, slowly rotate the disc through one revolution. Note the high and low readings on the dial as the rotor revolves. The difference between the high and low readings is the total rotor runout. If the rotor exceeds the maximum specification for runout, it will have to be removed for machining or replacement.
4 If the rotor has to be removed for machining or replacement, follow the instructions in Chapter 8 (4 x 4) or Chapter 11 for hub and bearing assembly removal.
5 After machining or replacement, install the rotor(s) as described in Chapter 8 or Chapter 11.
6 Install the brake caliper and brake pads as described in Sections 6 or 7 of this Chapter.

11 Master cylinder – removal, overhaul and installation

Removal

1 For safety reasons, disconnect the battery.
2 If equipped with manual (not power) brakes, disconnect the wires from the stoplight switch, located adjacent to the brake pedal. Remove the nut and shoulder bolt securing the master cylinder pushrod to the brake pedal.
3 Place newspapers, rags, etc. under the master cylinder to catch leaking brake fluid. Brake fluid will ruin paint.
4 Unscrew the brake pipes from the primary and secondary outlets

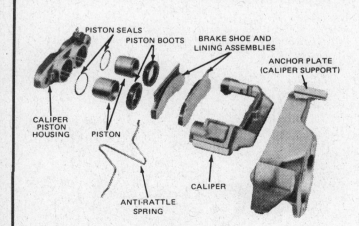

Fig. 9.18 Exploded view of heavy duty disc brake caliper (Sec 9)

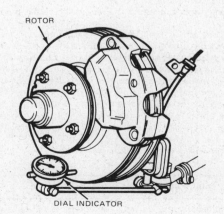

Fig. 9.19 Checking front disc runout with a dial indicator (Sec 10)

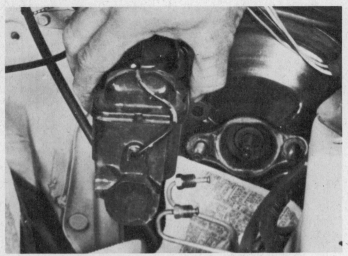
11.6 Removing the master cylinder from the servo unit. Note the newspapers to catch the fluid leakage

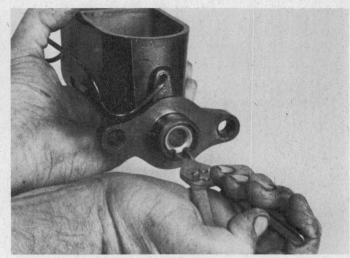
11.11 Removing the snap ring from the rear of the master cylinder

of the master cylinder. Plug the ends of the pipes to prevent any dirt from entering.

5   Remove the two screws securing the master cylinder to the firewall (or servo unit).

6   Pull the master cylinder forwards and lift it upwards from the vehicle. **Caution:** *Do not allow fluid to contact any paintwork as it will eat away the paint.*

Note: *It should be noted that new and rebuilt master cylinders are commonly available for these vehicles. If one of these is purchased, skip to Step 23 for installation instructions. If it is decided to overhaul the original unit, obtain an overhaul kit, which will contain all necessary parts, and then proceed as follows.*

Overhaul

7   Clean the exterior of the master cylinder and wipe dry with a non-fluffy rag.

8   Remove the filler cover and diaphragm (sometimes called gasket) from the top of the reservoir and pour out any remaining hydraulic fluid.

9   Remove the secondary piston stop bolt from the bottom of the master cylinder body.

10   Remove the bleed screw.

11   Depress the primary piston and remove the snap-ring from the groove at the rear of the master cylinder bore (photo). Remove the primary piston assembly.

12   *Do not* remove the screw that retains the primary return spring retainer, return spring, primary cup and protector on the primary piston. This is factory set and must not be disturbed.

13   Remove the secondary piston assembly.

14   *Do not* remove the outlet pipe seats, outlet check valves and outlet check valve springs from the master cylinder body.

15   Examine the bore of the cylinder carefully for any signs of scores or damage. If the imperfections are slight, a hone can be used to smooth the interior (photo). If damage is extensive, a new cylinder must be used.

16   If the rubber seals are swollen, or very loose on the pistons, suspect oil contamination in the system. Oil will swell these rubber seals and if one is found to be swollen it is reasonable to assume that all seals in the brake system need attention.

17   Thoroughly clean all parts in brake cleaner or alcohol. Ensure that the ports are clear.

18   All components should be assembled wet after dipping in brake assembly lube.

19   Carefully insert the complete secondary piston and return spring assembly into the master cylinder bore, easing the seals into the bore, taking care that they do not roll over. Push the assembly all the way in (photo).

20   Insert the primary piston assembly into the master cylinder bore.

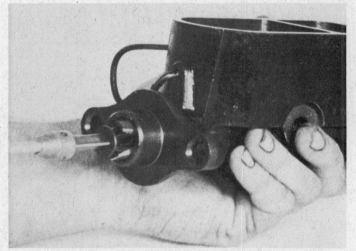
11.15 Using a hone to smooth the master cylinder bore

11.19 Inserting the assembled secondary piston into the master cylinder

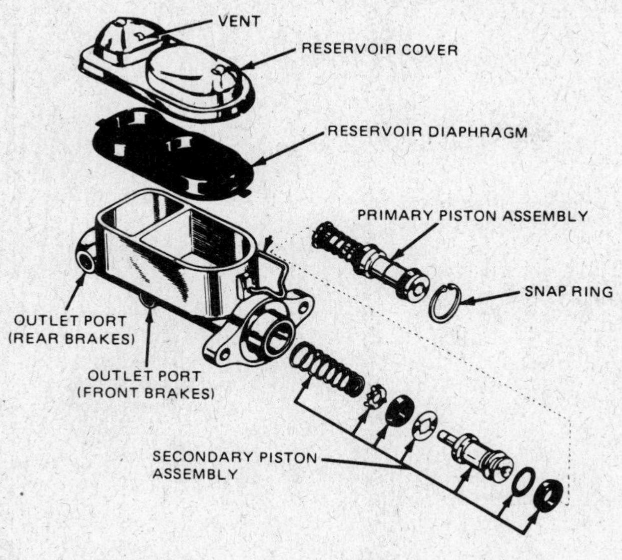

Fig. 9.20 Exploded view of master cylinder (Sec 11)

21 Push in the primary piston and tighten the secondary piston stop screw in the bottom of the cylinder.
22 Depress the piston again and install the snap-ring.

Installation
23 The master cylinder should be bled before it is installed. Fill the cylinder with fluid. Loosely install plugs in the outlet ports of the cylinder. Pump the primary piston until no air bubbles appear in the reservoir. Tighten the plugs and push on the piston. If the piston doesn't move, proceed with the installation. If it does move, continue the bleeding process until all of the air is displaced.
24 Check the pushrod-to-mounting face distance as shown. It may be necessary to turn the adjusting screw to achieve the correct dimension.
25 Installation of the cylinder is the reverse of removal. Bleed the hydraulic system after the cylinder is installed as described in Section 14.

12 Brake pressure differential valve – resetting and replacement

Resetting
1 If the light on the brake warning system goes on, a leak or problem has arisen in the braking system which must be corrected. Once the leak or problem has been repaired or if the hydraulic system has been opened up for brake cylinder overhaul or similar type repair, the pressure differential valve must be centralized. Once the valve is centralized, the brake light on the dash will go out.
2 To centralize the valve, first fill the master cylinder reservoir and make sure the hydraulic system has been bled (Sec 14).
3 Turn the ignition switch to On or Accessory. Slowly press the brake pedal down and the piston will center itself, causing the light to go out.
4 Check the brake pedal for firmness and correct operation.

Replacement
5 If the pressure differential valve has been determined to be defective or if it is leaking, it must be replaced. It is a non-serviceable unit and no repair operations are possible by the home mechanic.
6 Disconnect the brake warning light connector from the warning light switch.
7 Disconnect the front inlet and rear outlet pipe unions from the valve assembly. Plug the ends of the pipes to prevent loss of hydraulic fluid or the entry of dirt.
8 Remove the bolts and nuts securing the valve assembly to the center of the left-hand side chassis member.

9 Remove the valve assembly and bracket taking care not to allow any brake fluid to contact the paint as it is highly corrosive.
10 Installation is the reverse of removal.
11 Bleed the hydraulic system after the replacement valve has been installed.
12 Center the valve as described in Steps 1 through 4 above.

13 Hydraulic lines – inspection and replacement

1 The hydraulic system has a series of flexible rubber lines connecting the disc brake calipers and the rear axle fitting to metal lines running the length of the frame as well as connecting the differential valve and master cylinder. If an inspection (Chapter 1) reveals a problem in either a rubber hose or a metal line, this component must be replaced immediately for continued safe use of the vehicle.
2 Before replacing a line or hose, determine the cause of failure and remedy it or the hose or line will fail again. Often components such as exhaust pipes have come loose and are rubbing the line, causing the break or tear.
3 Replacement steel and flexible brake lines are commonly available from dealer parts dpartments and auto parts stores. **Caution:** *Do not, under any circumstances, use anything other than genuine steel or approved flexible brake hoses as replacement items.*
4 When removing any brake line or hose flare-nut fitting, always use the proper flare-nut wrenches when loosening and tightening the connections.
5 At the junction where a brake line meets a bracket supporting it and its connection, remove the spring clip with pliers or a vise-grip after loosing the connection.
6 Steel brake lines are usually retained along their span with clips. Always remove these clips completely before removing any brake line that they are supporting. Always replace these clips when replacing a metal brake line as they provide support and keep the lines from vibrating which will fatigue and eventually break the line.
7 Once a line has been replaced, the hydraulic system must be bled to rid the system of any air bubbles.

14 Hydraulic system – bleeding

1 When any part of the brake hydraulic system has been removed or disconnected for repair or servicing, the system must be bled to purge it of any air which may have entered.
2 The system must be in good condition with no leaks or loose fittings before any bleeding operation is attempted. If the master cylinder has been overhauled or a new one is being installed, bleed the master cylinder as described at the end of Section 11.
3 The system may be bled with either a pressure bleeder or manually, utilizing two people. Follow the instructions of the pressure bleeder manufacturer if you are using that system. Manual bleeding procedure is as follows:
4 On vehicles with disc brakes, a bleeder rod located on the pressure differential valve must be released to allow fluid to run to the front calipers. Vehicles with a gross vehicle weight rating under 6800 pounds must have the rod pulled out. Vehicles with a rating over 6800 pounds need the rod pushed in. Construct a tool like the one shown to retain the rod or use vise grips to maintain the rod in position during the bleeding process.
5 Fill the master cylinder with fluid to within $\frac{1}{4}$ inch of the top of the reservoirs. Keep the cylinders filled during the bleeding process. Cover the cylinder with a lint-free shop towel to prevent brake fluid from splashing on the painted surfaces and eroding them.
6 It may be necessary to raise the vehicle to gain access to the bleeder screws located at each brake cylinder or caliper. If this is necessary, support it securely before attempting this procedure.
7 Start with the wheel cylinder farthest from the master cylinder (right rear). Wipe the bleeder screw clean and install a tight-fitting section of rubber tubing over the fitting. The other end of the tubing should be placed into a container of new brake fluid. (Glass jars work well for this as they allow the person operating the bleeder to see any air bubbles coming from the hose).
8 Have the person assisting you sit in the driver's seat of the vehicle. Open the bleeder screw using a box-end or fitting wrench and have the assistant push the brake pedal down. Once the pedal reaches the

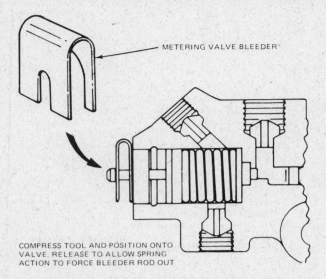

METERING VALVE BLEEDER

COMPRESS TOOL AND POSITION ONTO
VALVE. RELEASE TO ALLOW SPRING
ACTION TO FORCE BLEEDER ROD OUT

Fig. 9.21 A spring clip is used to force the bleeder rod out of the pressure differential during bleeding (Sec 14)

bottom of its travel, have him hold the pedal down while you close the bleeder valve. Have him release the brake pedal only after you have closed the valve tightly. Continue this sequence until only brake fluid and no air bubbles are being pushed from the hose into the container. It may be necessary to stop and fill the master cylinder reservoir from time to time as it must *not* be allowed to run dry.

9   Repeat this process at the next farthest brake cylinder from the master cylinder (left rear) and so on until you have covered all four wheels. At this time, the 'feel' at the brake pedal should be firm with no sponginess. Top off the master cylinder for the last time and replace the lid.

10   Once you have ascertained that the brake hydraulic system is free of air, release the bleeder rod and lower the vehicle to the ground. Check the brake pedal once again for feel before road testing the vehicle. Make the first few brake applications at low speeds to make certain the system is working properly and all valves and connections are tight.

11   If the brake warning light is on, center the differential valve as described in Section 12.

15 Vacuum booster unit – description

A servo is fitted into the brake hydraulic circuit in series with the master cylinder, to provide assistance to the driver when the brake pedal is depressed. This reduces the effort required by the driver to operate the brakes under all braking conditions.

The unit operates by vacuum obtained from the intake manifold and consists of a booster diaphragm and check valve. The servo and hydraulic master cylinder are connected together so that the servo piston rod acts as the master cylinder pushrod. The driver's braking effort is transmitted through another pushrod to the servo piston and its built-in control system. The servo piston does not fit tightly into the cylinder, but has a strong diaphragm to keep its edges in constant contact with the cylinder wall, thus assuring an air-tight seal between the two parts. The forward chamber is held under the vacuum conditions created in the intake manifold of the engine, and during periods when the brake pedal is not in use, the controls open a passage to the rear chamber, so placing it under vacuum conditions as well. When the brake pedal is pressed, the vacuum passage to the rear chamber is cut off and the chamber opened to atmospheric pressure. The consequent rush of air pushes the servo piston forward in the vacuum chamber and operates the main pushrod to the master cylinder.

The controls are designed so that assistance is given under all conditions and, when the brakes are not required, vacuum in the rear chamber is established when the brake pedal is released. All air from

the atmosphere entering the rear chamber is passed through a small air filter.

Under normal operating conditions the servo will give trouble-free service for a very long time. If, however, it is suspected that it is faulty, ie, increase in foot pressure is required to apply the brakes, it must be exchanged for a new servo. No attempt should be made to repair the old servo as it is not a serviceable item.

16 Vacuum booster unit – replacement

1   Remove the stoplight switch and actuating rod from the brake pedal as described in Section 19.
2   Working under the hood, remove the air cleaner from the carburetor and the vacuum hose from the servo.
3   Remove the master cylinder from the front of the servo and withdraw it sufficiently to allow removal of the servo.
Note: *It is not necessary to disconnect the hydraulic pipes from the master cylinder, but great care must be taken to avoid bending the pipes excessively.*
4   Remove the bolts securing the servo bracket to the engine compartment and lift the servo out of the vehicle.
5   Reinstall the servo using the reverse procedure to that of removal. If it was necessary to disconnect the hydraulic pipes, the braking system must be bled as described in Section 14.

17 Parking brake – description and adjustment

1   The parking brake system is operated by a foot pedal located at the very left of the driver's compartment. This mechanism operates a cable which is split into two cables at the mid-point of the vehicle. Each cable then runs to either side rear brake backing plate where it expands the rear brake shoes.
2   An equalizer bar with a threaded rod connected to the end of the primary cable is provided for adjustment purposes. Slack in the tension of the cables as they stretch is compensated by the threaded adjustment on this rod.
3   To adjust the parking brake mechanism, first raise the rear of the vehicle and support it securely.
4   Release the parking brake and put the vehicle into Neutral.
5   Loosen the locknut on the equalizer rod and slowly tighten the adjuster until the slack is taken out of the cables but the rear wheels will still turn freely. Check that the parking brake will engage in 3 to 6 clicks of the ratchet. Release the brake and make sure the wheels turn without dragging. Pull on each individual rear wheel cable to make sure it pulls and returns smoothly. Lubricate the cables with approved lubricant (Chapter 1).

18 Parking brake pedal and cables – removal and installation

1   The parking brake pedal and ratchet assembly is retained to the left side of the cab with two nuts on the engine side of the firewall and one bolt/nut combination underneath the dash panel.
2   To remove the pedal/ratchet assembly, remove the nuts from the studs of the assembly from the engine compartment side of the firewall. Remove the bolt and nut retaining the assembly to the underlip of the dashboard.
3   Pivot the assembly down far enough to gain access to the internal components. Remove the spring clip retaining the cable housing to the ratchet assembly bracket. Unhook the ball end of the cable from the cable pull lever. Remove the ratchet assembly.
4   The primary cable is retained to the body and chassis with a varying combination of clips and brackets. Follow the span of the cable and unbolt, unclip or disconnect any cables, retainers or springs. Note the location and type of retainer for installation purposes
5   The secondary cables of the parking brake system connect the brake shoe levers at the rear brakes to the equalizer bracket at the body midpoint. Some long wheelbase vehicles have additional intermediate cables which are merely extensions to compensate for extra chassis length.
6   The secondary and intermediate cables are removed by first removing the nut and locknut from the rod running through the brake equalizer bracket. Remove the return spring from the equalizer bracket.

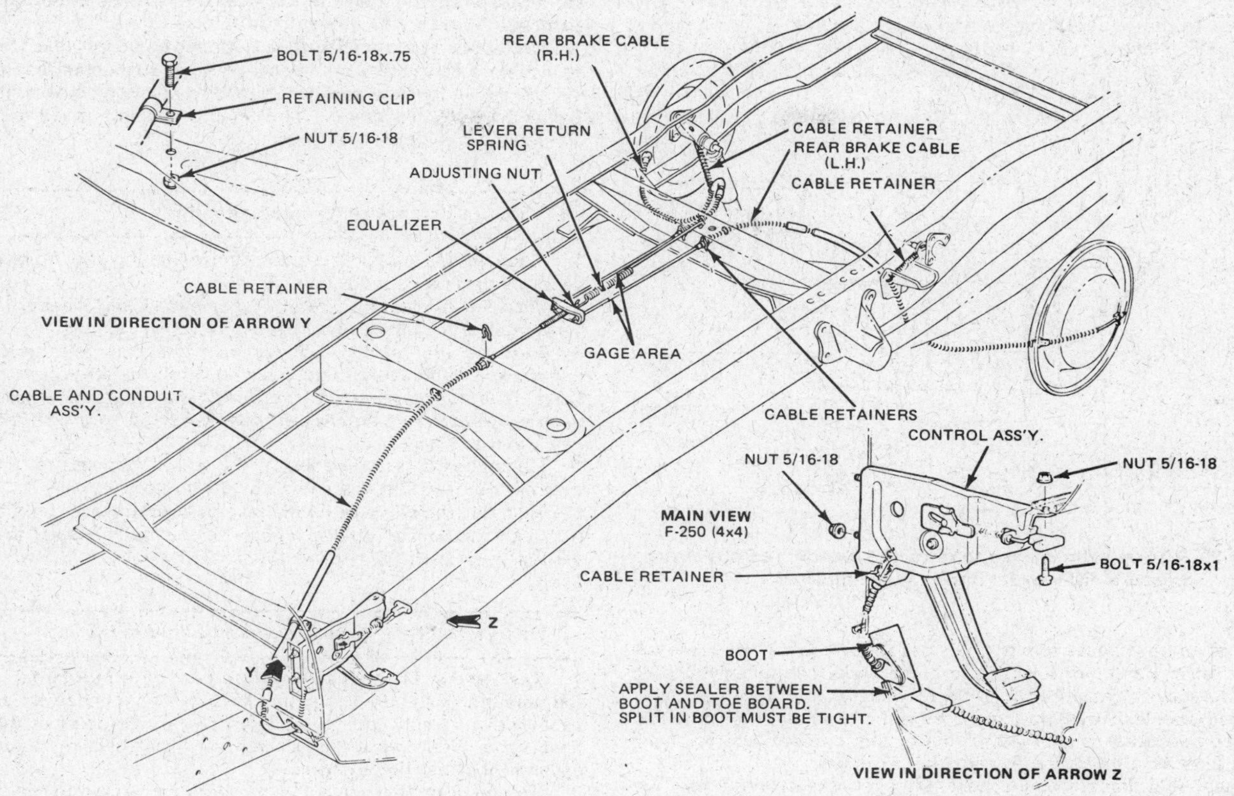

BOLT 5/16-18x.75

RETAINING CLIP

NUT 5/16-18

REAR BRAKE CABLE (R.H.)

LEVER RETURN SPRING

ADJUSTING NUT

EQUALIZER

CABLE RETAINER

VIEW IN DIRECTION OF ARROW Y

CABLE RETAINER
REAR BRAKE CABLE (L.H.)
CABLE RETAINER

CABLE AND CONDUIT ASS'Y.

GAGE AREA

CABLE RETAINERS

CONTROL ASS'Y.

NUT 5/16-18

NUT 5/16-18

MAIN VIEW
F-250 (4x4)

CABLE RETAINER

BOLT 5/16-18x1

BOOT

APPLY SEALER BETWEEN
BOOT AND TOE BOARD.
SPLIT IN BOOT MUST BE TIGHT.

Z

Y

VIEW IN DIRECTION OF ARROW Z

Fig. 9.22 Typical parking brake system (Sec 17)

Again, a combination of clips, springs and brackets will retain the length of these cables to the chassis and should be removed and kept in order for installation purposes. The rear brake drums and shoes must be removed to gain access to the ends of these cable. The ends of the cables can be removed through the rear brake backing plates by squeezing all of the retaining prongs together and pushing the cable and housing through the backing plates after unhooking the cable ends from the parking brake levers.

7   Installation is the reverse of removal. Lubricate any new or replacement cables thoroughly before installing them. Lubricate the ratchet of the pedal assembly before installing it. Adjust the cables as described in the previous Section after the cable and/or pedal assembly have been installed. Notice that the return spring attaches to the equalizer bar and a frame crossmember to provide proper pedal return action.

19 Brake pedal assembly – removal and installation

1   On vehicles equipped with a manual transmission, the brake pedal operates on the same shaft as the clutch pedal, and both pedals are removed as described in Chapter 7.
2   On automatic transmission models, disconnect the master cylinder pushrod and loosen the shoulder bolt nut. Slide the shoulder bolt to the right until the brake pedal and pedal bushings can be removed.
3   Replace the bushings if worn and install the pedal and pushrod using the reverse of the removal procedure.

20 Brakelight switch – adjustment

1   The brakelight switch is located under the dashboard directly above the brake pedal. It is activated by the pedal traveling away from its bottomed position which releases the plunger and closes an electrical circuit to the system. The switch is mounted in a metal bracket which can be bent to vary its position.
2   Make sure the switch is fully seated in its bracket. Use an assistant

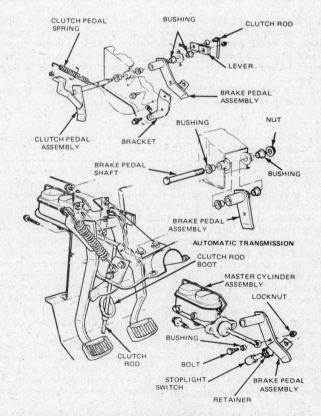

CLUTCH PEDAL SPRING

BUSHING

CLUTCH ROD

LEVER

BRAKE PEDAL ASSEMBLY

CLUTCH PEDAL ASSEMBLY

BRACKET

BUSHING

NUT

BUSHING

BRAKE PEDAL SHAFT

BRAKE PEDAL ASSEMBLY

AUTOMATIC TRANSMISSION

CLUTCH ROD BOOT

MASTER CYLINDER ASSEMBLY

LOCKNUT

BUSHING

CLUTCH ROD

BOLT

STOPLIGHT SWITCH

RETAINER

BRAKE PEDAL ASSEMBLY

Fig. 9.23 Brake pedal assembly including stoplight switch (Secs 19 and 20)

9

or a mirror to determine when the circuit is activated. A test light connected to the two terminals of the switch would also provide you with this information.

3   The switch should activate the brake circuit within the first $\frac{1}{2}$ inch travel of the brake pedal.

4   If the switch does not perform in this manner, bend the mounting bracket up or down to yield this action. Do not bend the bracket down to the point where it is preventing the pedal from returning fully.

5   The factory recommends that a 25-pound pull or less upward on the pedal is also sufficient to adjust the switch from a downward position. Again, make sure the switch is seated correctly in its bracket after performing this step.

Chapter 10 Chassis electrical system

Contents

Specifications

Windshield wiper blade-to-mounting clearance
    Bronco .... $\frac{1}{2}$ to $1\frac{1}{4}$ in
    Pick-up .... 1 to 2 in

1 General information

The electrical system is of the 12 volt, negative ground type.

Power for the lighting system and all electrical accessories is supplied by a lead/acid type battery which is charged by an alternator.

This Chapter covers repair and service procedures for the various lighting and electrical components not associated with the engine. Information on the battery, alternator, voltage regulator and starter motor can be found in Chapter 5.

It should be noted that whenever portions of the electrical system are worked on, the negative battery cable should be disconnected to prevent electrical shorts and/or fires.

2 Fuses and fusible links

1 The electrical circuis of the vehicle are protected by a combination of fuses, circuit breakers and fusible links.

2 The fuse box in most models is located underneath the dashboard, on the left side of the vehicle. It is easily accessible for fuse inspection or replacement without completely removing the box from its mounting.

3 Each of the fuses is designed to protect a specific circuit, and the various circuits are identified on the fuse panel itself.

4 If an electrical component has failed, your first check should be the fuse. A fuse which has 'blown' can be readily identified by inspecting the element inside the glass tube. If this metal element is broken, the fuse is inoperable and must be replaced with a new one.

5 When removing and installing fuses it is important that metal objects are not used to pry the fuse in or out of the holder. Plastic fuse pullers are available for this purpose.

6 It is also important that the correct fuse be installed. The different electrical circuits need varying amounts of protection, indicated by the amperage rating on the fuse.

7 At no time should the fuse be bypassed by using metal or foil. Serious damage to the electrical system could result.

8 If the replacement fuse immediately fails, do not replace again until the cause of the problem is isolated and corrected. In most cases this will be a short circuit in the wiring system caused by a broken or deteriorated wire.

9 In addition to fuses, the wiring system incorporates fusible links for overload protection. These links are used in circuits which are not ordinarily fused, such as the ignition circuit.

10 Although the fusible links appear to be of a heavier gauge than the wire they are protecting, this appearance is due to the heavy insulation. All fusible links are several wire gauges smaller than the

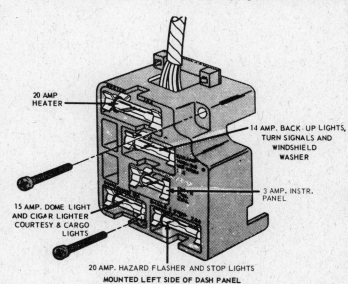

Fig. 10.1 Fuse block – 1973 and 1974 pick-ups (Bronco similar) (Sec 2)

10

wire they are incorporated into. They are color coded the same as the circuit they protect.

11 The exact locations of the four fusible links used may differ slightly but their protective circuits are the same.

12 The fusible links cannot be repaired, but rather a new link, of the identical wire size and special insulation type can be put in its place. This process is as follows:

13 Disconnect the battery ground cable.

14 Disconnect the fusible link from its electrical source.

15 Cut the damaged fusible link out of the wiring system. Do this just behind the connector. Some links have eyelet connectors and can be unbolted instead of cut.

16 Strip the insulation from the circuit wiring approximately $\frac{1}{2}$ inch.

17 Position connector on the new fusible link and crimp into place in the wiring circuit.

18 Use rosin core solder at each end of the new link to obtain a good solder joint.

19 Use plenty of electrical tape around the soldered joint. No exposed wiring should show.

20 Reconnect the fusible link at its source. Connect the battery ground cable. Test circuit for proper operation.

3 Light bulbs – replacement

Headlight

1 The headlights are replaceable sealed-beam type units. The high- and low-beam filaments are contained in the same unit. If one level of lighting fails, the entire unit must be replaced with a new one.

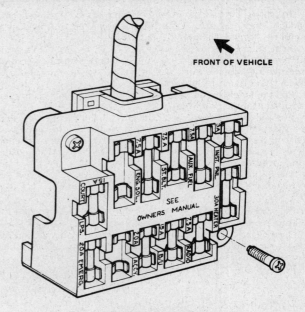

MOUNTED LEFT SIDE OF DASH PANEL

Fig. 10.2 Fuse block – 1976 on pick-ups (Bronco similar) (Sec 2)

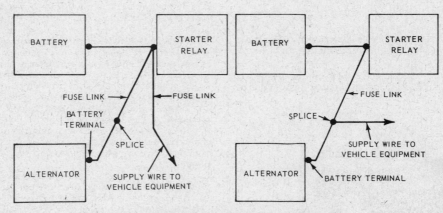

Fig. 10.3 Fusible link locations – typical (Sec 2)

Left – Light truck with charge indicator light   *Right – Light truck with ammeter and Bronco*

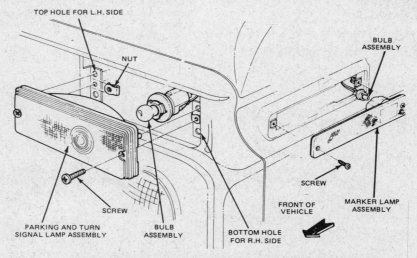

Fig. 10.4 Typical parking/side marker lights – exploded view (Sec 3)

2   To replace the headlight unit, first remove the screws retaining the headlight door (decorative trim ring surrounding the headlight). Be careful not to disturb the two headlight adjusting screws.

3   Remove the four retaining ring screws if the vehicle is equipped with a rectangular headlight unit. Loosen the retaining ring screws and rotate the ring counterclockwise to release it from the screws (if the vehicle has a round headlight unit).

4   Pull the headlight unit out far enough to allow access to the rear. Disconnect the plug from the unit.

5   Replace the headlight unit with one of the exact same size and type. Install the plug onto the prongs at the back of the unit. Place the bulb into the bucket with the large number embossed on the lens at the top. Make sure the alignment lugs cast into the unit are positioned in the recesses of the bucket.

6   Install the retaining ring.

7   Install the headlight trim ring.

Front parking lights

8   Remove the retaining screws from the (amber) parking light lens.

9   Replace the bulb with the exact same dual-filament combination type as you removed from the socket. The bulb should be turned counterclockwise for removal and clockwise for installation.

10   Install the parking light lens and tighten the screws until they are snug but not so tight that they crack the plastic lens.

Taillight and side marker lights

11   Remove the screws retaining the lens (and trim ring if so equipped) from the body. Pull the lens assembly out and turn the light bulb socket counterclockwise to remove it from the lens assembly.

12   Replace the bulb by turning it counterclockwise for removal and clockwise for installation.

13   Insert the bulb socket back into the lens assembly and turn it clockwise to secure it.

14   Replace the lens (and trim ring) and install the retaining screws. Don't overtighten the screws as they will crack the plastic lens.

Interior light

15   Remove the lens cover by unsnapping it (pick-ups) or unscrewing it (Broncos). Pull the bulb out of the clips and replace it with an exact duplicate. Install the lens cover.

KNOB RELEASE BUTTON

Fig. 10.5 Headlight switch knob release button location (Sec 4)

Dash lights

16   The bulbs illuminating the instruments and dash indicators are located at the rear of the instrument cluster. The cluster must be removed as described in Section 8 before the bulbs can be replaced. Once the cluster is out of the dash, the bulbs can be replaced by simply turning the holder counterclockwise and pulling the bulb from the holder. Installation is the reverse of removal.

---

4   Headlight switch – replacement

1   Disconnect the negative battery cable from the battery.

2   Remove the headlight switch control knob and shaft by reaching under the dashboard and pressing the knob release button located on the bottom of the switch. At the same time, pull the knob past the two On positions and out of the switch.

3   Unscrew the switch mounting nut and pull the switch out of the dash.

4   Remove the multi-connector from the switch.

5   Installation is the reverse of removal. Make sure the tang on the switch lines up with the slot in the dashboard for correct switch positioning. It is not necessary to push the release button to re-insert the knob and shaft assembly.

6   Check that the switch operates correctly after reconnecting the battery cable.

---

5   Turn signal switch – replacement

1   Disconnect the negative battery cable from the battery.

2   Remove the horn switch from the steering wheel. Most steering wheels have the switch retained from the rear with two Phillips-head screws.

3   Remove the steering wheel retaining nut. Mark the steering wheel and the post so they can be re-installed in the same relative position to each other. Do not use a punch, as it can damage the steering post.

4   Remove the steering wheel with a suitable puller.

5   Disconnect the turn signal indicator switch combination connector by lifting the lock tabs and carefully pulling it apart.

6   Unscrew the turn signal switch lever from the switch. A flat is provided on the shank of the lever to enable a wrench to fit it.

7   Record the color codes and locations of the wires as they lead into the combination connector. Remove each individual wire from the combination connector by releasing the tang on the terminal with a pointed tool.

8   Connect a pull wire to the end of the wiring harness after all of the wires have been removed from the connector.

9   Remove the screws retaining the switch assembly to the steering column. Remove the protective cover securing the wiring harness to the steering column.

10   Remove the switch and wires from the top of the steering column. Disconnect the pull wire from the end of the switch harness.

11   Installation is the reverse of removal. Check the operation of the turn signals and hazard flashers after the reassembly process has been completed.

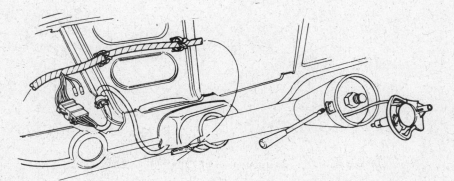

Fig. 10.6 Typical turn signal switch – exploded view (Sec 5)

10

6   Hazard switch – replacement

Refer to the previous Section for instructions on replacing the hazard switch (which is integral with the turn signal switch).

7   Wiper and washer system – description and replacement

Note: *The following procedure applies to pick-ups (all years) and Broncos manufactured after 1976. Earlier Broncos had direct drive wipers suspended from the windshield frame.*

1   The windshield wiper/washer system on Ford pick-ups consists of a motor with dual speed capabilities, linkages to convert rotary motion of the motor to oscillating movement at the blades and the wiper blades themselves. Windshield wiper blade replacement instructions can be found in Chapter 1. In addition, washer chores are handled by a plastic reservoir fitted with a pump which distributes washing fluid to a nozzle on each side of the windshield. A single control on the instrument panel next to the light switch activates both systems.

Wiper motor

2   Removal of the wiper motor should begin with removal of the battery negative cable.
3   From inside the cab, remove the radio (if so equipped).
4   Remove any components attached to the lower wiper bracket bolt.
5   Remove the wiper motor bracket retaining bolts.
6   Disconnect the wires leading to the wiper motor.
7   Remove the clip retaining the linkage to the motor shaft. Remove the linkage.
8   Remove the motor and bracket from the vehicle.
9   Installation is the reverse of removal. Make sure the motor works correctly after reassembly.

Linkage

10   Remove the wiper motor as described above.
11   Remove the instrument cluster as described in Section 8.
12   Remove the arm and blade assemblies from the shafts. To do this, swing the arm and blade away from the windshield and insert a $\frac{3}{32}$ inch pin through the hole provided for this purpose. Use a removal tool to pry the arm off the shaft. Do not use a screwdriver for this task.
13   Working through the instrument cluster opening, remove the bolts retaining the left pivot assembly. Remove the left pivot link assembly from under the instrument panel.

14   Remove the glovebox assembly which is retained by screws placed around the opening.
15   Working through the glovebox hole, remove the three bolts retaining the right pivot and link assembly to the cowl panel. Remove the pivot link assembly from under the instrument panel.
16   Installation is the reverse of removal. When re-installing the wiper arms, make sure the motor is in the parked position by allowing it to run a few cycles and turning it off. The shafts will then come to rest in the parked position. Install the blades with the prescribed clearance between them and the windshield lower molding or weatherstrip. Check the operation of the windshield wipers after assembly.

Switch

17   Remove the wiper switch knob with a hooked tool inserted in the rear to release the clip.
18   Remove the bezel nut by unthreading it from the switch. Remove the switch bezel.
19   Pull the switch out from the rear of the instrument panel.
20   Disconnect the plug-in wire connector from the switch and remove the switch.
21   Installation is the reverse of removal.

Washer reservoir and pump

22   The windshield washer reservoir and pump are located on the left inner fenderwell, inside the engine compartment. If the reservoir or the pump needs replacement, the reservoir may be removed by removing the three retaining screws and pulling the wiring connector out of the motor terminals.
23   To remove the pump from the reservoir, grasp the wall of the pump near the electrical terminals with a pair of pliers and pull the pump out of the reservoir. If the impeller and/or the seal come off of the motor during this operation, they may be reassembled.
24   Installation is the reverse of removal. Lubricate the outside of the pump seal with a dry lubricant such as powdered graphite. Align the tang on the motor with the groove on the reservoir before pushing the motor into the reservoir.

8   Instrument cluster – removal and installation

1   Remove the negative battery cable from the battery.
2   Remove the knobs from the radio (if so equipped).
3   Remove the heater control knobs and the wiper/washer knob with

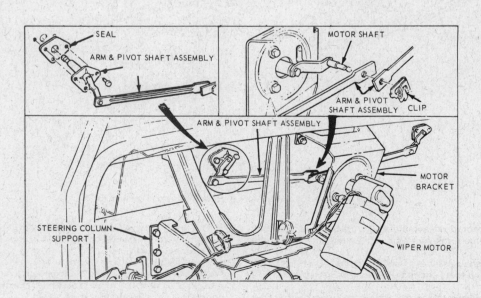

Fig. 10.7 Typical windshield wiper motor/linkage installation details (Sec 7)

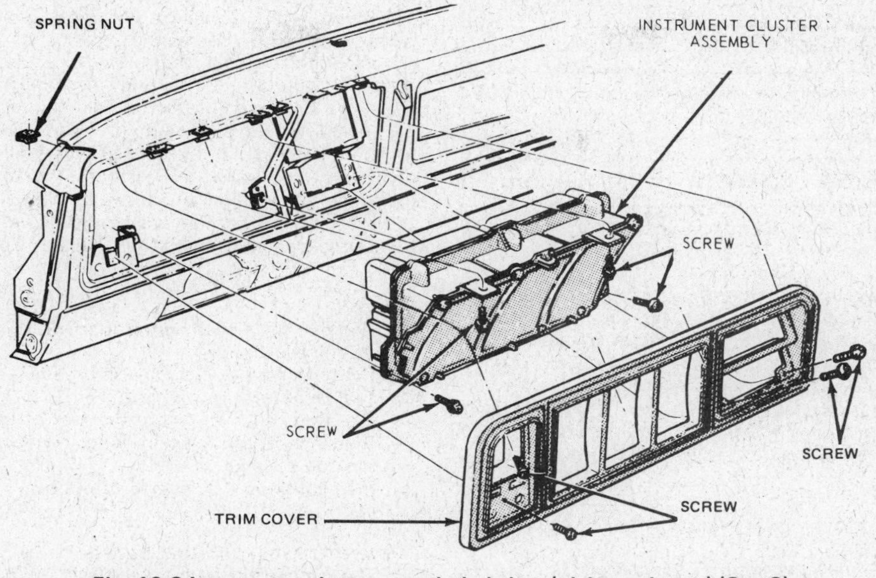

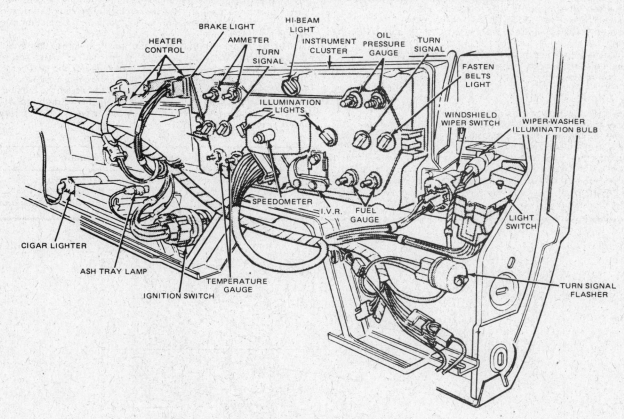

Fig. 10.8 Instrument cluster – exploded view (pick-up shown) (Sec 8)

Fig. 10.9 Instrument cluster – rear view (pick-up shown) (Sec 8)

10

a hook tool. Use the tool to release the spring loaded knob lock tab. Remove the auxiliary fuel tank switch (if factory equipped) from the heater control panel.

4   Remove the knob/shaft assembly from the light switch (Section 4).

5   Remove the nuts, washers and radio bezel from the radio shafts (if so equipped).

6   Remove the four screws along the top of the instrument cluster trim cover. Remove the screw beneath the headlight and wiper switch. Remove the two screws below the radio. Pull the cluster trim cover off of the dashboard.

7   Disconnect the air conditioning duct (if so equipped).

8   Remove the instrument cluster illumination light from between the light and wiper switches.

9   Remove the four instrument cluster retaining screws. Pull the cluster forward far enough to reach behind it and pry the retaining tab up to release the speedometer cable from the cluster. Remove the wire connector from the printed circuit board.

10 Remove the instrument cluster.

11 Installation is the reverse of removal. Check all instruments and controls for proper operation after the cluster has been re-installed.

9   Ignition switch – removal and installation

1   To remove the lock barrel of the ignition switch, insert the ignition key into the switch and insert a piece of wire into the hole in the front of the barrel.
2   Push the wire inward and turn the key counterclockwise past the Acc position, grip the key and withdraw the lock barrel from the switch assembly.
3   The lock barrel is not repairable and if faulty must be replaced.
4   To install the lock barrel, insert the key and turn it to the Acc position.
5   Push the barrel and key into the switch assembly until it is fully seated and then turn the key to the Lock position. Turn the key to check the operation of the different functions.
6   To remove the complete switch assembly from the instrument panel, use the notches to unthread the bezel nut retaining the switch to the panel. Withdraw the switch from the rear of the panel.
7   Insert the top of a small screwdriver under the finger-lift (heavy) side of the connector retaining clips. Pull the connector off the switch.

Installation

8   Install the wiring connector into the back of the switch with the alignment tab of the connector aligned with the slot in the switch.
9   Position the switch assembly in the instrument panel with the notch in the panel lined up with the groove in the switch. Thread the bezel nut onto the switch and tighten it.
10   Follow steps 4 and 5 above if the lock barrel has been removed. Reconnect the negative battery cable.

10   Battery – removal and installation

1   The battery is the heart of the entire electrical system and must be maintained properly. Battery maintenance and charging details can be found in Chapter 1.
2   Removal and installation of the battery is a simple process. Remove both battery cables from the posts of the battery. Use a battery terminal puller and never pry on the posts as they can be easily damaged. Remove the battery hold-down nuts and retaining bracket.
3   Lift the battery from the battery box with a tool designed for this task. Do not attempt to lift the battery by hand as it is heavy and often has a thin corrosive film of acid on its surface.
4   Installation is the reverse of removal. Coat the battery hold-down threads with petroleum jelly or a special terminal lubricant to prevent corrosion.

11   Neutral safety switch – replacement and adjustment

Bronco

1   Remove the downshift linkage return spring from the low/reverse servo cover.
2   To avoid damaging the inner lever shaft, apply penetrating oil to the outer lever retaining nut. After the penetrating oil has soaked for a sufficient time, remove the downshift outer lever retaining nut. Remove the lever.
3   Remove the two bolts retaining the switch to the transmission. Disconnect the two multiple wiring connectors. Remove the switch from over the shaft.
4   Install the Neutral safety switch over the shift shafts and install the two retaining bolts. Do not tighten the bolts.
5   Place the transmission shift lever in Neutral. Install a gauge pin made from a number 43 drill bit into the alignment holes of the switch.
6   Tighten the switch retaining bolts. Remove the gauge pin. Connect the two multiple wiring connectors.
7   The remainder of the installation procedure is the reverse of removal. Make sure the vehicle will start when the transmission selector is in Park or Neutral only.

Pick-up

8   Disconnect the switch wires at the plug connector. Remove the screws attaching the switch to the steering column and lift off the switch.
9   Position the switch on the column and install the screws.

Fig. 10.10 Ignition switch release pin hole location (Sec 9)

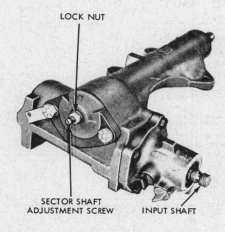

Fig. 10.11 Neutral safety switch adjustment details – Bronco (Sec 11)

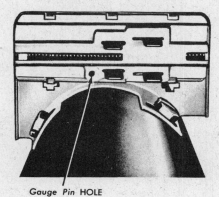

Fig. 10.12 Neutral safety switch gauge pin hole location – pick-up (Sec 11)

10   Hold the selector lever against the Neutral stop. Move the sliding block on the switch to the Neutral position. Working from the rear of the switch, insert a number 43 drill bit into the gauge pin hole.
11   Slide the switch, as necessary, to permit the actuating lever to contact the sliding block on the switch. Tighten the switch mounting screws and remove the drill bit.
12   Connect the switch wires and check for proper operation. The starter should operate only when the selector lever is in Park or Neutral.

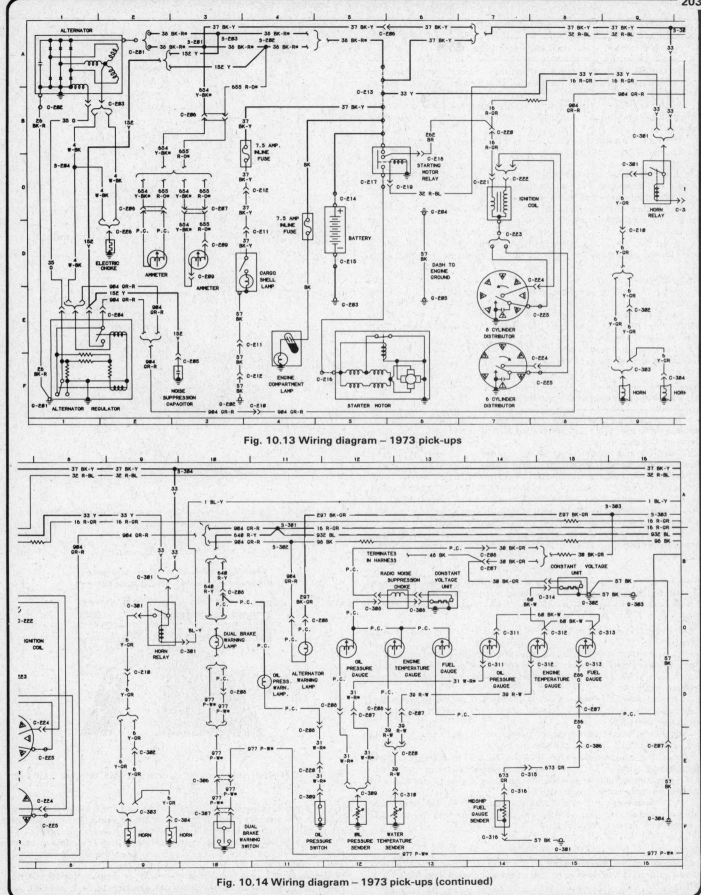

Fig. 10.13 Wiring diagram – 1973 pick-ups

Fig. 10.14 Wiring diagram – 1973 pick-ups (continued)

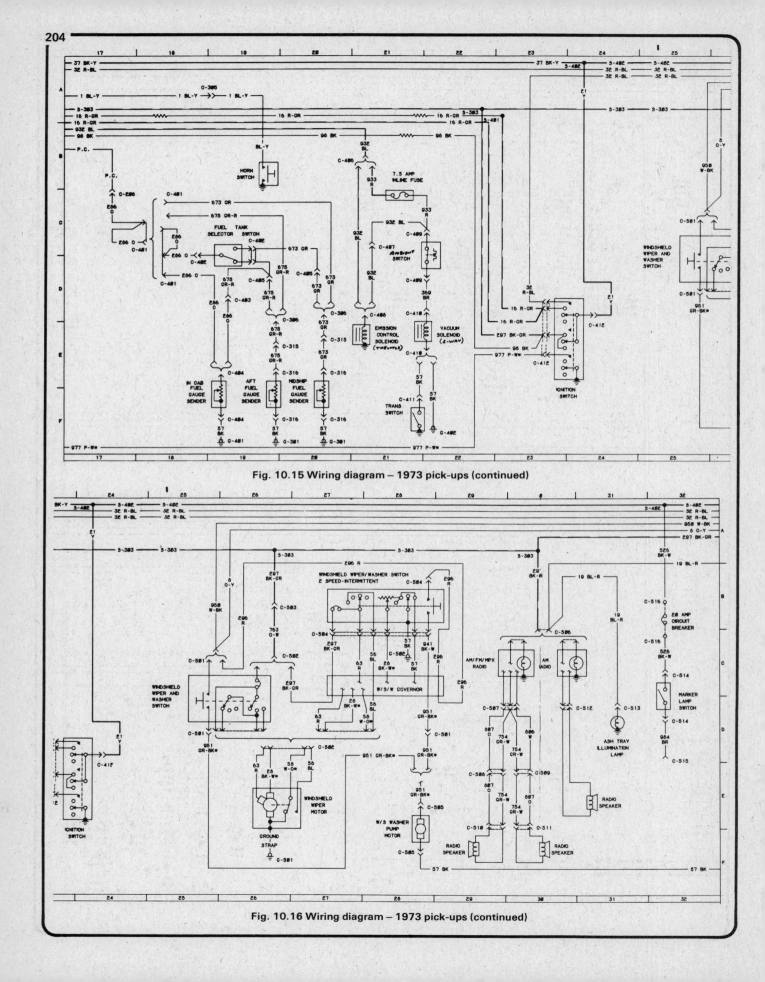

Fig. 10.15 Wiring diagram – 1973 pick-ups (continued)

Fig. 10.16 Wiring diagram – 1973 pick-ups (continued)

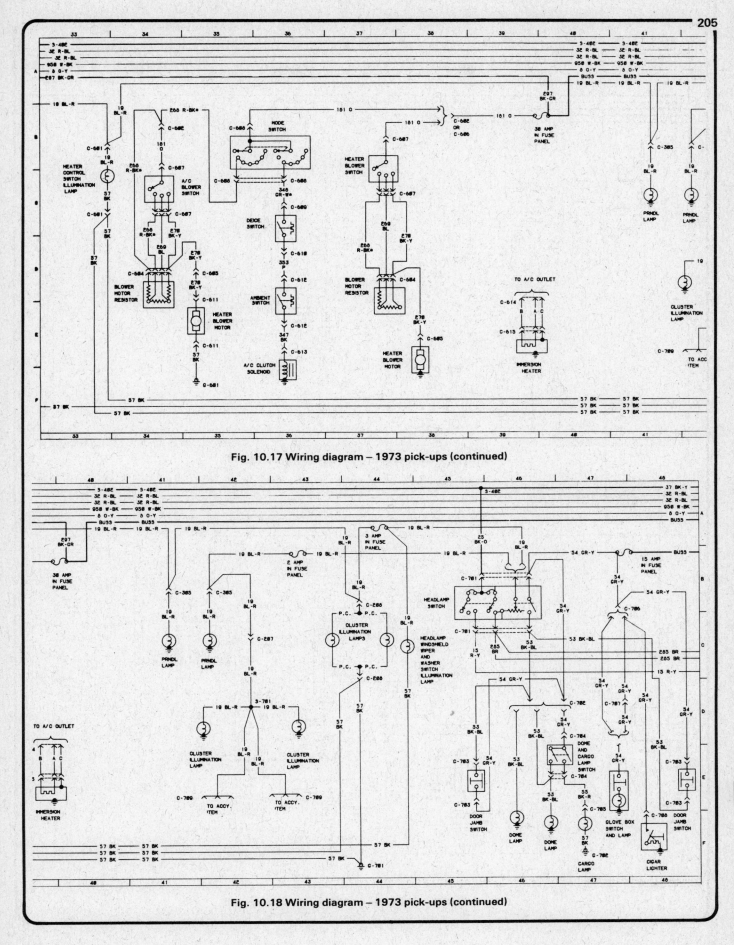

Fig. 10.17 Wiring diagram – 1973 pick-ups (continued)

Fig. 10.18 Wiring diagram – 1973 pick-ups (continued)

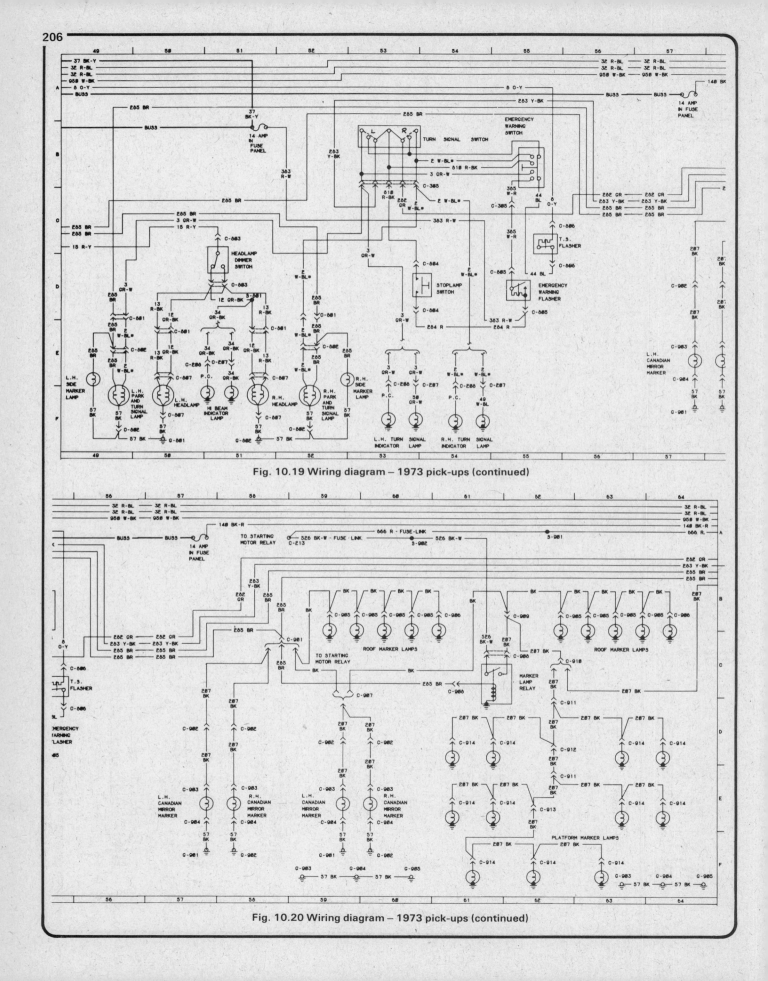

Fig. 10.19 Wiring diagram – 1973 pick-ups (continued)

Fig. 10.20 Wiring diagram – 1973 pick-ups (continued)

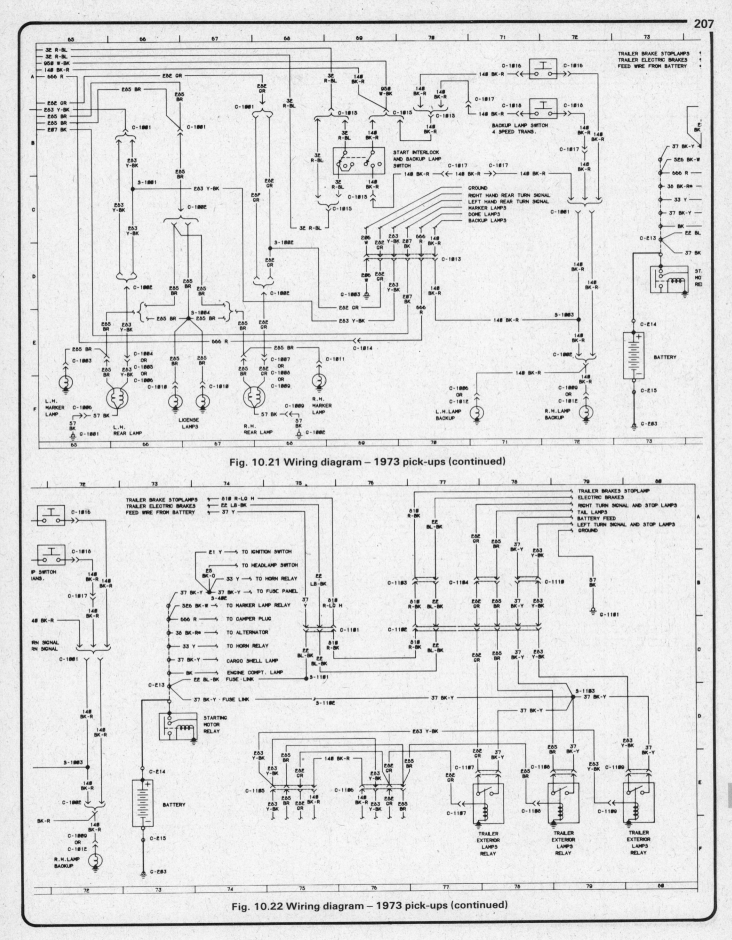

Fig. 10.21 Wiring diagram – 1973 pick-ups (continued)

Fig. 10.22 Wiring diagram – 1973 pick-ups (continued)

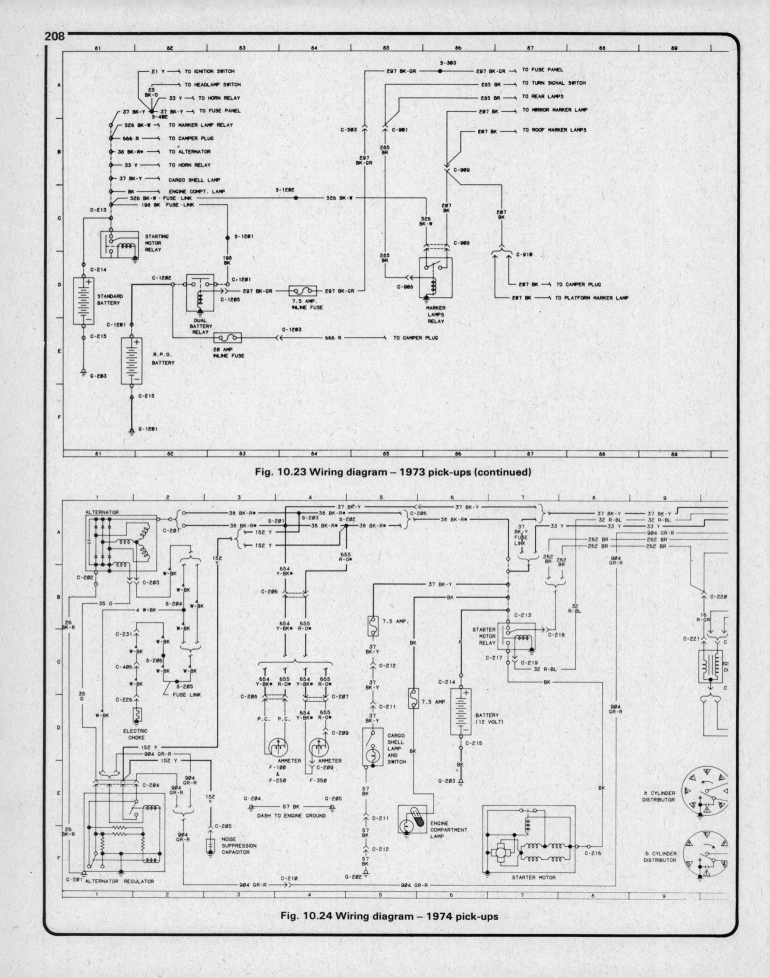

Fig. 10.23 Wiring diagram – 1973 pick-ups (continued)

Fig. 10.24 Wiring diagram – 1974 pick-ups

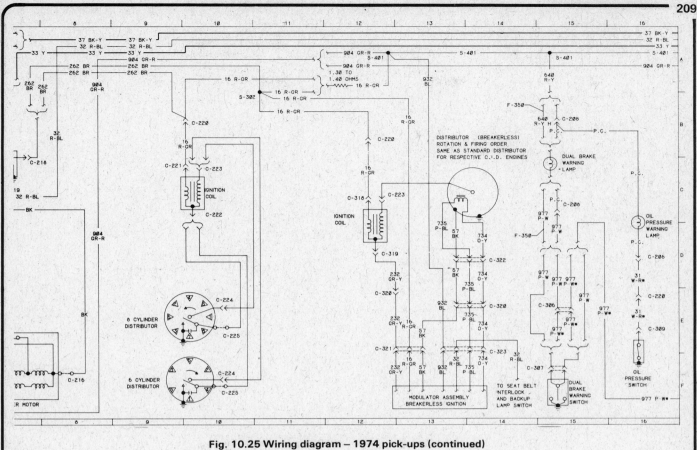

Fig. 10.25 Wiring diagram – 1974 pick-ups (continued)

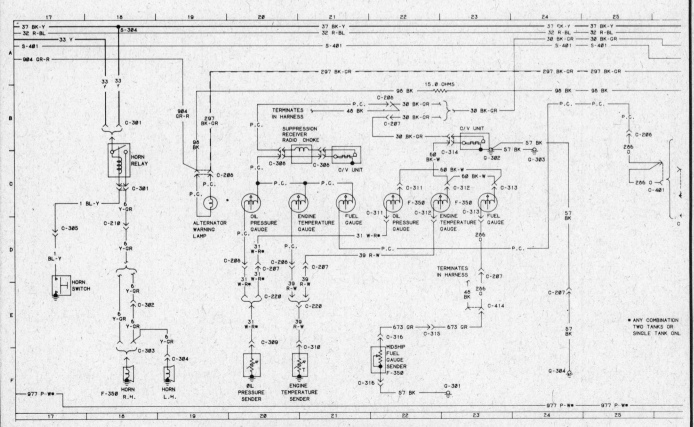

Fig. 10.26 Wiring diagram – 1974 pick-ups (continued)

10

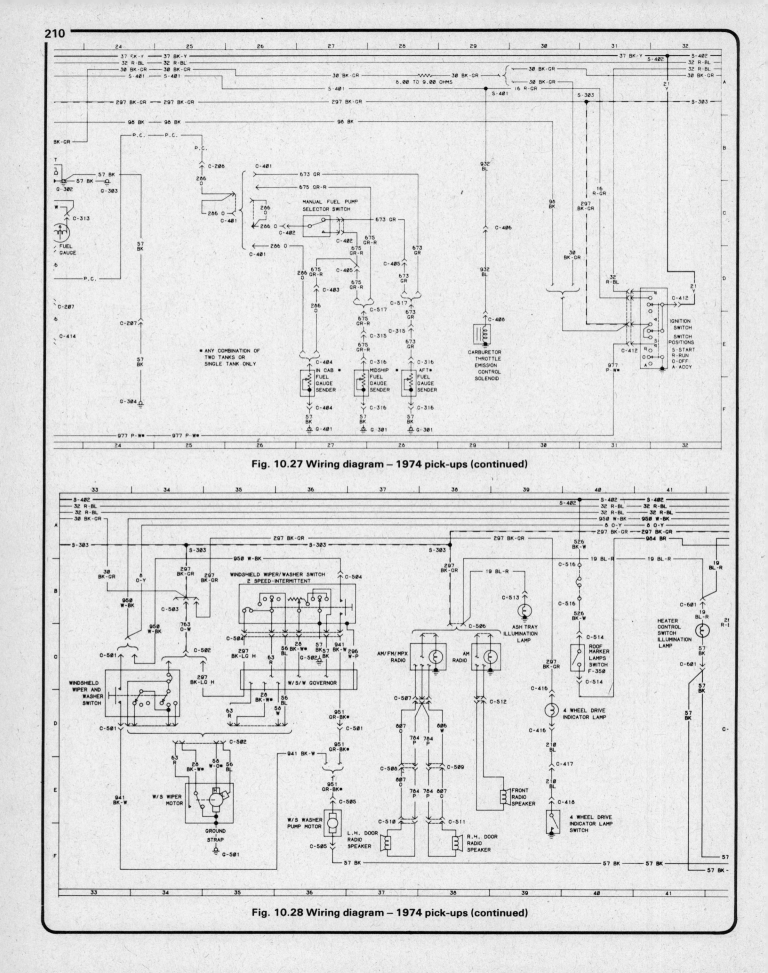

Fig. 10.27 Wiring diagram – 1974 pick-ups (continued)

Fig. 10.28 Wiring diagram – 1974 pick-ups (continued)

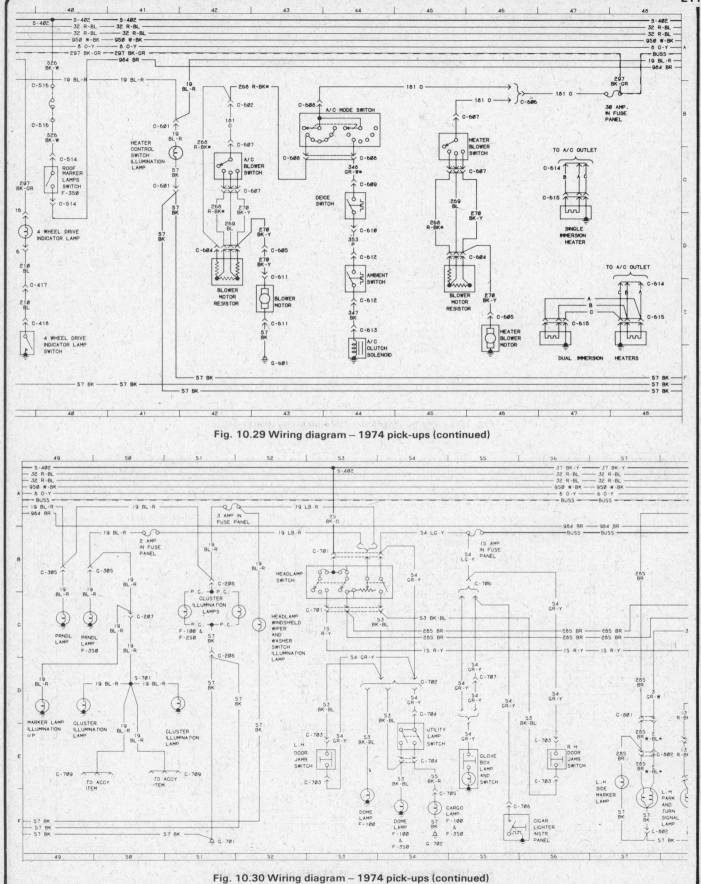

Fig. 10.29 Wiring diagram – 1974 pick-ups (continued)

Fig. 10.30 Wiring diagram – 1974 pick-ups (continued)

10

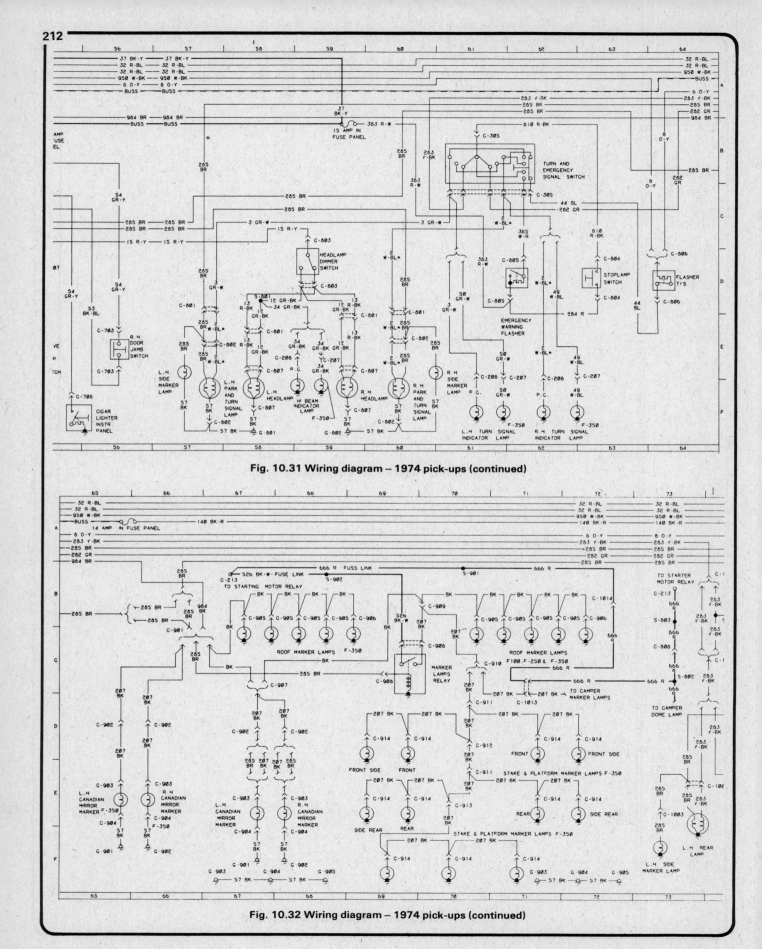

Fig. 10.31 Wiring diagram – 1974 pick-ups (continued)

Fig. 10.32 Wiring diagram – 1974 pick-ups (continued)

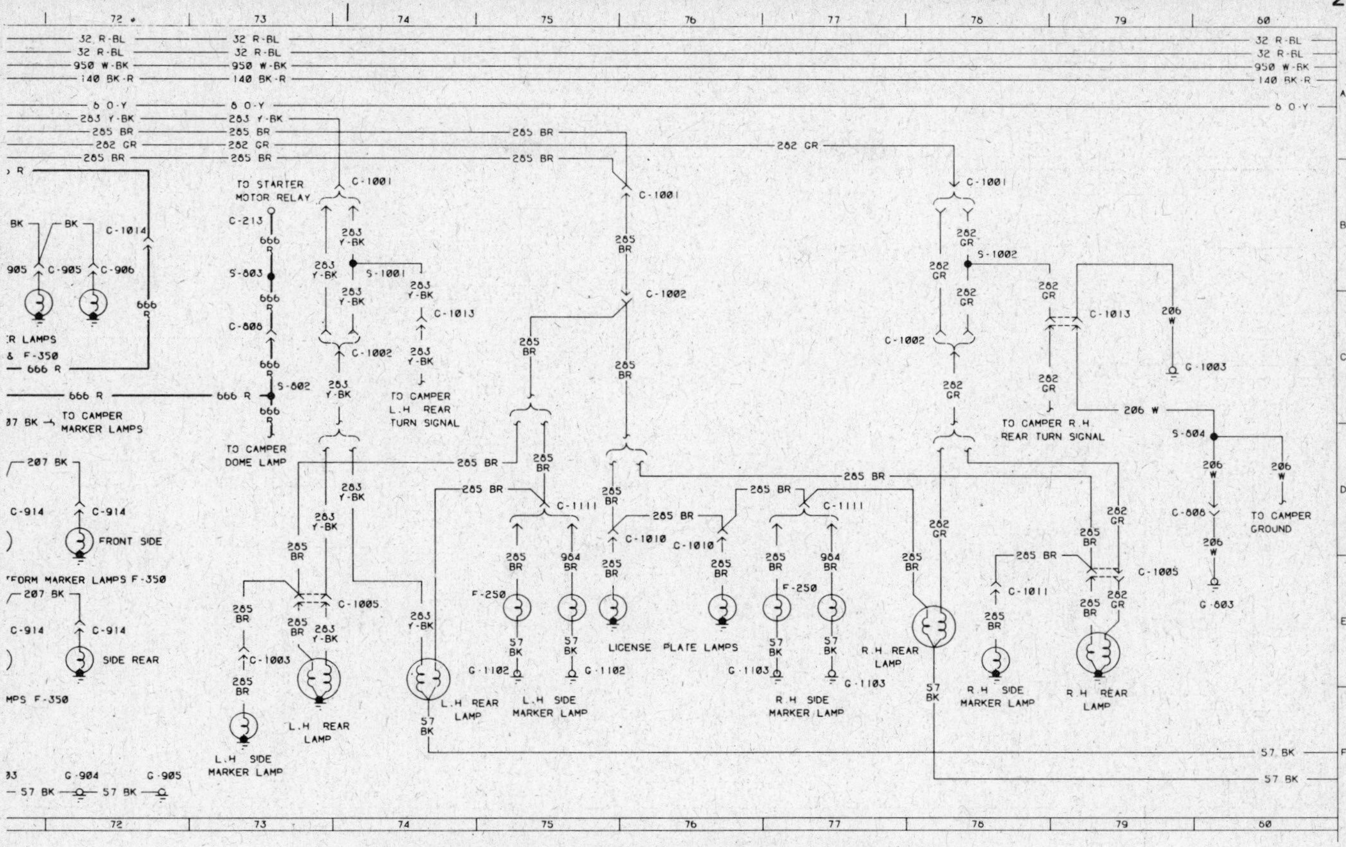

Fig. 10.33 Wiring diagram – 1974 pick-ups (continued)

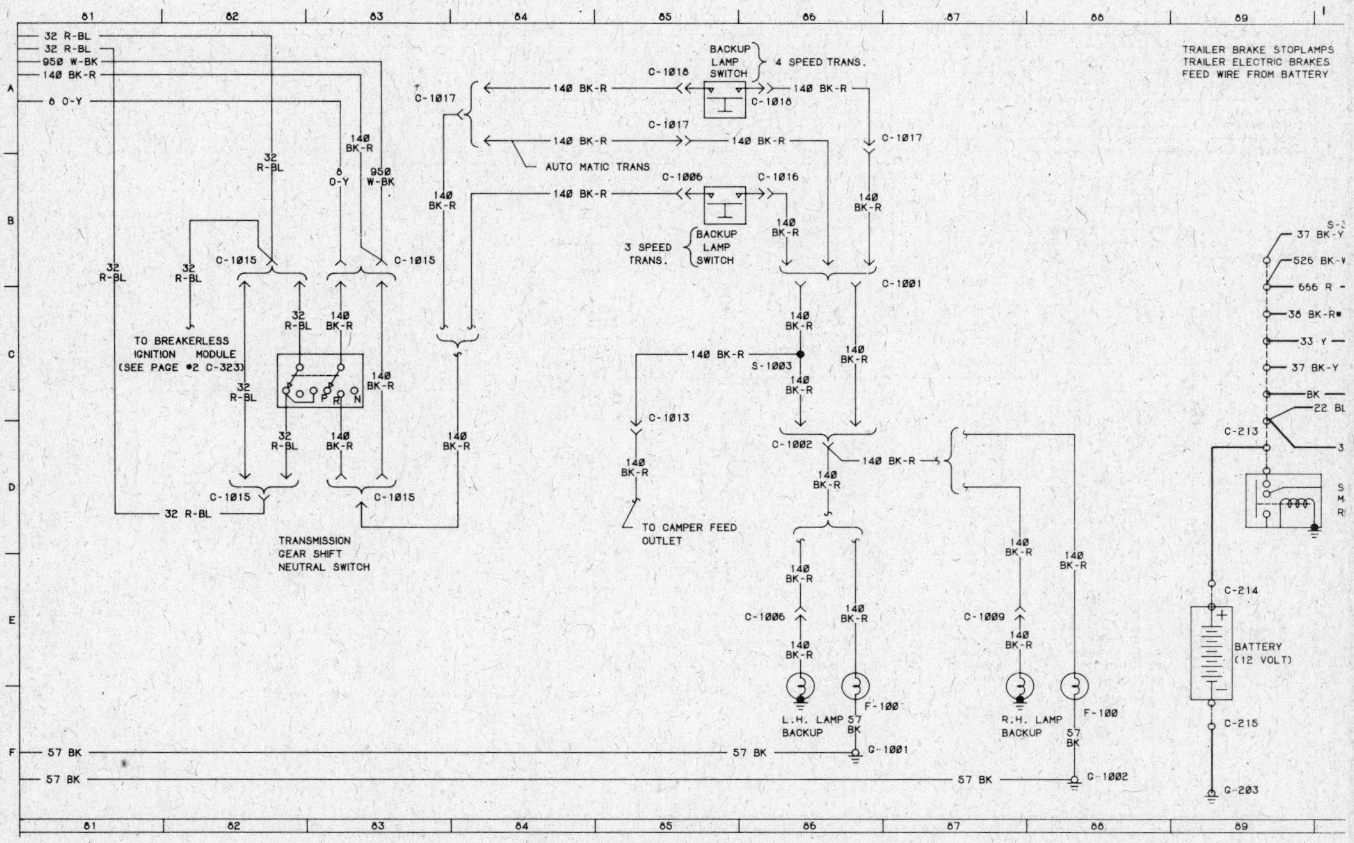

Fig. 10.34 Wiring diagram – 1974 pick-ups (continued)

10

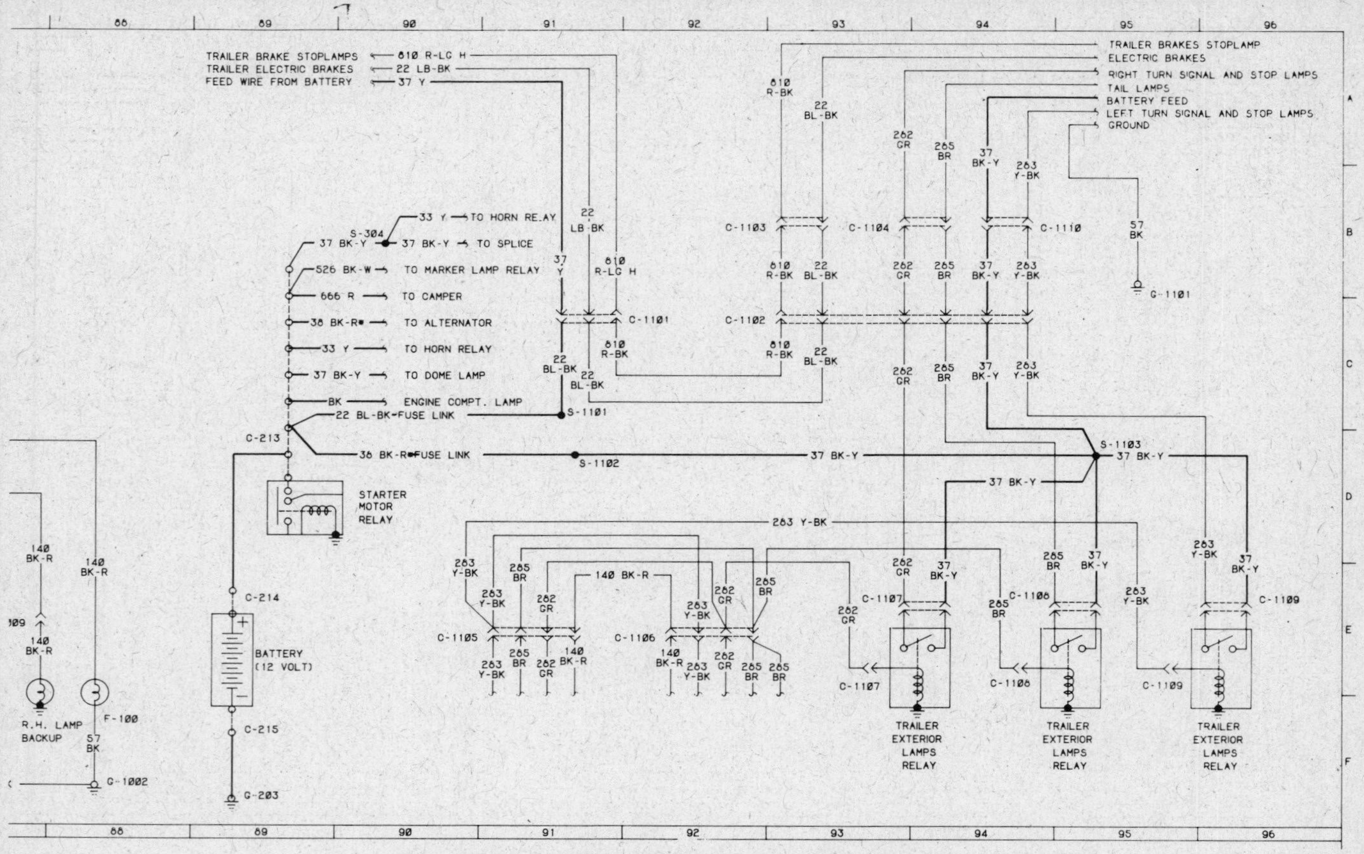

TRAILER BRAKE STOPLAMPS — 810 R-LC H
TRAILER ELECTRIC BRAKES — 22 LB-BK
FEED WIRE FROM BATTERY — 37 Y

TRAILER BRAKES STOPLAMP
ELECTRIC BRAKES
RIGHT TURN SIGNAL AND STOP LAMPS
TAIL LAMPS
BATTERY FEED
LEFT TURN SIGNAL AND STOP LAMPS
GROUND

33 Y → TO HORN RELAY
S-304
37 BK-Y — 37 BK-Y → TO SPLICE
526 BK-W → TO MARKER LAMP RELAY
666 R → TO CAMPER
38 BK-R → TO ALTERNATOR
33 Y → TO HORN RELAY
37 BK-Y → TO DOME LAMP
BK → ENGINE COMPT. LAMP
22 BL-BK-FUSE LINK
C-213
38 BK-R FUSE LINK
STARTER MOTOR RELAY
C-214
BATTERY (12 VOLT)
C-215
G-203

140 BK-R
909
140 BK-R
R.H. LAMP BACKUP
F-100
57 BK
G-1002

S-1101
S-1102   37 BK-Y
S-1103   37 BK-Y

TRAILER EXTERIOR LAMPS RELAY (×3)
C-1105 C-1106 C-1107 C-1108 C-1109
C-1101 C-1102 C-1103 C-1104 C-1110
G-1101

Fig. 10.35 Wiring diagram – 1974 pick-ups (continued)

S-303 297 BK-GR → TO FUSE PANEL
285 BR → TO LIGHT SWITCH
285 BR → TO REAR LAMPS
207 BK → TO MIRROR MARKER LAMP
207 BK → TO ROOF MARKER LAMPS

33 Y → TO HORN RELAY
S-304
37 BK-Y — 37 BK-Y → TO SPLICE
526 BK-W → TO MARKER LAMP RELAY
666 R → TO DOME LAMP
38 BK-R → TO ALTERNATOR
33 Y → TO HORN RELAY
37 BK-Y → CARGO SHELL LAMP
BK → ENGINE COMPT. LAMP
526 BK-W-FUSE LINK
198 BK-FUSE LINK
C-213
STARTER MOTOR RELAY
C-214
BATTERY (12 VOLT)
C-215
G-203
C-1201 C-1202 C-1205
DUAL BATTERY RELAY
297 BK-GR
7.5 AMP. INLINE FUSE
20 AMP INLINE FUSE
666 R → TO CAMPER PLUG
R.P.O. BATTERY (12 VOLT)
G-1201
S-1202 526 BK-W
S-1201
MARKER LAMPS RELAY
C-906 C-908 C-909 C-910
207 BK → TO CAMPER PLUG
207 BK → TO PLATFORM MARKER LAMP

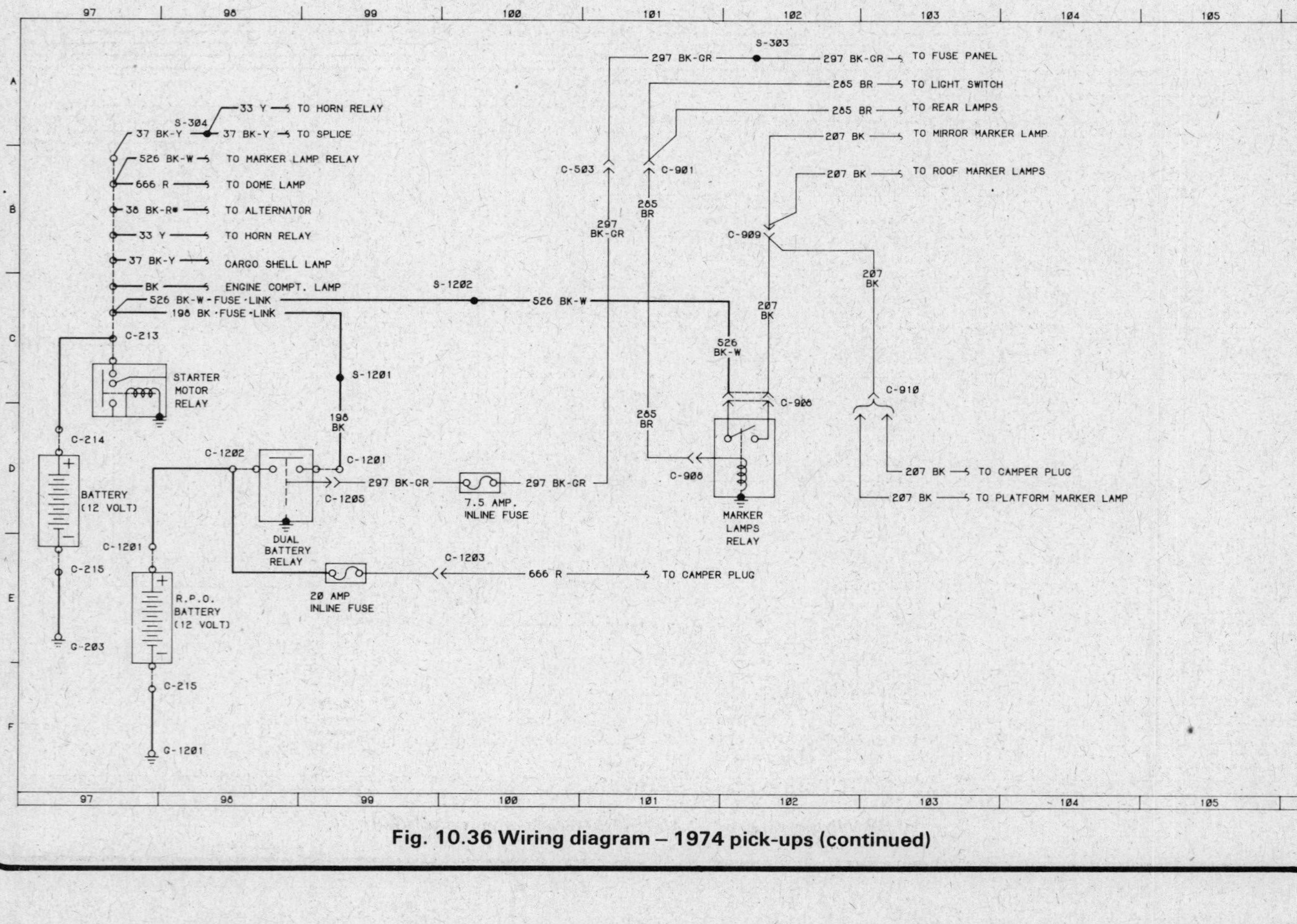

Fig. 10.36 Wiring diagram – 1974 pick-ups (continued)

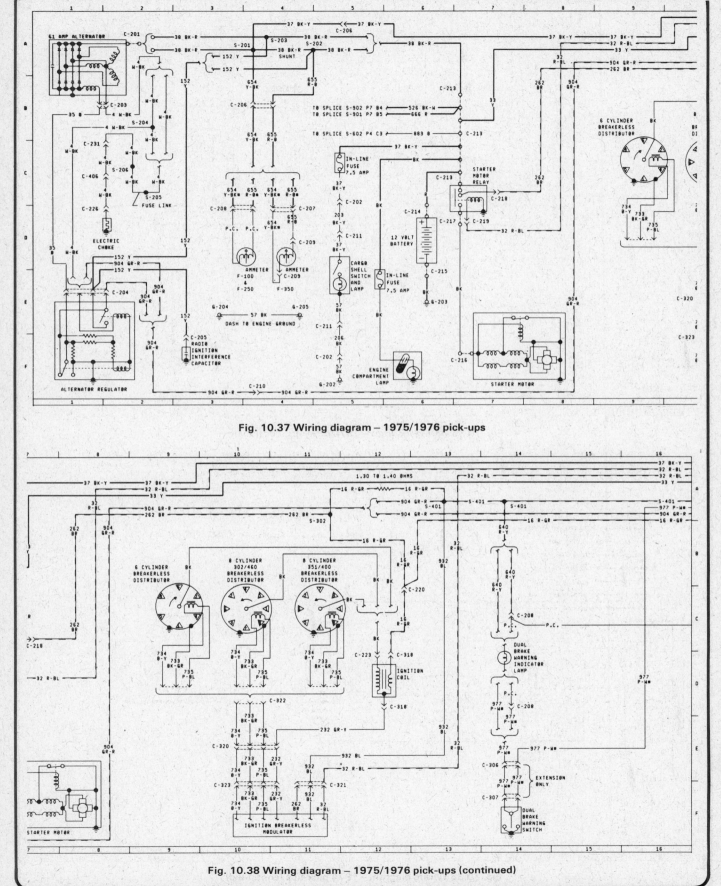

Fig. 10.37 Wiring diagram – 1975/1976 pick-ups

Fig. 10.38 Wiring diagram – 1975/1976 pick-ups (continued)

10

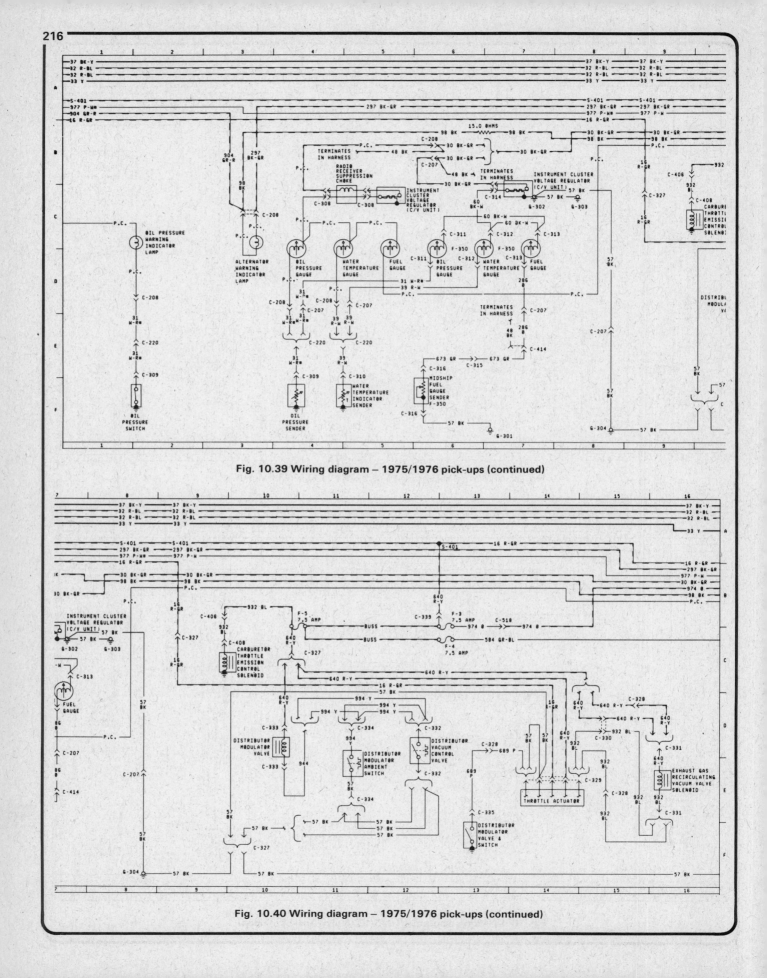

Fig. 10.39 Wiring diagram – 1975/1976 pick-ups (continued)

Fig. 10.40 Wiring diagram – 1975/1976 pick-ups (continued)

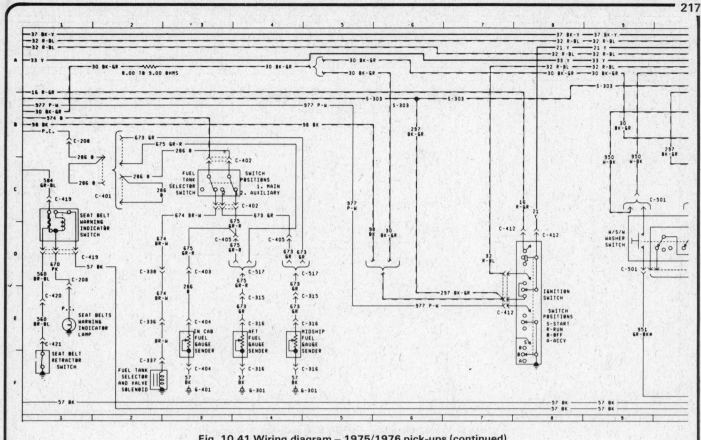

Fig. 10.41 Wiring diagram – 1975/1976 pick-ups (continued)

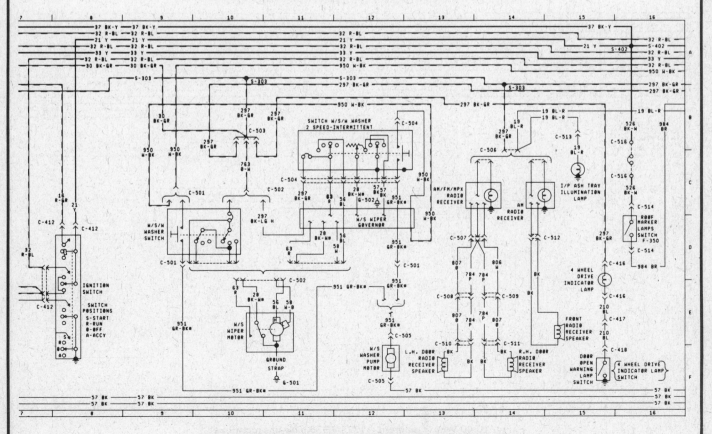

Fig. 10.42 Wiring diagram – 1975/1976 pick-ups (continued)

10

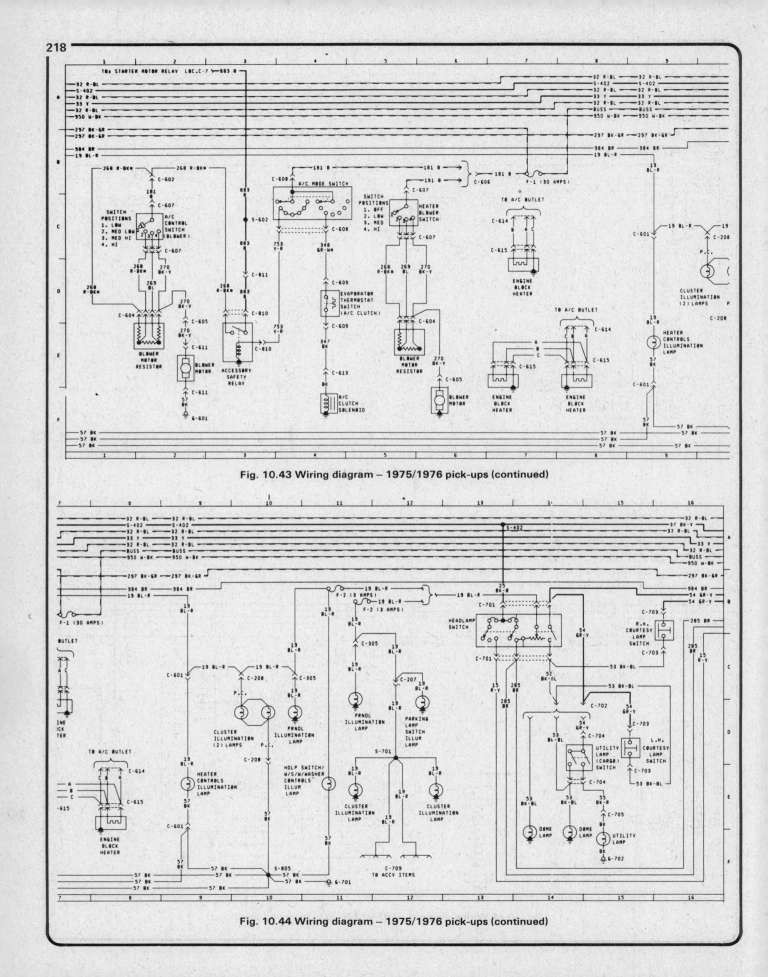

Fig. 10.43 Wiring diagram – 1975/1976 pick-ups (continued)

Fig. 10.44 Wiring diagram – 1975/1976 pick-ups (continued)

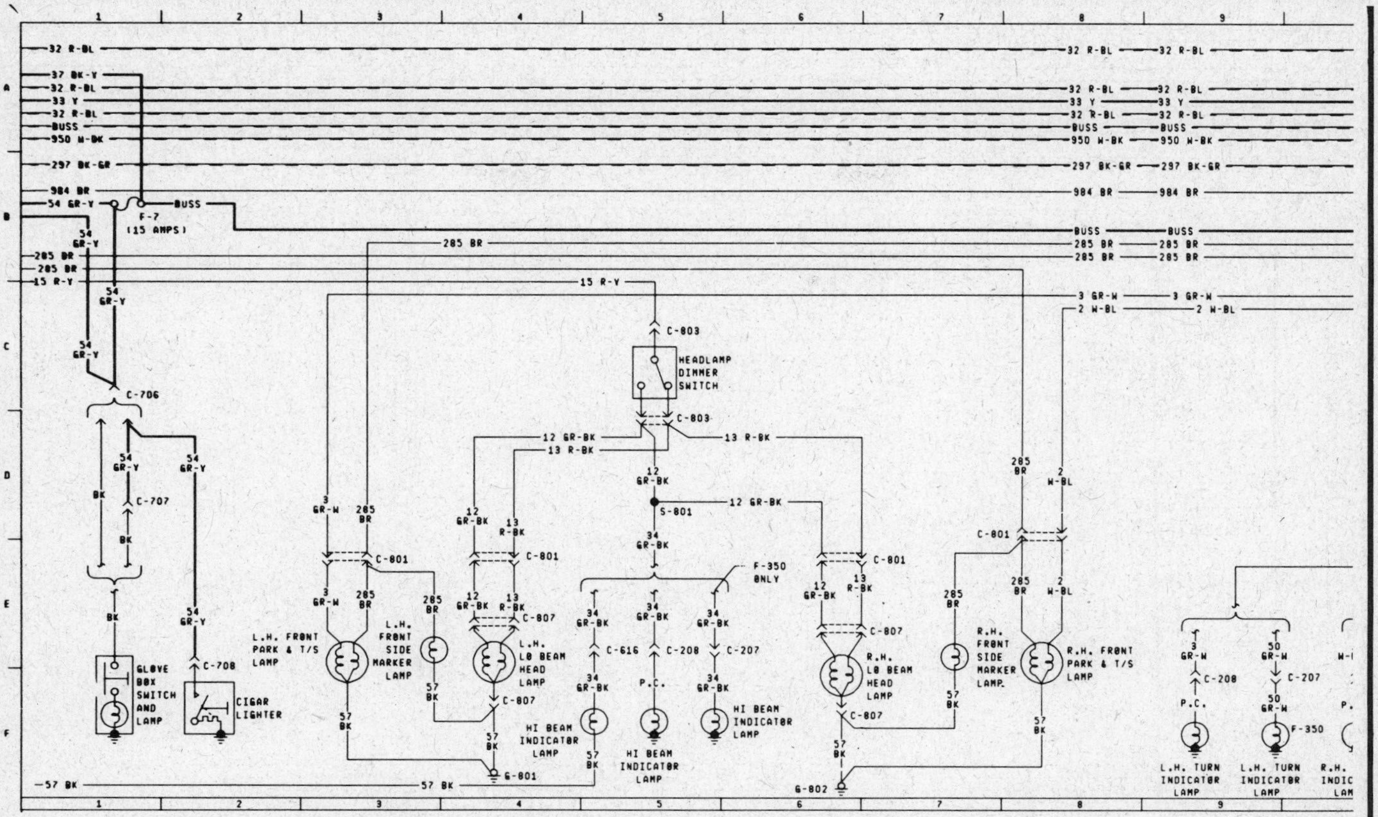

Fig. 10.45 Wiring diagram – 1975/1976 pick-ups (continued)

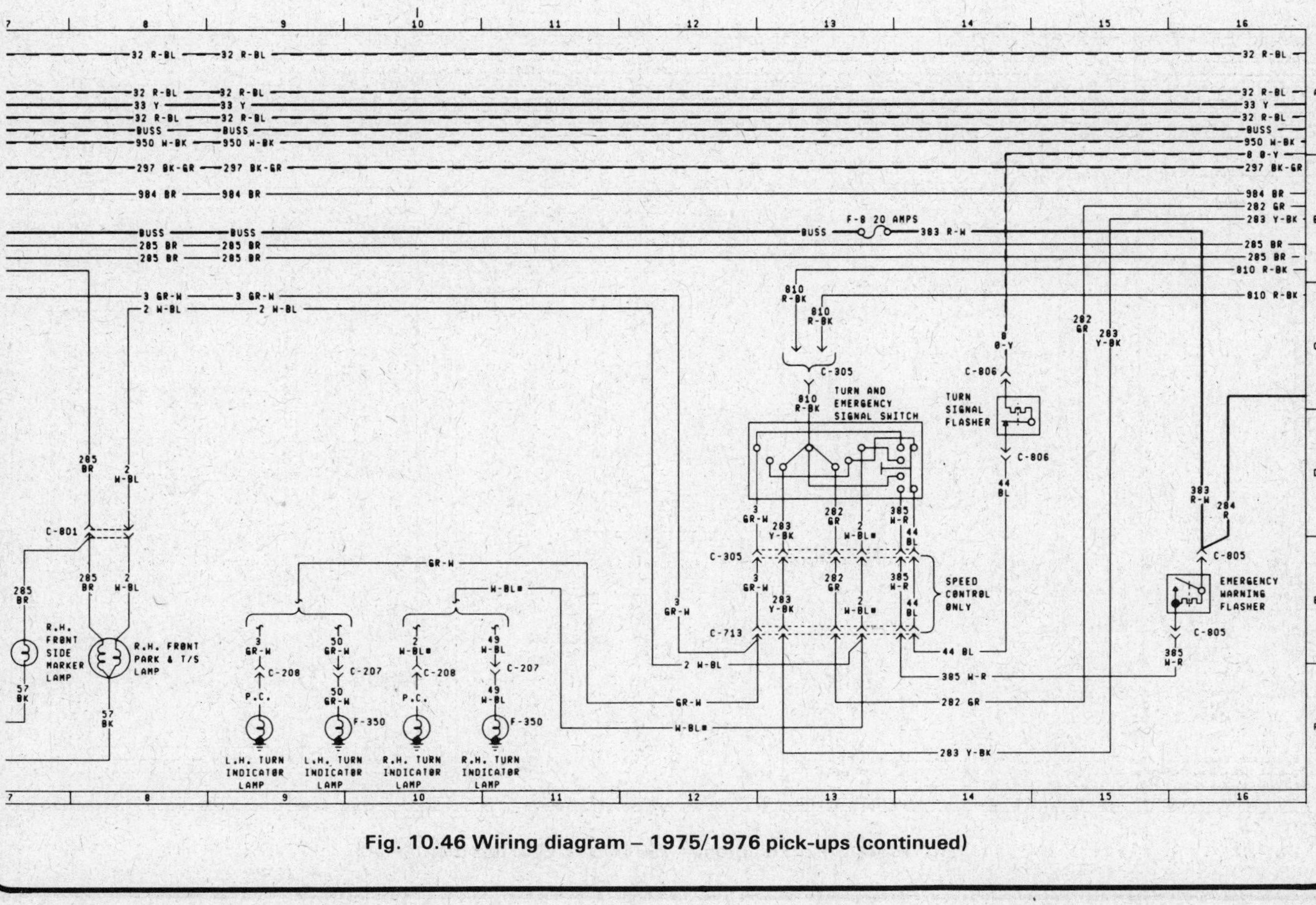

Fig. 10.46 Wiring diagram – 1975/1976 pick-ups (continued)

10

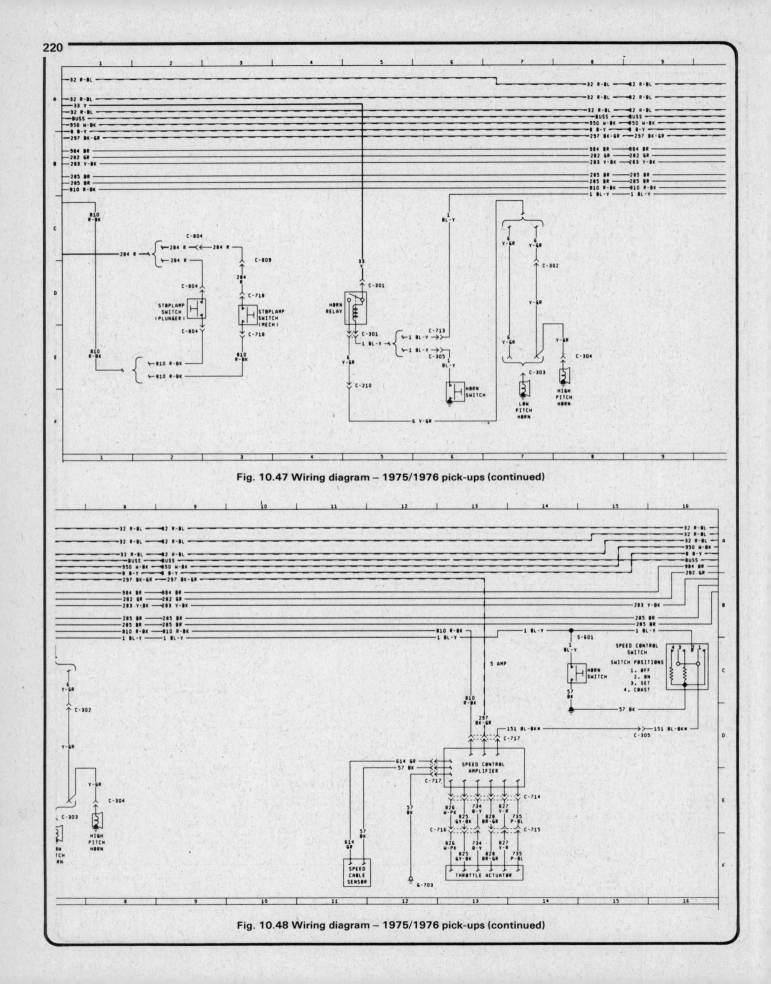

Fig. 10.47 Wiring diagram – 1975/1976 pick-ups (continued)

Fig. 10.48 Wiring diagram – 1975/1976 pick-ups (continued)

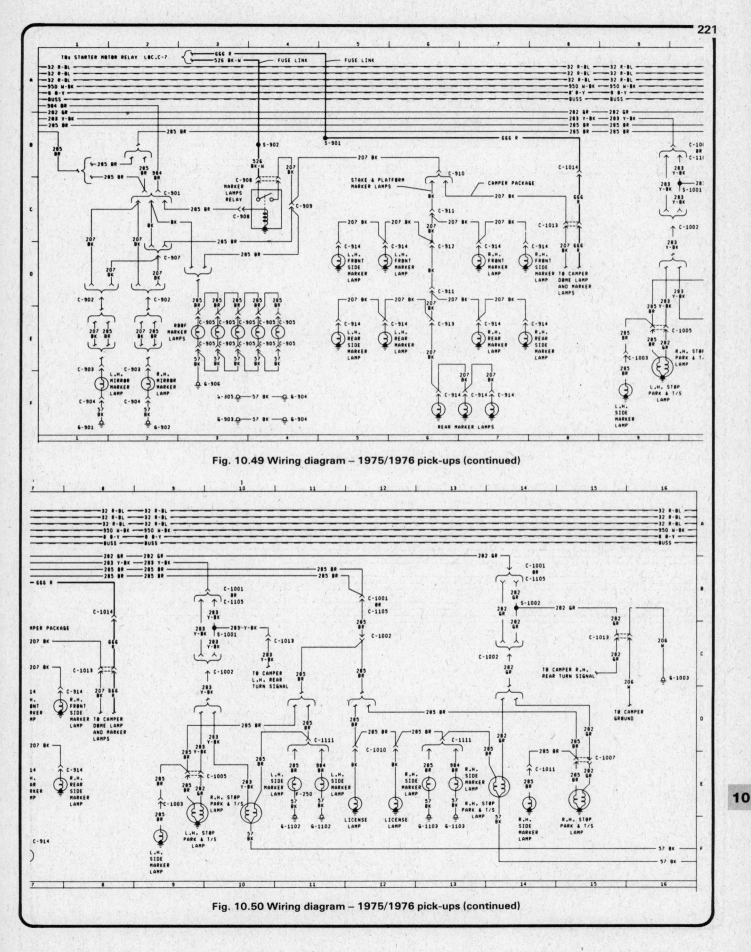

Fig. 10.49 Wiring diagram – 1975/1976 pick-ups (continued)

Fig. 10.50 Wiring diagram – 1975/1976 pick-ups (continued)

10

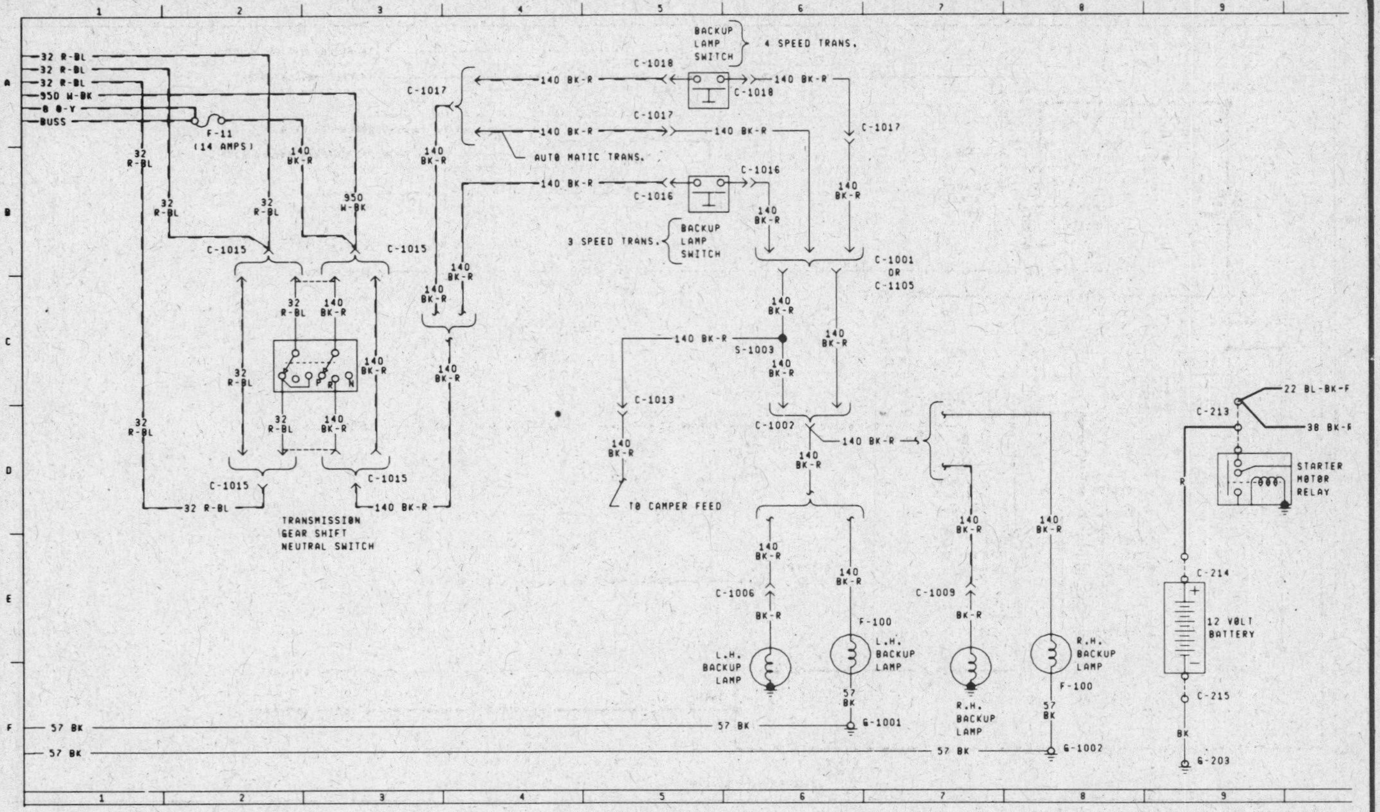

Fig. 10.51 Wiring diagram – 1975/1976 pick-ups (continued)

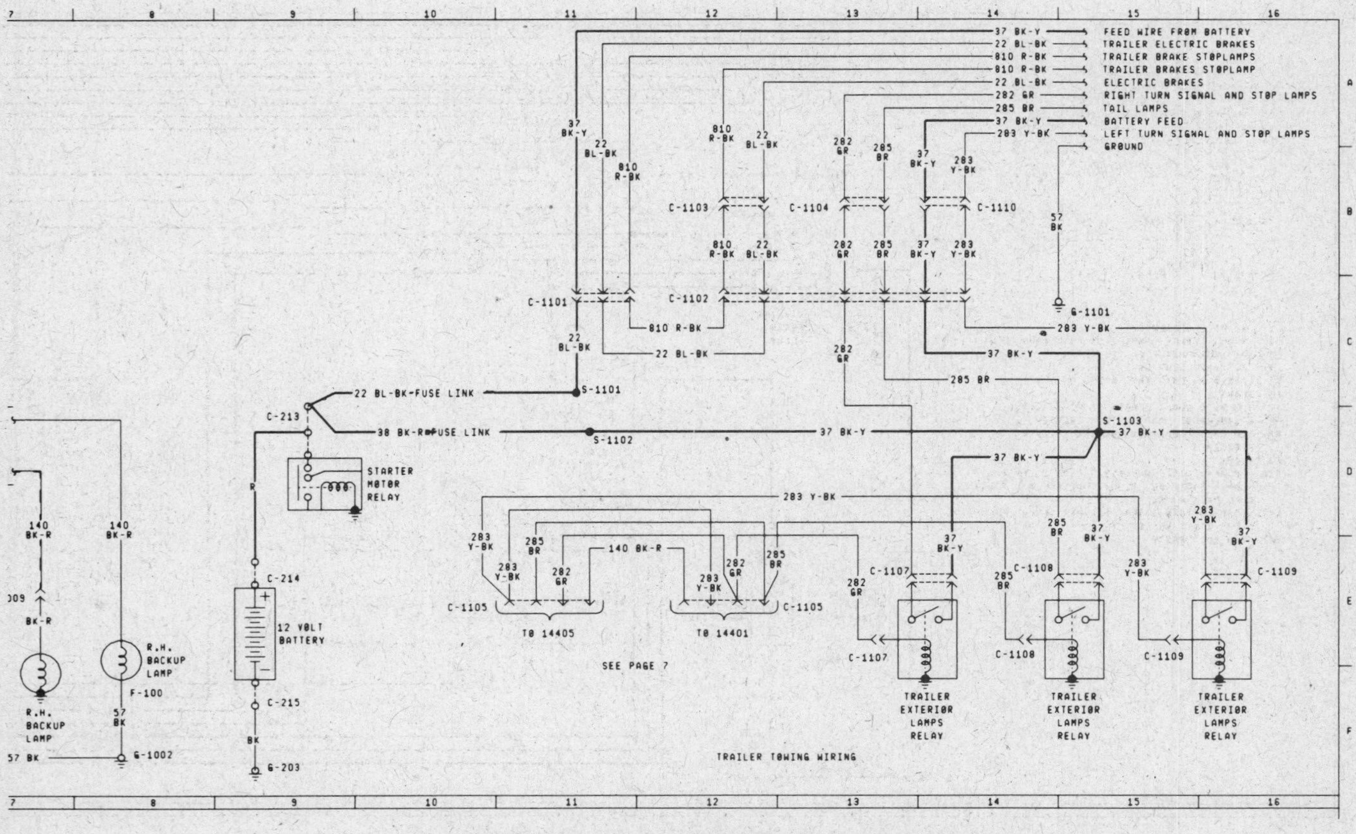

Fig. 10.52 Wiring diagram – 1975/1976 pick-ups (continued)

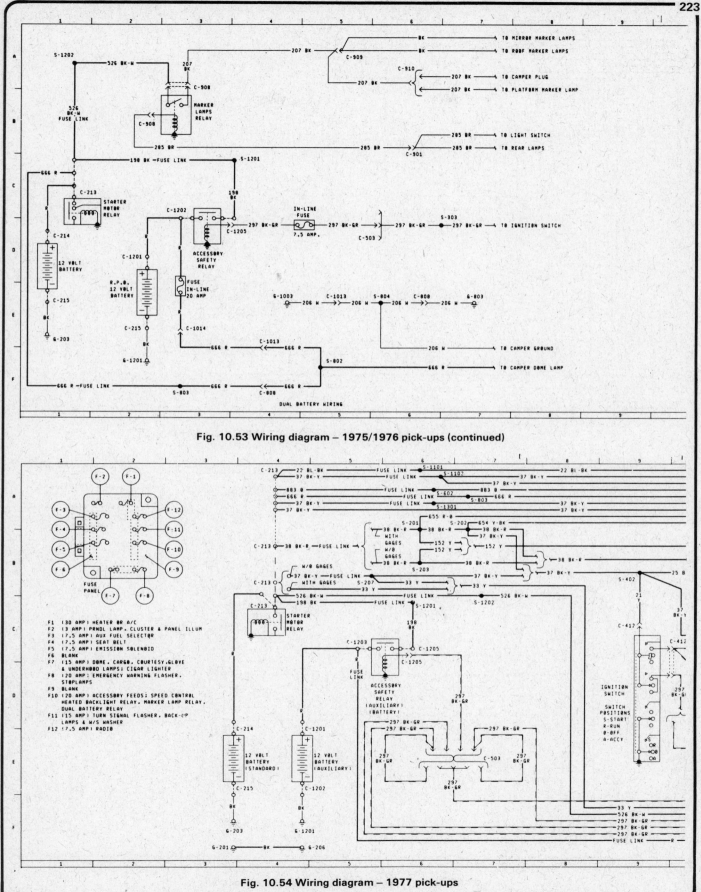

Fig. 10.53 Wiring diagram – 1975/1976 pick-ups (continued)

Fig. 10.54 Wiring diagram – 1977 pick-ups

10

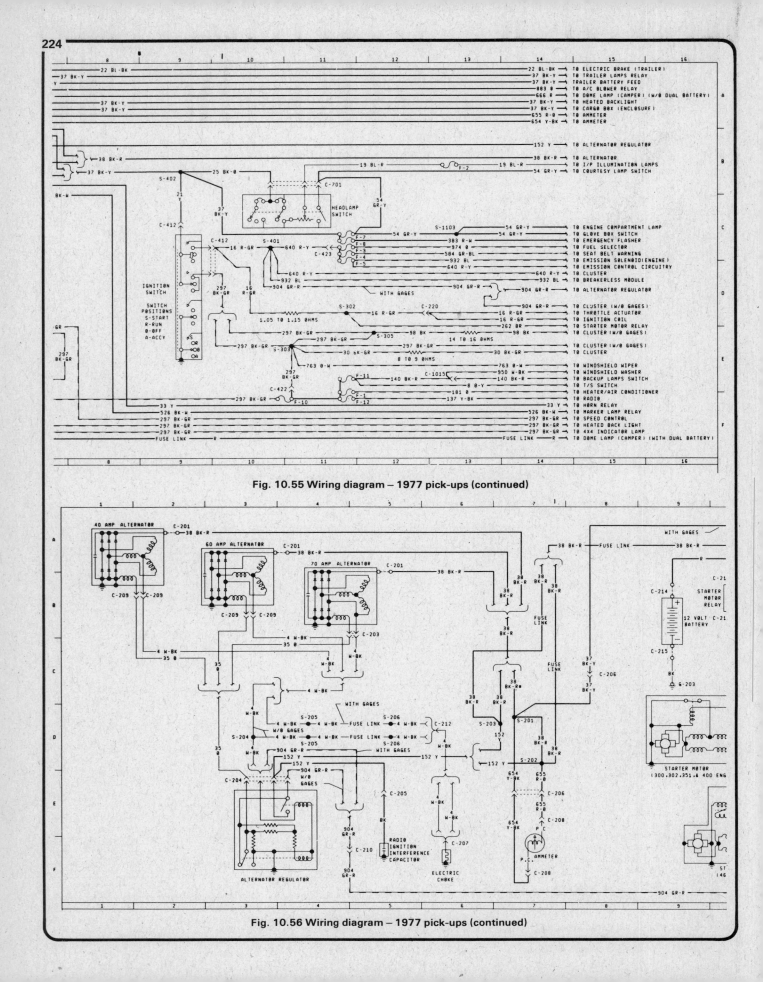

Fig. 10.55 Wiring diagram – 1977 pick-ups (continued)

Fig. 10.56 Wiring diagram – 1977 pick-ups (continued)

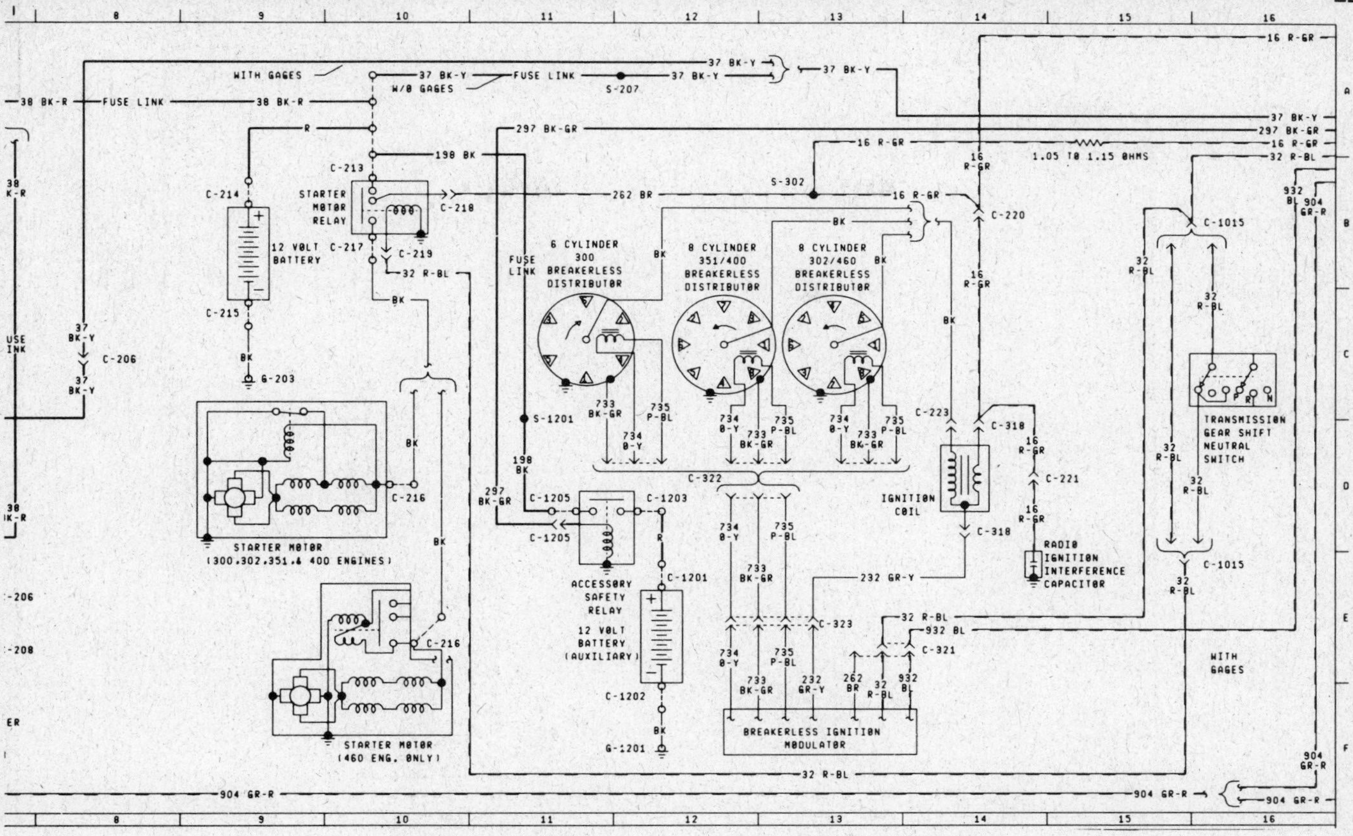

Fig. 10.57 Wiring diagram – 1977 pick-ups (continued)

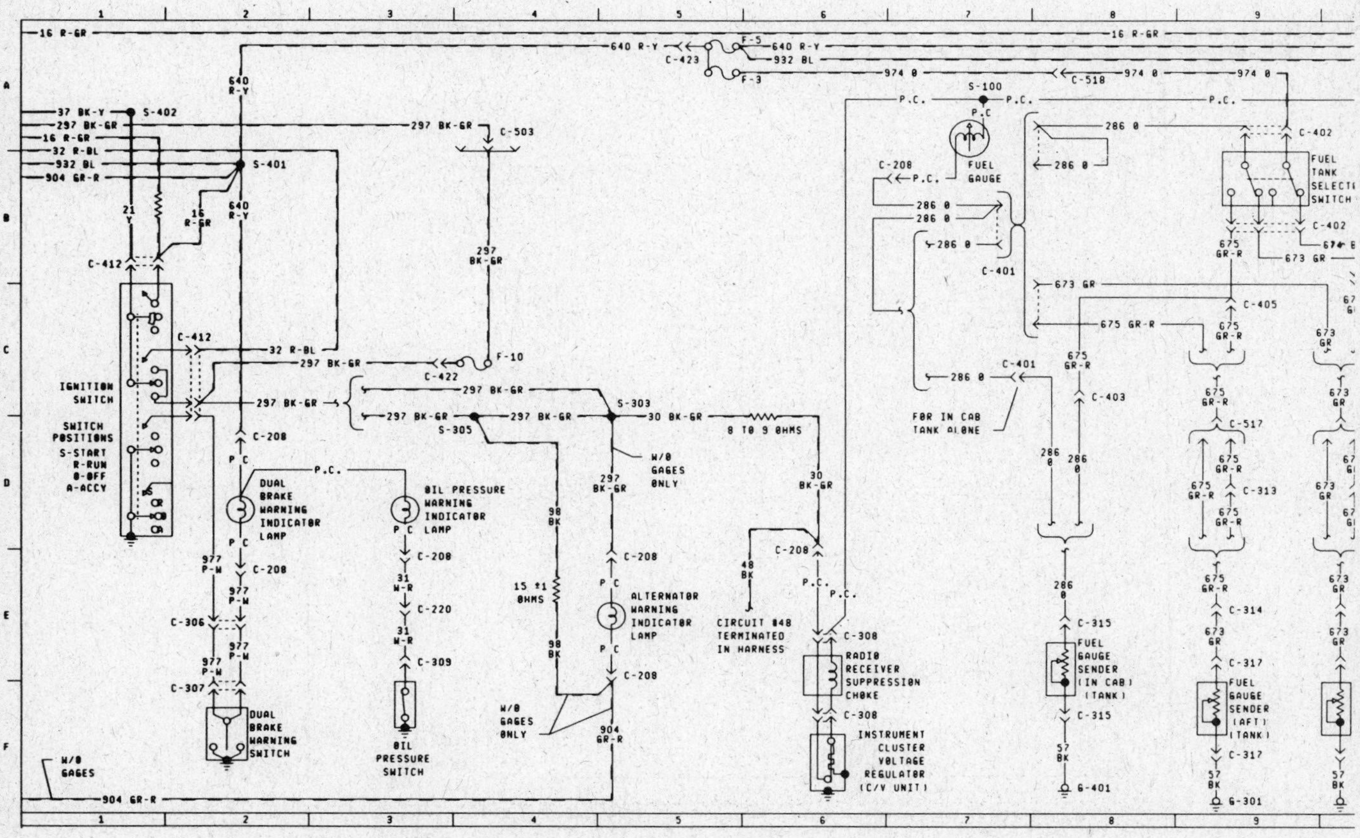

Fig. 10.58 Wiring diagram – 1977 pick-ups (continued)

10

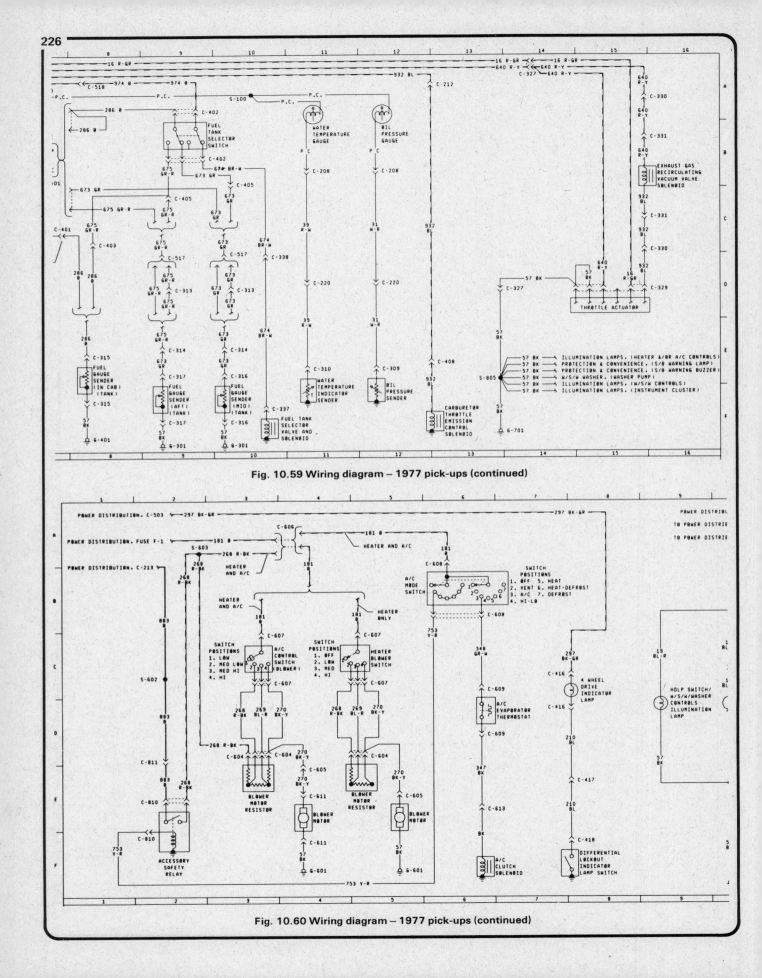

Fig. 10.59 Wiring diagram – 1977 pick-ups (continued)

Fig. 10.60 Wiring diagram – 1977 pick-ups (continued)

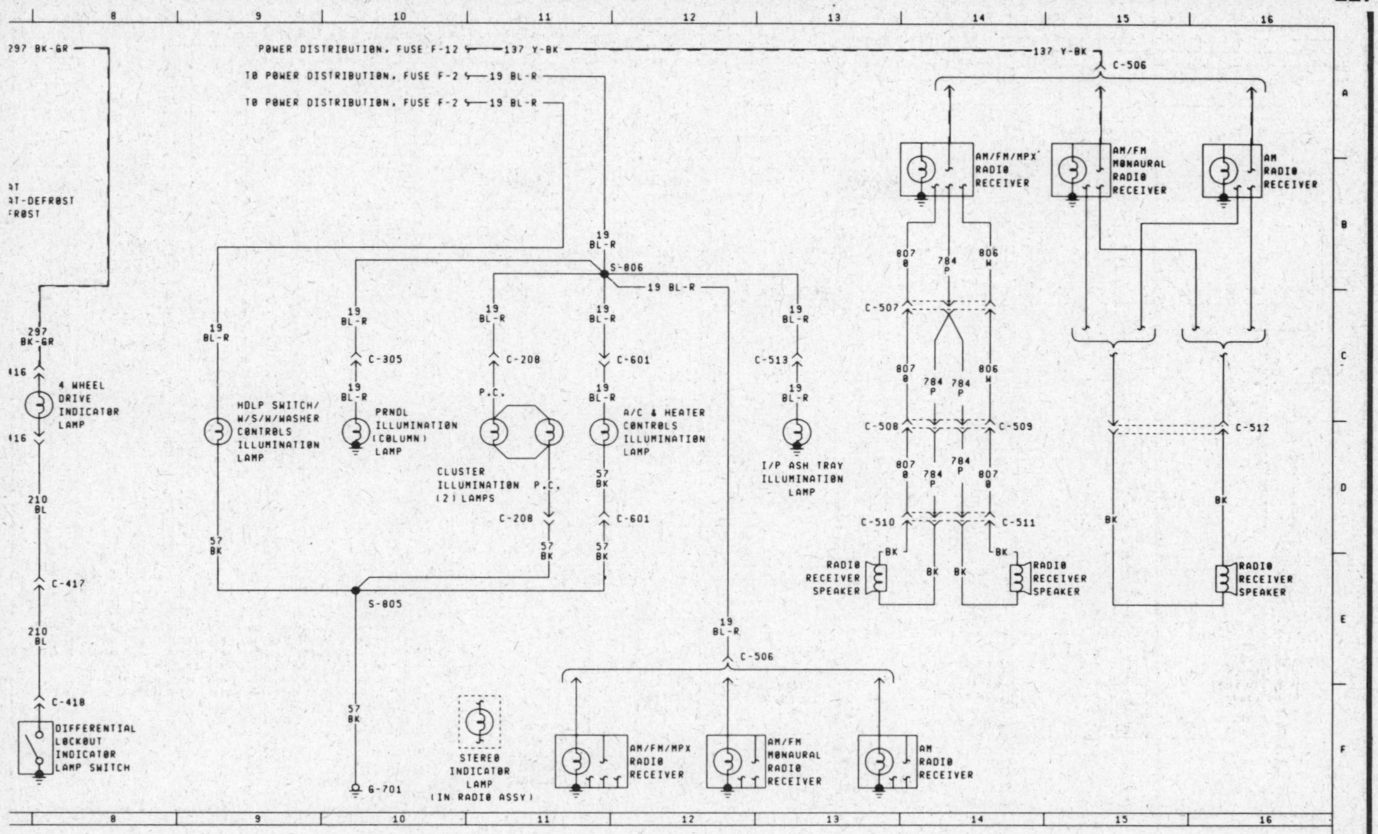

Fig. 10.61 Wiring diagram – 1977 pick-ups (continued)

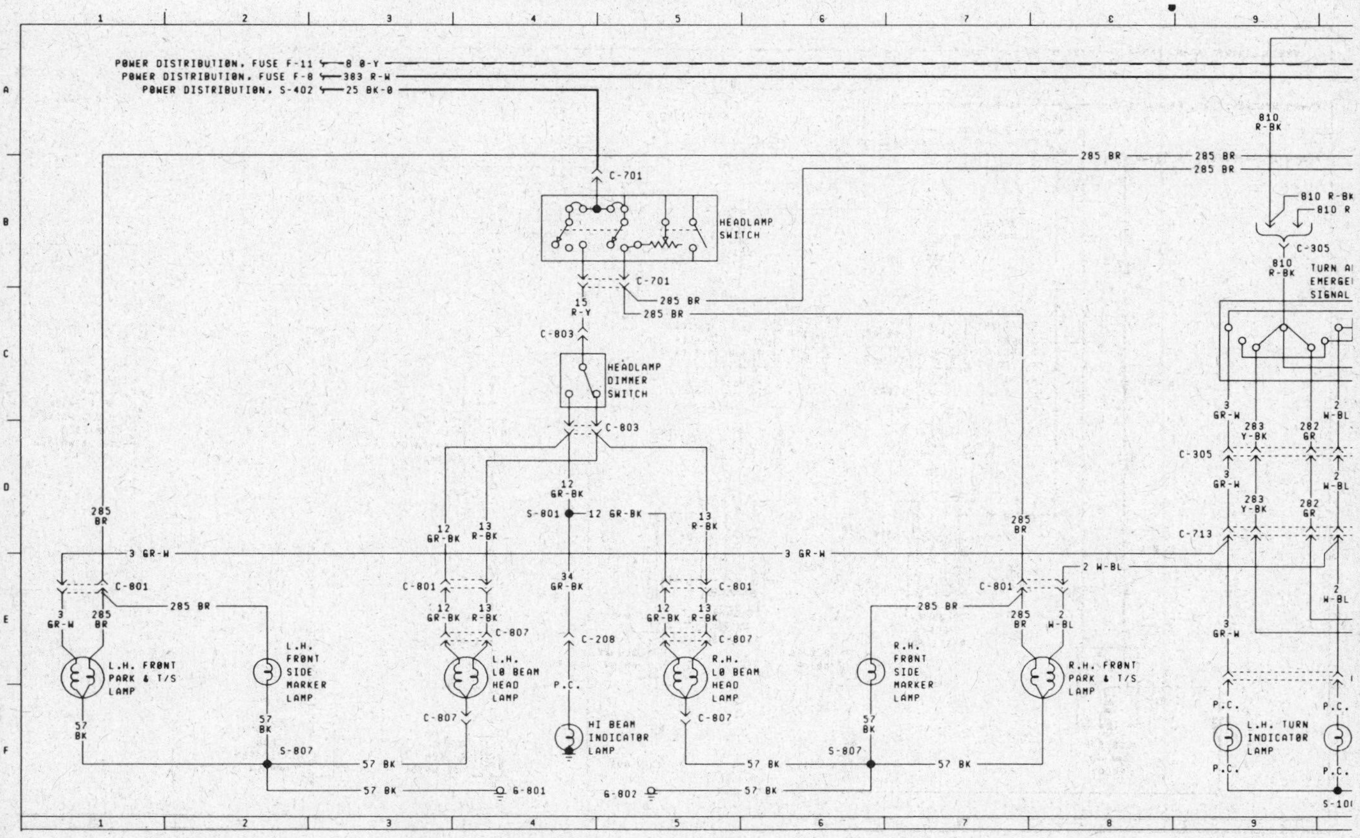

Fig. 10.62 Wiring diagram – 1977 pick-ups (continued)

10

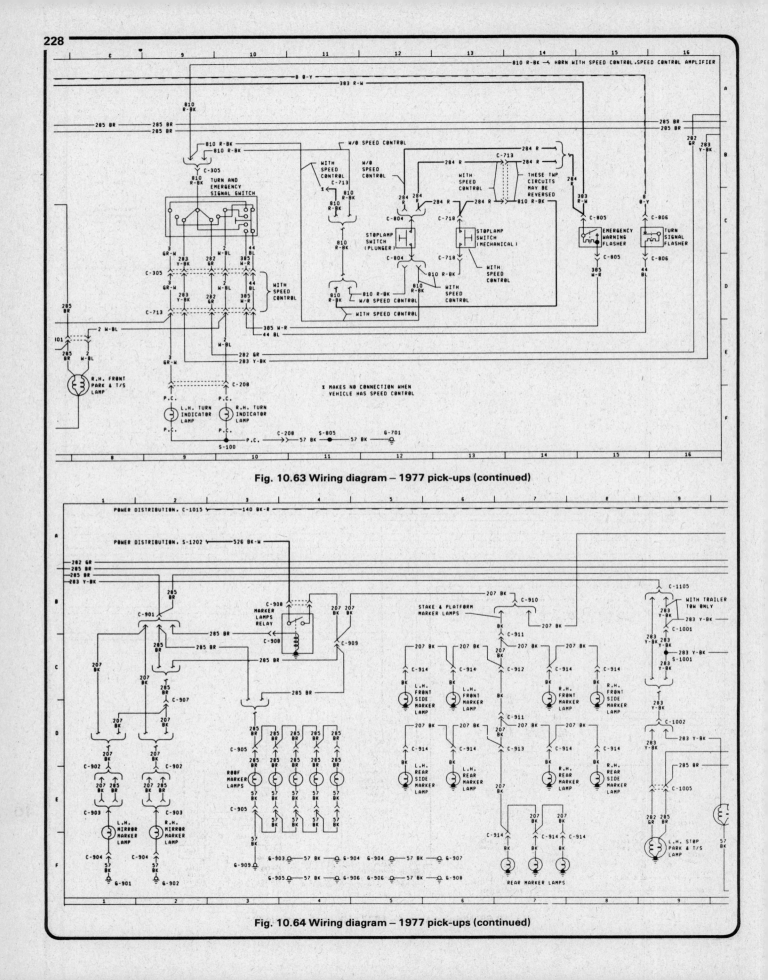

Fig. 10.63 Wiring diagram – 1977 pick-ups (continued)

Fig. 10.64 Wiring diagram – 1977 pick-ups (continued)

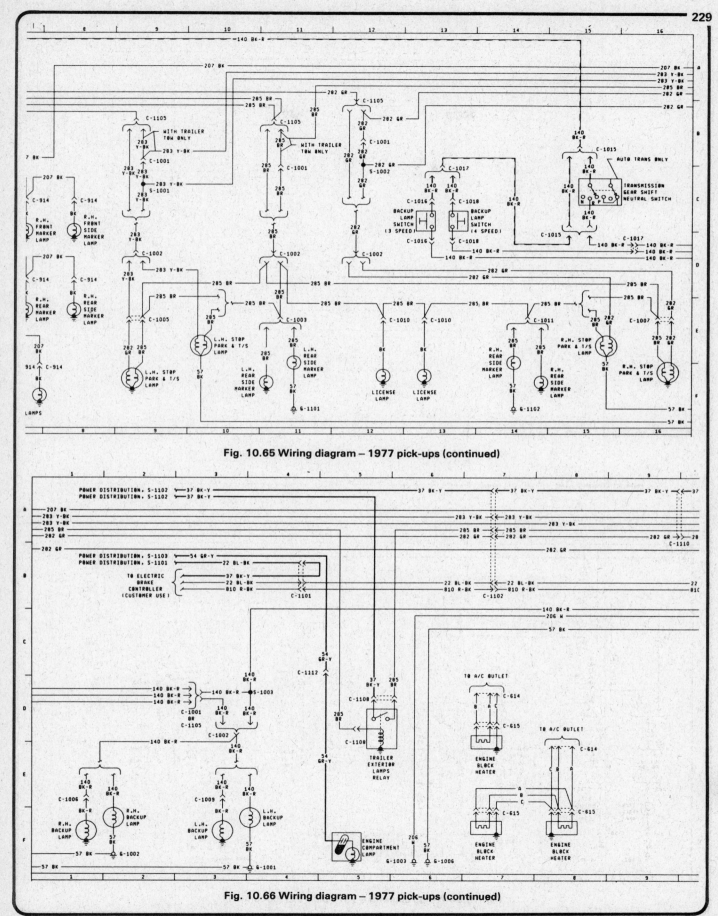

Fig. 10.65 Wiring diagram – 1977 pick-ups (continued)

Fig. 10.66 Wiring diagram – 1977 pick-ups (continued)

10

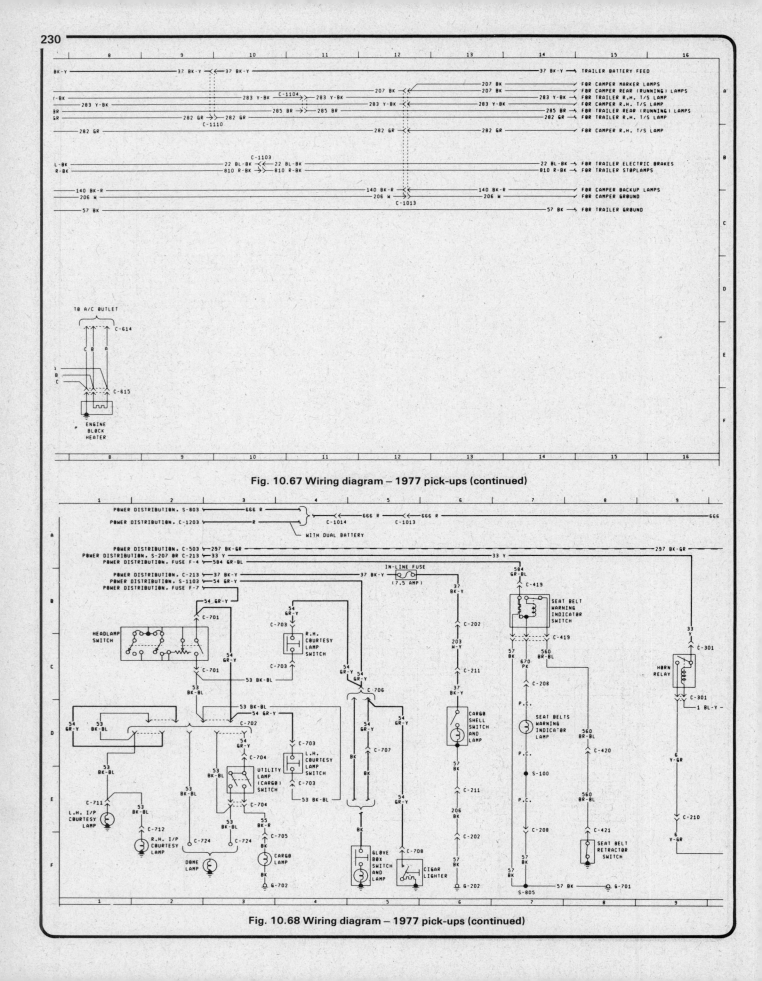

Fig. 10.67 Wiring diagram – 1977 pick-ups (continued)

Fig. 10.68 Wiring diagram – 1977 pick-ups (continued)

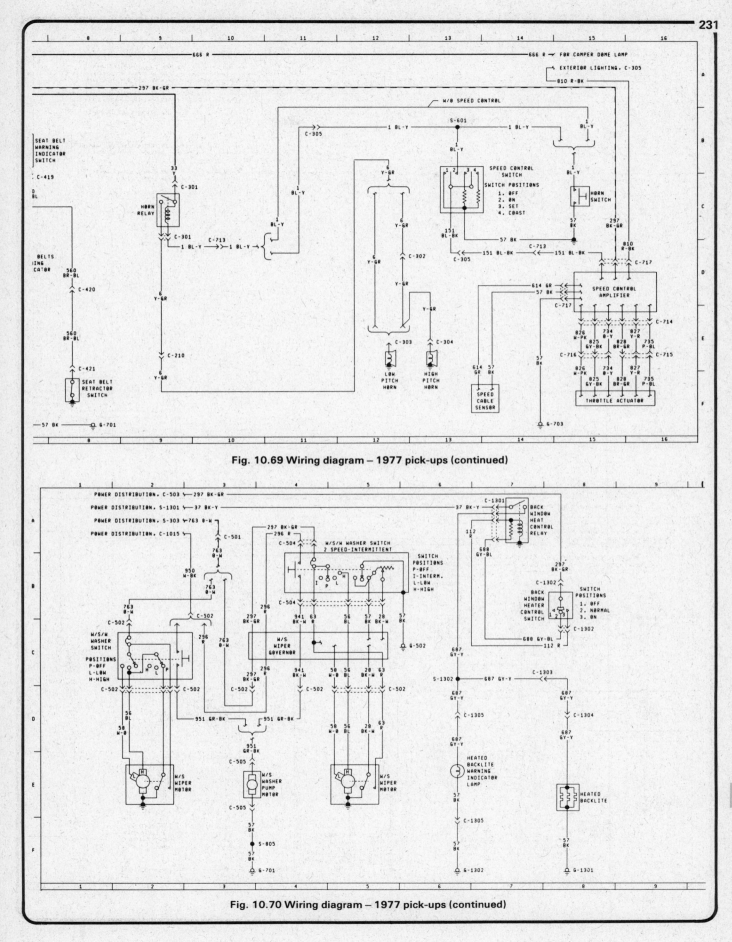

Fig. 10.69 Wiring diagram – 1977 pick-ups (continued)

Fig. 10.70 Wiring diagram – 1977 pick-ups (continued)

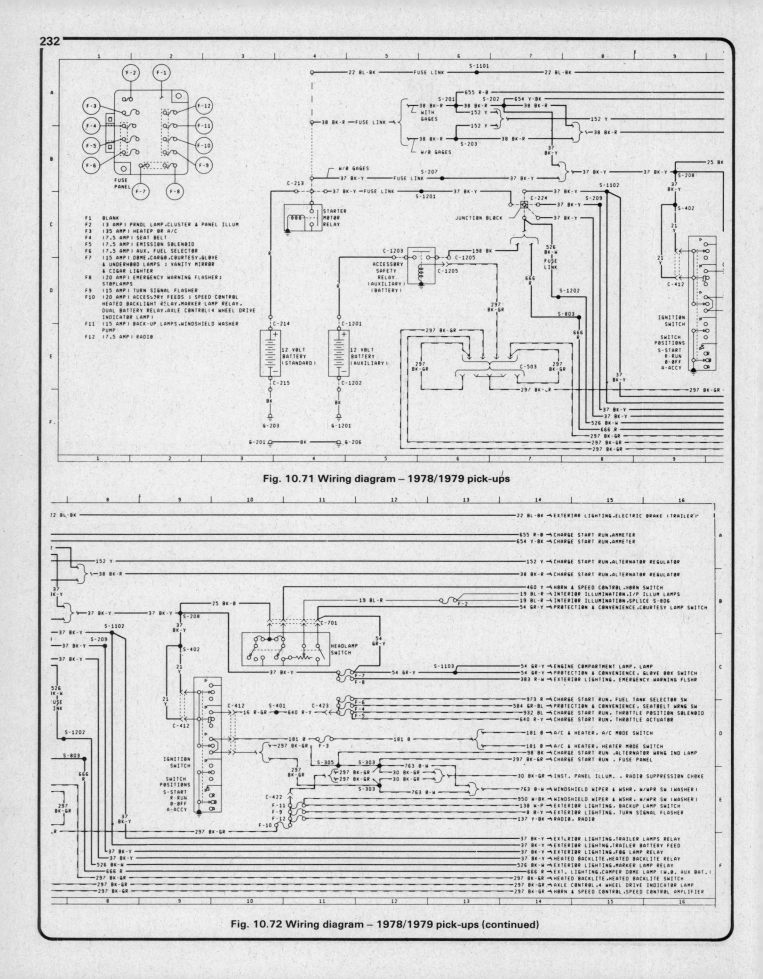

Fig. 10.71 Wiring diagram – 1978/1979 pick-ups

Fig. 10.72 Wiring diagram – 1978/1979 pick-ups (continued)

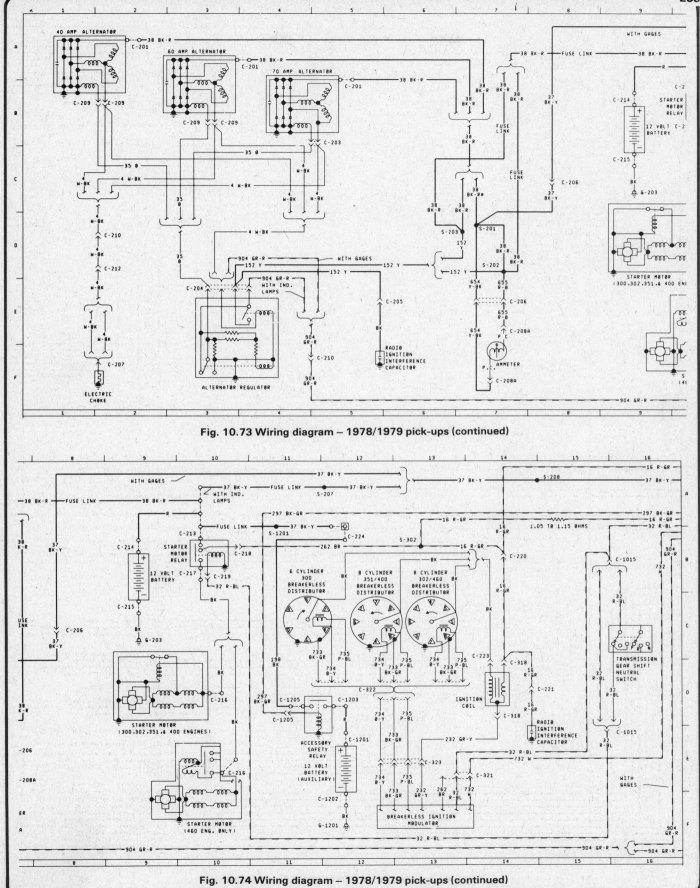

Fig. 10.73 Wiring diagram – 1978/1979 pick-ups (continued)

Fig. 10.74 Wiring diagram – 1978/1979 pick-ups (continued)

10

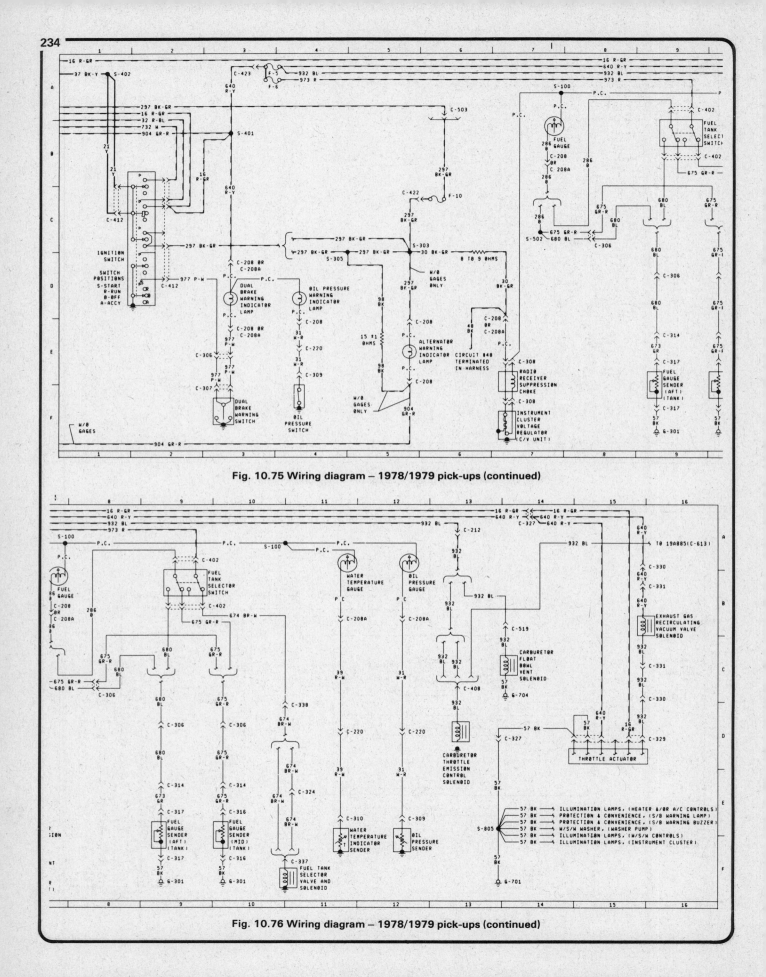

Fig. 10.75 Wiring diagram – 1978/1979 pick-ups (continued)

Fig. 10.76 Wiring diagram – 1978/1979 pick-ups (continued)

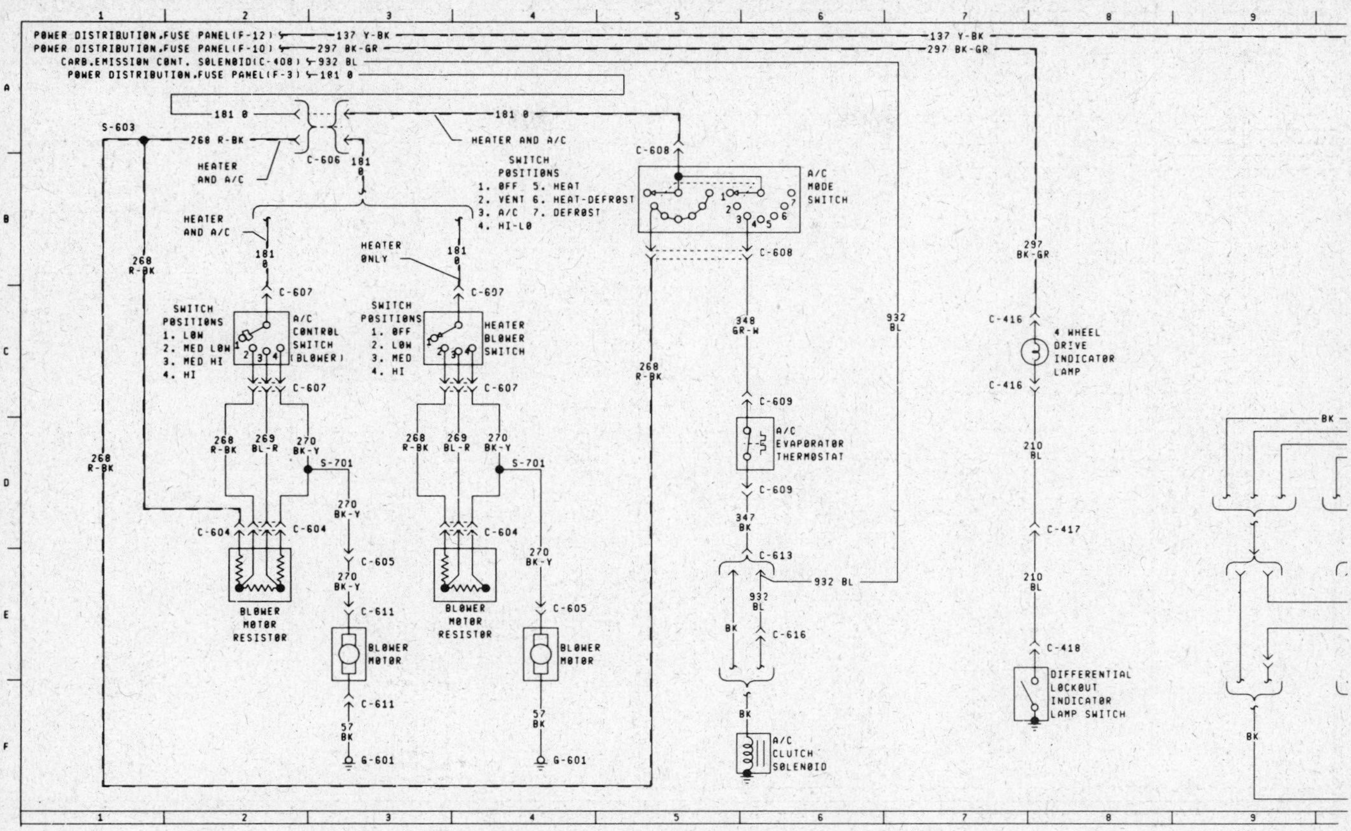

Fig. 10.77 Wiring diagram – 1978/1979 pick-ups (continued)

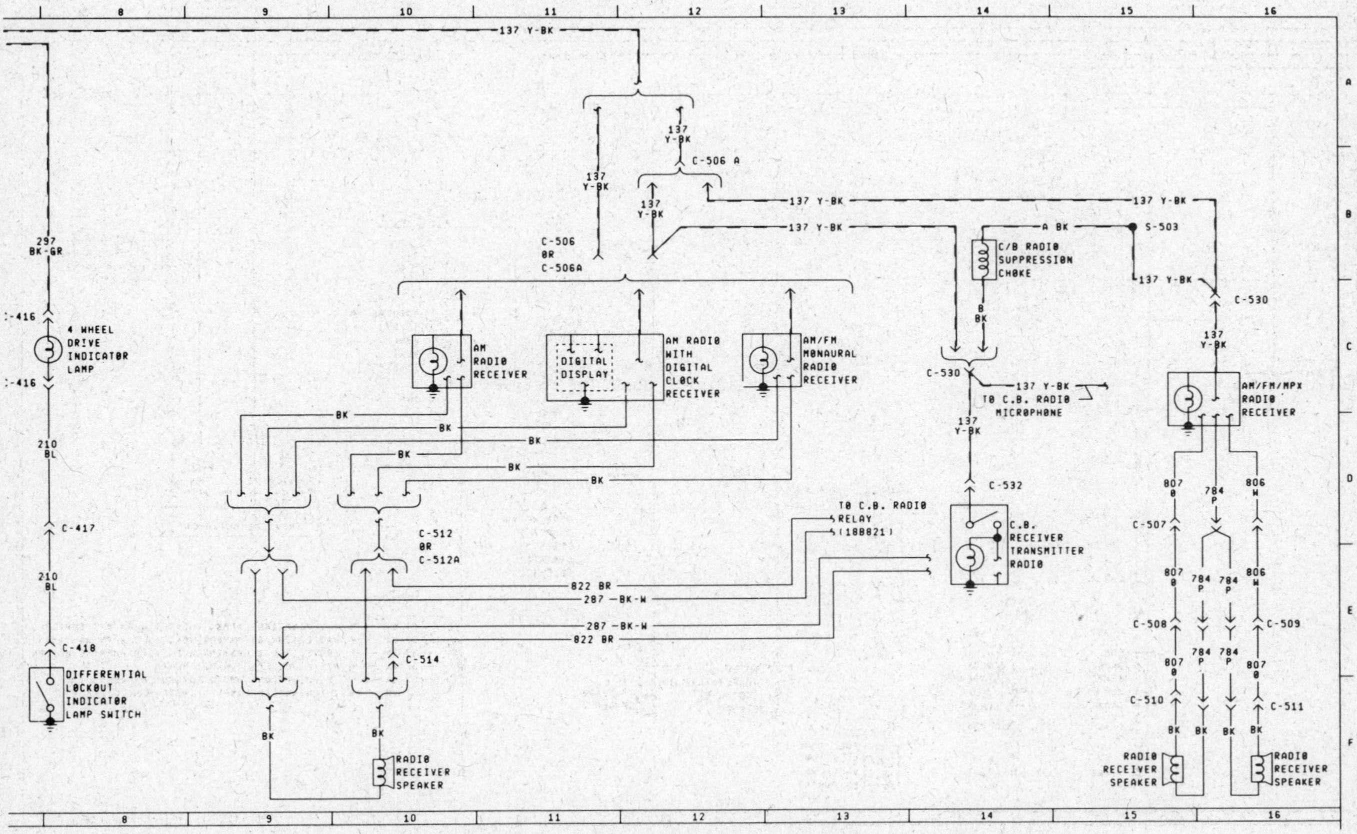

Fig. 10.78 Wiring diagram – 1978/1979 pick-ups (continued)

10

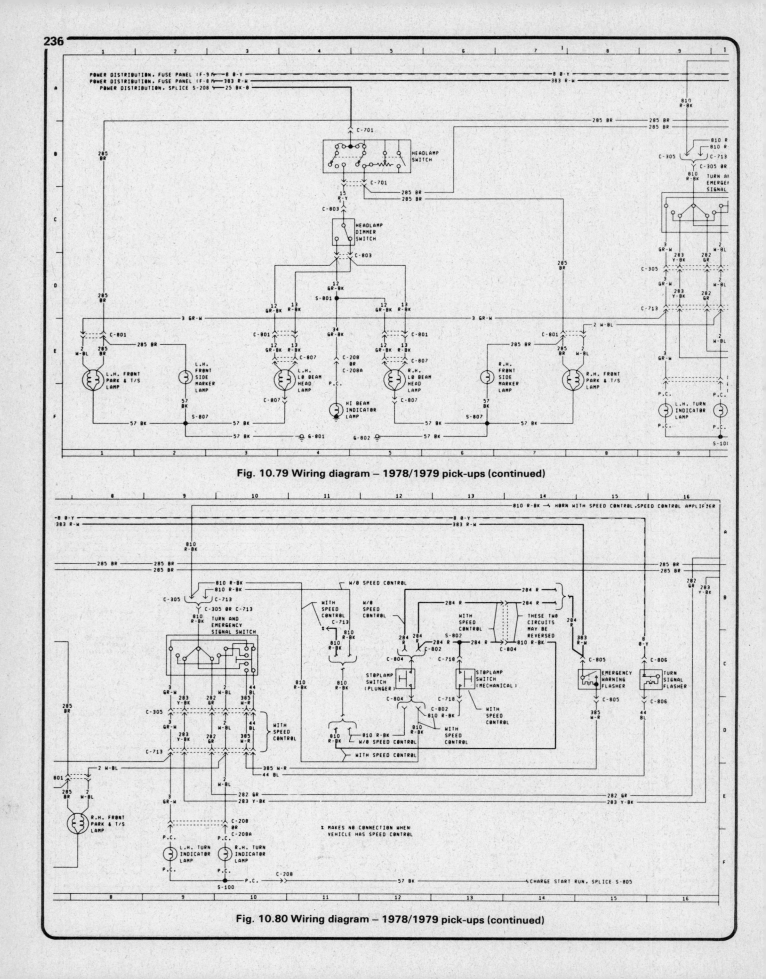

Fig. 10.79 Wiring diagram – 1978/1979 pick-ups (continued)

Fig. 10.80 Wiring diagram – 1978/1979 pick-ups (continued)

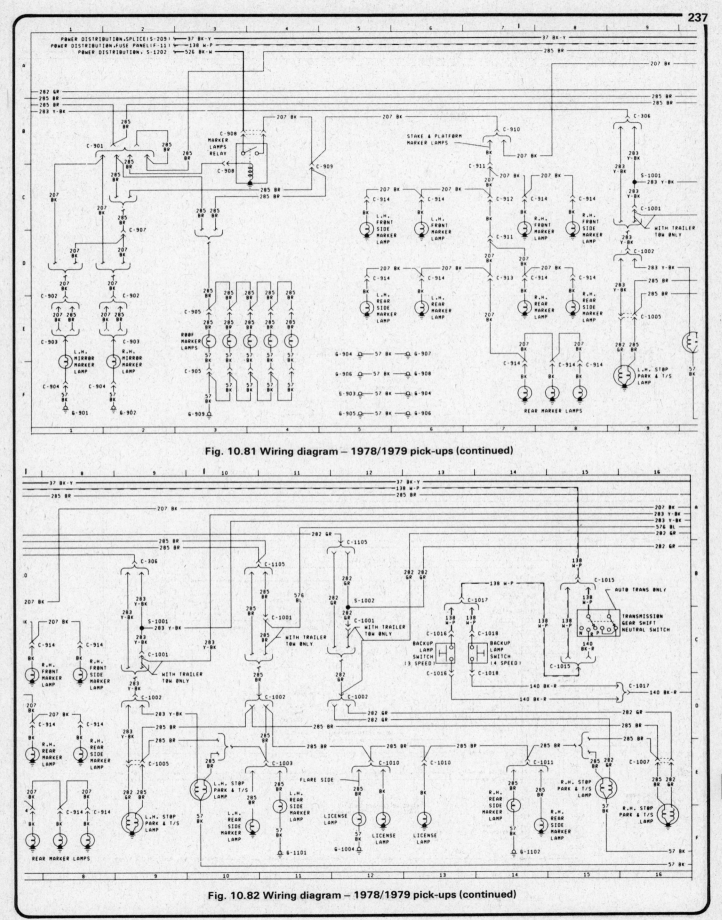

Fig. 10.81 Wiring diagram – 1978/1979 pick-ups (continued)

Fig. 10.82 Wiring diagram – 1978/1979 pick-ups (continued)

10

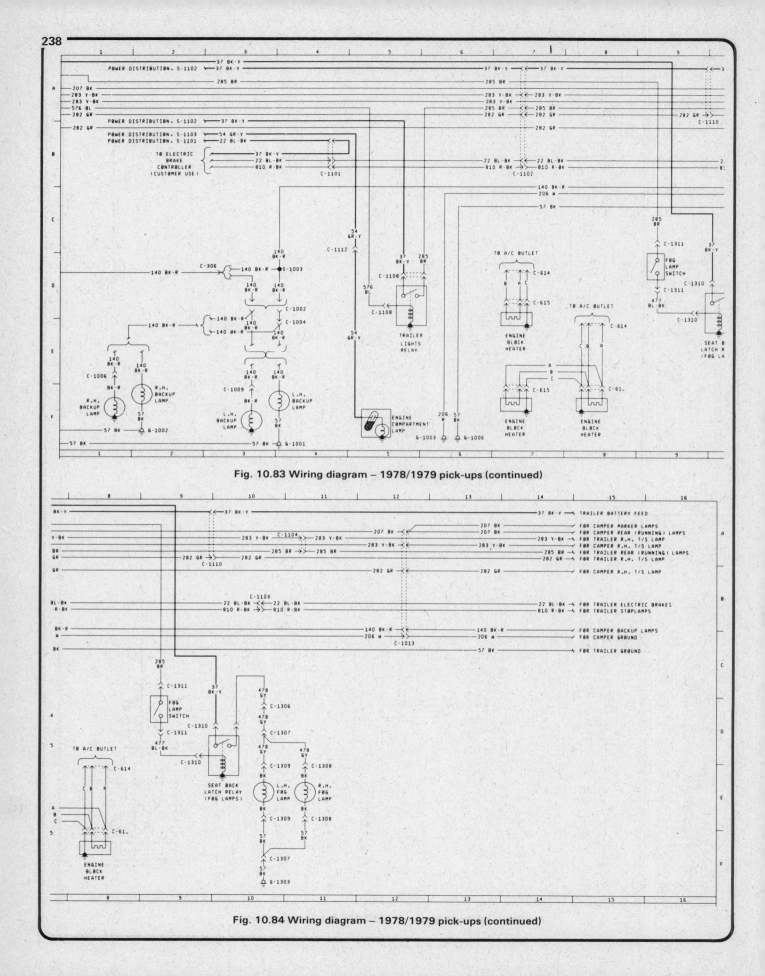

Fig. 10.83 Wiring diagram – 1978/1979 pick-ups (continued)

Fig. 10.84 Wiring diagram – 1978/1979 pick-ups (continued)

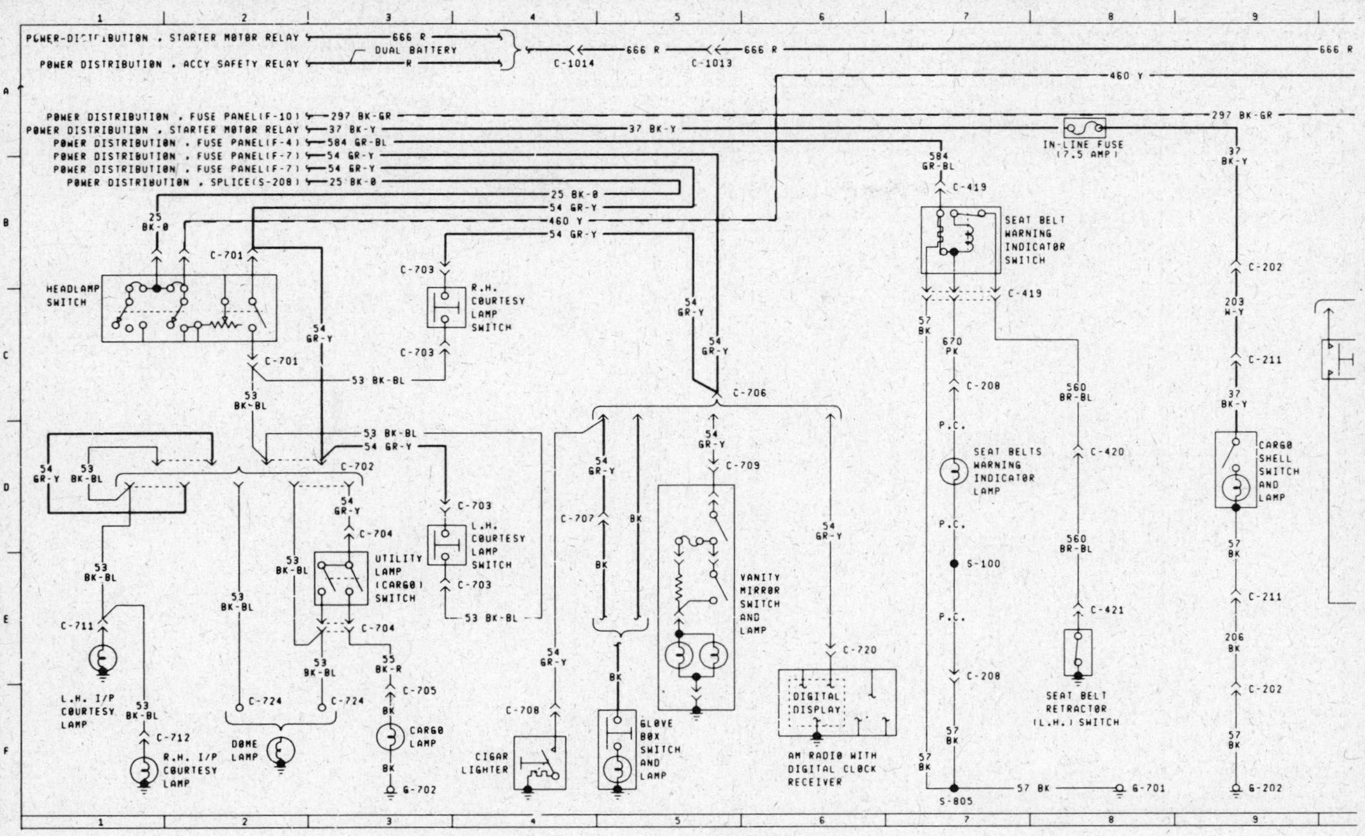

POWER DISTRIBUTION . STARTER MOTOR RELAY 666 R
POWER DISTRIBUTION . ACCY SAFETY RELAY
DUAL BATTERY
C-1014 C-1013
666 R 666 R 666 R
460 Y

POWER DISTRIBUTION . FUSE PANEL(F-10) 297 BK-GR
POWER DISTRIBUTION . STARTER MOTOR RELAY 37 BK-Y
POWER DISTRIBUTION . FUSE PANEL(F-4) 584 GR-BL
POWER DISTRIBUTION . FUSE PANEL(F-7) 54 GR-Y
POWER DISTRIBUTION . FUSE PANEL(F-7) 54 GR-Y
POWER DISTRIBUTION . SPLICE(S-208) 25 BK-0
37 BK-Y
297 BK-GR
IN-LINE FUSE (7.5 AMP)
584 GR-BL C-419
37 BK-Y

25 BK-0
54 GR-Y
460 Y
54 GR-Y

25 BK-0 C-701
HEADLAMP SWITCH
R.H. COURTESY LAMP SWITCH C-703
54 GR-Y
SEAT BELT WARNING INDICATOR SWITCH
C-419
57 BK 670 PK C-202 203 W-Y

C-701
53 BK-BL
C-703
54 GR-Y 54 GR-Y C-706 C-208
560 BR-BL C-211 37 BK-Y
C-202

53 BK-BL
53 BK-BL 54 GR-Y
C-702 C-709
54 GR-Y
L.H. COURTESY LAMP SWITCH C-703
SEAT BELTS WARNING INDICATOR LAMP
C-420
560 BR-BL
CARGO SHELL SWITCH AND LAMP

54 GR-Y 53 BK-BL
54 GR-Y
C-704
VANITY MIRROR SWITCH AND LAMP
S-100
57 BK

53 BK-BL 53 BK-BL C-703
UTILITY LAMP (CARGO) SWITCH
C-704 53 BK-BL
C-705
55 R
C-720
DIGITAL DISPLAY
C-208
C-421
SEAT BELT RETRACTOR (L.H.) SWITCH
206 BK C-202

C-711 C-724 C-724
L.H. I/P COURTESY LAMP 53 BK-BL
DOME LAMP C-708
CARGO LAMP
CIGAR LIGHTER
GLOVE BOX SWITCH AND LAMP
AM RADIO WITH DIGITAL CLOCK RECEIVER
57 BK
57 BK

C-712
R.H. I/P COURTESY LAMP
G-702
S-805 57 BK G-701 57 BK G-202

Fig. 10.85 Wiring diagram – 1978/1979 pick-ups (continued)

666 R 666 R → FOR CAMPER DOME LAMP
460 Y EXTERIOR LIGHTING, C-305
297 BK-GR 810 R-BK

IN-LINE FUSE (7.5 AMP)
37 BK-Y
460 Y
1 BL-Y S-601
C-305 BL-Y 1 BL-Y

SEAT BELT WARNING INDICATOR SWITCH
C-419
C-202
203 W-Y
C-301
HORN SWITCH
HORN RELAY
SPEED CONTROL SWITCH
SWITCH POSITIONS
1. OFF
2. ON
3. SET
4. COAST
HORN SWITCH
57 BK 297 BK-GR

C-211
37 BK-Y
C-301 C-713 1 BL-Y
151 BL-BK
57 BK
151 BL-BK C-713
810 R-BK
C-717

BELTS ING CATOR
560 BR-BL
C-420
CARGO SHELL SWITCH AND LAMP
57 BK
6 Y-GR
1 BL-Y
Y-GR
614 GR 57 BK
SPEED CONTROL AMPLIFIER
C-717

560 BR-BL
C-421
206 BK
C-211
C-202
C-210
C-303
C-304
LOW PITCH HORN
HIGH PITCH HORN
C-714
826 W-PK 734 O-Y 827 Y-R
825 GY-BK 828 BR-GR 735 P-BL
C-716 C-715

SEAT BELT RETRACTOR (L.H.) SWITCH
57 BK
1 BL-Y
614 GR 57 BK
SPEED CABLE SENSOR
57 BK
THROTTLE ACTUATOR
826 W-PK 734 O-Y 827 Y-R
825 GY-BK 828 BR-GR 735 P-BL

57 BK G-701 57 BK G-202 G-703

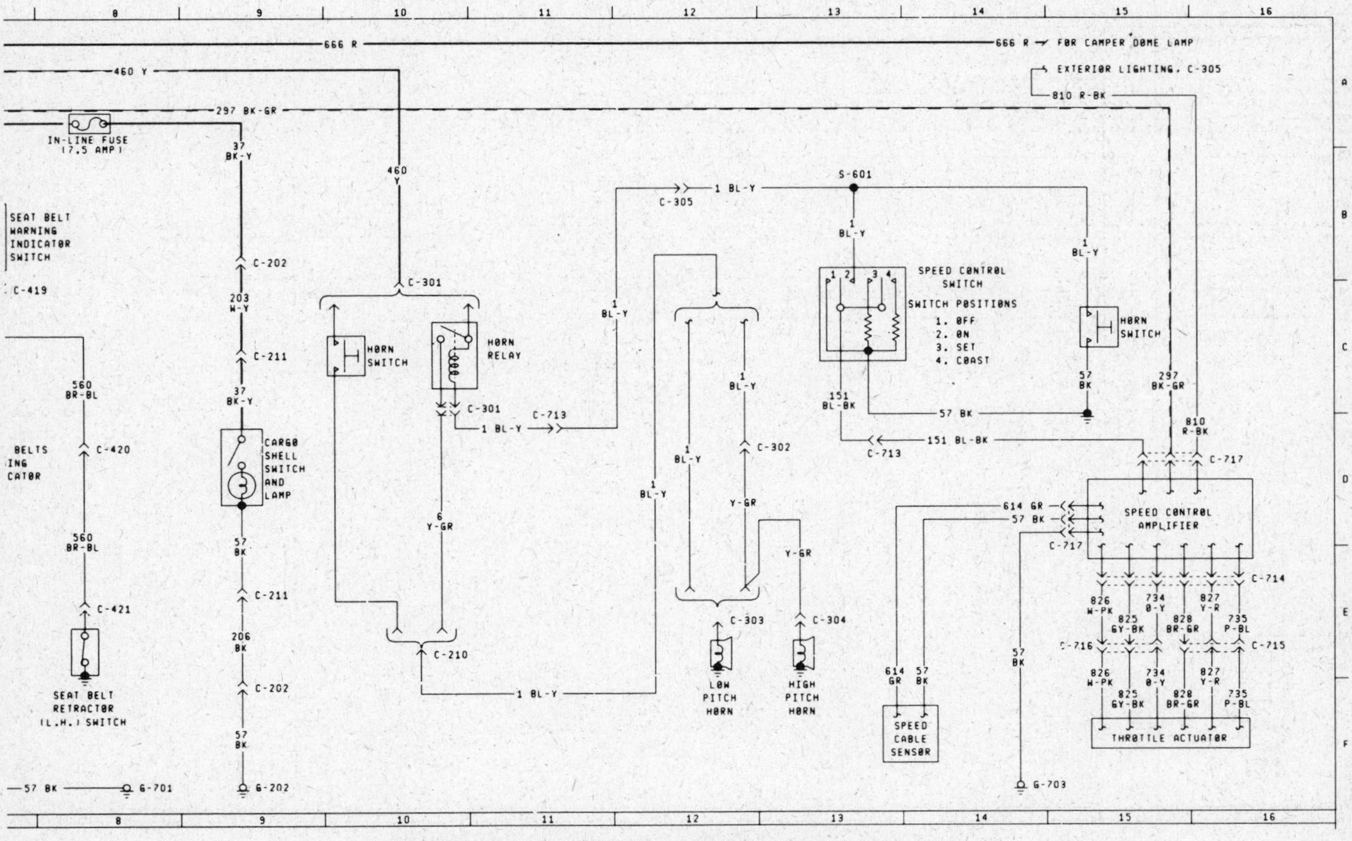

Fig. 10.86 Wiring diagram – 1978/1979 pick-ups (continued)

10

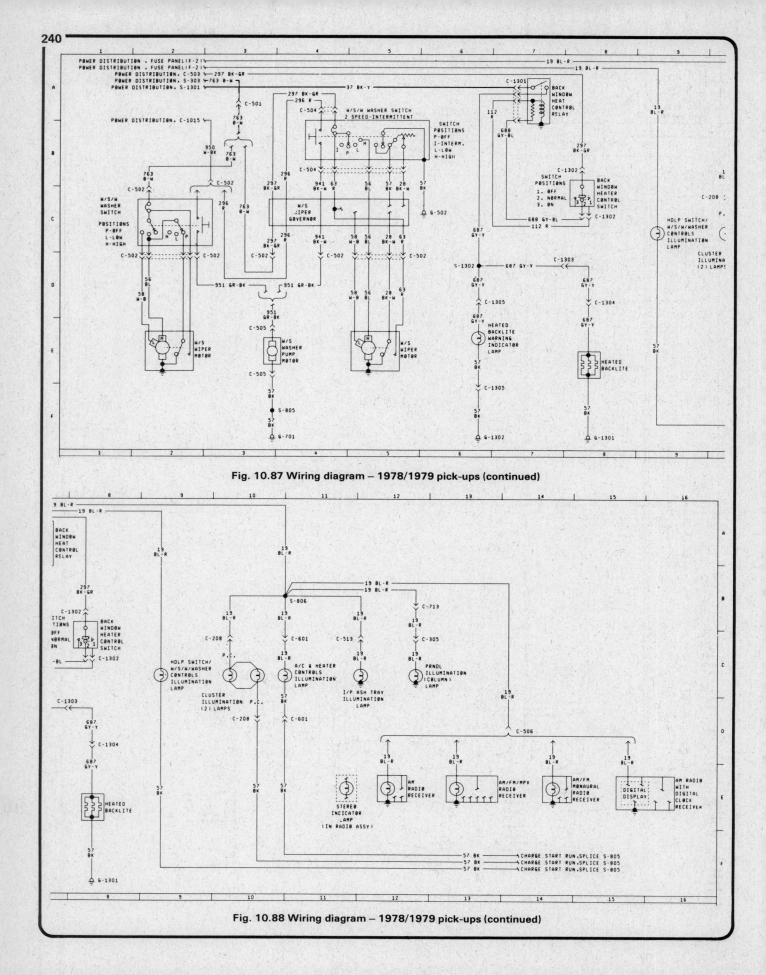

Fig. 10.87 Wiring diagram – 1978/1979 pick-ups (continued)

Fig. 10.88 Wiring diagram – 1978/1979 pick-ups (continued)

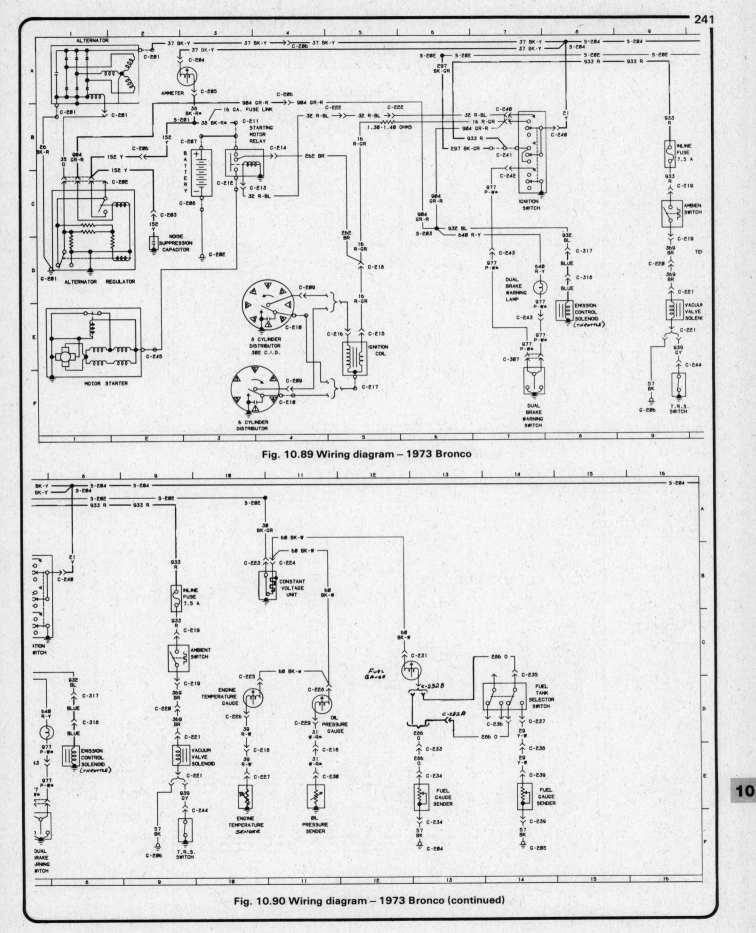

Fig. 10.89 Wiring diagram – 1973 Bronco

Fig. 10.90 Wiring diagram – 1973 Bronco (continued)

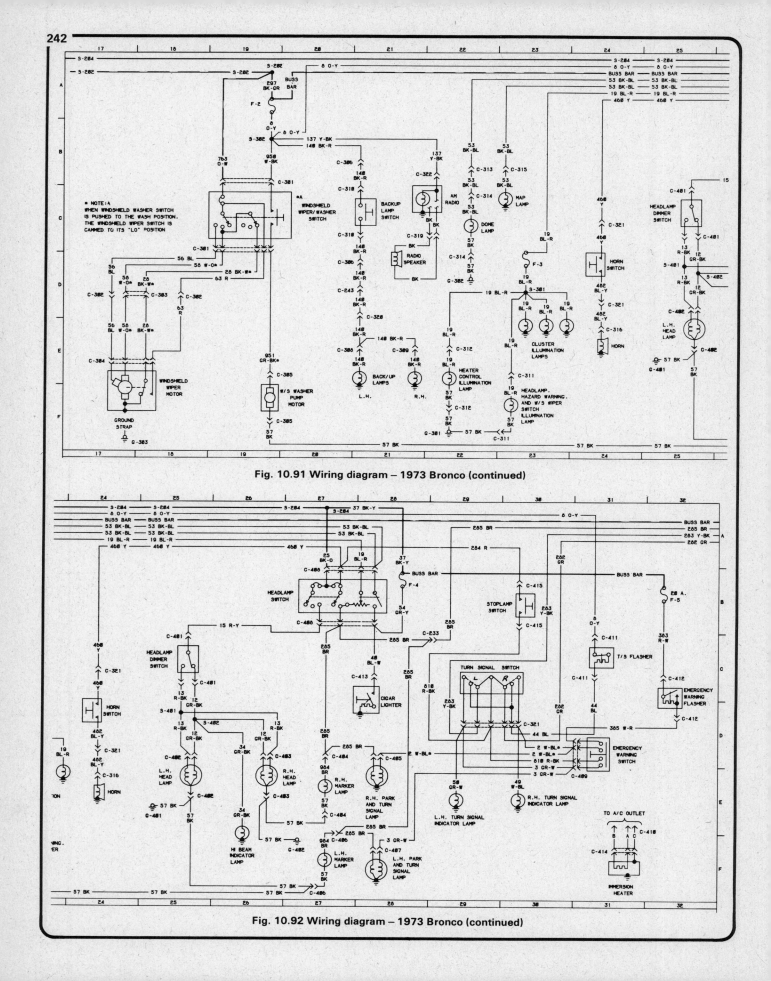

Fig. 10.91 Wiring diagram – 1973 Bronco (continued)

Fig. 10.92 Wiring diagram – 1973 Bronco (continued)

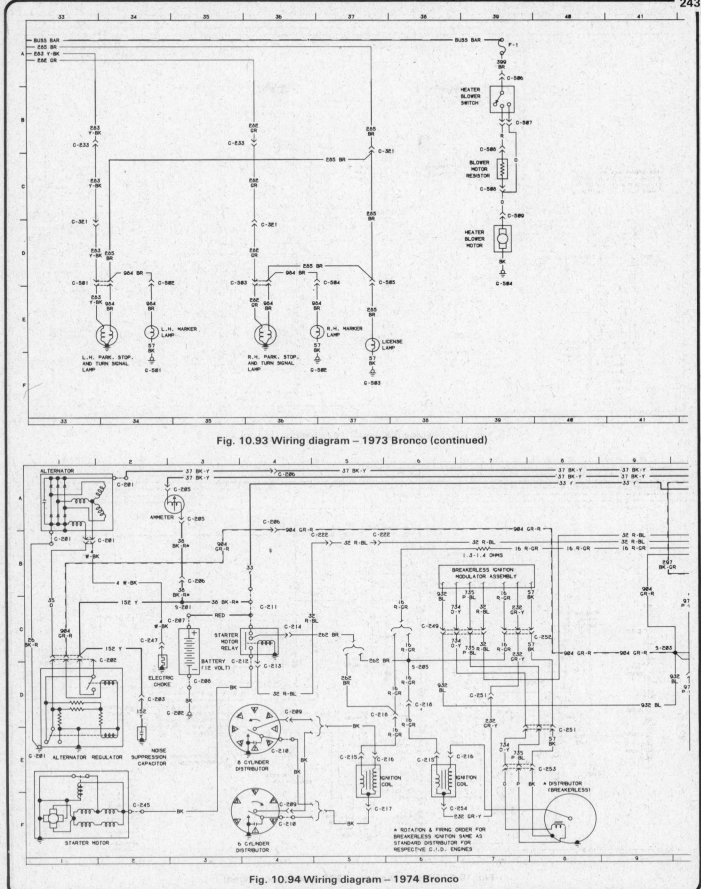

Fig. 10.93 Wiring diagram – 1973 Bronco (continued)

Fig. 10.94 Wiring diagram – 1974 Bronco

10

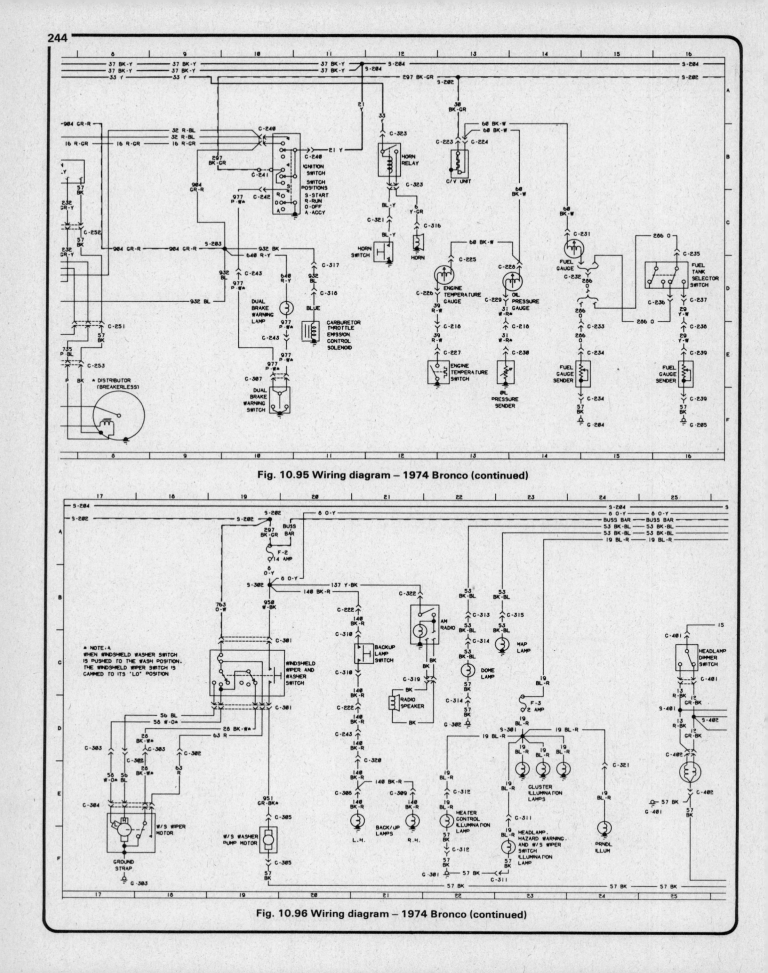

Fig. 10.95 Wiring diagram – 1974 Bronco (continued)

Fig. 10.96 Wiring diagram – 1974 Bronco (continued)

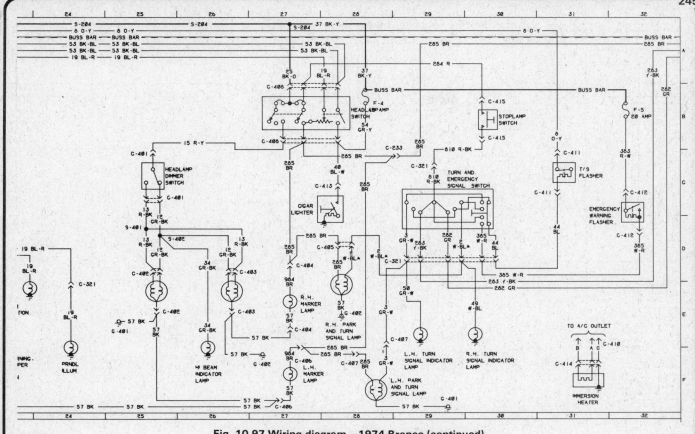

Fig. 10.97 Wiring diagram – 1974 Bronco (continued)

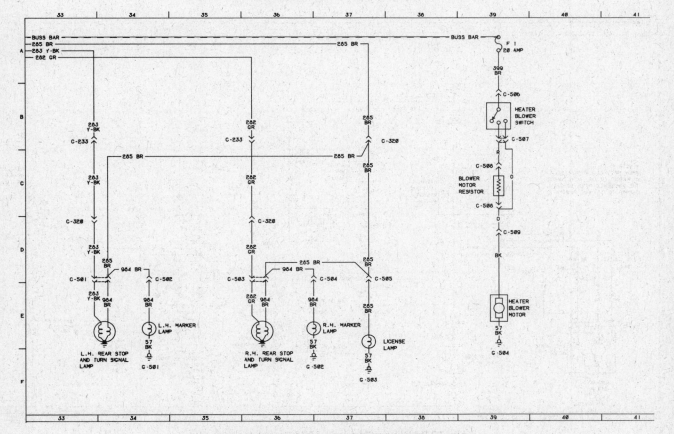

Fig. 10.98 Wiring diagram – 1974 Bronco (continued)

10

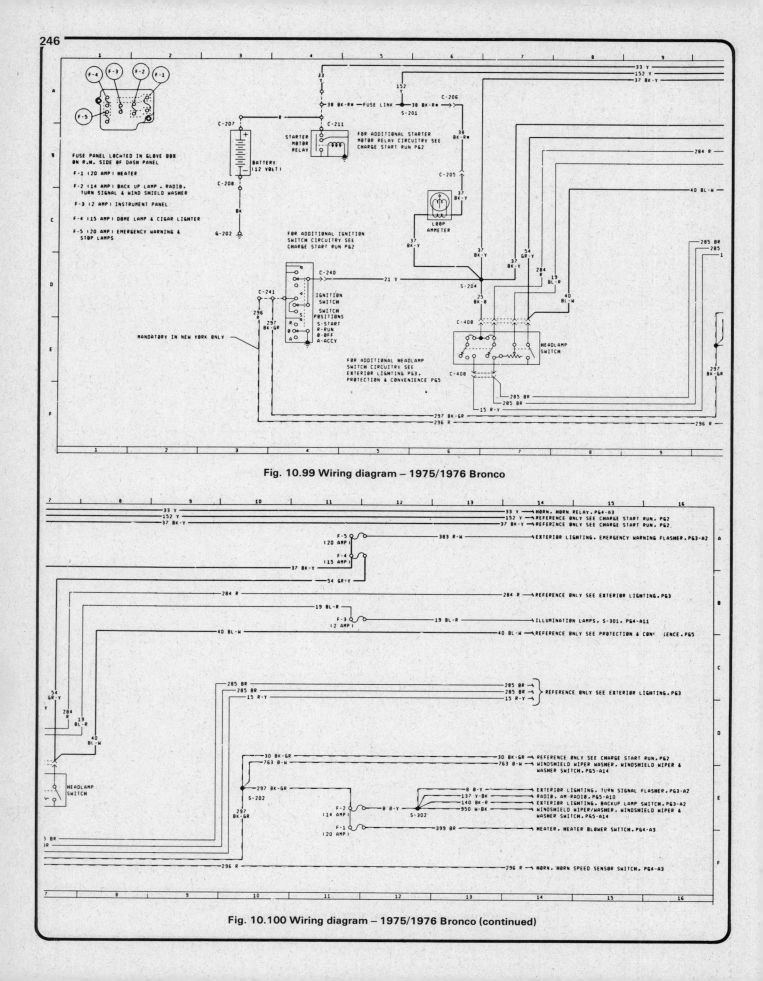

Fig. 10.99 Wiring diagram – 1975/1976 Bronco

Fig. 10.100 Wiring diagram – 1975/1976 Bronco (continued)

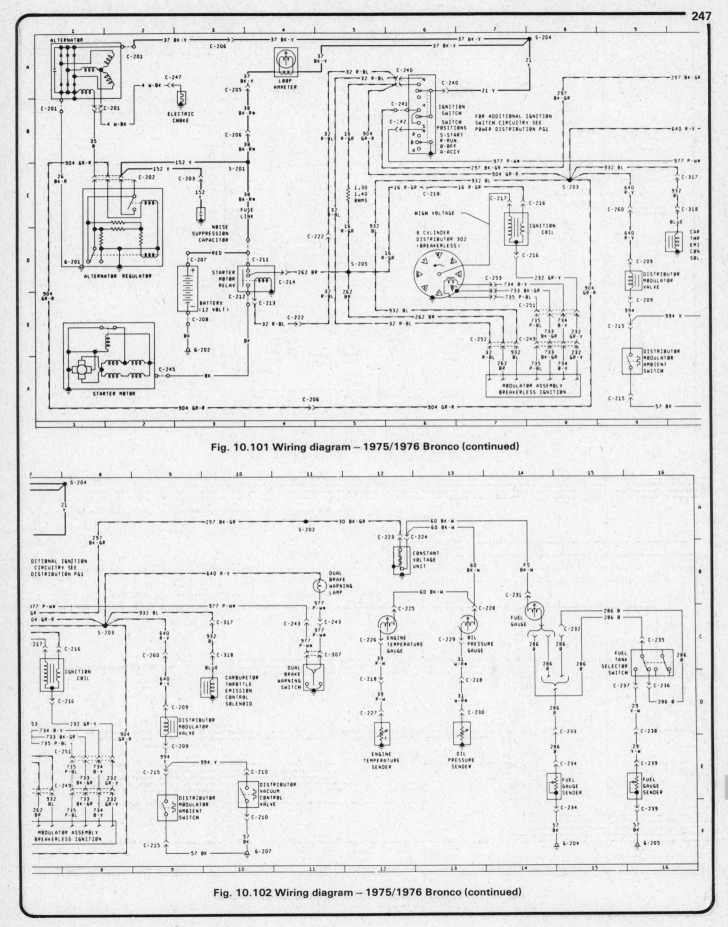

Fig. 10.101 Wiring diagram – 1975/1976 Bronco (continued)

Fig. 10.102 Wiring diagram – 1975/1976 Bronco (continued)

10

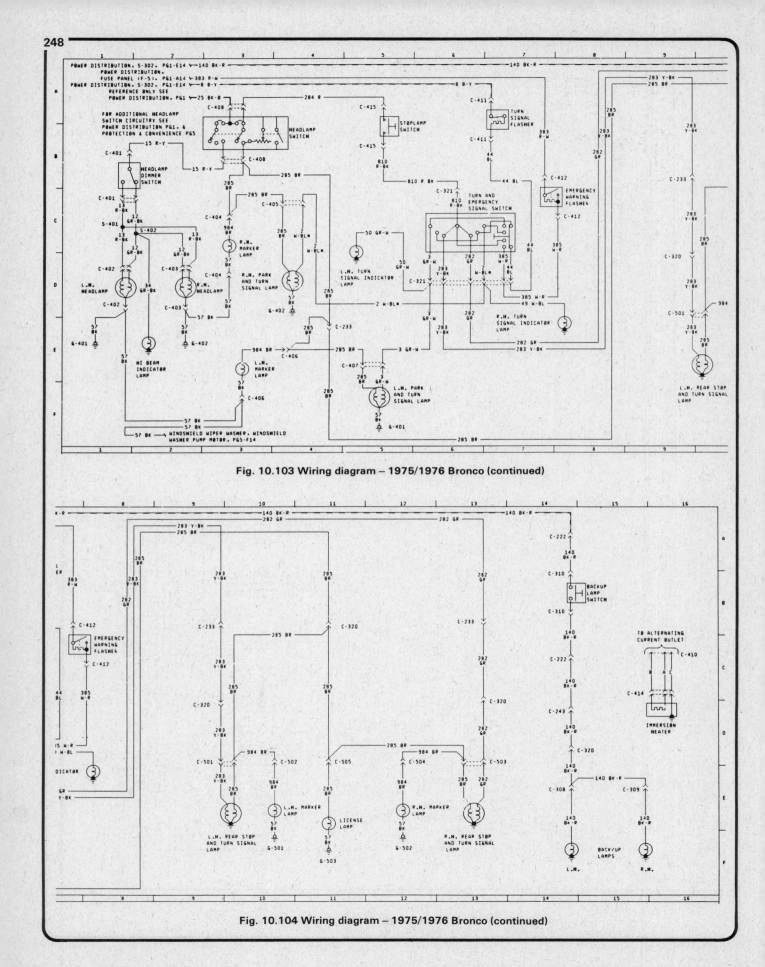

Fig. 10.103 Wiring diagram – 1975/1976 Bronco (continued)

Fig. 10.104 Wiring diagram – 1975/1976 Bronco (continued)

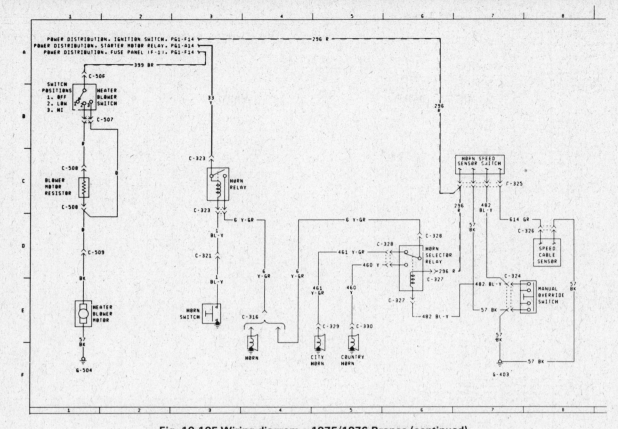

Fig. 10.105 Wiring diagram – 1975/1976 Bronco (continued)

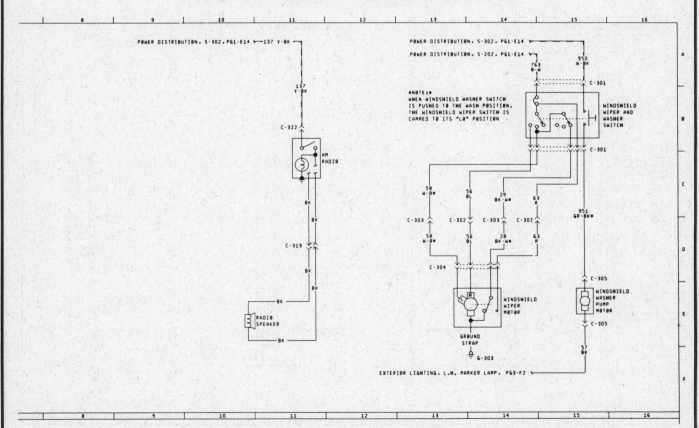

Fig. 10.106 Wiring diagram – 1975/1976 Bronco (continued)

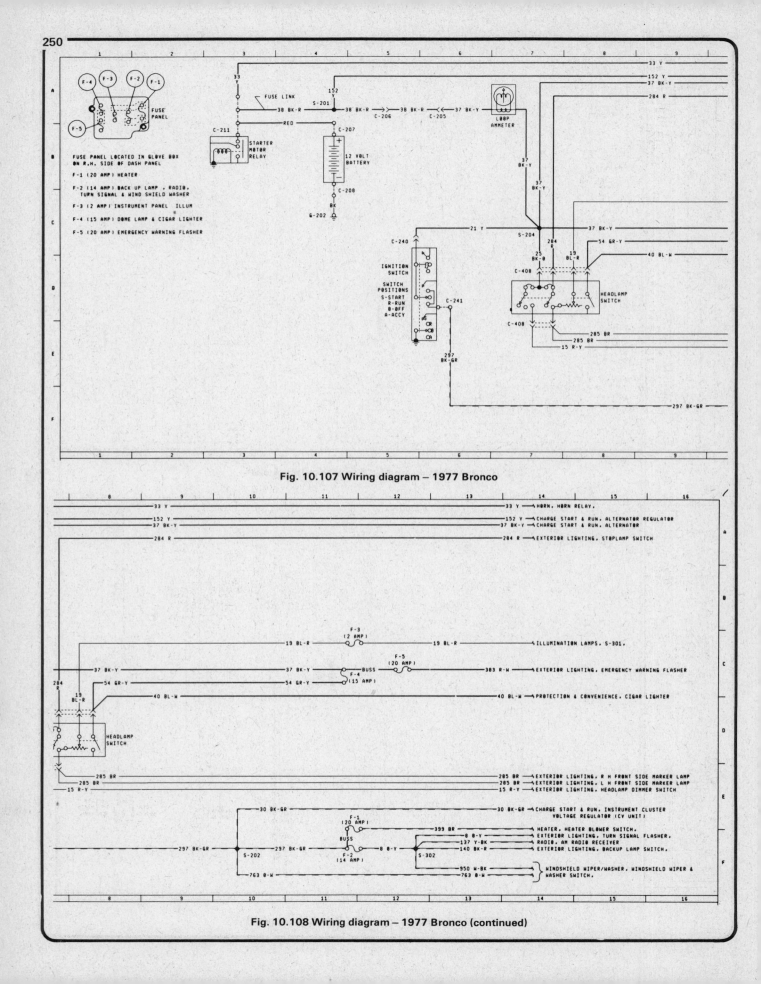

Fig. 10.107 Wiring diagram – 1977 Bronco

Fig. 10.108 Wiring diagram – 1977 Bronco (continued)

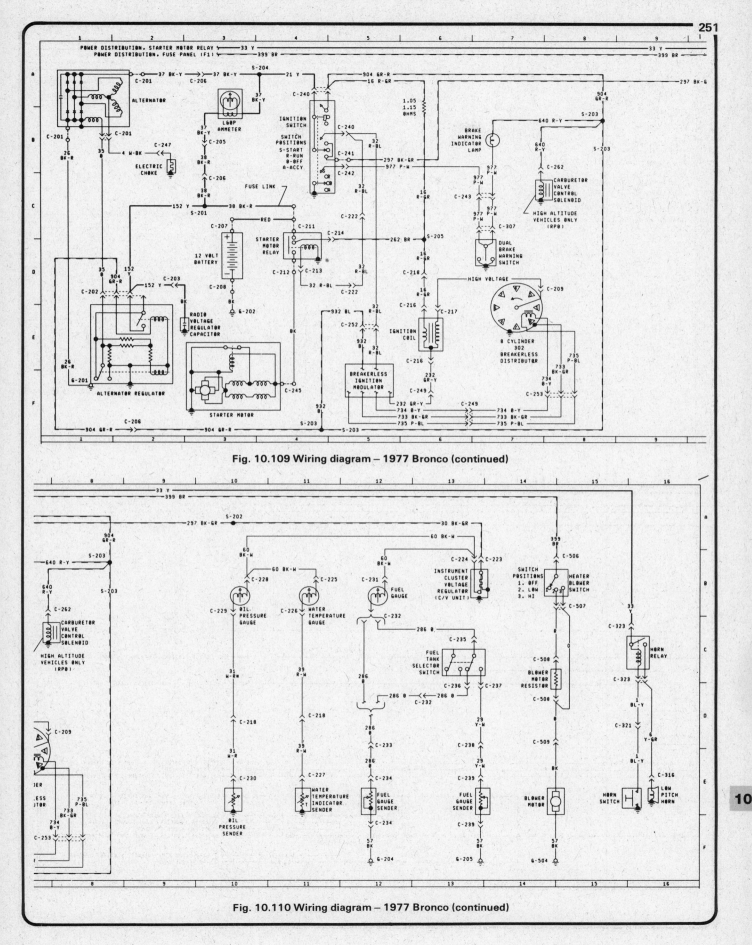

Fig. 10.109 Wiring diagram – 1977 Bronco (continued)

Fig. 10.110 Wiring diagram – 1977 Bronco (continued)

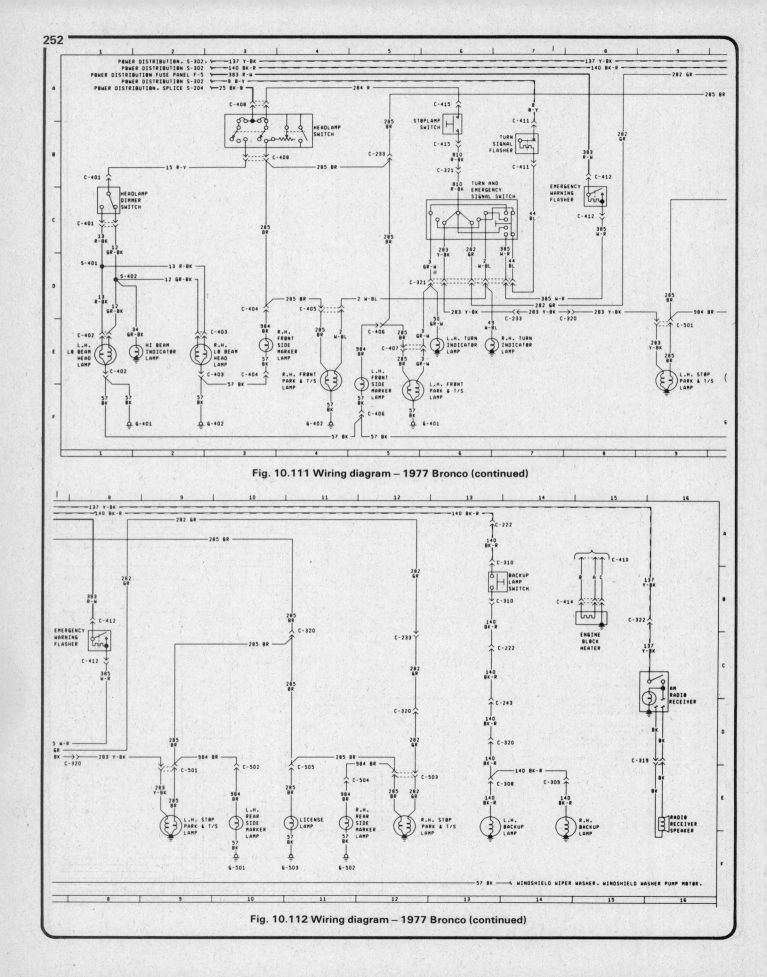

Fig. 10.111 Wiring diagram – 1977 Bronco (continued)

Fig. 10.112 Wiring diagram – 1977 Bronco (continued)

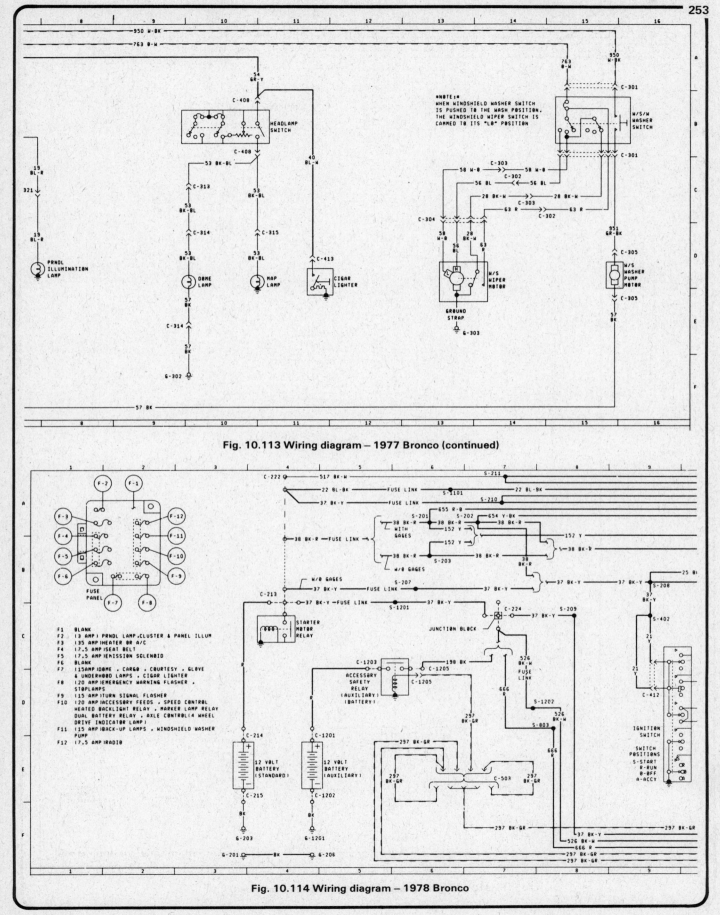

Fig. 10.113 Wiring diagram – 1977 Bronco (continued)

Fig. 10.114 Wiring diagram – 1978 Bronco

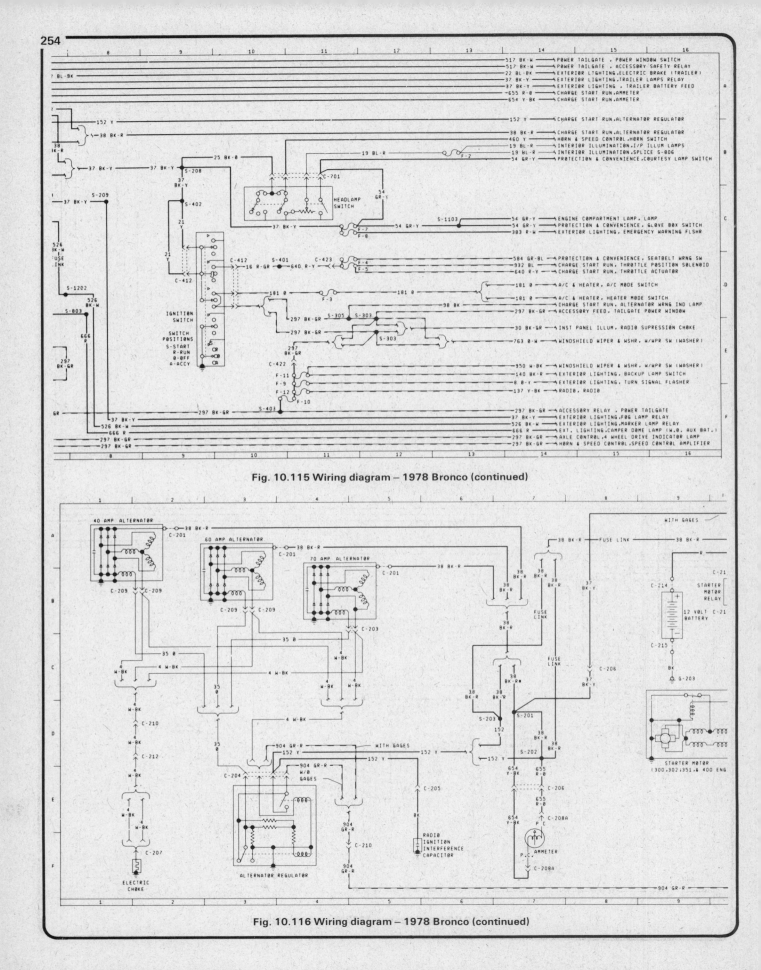

Fig. 10.115 Wiring diagram – 1978 Bronco (continued)

Fig. 10.116 Wiring diagram – 1978 Bronco (continued)

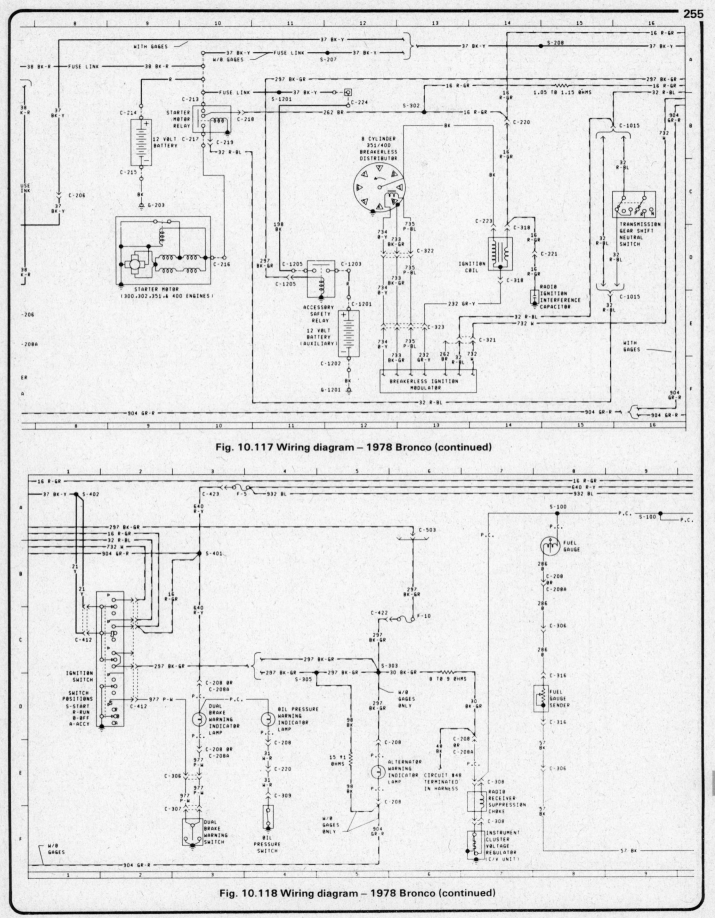

Fig. 10.117 Wiring diagram – 1978 Bronco (continued)

Fig. 10.118 Wiring diagram – 1978 Bronco (continued)

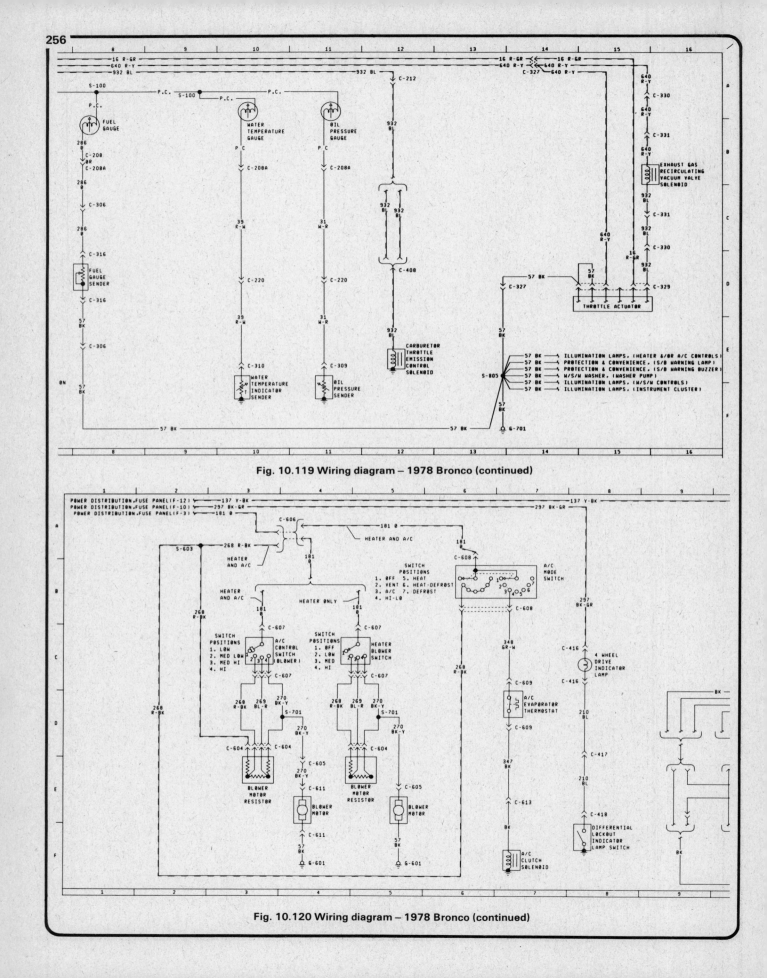

Fig. 10.119 Wiring diagram – 1978 Bronco (continued)

Fig. 10.120 Wiring diagram – 1978 Bronco (continued)

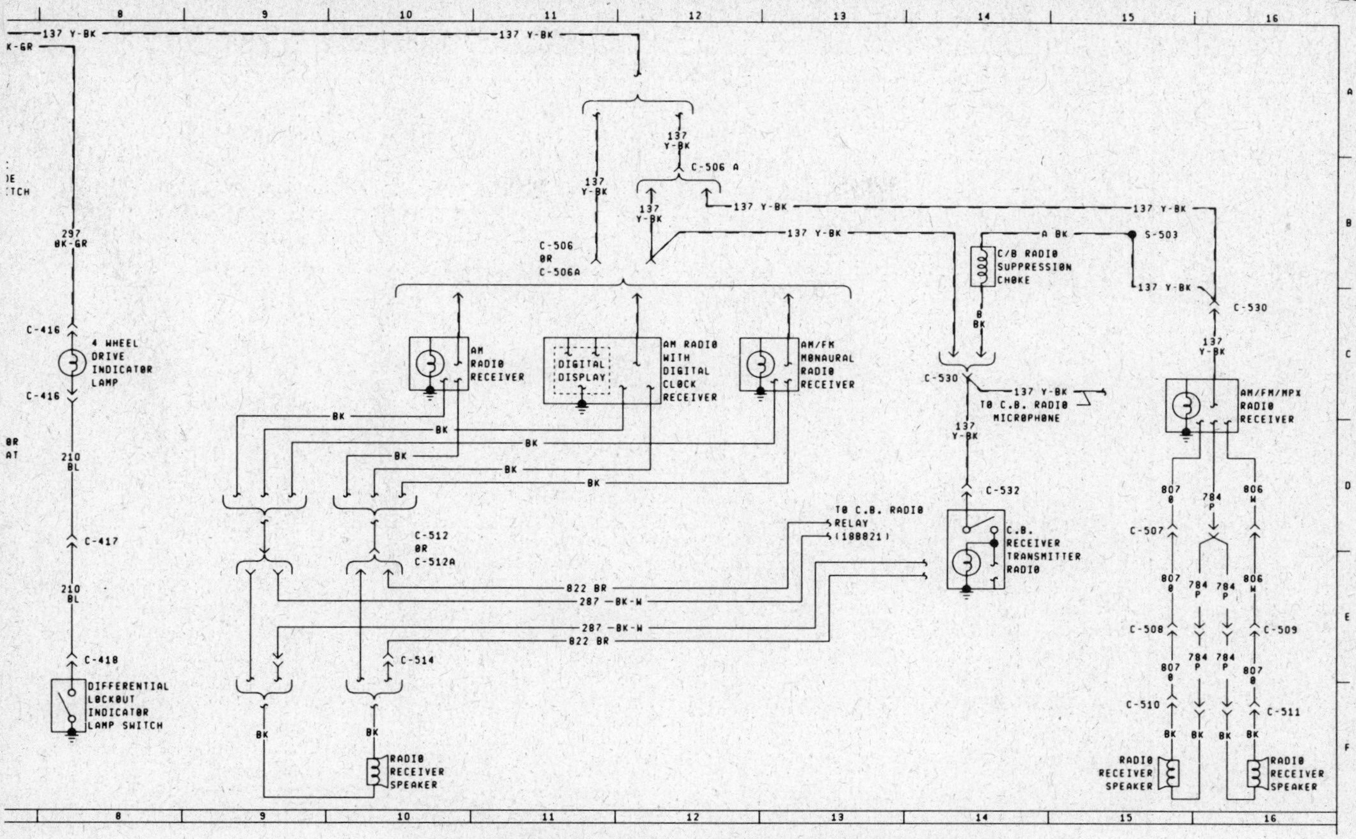

Fig. 10.121 Wiring diagram – 1978 Bronco (continued)

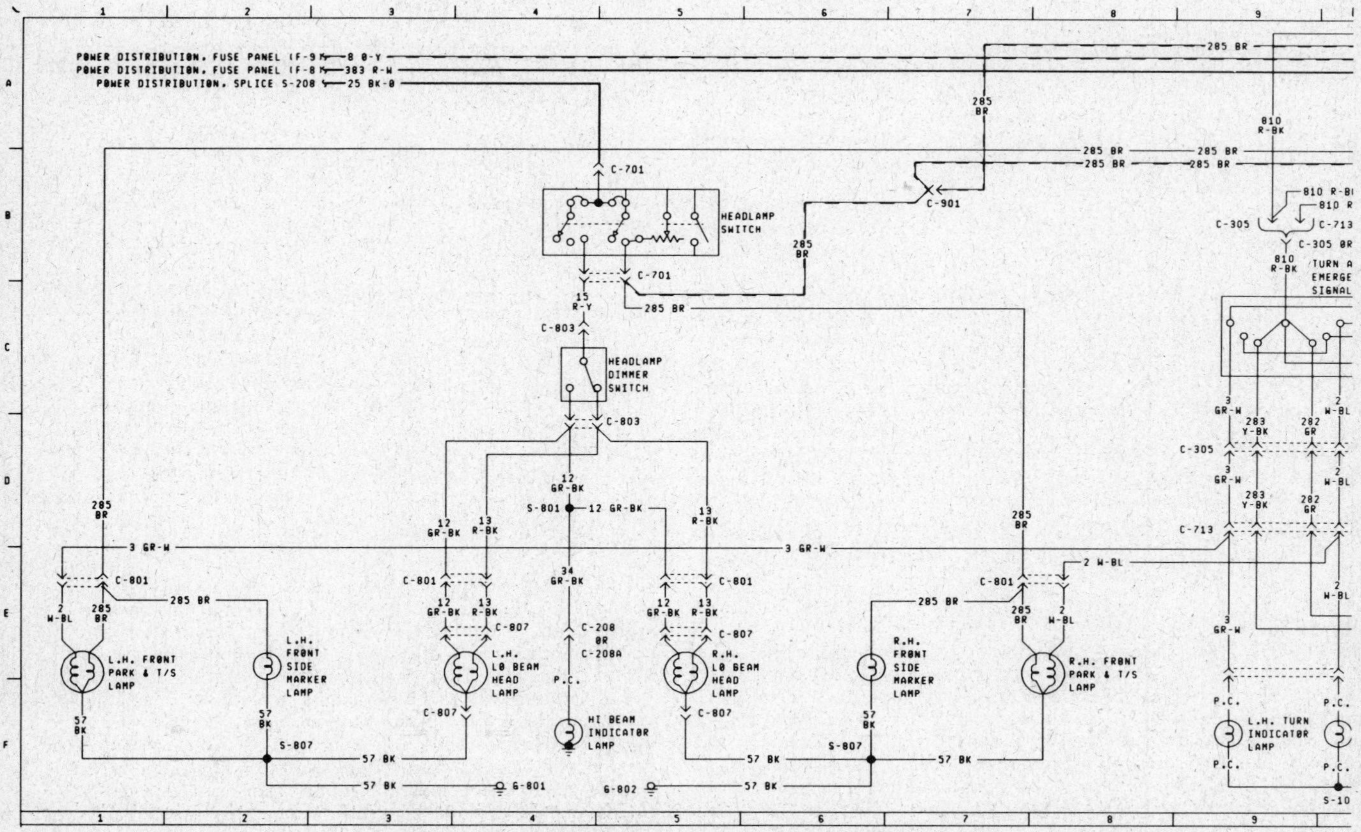

Fig. 10.122 Wiring diagram – 1978 Bronco (continued)

10

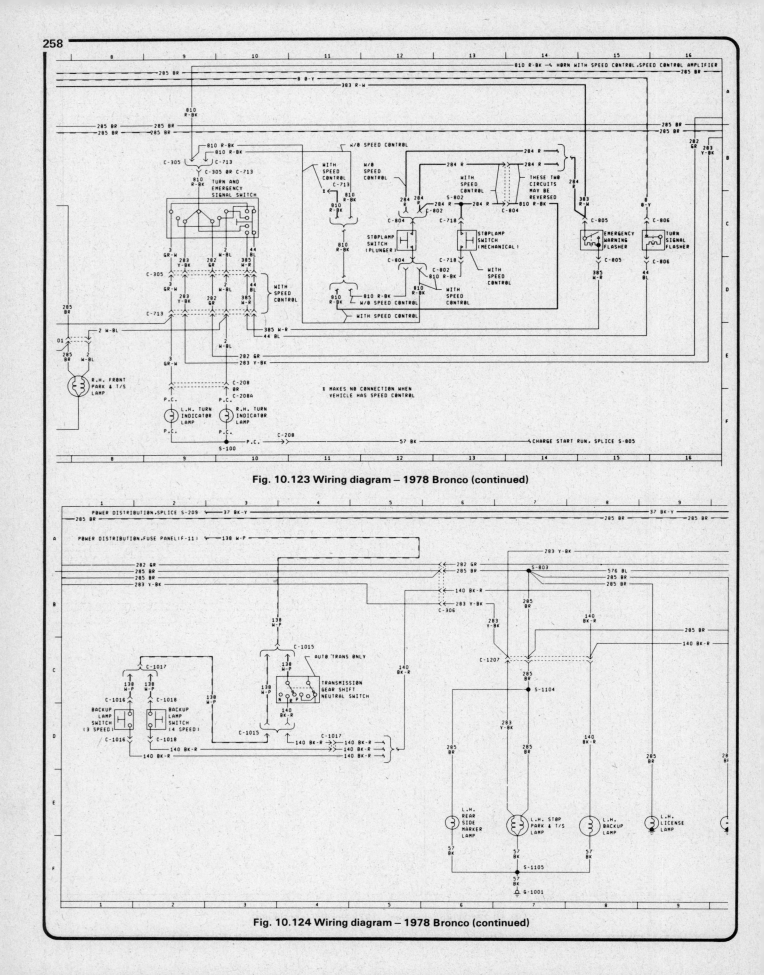

Fig. 10.123 Wiring diagram – 1978 Bronco (continued)

Fig. 10.124 Wiring diagram – 1978 Bronco (continued)

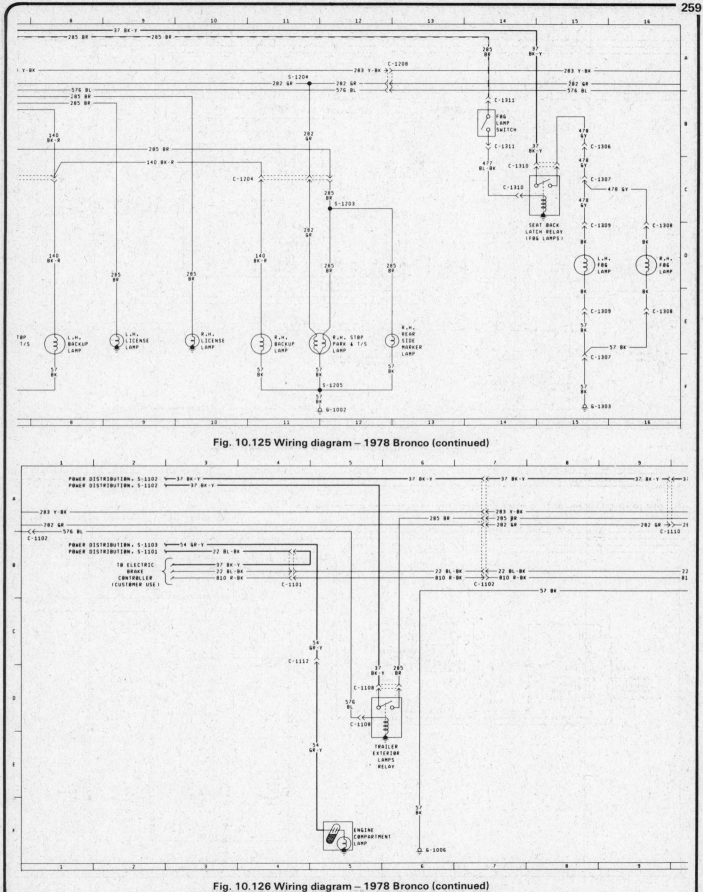

Fig. 10.125 Wiring diagram – 1978 Bronco (continued)

Fig. 10.126 Wiring diagram – 1978 Bronco (continued)

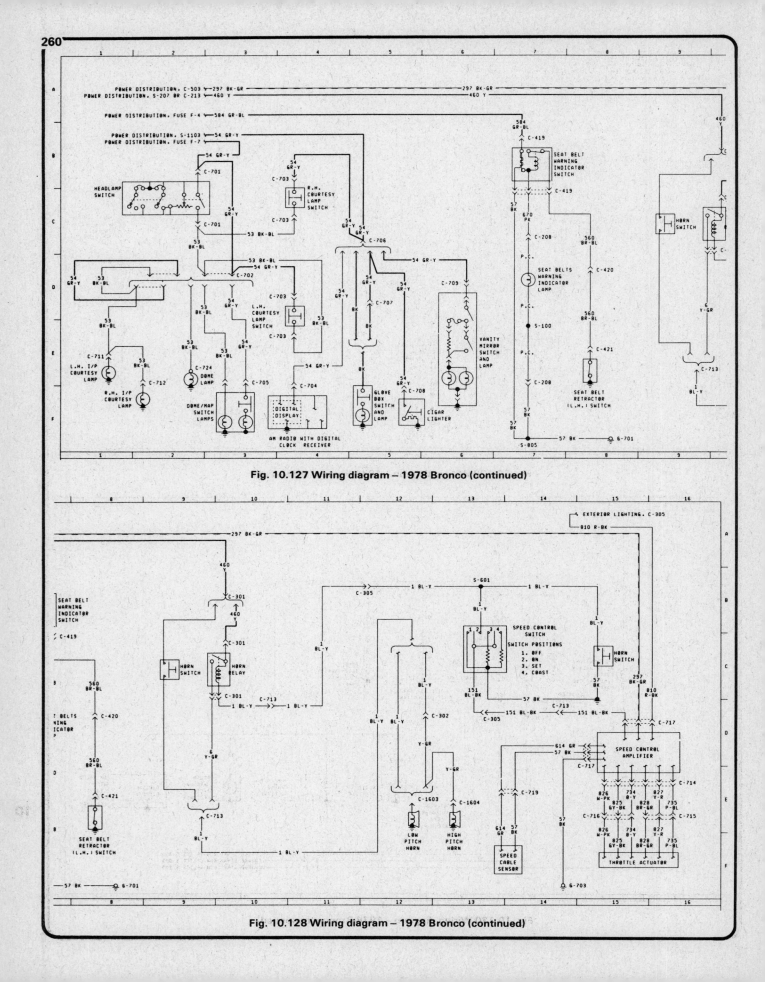

Fig. 10.127 Wiring diagram – 1978 Bronco (continued)

Fig. 10.128 Wiring diagram – 1978 Bronco (continued)

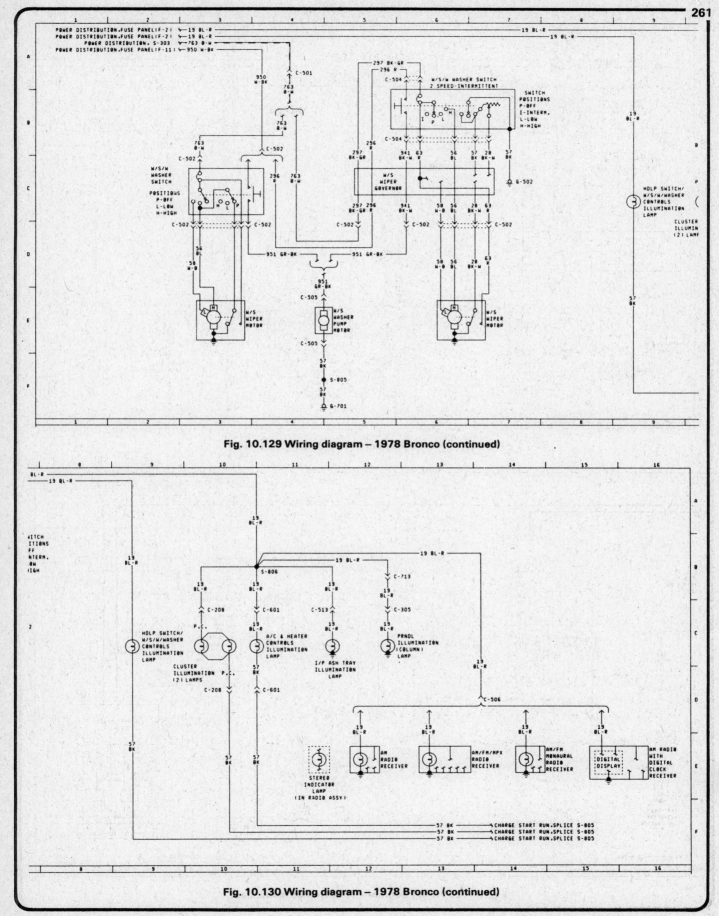

Fig. 10.129 Wiring diagram — 1978 Bronco (continued)

Fig. 10.130 Wiring diagram — 1978 Bronco (continued)

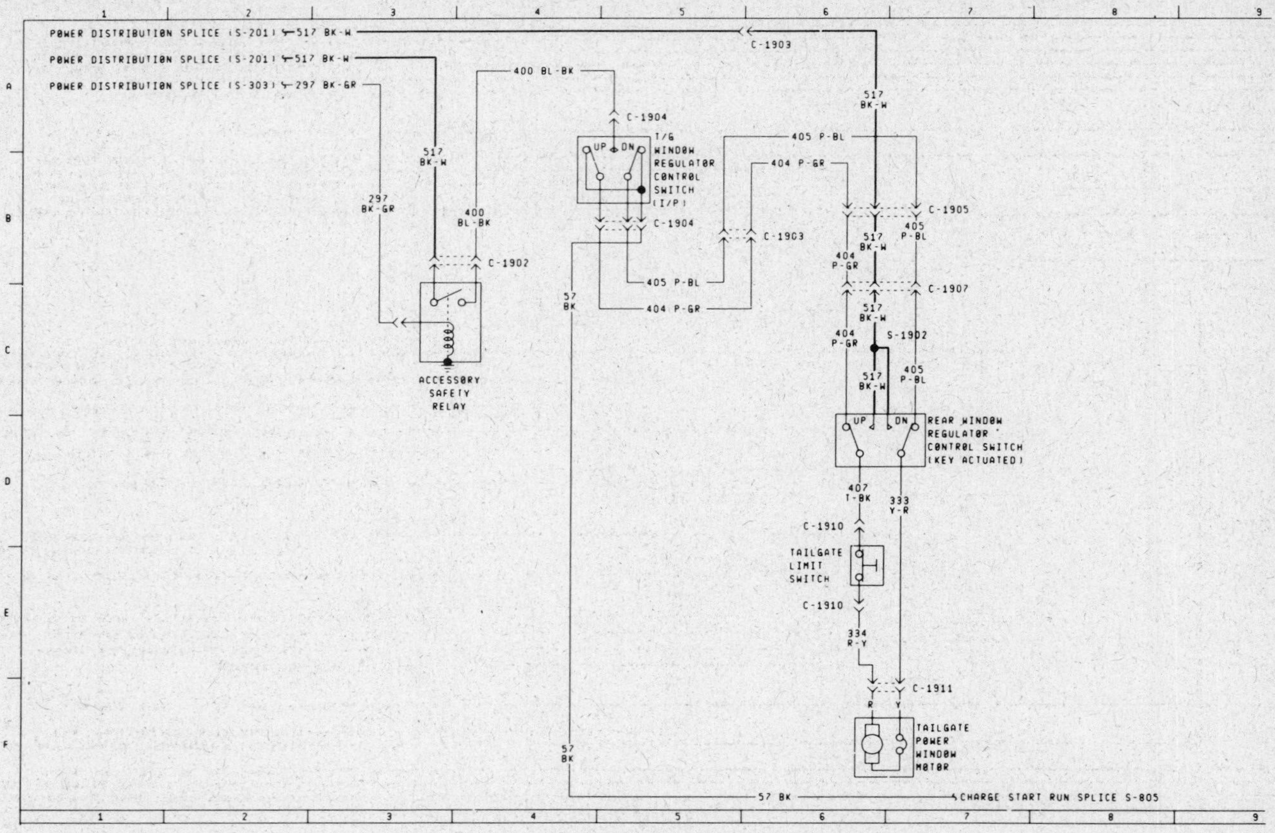

Fig. 10.131 Wiring diagram – 1978 Bronco (continued)

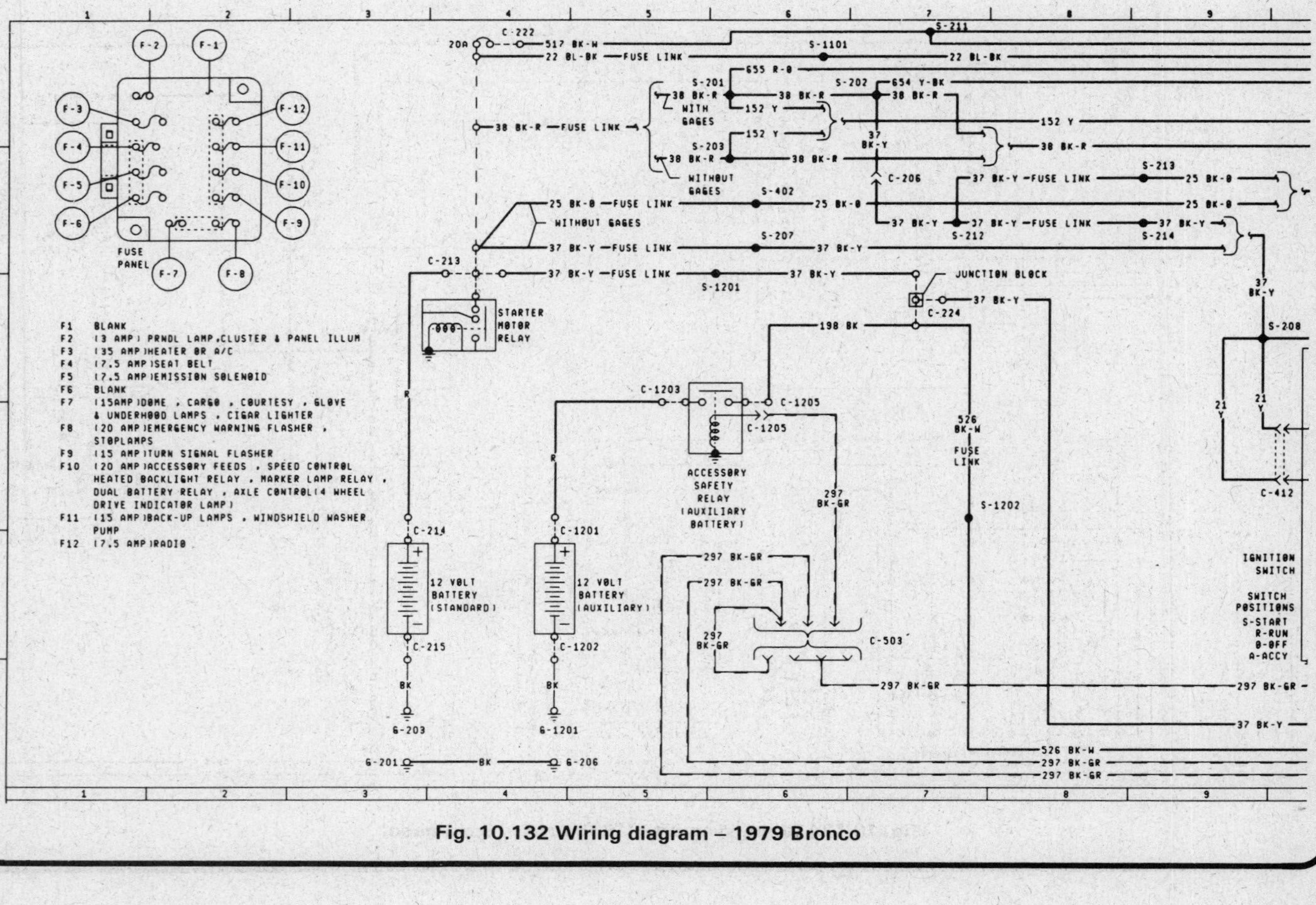

Fig. 10.132 Wiring diagram – 1979 Bronco

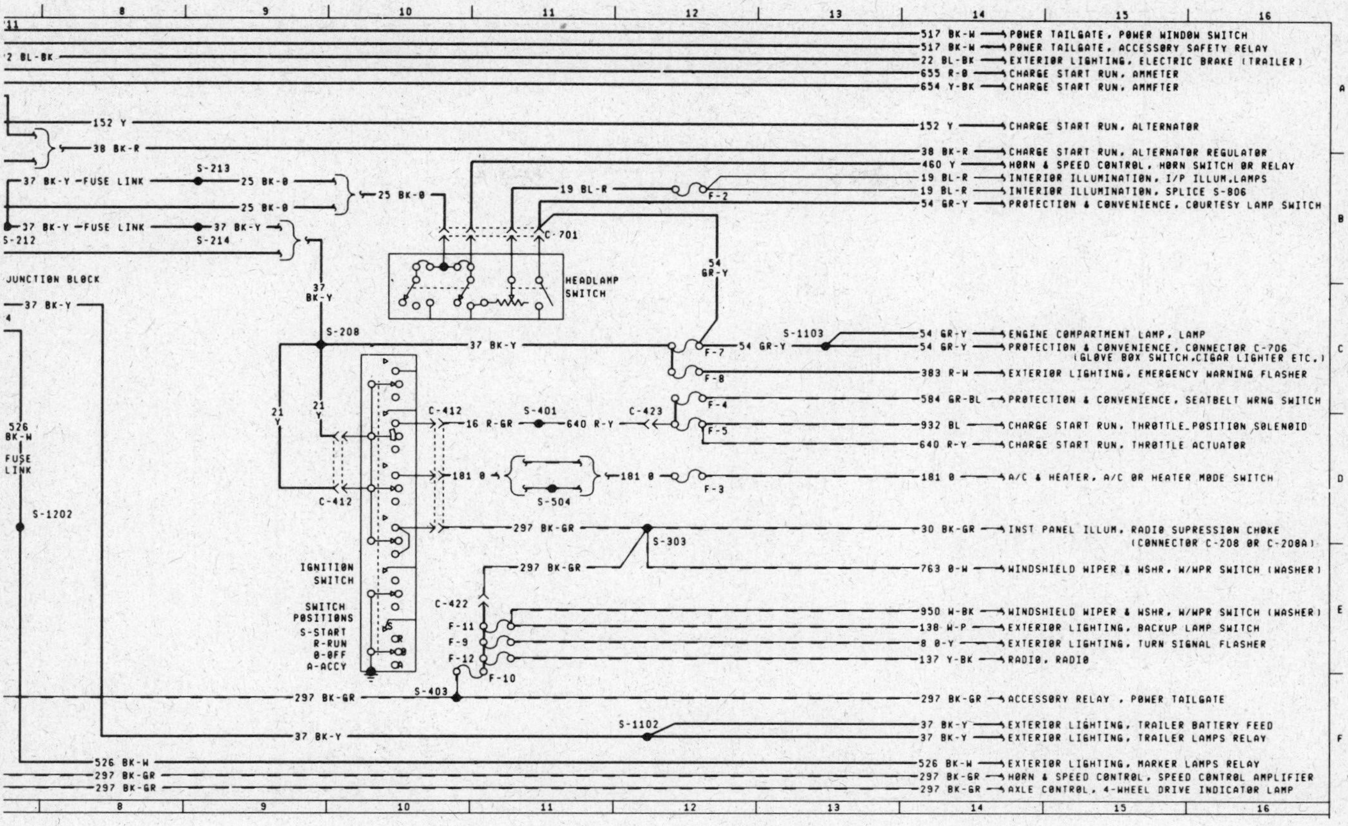

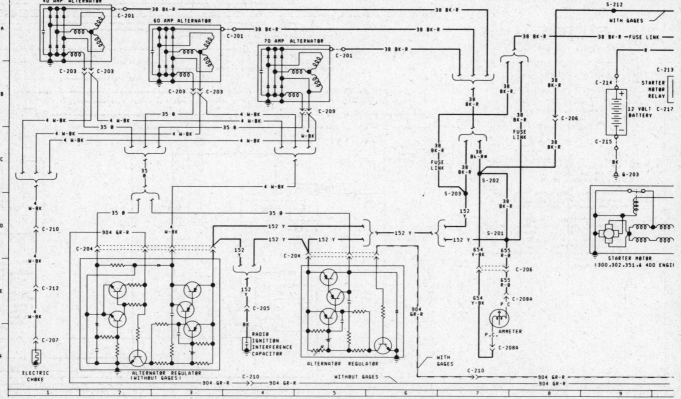

Fig. 10.133 Wiring diagram – 1979 Bronco (continued)

Fig. 10.134 Wiring diagram – 1979 Bronco (continued)

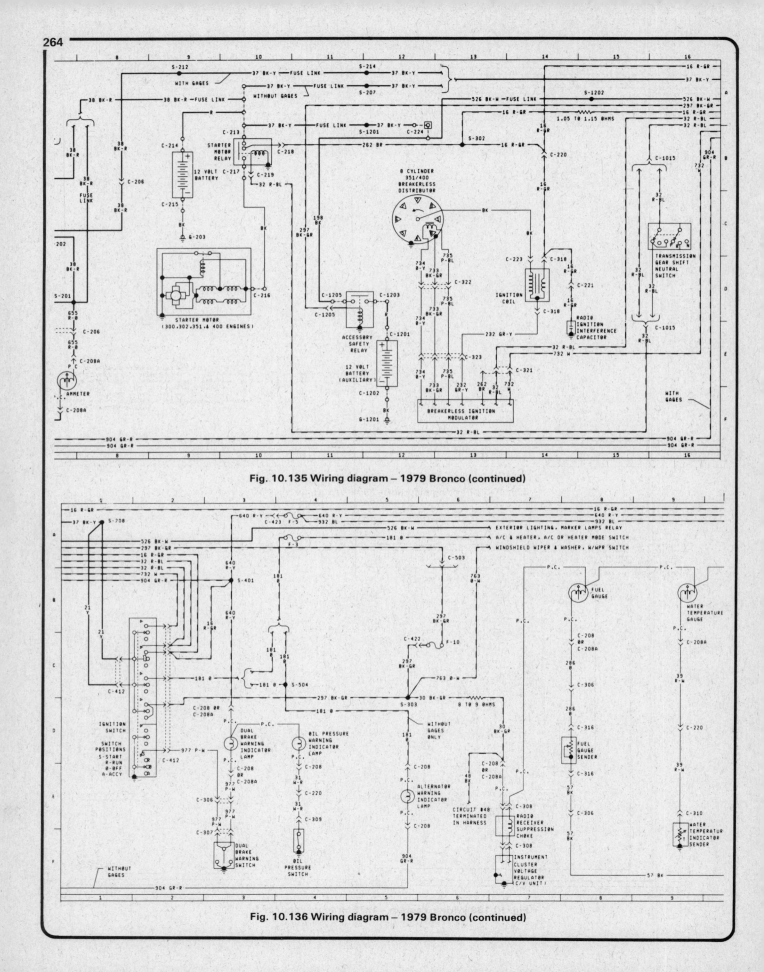

Fig. 10.135 Wiring diagram – 1979 Bronco (continued)

Fig. 10.136 Wiring diagram – 1979 Bronco (continued)

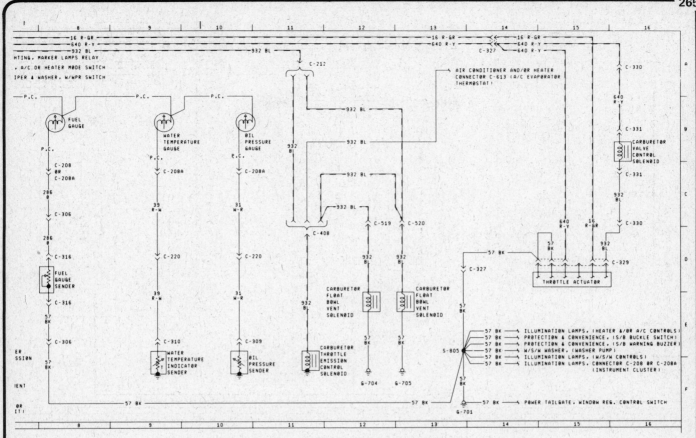

Fig. 10.137 Wiring diagram – 1979 Bronco (continued)

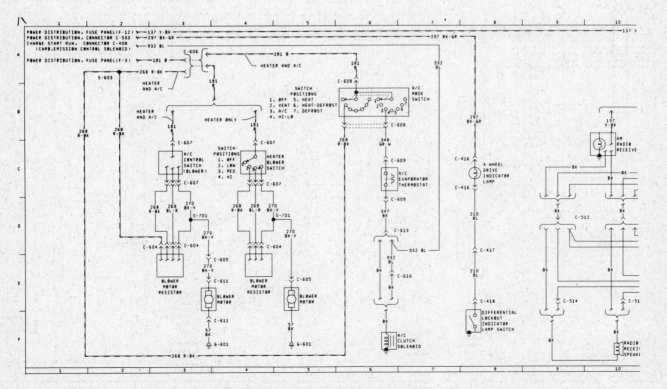

Fig. 10.138 Wiring diagram – 1979 Bronco (continued)

10

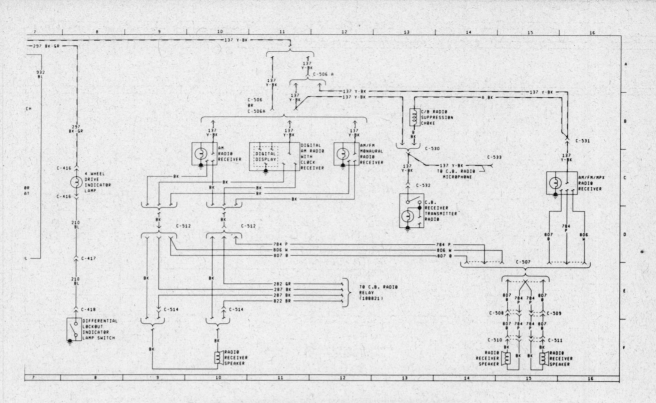

Fig. 10.139 Wiring diagram – 1979 Bronco (continued)

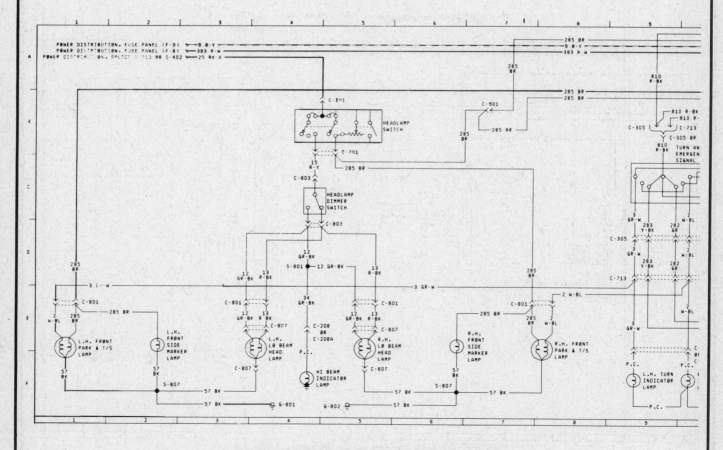

Fig. 10.140 Wiring diagram – 1979 Bronco (continued)

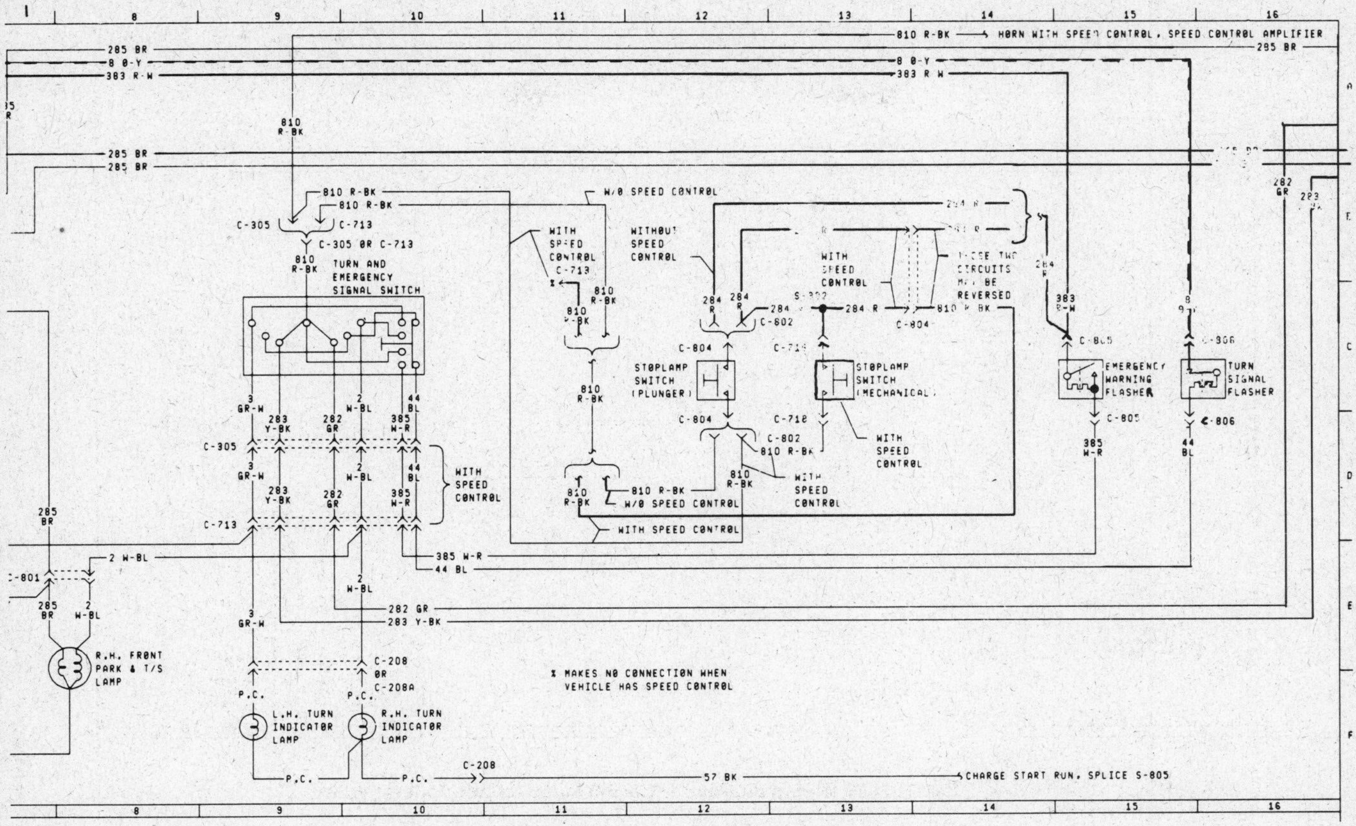

Fig. 10.141 Wiring diagram – 1979 Bronco (continued)

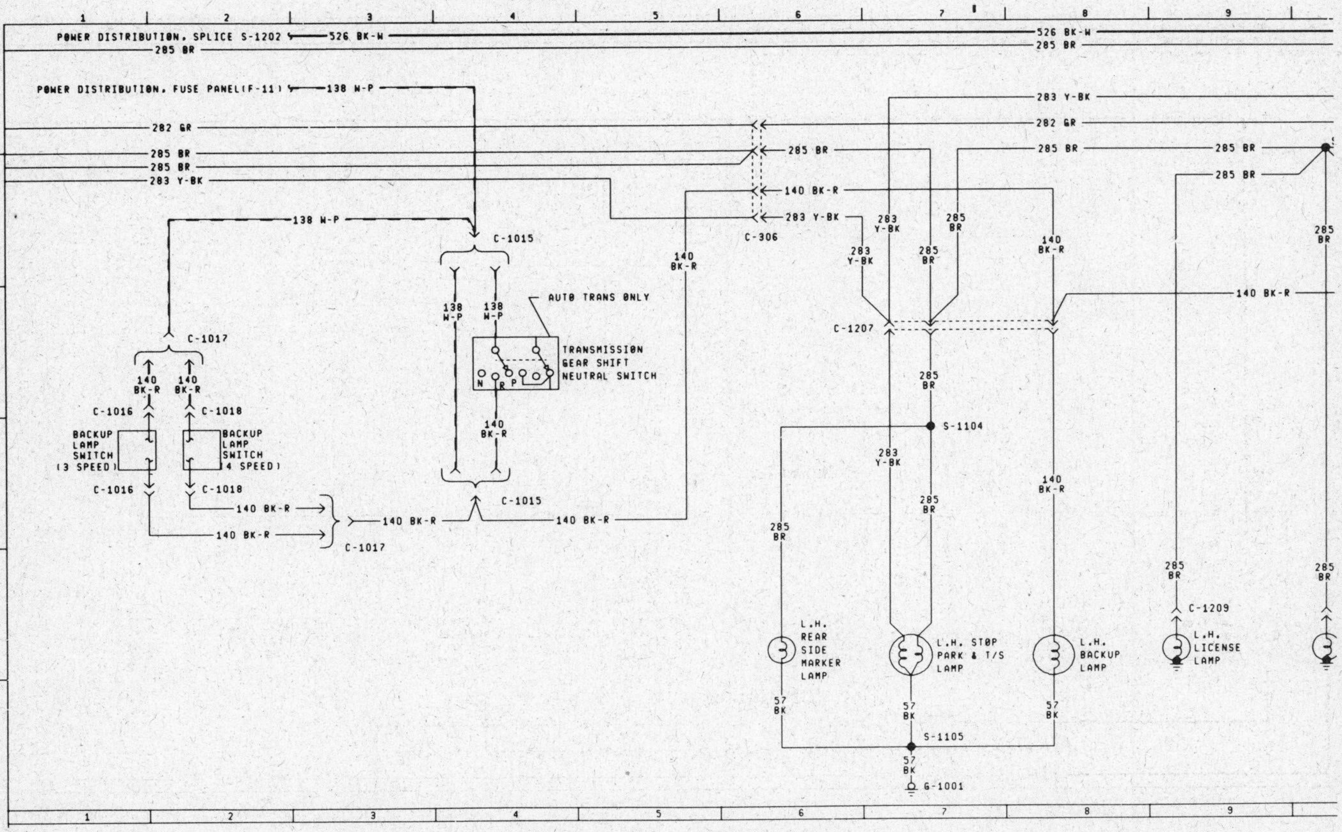

Fig. 10.142 Wiring diagram – 1979 Bronco (continued)

10

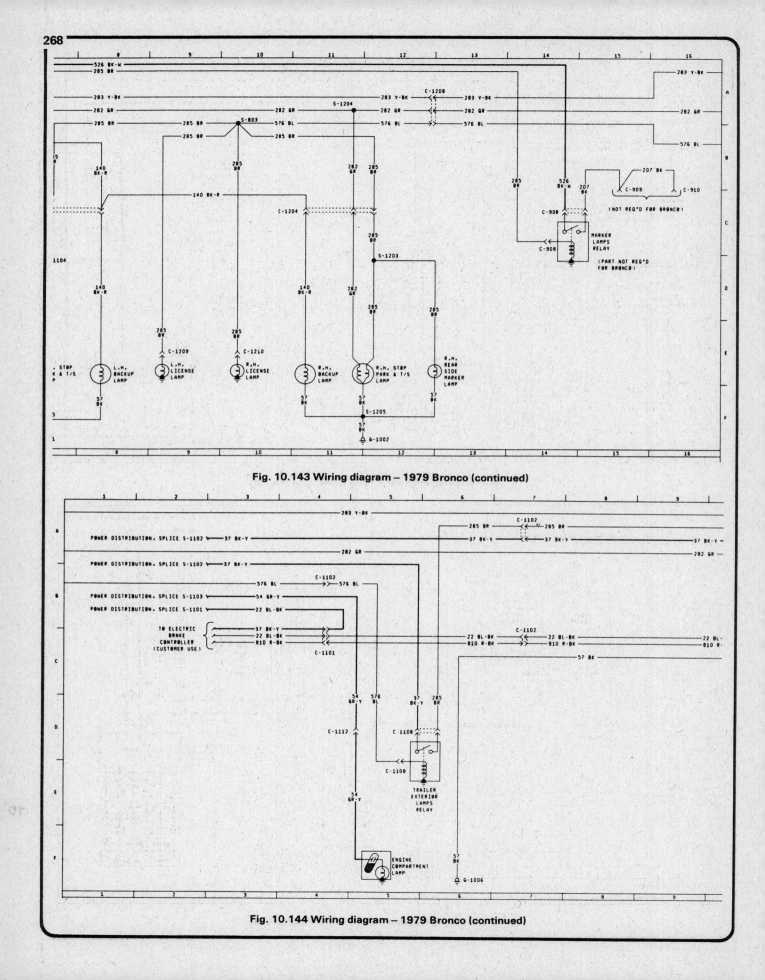

Fig. 10.143 Wiring diagram – 1979 Bronco (continued)

Fig. 10.144 Wiring diagram – 1979 Bronco (continued)

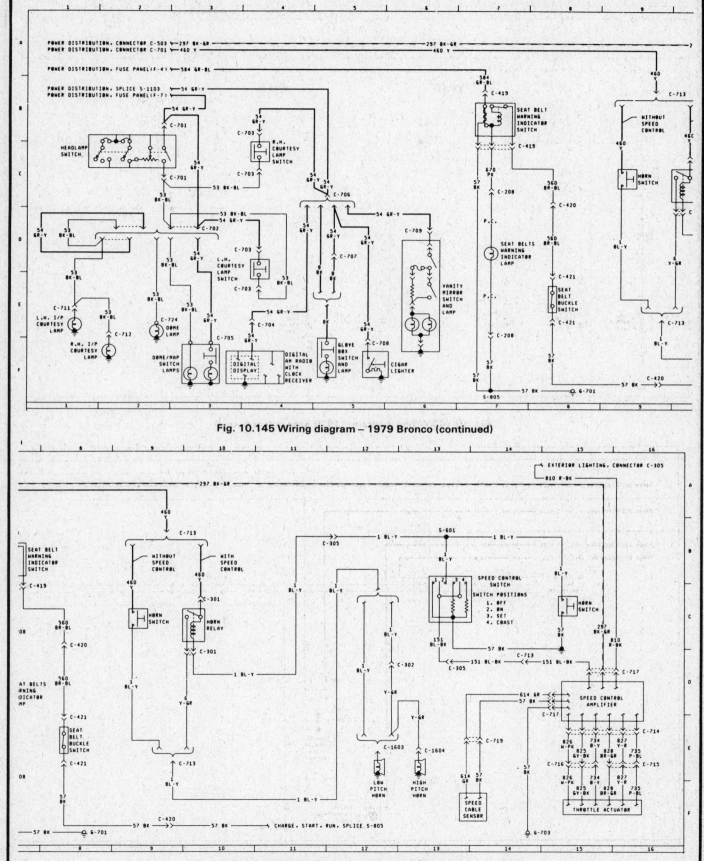

Fig. 10.145 Wiring diagram – 1979 Bronco (continued)

Fig. 10.146 Wiring diagram – 1979 Bronco (continued)

10

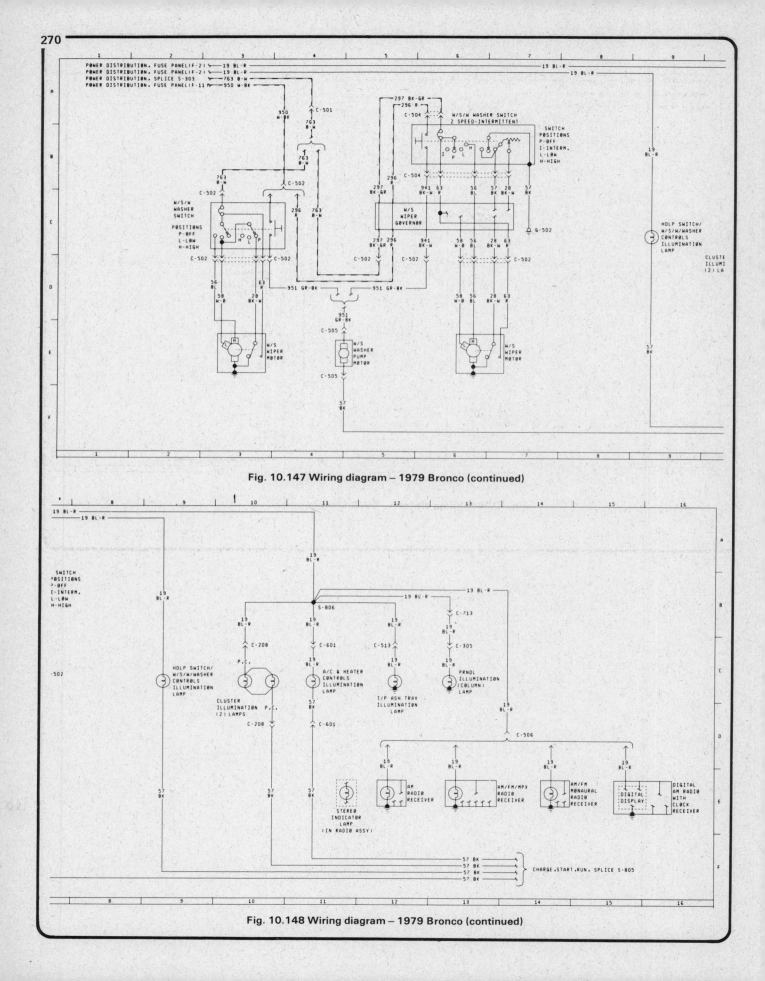

Fig. 10.147 Wiring diagram – 1979 Bronco (continued)

Fig. 10.148 Wiring diagram – 1979 Bronco (continued)

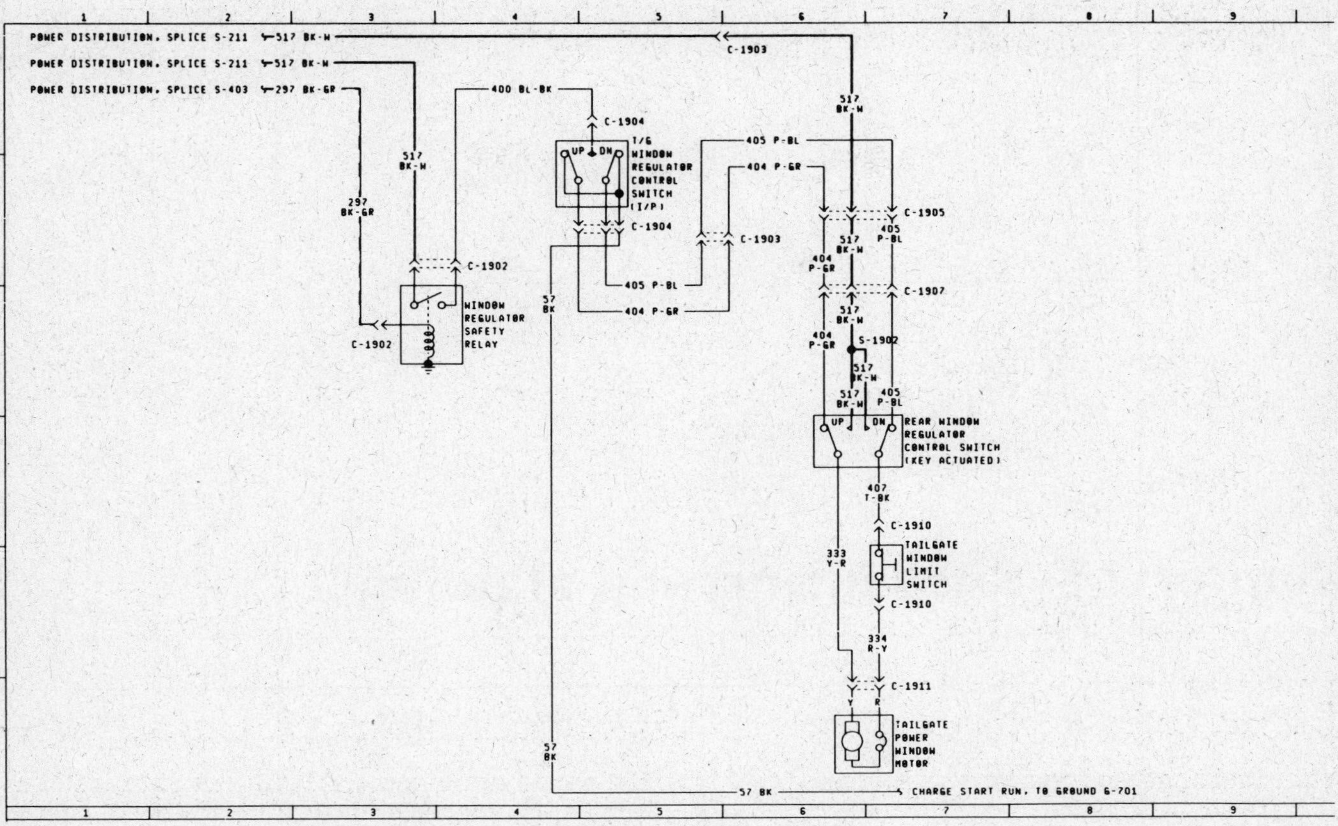

Fig. 10.149 Wiring diagram – 1979 Bronco (continued)

Chapter 11 Suspension and steering

Contents

Specifications

Front suspension

2-wheel drive	Twin I-beam axles with coil springs and telescoping shock absorbers
4-wheel drive	Leaf or coil spring with telescoping shock absorbers

Rear suspension type (all) .... Leaf spring with telescoping shock absorbers

Steering
Type
    F100, F250 and F350 manual .... Recirculating ball
    F100, F250, F350 and Bronco manual .... Worm and roller
    F100, F250 and F350 power assisted .... Ford integral worm and sector
    Bronco power assisted .... Saginaw integral
Fluid type .... Automatic transmission fluid Type F
Steering gear adjustment
    Ford integral power assisted
        Over-center position load .... 11 to 12 in-lb
    Saginaw power assisted
        Over-center torque limit .... 14 in-lb
    Worm and roller-type manual
        Worm and sector preload .... 5 to 10 in-lb
        Roller mesh load .... 12 to 21 in-lb
    Recirculating ball-type manual
        Mesh load (torque required to rotate the input shaft
        past center) .... 7 to 8 in-lb
        Steering gear on center preload .... 16 in-lb
        Worm bearing preload .... 3 to 8 in-lb
        Ball nut lash limit .... $1\frac{1}{4}$ in

Torque specifications

	ft-lb
Front suspension (2-wheel drive)	
Spring upper retainer-to-upper seat	
1974 thru 1975	10 to 40
1976 thru 1979	18 to 25
Shock absorber upper stud	15 to 25
Shock absorber-to-lower bracket	40 to 60
Shock lower bracket-to-radius arm	70 to 90
Spring lower retainer-to-seat	30 to 70
Radius arm-to-front axle	
1974	
F100 and F250	180 to 220
F350	350 to 500
1975 thru 1979	240 to 320
Radius arm-to-bracket	
1974	70 to 125
1975 thru 1979	80 to 120
Radius arm bracket-to-frame or crossmember	
1974	35 to 50
1975 thru 1979	70 to 90
Front axle-to-pivot bracket	120 to 150
Stabilizer bar link-to-bracket	40 to 60
Stabilizer bar link-to-bar	15 to 25
Stabilizer bar retainer-to-frame	15 to 25
Wheel spindle pin locking bolt nut	
1974	40 to 55
1975 thru 1979	38 to 64
Wheel spindle-to-steering link	50 to 75
Wheel spindle plug	35 to 50
Wheel spindle nut	17 to 25
Front suspension (4-wheel drive)	
Front spring-to-axle U-bolt	100 to 135
Front spring-to-hanger	90 to 130
Front spring shackle-to-shackle bracket	90 to 130
Shackle bracket-to-frame	20 to 30
Radius arm-to-bracket	80 to 120
Spring retainer-to-upper seat	
Bronco	18 to 25
F100	20 to 30
Track bar pivot-to-frame	110 to 130
Track bar pivot-to-axle	155 to 205
Lower spring seat-to-radius arm	45 to 55
Axle cap-to-radius arm assembly	90 to 110
Front shock bracket-to-frame	30 to 40
Front shock-to-lower bracket (Bronco, F100)	40 to 60
Upper shock stud	15 to 25
Front shock-to-lower bracket (F250)	15 to 25
Track bar bracket-to-frame (F100)	
$\frac{9}{16}$ in	50 to 70
$\frac{7}{16}$ in	30 to 40
Upper shock-to-bracket (F100)	40 to 60
Rear suspension	
Shock upper mounting	
F100 and F250 2-wheel drive and F100 4-wheel drive	15 to 25
F250, F350 and Bronco 4-wheel drive	40 to 60
Shock lower mounting (all)	40 to 60
Spring-to-axle U-bolt (all except Bronco)	
$\frac{1}{2}$ in	45 to 70
$\frac{9}{16}$ in	85 to 115
Bronco	45 to 60
Spring-to-front hanger	
$\frac{9}{16}$ in nut	75 to 105
$\frac{5}{8}$ in nut	150 to 190
Spring-to-rear hanger	
2-wheel drive	75 to 105
4-wheel drive	150 to 190
Steering (recirculating ball-type manual)	
Sector shaft cover bolt	17 to 25
Preload adjuster locknut	60 to 80
Meshload adjuster locknut	32 to 40
Lubricant fill plug (at least one thread must be exposed when tight)	3 to 9
Pitman arm nut (at least two threads must be visible after nut is installed)	170 to 230

11

Steering (worm and roller-type manual)
Cover bolts or nuts	18 to 22
Sector shaft cover	30 to 35
Sector adjuster locknut	16 to 20

Steering (Ford integral-type power assisted)
Sector shaft cover bolts	55 to 70
Mesh load adjuster locknut	35 to 45
Valve housing-to-gear housing screw	35 to 45
Pressure hose-to-gear	16 to 25
Return hose-to-gear	25 to 34
Hose clamps	1 to 2

Steering (Saginaw integral-type power assisted)
Sector shaft cover bolts	30 to 35
Mesh load adjuster locknut	30 to 35
Preload adjusting locknut	50 to 110
Hose clamps	1 to 2
Pitman arm-to-sector shaft nut	200 to 250

1 General information

The front suspension system of Ford light duty trucks (4 x 2) is unusual in design with its patented 'twin I-beam' layout. This design, with its two independent I-beam axles (one for each side) suspended by coil springs, has a number of advantages. The I-beam axles provide high strength and durability while the independent feature allows each side to absorb bumps and provide a smoother ride for passengers and cargo.

The outer wheel spindle of each axle is located by a radius arm mounted in rubber and damped by a hydraulic telescoping shock absorber. The inner ends of the I-beam are attached to a pivot bracket on the opposite side of the vehicle. This design provides for good suspension compliance and long spring travel.

The front suspension on 4 x 4 vehicles consists of a straight tubular drive-axle (Chapter 8) suspended by either coil springs (F100, F150 and Broncos) or semi-elliptical leaf springs (F250 and F350). Long wishbones locate the axle housing on coil spring equipped models while a transverse link provides lateral alignment control.

The rear suspension consists of leaf-type springs mounted to the axle with U-bolts. The springs are mounted to the frame by brackets and shackles and telescoping shock absorbers are used for damping.

Some models are equipped with sway bars at the front and/or rear as an option.

Several types of manual and power assisted steering gears are used and the steering wheel is connected through a collapsible shaft and flexible coupling. Some models incorporate a hydraulic damper in the steering linkage to reduce road shock at the steering wheel.

Due to the special techniques and tools required, several procedures involving the complicated assemblies such as power steering pumps and the front axle on 4-wheel drive vehicles are beyond the scope of the home mechanic. Consequently, only tasks which can be accomplished with standard tools and limited experience are described in this Chapter.

2 Wheels and tires – checking and rotation

Refer to Chapter 1, *Routine maintenance* for this procedure.

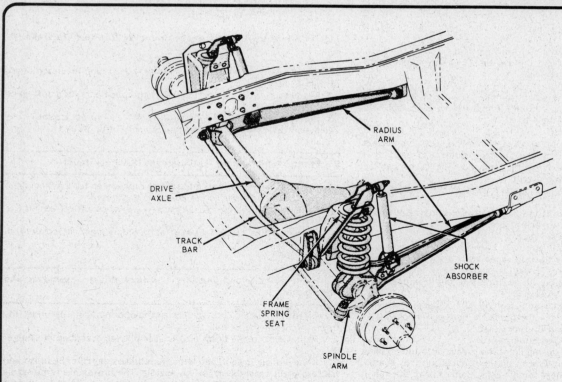

Fig. 11.1 Typical coil spring-type 4-wheel drive front suspension (Sec 1)

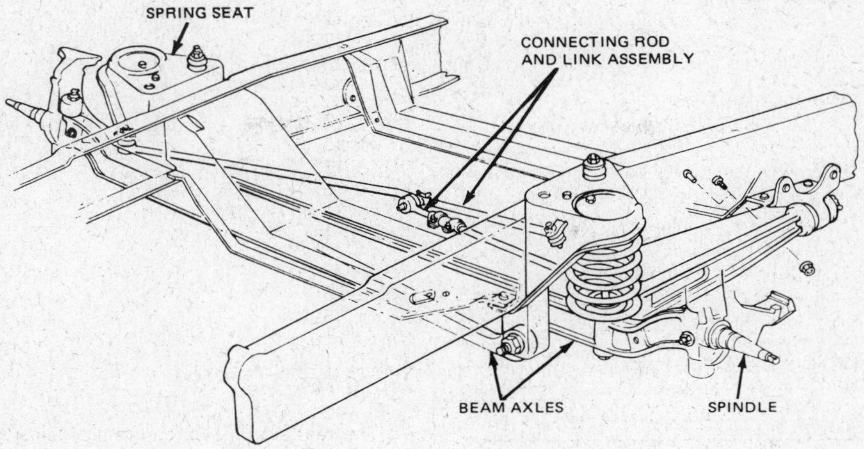

SPRING SEAT

CONNECTING ROD
AND LINK ASSEMBLY

BEAM AXLES   SPINDLE

Fig. 11.2 Typical 2-wheel drive twin I-beam front suspension layout (Sec 1)

3 Suspension – general checks

The suspension and steering mechanism requires lubrication maintenance as listed in Chapter 1. It should also be inspected periodically as described in Chapter 1. If you keep the suspension system lubricated and watch carefully for any damage that may arise from road hazards or accidents, your vehicle should provide good service over a long period of time and mileage.

4 Front wheel bearings (2-wheel drive) – removal, packing and installation

1   Chock the rear wheels, apply the parking brake, loosen the front wheel nuts, jack up the front of the vehicle and support it on jack stands. Remove the wheel.
2   Refer to Chapter 9 and detach the disc brake caliper (if so equipped).
3   Carefully remove the grease cap from the hub.
4   Withdraw the cotter pin and remove the nut lock, adjusting nut and plain washers from the spindle.
5   Remove the outer bearing.
6   Remove the hub from the wheel spindle.
7   Using a screwdriver or tapered drift, remove the grease seal. This seal must be replaced with a new one.
8   Remove the inner bearing.
9   Remove grease from the inner and outer bearing races and inspect for signs of wear, scratching or pitting. Damage of this kind means that the bearings and the races must be replaced. The races can be removed carefully with a tapered drift.
10 Clean the inner and outer bearings and wipe dry with a clean non-fluffy rag.
11 Carefully inspect the bearings for signs of wear or damage which, if evident, means that complete race assemblies must be obtained. Do not use a new bearing in an old race.
12 Clean the spindle and lubricate with fresh grease.
13 If the inner and/or outer bearing races were removed, the new ones should be installed using a suitable diameter drift.
14 Pack the inside of the hub with fresh grease until it is flush with the inside diameter of both bearing races.
15 Take each bearing assembly and clean off all old grease. Pack with fresh grease taking care to work the grease in between the rollers. A bearing packer should be used if at all possible.
16 Place the inner bearing in the inner race.
17 Apply a smear of grease to the lip of the grease seal and install it using a suitable diameter drift. Ensure that the seal is correctly seated.
18 Install the hub on the wheel spindle using care to keep the hub in a central position so that the grease retainer is not damaged.
19 Install the outer bearing. Follow this with the plain washer and adjustment nut.
20 Adjust the wheel bearing as described in Chapter 1.

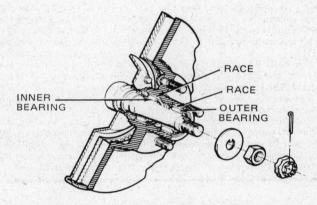

RACE

RACE

INNER
BEARING

OUTER
BEARING

Fig. 11.3 Front wheel bearing components (2-wheel drive) (Sec 4)

21 Install a new cotter pin and bend the ends around the castellations of the nut lock.
22 Install the grease cap by tapping it into position with a soft-faced hammer.
23 Refer to Chapter 9 and install the caliper (if so equipped).
24 Install the wheel and lower the vehicle to the ground.

5 Front wheel bearing – adjustment (2-wheel drive)

1   The front wheel bearing adjustment procedures for 2-wheel drive and 4-wheel drive vehicles are completely different.
2   Front wheel bearing adjustment on 2-wheel drive vehicles is described in Chapter 1.
3   4-wheel drive front wheel bearing adjustment is covered in Chapter 8.

6 Front spindle and bushing (2-wheel drive) – removal and installation

1   Raise the front of the vehicle and support it securely under the frame. Remove the wheel.
2   Remove the brake drum or disc assembly as described in Chapter 9.
3   If the vehicle is equipped with drum brakes, remove the brake and backing plate assembly from the spindle. The brakes are removed as described in Chapter 9. The brake backing plate is retained with four retaining bolts.
4   If the vehicle is equipped with disc brakes, remove the splash shield and the caliper anchor plate.

11

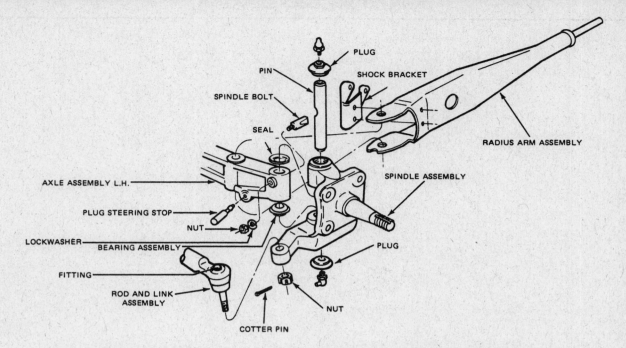

Fig. 11.4 Typical spindle and radius rod component layout (F250) (Secs 6 and 9)

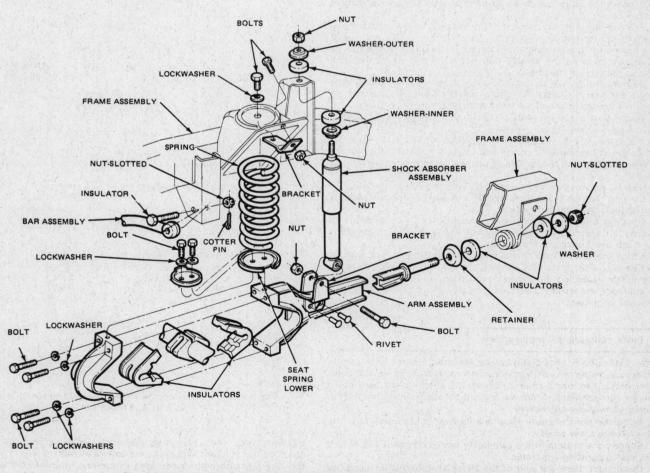

Fig. 11.5 Typical Bronco front suspension components (Secs 7, 9, 11 and 12)

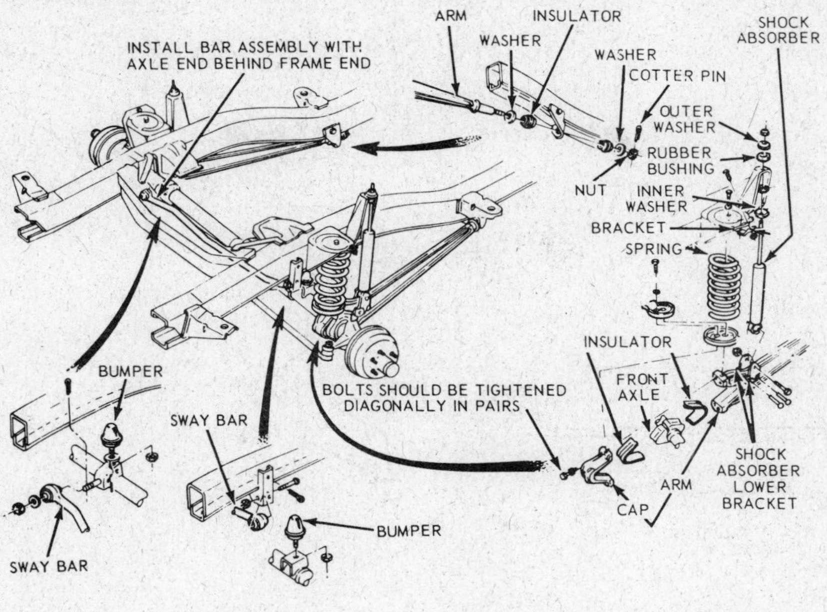

INSTALL BAR ASSEMBLY WITH
AXLE END BEHIND FRAME END

ARM
WASHER
INSULATOR
WASHER
COTTER PIN
SHOCK
ABSORBER
OUTER
WASHER
RUBBER
BUSHING
NUT
INNER
WASHER
BRACKET
SPRING
INSULATOR
FRONT
AXLE
SHOCK
ABSORBER
LOWER
BRACKET
ARM
CAP

BUMPER
SWAY BAR
BOLTS SHOULD BE TIGHTENED
DIAGONALLY IN PAIRS
BUMPER
SWAY BAR

Fig. 11.6 Typical 4-wheel drive front suspension components (Secs 7, 9, 11 and 12)

5   Remove the tie-rod end from the spindle assembly as described in Section 24.
6   Remove the nut and washer from the spindle bolt locking pin. Drive out the pin with a brass drift.
7   Remove the grease plugs from the top and bottom of the spindle bolt, and then drive the spindle bolt out from the top of the axle. Remove the spindle assembly.
8   Remove the grease seal and bushings from the spindle assembly using a suitable sized drift. Be careful not to damage the spindle.
9   Check the spindle bolt for wear and replace it if necessary.
10 Obtain new bushings, seals and a thrust bearing. Fit the bushings into the spindle assembly.
11 Place the spindle assembly in position on the axle. Pack the spindle thrust bearing with grease and insert it into the bottom of the spindle, ensuring that the lip side of the seal faces downward into the spindle.
12 Line up the notch in the spindle bolt with the hole in the axle and tap the bolt through the spindle and axle assembly until the notch is lined up with the hole in the axle.
13 Carefully drive a new locking pin through the axle and secure it with the nut and washer. Tighten the nut and install the grease plugs at the top and bottom of the spindle bolt.
14 Check that the spindle moves smoothly from lock-to-lock without any free-play. Then install the steering arm, back-plate, hub and brake assembly by reversing the removal procedure.
15 Lubricate the spindle assembly with grease. Install the wheel and check the alignment.

7   Front coil spring – replacement

Note: *Coil springs should always be replaced in pairs to maintain proper ride height and performance characteristics. As an additional safety precaution, use a chain to secure the spring to the axle during removal and installation. This will prevent the spring from flying out of position during the procedures.*

1   Raise the front of the vehicle and support it securely under the frame. Remove the wheels.
2   Support the bottom of the axle being worked on with a floor jack or similar supporting apparatus.
3   Disconnect the lower end of the shock absorber while using the jack to compress the spring and support the axle.
4   Remove the bolts holding the upper spring retainer to the frame. Remove the upper spring retainer.
5   Carefully lower the axle until the open end of the spring is

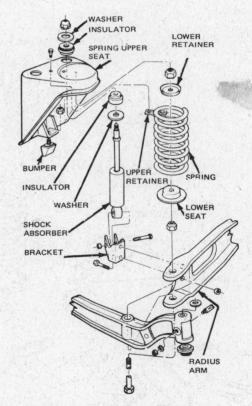

WASHER
INSULATOR
SPRING UPPER
SEAT
LOWER
RETAINER
BUMPER
INSULATOR
WASHER
SHOCK
ABSORBER
BRACKET
UPPER
RETAINER
SPRING
LOWER
SEAT
RADIUS
ARM

Fig. 11.7 Front suspension components (2-wheel drive) (Secs 7, 9, 11 and 12)

exposed. Drop the axle/spring assembly slowly as the coil spring could spring outward slightly as the axle is moved.
6   Use a socket and several long extensions to unfasten the lower spring retaining nut through the open end of the top of the spring. Remove the nut, washer, chain and spring from the axle.
7   To install, place the spring in position on the lower seat. Position it so that the end of the spring fits correctly into the recess of the upper

11

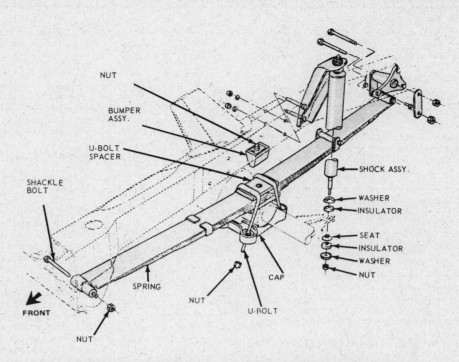

NUT

BUMPER ASSY.

U-BOLT SPACER

SHACKLE BOLT

SHOCK ASSY.

WASHER

INSULATOR

SEAT

INSULATOR

WASHER

NUT

SPRING

NUT

CAP

U-BOLT

FRONT

NUT

Fig. 11.8 Typical front leaf spring installation (4-wheel drive) (Secs 8 and 13)

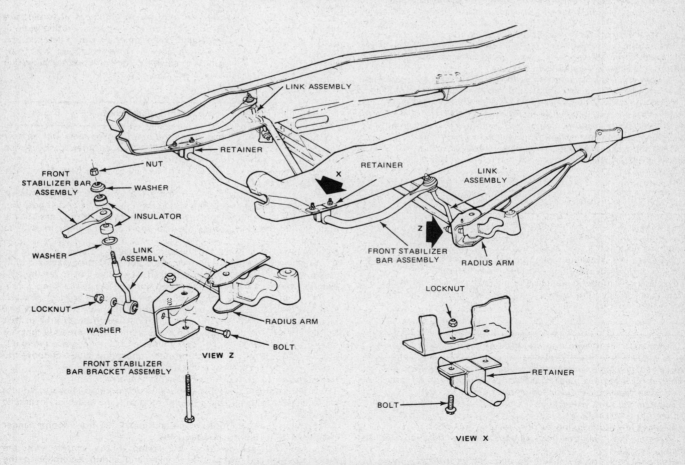

LINK ASSEMBLY

RETAINER

NUT

FRONT STABILIZER BAR ASSEMBLY

WASHER

INSULATOR

WASHER

LINK ASSEMBLY

LOCKNUT

WASHER

FRONT STABILIZER BAR BRACKET ASSEMBLY

RADIUS ARM

BOLT

VIEW Z

RETAINER

X

LINK ASSEMBLY

Z

FRONT STABILIZER BAR ASSEMBLY

RADIUS ARM

LOCKNUT

RETAINER

BOLT

VIEW X

Fig. 11.9 Typical sway bar installation (Sec 9)

spring cup. The spring can fit into a number of different positions, but the flat surface of the spring end must fit into the area where it is retained by the upper spring retainer.

8   Install the lower spring retainer washer and nut. Tighten the nut to the correct torque.

9   Raise the spring/axle combination until the spring top fits snugly against the upper spring cup. Work slowly and carefully to ensure that the spring is properly seated.

10 Install the upper spring retainer and retaining bolts. Tighten the retaining bolts to the correct torque.

11 Connect the lower end of the shock absorber.

12 Install the wheel. Lower the axle and remove the supporting device. Lower the vehicle to the ground.

8   Front suspension leaf spring – replacement

Some 4-wheel drive models are equipped with leaf-type front springs. Replacement procedures and cautions for these front springs are the same as those described in Section 13 for the rear leaf springs.

9   Radius arm – replacement

1   Jack up the front of the vehicle and support it securely.

2   Place a jack beneath the outer end of the axle and remove the wheel.

3   Disconnect the lower end of the shock absorber from the support bracket.

4   Remove the front spring using the method described in Section 7.

5   Remove the lower spring seat from the radius arm and then remove the nut and bolt securing the front of the radius arm to the axle.

6   Remove the nut, washer and rubber insulator from the rear end of the radius arm.

7   Push the front of the radius arm away from the front axle and withdraw it from the rear support bracket.

8   Remove the front retainer and rubber insulator from the rear of the radius arm and retrieve any shims that may be fitted.

9   Install the radius arm by reversing the procedure, ensuring that the rubber insulators are installed in the correct order. Tighten the radius arm-to-axle bolt to the specified torque and secure it with the cotter pin. Tighten the rear nut to the specified torque.

10 Have the front end wheel alignment checked by your dealer or a suitably equipped shop.

10   Stabilizer bar (front) – removal and installation

1   Jack up the front of the vehicle and support it.

2   Disconnect the left and right ends of the stabilizer bar from the link assemblies attached to the axle brackets.

3   Remove the brackets securing the bar to the chassis side members and remove the bar and links from the vehicle.

4   Replace any rubber bushings that are worn and install the bar by reversing the procedure. Ensure that the links are installed with the bend facing forward.

11   Front axle – removal and installation

Note: *The following procedure is for 2-wheel drive vehicles. 4-wheel drive front axle removal and installation is described in Chapter 8.*

1   Jack up the vehicle and support the frame securely.

2   Remove the front wheel spindle from the axle using the procedure described in Section 6.

3   Remove the front spring as described in Section 7.

4   Remove the stabilizer bar (if equipped) as described in the previous Section.

5   Remove the spring lower seat from the radius arm and remove the nut and bolt securing the front of the radius arm to the axle.

6   Remove the nut and bolt securing the end of the axle to the pivot bracket and withdraw the axle from beneath the vehicle.

7   Examine the bushings and pivot bolt for wear and replace it if

necessary. If the axle is bent, take it to a Ford dealer or alignment specialist with the necessary equipment for straightening it.

8   Install the axle by reversing the removal procedure. Tighten the nuts to the specified torque.

12   Front shock absorber – removal, inspection and installation

1   Chock the rear wheels, apply the parking brake, loosen the front wheel nuts, jack up the front of the vehicle and support it securely. Remove the wheel.

2   Undo and remove the nut, washer and bushing from the top end of the shock absorber.

3   Undo and remove the nut and bolt securing the bottom end of the shock absorber to the lower bracket.

4   Examine the shock absorber for signs of damage to the body, distorted piston rod, loose mounting or hydraulic fluid leakage which, if evident, means a new unit should be installed.

5   To test for shock absorber efficiency, hold the unit in a vertical position. Completely extend the piston rod and then invert the unit and completely compress it. Perform this sequence several times to work out any trapped air bubbles. Mount the bottom end of the shock absorber in a soft-jawed vise. Grasp the upper rod of the shock absorber, extend it fully and then contract it fully as rapidly as possible. The resistance should be smooth and uniform throughout the entire stroke in both directions. The resistance should be greater during the extension stroke than during the compression stroke. If there is erratic or notchy resistance during either stroke, or if the resistance is the same (or less) during the extension stroke, the shock absorbers should be replaced. The shock absorbers on each axle should have identical action and shock absorbers should always be replaced in pairs (on the same axle).

6   Installation is the reverse of removal. If old shock absorbers are being re-installed (after being checked for correct operating action), the bushings should be replaced if there are any signs of deterioration or wear. New shock absorbers always come equipped with new bushings. When installing new bushings, never compress them beyond the diameter of the steel washers retaining them.

13   Rear leaf spring – removal and installation

1   Chock the front wheels. Raise the rear of the vehicle and support the frame securely. Place a hydraulic floor jack or other similar device under the axle housing to support it.

2   Disconnect the lower end of the shock absorbers from their mounting brackets.

3   Place the supporting device under the axle housing and raise it until it just starts to deflect the spring from its fully extended position.

4   Loosen and remove the U-bolt retaining nuts. (If they are heavily rusted or corroded, you may have to apply a rust penetrant prior to their removal).

5   Remove the U-bolts and the spring retaining plates.

6   Slowly lower the axle housing with the supporting device until it clears the spring that is being removed. Take care not to let the axle drop too far as this could stretch and damage the brake line.

7   Remove the nuts from the upper and lower spring shackle. Remove the shackle bolts by driving them through the springs and bushings. If the bolts are to be re-used, use a soft brass drift so that the bolts won't be damaged. The manufacturer recommends that the bolts and nuts must be replaced whenever the springs are removed.

8   Remove the retaining nut from the front spring eyelet. Remove the bolt in the same manner as step 7.

9   Remove the spring from under the vehicle.

10 If the front bushing of the spring is deteriorated or worn, it must be replaced by a dealership or frame shop with the necessary hydraulic press and tools.

11 Position the spring into place and install the front spring hanger bolt. Loosely install the retaining nut.

12 Install the rear eyelet of the spring to the shackle with the retaining bolt and install the shackle and spring assembly to the bracket with the retaining bolt. Loosely install the retaining nuts

13 Raise the axle housing with the lifting apparatus and align the guide pin in the center of the spring with the hole on the axle housing mounting pad.

11

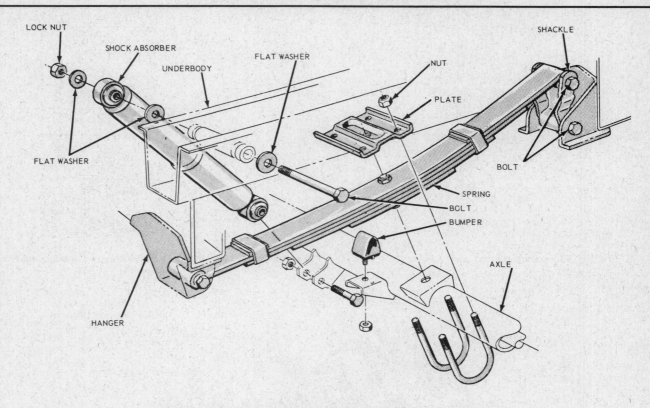

Fig. 11.10 Typical rear leaf spring installation (Secs 13 and 14)

14 Install the U-bolts, spring retaining plate and U-bolt retaining nuts. Make sure the U-bolts are evenly positioned.
15 Install the shock absorber lower mounting bolt and nut.
16 Raise the housing with the lifting apparatus until the vehicle's frame and body just begin to be supported, but are still resting on the jack stands.
17 Tighten the front spring mounting bolt and nut to the correct torque. Tighten the rear shackle retaining bolts and nuts to the correct torque. Tighten the U-bolt retaining nuts to the correct torque and also tighten the lower shock absorber mount.
18 Install the wheels. Check that the brakes are working properly and lower the vehicle to the ground. It is a good idea to recheck the torque on all of the mounting bolts and nuts after the vehicle has been driven for a few miles.

14 Rear shock absorber – removal and installation

1 Chock the front wheels. Raise the rear of the vehicle and support it securely.
2 Remove the shock absorber lower attaching nut and pull it free of the mounting bracket.
3 Remove the securing nut from the upper mounting stud and withdraw the shock absorber from the vehicle.
4 Examination and testing of the rear shock absorber is similar to that for the front shock absorber. Refer to Section 12.
5 Installation of the rear shock absorber is the reverse of removal, but be sure to tighten the mounting nuts to the specified torque.

15 Stabilizer bar (rear) – removal and installation

The optionally equipped stabilizer bar is usually found on 1976 thru 1979 F250, F350 and Bronco model rear suspensions. If the bar or bushings need replacement, the procedure for the front stabilizer bar replacement (Section 10) can be followed. Always replace any bushings that show signs of deterioration or wear.

16 Steering gearbox – checking and adjustment

1 Check the fluid reservoir level (if so equipped) and the steering linkage for wear if there is looseness present in the steering.
2 If the looseness is traceable to wear in the steering gearbox, adjust as follows:

F100, F250 and F350 2-wheel drive Ford integral-type power steering

3 Remove the Pitman arm and the steering wheel hub cover. Disconnect and plug the fluid return line at the reservoir.
4 Place the fluid return line in a suitable container and turn the steering wheel lock-to-lock several times to discharge all of the fluid from the steering gear.
5 Turn the shaft back 45° from the left stop and attach a torque wrench calibrated in inch-pounds to the steering wheel nut.
6 Rotate the steering gear about one eighth of a turn and then move it back across the center position several times. Loosen the adjuster nut and turn the adjuster screw until the specified torque reading is reached when the steering gear is rotated through the over-center position.
7 Hold the screw and tighten the nut.
8 Install the Pitman arm and steering wheel center cover. Reconnect the fluid return line and refill the reservoir.

Bronco Saginaw power steering

9 Perform the operations described in Steps 3 and 4.
10 Attach a torque wrench calibrated in inch-pounds to the steering wheel nut.
11 Rotate the steering shaft and check and record the torque wrench readings as follows:

a) *One half turn from the right and left stops*
b) *One half turn from the centered position on both left and right*
c) *The over-center position with the shaft rotated through 180° on each side of the centered position*

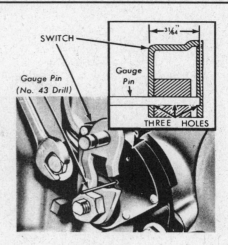

Fig. 11.11 Checking steering preload (Sec 16)

Fig. 11.12 Ford integral-type power steering gearbox adjustment (Sec 16)

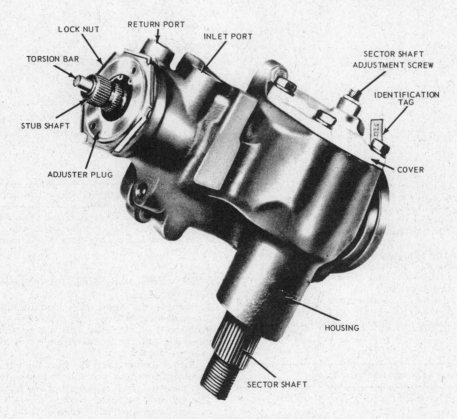

Fig. 11.13 Saginaw power steering gear (Sec 16)

12 The over-center torque readings should be four to five in-lbs greater than the end readings, not to exceed the limit found in the Specifications.

13 If the over-center load is out of specification, back the adjusting screw out fully and then turn it back to ½ turn. Rotate the steering shaft from lock-to-lock, counting the number of turns to locate the centered position. Use a torque wrench to move the shaft through the center of travel and record the highest reading.

14 Tighten the adjusting screw until the torque reading is three to six in-lbs higher than the highest reading in Step 13, with the total still not exceeding the specified limit. Tighten the locknut while holding the adjusting screw.

15 Perform the operations described in Step 8.

4-wheel drive manual worm and roller-type steering gear F100 and F250

16 Remove the Pitman arm and the horn button and install an inch-pound torque wrench on the steering wheel nut.

17 With the steering wheel turned all of the way to either the right or left lock, measure the torque necessary to keep the wheel moving at a constant rate for about one half turn. This measurement is the worm bearing preload.

18 If it is necessary to adjust the preload, this is accomplished by adding or removing shims between the worm shaft bearing retainer cover and the steering gear housing.

19 After installing the cover, check the lubricant level and then recheck the preload.

11

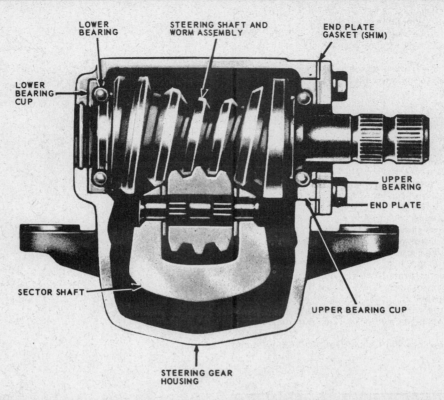

Fig. 11.14 Cutaway of worm and roller-type manual steering gear showing the adjusting shim location (Sec 16)

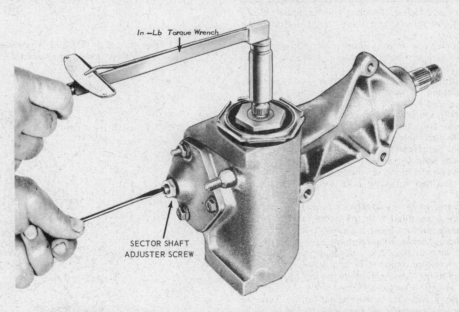

Fig. 11.15 Adjusting the sector mesh load on recirculating ball steering gear (Sec 16)

Bronco
20 Remove the steering gear.
21 Loosen the mesh and roller adjusting locknut and back out the adjusting screw two to three turns.
22 To determine the worm bearing preload, install an inch-pound torque wrench on the input shaft and rotate the shaft 1½ turns to either side of center.
23 If the preload is out of specification, add or subtract shims from between the steering gear cover and the housing.
24 Reinstall the cover and recheck the preload.
25 Check the roller mesh by installing the torque wrench to the input

shaft and determining the highest torque reading required to turn the steering wheel through the straight-ahead position.
26 To adjust the preload, loosen the locknut and turn the adjusting screw clockwise to tighten the mesh or counterclockwise to loosen it.
27 Hold the screw and tighten the locknut. Measure the preload of the roller mesh again, repeating the procedure until the measurement is within the specified limits.
28 Install the steering gear.

2-wheel drive recirculating ball-type manual steering
29 Remove the steering gear from the vehicle.

30 Loosen the sector shaft locknut and then back out the adjusting screw in a counterclockwise direction three full turns.

31 With an inch-pound torque wrench attached to the input shaft, turn the input shaft approximately $1\frac{1}{2}$ turns to each side of center and measure the torque reading.

32 This measurement is the bearing preload. If it is not within the limits, loosen the input shaft locknut and turn the bearing adjuster until the preload is within limits.

33 Tighten the locknut and recheck the preload.

34 Rotate the input shaft slowly and gently lock-to-lock. Turn the shaft about three turns back from the stop to center it.

35 Turn the sector shaft adjusting screw in a clockwise direction until the specified mesh load is obtained on the torque wrench when the input shaft is pulled over-center.

36 With the input shaft centered, apply a 15 in-lb torque load on the input shaft in both directions to check the lash between the ball nuts. Total travel should not exceed the Specifications.

37 Tighten the adjusting screw locknut and recheck the backlash.

38 After checking the steering over-center mesh load and preload, reinstall the steering gear so that the worm bearing preload can be checked and adjusted. Do not reinstall the Pitman arm at this time.

39 Remove the steering wheel horn assembly and turn the wheel fully to either the right or left full lock.

40 Install a torque wrench calibrated in inch pounds to the steering wheel nut. Turn the wheel and measure the torque required to move the wheel at a constant speed.

41 This measurement is the worm bearing preload and if it is out of the specified range, loosen the adjuster locknut and turn the screw to adjust the preload.

42 Tighten the locknut, recheck the preload and install the Pitman arm and horn cover.

17 Steering gearbox – removal and installation

1   Chock the rear wheels and loosen the front wheel lug nuts. Raise and support the front of the vehicle under the frame. Remove the wheels.

2   Remove the nut retaining the Pitman arm to the bottom of the steering gearbox. Have an assistant hold the steering wheel while you initially loosen this nut.

3   Mark the steering shaft lower coupling so that the two parts of the coupling can be reassembled in their original positions. Turn the steering to the straight-ahead position. Remove the retaining bolts from the lower flex coupling. Separate the two halves of the coupling.

3   Mark the Pitman arm and the steering shaft so they can be reassembled correctly. Use a suitable puller to remove the Pitman arm from the steering gearbox. Be careful when performing this operation as the arm can come loose from the shaft with great force.

4   Remove the retaining bolts from the steering gearbox. Support the box before you remove the last retaining bolt. Lower the steering gearbox from the vehicle.

5   Installation is the reverse of removal. Make sure the Pitman arm and the steering shaft are assembled with the same relationship to each other. If new component(s) are being installed, this relationship can be established as follows: center the steering gear by turning the steering shaft end from stop-to-stop and counting the number of revolutions. Working from either stop, back the steering shaft up exactly $\frac{1}{2}$ of the total revolutions. Center the steering linkage with the wheels pointing straight ahead. Install the Pitman arm.

6   Tighten all retaining bolts and nuts to the correct torque. Turn the steering wheel from stop-to-stop after all the work has been completed. Check for any signs of notchiness or binding. Install the wheels and lower the vehicle to the ground. Check the steering for correct operation while at a standstill before road-testing the vehicle.

18 Power steering system – general information

1   The power steering system available on Ford pick-ups and Broncos has a Ford Thompson-type pump that is belt driven from the crankshaft pulley. The pump has the rservoir built into it. This pump supplies fluid under pressure to a servo assisted recirculating ball-type steering box. Broncos (1973 through 1976) and 4 X 4 pick-ups of the

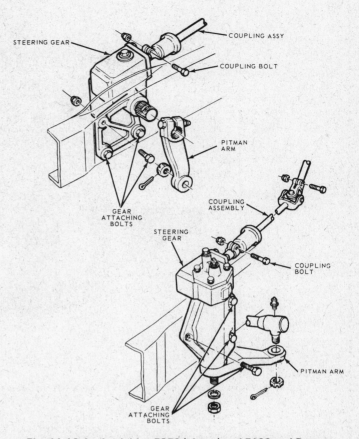

Fig. 11.16 4-wheel drive F250 (above) and F100 and Bronco (below) steering gear installation (Sec 17)

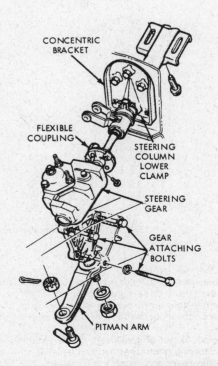

Fig. 11.17 Typical 2-wheel drive steering gear installation (Sec 17)

11

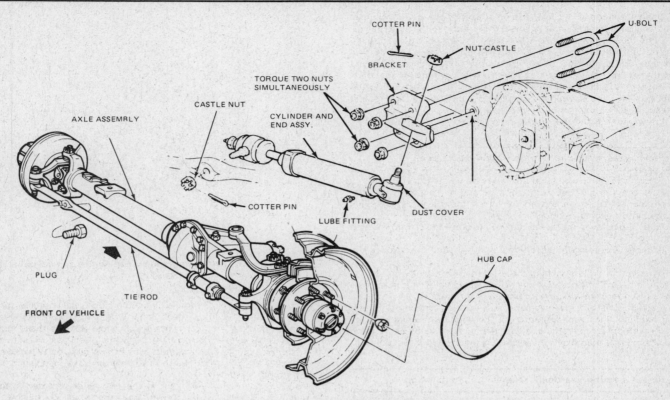

Fig. 11.18 Typical power cylinder installation (Sec 18)

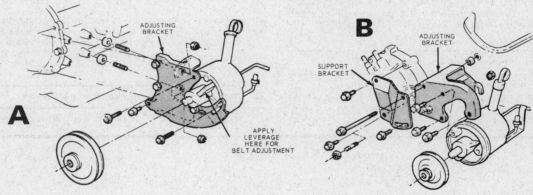

same years have a piston-type cylinder assisting the steering linkage, rather than the integral power steering box.

2   The integral servo assisted steering box transfers power through a piston attached to the end of the worm shaft. The degree of assistance is controlled by a spool valve attached to the steering input shaft.

3   Due to the complexity of the power steering system and the special tools required to work on the components, servicing and adjustments are limited to the items given in the following three Sections. Any other work should be referred to a dealership or repair shop specializing in this area of repair.

19 Power steering system – bleeding

1   The power steering system will need bleeding if air has gotten into the system while a component has been replaced or if leakage has caused the fluid level to drop. Make sure all of the components in the power steering system are working properly and that there are no leaks before attempting any type of bleeding.

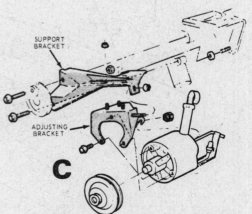

Fig. 11.19 Typical power steering pump installation

A   Six cylinder   C   360 and 390 V8
B   302 and 351 V8

2   Open the hood and check the fluid level in the pump reservoir (Chapter 1). Fill the system if necessary to bring it to the correct level.
3   Start the engine and allow the fluid to reach normal operating temperature. The system is bled by simply turning the steering wheel back and forth to the limit of each side's stops. Make sure you do not hold the steering at the stops as you can damage the components.
4   Recheck the fluid and inspect the reservoir for any signs of air bubbles. If air bubbles appear, repeat Step 3 until the system runs at a steady level with no air bubbles appearing.
5   Clean and reinstall the reservoir cap.

20 Power steering pump – removal and installation

1   Loosen the pump adjusting bolt and retaining bolts.
2   Push the pump in toward the engine, and remove the drivebelt.
3   Disconnect the power system fluid lines from the pump and drain the fluid into a suitable container.
4   Plug, or tape over, the end of the lines to prevent dirt from entering them.
5   If necessary, remove the alternator drivebelt(s) as described in Chapter 1.
6   Remove the bolts attaching the pump to the engine bracket and remove the pump. **Note:** *On some engine installations it may be necessary to remove the pump complete with bracket.*
7   Installation is a direct reversal of the removal procedure. Ensure that the fluid lines are tightened to the specified torque. Fill the system with an approved fluid, adjust the alternator drivebelt tension (see Chapter 1), then bleed the system, as described in Section 19.

21 Power steering gearbox – removal and installation

The procedure for removing the power steering box is similar to that described for the manual steering box, with the additional task of disconnecting the pump lines. When reinstalling, fill the system with an approved fluid, adjust the alternator drivebelt tension (see Chapter 1), then bleed the system, as described in Section 19.

22 Steering wheel – removal and installation

1   Disconnect the negative battery cable from the battery.
2   Remove the horn pad by withdrawing the two retaining screws from the underside of the steering wheel cross bar. If your vehicle is equipped with a sport steering wheel, the horn button is removed by

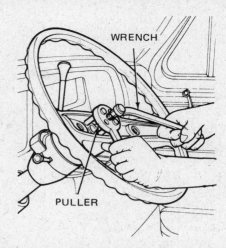

Fig. 11.20 Removing the steering wheel with a special puller (Sec 22)

depressing it evenly and turning it counterclockwise until the tabs release the button from the wheel. Either type of horn will have wires which have quick-disconnect clips on the ends. Release these clips and remove the pad or button from the wheel. Vehicles with cruise controls will have other connections which must also be withdrawn. Mark the steering wheel and the shaft so they can be re-installed in the same position.
3   Install a steering wheel puller at the two holes provided in the steering hub. Never attempt to withdraw the wheel by pulling or pounding on it with a hammer or similar object. Tighten the puller until the center bolt contacts the exact center of the steering shaft. Remove the steering wheel.
4   Installation is the reverse of removal. Install the steering wheel in the same position it was in unless it was removed for clear vision centering purposes. Tighten the retaining nut to the correct torque specification.

23 Steering linkage – removal and installation

1   Steering linkages for Ford pick-ups and Broncos come in many

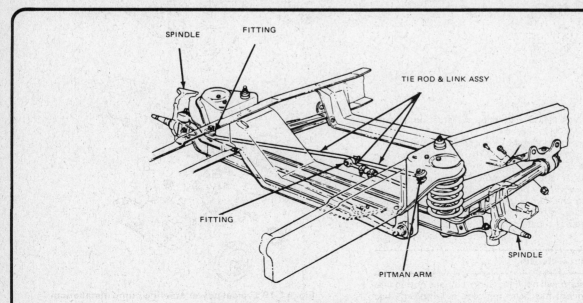

Fig. 11.21 Typical steering linkage layout (Sec 23)

11

configurations and combinations, depending on drive-axle, suspension type and load carrying capabilities. They are all of a common type and consist of a connecting link with either two ball-type links on either end or one ball-type link and a male or female thread.

2   If a linkage is bent or if the balljoint end is excessively worn, it must be replaced.

3   Any balljoint end can be removed after the cotter pin and retaining nut are first withdrawn. A 'pickle fork' designed for this job is the quickest and easiest method for removing this type of connection. However, the rubber dust seal is usually damaged with this type of tool and the seal should be replaced (even if the joint is being re-used). A balljoint end can also be removed with a puller. Use the jaws of the puller to grasp the housing of the component (Pitman arm, sector shaft, spindle arm, etc.). Situate the point of the screw onto the center of the bolt of the spherical end. Tighten the puller to put tension onto it and lightly tap the housing with a brass hammer to help break the joint free. Be careful not to damage either the joint or the housing.

4   If the threaded end of a linkage component is being removed, first mark the component so that the threads can be reinserted to the same exact depth. The vehicle will still need an alignment, but the setting will be close to original so the vehicle can be driven to the alignment facility.

5   Unscrew the component after releasing the bolts and nuts of the clamps. Install the new component to a depth matching the original part and install a retaining nut and new cotter pin to any spherical balljoints. Tighten the bolts and nuts on any clamps to the prescribed torque and have the vehicle's front end alignment checked.

24 Steering alignment – checking and adjustment

Note: *Since wheel alignment and testing equipment is generally out of the reach of the home mechanic, this section is intended only to familiarize the reader with the basic terms used and procedures followed during a typical wheel alignment job. In the event that your vehicle needs a wheel alignment check or adjustment, we recommend that the work be done by a reputable front-end alignment and repair shop.*

1   The three basic adjustments made when aligning a vehicle's front end are toe-in, caster and camber.

2   Toe-in is the amount the front wheels are angled in relationship to the centerline of the vehicle. For example, in a vehicle with zero toe-in, the distance measured between the front edges of the wheels is the same as the distance measured between the rear edges of the wheels. The wheels are running parallel with the centerline of the vehicle. Toe-in is adjusted by lengthening or shortening the tie-rods. Incorrect toe-in will cause tires to wear improperly by making them 'scrub' against the road surface.

3   Camber and caster are the angles at which the wheel and suspension upright are inclined to the vertical. Camber is the angle of the wheel in the lateral (side-to-side) plane, while caster is the angle of the wheel and upright in the longitudinal (fore-and-aft) plane. Camber angle affects the amount of tire tread which contacts the road and compensates for change in the suspension geometry when the vehicle is travelling around curves or over an undulating surface. Caster angle affects the self-centering action of the steering, which governs straight-line stability. Both camber and caster angles are designed into the front suspension of Ford pick-ups and Broncos and no provision is available to change them. In extreme cases, certain components may be bent by a shop with the proper equipment in order to correct the caster and camber on a vehicle that is severely out of line.

25 Steering damper – removal and installation

The steering damper is mounted to the steering linkage on some 4-wheel drive models. It is a specially calibrated shock absorber mounted horizontally to the frame on one end and to the steering cross linkage on the other end. The removal and installation procedure is the same as for a shock absorber with the exception of the location. When testing the damper, it should have the same resistance to compression as it does to extension. All other test and inspection procedures are the same as for a normal suspension shock absorber. Replace any worn or deteriorated grommets and tighten all retaining nuts or bolts to the specified torque.

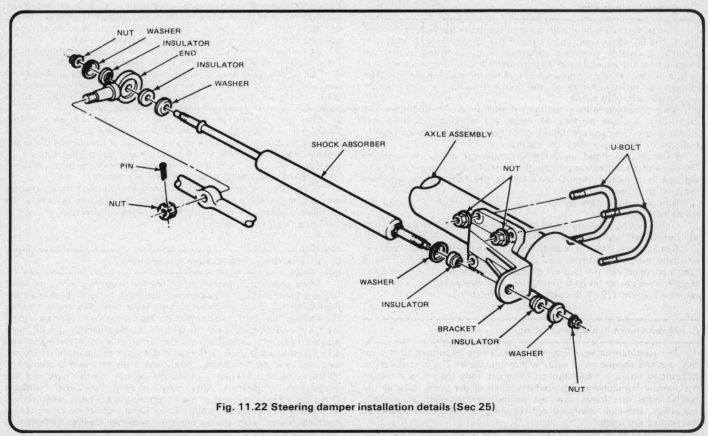

Fig. 11.22 Steering damper installation details (Sec 25)

Chapter 12 Bodywork

Contents

1 General information

Ford pick-ups are built with body-on-separate frame construction. The frame is ladder-type, consisting of two C-section steel side rails joind by a variable number of crossmembers. All crossmembers are riveted, with the exception of the one under the transmission which is bolted in to facilitate transmission removal and installation. The number of crossmembers in the frame depends on the vehicle wheelbase and load rating.

Body styles available range from standard cabs to super cabs and crew cab (4-door) models. All cabs are of single welded unit construction. The cabs are bolted to the frame and use rubber 'biscuit' mounts for noise and vibration isolation.

Front fenders, hood, inner fender panels and grilles are bolted to the cab and the radiator support at the front of the vehicle. The radiator support is a rubber 'donut' mounted to the front frame rails and retained by bolts.

Bumpers are bolted to the frame horns at the front and to the frame rails at the rear.

Doors, seats, dashboard and controls are all bolted to the cab and are individually replaceable.

Broncos are similarly constructed. However, the body comes in one type with different tops available. A short and long hardtop plus a soft top, round out the Bronco model configurations. The front inner fender wells are an integral part of the main body unit, as is the front radiator support (1973 through 1976 models).

2 Maintenance – body and frame

1   The condition of your vehicle's body is very important, as it is on this that the second hand value will mainly depend. It is much more difficult to repair a neglected or damaged body than it is to repair mechanical components. The hidden areas of the body, such as the fender wells, the frame, and the engine compartment, are equally important, although obviously not requiring as frequent attention as the rest of the body.

2   Once a year, or every 12 000 miles, it is a good idea to have the underside of the body and the frame steam cleaned. All traces of dirt and oil will be removed and the underside can then be inspected carefully for rust, damaged brake lines, frayed electrical wiring, damaged cables, and other problems. The front suspension components should be greased upon completion of this job.

3   At the same time, clean the engine and the engine compartment using either a steam cleaner or a water soluble degreaser.

4   The fender wells should be given extra attention, as undercoating can peel away and stones and dirt thrown up by the tires can cause the paint to chip and flake, allowing rust to set in. If rust is found, clean down to the bare metal and apply an anti-rust paint.

5   The body should be washed once a week (or when dirty). Thoroughly wet the vehicle to soften the dirt, then wash it down with a soft sponge and plenty of clean soapy water. If the surplus dirt is not washed off very carefully, it will in time wear down the paint.

6   Spots of tar or asphalt coating thrown from the road surfaces should be removed with a cloth soaked in solvent.

7   Once every six months, give the body and chrome trim a thorough wax job. If the chrome cleaner is used to remove rust on any of the vehicle's plated parts, remember that the cleaner also removes part of the chrome so use it sparingly.

3 Maintenance – upholstery and interior

Mats and carpets should be brushed or vacuum cleaned regularly to keep them clean. If they are badly stained, remove them from the vehicle for scrubbing or sponging and make sure they are dry before reinstalling. Seats and interior trim panels can be kept clean by wiping with a damp cloth. If they do become stained (which can be more apparent on light-colored upholstery) use a little liquid detergent and a soft brush to scour the grime out of the grain of the material. Do not forget to keep the headlining clean in the same way as the upholstery. When using liquid cleaners inside the vehicle, do not over wet the surfaces being cleaned. After cleaning, vinyl and plastic surfaces should be treated with any of the commercially available preservatives to prevent drying, cracking and fading. Clear instrument faces can be carefully wiped with a commercially available cleaner designed to remove tiny surface scratches and hazing.

4   Body repair – minor damage

See photographic sequences on pages 294 and 295.

Repair of minor scratches

If the scratch is very superficial, and does not penetrate to the metal of the bodywork, repair is very simple. Lightly rub the area of the scratch with a fine rubbing compound to remove loose paint from the scratch and to clear the surrounding paint of wax buildup. Rinse the area with clean water.

Apply touch-up paint to the scratch using a small brush. Continue to apply thin layers of paint until the surface of the paint in the scratch is level with the surrounding paint. Allow the new paint at least two weeks to harden, then blend it into the surrounding paint by rubbing with a very fine rubbing compound. Finally, apply a coat of wax to the scratch area.

Where the scratch has penetrated the paint and exposed the metal of the body, causing the metal to rust, a different repair technique is required. Remove any loose rust from the bottom of the scratch with a pocket knife, then apply rust inhibiting paint to prevent the formation of rust in the future. Using a rubber or nylon applicator, coat the scratched area with glaze type filler. If required, this filler can be mixed with thinner to provide a very thin paste which is ideal for filling narrow scratches. Before the glaze filler in the scratch hardens, wrap a piece of smooth cotton cloth around the top of a finger. Dip the cloth in thinner and then quickly wipe it along the surface of the scratch. This will ensure that the surface of the filler is slightly hollowed. The scratch can now be painted over as described earlier in this Section.

Repair of dents

When deep denting of the vehicle's bodywork has taken place, the first task is to pull the dent out until the affected area nearly attains its original shape. There is little point in trying to restore the original shape completely as the metal in the damaged area will have stretched on impact and cannot be reshaped fully to its original contours. It is better to bring the level of the dent up to a point which is about $\frac{1}{8}$ in below the level of the surrounding metal. In cases where the dent is very shallow, it is not worth trying to pull it out at all.

If the underside of the dent is accessible, it can be hammered out gently from behind using a mallet with a wooden or plastic head. While doing this, hold a suitable block of wood firmly against the metal to absorb the hammer blows and thus prevent a large area of the metal from being stretched out.

If the dent is in a section of the body which has double layers, or some other factor making it inaccessible from behind, a different technique is in order. Drill several small holes through the metal inside the damaged area, particularly in the deeper sections. Screw long self-tapping screws into the holes just enough for them to get a good grip in the metal. Now the dent can be pulled out by pulling on the protruding head of the screws with a pair of locking pliers.

The next stage of the repair is the removal of the paint from the damaged area and from an inch or so of the surrounding 'sound' metal. This is accomplished most easily by using a wire brush or sanding disc in a drill motor, although it can be done just as effectively by hand with sandpaper. To complete the preparation for filling, score the surface of the bare metal with a screwdriver or the tang of a file (or drill small holes in the affected area). This will provide a really good 'key' for the filler material. To complete the repair, see the Section on filling and painting.

Repair of rust holes or gashes

Remove all paint from the affected area and from an inch or so of the surrounding 'sound' metal using a sanding disc or wire brush mounted in a drill motor. If these are not available a few sheets of sandpaper will do the job just as effectively. With the paint removed you will be able to determine the severity of the corrosion and therefore decide whether to replace the whole panel if possible, or to repair the affected area. New body panels are not as expensive as most people think and it is often quicker and more satisfactory to install a new panel than to attempt to repair large areas of rust.

Remove all trim pieces from the affected area (except those which will act as a guide to the original shape of the damaged body ie. headlamp shells etc). Then, using metal snips or a hacksaw blade, remove all loose metal and any other metal that is badly affected by rust. Hammer the edges of the hole inwards to create a slight depression for the filler material.

Wire brush the affected area to remove the powdery rust from the surface of the metal. If the back of the rusted area is accessible, treat it with rust-inhibiting paint.

Before filling can be done it will be necessary to block the hole in some way. This can be accomplished with sheet metal riveted or screwed into place, or by stuffing the hole with wire mesh.

Once the hole is blocked off the affected area can be filled and painted (see the following section on filling and painting).

Filling and painting

Many types of body fillers are available, but generally speaking body repair kits which contain filler paste and a tube of resin hardener are best for this type of repair work. A wide, flexible plastic or nylon applicator will be necessary for imparting a smooth and contoured finish to the surface of the filler material.

Mix up a small amount of filler on a clean piece of wood or cardboard (use the hardener sparingly). Follow the maker's instructions on the packackage, otherwise the filler will set incorrectly.

Using the applicator, apply the filler paste to the prepared area. Draw the applicator across the surface of the filler to achieve the desired contour and to level the filler surface. As soon as a contour that approximates the correct one is achieved, stop working the paste. If you continue, the paste will begin to stick to the applicator. Continue to add thin layers of filler paste at 20-minute intervals until the level of the filler is just proud of the surrounding metal.

Once the filler has hardened, excess can be removed using a body file. From then on, progressively finer grades of sandpaper should be used, starting with a 180-grit paper and finishing with 600-grit wet-and-dry paper. Always wrap the sandpaper around a flat rubber or wooden block, otherwise the surface of the filler will not be completely flat. During the sanding of the filler surface the wet-and-dry paper should be periodically rinsed in water. This will ensure that a very smooth finish is produced in the final stage.

At this point, the repair area should be surrounded by a ring of bare metal, which in turn should be encircled by the finely feathered edge of the good paint. Rinse the repair area with clean water until all of the dust produced by the sand operation has gone.

Spray the entire area with a light coat of primer. This will reveal any imperfections in the surface of the filler. Repair these imperfections with fresh filler paste or glaze filler and once more smooth the surface with sandpaper. Repeat this spray-and-repair procedure until you are satisfied that the surface of the filler and the feathered edge of the paintwork are perfect. Rinse the area with clean water and allow to dry fully.

The repair area is now ready for painting. Paint spraying must be carried out in warm, dry, windless and dustfree atmosphere. These conditions can be created if you have access to a large indoor working area, but if you are forced to work in the open, you will have to pick your day very carefully. If you are working indoors, dousing the floor in the work area with water will help to settle the dust which would otherwise be in the air. If the repair area is confined to one body panel, mask off the surrounding panels. This will help to minimise the effects of a slight mis-match in paint color. Trim pieces such as chrome strips, door handles, etc., will also need to be masked off or removed. Use masking tape and several thicknesses of newspaper for the masking operations.

Before spraying, shake the paint can thoroughly, then spray a test area until the technique is mastered. Cover the repair area with a thick coat of primer. The thickness should be built up using several thin layers of primer rather than one thick one. Using 600-grit wet-or-dry sandpaper, rub down the surface of the primer until it is very smooth. While doing this, the work area should be thoroughly rinsed with water, and the wet-or-dry sandpaper periodically rinsed as well. Allow the primer to dry before spraying additional coats.

Spray on the top coat, again building up the thickness by using several thin layers of paint. Begin spraying in the center of the repair area and then, using a circular motion, work out until the whole repair area and about two inches of the surrounding original paint is covered. Remove all masking material 10 to 15 minutes after spraying on the final coat of paint. Allow the new paint at least two weeks to harden, then using a very fine rubbing compound, blend the edges of the paint into the existing paint. Finally, apply a coat of wax.

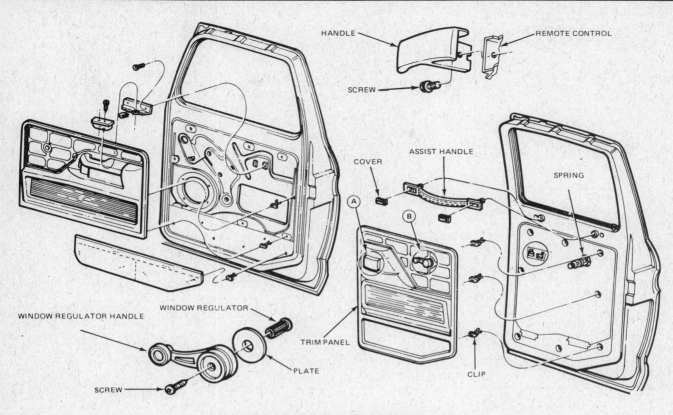

Fig. 12.1 Typical door trim panel – exploded view (Sec 7)

5 Body and frame repairs – major damage

1 Major damage must be repaired by an auto body shop equipped to perform body and frame repairs. These shops have available the welding and hydraulic straightening equipment required to do the job properly.

2 If the damage is extensive, the frame must be checked for proper alignment or the vehicle's handling characteristics may be adversely affected and other components may wear at an accelerated rate.

3 Due to the fact that all of the major body components (cab, hood, bed, (fenders etc.) are separate and replaceable units, any seriously damaged components should be replaced rather than repaired. Sometimes these components can be found in a wrecking yard that specializes in used vehicle components (often at a considerable saving over the cost of new parts).

6 Maintenance – hinges, locks and latches

Instructions for lubricating and maintaining these components can be found in Chapter 1, Sec 19.

7 Door trim panel and hardware – removal and installation

Note: *The following procedure is for pick-ups and Broncos 1978 and newer. The door panel of earlier model Broncos is retained by screws and clips which are obvious as you look at the panel.*

Removal

1 Remove the two screws retaining the door armrest finger plate. Remove the plate.

2 Remove the window crank, which is retained by one screw. Remove the scuff disc from beneath the crank handle.

3 Remove the single screw retaining the inner door handle to the plate. Remove the inner door handle.

4 Remove the eight door trim panel retaining clips (three on the top and bottom and one on each side) with a putty knife or similar tool. Make sure you engage the clip and not the panel with the tool as the panel can be damaged if you pry on it in order to pull a clip out of the door.

Installation

5 Make sure that the clips are in good condition and located in the proper recess of the door panel. Place the panel in position and start the clips into their holes one by one. You may have to push each clip in firmly with your hand, but never use a hammer or excessive force. If the clip will not go into the door readily, it is either out of line or defective.

6 Install the remaining components removed in steps 1 through 3 in reverse order.

8 Vent window assembly – removal and installation

Pick-ups and 1978 and 1979 Broncos

1 Remove the door trim panel as described in the previous Section.

2 Remove the retaining nut from the front window run stud.

3 Remove the three vent window assembly retaining screws from the front of the upper door edge.

4 Lower the door glass to the bottom of its travel.

5 Pull the glass run out of the upper run retainer next to the vent window division bar. Pull the glass run out just far enough to allow the vent window assembly to be removed.

6 Tilt the vent window and the division bar assembly toward the rear of the door. Carefully guide the assembly up and out of the door.

7 Installation is the reverse of removal.

1973 thru 1977 Broncos

8 Remove the access panel from the door.

9 Remove the lower glass stop from the door.

10 Lower the glass to the bottom of the run.

12

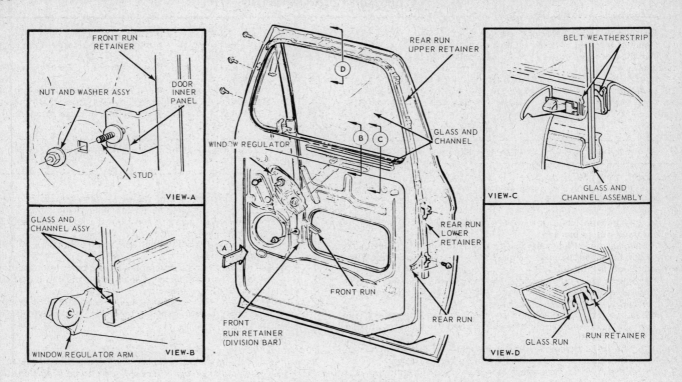

Fig. 12.2 Pick-up door glass and regulator installation details (Sec 9)

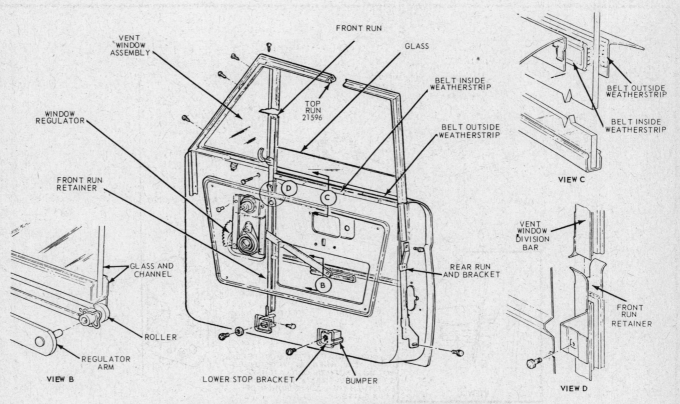

Fig. 12.3 Bronco door glass and regulator installation details (Sec 9)

11 Remove the inner belt weatherstrip.
12 Remove the vent window retaining screws.
13 Pull the door glass top run down and away from the vent window assembly.
14 Lift the vent window assembly up and out of the door.
15 Installation is the reverse of removal. If only the glass needs to be replaced, remove the assembly and have a glass shop install new glass in it.

9 Window regulator and door glass – removal and installation

Pick-ups and 1978 and 1979 Broncos
1 Remove the door trim panel as described in Section 7.
2 Remove the vent window assembly as described in the previous Section.
3 Rotate the front edge of the glass forward and down and lift the glass up and out of the door.
4 If the glass needs replacement, it must be removed and new glass installed in the glass channel by a glass shop with the special tools and skills required for this job.
5 To remove the regulator assembly, remove the retaining screws. Lift the regulator assembly out of the door through the access panel.
6 Installation is the reverse of removal.
7 When inserting the glass and channel into the door, make sure that the regulator arm roller is positioned correctly in the glass channel slot.
8 After the glass assemblies are all installed but before the water-shield or inner trim are in place, adjust the glass as follows.
9 Lower the glass to the bottom of its run. Check that the top edge of the glass is even with the opening line. If it is not, loosen the regulator retaining screws and move the regulator to the position necessary to provide this alignment. Re-tighten the retaining screws and install the trim panel and watershield.

Bronco (1973 thru 1977)
10 Remove the vent window assembly as described in the previous Section.
11 Disconnect the roller from the regulator arm. Remove the roller from the glass channel.
12 Lift the glass and channel assembly up and out of the door.
13 Installation is the reverse of removal. Lubricate the window regulator roller, shaft and guide with the proper lubricant.

10 Door handle (outside) and lock cylinder – removal and installation

Door handle
1 Remove the inner door trim panel as described in Section 7. Remove the plastic watershield from the inside of the door.
2 Disconnect the latch actuator rod from the hole on the inside of the door handle assembly.
3 Using a socket and small ratchet, remove the retaining nuts from the door handle assembly.
4 Remove the door handle assembly and the pads from the door.
5 If the handle is being replaced, transfer the pads and the actuator rod clip to the new handle assembly.
6 Installation is the reverse of removal. Check the handle assembly for correct operation before installing the inner door watershield and panel.

Lock cylinder
Note: *If a lock cylinder is being replaced, it should be replaced in both doors and the ignition cylinder. These cylinders come in sets and allow the vehicle to be unlocked and driven with one key.*
7 Roll the window all the way up.
8 Remove the inner door trim panel and watershield as described in Section 7.

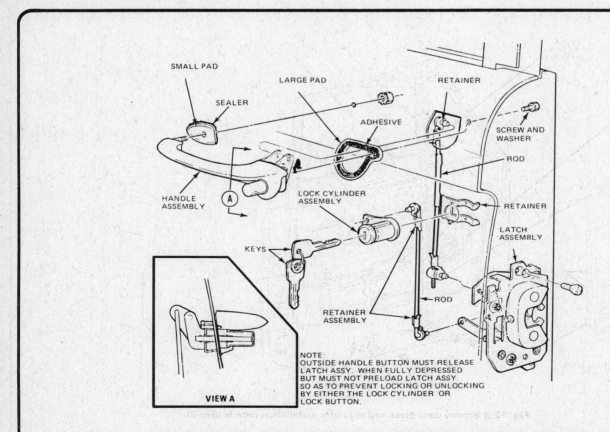

NOTE:
OUTSIDE HANDLE BUTTON MUST RELEASE LATCH ASSY. WHEN FULLY DEPRESSED BUT MUST NOT PRELOAD LATCH ASSY. SO AS TO PREVENT LOCKING OR UNLOCKING BY EITHER THE LOCK CYLINDER OR LOCK BUTTON.

SMALL PAD
SEALER
LARGE PAD
ADHESIVE
RETAINER
SCREW AND WASHER
ROD
HANDLE ASSEMBLY
LOCK CYLINDER ASSEMBLY
RETAINER
LATCH ASSEMBLY
KEYS
RETAINER ASSEMBLY
ROD
VIEW A

Fig. 12.4 Typical door hand and lock mechanism – exploded view (Bronco shown) (Sec 10)

12

9   Disconnect the lock actuating rod from the lock control link clip.
10   Slide the lock cylinder retaining clip out of the groove in the lock cylinder. Remove the lock cylinder from the outside of the door.
11   Installation is the reverse of removal. Be careful when re-installing the watershield to ensure that it fits tightly to the door and is not torn or deformed in any way. If this shield is not watertight, it can cause an accumulation of water inside of the door and eventual rusting. It is sometimes necessary to reglue the lip of the seal.

11 Windshield glass – replacement

Note: *Due to the chance of glass breakage and/or damage to the paint and body, we recommend that you have the windshield replaced by a glass shop or dealership. If you are going to perform this task yourself, you will need a helper.*

1   Remove the windshield wiper arms and blades.
2   Remove the inside rear view mirror and bracket. If you are replacing the windshield, you will need to purchase a special bonding kit and mount which comes with instructions.
3   Work around the inner lip of the windshield weatherstrip and loosen it from the body. If there is any sealant present you should cut it with a piano wire or blade. Be very careful not to damage the weatherstrip.
4   Using the palms of your hands, push the windshield out of the windshield opening from inside the vehicle. Your helper can be stationed outside of the vehicle to keep the windshield from falling forward and damaging the body. A second helper on the inside can help provide an even pushing force.
5   Remove the moldings (if so equipped) from the weather-stripping.
6   Remove the weatherstripping from the glass.
7   Inspect the weatherstripping for any signs of damage. Cracks,

rotting or any other form of deterioration is cause for replacement.
8   Clean the glass (if used) and the opening in the cab of any old sealer or weatherstripping material.
9   Apply an approved sealer (Ford 19563 or equivalent) to the windshield opening flange.
10   Place the weatherstripping on the windshield in the correct position. Install the moldings (if so equipped) into the windshield weatherstripping.
11   Insert a strong draw cord (nylon clothesline works well) into the pinch weld opening of the weatherstrip, starting at the bottom center of the glass. Leave approximately a foot of cord at the end and insert the cord around the entire circumference of the weatherstrip until you reach the bottom center point from the other side.
12   Place the windshield and weatherstrip/cord assembly into the windshield opening. Make sure both free ends of the draw cord are inside of the opening and not pinching or binding.
13   While your assistant applies even open palm hand pressure to the outside of the windshield, pull the drawcord to the inside of the cab. This will pull the lip of the weatherstrip over the windshield opening flange. Work slowly and proceed on one side of the bottom to the corner, then work from the center toward the other side. Pull each lower corner into place and continue alternating this way until the windshield weatherstrip is completely pulled in and the cord can be withdrawn at the top center of the windshield opening.
14   Install the rear view mirror and bracket.
15   Leak check the windshield and seal any leaks with windshield sealant. If your weatherstrip was in good condition and the installation was performed correctly very little if any sealant should be needed.
16   Install the windshield wiper arms and blades.

12 Rear window glass – replacement

The rear window glass in pick-ups is replaced in a manner similar

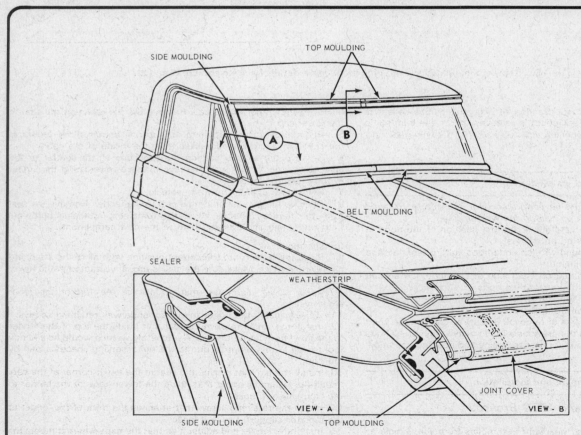

Fig. 12.5 Windshield glass and molding installation details (pick-up shown) (Sec 11)

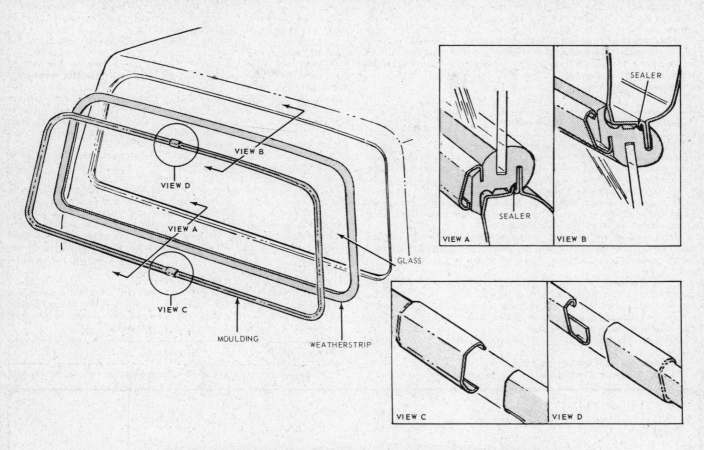

Fig. 12.6 Rear window glass and molding installation details (pick-up shown) (Sec 12)

to the windshield replacement (Section 11). The only difference is that the outer molding (if so equipped) is removed before the window is withdrawn from the cab opening and installed after the new glass and weatherstrip are in place.

13 Hood – removal and installation

Note: *This procedure must be performed with two people to avoid damaging the component or injuring the worker.*
1 With the hood open, carefully scribe the position of the hood in relationship to the hinges on both sides.
2 If the vehicle is equipped with an underhood light, disconnect the light loom at the plug connector.
3 With one person situated on each side of the hood, loosen and remove the two hood-to-hinge retaining bolts on each side.
4 Pivot the nose of the hood down slowly until the assembly is level and remove it towards the front of the vehicle.
5 Installation is the reverse of removal. Be sure to position the hood carefully and align it with the previously made marks. Tighten all bolts securely and check the hood for proper closing and opening operation.

14 Front fenders – removal and installation

Pick-ups and 1978 and 1979 Broncos
Removal
1 Remove the grille and headlight assemblies from the vehicle as described in the following Section.
2 Clean all the dirt and road debris from the fender retaining bolts.
3 Remove the screws retaining the front of the fender(s) to the radiator support.
4 Remove the screw retaining the lower bottom portion of the

fender to the corner of the cab. Remove the pin retaining the seal to the lower cab corner.
5 Remove the screw retaining the top rear corner of the fender to the cowl. This screw is accessible from the inside of the cab.
6 Remove the screws holding the top edge of the fender to the galvanized inner fender well. Remove the screws retaining the fender to the radiator support.
7 Remove the fender from the vehicle.
8 Remove the pins retaining the seal to the fender. Remove the seal from the fender. Remove all of the remaining attaching hardware from the fender and transfer them to the new component.

Installation
9 Place the fender into the correct position with all of the attaching hardware in place. Make sure the seal is properly situated at the lower rear edge.
10 Apply sealer along the mating face of the top of the inner fenderwell.
11 Loosely install the upper fender-to-fenderwell retaining screws.
12 Install the single retaining screw that holds the top of the fender to the cowl from inside the cab. A ratcheting wrench would be a handy tool to use in this situation due to the tight working space caused by the door.
13 Install the pin that retains the seal to the lower corner of the cab. Install the retaining screw that holds the lower edge of the fender to the cab. Leave it loose.
14 Install the retaining screw that attaches the front of the fender to the radiator support. Leave it loose.
15 Install the fender and adjust it so that the gaps where it meets the hood, grille and cab/door are equal. Have a helper hold the fender in this position while you tighten all of the retaining screws and fasteners.
16 Install the grille and headlight assemblies as described in the following Section.

12

These photos illustrate a method of repairing simple dents. They are intended to supplement *Body repair - minor damage* in this Chapter and should not be used as the sole instructions for body repair on these vehicles.

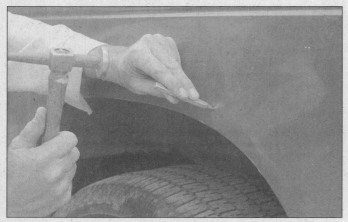

1   If you can't access the backside of the body panel to hammer out the dent, pull it out with a slide-hammer-type dent puller. In the deepest portion of the dent or along the crease line, drill or punch hole(s) at least one inch apart . . .

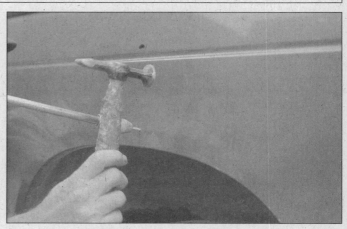

2   . . . then screw the slide-hammer into the hole and operate it. Tap with a hammer near the edge of the dent to help 'pop' the metal back to its original shape. When you're finished, the dent area should be close to its original contour and about 1/8-inch below the surface of the surrounding metal

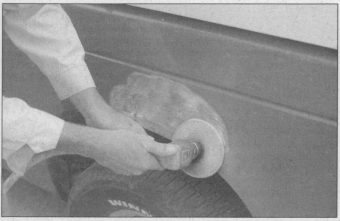

3   Using coarse-grit sandpaper, remove the paint down to the bare metal. Hand sanding works fine, but the disc sander shown here makes the job faster. Use finer (about 320-grit) sandpaper to feather-edge the paint at least one inch around the dent area

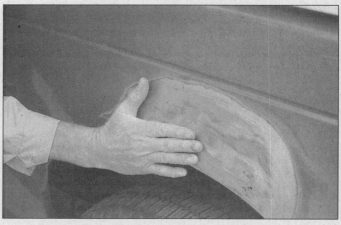

4   When the paint is removed, touch will probably be more helpful than sight for telling if the metal is straight. Hammer down the high spots or raise the low spots as necessary. Clean the repair area with wax/silicone remover

5   Following label instructions, mix up a batch of plastic filler and hardener. The ratio of filler to hardener is critical, and, if you mix it incorrectly, it will either not cure properly or cure too quickly (you won't have time to file and sand it into shape)

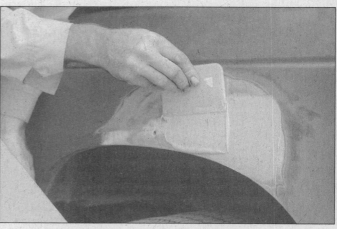

6   Working quickly so the filler doesn't harden, use a plastic applicator to press the body filler firmly into the metal, assuring it bonds completely. Work the filler until it matches the original contour and is slightly above the surrounding metal

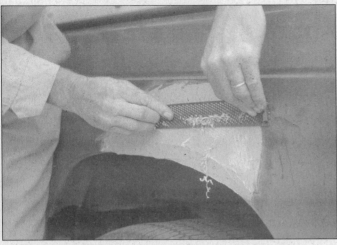

7   Let the filler harden until you can just dent it with your fingernail. Use a body file or Surform tool (shown here) to rough-shape the filler

8   Use coarse-grit sandpaper and a sanding board or block to work the filler down until it's smooth and even. Work down to finer grits of sandpaper - always using a board or block - ending up with 360 or 400 grit

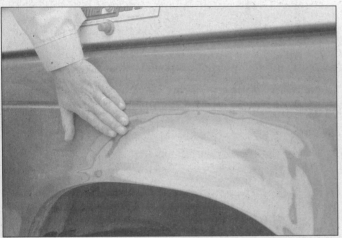

9   You shouldn't be able to feel any ridge at the transition from the filler to the bare metal or from the bare metal to the old paint. As soon as the repair is flat and uniform, remove the dust and mask off the adjacent panels or trim pieces

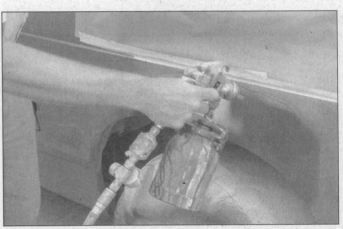

10   Apply several layers of primer to the area. Don't spray the primer on too heavy, so it sags or runs, and make sure each coat is dry before you spray on the next one. A professional-type spray gun is being used here, but aerosol spray primer is available inexpensively from auto parts stores

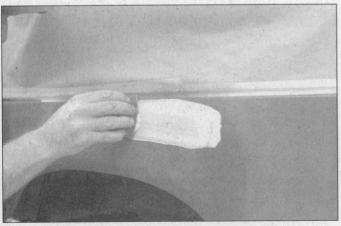

11   The primer will help reveal imperfections or scratches. Fill these with glazing compound. Follow the label instructions and sand it with 360 or 400-grit sandpaper until it's smooth. Repeat the glazing, sanding and respraying until the primer reveals a perfectly smooth surface

12   Finish sand the primer with very fine sandpaper (400 or 600-grit) to remove the primer overspray. Clean the area with water and allow it to dry. Use a tack rag to remove any dust, then apply the finish coat. Don't attempt to rub out or wax the repair area until the paint has dried completely (at least two weeks)

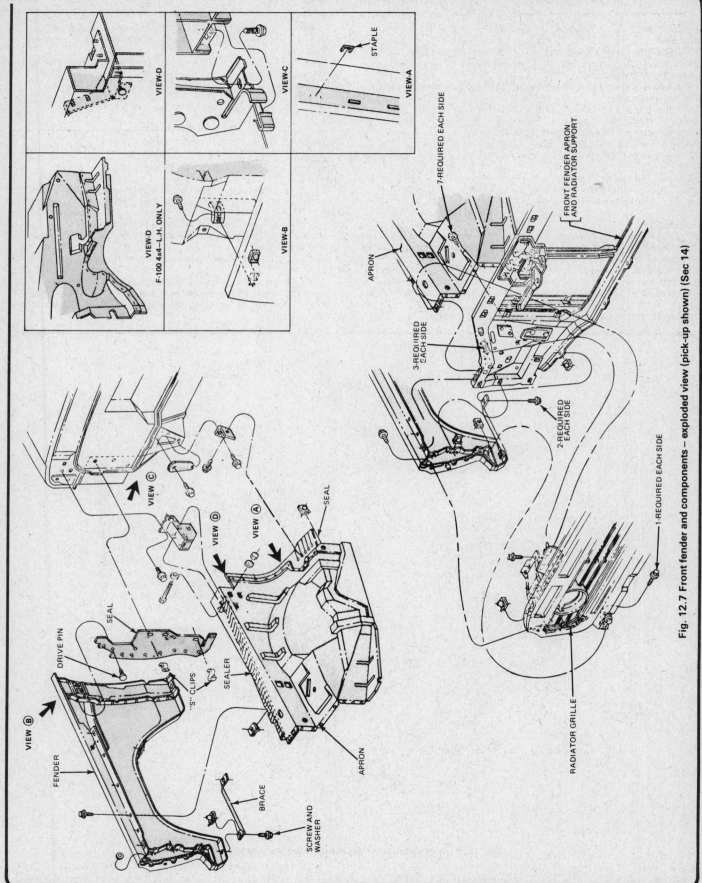

VIEW-D

VIEW-C

STAPLE

VIEW-A

VIEW-D
F-100 4x4 – L.H. ONLY

VIEW-B

FRONT FENDER APRON
AND RADIATOR SUPPORT

7-REQUIRED EACH SIDE

APRON

3-REQUIRED
EACH SIDE

2-REQUIRED
EACH SIDE

1-REQUIRED EACH SIDE

RADIATOR GRILLE

VIEW C

VIEW D

VIEW A

SEAL

SEAL

DRIVE PIN

SEAL

"S" CLIPS

SEALER

VIEW B

FENDER

BRACE

SCREW AND
WASHER

APRON

Fig. 12.7 Front fender and components – exploded view (pick-up shown) (Sec 14)

1973 thru 1977 Broncos
Removal

17 Raise the hood and secure it to the windshield with the clip.

18 Remove the screws that hold the fender to the grille from the underside of the fender.

19 Remove the screws that retain the fender to the inner fenderwell and radiator support.

20 From the fender flange, remove the screw that retains the front fender to the fender bracket.

21 With the vehicle's door open, remove the three screws that hold the fender to the cowl hinge pillar.

22 Remove the screw that holds the rear fender bracket to the fender skirt.

23 Have a helper hold the fender in position. Remove the screws that retain the top side of the fender to the side apron.

24 Remove the fender from the vehicle.

Installation

25 Apply a bead of sealer to the fender mating surface side of the inner fender apron. Also apply sealer to the front and rear mating surfaces of the fender.

26 Have a helper hold the fender in the correct position and install the retaining screws holding the fender to the top of the side apron.

27 Install the three screws that hold the fender to the cowl hinge pillar.

28 Install the screws that hold the apron and the radiator support.

29 Secure the fender to the grille with the retaining screws.

30 Install the screws that hold the front and rear fender brackets to the fender.

31 Have your helper hold the fender in correct alignment and tighten all of the fasteners.

32 Lower the hood.

15 Grille – removal and installation

Pick-ups and 1978 and 1979 Bronco
Removal

1 The grille assembly consists of an aluminum outer shell with one insert made of plastic (1978 and 1979) or two plastic inserts (1973 through 1977). Each insert is retained to the outer shell with several Phillips head screws. Remove the grille insert(s).

2 Remove the four screws on each side retaining the outer grille shell to the fenders.

3 Remove the four retaining screws along the bottom of the grille shell.

4 Remove the bolts retaining the grille outer shell to the radiator support. These retaining bolts are positioned on each end of the grille.

5 Remove the bolts securing the upper mounting bracket to the grille outer shell.

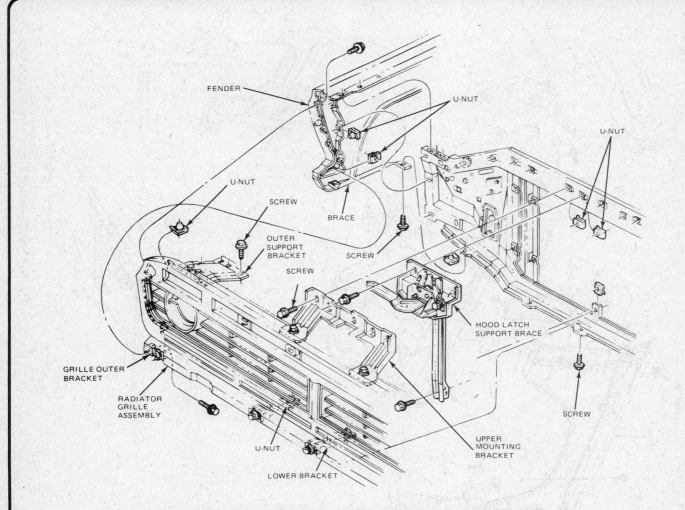

Fig. 12.8 Grille installation details (pick-up shown) (Sec 15)

12

6   Disconnect the parking light wires after noting the positions of each plug for installation purposes.
7   Remove the grille assembly.

Installation
8   Transfer all clips, mounting brackets and hardware from the old assembly to the new one.
9   Position the grille assembly into place on the front of the radiator support.
10 The remainder of the installation procedure is the reverse of removal.

1973 thru 1977 Broncos
Removal
11 Unlatch and raise the hood. Secure the hood to the windshield with the clip.
12 From beneath the front fenders, remove the five screws per side that retain the grille to the front fenders.
13 Mark the light connectors for installation purposes. Disconnect the headlight and parking light wiring connectors.
14 Remove the retaining screws holding the left and right headlight rims to the grille.
15 Remove the six retaining screws that hold the headlight adjusting rings to the grille brackets. Remove both headlight assemblies along with the retaining springs.
16 Remove the three retaining bolts holding the hood latch bracket to the top rail of the radiator support.
17 Remove the grille assembly.
18 Remove the four bolts retaining the hood latch to the grille bracket. Remove the latch.
19 Remove the four nuts and lock washers securing the left and right parking light assemblies to the grille. Remove the assemblies.

Installation
20 Installation is the reverse of removal. Align the headlights (Chapter 1) before installing the headlight rings. Test the lights for proper operation after the new grille assembly has been installed.

---

16 Tailgate – removal and installation

Note: *It is much easier to perform the tailgate removal and installation procedure with a helper.*

Trucks and early Bronco models
1   Unhook the support chains on narrow-box models. Rotate the support straps over-center and release the strap from the stud on wide-box models.
2   Unbolt the two retaining bolts holding each tailgate hinge (narrow-box requires only one side hinge removal). Lift the tailgate up and out of the channel at the rear of the bed.
3   Installation is the reverse of removal. Coat the hinge with grease before installing the tailgate.

Later Bronco models
4   Lower the tailgate. Disconnect the cables at the tailgate.
5   Unplug the electrical connector for the tailgate window.
6   Support the tailgate and unbolt the torsion bar retainer from the body.
7   Remove the three bolts from each tailgate hinge and detach the tailgate from the vehicle.
8   Installation is the reverse of removal. Apply grease to the hinges and to the torsion bar contact areas.

---

17 Bumpers – removal and installation

1   The bumpers installed on Ford pick-ups vary in style and design, depending on year of manufacture and order specifications. Some bumpers also incorporate bumper guards and/or push bar or brush guards.

Removal
2   Removal on all models is achieved by unbolting the four bolts (two per side) for the front bumpers. Rear bumpers have a more variable type of mounting but they must always include four or six bolts retaining intermediate brackets to the frame rails. The bumpers are then removeable from the intermediate brackets with another group of bolts through the bumper and brackets. Some rear models also have a license plate light incorporated in them. The wiring loom for the light must be unplugged before the bumper can be withdrawn from the vehicle.

Installation
3   Installation is the reverse of removal. Install all mounting bolts loosely and make sure the bumper is aligned before tightening the bolts securely.

Conversion factors

Length (distance)

Inches (in)	X 25.4	= Millimetres (mm)	X 0.0394	= Inches (in)
Feet (ft)	X 0.305	= Metres (m)	X 3.281	= Feet (ft)
Miles	X 1.609	= Kilometres (km)	X 0.621	= Miles

Volume (capacity)

Cubic inches (cu in; in³)	X 16.387	= Cubic centimetres (cc; cm³)	X 0.061	= Cubic inches (cu in; in³)
Imperial pints (Imp pt)	X 0.568	= Litres (l)	X 1.76	= Imperial pints (Imp pt)
Imperial quarts (Imp qt)	X 1.137	= Litres (l)	X 0.88	= Imperial quarts (Imp qt)
Imperial quarts (Imp qt)	X 1.201	= US quarts (US qt)	X 0.833	= Imperial quarts (Imp qt)
US quarts (US qt)	X 0.946	= Litres (l)	X 1.057	= US quarts (US qt)
Imperial gallons (Imp gal)	X 4.546	= Litres (l)	X 0.22	= Imperial gallons (Imp gal)
Imperial gallons (Imp gal)	X 1.201	= US gallons (US gal)	X 0.833	= Imperial gallons (Imp gal)
US gallons (US gal)	X 3.785	= Litres (l)	X 0.264	= US gallons (US gal)

Mass (weight)

Ounces (oz)	X 28.35	= Grams (g)	X 0.035	= Ounces (oz)
Pounds (lb)	X 0.454	= Kilograms (kg)	X 2.205	= Pounds (lb)

Force

Ounces-force (ozf; oz)	X 0.278	= Newtons (N)	X 3.6	= Ounces-force (ozf; oz)
Pounds-force (lbf; lb)	X 4.448	= Newtons (N)	X 0.225	= Pounds-force (lbf; lb)
Newtons (N)	X 0.1	= Kilograms-force (kgf; kg)	X 9.81	= Newtons (N)

Pressure

Pounds-force per square inch (psi; lbf/in²; lb/in²)	X 0.070	= Kilograms-force per square centimetre (kgf/cm²; kg/cm²)	X 14.223	= Pounds-force per square inch (psi; lbf/in²; lb/in²)
Pounds-force per square inch (psi; lbf/in²; lb/in²)	X 0.068	= Atmospheres (atm)	X 14.696	= Pounds-force per square inch (psi; lbf/in²; lb/in²)
Pounds-force per square inch (psi; lbf/in²; lb/in²)	X 0.069	= Bars	X 14.5	= Pounds-force per square inch (psi; lbf/in²; lb/in²)
Pounds-force per square inch (psi; lbf/in²; lb/in²)	X 6.895	= Kilopascals (kPa)	X 0.145	= Pounds-force per square inch (psi; lbf/in²; lb/in²)
Kilopascals (kPa)	X 0.01	= Kilograms-force per square centimetre (kgf/cm²; kg/cm²)	X 98.1	= Kilopascals (kPa)
Millibar (mbar)	X 100	= Pascals (Pa)	X 0.01	= Millibar (mbar)
Millibar (mbar)	X 0.0145	= Pounds-force per square inch (psi; lbf/in²; lb/in²)	X 68.947	= Millibar (mbar)
Millibar (mbar)	X 0.75	= Millimetres of mercury (mmHg)	X 1.333	= Millibar (mbar)
Millibar (mbar)	X 0.401	= Inches of water (inH₂O)	X 2.491	= Millibar (mbar)
Millimetres of mercury (mmHg)	X 0.535	= Inches of water (inH₂O)	X 1.868	= Millimetres of mercury (mmHg)
Inches of water (inH₂O)	X 0.036	= Pounds-force per square inch (psi; lbf/in²; lb/in²)	X 27.68	= Inches of water (inH₂O)

Torque (moment of force)

Pounds-force inches (lbf in; lb in)	X 1.152	= Kilograms-force centimetre (kgf cm; kg cm)	X 0.868	= Pounds-force inches (lbf in; lb in)
Pounds-force inches (lbf in; lb in)	X 0.113	= Newton metres (Nm)	X 8.85	= Pounds-force inches (lbf in; lb in)
Pounds-force inches (lbf in; lb in)	X 0.083	= Pounds-force feet (lbf ft; lb ft)	X 12	= Pounds-force inches (lbf in; lb in)
Pounds-force feet (lbf ft; lb ft)	X 0.138	= Kilograms-force metres (kgf m; kg m)	X 7.233	= Pounds-force feet (lbf ft; lb ft)
Pounds-force feet (lbf ft; lb ft)	X 1.356	= Newton metres (Nm)	X 0.738	= Pounds-force feet (lbf ft; lb ft)
Newton metres (Nm)	X 0.102	= Kilograms-force metres (kgf m; kg m)	X 9.804	= Newton metres (Nm)

Power

Horsepower (hp)	X 745.7	= Watts (W)	X 0.0013	= Horsepower (hp)

Velocity (speed)

Miles per hour (miles/hr; mph)	X 1.609	= Kilometres per hour (km/hr; kph)	X 0.621	= Miles per hour (miles/hr; mph)

Fuel consumption*

Miles per gallon, Imperial (mpg)	X 0.354	= Kilometres per litre (km/l)	X 2.825	= Miles per gallon, Imperial (mpg)
Miles per gallon, US (mpg)	X 0.425	= Kilometres per litre (km/l)	X 2.352	= Miles per gallon, US (mpg)

Temperature

Degrees Fahrenheit = (°C x 1.8) + 32

Degrees Celsius (Degrees Centigrade; °C) = (°F - 32) x 0.56

*It is common practice to convert from miles per gallon (mpg) to litres/100 kilometres (l/100km), where mpg (Imperial) x l/100 km = 282 and mpg (US) x l/100 km = 235

Index

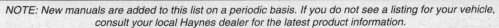 

Haynes Automotive Manuals

NOTE: New manuals are added to this list on a periodic basis. If you do not see a listing for your vehicle, consult your local Haynes dealer for the latest product information.

ACURA
*1776 **Integra & Legend** all models '86 thru '90

AMC
Jeep CJ - see JEEP (412)
694 **Mid-size models,** Concord, Hornet, Gremlin & Spirit '70 thru '83
934 **(Renault) Alliance & Encore** all models '83 thru '87

AUDI
615 **4000** all models '80 thru '87
428 **5000** all models '77 thru '83
1117 **5000** all models '84 thru '88

AUSTIN
Healey Sprite - see MG Midget Roadster (265)

BMW
*2020 **3/5 Series** not including diesel or all-wheel drive models '82 thru '92
276 **320i** all 4 cyl models '75 thru '83
632 **528i & 530i** all models '75 thru '80
240 **1500 thru 2002** all models except Turbo '59 thru '77
348 **2500, 2800, 3.0 & Bavaria** all models '69 thru '76

BUICK
Century (front wheel drive) - see GENERAL MOTORS (829)
*1627 **Buick, Oldsmobile & Pontiac Full-size (Front wheel drive)** all models '85 thru '95
Buick Electra, LeSabre and Park Avenue; Oldsmobile Delta 88 Royale, Ninety Eight and Regency; Pontiac Bonneville
1551 **Buick Oldsmobile & Pontiac Full-size (Rear wheel drive)**
Buick Estate '70 thru '90, Electra'70 thru '84, LeSabre '70 thru '85, Limited '74 thru '79
Oldsmobile Custom Cruiser '70 thru '90, Delta 88 '70 thru '85,Ninety-eight '70 thru '84
Pontiac Bonneville '70 thru '81, Catalina '70 thru '81, Grandville '70 thru '75, Parisienne '83 thru '86
627 **Mid-size Regal & Century** all rear-drive models with V6, V8 and Turbo '74 thru '87
Regal - see GENERAL MOTORS (1671)
Skyhawk - see GENERAL MOTORS (766)
Skylark '80 thru '85 - see GENERAL MOTORS (38020)
Skylark '86 on - see GENERAL MOTORS (1420)
Somerset - see GENERAL MOTORS (1420)

CADILLAC
*751 **Cadillac Rear Wheel Drive** all gasoline models '70 thru '93
Cimarron - see GENERAL MOTORS (766)

CHEVROLET
*1477 **Astro & GMC Safari Mini-vans** '85 thru '93
554 **Camaro V8** all models '70 thru '81
866 **Camaro** all models '82 thru '92
Cavalier - see GENERAL MOTORS (766)
Celebrity - see GENERAL MOTORS (829)
625 **Chevelle, Malibu & El Camino** all V6 & V8 models '69 thru '87
449 **Chevette & Pontiac T1000** '76 thru '87
550 **Citation** all models '80 thru '85
*1628 **Corsica/Beretta** all models '87 thru '95
274 **Corvette** all V8 models '68 thru '82
*1336 **Corvette** all models '84 thru '91
1762 **Chevrolet Engine Overhaul Manual**
704 **Full-size Sedans** Caprice, Impala, Biscayne, Bel Air & Wagons '69 thru '90

Lumina - see GENERAL MOTORS (1671)
Lumina APV - see GENERAL MOTORS (2035)
319 **Luv Pick-up** all 2WD & 4WD '72 thru '82
626 **Monte Carlo** all models '70 thru '88
241 **Nova** all V8 models '69 thru '79
*1642 **Nova and Geo Prizm** all front wheel drive models, '85 thru '92
420 **Pick-ups '67 thru '87** - Chevrolet & GMC, all V8 & in-line 6 cyl, 2WD & 4WD '67 thru '87; Suburbans, Blazers & Jimmys '67 thru '91
*1664 **Pick-ups '88 thru '95** - Chevrolet & GMC, all full-size pick-ups, '88 thru '95; Blazer & Jimmy '92 thru '94; Suburban '92 thru '95; Tahoe & Yukon '95
*831 **S-10 & GMC S-15 Pick-ups** all models '82 thru '93
*1727 **Sprint & Geo Metro** '85 thru '94
*345 **Vans - Chevrolet & GMC,** V8 & in-line 6 cylinder models '68 thru '95

CHRYSLER
2114 **Chrysler Engine Overhaul Manual**
*2058 **Full-size Front-Wheel Drive** '88 thru '93
K-Cars - see DODGE Aries (723)
Laser - see DODGE Daytona (1140)
*1337 **Chrysler & Plymouth Mid-size** front wheel drive '82 thru '93
Rear-wheel Drive - see Dodge Rear-wheel Drive (2098)

DATSUN
402 **200SX** all models '77 thru '79
647 **200SX** all models '80 thru '83
228 **B - 210** all models '73 thru '78
525 **210** all models '78 thru '82
206 **240Z, 260Z & 280Z** Coupe '70 thru '78
563 **280ZX** Coupe & 2+2 '79 thru '83
300ZX - see NISSAN (1137)
679 **310** all models '78 thru '82
123 **510 & PL521 Pick-up** '68 thru '73
430 **510** all models '78 thru '81
372 **610** all models '72 thru '76
277 **620 Series Pick-up** all models '73 thru '79
720 Series Pick-up - see NISSAN (771)
376 **810/Maxima** all gasoline models, '77 thru '84
Pulsar - see NISSAN (876)
Sentra - see NISSAN (982)
Stanza - see NISSAN (981)

DODGE
400 & 600 - see CHRYSLER Mid-size (1337)
*723 **Aries & Plymouth Reliant** '81 thru '89
1231 **Caravan & Plymouth Voyager Mini-Vans** all models '84 thru '95
699 **Challenger & Plymouth Saporro** all models '78 thru '83
Challenger '67-'76 - see DODGE Dart (234)
236 **Colt** all models '71 thru '77
610 **Colt & Plymouth Champ (front wheel drive)** all models '78 thru '87
*1668 **Dakota Pick-ups** all models '87 thru '93
234 **Dart, Challenger/Plymouth Barracuda & Valiant** 6 cyl models '67 thru '76
*1140 **Daytona & Chrysler Laser** '84 thru '89
*545 **Omni & Plymouth Horizon** '78 thru '90
*912 **Pick-ups** all full-size models '74 thru '91
*556 **Ram 50/D50 Pick-ups & Raider and Plymouth Arrow Pick-ups** '79 thru '93
2098 **Dodge/Plymouth/Chrysler** rear wheel drive '71 thru '89
*1726 **Shadow & Plymouth Sundance** '87 thru '93
*1779 **Spirit & Plymouth Acclaim** '89 thru '95
*349 **Vans - Dodge & Plymouth** V8 & 6 cyl models '71 thru '91

EAGLE
Talon - see Mitsubishi Eclipse (2097)

FIAT
094 **124 Sport Coupe & Spider** '68 thru '78
273 **X1/9** all models '74 thru '80

FORD
*1476 **Aerostar Mini-vans** all models '86 thru '94
788 **Bronco and Pick-ups** '73 thru '79
*880 **Bronco and Pick-ups** '80 thru '95
268 **Courier Pick-up** all models '72 thru '82
2105 **Crown Victoria & Mercury Grand Marquis** '88 thru '92
1763 **Ford Engine Overhaul Manual**
789 **Escort/Mercury Lynx** all models '81 thru '90
*2046 **Escort/Mercury Tracer** '91 thru '95
*2021 **Explorer & Mazda Navajo** '91 thru '95
560 **Fairmont & Mercury Zephyr** '78 thru '83
334 **Fiesta** all models '77 thru '80
754 **Ford & Mercury Full-size,** Ford LTD & Mercury Marquis ('75 '82); Ford Custom 500,Country Squire, Crown Victoria & Mercury Colony Park ('75 thru '87); Ford LTD Crown Victoria & Mercury Gran Marquis ('83 thru '87)
359 **Granada & Mercury Monarch** all in-line, 6 cyl & V8 models '75 thru '80
773 **Ford & Mercury Mid-size,** Ford Thunderbird & Mercury Cougar ('75 thru '82); Ford LTD & Mercury Marquis ('83 thru '86); Ford Torino,Gran Torino, Elite, Ranchero pick-up, LTD II, Mercury Montego, Comet, XR-7 & Lincoln Versailles ('75 thru '86)
*654 **Mustang & Mercury Capri** all models including Turbo. Mustang, '79 thru '93; Capri, '79 thru '86
357 **Mustang V8** all models '64-1/2 thru '73
231 **Mustang II** 4 cyl, V6 & V8 models '74 thru '78
649 **Pinto & Mercury Bobcat** '75 thru '80
1670 **Probe** all models '89 thru '92
*1026 **Ranger/Bronco II** gasoline models '83 thru '93
*1421 **Taurus & Mercury Sable** '86 thru '94
*1418 **Tempo & Mercury Topaz** all gasoline models '84 thru '94
1338 **Thunderbird/Mercury Cougar** '83 thru '88
*1725 **Thunderbird/Mercury Cougar** '89 and '93
344 **Vans** all V8 Econoline models '69 thru '91
*2119 **Vans** full size '92-'95

GENERAL MOTORS
*829 **Buick Century, Chevrolet Celebrity, Oldsmobile Cutlass Ciera & Pontiac 6000** all models '82 thru '93
*1671 **Buick Regal, Chevrolet Lumina, Oldsmobile Cutlass Supreme & Pontiac Grand Prix** all front wheel drive models '88 thru '95
*766 **Buick Skyhawk, Cadillac Cimarron, Chevrolet Cavalier, Oldsmobile Firenza & Pontiac J-2000 & Sunbird** all models '82 thru '94
38020 **Buick Skylark, Chevrolet Citation, Olds Omega, Pontiac Phoenix** '80 thru '85
1420 **Buick Skylark & Somerset, Oldsmobile Achieva & Calais and Pontiac Grand Am** all models '85 thru '95
*2035 **Chevrolet Lumina APV, Oldsmobile Silhouette & Pontiac Trans Sport** all models '90 thru '94
General Motors Full-size Rear-wheel Drive - see BUICK (1551)

GEO
Metro - see CHEVROLET Sprint (1727)
Prizm - see CHEVROLET Nova (1642)
*2039 **Storm** all models '90 thru '93
Tracker - see SUZUKI Samurai (1626)

GMC
Safari - see CHEVROLET ASTRO (1477)
Vans & Pick-ups - see CHEVROLET (420, 831, 345, 1664)

(Continued on other side)

---

* Listings shown with an asterisk (*) indicate model coverage as of this printing. These titles will be periodically updated to include later model years - consult your Haynes dealer for more information.

Haynes North America, Inc., 861 Lawrence Drive, Newbury Park, CA 91320 • (805) 498-6703

Haynes Automotive Manuals (continued)

NOTE: New manuals are added to this list on a periodic basis. If you do not see a listing for your vehicle, consult your local Haynes dealer for the latest product information.

HONDA

351	**Accord CVCC** all models '76 thru '83
1221	**Accord** all models '84 thru '89
2067	**Accord** all models '90 thru '93
42013	**Accord** all models '94 thru '95
160	**Civic 1200** all models '73 thru '79
633	**Civic 1300 & 1500 CVCC** '80 thru '83
297	**Civic 1500 CVCC** all models '75 thru '79
1227	**Civic** all models '84 thru '91
*2118	**Civic & del Sol** '92 thru '95
*601	**Prelude CVCC** all models '79 thru '89

HYUNDAI

*1552	**Excel** all models '86 thru '94

ISUZU

*1641	**Trooper & Pick-up**, all gasoline models Pick-up, '81 thru '93; Trooper, '84 thru '91

JAGUAR

*242	**XJ6** all 6 cyl models '68 thru '86
*478	**XJ12 & XJS** all 12 cyl models '72 thru '85

JEEP

*1553	**Cherokee, Comanche & Wagoneer Limited** all models '84 thru '93
412	**CJ** all models '49 thru '86
50025	**Grand Cherokee** all models '93 thru '95
*1777	**Wrangler** all models '87 thru '94

LINCOLN

2117	**Rear Wheel Drive** all models '70 thru '95

MAZDA

648	**626** Sedan & Coupe (rear wheel drive) all models '79 thru '82
*1082	**626 & MX-6** (front wheel drive) all models '83 thru '91
267	**B Series Pick-ups** '72 thru '93
370	**GLC Hatchback** (rear wheel drive) all models '77 thru '83
757	**GLC** (front wheel drive) '81 thru '85
*2047	**MPV** all models '89 thru '94
	Navajo-see Ford Explorer (2021)
460	**RX-7** all models '79 thru '85
*1419	**RX-7** all models '86 thru '91

MERCEDES-BENZ

*1643	**190 Series** all four-cylinder gasoline models, '84 thru '88
346	**230, 250 & 280** Sedan, Coupe & Roadster all 6 cyl sohc models '68 thru '72
983	**280 123 Series** gasoline models '77 thru '81
698	**350 & 450** Sedan, Coupe & Roadster all models '71 thru '80
697	**Diesel 123 Series** 200D, 220D, 240D, 240TD, 300D, 300CD, 300TD, 4- & 5-cyl incl. Turbo '76 thru '85

MERCURY

See FORD Listing

MG

111	**MGB** Roadster & GT Coupe all models '62 thru '80
265	**MG Midget & Austin Healey Sprite** Roadster '58 thru '80.

MITSUBISHI

*1669	**Cordia, Tredia, Galant, Precis & Mirage** '83 thru '93
*2097	**Eclipse, Eagle Talon & Plymouth Laser** '90 thru '94
*2022	**Pick-up & Montero** '83 thru '95

NISSAN

1137	**300ZX** all models including Turbo '84 thru '89
*1341	**Maxima** all models '85 thru '91
*771	**Pick-ups/Pathfinder** gas models '80 thru '95
876	**Pulsar** all models '83 thru '86
*982	**Sentra** all models '82 thru '94
*981	**Stanza** all models '82 thru '90

OLDSMOBILE

	Bravada - see CHEVROLET S-10 (831)
	Calais - see GENERAL MOTORS (1420)
	Custom Cruiser - see BUICK Full-size RWD (1551)
*658	**Cutlass** all standard gasoline V6 & V8 models '74 thru '88
	Cutlass Ciera - see GENERAL MOTORS (829)
	Cutlass Supreme - see GM (1671)
	Delta 88 - see BUICK Full-size RWD (1551)
	Delta 88 Brougham - see BUICK Full-size FWD (1551), RWD (1627)
	Delta 88 Royale - see BUICK Full-size RWD (1551)
	Firenza - see GENERAL MOTORS (766)
	Ninety-eight Regency - see BUICK Full-size RWD (1551), FWD (1627)
	Ninety-eight Regency Brougham - see BUICK Full-size RWD (1551)
	Omega - see GENERAL MOTORS (38020)
	Silhouette - see GENERAL MOTORS (2035)

PEUGEOT

663	**504** all diesel models '74 thru '83

PLYMOUTH

	Laser - see MITSUBISHI Eclipse (2097)
	For other PLYMOUTH titles, see DODGE listing.

PONTIAC

	T1000 - see CHEVROLET Chevette (449)
	J-2000 - see GENERAL MOTORS (766)
	6000 - see GENERAL MOTORS (829)
	Bonneville - see Buick Full-size FWD (1627), RWD (1551)
	Bonneville Brougham - see Buick (1551)
	Catalina - see Buick Full-size (1551)
1232	**Fiero** all models '84 thru '88
555	**Firebird** V8 models except Turbo '70 thru '81
867	**Firebird** all models '82 thru '92
	Full-size Front Wheel Drive - see BUICK Oldsmobile, Pontiac Full-size FWD (1627)
	Full-size Rear Wheel Drive - see BUICK Oldsmobile, Pontiac Full-size RWD (1551)
	Grand Am - see GENERAL MOTORS (1420)
	Grand Prix - see GENERAL MOTORS (1671)
	Grandville - see BUICK Full-size (1551)
	Parisienne - see BUICK Full-size (1551)
	Phoenix - see GENERAL MOTORS (38020)
	Sunbird - see GENERAL MOTORS (766)
	Trans Sport - see GENERAL MOTORS (2035)

PORSCHE

*264	**911** all Coupe & Targa models except Turbo & Carrera 4 '65 thru '89
239	**914** all 4 cyl models '69 thru '76
397	**924** all models including Turbo '76 thru '82
*1027	**944** all models including Turbo '83 thru '89

RENAULT

141	**5 Le Car** all models '76 thru '83
	Alliance & Encore - see AMC (934)

SAAB

247	**99** all models including Turbo '69 thru '80
*980	**900** all models including Turbo '79 thru '88

SATURN

2083	**Saturn** all models '91 thru '94

SUBARU

237	**1100, 1300, 1400 & 1600** '71 thru '79
*681	**1600 & 1800** 2WD & 4WD '80 thru '89

SUZUKI

*1626	**Samurai/Sidekick and Geo Tracker** all models '86 thru '95

TOYOTA

1023	**Camry** all models '83 thru '91
92006	**Camry** all models '92 thru '95
935	**Celica Rear Wheel Drive** '71 thru '85
*2038	**Celica Front Wheel Drive** '86 thru '92
1139	**Celica Supra** all models '79 thru '92
361	**Corolla** all models '75 thru '79
961	**Corolla** all rear wheel drive models '80 thru '87
*1025	**Corolla** all front wheel drive models '84 thru '92
636	**Corolla Tercel** all models '80 thru '82
360	**Corona** all models '74 thru '82
532	**Cressida** all models '78 thru '82
313	**Land Cruiser** all models '68 thru '82
*1339	**MR2** all models '85 thru '87
304	**Pick-up** all models '69 thru '78
*656	**Pick-up** all models '79 thru '95
*2048	**Previa** all models '91 thru '93
2106	**Tercel** all models '87 thru '94

TRIUMPH

113	**Spitfire** all models '62 thru '81
322	**TR7** all models '75 thru '81

VW

159	**Beetle & Karmann Ghia** all models '54 thru '79
238	**Dasher** all gasoline models '74 thru '81
*884	**Rabbit, Jetta, Scirocco, & Pick-up** gas models '74 thru '91 & Convertible '80 thru '92
451	**Rabbit, Jetta & Pick-up** all diesel models '77 thru '84
082	**Transporter 1600** all models '68 thru '79
226	**Transporter 1700, 1800 & 2000** all models '72 thru '79
084	**Type 3 1500 & 1600** all models '63 thru '73
1029	**Vanagon** all air-cooled models '80 thru '83

VOLVO

203	**120, 130 Series & 1800 Sports** '61 thru '73
129	**140 Series** all models '66 thru '74
*270	**240 Series** all models '76 thru '93
400	**260 Series** all models '75 thru '82
*1550	**740 & 760 Series** all models '82 thru '88

TECHBOOK MANUALS

2108	**Automotive Computer Codes**
1667	**Automotive Emissions Control Manual**
482	**Fuel Injection Manual, 1978 thru 1985**
2111	**Fuel Injection Manual, 1986 thru 1994**
2069	**Holley Carburetor Manual**
2068	**Rochester Carburetor Manual**
10240	**Weber/Zenith/Stromberg/SU Carburetors**
1762	**Chevrolet Engine Overhaul Manual**
2114	**Chrysler Engine Overhaul Manual**
1763	**Ford Engine Overhaul Manual**
1736	**GM and Ford Diesel Engine Repair Manual**
1666	**Small Engine Repair Manual**
10355	**Ford Automatic Transmission Overhaul**
10360	**GM Automatic Transmission Overhaul**
1479	**Automotive Body Repair & Painting**
2112	**Automotive Brake Manual**
2113	**Automotive Detaiing Manual**
1654	**Automotive Eelectrical Manual**
1480	**Automotive Heating & Air Conditioning**
2109	**Automotive Reference Manual & Illustrated Dictionary**
2107	**Automotive Tools Manual**
10440	**Used Car Buying Guide**
2110	**Welding Manual**

SPANISH MANUALS

98905	**Códigos Automotrices de la Computadora**
98915	**Inyección de Combustible 1986 al 1994**
99040	**Chevrolet & GMC Camionetas** '67 al '87 Incluye Suburban, Blazer & Jimmy '67 al '91
99041	**Chevrolet & GMC Camionetas** '88 al '95 Incluye Suburban '92 al '95, Blazer & Jimmy '92 al '94, Tahoe y Yukon '95
99075	**Ford Camionetas y Bronco** '80 al '94
99125	**Toyota Camionetas y 4-Runner** '79 al '95

* Listings shown with an asterisk (*) indicate model coverage as of this printing. These titles will be periodically updated to include later model years - consult your Haynes dealer for more information.

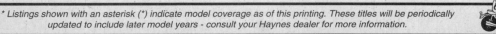

Over 100 Haynes motorcycle manuals also available

2-96

Haynes North America, Inc., 861 Lawrence Drive, Newbury Park, CA 91320 • (805) 498-6703